NEHRU
A Political Biography

Jawaharlal Nehru in 1956

NEHRU

A Political Biography

MICHAEL BRECHER

LONDON
OXFORD UNIVERSITY PRESS
NEW YORK   BOMBAY   TORONTO
1959

Oxford University Press, Amen House, London, E.C.4

GLASGOW NEW YORK TORONTO MELBOURNE WELLINGTON
BOMBAY CALCUTTA MADRAS KARACHI KUALA LUMPUR
CAPE TOWN IBADAN NAIROBI ACCRA

PRINTED IN GREAT BRITAIN
BY WESTERN PRINTING SERVICES LTD BRISTOL

To my
Father and Mother

PREFACE

Time moves swiftly in contemporary Asia. At the turn of the century Western Powers held sway almost without challenge. Since then new ideas and forces have come to the surface, inducing change among the ancient peoples of the area. The result has been the still-unfinished Asian Revolution, worthy of study not only for its human interest but also because it has shattered the traditional relations between Asia and the West. The present work is, in part, an attempt to view that revolution in its Indian setting. The story is many-sided and complex. Many persons played a notable role. But only one, Jawaharlal Nehru, links the years of promise and fulfilment, of nationalist agitation and national construction. Indeed, the life of Nehru is admirably suited to serve as the binding thread in an account of recent Indian history and politics. Hence, I have employed the technique of biography to shed light on political events, ideas, and movements. At the same time I have used the Indian revolution as the background for a study of Nehru the man and the statesman. The book is, then, both a biographical history and a political biography.

The approach is chronological and topical, covering the period from the 1880's to the summer of 1958 and ranging widely over the panorama of Indian politics. All this is preceded by a portrait of Nehru in his seventieth year, a study of his personality and character, of his mood and popularity, and of his manner of living. His relationship with Mahatma Gandhi looms large in the first half of the book, along with comments on other men and conditions moulding his outlook on life—the influence of his father, of Harrow and Cambridge, and of Western and Indian cultures. I have also attempted to take the reader through the various stages along Nehru's road to fame and power and to examine the friendships and antagonisms of the past forty years, as well as the shifting composition of the 'inner circles' surrounding Nehru since 1947. These and other themes are viewed against the background of India's struggle for independence, in which Nehru played a vital role. There are glimpses, too, of a galaxy of men who crossed the

Indian stage, including Churchill and Roosevelt, Attlee and Mountbatten, Cripps and Halifax, Patel and Bose, and Jinnah. Considerable attention is devoted to the year of decision, 1947, at once the year of triumph (independence) and anguish (partition) in the life of Nehru and India. The first eleven years of Nehru's leadership and India's freedom are treated extensively in the second half of the book. Finally, despite the admonitions of scholarly friends, I indulge in speculations on the future.

A biography of a living statesman can never be entirely satisfactory. Some of the source materials are not available, some major themes in the plot remain incomplete, and one's judgements do not have the benefit of perspective. Yet there are compensations: the opportunity to talk at leisure with men who have lived through and have helped to shape the events analysed in this book, especially important because Indians, for the most part, are reluctant to write memoirs; the opportunity to capture the spirit of a society in motion and of the man about whom one is writing; and the possibility of breaking new ground. Future historians will undoubtedly reveal inadequacies in the narrative and errors in judgement for which I alone claim full responsibility. Some persons may well criticize my interpretation of complex events, notably those relating to independence and partition. To those who may wish to take issue with anything that follows, I wish to record that my conclusions have been drawn from whatever evidence I had at my disposal; further, that it was not my intention to question motives, only to record events and evaluate their meaning and significance.

If this book provides some clues to the tortuous course of recent Indian history and politics it will have served one major purpose. If it succeeds, at least in small measure, in making Nehru more intelligible to his admirers and critics alike, it will have served another. If it provides some insight into the role of the outstanding individual in history, it will have accomplished a third goal. Finally, I hope that it may contribute to the understanding of the state of mind among 'the uncommitted billion'. I leave the final verdict on Nehru to the historians. My concern is with the living, with the actions of statesmen when and as they take place, and with their implications.

Many have contributed to the making of this book. The Nuffield Foundation made possible the basic research by the award of a Travelling Fellowship which enabled me to spend the academic year 1955–6 in England and India. McGill University kindly granted a year's leave of absence and the McGill Research Committee assisted me to return briefly to India at the beginning of 1958. The Canadian Social Science Research Council was generous in its support of this return visit to complete my research.

To Jawaharlal Nehru I am indebted for many kindnesses: for allowing me to spend three days on tour with him in a relaxed and informal atmosphere; for consenting to unrehearsed interviews in June 1956 and for allowing me to use the verbatim record as I saw fit (many selections have been inserted in the text); for agreeing to a lengthy interview at the beginning of 1958; for granting me permission to read 250 of his unpublished letters, and to quote extracts from them (while my book was in the press, most of these letters appeared in a book by Nehru entitled *A Bunch of Old Letters*); and, more generally, for providing such a fascinating subject for study and analysis.

I wish to express my appreciation to the Earl Mountbatten of Burma for permission to use extracts from lengthy interviews with him in the autumn of 1955; to Sir Frederick James for permission to quote directly from his unpublished memoir on Pandit Motilal Nehru; and to Dr. Syed Mahmud, former Minister in the Indian Ministry of External Affairs and an old friend of Nehru, for permission to read and quote extracts from about 150 letters exchanged with the Prime Minister between 1921 and 1951. I also wish to thank Professor C. H. Phillips, Director of the School of Oriental and African Studies, for his sympathetic interest in the project and for making available the valuable facilities of the School.

Dr. P. C. Chakravarti, Professor of International Affairs at Jadavpur University, very kindly guided me through the voluminous and valuable files of the incomplete 'History of the Freedom Movement Project' in New Delhi, and the Ministry of Home Affairs of the Government of India granted me permission to use some of these materials, along with other unpublished sources in the National Archives of India relating to the pre-Independence period.

The library staffs at India House, London, Chatham House, London, and the All-India Congress Committee office, New Delhi, were very helpful and courteous. In the final stages, Mrs. N. Reiss and other members of the Reference Section of McGill's Redpath Library helped in tracking down misplaced footnote references and bibliographical materials. I also owe a special debt to the officers of the Oxford University Press for their helpful editorial assistance.

Friends and colleagues were generous with their time and advice. One in particular, who regrettably seeks anonymity, read the entire manuscript with great care and expert knowledge and provided invaluable comments at every stage of the work. Although his views were not always accepted, they compelled me to rethink my interpretations. The bulk of an earlier draft was also read, with much benefit to the author, by Mark Gayn and by Freda and B. P. L. Bedi of New Delhi. Specific chapters have undergone the careful scrutiny of my colleagues, Professors Irving Brecher, Keith Callard, and Saul Frankel, and of Professor Richard L. Park of the University of California. To many friends on three continents I owe a debt for their sympathetic interest in the book during the past four years.

The reader will notice many references to anonymous persons. This technique was used because of the request of certain persons that their names not be associated directly with controversial statements. However, a selection of the four hundred persons interviewed is listed in the bibliographical section.

Wherever quotations are not supported by specific documents, they are based on the author's notes taken immediately after each interview. In those instances where the person is identified, I wish to absolve him from any responsibility for the direct speech.

Most of all, I owe a profound debt of gratitude to my wife. She cheerfully undertook a year of travel to far-off lands with two small children under the most trying conditions. At every stage she was a source of inspiration and encouragement. She read and re-read the manuscript with a critical eye, constantly forcing me to present my ideas clearly and to reassess my conclusions. Patient and determined, she was a devoted companion on the long voyage of discovering Nehru and India. As on an earlier venture in scholarship, her contributions to this book were greater than even she realizes.

MICHAEL BRECHER

McGill University
Montreal
November 1958

CONTENTS

LIST OF ILLUSTRATIONS

MAPS

CHAPTER I

Portrait of the Man

NATURE and circumstance were kind to Jawaharlal Nehru. He was born into the Kashmiri Brahmin community, the most aristocratic sub-caste in the Hindu social system. His father was a distinguished and wealthy barrister, modern, urbane, highly cultivated and lavishly generous. As an only son—and the only child for eleven years—Jawaharlal was the focus of concentrated affection. He had, too, the leisure and learning of an English aristocrat in the secure atmosphere of the Edwardian Age—private tutors, Harrow, Cambridge and the Inner Temple. When he was drawn to the political arena soon after his return to India, his path was eased by the guidance and support of his father and Gandhi. Prime Minister Nehru recalled this head-start in a modest portrait of his past seen forty years later. 'My growth to public prominence, you know, was not by sharp stages. It was, rather, a steady development over a long period of time. And if I may say so,' he added dryly, 'I began at a fairly high level.'[1]

Nehru was also favoured with a strikingly handsome appearance, both by Indian and Western standards. Pictures of him at the age of twenty or sixty reveal the slim, chiselled features which stamp the Kashmiri Brahmin. The later ones reveal much more: expressive eyes, sometimes pensive or sharp with irritation or gay and self-satisfied and, at other times, intent and alight with resolve; the high, full temples suggestive of two of Nehru's outstanding qualities—stubbornness and intellectual curiosity; the wide mouth and sensuous lips which pout shamelessly during moments of ill-temper; the soft-moulded chin; and the long, delicate fingers. His smile is captivating, at times disarming. His face is oval-shaped and his profile classic Greek, making Nehru one of the most photogenic statesmen of the century. He exudes the magnetic charm which has swiftly won individuals and crowds alike. Although he lacks the emphasis of height—he

[1] To the author in New Delhi on 30 January 1958.

is about 5 ft. 8 in.—his straight back and good posture express the vigour and youthfulness for which he was justly famous. With years and especially since 1956 the lines of age have begun to score his face. Nevertheless, he remains on the eve of his Biblical three score and ten an unusually attractive man.

The benefits of aristocratic background and education were not without price. Security was accompanied by an overweening paternalism which hindered his growth to self-reliance. This tendency to depend on a strong, decisive and older man became a marked feature of Nehru's character in his adult life. Even before the death of his father in 1931 he had already transferred this dependence in large measure to Gandhi, who served as guide, counsellor and father-confessor in matters both political and personal. After Gandhi's death the habit continued but in a less pronounced manner. Indeed, it was not until his early sixties that Nehru emerged completely from the shadow of the two men who exercised more influence on his character than all other persons.

The legacy of that habit is still visible. Despite his power and prestige, Nehru continues to exhibit a lack of confidence about the right course of action. Perhaps the most notable example in recent years was his weak handling of the vexed issue of States Reorganization. In part, his vacillations are due to the intellectual in Nehru who sees all points of view and therefore hesitates to act boldly lest he destroy that element of 'good' which he thinks all viewpoints possess. But in large measure this indecisiveness must be traced to the circumstances in which his character was moulded.

Other elements in his background helped to shape the character of Jawaharlal Nehru. Alone among Indian nationalist leaders of his generation he was a true aristocrat. Nehru detests the waste and iniquities of the caste system but he cannot escape the indelible mark of his caste origin. He remains a Brahmin with everything that this status connotes. All who have known him through the years, whether intimately or casually, have detected this inbred superiority which clings to the Brahmin *malgré lui*.

His education in the West marked him in other ways. For one thing, it set him apart from his colleagues in the Indian National Congress, a solitary figure in a middle-class, traditional-minded General Staff, guiding a petty-bourgeois and peasant army. Although he accepted the stern discipline imposed by Gandhi and functioned as a member of a team, Nehru's approach to strategy and tactics revealed the Western rationalist. This explained, in part, the constant struggle as he fought to reconcile his own conception of the right line of action with that of Gandhi, notably in the methods of pursuing civil disobedience and the timing and reasons for suspension of direct action in 1922 and 1933. In a wider sense it made Nehru alien in his own society, a Hindu out of tune with Hinduism, 'a queer mixture of the East and the West, out of place everywhere, at home nowhere'.[1] In this respect his was merely an extreme case in a whole class of young, Westernized intellectuals. But as the first to achieve prominence he carried a heavy burden of adjustment. In his later years Nehru acquired a deeper appreciation of Indian history and philosophy and enriched the bases for subsequent thought and action. *The Discovery of India*, written during his long war-time imprisonment at the age of fifty-five, is the clearest evidence of this adjustment.

From his father Nehru acquired an intense pride frequently asserted in his public life. Here lies the root of his resentment against British rule—for Nehru's initial response to politics was emotional, not intellectual. Anything that smacks of racialism produces instinctive anger, as the Suez War of 1956 amply revealed. So too does rampant discrimination in South Africa. His pride often flashes out in imperious behaviour, another gift from Motilal Nehru. In recent years, however, this characteristic has been less in evidence. His volatile temper, too, has been moderated. He is quick to anger, but his outbursts are usually short-lived; and he rarely bears a grudge against those who experience his momentary fury. It is a release from nervous tension and the 'normal' reaction of an over-sensitive man to any act which violates his high standards of integrity, morality and efficiency. Nehru is a perfectionist, in the Western sense, which compounds the sources of irritation with people and things about him.

Nehru is a most affable and charming man. Indeed, he has the gift rare among statesmen of inspiring genuine regard and

<hr />

[1] Nehru, J., *Toward Freedom: The Autobiography of Jawaharlal Nehru* (John Day, 1942), p. 353. Unless otherwise indicated, all subsequent references to the autobiography are taken from this edition.

affection from persons ranging the whole spectrum of political opinion at home and abroad. But an inner quality of aloofness prevents him from reciprocating, even with colleagues of long standing. His early life in Allahabad strengthened a natural reticence and so did a British public-school education. Nehru himself underlined this element in his make-up in a letter to an Indian friend: 'Yes, we did not discuss personal matters. You ought to know me sufficiently to realize that I never discuss them unless the other party takes the initiative. I would not do so even with Kamala [his wife] or Indu [his daughter]. Such has been my training.'[1] So it continues down to the present day.

This quality should not be construed as mistrust or indifference to the welfare of others. On the contrary, Nehru is sustained in trial by a strong faith in man. Moreover, colleagues, friends, and subordinates speak in glowing terms of his kindness and consideration, in matters vital and trivial. There is the story of a salary increase given to his servants during the second world war because their responsibilities had increased when he went to prison! According to one official who has worked closely with the Indian Prime Minister for some years, 'Nehru is not a demonstrative person; in that respect he is very much the English public school type. He will never tell you that he appreciates your work but he shows his affection and kind-heartedness in indirect ways.' He then related an incident that occurred when he was accompanying Nehru on a state visit. Because the Prime Minister was ill, the day's programme was shelved, and the party returned to their quarters. Dinner was hurriedly brought to Nehru but he refused to begin until his aide was attended to.[2]

I saw a similar incident on a tour with Nehru in 1956. As we were about to breakfast one morning the Prime Minister turned to his security chief and asked, 'Where is X? Why doesn't he join us?' X was a very junior typist on his staff. Only when he was assured that the person concerned was being looked after did Nehru proceed with his meal. Prestige and power do not seem to have hardened Nehru or made him

[1] To Dr. Syed Mahmud, 24 November 1933. Unpublished Nehru-Mahmud Correspondence.
[2] Related to the author in New Delhi in January 1958 by a person who wishes to remain anonymous.

neglect those little acts of kindness for which he was well known in pre-Independence days.

Nehru's natural reserve makes him feel uneasy in the company of a few, detached, almost withdrawn from those about him. An intangible but very real barrier seems to assert itself. But not so in the presence of a crowd. There his personality is transformed. He becomes alive, relaxed, uninhibited, as if infused with the collective energy of the group. He never loses himself completely, for the aristocrat in his make-up prevents a complete fusion with the mass. He is in the crowd but never of it, stimulated but not absorbed.

For twenty-five years or more he has been the idol of the Indian masses, second only to Gandhi. They literally adore him, with a vivid affection and hero-worship. From distant villages they come in thousands to hear him, more to see him, to have a *darshan* (communion) with their beloved 'Panditji', successor to the Mahatma, champion of the oppressed, symbol of the new India of their vague dreams. They may not understand everything he says, but no matter. He has come to talk to them, to inspire them and to make them forget, even for a little while, their misery and their problems. And he, in turn, feels a bond with the masses. They are not simply the clay with which to fashion a new society, his primary goal since Independence. Their simplicity and credulity and belief in him draw him out from the shell of reticence which normally encases his personality in the city. Their faith touches his vanity, giving him a sense of power—power to alter the grim poverty which they have always known. But most of all they provide him with an inexhaustible source of energy which enables Nehru to maintain his incredible pace of work.

Remarkable indeed is the mutual impact of Nehru and the crowd. They seem to transmit waves of energy to him by virtue of their presence and their constantly expressed faith in his leadership. The larger the audience the more exhilarated he feels, the more determined he becomes to persevere in the face of great odds. By periodic tours and almost daily speeches before crowds, large and small, his storehouse of energy is constantly replenished, not depleted. He, in turn, transmits his buoyant enthusiasm and irrepressible optimism to the masses, maintaining the precarious 'hope level' which enables them to press ahead in the long, difficult task of improving their way of life.

No one has recognized this unusual emotional link between Nehru and the masses better than the Prime Minister himself. 'When I am in Delhi', he told a group of political workers some years ago, 'a terrible feeling comes to me about this lack of contact with the people. When I get that feeling I rush out and meet people.'[1] The basic reason for his frequent excursions to the countryside he explained in these words: 'Delhi is a static city with a dead atmosphere. . . . I go out and see masses of people, my people, your people, and derive inspiration from them. There is something dynamic and something growing with them and I grow with them. I also enthuse with them.'[2]

*　　*　　*　　*

Some personal insight into this and other aspects of Nehru's character emerged from my tour with the Indian Prime Minister in the spring of 1956. It was dark and pleasantly cool on that early March morning when I drove through the deserted streets of the capital towards Palam Airport. To the surprise of everyone, Nehru was late in arriving, just a few minutes; but even this is a rare occurrence, for the Indian leader is typically Western in his mania for punctuality. As one colleague of very long standing remarked, 'he insists that his programme at all times be orderly, with precise arrangements for every function and appointment. Punctuality and discipline are things which he prizes very highly. Nehru is not averse to relaxation and leisure, but these too must be fitted into an orderly schedule. He detests wastage of time and must fill his day with purposeful activity. By comparison, however, Gandhi was a much more ruthless disciplinarian.'[3]

After brief, formal introductions, we boarded the luxurious Viscount which had been purchased recently for his official travels and headed south to Hyderabad City on the first lap of

---

[1] Address to the Tamilnad (Madras) Political Conference, 3 October 1953. *Congress Bulletin*, Nos. 10 and 11, October–November 1953, p. 312.

[2] To a conference of irrigation and power engineers in New Delhi, 17 November 1952. *Express* (Bombay), 18 November 1952.

[3] Related to the author in New Delhi in January 1958 by a person who wishes to remain anonymous.

our journey. A very small party accompanied the Prime Minister from Delhi, but we were joined later by various colleagues and friends. The faithful Hari was there, of course, Hari who had been adopted by Motilal Nehru more than fifty years ago and has served as the 'young Nehru's' devoted valet since the early 1930's. So too was a member of Nehru's personal staff, one of the battery of private assistants who transcribe his perennial flow of words. Two unobtrusive security agents and a photographer for Indian Newsreels rounded out the group.

The flight was swift and uneventful. Nehru withdrew immediately to the private compartment which serves as bedroom, sitting-room and office during his travels within India and abroad. There he passes the time in one of three ways: dictating letters, minutes and memoranda; reading official files or a book which has lain by his bed in Delhi, neglected for want of time; or resting his weary mind and body. On this occasion he slept throughout the two-hour flight which followed a week of conferences with the American, French and British Foreign Ministers who had descended upon the capital in rapid succession. His penchant for sleep while travelling is well known.

Presently we found ourselves at Begumpet Airport on the outskirts of Hyderabad City where the local élite had gathered to pay their respects to the uncrowned king of the Indian Republic. Among them were Ramkrishna Rao, then Chief Minister of Hyderabad and later Governor of Kerala; the charming Padmaja Naidu, whose friendship with Nehru is deep and abiding; the scholarly Shriman Narayan (Agarwal), a long-time General-Secretary of the Congress; the handsome, polished, and competent G. K. Handoo, then Deputy-Director of the Intelligence Bureau in the Home Ministry, who carried with apparent ease the tremendous responsibility of guarding Nehru's life; and the aged Nizam of Hyderabad, one of the most unprepossessing-looking men in the public eye. Dressed in simple and slovenly clothes, he looked more like a peon than the man with a fortune worth two billion dollars.

After the usual garlanding ceremony, with the ubiquitous photographers surrounding the Prime Minister like ants, we were herded into a caravan of old American cars for the short trip to the railway station. A large crowd patiently awaited the arrival of their hero. As his open car approached the entrance a mighty roar went up, 'Pandit Nehru ki jai, Pandit Nehru ki jai' ('Hail Pandit Nehru, Hail Pandit Nehru'). Unlike the throngs in totalitarian states, this was a spontaneous crowd expressing genuine affection for India's first citizen. Being accustomed to this adulation for the past twenty-five years, Nehru took it in his stride, smiling to the crowd and reciprocating their warm greeting with the traditional *namaste* salutation—holding his hands together palm to palm and moving them towards his forehead.

Further evidence of this hero-worship was provided during the lengthy journey by car along the dusty roads of rural Hyderabad. At one large village a crowd of 10,000 had gathered to greet the Prime Minister. As our caravan rounded the bend they broke into a frenzied run towards the opposite side in order to get another look at him. The race for a *darshan* was like an instinctive, compelling drive, a craving for association with an exalted man, however brief. Throughout the journey there was a mumble among the crowds along the route, which was translated for my benefit. 'We saw him, we saw him', they were saying in ecstasy to their families. In the evening, on the return journey, the road was again lined with people. There was not the slightest possibility of seeing Nehru, for he was in a closed car travelling at fifty miles per hour in the dark. Yet they stood patiently to see the car go by. And frequently there arose the cry, 'Pandit Nehru ki jai'.

Watching this scene and others like it in the next few days recalled to memory some passages in a vivid 'portrait of Nehru' which was published anonymously in 1937:

Jawaharlal ki jai! [Hail Jawaharlal!] The Rashtrapati [President] looked up as he passed swiftly through the waiting crowds; his hands went up, and his pale, hard face was lit up with a smile. . . . The smile passed away and the face became stern and sad. Almost it seemed that the smile and the gesture accompanying it had little reality; they were just tricks of the trade to gain the goodwill of the crowd whose darling he had become. Was it so? Watch him again. Is all this natural, or the carefully thought out trickery of the public man? Perhaps it is both. . . . Steadily and persistently he goes on increasing his personal prestige and influence. . . . From the Far North to Cape Comorin he has gone like some triumphant Caesar, leaving a trail of glory and a legend behind him. Is all this just a passing fancy which amuses him . . . or is it his will to power that is driving him from crowd to crowd. . . . What if the fancy turns? Men like Jawaharlal, with all their great capacity for great and good work, are unsafe in a democracy. He calls himself a democrat and a socialist, and no doubt he does so in all earnestness . . . but a little twist and he might turn into a dictator. . . . Jawaharlal cannot become a fascist. . . . He is too much an aristocrat for the crudity and vulgarity of fascism. His very face and voice tell us that. . . . And yet he has all the makings of a dictator in him—vast popularity, a strong will, energy, pride . . . and with all his love of the crowd, an intolerance of others and a certain contempt for the weak and inefficient. His flashes of temper are well known. His overwhelming desire to get things done, to sweep away what he dislikes and build anew, will hardly brook for long the slow processes of democracy. . . . His conceit is already formidable. It must be checked. We want no Caesars.

The purpose of this critique was to persuade the Indian National Congress not to re-elect Nehru as President for a third successive term. The author—Jawaharlal Nehru.[1]

Most of the qualities mentioned in this remarkable self-analysis are still with Nehru: his command of the crowd; the actor's finesse in the centre of the stage; popularity; prestige; influence; impatience, and the like. Some have been tempered by time and experience; his outbursts of anger are less conspicuous, and he has acquired a greater measure of tolerance and sympathy for the failings of others. Perhaps the most important trait suggested in his self-portrait has been belied by Nehru's own actions since Independence. He still possesses 'the makings of a dictator' but he is no Caesar. Jawaharlal *is* safe in a democracy. In fact, the Indian experiment in constitutional democracy owes more to Nehru than to anyone else or to any combination of factors. Aware of his autocratic tendencies, he has striven—successfully—to curb them lest India revert to the condition of benevolent despotism. Few men with these talents could have resisted the inducements to exercise dictatorial powers. Some frustrated Indians regret his reluctance to do so. Some Westerners would do well to appreciate this aspect of Nehru's leadership.

[1] This article first appeared as 'The Rashtrapati' by 'Chanakya' in *The Modern Review* (Calcutta), vol. 62, November 1937, pp. 546–7. The quoted passages are taken from excerpts which were reprinted in *Toward Freedom*, Appendix E, pp. 436–7.

Lunch was an informal affair in the Prime Minister's 'private car', very modest by any standards. To Miss Naidu, Rao and Narayan he said in a good-natured tone, 'You vegetarians go off to that side', while Handoo and I joined him for a mixed Indian-Western meal. Unlike Gandhi, Nehru has no fads regarding food. Typically, he partakes of both Indian and European dishes, with a preference for the latter, particularly English cuisine. His tastes were spelled out in an official note from his Delhi office in an effort to reduce the ostentation which greeted him everywhere in the land: 'The Prime Minister is anxious that no special and out-of-the-way arrangements might be made for his meals. He would like to have the normal food of the place he visits. The only thing that might be remembered is that he likes as simple food as possible, whether Indian or after the European style, and that he is not used to spices and chillies at all. While he eats meat, he does so sparingly and has far more vegetables. He likes a full vegetarian meal. . . . Normally he takes coffee with hot milk in the morning and a cup of weak tea in the afternoon.'[1] His distaste for lavish displays of any kind was illustrated by his response to a silver- and gold-plated chair presented to him at a public meeting: 'What is this?' he exclaimed. 'I hate this show. Take it away.'[2]

After lunch and conversational pleasantries Nehru retired for a brief nap. At that point there occurred an amusing but rather significant episode. One member of the group suggested a change in the itinerary so as to reduce the Prime Minister's discomfort. It was absurdly simple—to spend more time on the train the following day in order to shorten the dusty journey by car to the rendezvous with Vinoba Bhave in a remote village. Anywhere else in the world the staff would have done this without consulting the Prime Minister—but not in India. For half an hour the pros and cons were weighed with due solemnity. 'Why not do it without bothering him?' I interjected. 'Oh no', was the sober reply. 'He has already seen the itinerary and might become irritated by any change.' Finally the great decision was made—to let sleeping dogs lie, even though the change would have been wiser.

[1] Issued on 18 June 1956. A copy was made available to the author by a member of the Prime Minister's Secretariat.
[2] *The Hindu* (Madras), 15 July 1954.

At last we arrived in Nizamabad for the conference of the *Bharat Sevak Samaj* (National Service Organization). Ostensibly this was the primary purpose of the tour, though the meeting with Vinoba was far more important. The local political gentry were assembled in full force, along with Gulzir Lal Nanda, the Minister for Planning. We were also joined by a person with the designation D.I.G.C.I.D. (Deputy Inspector-General of Police, Criminal Investigation Department), a nervous little man who rushed to and fro lest evil befall the first citizen of India.

Nehru spoke twice in the afternoon, first to the delegates who had come from all over India and later to about 100,000 peasants who had trudged from surrounding villages to see and to hear their hero. He was in excellent form, speaking in his typical conversational manner. As soon as the star attraction came forward to address the delegates he was surrounded by photographers. He was patient for a few moments but then waved them aside with annoyance. The following day he demonstrated his quick and sometimes petulant temper more emphatically. As he emerged from the private conclave with Vinoba he was approached indirectly for a statement to the press. 'I won't be bullied by these people. Who do they think they are? Who asked them to come?' Then, after a brief pause, 'What do they want anyway?'

The highlight of his speech to the delegates was a derisive reference to the *sadhus* (Hindu holy men) who were trying to curry favour by mobilizing their ranks for 'national service'. Nehru remarked at one point that there were 50 lakhs (hundred thousands) of *sadhus* in 1931 and 78 lakhs at present. A prominent *sadhu*, sitting on the dais, interjected that there were only 10 lakhs now. 'What happened to the rest of them?' the Prime Minister asked. 'Did they go to Pakistan?' The audience roared with laughter and Nehru himself joined in, slapping his knee in delight.

The scene then shifted to the huge throng of peasants waiting for a *darshan* of 'Panditji'. There they sat, passive and quiet, stretched out as far as the eye could see. They had assembled early in the morning and had waited patiently for six hours or more in the burning heat—it was well over 100 degrees. They were not disappointed, for Nehru took them into his confidence and communicated his sympathy with their problems. Even though they could not understand his language—he spoke in Hindustani and his words were translated into Telugu—they watched him intently, as if transfixed by his presence.

To observe Nehru talking *with* his people makes it possible to penetrate the intangibles of his popularity. There he stands in his typical pose, bent slightly forward as he surveys the audience, his hands now resting on the podium, now gripping the microphone, sometimes folded behind him, with a crumpled handkerchief tucked up his right shirt sleeve. He is no natural orator and rises to great heights only on rare occasions, such as on Independence Day and the death of Gandhi. His voice is soft and relaxed. He does not rouse his listeners by thundering pronouncements. He talks to them like a teacher to his pupils, showing them the errors of their ways, pointing out the proper path of conduct, stressing the need for discipline, hard work, unity, tolerance and faith, drawing on the inspiration of Gandhi and the freedom struggle, painting a picture of the India of the future, pledging himself to their welfare, calling for rededication to the cause of a good society.

Candour and spontaneity are the outstanding qualities of his speech. He talks as he thinks and feels at the moment. He thinks aloud, sharing his ideas as they develop. His words flow as in a stream of consciousness and therefore into endless side channels. He comes to his main points very slowly and indirectly, his words reflecting the variety of thoughts and emotions which filter through his mind as he speaks. The result is a rambling, verbose, repetitive and, very often, woolly speech, especially in the last few years. This is inevitable because of the mode of his public speaking. Nor is Nehru's habit of thinking aloud about all manner of subjects confined to the village crowd. Whether it be in Parliament or to a party gathering, before a group of sophisticated intellectuals or university students, among foreign visitors or even at a press conference, his approach remains the same. His speeches, then, provide insight into his way of thinking as well as the content of his views.

Nehru speaks in public more frequently than any statesman of the age. And the vast majority of his speeches are extemporaneous. Indeed, since 1947 less than a dozen were prepared statements, according to his secretariat. It was not always so.

Until the early 'forties his important speeches were thoroughly prepared and were models of clarity, such as his presidential addresses to the Congress in 1929, 1936 and 1937. Later, however, the pressure of time, combined with the practice of almost daily speeches, made spontaneity inescapable.

There are some who decry the free flow of ideas and the endless number of Nehru's speeches. There can be no doubt that they would benefit from greater organization and clarity. But this would require a marked reduction in his public appearances. And this he is reluctant to make. One reason is that in a predominantly illiterate society the spoken word is the most effective means of communication between the governors and the governed. Another is the legacy of the pre-Independence period when Gandhi and Nehru created a personal bond with the Indian people by incessant tours of the countryside. Moreover, Nehru feels strongly that only in this manner can he continue to feel the pulse of the common man. By constantly appearing before different segments of society he also acts as a great unifying force, helping to weld them into a national unit. Finally, as suggested earlier, he needs the crowd, perhaps no less than they need him.

The tour also revealed Nehru's penchant for reading. Books were a constant companion on his travels before Independence. It was comforting to have them, he used to say, even if he could not read them all. The habit of earlier days and his very strong attachment continue.

During this particular outing from the capital he was absorbed by Dr. Oppenheimer's *Science and the Common Understanding*. The literature of science is, indeed, his favourite reading—almost a passion with him. In part this must be traced to his education at Cambridge, as indicated in a chance remark over lunch: 'Where I differ from Indian Socialists is that I have a scientific background and am more aware of the impact of science on social evolution.' Over the years he has acquired little interest in fiction. But he is still a great admirer of English poetry. According to one of his subordinates, a collection of Keats is always close by. 'He constantly talks about the lack of time to read; in fact he bemoans it.'[1] This has been part of the price of

[1] To the author in New Delhi in January 1958 by a person who wishes to remain anonymous.

power and responsibility. Yet he continues to find time, almost daily for a half-hour or more before he retires and while travelling.

Despite the arduous road journey the Prime Minister showed no signs of fatigue. Throughout the tour, in fact, he demonstrated a youthful vigour which seemed astonishing for a man in his mid-sixties. Upon reflection, however, this is not too surprising, partly because of the rejuvenative process resulting from direct contact with the masses and partly because this excursion to the countryside was in the nature of a holiday when compared with his normal schedule in Delhi. Indeed, Nehru's daily routine on the eve of his seventieth year is such that few men twenty years his junior could stand the strain.

*   *   *   *

During the winter months he rises at 6.30 in the morning. The next hour is devoted to a glance at the Delhi press and yoga exercises. Many are the stories of Nehru standing on his head. Suffice it to note that he continues to do so, in fact, for a longer period than in the past. The habit of daily morning exercise dates to the 1920's, and Nehru retains the firm belief that it is essential to his physical health, so much so that the fifteen-minute period has been doubled since the beginning of 1957. Furthermore, the exercises are more elaborate than before and are done under the guidance of a master of yoga who took the initiative and approached the Prime Minister.

By 7.30 he is ready to meet the formidable challenge of a typical day. It begins with half an hour in his private study reading cables that arrived during the night and signing papers and letters dictated the previous evening. So heavy is his correspondence and comments on sundry matters of state that typists work around the clock to keep up with the flow of words.

Breakfast generally takes no more than fifteen minutes, for Nehru does not believe in tarrying over meals. Usually it is of the typical Western variety—with fruit juice, cereal, eggs, toast and coffee. His daughter, Indira, who lives at the Prime Minister's Residence, is almost always present, along with her two sons when on holiday from school. Frequently there are guests of one kind or another, persons whom Nehru feels he must see but whom he cannot fit into his schedule for the day. For the most part they are friends and political colleagues, people who will not be slighted by an informal chat. Occasionally foreigners seeking an interview or acquaintances revisiting India are invited to the breakfast table.

From his living-quarters he descends to the office on the ground floor at about 8.15. (In the summer this would be at 7.45; the entire schedule is put back half an hour.) There are always people to see him, 'gate-crashers' who try to catch him before he leaves the Residence. They may be peasants with grievances, politicians with requests or just sightseers. Sometimes they take fifteen minutes, sometimes less. Then he pays a brief visit to his four pet pandas, exquisite-looking Himalayan cat-bears which are kept in a specially constructed cage behind the Residence, surrounded by the lovely pleasure-gardens which add lustre to the estate. Nehru is very keen about them as he is about most animals, and about nature in all its forms.

The effect of nature on Jawaharlal is well known. Indeed, it finds expression even in his political writings. In a letter to the Presidents of the Provincial Congress Committees from Simla, at the foothills of the Himalayas, he remarked: '[It is] not so much because of the cooler climate but rather what I might call the feel and the look of the place. There is something soothing and solid about a mountain and its deep valleys. . . . Time and space assume a different perspective and the problems of today do not appear quite so overwhelming, as they do in the plains below.'[1] Neither age nor power has blunted Nehru's sensitive responses.

By 9 o'clock he is at his desk in the Ministry of External Affairs, located in the South Block of Delhi's reddish-sandstone Secretariat. With the President's House (*Rashtrapati Bhawan*) in the background these government buildings are an impressive but dull sight, a legacy of the British *Raj*. They stand in splendour at the head of Kingsway (*Rajpath*) which leads down to the war memorial of India Gate.

When Parliament is not in session Nehru remains at his office in External Affairs throughout the day, i.e. from 9 until 1.30 and, after lunch, from about 2.45 until 6.30 or 7. There he receives diplomats, visiting dignitaries, Cabinet colleagues and

---

[1] 26 May 1954. *Congress Bulletin*, No. 4, May 1954, pp. 157–8.

party workers in a seemingly endless flow. There he pores over a mountain of files and deals with many matters requiring immediate decision, either domestic or foreign. Interviews and paper work are co-ordinated in a pattern which enables the Prime Minister to use every moment to advantage. Appointments are fixed on the half-hour; many of them, however, are brief courtesy calls, and others frequently do not occupy the allotted time. Between appointments Nehru dictates unceasingly to stenographers who are constantly at his beck and call. This, indeed, is the key to his formidable pace of work—stenographers stand by at all times and at all places: in his offices at External Affairs and Parliament, at his Residence and in his makeshift headquarters while on tour. Moreover, Nehru invariably takes notes while persons are talking with him so that he can take action immediately following the interview.

During parliamentary sessions the pattern of work remains essentially the same, but the physical locale shifts from the Secretariat to the Prime Minister's office in the parliament building a few minutes away by automobile. The legislature convenes at 11 a.m. If it is a question hour he remains in the House until noon; if an unimportant matter is on the floor, he leaves after fifteen minutes or a half-hour; during a key debate, especially on foreign affairs, he stays on until its conclusion. For the remainder of the day he conducts affairs from his office on the second floor of Parliament. Here, the routine of file-reading, conferences, interviews and dictation is repeated. Because of the pressure of time during the session, Cabinet meetings, party conclaves and the like are held before 11 in the morning or at his home in the evening.

When he returns to the Residence at 6.30 or 7 in the evening more appointments are waiting. Normally, they are fixed at quarter-hour intervals and continue until 8.30; between interviews he takes up the broken thread of dictation. Dinner varies from the purely informal family gathering—a rare occurrence— to the formal state banquet in honour of a distinguished guest. Colleagues or diplomats whom he could not see during the crowded day are frequently invited to dinner at the Residence. On these occasions he will remain a full hour or more; at state functions he is usually engaged until about 10.30 in the evening. In either event he returns to his desk at home and carries on with affairs of state until midnight or later. Previous to 1957 he continued until 1 or 1.30 and then read until 2 a.m. Since that time, however, he has reduced the normal daily workload one hour at night. This concession was made, not at the request of doctors, but in response to persistent pleas of family and friends and because of his desire to conserve his energy for the years ahead.

Such has been the normal routine of Jawaharlal Nehru since Independence. The only discernible changes—since the beginning of 1957—are the longer and more elaborate yoga exercises in the morning and a one-hour reduction in the workload, a minor concession indeed for a man approaching seventy. There are, of course, frequent public appearances in Delhi. And while on tour the schedule is of necessity more flexible. Nevertheless, the workload is not fundamentally different. The average workday is about seventeen hours, with about five hours' sleep and, in the summer months, a half-hour rest after lunch. This routine applies seven days a week, fifty-two weeks a year.

Not that Nehru is, in principle, averse to holidays. Prior to Independence he loved to wander in the hills and valleys of Kashmir or in the Kulu valley of the Punjab or in the isolated splendour of the Himalayas viewed from the hill stations of the United Provinces. But the demands of public office have pressed him forward relentlessly, with little time for leisure and relaxation. Aside from a one-week rest on the Indian cruiser *Delhi* *en route* to Indonesia in 1950 and the occasional two- or three-day stay at a hill station, in response to the prodding of his daughter, Nehru had no holiday from 1947 to 1958. And even when in the hills he does not rest; there are speeches to the local population, inauguration ceremonies, correspondence and party gatherings.

This pace would have felled most men somewhere along the road. Certainly, few statesmen pursue their work with such unremitting vigour. What makes it possible is Nehru's storehouse of energy and the benefits of extraordinarily good health. 'I have always attached importance to bodily health and physical fitness', he wrote from prison in the early 'thirties.[1] This is not surprising in the light of family experience. During his formative years at home his mother was fragile and sickly,

---

[1] 'Prison-Land' in *Recent Essays and Writings*, p. 88.

indeed, a semi-invalid throughout her adult life. Later he had to stand by helplessly while his wife struggled in vain against the ravages of tuberculosis. And his only child, Indira, has never enjoyed robust health. Hence, in time, Nehru's concern became a veritable compulsion, a stimulus to guard against severe illness. His addiction to yoga exercises is a continuing reflection of this concern. So too is the exacting care for his physical well-being.

In this ceaseless preventive battle he has been remarkably successful. Nature was kind, endowing him with a resilient and powerful constitution able to cope with the privations of long years in prison. His only known serious illnesses were a severe bout of typhoid in 1923 and a brief attack of pleurisy in prison during the spring of 1934. Since Independence Nehru has rarely been compelled to cancel an engagement because of indisposition. The odd cold, fatigue and an occasional bout of fever, as on the eve of his departure for China in the autumn of 1954, have been the extent of his sickness. It is this bountiful good health which enables him to maintain his furious pace of activity.

What makes it necessary lies more in the realm of speculation. The heart of the matter would appear to be Nehru's temperament: among contemporary statesmen he is perhaps the supreme individualist, a man who feels compelled to do things himself. This was true during the struggle for independence when, by his own admission, Nehru as Congress President also 'functioned often as a secretary or a glorified clerk'.[1] This has also been true of Nehru as Prime Minister. He frequently expresses dissatisfaction with administrative arrangements for a party conclave, the programme at a ceremonial function or the proposed itinerary for one of his tours. His attention to trivia is startling for a man in his position. He continues to act as Congress draftsman, but party resolutions are less important now and could be entrusted to his colleagues. Nehru also insists on handling his vast correspondence direct with the result that he writes thousands of letters a year. And on the minutest affairs of party and government he must be informed. It is not because he desires to occupy the centre of the stage at all times, though his vanity is ill-concealed. Rather, his enthusiasm and

---

[1] Letter to Subhas Bose, 3 April 1939. Unpublished Nehru Letters.

curiosity get the better of him. Indeed, he seems to derive great pleasure from meticulous care about all manner of unimportant things.

Much more than temperament, however, is responsible for Nehru's all-embracing direction of affairs. For one thing, he is acutely conscious of his place in history and is driven to act in all spheres so as to hasten the attainment of his goals. For another, he has never forgotten the disappointments of the 'thirties which led him to write, 'one must journey through life alone; to rely on others is to invite heartbreak'.[1] Moreover, Nehru is essentially a Westerner in his intellectual make-up, and an impatient one at that. He becomes easily annoyed at evidence of inefficiency or an unruly audience and feels constrained to put things right. Lack of order and organization irritate him, as does the Indian indifference to time. Thus in his mission to transform Indian society he feels obliged to act at every level.

Even if he were not so inclined, however, objective circumstance would impose similar pressures. The sense of dependence on Nehru since 1947 is no less apparent than was that of Nehru and others on Gandhi during the freedom struggle. This is due partly to the authoritarian tradition of India, partly to Nehru's status as Gandhi's successor, and partly to his towering position among his colleagues—with the sole exception of Sardar Patel who shared the summit of Indian political power until his death in 1950.

Nehru holds more offices than that of Prime Minister, and even in this position he can hardly be termed 'first among equals'; a more apt description would be 'a giant among pygmies'. He is also the last hero of the freedom struggle, the continuing expression of the movement which fought a successful non-violent war of independence. For the Congress, now in decline, he alone separates the party from electoral defeat. And to the masses he alone seems to offer the promise of a higher standard of living (except for twelve million who voted Communist in 1957). The effect has been to place Nehru on a pedestal, to rely on him for guidance, direction and decision. Colleagues and subordinates feel the necessity of consulting him on a host of issues which should never reach the desk of a Prime Minister, partly because they do not want to risk incurring his

---

[1] *Toward Freedom*, p. 312.

displeasure by making a decision which might be objectionable
to the 'P.M.', partly because he has set the pattern by involving
himself in matters beyond his normal jurisdiction, and partly
because it is obviously easier to let 'Panditji' himself bear the
responsibility. Members of the Congress High Command have
been in the habit of consulting Nehru for thirty years or more;
it is comforting to have his advice today as well.

The extent of his personal involvement in trivia has become
ludicrous, as the following example reveals. While driving

R. K. Laxman: *The Times of India* 27.7.1956

through an exclusive residential area of New Delhi, Nehru
noticed, to his dismay, that laundry was being displayed in
public. Once back in his office he asked the Delhi Municipal
Committee for an explanation; the 'reason' was that the town-
planners had not made ample provision for laundering facilities
along the banks of the Jumna River. Further investigation
showed that the *dhobi* (washerman) union had sought improvements, but in vain. At that point the Prime Minister exploded.
The long-delayed decision was made and a blot on the capital's
appearance was removed.

Nehru has an array of positions of responsibility in the Government and the Congress. Since 1947 he has been Prime Minister and Foreign Minister of India, as well as Head of the Atomic Energy Department; since 1950 he has served as Chairman of the Planning Commission; from 1951 to 1954 he also held the time-consuming post of Congress President, and throughout the period he has served on the party's Working Committee. On various occasions he has filled a gap created by the death or resignation of a Cabinet colleague. In 1953 he held the Defence portfolio for a few months following the death of Gopalaswami Ayyangar; in 1956, the Finance portfolio when C. D. Deshmukh left the Cabinet, and again in 1958 after the resignation of T. T. Krishnamachari.

*   *   *   *

The tenth year of Independence, 1956–7, was, in many respects, a turning-point in the life of Nehru. It was a year of turmoil following a period of relative calm, a year of continuous crisis which tried his faith as no other time since the aftermath of Partition. A few months earlier had come the storm of States Reorganization (SRC) which undermined the foundations of Indian unity—riots in Central India and Orissa, violence and bloodshed in Bombay, tension between Sikh and Hindu in the Punjab, threats and squabbling over the Bengal-Bihar border area. For Nehru it was a bitter personal blow. How often had he preached the virtues of unity to his people. Yet at the first severe test they had failed him. To some extent his own indecision was responsible for the sad chain of events. Nevertheless, the outburst of regional and communal passions augured ill for the future of India.

Amidst the reverberations of SRC came the Hungarian uprising and the spectacle of Soviet repression. This, too, was an event for which he was unprepared. Had not the Russians loudly trumpeted their support for 'peaceful coexistence', non-intervention and the *Panch Shila* (Five Principles) during the tumultuous reception accorded him in Moscow only sixteen months earlier? How could they violate their pledge with such impunity? Did this not make a mockery of the 'Geneva spirit' of 1955 which seemed to offer the prospects of a new era in international relations? At first the lack of direct knowledge and Soviet flattery inclined him to disbelieve Western reports of Russian perfidy and ruthlessness. But as the evidence accumulated he moved towards a mild censure of Soviet actions, reluctantly it appeared, for he did not want to believe that they would act so brazenly against a people struggling for freedom. His own performance during this tragic affair disappointed many persons, both within India and abroad. This was not the Nehru who had spoken so eloquently for oppressed peoples everywhere in the years gone by.

The decline of faith in Soviet sincerity was coupled with a mixture of anger and sadness as the British assault on Suez unfolded. Was this not a symbol of Western Imperialism reborn? Was this the behaviour to be expected from the leader of a commonwealth which India had joined as an independent state? The deep wounds of the past, which had healed so slowly, were now reopened by what he considered to be a dastardly act against a weak, non-white people asserting its rights. Yet along with this disappointment came a more friendly disposition towards the United States which censured its allies and seemed to champion the Egyptian cause.

A few months later the Indian general elections brought new sources of anxiety. The Congress was returned to power at the Centre and in all but one of the States. The results, however, were not entirely reassuring. The Communists had come to power in Kerala through the ballot box; and though they secured only 35 per cent. of the vote they had broken the Congress monopoly of political power. Moreover, they showed disturbing signs of strength in the country as a whole and emerged as the undisputed second party capable of attracting widespread support. Even more disquieting was the evidence of how deep was the rot which had penetrated the once-mighty Congress. Factional strife reached alarming proportions; the struggle for personal power and prestige at all levels in the party continued apace; the leadership was old and tired, and efforts to recruit many good young people were failing. Only Nehru, the ever-receding association with the freedom movement and a nation-wide, often corrupt, machine seemed to hold the Congress together. It was a sick party, with no signs of vitality, while the leading opponent was disciplined, vigorous and united. What would happen to the experiment in constitutional government once Nehru passed from the scene? The future looked bleak as he surveyed the results of the 1957 elections.

There was little time to ponder the long-term significance of the elections. Suddenly, it appeared, India was confronted with a twofold economic crisis, the most alarming since Independence. On the one hand, floods and drought had played havoc with food production, causing serious hardship in many parts of the country and had depleted the slender reserves of foreign exchange. At the same time, large imports, many of them unnecessary consumer goods, also helped to cause a grave shortage of foreign exchange—precisely at a time of need for industrial development projects. Only two years earlier India appeared to have almost reached self-sufficiency in food, a pre-condition to economic progress. And only one year before, the Second Five Year Plan had been launched with high hopes of success. Now the Plan was in jeopardy unless the staggering sum of $1·4 billion could be raised abroad as loans or gifts. The spectre of failure on the vital economic front began to haunt Indian minds. Even if the short-term financial problem were solved, the crisis indicated how steep and rocky was the road to economic development. Thus, as India moved into the second decade of independence Nehru had ample reason for concern.

The effect of these crises on the Prime Minister was profound. His buoyant spirit and vivid enthusiasm of earlier years have been less in evidence since 1956. They have largely given way to a more sober appreciation of the facts of Indian and international life. It is as if Nehru discovered India afresh, not in a romantic setting as in the past but in all its harsh realities. With this rediscovery there came a deeper insight, a greater awareness of the intractable nature of certain problems and the impossibility of changing such deep-rooted institutions as caste overnight. The result has been a tendency to be less agitated about these things in public, for he realizes that shouting alone is not enough. As one person, who knows the Prime Minister intimately, remarked, 'he is now seeking footholds to scale the walls instead of smashing his head against the walls, as in the past'.[1]

[1] To the author in New Delhi in January 1958 by a person who wishes to remain anonymous.

The 'new' Jawaharlal is less confident about the future, less exuberant and less temperamental than the 'old'. He has mellowed a great deal. His outbursts of anger and irritation are much less frequent. He is inclined to be more patient with colleagues and subordinates, and more tolerant of human failings. An air of almost philosophic calm appears to have descended upon the mercurial Indian leader. Typical of the change was an incident on a tour of Rajasthan in 1957. New stamps had been issued to commemorate the union of the Rajput princely States, and Nehru asked a member of his staff to get a set. At breakfast one day he was informed that his subordinate had forgotten the request. The Nehru of years gone by would undoubtedly have shown extreme and loud displeasure. On this occasion, however, he merely remarked quietly, 'Let's stop at the post office and I will get them myself.'[1]

The spark is not yet gone. Given the right stimulus, he can still respond pungently; but on the whole he is more restrained. It would be wrong to infer that Nehru is a defeated man. Rather, he is wiser, less quick to anger and more balanced in his attitude to men and affairs. This is true not only of India's internal problems but also of the international situation. More particularly, he appears to have fewer illusions about the Soviet Union and greater regard for the United States, partly because of the Hungarian tragedy and Suez War, and partly because of his unexpectedly warm reception in America and his conversations with President Eisenhower at the end of 1956. In sum, the crises of 1956–7 produced a rounding off of the edges and, ironically, a greater sense of inner calm in the face of external turmoil.

Inevitably the advancing years have deepened his sense of loneliness. One by one fellow pilgrims to independent India have passed from the scene, including the few persons with whom Nehru had a genuine intellectual and emotional friendship: first Gandhi and then Sarojini Naidu, the 'nightingale of the Congress'; then Rafi Kidwai, and most recently Maulana Azad. The few colleagues of long standing who remain either were never intimate friends, like the President of India, Dr. Rajendra Prasad, or have drifted away for various reasons, like Rajagopalacharia, who indulges in Olympian criticism from

[1] To the author in New Delhi in January 1958 by a person who wishes to remain anonymous.

his retreat in the south, and Jaya Prakash Narayan, the former Socialist leader, whom many considered Nehru's heir-apparent until the mid-1950's. Nor have younger men emerged to fill this vacuum, even in part.

Nehru has always loved to indulge in quick repartée. Nor is he averse to gaiety and laughter. But the occasions for such pleasure have become fewer in recent years. Apart from family birthday parties, including his own, the only setting in which his *joie de vivre* readily comes to the fore is in the company of children, notably his daughter's two sons, Rajiv and Sanjay. Until a few years ago they lived at his home with their mother and provided a constant source of joy and relaxation. Even now, during holidays from school, they add a much-sought element of lightheartedness to the otherwise forbidding atmosphere of the palatial Residence.[1]

Nehru's attachment to children is well known. Their candour and honesty are refreshing, their exuberance contagious. His shyness seems to evaporate as he descends to their level and joins them in carefree play. Never is he more relaxed than with youngsters, whether at a house party or at the National Stadium in Delhi on November 14th, his birthday, celebrated as Children's Day since 1954. 'Chacha Nehru', uncle Nehru, they call him, and his face glows as he watches them, the future hope of India. Their continued faith in him is also a source of happiness, and he responds with spontaneous affection. In recent years he has developed the habit of writing warm and sensitive letters to the children of India and the world.[2]

Another result of 'the year of crisis' was the beginning of disenchantment with Nehru's political leadership. The masses continued to adore him. But in the vocal section of India's

[1] It was at Lord Mountbatten's suggestion that Nehru moved to the former home of British Commanders-in-Chief which stands at one end of South Avenue, facing the even gloomier, museum-like *Rashtrapati Bhawan*, the former Viceroy's Palace and now the President's home. Many Indians deplored his decision to abandon the modest, intimate bungalow at 17 York Road for the sumptuous surroundings of the Residence, among other reasons, because of the example set for other public servants. In 1957, as part of an economy drive, a decision was reached in principle to construct a rather simple, five-bedroom home for the Prime Minister in the grounds of the Residence.

[2] See for example his letters in *Shankar's Weekly* (New Delhi), 3 December 1949 and 26 December 1950 (Children's Numbers). Reprinted in *Jawaharlal Nehru's Speeches 1949–1953*, pp. 439–41 and pp. 442–4 respectively. See also his letter in December 1957 reprinted in *Weekend Magazine* (Montreal), 21 December 1957, p. 7.

population questioning and critical voices multiplied. Some focused on his vacillation during States Reorganization, others on his initial rationalization of the Soviet onslaught on Hungary; some commented on his alleged inability to put the Congress house in order, and still others were dissatisfied with his handling of the economic problem. The novelty of this attitude lay in the crucial and unhealthy fact that prior to 1956 criticism of Nehru had been virtually non-existent—except for the extreme Right and Left wings of the political spectrum.

Since then he has not been accorded such widespread adulation. The conviction of indispensability has ebbed. Indeed, it became fashionable for intellectuals and middle-class Indians openly to criticize him, a healthy development for Indian democracy. The decline in popularity has been marginal in numbers and influence. But even this contributed to the change in mood, weakening, however imperceptibly, his drive and dedication. Beyond specific issues, there was a somewhat muted feeling that after ten years in power Nehru should give younger men an opportunity to bear some of his responsibilities. Yet, when he expressed the desire to resign as Prime Minister in the spring of 1958, there was an outcry among his party followers, and he was persuaded to yield.

Despite the strain of recent years, Nehru retains a zest for life and an abundant supply of energy. He retains, too, his love of nature, his fondness for animals—like the pandas and tiger cub which have offered pleasant diversions at the Residence—and his interest in games. Whenever he goes to the hills, he indulges his childhood pleasure in riding and walking. Nevertheless, he has aged considerably since 'the year of crisis'. He tires more quickly than before, according to colleagues, and he has begun to show signs of marked fatigue. No longer does he bound up the stairs to his office in the Ministry three at a time. He moves more slowly and reacts less quickly than the Nehru of old. The river of time, which seemed to stand still for him mentally and physically until a relatively advanced age, has moved at a rapid pace since 1957.

*   *   *   *

The change in Nehru's mood, the decline in popularity, the ageing process in recent years—all this became apparent to a foreign observer in India at the beginning of 1958. These insights were gleaned from interviews with well-informed Indians, from the press and from the atmosphere of India. Most of all they emerged from another lengthy interview with the Indian Prime Minister which I was privileged to have.[1]

When I was ushered into his spacious office in External Affairs he was standing behind a huge, neat desk, poring over some papers. The first impression was that age had caught up with him at last, that he had begun to look elderly. A handsome man still, but no longer with the youthful appearance which I recalled vividly from my first meeting with him two years earlier. The lines on his face were more pronounced, the eyes seemed sadder, the general expression was one of fatigue. He moved slowly to his seat, placed his hands under his chin and waited for me to begin. His mind seemed far away, preoccupied with one or another of the many problems besetting India in this, the eleventh year of independence.

After glancing at a list of prepared questions he moved forward in his chair, a faded rose prominently displayed in his brown *achkan* jacket.[2] A sword-like letter-opener in his left hand served as a diversion while he thought aloud in his usual manner. This time, however, he spoke more slowly and softly, with longer lapses for thought. As he reflected on the past and the future he moved the 'sword' in and out of its scabbard, an apparent outlet for nervous energy. Frequently his right hand was raised to his head in a stroking motion. He seemed fidgety throughout the hour-long interview. At times he moved forward and stared straight ahead as he spoke; at other times he sat back in his chair while his mind wandered back to the great events in his growth to public prominence. His monologue added little to the known record, but it was a moving perform-

---

[1] The following account is based on the author's notes, taken immediately after the interview.

[2] For some years Nehru has always worn a rose in the button-hole of his tunic. The habit began as the result of a curious incident. One morning, as he was leaving the Residence for his office, an admirer tried to present him with a rose. At first she was prevented from doing so by the guards. But the lady persisted. Every morning she waited at the gate with a fresh flower. She was finally rewarded; Nehru accepted the gracious gesture. When the gardener at the Residence noticed this he assumed that the Prime Minister was fond of wearing flowers in his tunic. Hence he prepared a fresh rose each morning from the lovely gardens in the estate. The habit has continued ever since, even when Nehru is away from the capital.

ance, an intensely human self-analysis by an extraordinary person.

He swung his chair to the side and ran his fingers through his fringe of white hair. There was a pensive, withdrawn expression on his face as he searched out the past, the long, eventful road to his position of eminence in India and the world at large. After what seemed like an unusually long silence, a slight, almost embarrassed smile appeared, his eyes lit up, and the glow of pride transformed his expression of fatigue. One could almost observe his memory at work, with an endless flow of impressions, of persons and places and experiences in the moulding of his character and outlook—and the moulding of independent India.

He began, somewhat self-consciously, by referring to the special position he occupied at the outset of his career by virtue of his father's prominence and Gandhi's fondness for the young man. 'At that time I didn't think very much about myself', he continued. 'We were so involved in the struggle, so wrapped up in what we were doing that I had little time or inclination to give thought to my own growth.' His words exuded warmth, sincerity and humility. They were simple words, gentle words, gently spoken in an honest portrait of his past.

Certain landmarks are deeply rooted in Nehru's memory. The first to be mentioned was *Jallianwalla Bagh*—the Amritsar Tragedy in 1919—the effect of which has been feelingly described in his autobiography. Along with this, 'my visit to the villages'—his discovery of the peasant in 1920—and 'my first close contact with Gandhi'. In 1920–1, 'I lived my intensest,' he continued, referring to the first civil disobedience campaign. Then came prison, 'a period with no peaks of experience'. Despite the sharp change from a life of activity and fulfilment, 'I adjusted very well. I have that capacity, you know. I was much less agitated than my colleagues by events outside; there was nothing I could do about it so why get involved. I was interested, of course, but I adjusted very well to the changes which prison brought.' Later, he returned to his prison experience. As he talked freely, he conveyed more poignantly than anything he has written the lasting effects of the nine years of enforced isolation from the outside world. 'I did a lot of reading and writing', he remarked casually. He also learned the art of self-discipline and used his time to think through the next phase of the struggle for Indian freedom. There was no hint in his words of anger at his captors, nothing to suggest that his experience had produced resentment. A Gandhian spirit of forgiveness seemed to permeate his attitude as he reflected on the lonely days and nights behind the walls. But he has not forgotten them.

The next milestone was the Lahore Congress in 1929 'which remains vivid in my memory'. Understandably so, for this was the year Nehru came of age politically, the first time he was elected Congress President. Suddenly he remembered his European sojourn in 1926–7, 'which gave me time to think, to broaden my outlook, to see India from afar, to think on life itself. Until then I was so involved in Indian affairs that I had little time to think about the broad world or about life's problems in general.'

He turned next to 'whither India', to the probable course of Indian society in the next generation. His tone was one of cautious optimism, but clearly optimistic. 'We shall certainly have our ups and downs, but I have no doubt that we shall go forward, perhaps a little more slowly than we should like, but forward none the less.'

Nehru is one of those men who refuse to lose hope. He has had good reasons to be disappointed with the trend of many events in India and abroad. His faith in man—everywhere—remains. He has moments of doubt, but his deep belief in the ability and desire of India and the world to solve their problems dispels misgivings. Caste would gradually fade away, he said, though the process would be slow. So too with economic development which might proceed less quickly than he and others would like. Although tired and seemingly aware that he may have entered the final stage of his public life, Nehru showed that he retains a determined faith in the future.

Little time remained, for he had dealt with his early life at leisure. But he seemed oblivious of the clock and began a discourse on the world situation. I asked if he had reason to feel optimistic in the light of the preceding year. 'There are some hopeful features', he began, seizing upon the brighter side of the picture. 'Take Hungary, for instance. The events of 1956 show that Communism, if it is imposed on a country from outside, cannot last. I mean to say [a characteristic expression] if Communism goes against the basic national spirit, it will not be accepted. In those countries where it has allied itself with nationalism it is, of course, a powerful force. As in China; in Russia, too.

'The events in Suez also brought out an important fact. It is no longer possible for strong, former colonial powers to return to areas they once ruled.' His discussion of Suez underlined the continuing influence of Colonialism on his thought.

He then turned to Eastern Europe. He seemed convinced that the Russians would ease their grip on the entire area 'once this wretched Cold War is ended'. 'Once, perhaps, Eastern Europe was of benefit to Russia, economically and strategically. But now—well, look at Hungary—and Poland. It is a major cost to the Russians; strategically, it is of little value, and they have lost a great deal in world opinion. They will give it up, but not as long as they feel threatened.'

That the Soviets still labour under the psychology of siege, Nehru appeared to believe at the beginning of 1958. 'As Khrustchev said to me, "for forty years we have had to defend ourselves". They have never had a chance to settle down. If only they were allowed to do so, this fear would give way and then they could give up their hold on Eastern Europe.' This remark was ventured three months after the launching of the first Soviet satellite. It provided insight into the point of departure for Indian policy-making regarding European problems and Nehru's attitude to the Cold War which he clearly regarded as the great evil.

This was further clarified by his observations on military pacts and Western policy, particularly the idea of bargaining from strength. 'I cannot see the value of a military approach to these problems. This approach can no longer solve any problems. Besides, I do not see why some people in the West think the Russians are out to conquer other peoples. They are not interested in this. It is only when a neighbour is hostile that they try to weaken it. The Russian people want peace. So do the Americans. In fact, they are so similar, the Russians and the Americans. If only they could agree to end the Cold War.'

On the world situation in general he made the following comment, more revealing of his personality than the subject itself.

'Viewed logically, there is much to be pessimistic about—but looked at in a human way there is a good deal to be optimistic about.' By this he meant, as he later elaborated, that people everywhere were yearning for peace and that the force of public opinion in all lands would make itself felt, as the awful consequences of nuclear war became understood; and they were now understood by thinking people everywhere. On this note the interview came to a close.

Nehru had aged since I last saw him in Ottawa a year before. He also seemed more mellow, more troubled, more tired. But the most vivid impression was a quality of deep sincerity, a human touch which breathes warmth and tenderness. Throughout the interview I felt that here was a sensitive man who had succeeded in absorbing the shocks of life without coarsening his mind, character and personality.

CHAPTER II

The Young Brahmin

INDIA in the 1880's was a land of relative tranquillity. The flames which had fired the Rebellion of 1857 had long since been extinguished. The Moghul Court in Delhi, symbol of the revolt and heir to an illustrious dynasty, finally made its exit from the stage of Indian history. So too did the East India Company, that remarkable private corporation which conquered the sub-continent for Crown and Investor. The Company had sown the seeds of discontent and had, therefore, been swept away in the aftermath of rebellion. In 1858, direct Crown rule was imposed on British India. Along with this constitutional change came a complete reversal of the Company's policies, in an effort to pacify the dominant groups in Indian society—the princes, the Brahmins and the landlords.

Hostility to the princes and annexation of their territories, which had marked the last phase of Company rule, were replaced by unqualified support for the princely order. The policy of social reform, which had threatened the prestige and time-honoured prerogatives of the Brahmin (priest) caste, gave way to social conservatism. And the expropriation of certain estates, which had aroused the fear and wrath of the landed gentry, was terminated by the new dispensation. By these abrupt and fundamental changes in imperial policy, the three most influential groups in Indian society were rallied to the British connection, a loyal aristocracy whose interests and privileges were identified with the perpetuation of British rule. The spearhead of the Rebellion, the army, was also transformed into a reliable instrument of British power. Thus, when Queen Victoria was proclaimed Empress of India in 1877, amidst the pomp and splendour of a Delhi Durbar, British power in India was at its peak.

The white *sahib* was lord of all he could survey. From the Himalayas in the north to Cape Comorin, from Kathiawar in the west to the borders of Burma, he ruled unchallenged, set the standards for law and morality, and occupied positions of un-rivalled status and influence. A new super-caste had been imposed on the traditional social structure. It was a narrow world, in which self-imposed segregation prevailed, social contact being confined to members of the ruling race. There was, too, a sense of civilizing mission. It seemed inconceivable that Indians could ever master the complexities of self-government, and the 'white man's burden' provided a satisfying rationalization for those who wielded enormous power over millions of 'natives'. It was the hey-day of the *Raj*.

And yet, beneath the surface of secure British power the rumblings of discontent could be heard in the late 1870's and early 1880's. The peasantry, then as now the largest class in Indian society, did not pose a serious threat at the time, for it lacked political consciousness, organization and leadership. But a serious famine in 1877, coinciding with the costly Durbar attending Queen Victoria's assumption of the imperial title, roused the slumbering peasant masses, creating the fear of an agrarian revolt. Curtailment of freedom of the press and other unpopular legislative enactments of the period caused dissatisfaction among the urban élite, which was in the process of formation during the last half of the nineteenth century. Indeed, far more important than these specific events was the growth of new classes in Indian society, largely as a result of the very character of British rule.

The growing needs of the bureaucracy, with the expansion of governmental activities, and the new professions of law, medicine and teaching, inspired by the British, were creating a Western-type intelligentsia which was imbibing the spirit of English liberalism and the ideas of national freedom then sweeping Europe. By the 1880's it was beginning to make its voice heard, haltingly and timidly at first but in the direction of political reform. Parallel with its growth was the creation of a new merchant-industrial class as a result of the economic penetration of the interior by means of railways, the growth of trade and commerce, and the greater integration of India into the world economy following the opening of the Suez Canal. With the emergence of these classes the foundations of a nationalist movement were laid—though few were aware of its significance at the time. The intellectuals were to provide its leadership, and the merchant-industrialists the necessary funds, without

C

which an effective political organization could not be built. In time their message was to reach the peasantry, and ultimately they were to attain complete independence.

The origins of national consciousness in modern India are to be found in Bengal, the area which had the longest contact with British rule and the most highly developed political awareness in the sub-continent. From the early part of the nineteenth century onwards, various organizations, such as the *Brahmo Samaj* (Brahmin Society), founded in 1828, and the Indian Association, founded in 1875, had come into being as forums for the expression of views by Hindu reformers and the intelligentsia respectively. Gradually the idea of a representative, national body took root and, in 1885, the Indian National Congress was formed. The initiative for its creation was taken by an Englishman, Alan Octavian Hume, a retired member of the Indian Civil Service, with the blessing of the Viceroy, Lord Dufferin.

At its inception and, indeed, for the first twenty years of its existence, the Congress was an unimpressive body. Only seventy-two delegates, almost all from the new professions, gathered in Bombay for the first session. The speeches, all of them in English, abounded in expressions of loyalty to the Crown. The demands were of a peripheral nature, focusing on minor administrative reforms which would enable the intelligentsia to play a more active role in public affairs. The early Congress leaders were anxious for greater prestige and influence, but within the framework of the existing régime. Many years were to elapse before the vision of independent India was to capture the imagination of the Congress and the millions whom it came to represent. Yet the intelligentsia had made its appearance on the stage of Indian politics. From its ranks were to be drawn all the great figures of the nationalist movement: Gokhale and Tilak from Maharashtra; Gandhi and Patel from Gujarat; Motilal Nehru from the United Provinces; C. R. Das and Subhas Bose from Bengal; and Lajpat Rai from the Punjab. From the intelligentsia, too, came the most romantic and heroic figure in modern Indian history, Jawaharlal Nehru.[1]

*   *   *   *

[1] In historical analysis it is inherently difficult to prevent hindsight from creeping into the interpretation of events. It may well be that some of the aspirations attributed here to Indian nationalists in the early stage of their struggle for freedom found

While the Congress was making its inauspicious début, in an atmosphere of quiescence and submissiveness, a young, unknown lawyer named Motilal Nehru was beginning his practice at the High Court in Allahabad, a sleepy town in the United Provinces, more famous for pilgrimage than for politics. He had come there from Kanpur after three years of apprenticeship and was soon to establish a reputation as a brilliant and successful barrister.

The Nehrus are Brahmins, Kashmiri Brahmins, the élite group in Hindu society. It is a small community but renowned for its tradition of learning, its handsome men and delicately beautiful women—and its inordinate pride. The Allahabad branch of the family was seven generations removed from its ancestral home. But like his son, Jawaharlal, Motilal was proud of his origins in the fabled Valley of Kashmir, so much so that Allahabad was a place of self-exile from their beloved homeland.

It was early in the eighteenth century, around the year 1716, that one of Motilal's forbears, a distinguished Sanskrit and Arabic scholar, Raj Kaul by name, migrated to the plains at the invitation of the reigning Moghul Emperor. In the feudal tradition of the age, he was given a small estate beside a canal, on the outskirts of Delhi. From this fortuitous circumstance derives the present family name—Nehru from *nahar*, the Urdu word for canal. For some time the family was known as Kaul-Nehru; later, the original name was dropped.

As long as the Moghuls reigned in Delhi—they had ceased to rule effectively by the middle of the eighteenth century—the Nehrus remained in the imperial capital, occupying positions of greater or lesser importance in the administration. Motilal's father, Pandit Ganga Dhar Nehru, was the *Kotwal* (police chief) of Delhi; his grandfather served as the first legal adviser to the East India Company at the royal court. But with the ignominious demise of the Moghuls, after the collapse of the Rebellion, the Nehrus migrated to Agra, the site of that magnificent monument to Moghul architectural genius, the Taj Mahal. It

their full expression only many years later. A conscious effort has been made to limit the telescoping of events to the minimum required by clarity and brevity in a background survey of this kind. In any event, it seems reasonable to suggest that the general *spirit* of early nationalist hopes has been captured by the above account.

was there that Motilal Nehru was born, on 6 May 1861, the same day as Rabindranath Tagore, the greatest poet of modern India.

Motilal was a posthumous child. In the tradition of the Hindu joint family he became the responsibility of his elder brothers, notably Nandlal Nehru, a moderately successful lawyer at the High Court in Agra. When the Court moved to Allahabad, the family migrated to this quiet, provincial town, known in ancient times as Prayag. Allahabad is famous as the point of convergence of the holy Ganges and Jumna Rivers—and the legendary Saraswati. Here millions gather annually for the *Magh Mela* ceremony and, every twelve years, for the mammoth *Kumbh Mela* festival.

Until the age of twelve Motilal was educated at home, largely in Persian and Arabic. This was somewhat unusual for Brahmins, except in the United Provinces where the fusion of Hindu and Muslim cultures had reached its peak. In time this unique cultural blend was to exert a profound influence on Motilal's son. Thereafter, Motilal attended the Government High School in Kanpur and Muir Central College in Allahabad. There, under the influence of his English professors, he began to admire Western ideas and ways of living. However, Motilal failed to take the B.A.; he wrote the first exam but absented himself from the others in the erroneous belief that he had started badly. Despite this handicap he sat for the *vakil* (lawyer) examinations and led his class. Then, after his apprenticeship in Kanpur, he settled down in Allahabad in 1886 to practise law at the High Court. The death of his brother the following year was a grievous blow and placed the burden of family responsibility on the young man of twenty-six. By sheer talent and a capacity for prolonged and concentrated work, Motilal rose rapidly in his profession. Within a few years he was recognized as one of the outstanding lawyers in Allahabad. It was there that his only son was born, on 14 November 1889. His name: Jawaharlal, the red jewel.

His parents doted upon the youngster, and with good reason. He was the first child to survive, and Indians attach great importance to an assurance of continuity in the family name. There had been much tragedy in Motilal's married life prior to the arrival of Jawaharlal. He had been married once before, there had been a child, and both mother and child had died. A child had been born to Motilal and his second wife but it too had died in infancy. Hence Jawaharlal was the object of their complete devotion and love. And as the only child of a wealthy barrister for eleven years—his sister Swarup, better known as Mrs. Vijaya Lakshmi Pandit, was born in 1900—he was spoiled in a princely fashion.

Until Jawaharlal was three the family lived in the city proper, near the *chowk* (market), amidst congestion and crowds. Then, as Motilal's practice became increasingly lucrative, it moved to the Civil Lines, the exclusive residential area where Europeans lived in splendour. Only one other Indian family lived there at the time. The Nehru home at 9 Elgin Road was unpretentious, but luxurious compared to those of almost all other Indians in Allahabad. In 1900, when Jawaharlal was ten, his father purchased a palatial home which he named *Anand Bhawan* (Abode of Happiness). Thus, for all practical purposes, the young Nehru lived in comfortable surroundings throughout the formative period of his life. No less important was the fact that, apart from the period of infancy, he lived amongst Europeans until the age of twenty-two, first in Allahabad, then at Harrow, Cambridge and in London. And even at home the atmosphere was more typically English than Indian, for Motilal Nehru, like most of the intelligentsia of his generation, admired everything British and was inclined to emulate their ways.

In his early education, too, the young Nehru was subjected to European influences. Perhaps because of his own experience, Motilal was opposed to the education of his children in public schools. As one of his daughters later related, he thought it more appropriate for them 'to have lessons in solitary grandeur with a governess'.[1] From the pre-school age until he left for England at the age of fifteen Nehru was trained at home by private tutors, most of them British. His education in Indian languages was not entirely neglected, however. Learned Brahmins were assigned to teach him Hindi and Sanskrit, but apparently without much success. As Jawaharlal wrote, 'after many years' effort the Pandit managed to teach me extraordinarily little, so little that I can only measure my pitiful knowledge of Sanskrit with the Latin I learned subsequently at Harrow'.[2]

[1] Hutheesingh, Krishna Nehru, *With No Regrets*, p. 22.   [2] *Toward Freedom*, p. 28.

The education of the young Brahmin in Allahabad had a pronounced English bias. As a result, though 'I was filled with
resentment against the alien rulers of my country who mis-
behaved . . . I had no feeling whatever, so far as I can remember, against individual Englishmen. . . . In my heart I rather
admired the English.'[1]

Life at home was not unpleasant for the young Jawaharlal.
An atmosphere of luxury and security pervaded *Anand Bhawan*.
Motilal loved life and lived it in the patrician manner. Every
material comfort was available, including the latest scientific
gadgets of the age. There were two swimming-pools, one in the
palatial garden, another in the house itself. One of the more
impressive stables in India enabled the young Nehru to become
a proficient horseman and to develop a taste for riding which
persisted throughout his adult life. In his urge to imitate
Western habits, and perhaps to satisfy an inner need for recognition, Motilal imported the first motor-car into India. Nothing
was spared in his effort to transplant to provincial Allahabad
the standards and ways of life prevailing in the country estates
of English aristocrats. He entertained royally, English officials
as well as Indians, both Hindu and Muslim, and maintained
three separate kitchens to satisfy the diverse needs of his guests.

For Jawaharlal, nothing was beyond reach. His every whim
was catered for by an army of servants. Motilal clearly intended
to raise his son in the image of an English gentleman. To a large
extent he succeeded. And yet, Jawaharlal was a lonely child.
There were many children at *Anand Bhawan*, including his
cousins, Brijlal, Mohenlal and Shyamlal Nehru, but no one of
his own age. Moreover, his father's insistence on a private
education isolated him from schoolboys in the neighbourhood.
He was, too, a shy and diffident boy, qualities which were enhanced by this 'splendid isolation'.

Of his parents, Jawaharlal's father exerted much the more
pronounced influence. Motilal was entirely a self-made man,
with all the virtues and vices of that type. He was proud,
strong-willed, imperious, and possessed of a ferocious temper.
He fitted the image of a patriarch perfectly, expected obedience,
and dominated all those about him. Excessively generous, he
earned vast sums of money and spent most of it on his family.

[1] *Toward Freedom*, p. 21.

All who knew him agree that he was a formidable and commanding figure, in appearance very much like a Roman senator, with a remarkable strength of character and rock-like will. Motilal had little imagination and was in no sense an original thinker, but he possessed an uncommon common sense. He was intensely practical, and disdainful of theoretical subtleties. He was not particularly eloquent, but he was lucid, logical, precise, witty and sarcastic, interspersing his remarks with pointed quotations from Persian and Arabic poetry. He was affable among friends and guests, and an entertaining raconteur. He was, according to all who knew him, a complete man, with many-sided interests and activities. In every sphere of life in which he was interested he towered above those about him. He was acknowledged to have no peer at the Allahabad Bar; he set the fashion for contemporaries of his class; he was more advanced than anyone else in the United Provinces in his liberal social ideas; and he was responsible for a secular outlook in the Congress organization of his province.

Typical of the attitude of British officials in India who knew him is a portrait of Motilal Nehru by Sir Frederick James, sometime Finance Member of the Viceroy's Executive Council:

He was a nationalist, but a cosmopolitan; at home in any society and with every race. He was a distinguished lawyer and a powerful advocate; also a man of charm, culture and tolerance. He represented in many respects the highest type of civilization. He was, in fact, a Grand Seigneur—such as those who have appeared in all the great epochs of history. . . . I remember particularly his exquisite courtesy and delightful deference to youth. No wonder he was adored by his family. He was the perfect host. His hospitality was generous and of a high order. . . . His home, which was always open, was the Mecca of all who enjoyed the good things of life and who looked to him as a great lawyer and national leader. Motilal had the dignified, clear-cut features and fair skin of a Kashmiri Brahmin of ancient lineage. He was always immaculate in dress whether in European or Indian style. . . . What struck me most [about his speeches in the legislature] was his tolerance towards his political enemies. No querulousness, irritation or bitterness marred his reasoned statement of his case, whether legal or political. . . . Motilal was generous in everything that he did. There were no half-measures.[1]

[1] Extracts from an unpublished memoir kindly made available to the author by Sir Frederick in London in October 1955.

All of Motilal's children acknowledged his predominant influence within the family. Mrs. Pandit offered the following reflections: 'In the formative period of our lives, it was father who played the dominant role. He had a magnetic personality, domineering, yes, but not with the family. With us, he was kind and thoughtful, a person who drew everyone to him, who commanded respect.' She then related that 'in the evening, after a hard day at the office, father would have his cocktail—a rare thing in those days but he was very westernized—would laugh and joke and demand that all of us participate in the proceedings whether we were five or twenty or fifty. All of us acknowledged his place in the family, a joint family it was then.'[1]

Similar views were expressed by Mrs. Krishna Hutheesingh, the youngest of Motilal Nehru's children. Some years ago, in a fragment of an autobiography, she described her father 'as a tower of strength to his children . . . with a certain grandeur and magnificence that was bound to command the respect of all who knew him. . . . His one fault was his temper . . . a fault handed down to him from a long line of ancestors and not one of us is immune from it. Perhaps his only weakness was his amazing love for his children. . . . Whilst he was alive, we lived a happy, carefree life, knowing he was there to guard and protect us.'[2]

Jawaharlal's attitude to his father was ambivalent. He, too, experienced this sense of security radiating from Motilal's personality. He 'admired [his] father tremendously', saw him as 'the embodiment of strength and courage and cleverness', and wrote of him as the ideal to which he aspired. 'But much as I admired him and loved him I feared him also. I had seen him lose his temper . . . he seemed to me terrible then, and I shivered with fright, mixed sometimes with resentment, at the treatment of a servant. His temper was indeed an awful thing, and even in after years I do not think I ever came across anything to match it. . . . But, fortunately, he had a strong sense of humour also and an iron will and he could control himself as a rule. . . .'[3]

Many years later, on the ninety-fifth anniversary of his father's

---

[1] To the author in London in October 1955.
[2] Hutheesingh, op. cit., pp. 75–77.
[3] *Toward Freedom*, pp. 21–22.

birth, Jawaharlal referred to him as 'something like a Renaissance prince. . . . Maybe, in times of trouble in the earlier days, he might have been a founder of some principality. . . . He created naturally a very great impression on me not only because he was my father, but because he was what he was. . . . You might say that whenever he went to a gathering he became the centre of that gathering.' It was his father's perseverance and strength of character that stood out in Nehru's mind. 'I have no doubt that he would have succeeded in any other activity of life which he had undertaken. In normal times, he would have remained a successful lawyer, maybe a successful politician too. But in abnormal times he would have risen to the top.'[1]

The contrast between father and son in those early days, and the atmosphere of his home life in Allahabad left lasting impressions on Jawaharlal Nehru. The shy, reticent, aesthetically-inclined son stood in awe of his father's personality. Emotionally his growth was stunted by Motilal's all-embracing strength. There was no inducement to make decisions, for his father provided the symbol and substance of security. Doubt and vacillation date from this early association with his father. So, too, it would appear, does his respect for decisive and strong men— men such as Gandhi and Mountbatten, men who acted boldly and swiftly, men of perseverance and self-confidence. Thus, too, the duality in his later years, of lucid thought along with constant doubt about the appropriate course of action.

From his father Jawaharlal inherited or acquired certain qualities which remain embedded in his personality. Among these were pride—pride in his own achievements, in his family, in his Kashmiri ancestry and in his people; a fierce temper, though like his father he learned to control it in his later years; magnetic charm; and a somewhat haughty, imperious attitude to his colleagues.

Still another legacy of his home in Allahabad was a broad secular outlook, one of Nehru's significant contributions to the nationalist movement and readily apparent in his voluminous writings and speeches. Three cultural strands pervaded *Anand Bhawan* and provide the key to the atmosphere in which the young Nehru spent his formative years. Although not a religious

[1] An interview with Prime Minister Nehru, on All-India Radio, 5 May 1956.

man, Motilal adhered to certain Hindu customs regarding family and social matters, largely out of deference to his wife who retained her orthodox beliefs throughout her life. The predominant Indian influence was Moghul culture which prevailed in the western parts of the United Provinces, and still does to a considerable degree. Motilal knew Persian and Arabic much better than either Sanskrit or Hindi; in fact, like so many of his contemporaries, he had contempt for Hindi. There was, too, the intellectual and social influence of the West; the English language, which was like a mother tongue to Jawaharlal; English dress, which he shed only after he joined Gandhi's movement at the age of thirty; and the manners of the English aristocrat, many of which have remained a part of his make-up. Of all the Indian languages the only one which Nehru has mastered with reasonable competence is Urdu, the Moghul derivative of Persian and Hindi. And he has always felt more at ease in English, for both the written and spoken word. In fact, all his works have been written in English, in a fluent, sensitive style.

Both parents were immensely proud of their son, though his mother was much more demonstrative in her show of affection. For her, he could do no wrong; and even after the arrival of her two daughters, Jawaharlal remained the favourite. Of Swarup Rani Nehru little has been written. Like her children during their formative years, she lived in the shadow of the benevolent and towering patriarch that was Motilal Nehru. Unlike the Nehrus, hers was an orthodox family which had descended to the plains from the Valley of Kashmir only two generations before. She had little formal education, as was customary for women at the time, never spoke English well, and never fully approved her husband's Western habits, though she adjusted to them in time. According to her elder daughter, 'Mother was a charming and delicate person, a fragile woman, afflicted with ill-health; she was a good, gentle Hindu wife whose life was wrapped around that of her husband. Yet, as I think back, I realize now that mother did influence us all, though indirectly.'[1]

From her marriage, at the age of thirteen, she occupied a submissive but none the less vital role in the Nehru home, dominated first by her in-laws, then by her husband, and later by her

---

[1] Related to the author in London in October 1955.

children. Of fair complexion and hazel eyes, she was tiny and doll-like with small beautifully shaped hands and feet. She was born and bred in luxury and was pampered by everyone about her. Life had been kind to Swarup Rani Nehru. She had a devoted husband, a famous name, wealth, leisure, comfort and three children upon whom she could dote to her heart's content. Yet, later in life, she became a semi-invalid and was confined to her bed for many months at a time. Most of her life was absorbed in her children and home. However, with the traumatic change in the Nehru way of living in 1920, when her husband and son joined Gandhi's non-co-operation movement, she gave up many comforts and joined in the fray, even to the extent of participating in demonstrations and courting arrest.

There are few references to his mother in Nehru's lengthy autobiography. Partly because of his father's preoccupation with work, partly because of the boy's fear, and partly because of his mother's unconcealed and protective love, Jawaharlal was drawn to her in the early years. To some extent he sought compensation for his father's domination. 'I had no fear of her, for I knew that she would condone everything I did, and, because of her excessive and indiscriminating love for me, I tried to dominate over her a little. I saw much more of her than I did of father, and she seemed nearer to me, so I would confide in her when I would not dream of doing so to father.'[1] Yet it is doubtful that she exerted more than a token influence on the formation of her son's character and outlook.

The young Nehru's leisure hours were whiled away in a variety of activities—swimming, cricket, tennis, riding and the like. He enjoyed an occasional dip in the Ganges, not because of any spiritual sustenance but because of the joy derived from communion with crowds. There were, too, visits to temples and the many Hindu festivals, which provided much enjoyment but to which he attached no religious significance. In fact, of religion proper he had only 'hazy notions' and tried to emulate the casual attitude of his father and elder cousins. 'It seemed to be a woman's affair', he wrote of his early indifference to religious beliefs. Later this was to blossom into agnosticism, though since the mid-1940's he has been more conscious of the role of religion. Occasional journeys to distant towns for a family marriage

[1] *Toward Freedom*, p. 22.

were times of excitement, opportunities to enjoy freedom from the normal routine. At home, he imbibed some of the classics of Hindu mythology from his aunts, and listened with delight to the stories of the 1857 Rebellion and the romantic fables which were related with all the embellishments by a kindly family retainer, Munshi Mubarak Ali. It was this early association with Muslims at home and the composite environment of life in Allahabad that shaped his attitude to Muslims in particular and the communal problem in general during his adult life.

What the young Nehru lacked above all was companionship. He found himself surrounded by his elders, people who could instruct, discipline and guide but who could not share his youthful world. His father spent very little time with him and, in any event, was too forbidding and aloof to be a confidant. His mother was a refuge to some extent. His tutors provided a formal education. But in his early years Jawaharlal suffered from a lack of friends with whom to exchange ideas and to enjoy the carefree days of youth. This, too, had a lasting effect, for in his adult life Nehru never confided completely in anyone, except Gandhi. Nor did he ever develop intimate friendships or a sense of complete trust in any of his colleagues.

Among his tutors, only one, Ferdinand T. Brooks, had any significant effect on the young Nehru's outlook and aesthetic tastes. Of mixed Irish and French extraction, Brooks was a moody, sensitive, gifted young man of twenty-six when he joined the Nehru household. He was also a devout follower of theosophy and had been recommended to Motilal by one of the leading exponents of this hybrid religion, Mrs. Annie Besant, the grand old lady of Indian nationalism. Jawaharlal was ten years old at the time.

Under Brooks's inspiration he developed a taste for serious reading which he retained throughout his life. Like many boys of his age in the West, Nehru derived much pleasure from the fables of Lewis Carroll, the Kipling stories, the adventures of Don Quixote, and the more serious real-life adventures of the great explorers at the turn of the century. Mark Twain and Sherlock Holmes also intrigued his youthful mind, as did the writings of Dickens, Scott, and Thackeray. It seems to have been a most unusual education for a young Brahmin in Allahabad. And so it was. But it was an experience shared by many upper- and middle-class Indians of the time. This period witnessed, as well, the beginnings of a deep attachment to English poetry. Nehru remains basically an intellectual with highly developed literary tastes, thrust into the arena of public affairs by force of circumstances.

From Brooks he also acquired an avid interest in science. It was probably due to this initial experience, and the laboratory which they set up at *Anand Bhawan*, that Nehru decided to specialize in the natural sciences at Cambridge some years later.

Inevitably the tutor's spiritual bent penetrated the curious and receptive mind of his pupil. Although his home atmosphere was predominantly secular, except for the influence of the women, Jawaharlal began to read, with respect, the Hindu classics, such as the *Bhagavad Gita* and the *Upanishads*. It was but natural that he should be attracted to his tutor's faith as well. And so there occurred, at the age of thirteen, the young Nehru's flirtation with theosophy, partly under the influence of Brooks and partly due to the stirring speeches of Mrs. Besant in his home town. His father was amused but did not object; he, too, had been a brief convert. Jawaharlal was initiated into the Theosophical Society by Mrs. Besant herself, probably as a mark of respect to Motilal, already a name to conjure with. But his infatuation was short-lived. Soon afterwards Brooks parted from the Nehrus because Motilal was concerned about his austere and spiritual influence on his son. With his departure the young Nehru's attachment to theosophy faded rapidly. But Brooks's legacy to Jawaharlal, an awakened interest in literature and science, remained.

*   *   *   *

The time was rapidly approaching when the young Nehru would have to leave the sheltered atmosphere of *Anand Bhawan*, for the potentialities of private tutorial instruction had been exhausted. As an admirer of the West and the English aristocracy in particular, Motilal had long ago decided that his son should attend an exclusive British public school before proceeding to the university. Thus it was that when Jawaharlal was fifteen, in the month of May 1905, the Nehru family embarked for England—and Harrow—where Motilal had succeeded in arranging his son's admittance.

It was the first time that Jawaharlal Nehru was on his own, cast adrift from the secure moorings of home and family. He remained at the famous public school for two years, a period in his life which was relatively uneventful but not unhappy. He was a quiet, reserved, studious boy who passed through Harrow without much difficulty but did not leave any particular mark. By his own admission he managed to fit into the school life but 'was never an exact fit'.

Research into the Harrow archives and conversations with some of his classmates have revealed very little indeed. Only those who took an active interest in school sports were likely to leave a lasting impression on their contemporaries—and the shy Jawaharlal was not the rugger type. Yet he was not entirely averse to games: in 1906, in the track and field competition for the Headmaster's House, to which he belonged, Jawaharlal won the half-mile race and was placed third in the mile event. More noteworthy, he was awarded the prize for topping the examination list in his form during the third term in 1905 and again in the first term of 1906. One of these prizes was the first volume of Trevelyan's biography of Garibaldi which he devoured along with the rest of the trilogy. Already a streak of romantic idealism was apparent in Nehru's outlook, for 'visions of similar deeds in India came before me, of a gallant fight for freedom. . .'.[1] Among his other interests were local British politics and the pioneering developments in aviation. In his autobiography he recalled having written to his father, anticipating a week-end visit to India by air.

The boys at Harrow, then as now, included sons of many distinguished English families. There were as well a few representatives from various countries in the Empire, among them four or five Indians such as the last Maharaja of Kapurthala and a son of the reigning Gaekwar of Baroda. Of his British contemporaries, there were two who later achieved distinction in public life, Field-Marshal Alexander and Sir Walter Monckton. Neither had any vivid recollections of Nehru at Harrow, even though Alexander was also in the Headmaster's House. Nor did Jawaharlal contribute anything to the school magazine, *The Harrovian*. And unfortunately, none of his school essays survived the half-century since he was there.

[1] *Toward Freedom*, p. 32.

Restlessness and a feeling of dissatisfaction with the atmosphere of Harrow, particularly the narrow interests of his fellow boys, impelled the young Nehru to hasten his departure for the university. Yet it was with misgivings that he said farewell, because like so many Harrovians before and after him Jawaharlal became imbued with the Harrow tradition. Indeed, he retained an emotional attachment to his public school down through the years of struggle and more so since Indian independence. Whenever his permission was sought to enable sons of Indian princes to attend his *alma mater* after 1947 he was most accommodating. More recently, Nehru's association with Harrow provided the setting for an act of some political significance.

All through India's freedom struggle Sir Winston Churchill remained steadfast in his opposition to the transfer of power to 'men of straw', as he termed the Congress leaders. His insulting remarks about Gandhi—'that half-naked fakir', he called him in 1931—and his passionate defence of the British *Raj* had made him a symbol of the most reactionary aspects of British life in the eyes of most Indian nationalists. In the early 1950's, however, Churchill was Prime Minister of Great Britain while Nehru was Prime Minister of India, and India was now a full-fledged member of the Commonwealth. There were some who felt that a reconciliation between the two great protagonists would strengthen Commonwealth relations. Although they differed in many respects, both wore the same old school tie. And so a group of Old Harrovians arranged a dinner in Nehru's honour during one of his many visits to London, early in 1953.

Churchill consented to attend and to propose Nehru's health. Unfortunately, he was called away at the last moment to an unavoidable state function. Sir Walter Monckton substituted for Churchill; hopes of a reconciliation were rapidly fading. But soon after Nehru replied to the toast word was received from Churchill that he would be able to come, even at that late hour, if it were still desired. Churchill was at his best. He paid tribute to Nehru's courage and integrity. He spoke rapturously about Nehru's magnanimity in remaining within the Commonwealth after the experience of subjection. Nehru accepted the gesture and the formal reconciliation took place.[1] It is doubtful,

[1] Related to the author by Sir Walter Monckton in London in October 1955.

however, that the emotional antagonisms of thirty years could be waved away by a few generous words, even by two Harrovians.

Nehru went up to Cambridge in the autumn of 1907, at a time when the awful spectre of war was still remote, when England basked in the glory of the Edwardian era, when the Empire was firmly established in the far-flung corners of the earth, and when the first stirrings of serious nationalist agitation were causing a storm in India. Three years he remained, three idyllic years in the peaceful, stimulating atmosphere of one of the world's great centres of learning. They were years of mental growth, of comfort and pleasant living. By one of those quirks of fate he was enrolled at Trinity College, famous among other things as the training ground of Prime Ministers.

His formal studies were in the natural sciences, chemistry, geology and botany, but his intellectual interests ranged far and wide—into literature, philosophy, economics, politics, history and Greek poetry. No one exerted a very marked influence, but George Bernard Shaw, Bertrand Russell, John Maynard Keynes and some of the scientific lecturers stimulated his thought. It was at Cambridge, too, that Jawaharlal first came into contact with socialist ideas; Fabianism was then very much in the air. But his interest was of the dilettante variety. Twenty years were to elapse before Nehru began to acquire a serious understanding of, and a genuine attraction to, socialism. At Cambridge it was still very academic.

In his adult life the figure of Jawaharlal Nehru was to loom large on the stage of Indian and world politics. It is perhaps surprising, therefore, that his political consciousness developed very slowly. Indeed, it was not until the political ferment in India towards the end of the first world war and, more particularly, until the coming of Gandhi in 1919, that Nehru began to take an active role in public affairs. During his adolescent and student days his emotions were aroused by certain dramatic events, but an intellectual response was late in coming.

In narrating the story of his life, he recalls his sympathies with the Boers and his 'high good humour' at the news of the decisive Japanese naval victory over the Russians at Tsushima in the spring of 1905, on the eve of his entry into Harrow. Sympathy for the underdog, a vital factor in his later attraction to socialism, would seem to have been at the root of these attitudes. While still at Harrow, and more so at Cambridge, he was distraught by the partition of Bengal which took place in 1905 and sympathized with the agitation to revoke this act.

Of his political thoughts and moods while at Cambridge, Prime Minister Nehru remarked fifty years later: 'So far as political matters were concerned, I was, if I may say so, an Indian nationalist desiring India's freedom and rather inclined, in the context of Indian politics, to the more extreme wing of it, as represented then by Mr. Tilak. I felt like any average Indian student would feel. There was nothing peculiar about it.'[1]

It was over this issue that he and his father first clashed on political matters, a conflict which was to continue unabated and with much agony until Motilal decided to join Gandhi in 1920, partly under the influence of his son. For Motilal began as a Moderate, while his son was immediately attracted to the Extremists, as they were then called. The elder Nehru came to politics rather late because of his preoccupation with his career. And when he did so, his legal background led him inevitably to the constitutionalist approach to political reform. Moreover, many of the Moderate leaders were personal friends. The disagreement at this stage was highlighted by a letter from Jawaharlal to his father criticizing his views as likely to please the British Government. But during his stay in England the young Nehru devoted very little thought to politics, Indian or other.

Cyrenaicism was then the rage, and Jawaharlal was inclined to its philosophy of pleasure. Life was pleasant and to be enjoyed. There were no religious inhibitions to mar this excursion into a soft and easy living. His allowances were ample, his responsibilities a thing of the future. There was a mood of optimism all about him, fostered by the Edwardian illusion about steady progress in all matters material, and thus no incentive to treat the problems of India or the world in any but a 'mock-serious' manner. It was for Jawaharlal a period of exuberant adolescence. 'I enjoyed life, and I refused to see why I should consider it a thing of sin . . . [The ideas that I was exposed to] were just vague fancies that floated in my mind and in this process left their impress in a greater or less degree. I did not worry myself at all about these speculations. Work and

[1] To the author in New Delhi on 6 June 1956.

games and amusements filled my life, and the only thing that disturbed me sometimes was the political struggle in India.'[1]

As at Harrow, Nehru did not impress his contemporaries. Indian classmates recall him as a typical public-school product, polished, urbane, somewhat snobbish, characteristics which were understandable in view of his way of life in Allahabad and Harrow. There was no evidence yet of his future greatness. Nor did he reveal any flair for public speaking. In the Indian student group at Cambridge, the *Majlis*, he rarely participated in the debates, and in his college debating society he often paid a fine imposed on those who did not speak at least once during a term.

However, as noted earlier, his Cambridge experience had a lasting influence on Nehru and on his place in the Indian nationalist movement. Nehru himself testified to this in a remarkable statement before an Allahabad Court in 1922, on the eve of his second imprisonment: 'Less than ten years ago, I returned from England after a long stay there. . . . I had imbibed most of the prejudices of Harrow and Cambridge, and in my likes and dislikes I was perhaps more an Englishman than an Indian. I looked upon the world almost from an Englishman's standpoint . . . as much prejudiced in favour of England and the English as it was possible for an Indian to be.'[2] More than thirty years later he told the members of the Cambridge Union that wherever he goes he tries to make himself receptive, and 'coming to England it is far easier for me, because a part of me, a fairly important part of me, has been made by England, by Cambridge'.[3]

He took his degree in the summer of 1910, with second-class honours in the natural science tripos. As his university days were drawing to an end the question of an appropriate career arose. It is ironic, in view of subsequent developments, and indicative of the depth of his Britishness, that serious consideration was given to the I.C.S. (Indian Civil Service), the 'steel-frame' of the British *Raj*. The idea was finally abandoned, largely because of expediency. Such a choice would have necessitated an extension of his sojourn in England, for he was

[1] *Toward Freedom*, p. 34.
[2] Dwivedi, R. (ed.), *The Life and Speeches of Pandit Jawahar Lal Nehru*, pp. 4–5.
[3] *Manchester Guardian*, 11 February 1955.

still under-age, and a career in the I.C.S. would have involved almost constant absence from his family within India. There was, too, Motilal's preference for the law. Thus in the autumn of 1910 the young Nehru went down to London to read for the Bar at the Inner Temple.

During his two years in London Nehru lived the life of an English gentleman, applying his philosophy of Cambridge days to the full. He was a very handsome, slim young man, with black hair and a moustache, debonair in his Bond Street clothes. He frequented the proper clubs and restaurants, whiled away his time at the theatre and at social functions of the young aristocrats. His law studies took up relatively little time, as did serious intellectual pursuits, though he dabbled in Fabian ideas and was interested in the suffragette movement. In the summer he did Europe, as was fashionable then and now. Motilal was generous, and the young Nehru passed his London days in a merry-go-round of mundane pleasures. So wealthy was his father at the time that Jawaharlal was able to return to India twice for the summer vacation, in 1906 and 1908. Soon after completing his degree he visited Ireland, from which dates his emotional sympathy with the Irish struggle against the British.

He was called to the Bar in 1912. With his education complete, he returned to India after seven formative years in the country against which he was to struggle much of his adult life, and at whose hands he was to undergo imprisonment for nine years. But this was in the future. At that time, Nehru was merely a polished aristocrat, in a triple sense: he was a Kashmiri Brahmin; he was the son of a distinguished and wealthy lawyer; and he had acquired the manners and habits of an English nobleman. 'I am afraid', he wrote about himself on his return to India, 'I was a bit of a prig with little to commend me.'[1]

*   *   *   *

The India to which Nehru returned in the late summer of 1912 was not fundamentally different from that which he had left seven years earlier. The British were still undisputed masters of the sub-continent. Political consciousness was still confined to the intelligentsia in the cities, though the lower

[1] *Toward Freedom*, p. 39.

middle class had been aroused by Tilak and the anti-partition agitation in Bengal from 1906 to 1910. The Congress had been rent asunder by the basic conflict between Moderates and Extremists, led by Gokhale and Pherozeshah Mehta and Tilak respectively; but after the split at Surat in 1907 the Moderates had re-established control of the party machine, primitive as it was at the time. Indeed, the Congress remained a timid annual gathering of the English-speaking intelligentsia, loyal to the British connection and seeking India's salvation through gradual political and social reform under the guidance of their foreign rulers. By means of a judicious concession to these professional classes, in the form of the Morley-Minto reforms of 1909 which granted increased Indian representation in the Legislative and Executive Councils, London had rallied the Moderates to a strong, pro-British view. The Extremists had been subdued and their leaders were in prison, like Tilak, or in self-imposed exile, like the great mystic philosopher, Aurobindo Ghose. Just prior to Nehru's return the cause of the violent agitation had been removed by the reunion of eastern and western Bengal. By way of concession to the Muslims, who had pressed for partition originally, the capital of British India was transferred from Calcutta to Delhi, near the main concentration of Muslims in north-west India. The peasant masses continued to slumber. Gandhi was still in South Africa, experimenting with his technique of political action which was later to transform his native land. For all of these reasons India in 1912 posed a picture of political apathy.

Within his own family little had changed. Another sister had arrived in his absence, Krishna by name, or Betti as she was called. Swarup, the beautiful one, or Nan as she was nick-named, was now twelve, but the difference in age between Jawaharlal and his sisters prevented any real communion with them. Motilal's practice was as lucrative as ever, and *Anand Bhawan* had become the social centre of Allahabad. Here the leading lawyers and journalists of the town gathered to talk shop and exchange ideas about the shifting currents of political thought.

After London, Allahabad must have seemed terribly provincial to the young Nehru. Far from the principal centres of Indian political and intellectual life, it had a quaint but depressing atmosphere. Time moved slowly, and the scope of activity was severely limited: the club; family gatherings at *Anand Bhawan*; and the Bar library, for the young Nehru began to practise his profession soon after his return. 'Gradually the life I led', he wrote, 'began to lose all its freshness, and I felt that I was being engulfed in a dull routine of a pointless and futile existence. . . . Decidedly the atmosphere was not intellectually stimulating, and a sense of the utter insipidity of life grew upon me.'[1]

Nor was his legal practice inspiring or inspired. For eight years Jawaharlal carried on his profession in a desultory fashion. His qualifications and assets were formidable indeed—intelligence, a legal training at one of the great English inns of court, and the benevolent guidance of Motilal, the acknowledged leader at the Allahabad High Court. His father had great ambitions for Jawaharlal and hoped that his son would succeed him as dean of the profession. In fact, Motilal kept a two-volume album of his son's activities, significantly entitled 'From the Cradle to the Bar' and 'From the Bar—' respectively. But his expectations and dreams were doomed to disappointment.

The young Nehru showed little initiative or promise at the Bar. He remained a junior to his father, rarely pleaded a case on his own, and made no impression on his colleagues. Even had he not been drawn away to the political arena it is doubtful whether he would have been more than moderately successful. For such a high-strung, sensitive personality could not adjust to the drab, dismal surroundings of Indian law courts at the time.[2] Many years later Nehru recalled this period of his life without any enthusiasm: 'There was little that was inviting in that legal past of mine, and at no time have I felt the urge to revert to it.'[3]

During these years he lived a leisured and lordly life in the atmosphere of *Anand Bhawan*. Like many young men of his class he indulged in armchair politics. But there was little active and sustained interest. The conditions were not yet ripe for his complete involvement in the freedom struggle; in fact, it was not yet a genuine struggle for freedom; rather, a debating

---

[1] *Toward Freedom*, p. 40.

[2] Based upon K. N. Katju's recollections of this period, published in the *Hindusthan Standard* (Calcutta), 14 November 1949, on the occasion of Nehru's birthday, and on conversations with various persons.

[3] 'The Mind of a Judge', September 1935, in *India and the World*, p. 130.

society of cautious intellectuals. These were years of war, but the battle-fronts were remote and the war aims of the Allies failed to capture the imagination of Indian nationalists. Like most Indians at the time Nehru derived vicarious pleasure from news of German victories. His attitude was ambivalent, for he admired the British but resented their domination of his native land. Only France, which symbolized revolutionary spirit and national freedom, called forth his sympathies.

Nehru's early ventures into the political arena were amateurish. At the end of 1912 he attended the Bankipore session of the Congress; he found the submissive and loyalist mentality utterly depressing. He toyed with the idea of joining the Servants of India Society, a prominent welfare organization dedicated to the regeneration of Indian life. However, its political orientation was too moderate for his temperament. He joined the United Provinces Congress organization in 1913 but remained inactive for some time. Two years later there occurred his first active participation in Indian politics, as secretary of a fund drive for Indians in South Africa, initiated by Gokhale. It was in 1915, too, that Jawaharlal made his first public speech. Until that time his diffidence prevented him from taking the plunge. So pleasantly surprised were those who knew him that Dr. Tej Bahadur Sapru, a prominent lawyer and intimate friend of Motilal, later the leader of the Indian Liberals (Moderates), embraced him on the dais at the conclusion of his speech. Aside from his natural reserve, his inadequacy in Hindi was a barrier to his contact with non-English-speaking Indian audiences. During this period, too, he participated in the agitation against the system of indentured labour for Indians in Fiji. But none of these activities was more than peripheral to his essentially placid life.

It was not until 1917 that Nehru was genuinely moved by political events within India. Home Rule Leagues had been established the previous year by Tilak and Mrs. Besant, a marked departure from the passive and loyalist outlook of the Indian National Congress at the time. Then, at the historic Lucknow session of the Congress at the end of 1916, the Moderates and Extremists, who had parted bitterly nine years earlier, were reunited in the common cause. Another event of even greater political significance occurred at Lucknow; the Congress

and the Muslim League, later to become the great protagonists in the drama which culminated in the partition of India,
joined hands in a demand for virtual Dominion status on the
basis of a scheme for the representation of Hindus and Muslims
in the various legislatures. Ironically, the 'ambassador of
Hindu-Muslim unity' at that time was Mohammed Ali Jinnah,
later to become the 'Father of Pakistan'.

Nehru could hardly have been impervious to the Lucknow
Pact, as the Congress-League scheme was called, for it was
hammered out at *Anand Bhawan*, the first of many important
political developments associated with the Nehru family home.
Indeed, *Anand Bhawan* was to become the virtual headquarters
of the Congress. Motilal donated his home 'to the nation' in
1930 and, thereafter, as *Swaraj Bhawan* (Abode of Freedom), it
housed the office of the All-India Congress Committee (A.I.C.C.)
until Independence. Nehru was present at Lucknow as a
member of the important Subjects Committee but he did not
address the session; nor was his role of any consequence. By
contrast, his father was a prominent figure in the Congress
deliberations at the time, as he was to remain until his death in
1931. Throughout that period Jawaharlal was overshadowed
by his father, among others, certainly until 1929, when he succeeded him as Congress President.

Of all the events in the war-time period the one which stirred
him most was the internment of Mrs. Besant on 16 June 1917.
Six days later the Allahabad branch of the Home Rule League
was formed, with Jawaharlal as joint secretary.[1] Almost at
once the scope and nature of politics in the United Provinces
underwent a radical transformation. For the first time since his
return to India an atmosphere and an issue were created which
could galvanize young men to some form of political action.
Moreover, Mrs. Besant was an intimate friend of the family
who had exerted considerable influence on Nehru, both in his
childhood—the theosophy episode—and during this war-time
period of mental growth.

Jawaharlal threw himself enthusiastically into the Home
Rule agitation, his action conforming to his outlook at the time.
'I was a pure nationalist,' he wrote of this period, 'my vague

---

[1] Nehru also joined Tilak's League but devoted most of his attention to Mrs.
Besant's organization. Motilal later became president of the Allahabad branch.

socialist ideas of college days having sunk into the background. . . . Yet fresh reading was again stirring the embers of
socialistic ideas in my head. They were vague ideas, more
humanitarian and utopian than scientific.'[1] Throughout his
adult life these two ideologies, nationalism and socialism, were
to vie for primacy in his thought and action. As in this early
phase, nationalism was invariably to be the more compelling
motive of his decisions, though he has consistently maintained
his allegiance to both.

*   *   *   *

It was on the eve of his first appearance on the active political
stage that Jawaharlal Nehru was married. He was then twenty-
six and among the most eligible young men in all of India—a
Kashmiri Brahmin and the son of a prominent, wealthy lawyer.
He was also handsome, polished and highly educated. It was
an arranged marriage, for a love marriage in the Western tradition was rare in India at that time.

Because of these qualifications, proposals of marriage began
coming to the Nehru family while he was still in England.
Motilal finally chose Kamala Kaul, daughter of a prosperous
Kashmiri businessman of the same caste, whom he saw one
day at a wedding reception. She was seventeen, tall, slim, with
classic Kashmiri features, and the picture of health at the time
of her marriage. To Nehru's misfortune Kamala's appearance
of health proved to be tragically deceptive. She was also shy,
somewhat awkward in social company, and like him, sensitive
and high-strung. Coming as she did from an orthodox family,
she was educated in the traditional Hindu manner. From the
beginning there was an intellectual gap between them but with
the passage of time she more than compensated for this with
her understanding, sympathy and devotion to her husband.
Although she was overshadowed by Jawaharlal throughout
their married life, she later revealed much courage and inner
strength, which won the admiration of all who knew her.

The marriage took place in Delhi, in February 1916, after
Kamala had spent a few months in Allahabad under the tutor-
ship of the governesses of Nan and Betti. It was a lavish affair,
with pomp and splendour. Motilal arranged for a special train

---

[1] *Toward Freedom*, p. 44.

to take 300 guests to the capital where a city of tents, known as 'The Nehru Wedding Camp', was established.

At first it was difficult for Kamala to fit into the Westernized surroundings of *Anand Bhawan*. However, after the fundamental change in the manner of family living with the decision to join Gandhi in 1920, she succeeded in adjusting herself. She followed her husband dutifully and gracefully even though it meant giving up a life of luxury. She was a favourite of Motilal —causing some jealousy on the part of Jawaharlal's elder sister. Her only child, Indira Priyadarshini, better known as Mrs. Indira Gandhi, was born on 19 November 1917. It was at that time that the first evidence of Kamala's fatal disease appeared.

As his attraction to politics increased, Nehru devoted less and less attention to the Bar. An alternative interest had kindled his imagination, and without regret his legal practice faded away. Like many of the Moderates, his father had been moved by the internment of Mrs. Besant and had been driven to a more radical course of action, as reflected in his espousal of the Home Rule League demands. But he was still basically a constitutionalist and was to remain so until the very end, even though he joined Gandhi and supported civil disobedience. In any event he was not given to the highly emotional responses of his son and was prepared to change his political outlook only very slowly, after prolonged and careful deliberation. He was far from convinced about the wisdom of agitational politics at this time and looked with disfavour upon Jawaharlal's enthusiasm for the Extremist approach. Political tension grew steadily between father and son.

And yet Jawaharlal's involvement in the nationalist movement was still far from complete. His urge to political action had been aroused, but that urge remained partially expressed until Mahatma (Great Soul) Gandhi appeared on the scene.

CHAPTER III

'And then came Gandhi'

MOHANDAS KARAMCHAND GANDHI, revered throughout the land as 'Father of the Nation', was India's most illustrious son since the Buddha. Unlike Jawaharlal, the Mahatma came from a relatively plebeian social background, though his family was cultured and well-to-do by Indian standards. The Gandhis belong to the *Vaishya* caste, third highest of the four traditional Hindu castes; their sub-caste, the *Modh Bania*, has long been identified with money-lending and commerce, an object of derision and envy in Indian society. Yet both his father and grandfather had served with distinction as Chief Minister of Porbander, a tiny princely State in the Kathiawar peninsula of western India. It was there, on 2 October 1869, that the Mahatma was born.

The young Gandhi was physically weak, timid and self-conscious. Like his most prominent political disciple he admired and feared his father and, for a brief period, was inclined towards atheism. In both respects the long-range consequences on Gandhi and Nehru were fundamentally different. So too was the impact of their educational experience in England.

Gandhi completed his university studies in Bombay and then proceeded to London to read for the Bar at the Inner Temple —in the very year that Nehru was born. Both men lived and dressed like fashionable young Englishmen of the day. Both imbibed the spirit of English law and the sense of British justice. But whereas Nehru was profoundly influenced by his contact with British culture, habits and thought-processes, Gandhi remained essentially untouched by the experience.

Nehru had gone to England as a young boy whose home life was permeated with the modern, secular, aristocratic atmosphere of the West. His real mother-tongue was English, as were most of his tutors in Allahabad, and his formal education was absorbed entirely in the environment of upper-class England. Seven years at Harrow, Cambridge and London deepened his attachment to the British way of life, with the result that he returned to his native land 'more an Englishman than an Indian'. By contrast, Gandhi spent his formative years in an orthodox Hindu home and was educated in Indian schools. Although he learned English at school, his mother-tongue was Gujarati. And by the time he left for England his personality and outlook had already been fashioned by his traditional Indian environment. Thus, two years in London were but a passing phase for the Mahatma. They provided him with a legal training but did not leave any lasting imprint on his character, thought-processes or way of life. He returned to India in 1891 basically unchanged, entirely an Indian, in no sense an Englishman.

After a few years at the Bar Gandhi was invited to South Africa, to plead a case on behalf of the Indian community against discriminatory legislation enacted by the Transvaal Government. He expected to remain a year but stayed on for almost twenty. It was there that he experimented successfully with his novel method of political action, *satyagraha* or non-violent non-co-operation, a technique which was later to revolutionize Indian politics and to galvanize millions into action against the British *Raj*. He returned to India in 1915 but remained a relatively passive and silent spectator of events for the next three years.

Within the Congress he was looked upon with a curious combination of respect, for his South African exploits, and disdain, for his non-conformist approach to political and social problems. Sensing the gap between the urban-dominated Congress and the Indian masses, he turned to the countryside as a champion of the oppressed peasant. His triumphant campaign in support of indigo plantation workers in 1918 and his leadership of an agrarian struggle in Gujarat began to rouse the peasants from their deep-rooted apathy and heralded the arrival of a new force in Indian politics. But conditions were not yet ripe for his acceptance by the staid constitutionalists who still controlled the Congress: as long as the world war continued, a virtual moratorium on serious political action was in force, though the Home Rule Leagues were allowed to function. Yet the coming of Gandhi to the fore could not be stayed much longer.

At first glance, it seems strange that the young Nehru, with his aristocratic bearing, his Western outlook, his life of leisure, should have been attracted to the Mahatma, with his simple habits of living, his orthodoxy and his stress on the peasant, about whom Jawaharlal knew nothing at this stage. And, indeed, he was not over-impressed upon first meeting Gandhi at the end of 1916. 'All of us admired him for his heroic fight in South Africa, but he seemed very distant and different and un-political to many of us young men.'[1] What brought them to-gether was a fortuitous set of circumstances, for Gandhi's emerging prominence on the Indian political stage occurred at a time of transition in the life of Jawaharlal Nehru and at a critical juncture in the history of the nationalist movement.

As the first world war drew to a close, the temper of discon-tent and eager anticipation became increasingly felt on the Indian scene. The principle of self-determination for all peoples, proclaimed by President Wilson in his Fourteen Points, stirred the imagination of the intelligentsia. Closer to home, its hopes and expectations had been raised by the British pledge of ultimate self-government for India, contained in the Montagu Declaration of 1917, a landmark in the history of the *Raj*. The first instalment of self-government was promised soon after the war; proposals to this effect were anxiously awaited. War-time lethargy was giving way to a new wave of political conscious-ness.

A similar ferment was evident among other classes of Indian society for, as elsewhere in the world, the war served as a catalyst to social and economic change. Inflation and the shortage of consumer goods had produced widespread dissatis-faction. The forced pace of industrialization had enhanced the influence and aspirations of Indian businessmen. Returning soldiers were beginning to demand equality of treatment and a better way of life. Even the dormant peasantry showed signs of unrest. And in the Punjab, in northern India, revolutionary groups like the *Ghadr* Party were actively challenging British authority. Such was the political state of India when the Mon-tagu-Chelmsford Report on constitutional reforms was published in June 1918.[2]

A special session of the Congress was held in Bombay to con-

---

[1] *Toward Freedom*, p. 44.   [2] Cmd. 9109, 1918.

sider the proposals—and curious proposals they were. By way of experiment, partial self-government was recommended for the provinces. The principle of dyarchy it was termed: certain matters would be placed under the jurisdiction of a 'cabinet' of Indian ministers drawn from an elected legislature while others, 'reserved subjects', would remain under the control of the Governor and his advisory Executive Council. To the British, this was an appropriate introduction to responsible government in the sub-continent. To most Indian nationalists, however, it was a paltry concession, far short of the expectations raised by the Montagu Declaration. Thus, the Congress demanded 'self-government within the Empire', asserted that India was ready for responsible government, and requested the abandonment of the notion of dyarchy, which would have left the central government and most vital provincial matters under the exclusive jurisdiction of the existing régime. It also demanded fiscal autonomy for India and a declaration of Indian rights, and reaffirmed the Lucknow Pact (Congress–Muslim League agreement of 1916) as the preferred basis for the composition of the legislatures, federal and provincial.

And yet this was hardly a revolutionary group, in any sense of the term. 'God Save the King' was inscribed over the entrance to the pavilion, and the Congress tendered 'its most loyal homage to His Gracious Majesty the King-Emperor'. The constitutional Old Guard was still in control, and the habit of co-operation was too deeply ingrained to permit anything more drastic than polite criticism. Only a traumatic experience and a dramatic call to action could set the Congress—and the young Nehru—on a new path.

* * * *

The necessary shock was provided early in 1919 by the Rowlatt Bills and the Amritsar Tragedy; the leadership, by Gandhi. To many, the Rowlatt Bills seemed like a tragic omen of renewed repression, for they granted sweeping powers of preventive detention or enforced residence on all suspected political agitators. They were received with dismay by every section of Indian public opinion. But only Gandhi responded with a direct challenge. He first requested the Viceroy to withhold his assent from the 'black bills', as they were called. When this appeal failed he formed a *Satyagraha* Society, whose members were pledged to disobey the law as a symbol of passive resistance. To galvanize mass support for this act of defiance he proclaimed 6 April *Satyagraha* Day, a day of *hartal* (suspension of all business), a day of fasting, a day of mass meetings to protest against the hated legislation. In major cities and provincial towns alike the call to non-co-operation evoked a widespread response. The demonstrations were peaceful on the whole, but minor clashes with the police occurred.

The main centre of unrest in the aftermath of the war was the Punjab, 'the land of the five rivers', the home of the Sikhs and the reservoir of the Indian Army. Indeed, it was primarily against the upsurge of revolutionary agitation in this province that the Rowlatt Bills were passed. The spark which set the Punjab ablaze in 1919 occurred on 10 April, when two popular Congress leaders, Drs. Kitchlew and Satyapal, were summoned by the District Magistrate of Amritsar and were then held incommunicado. As word drifted through the bazaars, crowds gathered quickly and began to march to the Civil Lines, the European and upper-class Indian section of the town, to demand their release. Police barred their way, a skirmish occurred, and a few demonstrators were killed. Bitter and angry, the others marched back to the city and retaliated with arson and mob violence, in which five Europeans were killed. A few days later similar scenes of violence occurred in the nearby towns of Gujaranwala and Kasur. Martial law was proclaimed, and all public meetings were banned in Amritsar. Tension mounted hourly.

In the heart of the city is a public park known as *Jallianwalla Bagh*, enclosed on three sides by high walls which form the boundaries of adjoining houses. The only exit is wide enough to allow but a few persons to pass at a time. Despite the ban on public gatherings, the Congress organized a mammoth meeting on 13 April, the Hindu New Year Day. An estimated 20,000 people gathered in the *Bagh*. Suddenly there appeared at the entrance 150 soldiers under the command of General Dyer. The crowd was ordered to disperse, but there was no way out; the military blocked the only exit. Within three minutes, an order was given to fire at point-blank range on the unarmed mass. Panic enveloped the crowd; they were caught in a veritable graveyard. Some tried to scale the eight-foot walls, but in vain. A hail of bullets cut them down. Blood flowed freely on that tragic day.

According to the Hunter Commission of Inquiry, 379 were killed and about 1,200 were wounded. The only reason the others were spared, according to Dyer's own testimony before the Commission, was that he had exhausted his ammunition.[1] It was perhaps the worst crime in the annals of British rule in India, a massacre of defenceless people who could not even seek cover from the merciless attack. Matters were not improved when the Lieutenant-Governor of the Punjab, Sir Michael O'Dwyer, gave his official approval.

In his determination to 'teach the natives a lesson' Dyer ruled Amritsar with an iron hand. Public floggings were not infrequent. Detention of all nationalist leaders was the order of the day. But the most degrading measure was a 'crawling order' imposed on all Indians who passed a narrow lane in the city where a medical missionary, Miss Sherwood, had been assaulted during the disturbances. The humiliation of crawling on all fours to and from one's home, for many lived in this lane, was not to be forgotten or forgiven by those who were subjected to this indignity, or indeed, by any sensitive Indian. These were tense days in Amritsar, and a wave of anger swept the land. *Jallianwalla Bagh* became hallowed ground and the shooting a day of remembrance for the Congress.

The British were to pay dearly. As one well-known British historian of the sub-continent remarked, the Amritsar tragedy was 'a turning-point in Indo-British relations almost as important as the Mutiny [1857]' primarily because of 'the assumption, implied in the behaviour of responsible Englishmen and in their evidence before the Hunter Commission, that Indians could and should be treated as an inferior race'.[2] A former senior member of the Indian Civil Service (I.C.S.) put the issue more pungently: '. . . from now onwards the whole situation was changed. Government had been carried on with the consent—

---

[1] Two reports were submitted by the Hunter Commission, the Majority Report by the four British members, the Minority Report by the three Indian members. Both accepted the above-noted account of Dyer's action and the casualty figures. See Cmd. 681, 1920.

[2] Thompson, Edward & Garratt, G. T., *Rise and Fulfilment of British Rule in India*, p. 610.

usually apathetic and half-hearted, but still consent—of the governed. That consent was now changed to active mistrust.'[1]

The Punjab tragedy roused Indians as no other act since the Rebellion of 1857. For Nehru, along with many others, it was a profound insult to the national honour, pride and self-respect. The Amritsar Tragedy in particular was for him the first great shock as an Indian, and as such it provoked an instinctive response. The intensity of his resentment was undoubtedly due, in part, to the fact that it violated all that he had absorbed and admired about British justice and liberal idealism during his seven years in England. Indeed, it was under this emotional impact that the young Nehru plunged into politics with vigour and enthusiasm.

When he first learned about Gandhi's proposed *Satyagraha* Society his reaction 'was one of tremendous relief. Here at last was a way out of the tangle, a method of action which was straight and open and possibly effective. I was afire with enthusiasm and wanted to join . . . immediately. I hardly thought of the consequences—law-breaking, jail-going, etc.— and if I thought of them I did not care.'[2] How vast a change in Nehru's outlook! Just six months earlier, he had attended the special Congress session at Bombay. According to one of Jawaharlal's oldest political colleagues, both he and his father left 'no doubt that they attended the meeting with a certain air of condescension'.[3] He was still very much an Englishman living in the placid atmosphere of *Anand Bhawan*, almost impervious to public affairs, though he had participated in the Home Rule League agitation in 1917. It was not until the Punjab shootings and the coming of Gandhi, with his 'revolutionary' approach to political action, that Jawaharlal was impelled to join in the fray.

And yet, in deference to his father's wish, the young Nehru did not plunge into Gandhi's movement immediately. Motilal was opposed to the idea of non-co-operation at that stage and was horrified by the thought of his son going to prison. There were lengthy discussions at home. Heated words passed between father and son, and the atmosphere became increasingly

---

[1] Woodruff, Philip, *The Men Who Ruled India: The Guardians*, vol. ii, p. 243.
[2] *Toward Freedom*, p. 48.
[3] Sitaramayya, P., 'Memories of Jawahar' in *Bombay Chronicle*, 14 November 1949.

'Nehru Abhinandan Granth: A Birthday Book'

1. In 1894, aged five

2. At the time of the Upanayana (sacred thread) ceremony
in 1902

tense. According to his youngest child, Motilal 'was furious with Jawahar for joining Gandhi. Once, in a rage, he ordered [his son] out of the house.'[1] The clash was particularly distressing because of their genuine affection for each other. Unknown to his son, Motilal tried to sleep on the floor to imagine what prison life would be like. Jawaharlal loved his father, respected his judgement and was loath to hurt him. Hence he procrastinated: 'For many days there was this mental conflict . . . night after night I wandered about alone, tortured in mind and trying to grope my way out.'[2] Finally Gandhi's intervention was sought by the elder Nehru, and Jawaharlal was persuaded to relent, temporarily, in order not to upset his father. He was then almost thirty, but the bond with his father was so strong that his decisions were not his own.

The cleavage lasted about eighteen months, for Motilal was a proud man, set in his ways and temperamentally unsuited to the novelty of non-co-operation, while Jawaharlal's enthusiasm remained undiminished. Gradually, however, the elder Nehru's opposition waned. And ultimately he succumbed to the Mahatma's persuasive arguments and his son's passionate devotion to Gandhi's cause. 'It was', said Jawaharlal many years later, 'a tremendous struggle for him [his father] to uproot himself and to fit himself into this new environment.'[3] As for the conversions, 'it was perhaps a triangle: Mr. Gandhi, my father and myself; each influencing the other to some extent. But principally, I should imagine, it was Gandhi's amazing capacity to tone down opposition by his friendly approach. . . . Secondly, our closer association . . . brought out that Gandhi was not only a very big man and a very fine man, but also an effective man. . . . [No less important, father] was forced to think because of my own reaction. I was his only son; he was much interested in me.'[4]

The political reconciliation between father and son was greatly assisted by the chain of circumstances. Only a month after their initial clash came news of the Amritsar Tragedy and

[1] Hutheesingh, 'Nehru and Madame Pandit' in *Ladies' Home Journal*, January 1955, p. 77.
[2] *Toward Freedom*, p. 48.
[3] Talk on All-India Radio, 6 May 1956, on the occasion of the ninety-fifth birthday anniversary of Motilal Nehru.
[4] Mende, Tibor, *Nehru: Conversations on India and World Affairs*, pp. 22–24.

D

its degrading by-products in the Punjab. It was a shattering experience for both Nehrus causing a disenchantment with the British sense of justice. Motilal's opposition to *satyagraha* softened, and the road was thereby paved for the young Nehru's full-fledged entry into the political arena.

Of his own initial reaction Jawaharlal wrote, 'helplessly and impotently, we who were outside waited for scraps of news [martial law was then in force], and bitterness filled our hearts'.[1] As so often in the future it was the callous and ignoble behaviour of the British more than the act of killing which stirred him to anger. Many years later, when he reflected upon the action of the House of Lords and others in condoning General Dyer's behaviour, he wrote, 'I realized then, more vividly than I had ever done before, how brutal and immoral imperialism was and how it had eaten into the souls of the British upper-classes.'[2] It was this mood of anger and disillusionment, even more than Gandhi's call to action, which drew him to the nationalist cause.

The slaughter at *Jallianwalla Bagh* was a landmark in Nehru's life in still another sense: it brought him into direct personal contact with the *worst* features of British rule and with the sufferings of his own people as a result of British brutality. Early in June 1919 the Congress established a committee of inquiry into the Punjab disturbances. Many of the outstanding nationalist leaders of the day were active members, including Gandhi, Motilal, Pandit Malaviya and C. R. Das. The younger Nehru assisted Das who was in charge of the Amritsar area, the heart of the atrocities. The experience left indelible marks, probably more so than in the case of the older men. Only recently had he returned from an idyllic association with British culture which he admired enormously. Moreover, during this episode he was brought into close contact with the Mahatma for the first time. Gandhi's assessment of the situation proved to be accurate. As a result, 'faith in his political insight grew in me'.[3]

At the end of 1919 the Congress met in annual session at Amritsar, a symbolic act of defiance of the *Raj*. Motilal Nehru presided, but Gandhi was rapidly emerging as the dominant

---

[1] *Toward Freedom*, p. 49.

[2] 'Quetta', written in prison in August 1935. *India and the World*, p. 147.

[3] *Toward Freedom*, p. 50.

figure. He was already the hero of the masses, though still un-accepted by the Old Guard, including the elder Nehru himself. Jawaharlal was present but as a passive spectator of events, while his father held the stage.

Ironically, it was Gandhi, the exponent of non-co-operation, who pressed for moderation. Despite *Jallianwalla Bagh* he favoured acceptance of the Montagu-Chelmsford Reforms, though acknowledging their inadequacy. As for the atrocities, he told the delegates, 'the Government went mad at the time; we went mad also at the time. I say, do not return madness with madness, but return madness with sanity and the whole situation will be yours.'[1] Here in essence was the Mahatma's philosophy of *satyagraha*.

Nineteen-twenty was a year of gestation in Indian politics, the lull before the storm. A new issue blazed across the Indian horizon and stirred the emotions of the Muslim community— the *Khilafat* agitation. It was a curious but none the less signifi-cant political phenomenon, with highly charged spiritual over-tones relating to the Khaliphate, the highest religious office in the Islamic world. The defeat of Turkey in the first world war caused genuine disquiet among many Indian Muslims. More particularly, the Allied decision to dismember the Ottoman Empire and to disband the office of Khaliph aroused anger and hostility, partly because it violated a pledge of Lloyd George during the war and partly because it was taken as an insult to their religious beliefs. Deputations were sent to the Viceroy and even to London, but in vain.

The result was the creation of a powerful politico-religious movement headed by the Ali brothers, Mohammed and Shau-kat. More important, this episode led to an alliance between the Congress and the Muslims, always a source of concern for the ruling power. Gandhi correctly perceived the measure of Muslim feeling on the *Khilafat* issue and succeeded in combining forces on the two entirely unrelated questions of 'the Punjab Wrongs' and the preservation of the Khaliphate. Under-pinning these sources of discontent was the positive goal of *swaraj*, self-rule or independence. The stage was being set for the first civil disobedience campaign. It was a slow process, for Gandhi insisted on the acceptance of non-violence as the sole

[1] As quoted in Sitaramayya, P., *History of the Indian National Congress*, vol. i, p. 181.

method of political action, an alien doctrine to Islam. But before the year was out the *Khilafat* leaders were won over by the Mahatma—indeed, even before the principal leaders of the Congress.

*   *   *   *

Jawaharlal Nehru did not play an important part in these developments. He was still a newcomer to the political arena and was entirely overshadowed by the older leaders of the Congress. Yet 1920 was marked by an episode of great significance in his growth to maturity—his first direct contact with the Indian peasant. Until then his outlook and experience had been confined to the intelligentsia of the cities, tiny islands in the ocean of Indian peasantry. Strange that this landmark in his life should have occurred by accident.

Like other members of the Indian élite, the Nehrus were in the habit of spending part of every summer in the hills, away from the extreme heat that parches the plains and dulls the mind. In May 1920 Jawaharlal, his wife, and his mother were on holiday in Mussourie, queen of India's hill stations, in the eastern United Provinces. By chance, an Afghan delegation, negotiating peace terms after the third Afghan War, was staying at the same hotel. There was no contact between them for a month. But suddenly, the young Nehru was asked by the District Magistrate to give a formal pledge that he would refrain from any association with the Afghans. Since it 'went against the grain' he refused, and was therefore compelled to leave the area. Such was the setting for Nehru's discovery of the peasant —his way of life, his problems, his fears and his hopes.

Soon after he returned to Allahabad, a delegation of oppressed peasants from the Partabgarh District of Oudh walked to the city in the hope of enlisting the sympathy and support of prominent politicians. Jawaharlal agreed to return with them to their villages for a first-hand inquiry. There he discovered a whole new world. 'We found the whole countryside afire with enthusiasm and full of a strange excitement. . . . I was filled with shame and sorrow—shame at my own easygoing and comfortable life and our petty politics of the city which ignored this vast multitude of semi-naked sons and daughters of India, sorrow at the degradation and overwhelming poverty of India.

A new picture of India seemed to rise before me, naked, starving, crushed, and utterly miserable. And their faith in us, casual visitors from the distant city, embarrassed me and filled me with a new responsibility that frightened me.'[1] From this experience dates Nehru's interest in, and awareness of, the Indian masses, a key to his great political power in later years.

In many respects this was an educational experience. Not only did it broaden his horizon, with a new vision of his native land. It also gave him insight into the meaning of poverty, totally alien to his own life experience, and provided him with the emotional basis for his later conversion to socialism. Like the Amritsar Tragedy, his march through the sun-baked fields of the Indian countryside was a moving experience. His sympathy for the underdog, one of the key motives of his subsequent behaviour in politics, was aroused by the sub-human conditions of life which he observed in 1920 for the first time. Moreover, his discovery of the peasant tempered his shyness and removed the mental block to public speaking.

The village crowd provided an ideal setting for a novice in this art. It also necessitated a simple and lucid form of expression. From that early experience dates Nehru's conversational method of public speech, his tendency to speak to his people 'like a schoolmaster; to try to explain things to them in as simple a language as possible; not to deliver, well, I can't deliver them, fiery orations, but just trying to get them to think and to understand'.[2]

Jawaharlal's discovery of the *kisans* (peasants) spurred him to action on their behalf and occupied much of his leisure time during 1920–1. Typical of the incidents which influenced his thought on the agrarian question was that which occurred near the town of Rae Bareli in the United Provinces early in January 1921. Thousands of peasants marched on the town to protest against the detention of their leaders by the police. They gathered on the opposite bank of the river flowing by the town but were barred from further advance by armed police and troops. Nehru hurried to the scene with the intention of avoiding violence—he was then a complete convert to the Mahatma's

---

[1] *Toward Freedom*, pp. 56–57.
[2] Related to the author in New Delhi on 13 June 1956.

doctrine of non-violence—but he was prevented from crossing the bridge by the local magistrate. The authorities demanded that the demonstrators disperse, to which they were agreeable on condition that Nehru were allowed to appear before them. Their request being refused, the peasants stood fast. Police firing followed, and many died or were wounded. Jawaharlal remained behind to supervise relief for the injured and later collected funds in Allahabad for the affected families.

It was this and similar experiences that strengthened his hostility to the British *Raj*: such behaviour by the foreign rulers struck him as immoral and callous in the extreme. At the same time, his reputation as a friend of the *kisan* spread into the interior where serious agrarian agitation continued for more than a year. From that time onwards Jawaharlal's conception of the good society included a fundamental transformation of conditions in the Indian countryside. Some years later, socialism was to provide an intellectual response to this aversion to poverty.

*   *   *   *

In the meantime, preparations for civil disobedience had been completed. Strangely enough, it was the *Khilafat* Committee that took the lead; 1 August 1920 was proclaimed the date for the inauguration of non-co-operation. On that very day the last serious rival to Gandhi's leadership in the Congress, Lokmanya Tilak, died in Bombay. By chance, the younger Nehru and Gandhi were on tour in the nearby province of Sind. They hastened to Bombay, arriving just in time to pay homage to the man who is honoured throughout India as one of the giants of the nationalist movement, the man who stirred the nation as early as 1906 with his dramatic dictum, '*Swaraj* (freedom) is my birthright.'

The following month the Congress met in special session at Calcutta to frame its policy on the oft-debated issue of non-co-operation. A new atmosphere pervaded its deliberations, a sense of impending change from the cautious, timid, rather exclusive debating society of earlier years. The Gandhi era in Indian politics was about to begin. Hindustani and other Indian languages vied with English as the medium of debate for the first time. *Khaddar* (home-spun cotton cloth) was more in evidence, and delegates from the lower middle-class were coming to the fore.

But it was not clear sailing for the Mahatma. Almost all the prominent leaders were still opposed or were sceptical of *satyagraha*, persons like Das from Bengal, Lajpat Rai from the Punjab, the redoubtable Mrs. Annie Besant, and Mohammed Ali Jinnah, founder of Pakistan, who was then an active member of the Congress. Only one of the Old Guard broke ranks and sided with Gandhi—Motilal Nehru. It had been a slow process, but the elder Nehru finally cast his lot with militant nationalism. His defection was sufficient to turn the scales. Non-co-operation became official Congress policy, though many senior Congressmen remained unconvinced.

The Mahatma's programme was simple and seemingly negative in character. In essence it consisted of a triple boycott—of the impending elections under the Government of India Act of 1919, of Government schools and colleges, and of the law courts. To the surprise of many, both officials and Congressmen, almost two-thirds of the electors stayed away from the polls in November 1920. Thus, when the Congress held its regular annual session in Nagpur at the end of the year the critics were won over. So persuasive was Gandhi, even among the older men, that C. R. Das, who had gone to Nagpur with the avowed intention of undoing the Calcutta resolution, with hundreds of delegates brought at his own expense, succumbed after an all-night discussion with the Mahatma.

The Nagpur session proved to be a landmark in many respects. Gandhi's undisputed leadership was acknowledged for the first time. Moreover, the Congress goal was officially changed to 'the attainment of Swaraj . . . by all legitimate and peaceful means', a radical departure from the previous goal of 'self-government within the Empire'. The Mahatma was 'delightfully vague' about the meaning of *swaraj*, which could be interpreted as Dominion status or complete independence. But the use of a Hindi term to describe the nationalist objective evoked an emotional response from large masses of people to whom the Western expression, self-government, was utterly foreign and devoid of significance. This was Gandhi's way, to convey ideas in traditional Indian symbols and thereby to reach the masses. Hence *swaraj* and *satyagraha*, not self-government and non-co-operation. Thus, too, the emphasis on *khaddar*, his simple way of life, his renunciation and his founding of an *ashram* (a commune of teacher and disciples). All this appealed to the tradition-bound peasants, the overwhelming majority of India's population.

As a result of this change in the Congress creed and the re-affirmation of *satyagraha*, Mohammed Ali Jinnah resigned from the party, never again to return. In perspective, his departure was of enormous political significance, for in later years it was he who provided the dynamic and successful leadership of the movement in favour of Pakistan. But by far the most important development at Nagpur in 1920 was the refashioning of the Indian National Congress along mass lines. From that time dates the present party structure, one of Gandhi's major con-tributions to the struggle for independence.

At the apex of the organizational pyramid was the Annual Session, the 'legislature' of the Congress 'government', where, in theory, major policy decisions were to be taken. India was divided into twenty-one 'provinces' based on linguistic groups, each headed by a Provincial Congress Committee (P.C.C.). The 'provinces', in turn, were sub-divided into districts, *taluqs*, towns and villages, each lower body electing delegates to the committee immediately above it, ultimately to the All-India Congress Committee (A.I.C.C.), the highest executive organ in the party. The A.I.C.C., with a membership of three to four hundred, conducted all Congress business between the annual sessions and was given wide discretion to frame rules not covered or inconsistent with the constitution. It also elected the Working Committee, the real decision-making organ of the Congress. Popularly known as the High Command, it consisted of the President, the General-Secretaries, the Treasurer and about a dozen others. The President was elected annually by the P.C.C.s but remained only one of the élite, first among equals—with Gandhi as super-president until 1947.

With these constitutional changes, the entire basis of Indian politics was revolutionized. The Congress was transformed from an upper-class urban club into a nation-wide mass organization capable of penetrating to the grass roots, to the village, the heart of Indian society: 1920, therefore, represents the great divide in the history of Indian nationalism—the emergence of a new leader, a new method of political action, a more advanced goal and a mass party which in time was to rally millions to the cause of Indian freedom. The way was now paved for the first civil disobedience campaign.

The campaign lasted about fourteen months but it gathered momentum very slowly. Indeed, the response was discouraging until the autumn of 1921. The overwhelming majority of students remained at their desks. Only a few lawyers heeded the Mahatma's call to give up their practice, the most noteworthy being C. R. Das and Motilal Nehru. There were scattered demonstrations and *hartals*, and a torrent of words enjoining the masses to rally to *satyagraha*. But deep-rooted inertia, fear and scepticism prevented most from taking the plunge.

The first event of any consequence was the arrest of the Ali brothers in mid-September 1921, for a fiery speech delivered by Mohammed Ali inciting Muslim soldiers to sedition. Gandhi seized upon this issue and openly espoused the view of the *Khilafat* leaders. 'Only a Mussulman divine can speak for Islam,' he wrote at the time, 'but speaking for Hinduism and speaking for nationalism, I have no hesitation in saying, that it is sinful for anyone, either as soldier or civilian, to serve this Government which has proved treacherous to the Mussulmans of India and which has been guilty of the inhumanities of the Punjab. . . . Sedition has become the creed of the Congress. . . . Non-co-operation, though a religious and strictly moral movement, deliberately aims at the overthrow of the Government . . .'[1] To leave no doubt about his intention, the Mahatma instructed his followers to repeat Mohammed Ali's speech at hundreds of special meetings on 21 October.

The challenge to legal authority was unmistakable, but the Government hesitated to take action against him, in fear of provoking a major onslaught on the *Raj*. For despite the undramatic character of non-co-operation thus far, Gandhi's influence had spread to almost all sections of the Indian people. Such was the sober assessment of Dr. Tej Bahadur Sapru, the pro-Government leader of the Liberals, in a confidential letter to the Home Member of the Viceroy's Executive Council:

The question as to whether we should arrest and prosecute him [Gandhi] is not so much a question of law as it is one of political

[1] *Young India* (Ahmedabad), 29 September 1921.

expediency. . . . During the last twelve months or so, his influence
has extended over a much larger area than perhaps we can realise.
The masses may not understand exactly the full significance of his
propaganda or the meaning of Swaraj, but he has been eminently
successful in exploiting their discontent . . . and enlisting their active
sympathy and support on his side. He is not a mere politician in the
eyes of the masses. He has all the sanctity of a holy man attached to
him, and therein lies, to my mind, the secret of his hold and also the
danger of it. To the Muhammedans he has made himself invaluable. . . . Probably the landed classes [are the only disturbed ele-
ment]. . . . As against them, however, we should set off the moneyed
classes in Bombay, and to a certain extent the Marwari community
in Calcutta. With the labouring classes, he and his party unquestionably wield a most powerful influence which cannot be ignored.
Even those who differ from him among the Moderate [Liberal] party
respect him for his personal character. . . . I have also grave doubt as
to whether we would be able to carry even the Assembly with us in
regard to this matter [the arrest of Gandhi].[1]

Thus did Gandhi inspire his countrymen as early as 1921.

*   *   *   *

Nehru was present at the Nagpur session of 1920 but did not
participate in the proceedings. However, as the campaign unfolded in the early months of 1921, he was filled with elation.
'Many of us . . . lived in a kind of intoxication', he wrote about
this phase of his life. 'We were full of excitement and optimism
and a buoyant enthusiasm. We sensed the happiness of a person crusading for a cause. We were not troubled with doubts
or hesitation; our path seemed to lie clear in front of us, and we
marched ahead. . . . Above all, we had a sense of freedom. . . .
What did we care for the consequences? Prison? We looked
forward to it; that would help our cause still further. . . .
[There was] also an agreeable sense of moral superiority over
our opponents, in regard to both our goal and our methods.'[2]
Indeed, he was so absorbed in the struggle that he ignored
certain unattractive features of the campaign. Like all true
converts, he had absolute faith in his leader and his cause.
    Upon reflection, he recorded his distress at the religious over-

---

[1] Letter to Sir William Vincent, K.C.S.I., on 9 October 1921. Published with
the permission of the Ministry of Home Affairs, Government of India.
[2] *Toward Freedom*, p. 69.

tones of the 1921 campaign: Gandhi's habit of invoking traditional symbols to win mass support and the strange admixture of politics and religion, the artificial unity which Gandhi had forged out of diverse discontents in the aftermath of the war. He was also disturbed by the lack of a clear-cut ideology. 'But I was powerless to intervene [and] I was too full of my work and the progress of our movement to care for such trifles as I thought at the time they were.'[1] Imperceptibly, too, he found himself drawn to religion, more so than at any time in his early life. As he recalled this period many years later, 'I should imagine that in the early 'twenties I was much more powerfully influenced by him [Gandhi] than I was a few years later when I started questioning about violence and non-violence.'[2]

What was it, then, that attracted Nehru to the Mahatma? Many persons testify to Gandhi's magnetic personality. But that magnetism required an appropriate setting to be effective. Gandhi arrived upon the Indian political scene at a propitious moment, at a time when the nationalist movement was devoid of imaginative thought or leadership. There were only two recognized methods of political action, according to Nehru: terrorism, 'which I could not accept', and constitutionalism, 'which offered no hope of success'. Gandhi created a new mood and provided a way out, novel and untested, but potentially capable of breaking the deadlock and achieving the desired results. As Prime Minister Nehru put it thirty-five years later, 'We saw him functioning, functioning with success. It was so different from our method, the normal political method of a nationalist movement, which shouted a great deal and did little. Here was a man who didn't shout at all. He spoke softly and gently, and put forward what he thought were his minimum demands, and stuck to them. There was an element of great strength about it.'[3] Beyond that were Gandhi's extraordinary courage in the face of a mighty empire, his serenity, his pledge to free India through *satyagraha*, and his genuine renunciation of material comfort, which appealed to intellectuals and the masses alike.

The Mahatma's personal influence at that time was remarkable. Jawaharlal gave up smoking for five years and even

[1] Ibid., p. 72.
[2] To the author in New Delhi on 6 June 1956.   [3] Ibid.

flirted with vegetarianism, though only for a brief period. He began reading the *Bhagavad Gita* afresh, with its emphasis on right action, caring less for the consequences. His faith in the importance of means dates to this period, as does his stress on the ethical side of politics. In the broadest sense, his life was simplified and spiritualized. The Mahatma's spell was all-embracing.

Calm and serene, yet firm and decisive, drawing people from all walks of life, Gandhi the man was a model of behaviour for Nehru and provided all or nearly all the answers. Yet it was not only the Mahatma who caused this feeling of exhilaration. The opportunity of action, the goal of national freedom, and the conviction that a new India could arise from the struggle—these pressed Nehru forward.

*   *   *   *

Throughout the first civil disobedience campaign Jawaharlal was General Secretary of the United Provinces P.C.C., a not unimportant position then as now. All his energies were devoted to the struggle: the innumerable committee meetings; the establishment of Congress branches throughout the province; the drafting of memoranda; the organization of *hartals* and demonstrations; public speeches by the score; and visits to the countryside, in an effort to broaden the basis of support for non-co-operation. Like the Russian *Narodniks* in the 1870's, the Congressmen of 1921 turned to the village as the hope for a genuine renaissance and the key to political success.

Although he had discovered the *kisan* earlier, this was Nehru's first prolonged association with the rural masses. It was a fruitful and wholly satisfying experience, a vital formative influence. For he felt 'the power of influencing the mass [and] began to understand a little the psychology of the crowd, [and] . . . felt at home in the dust and discomfort . . . though their want of discipline often irritated me. . . . I took to the crowd, and the crowd took to me, and yet I never lost myself in it; always I felt apart from it', a trait Nehru retained over the years.[1] So involved did he become that every other association was virtually ignored, including family and friends. It was an especially difficult time for Kamala.

[1] *Toward Freedom*, p. 76.

Tension mounted steadily in the autumn of 1921 and reached its peak with the arrival of the Prince of Wales (later the Duke of Windsor) for a goodwill visit, on 19 November. Gandhi proclaimed a nation-wide *hartal*. To the surprise and consternation of many it was a remarkable success, though marred by violence in Bombay, which the Mahatma castigated severely. At that point the Government struck, and struck hard. Congress volunteer organizations were outlawed, and a policy of mass arrests was introduced. In the next few months about 30,000 nationalists were sent to prison, most of them for short terms. The trek to jail, later to become a torrential flow, had begun. Both Nehrus were among those seized in the first round-up of prominent Congressmen. They were arrested on the evening of 6 December at *Anand Bhawan* and were sentenced to six months' imprisonment, Motilal for membership of an illegal organization, Jawaharlal for handing out notices of a *hartal*. The younger Nehru's 'offence' turned out to be a perfectly legal act, and so he was released after three months.

While they were in prison the political situation was transformed—by Gandhi's abrupt decision to terminate civil disobedience. It was a strange and unexpected development. But the Mahatma's actions were often unintelligible both to his followers and opponents. On 4 February 1922 he issued a directive for mass civil disobedience throughout the country. Almost everywhere the response was non-violent in character. But in the remote village of Chauri Chaura, in the United Provinces, an unfortunate incident occurred. An exuberant crowd of Congress volunteers, backed by a thousand peasants, came into conflict with the authorities. The police fired, and the crowd retaliated by burning down a police station with about half a dozen policemen inside; altogether, twenty-two policemen were killed in the fracas. Gandhi was appalled by this violation of his creed. He announced that the Indian people were not yet ready to wage a non-violent struggle and summarily called off the campaign.

Without exception the Mahatma's colleagues were stunned by his decision. Many were hurt and angry. 'What troubled us even more', wrote Nehru about these events, 'were the reasons given for this suspension and the consequences that seemed to flow from them. . . . If [the cessation of the struggle] was the inevitable result of a sporadic act of violence, then surely there was something lacking in the philosophy and technique of a non-violent struggle. . . . Must we train the three hundred and odd millions of India in the theory and practice of non-violent action before we could go forward?'

In time these initial doubts led to serious questioning about the merits of *satyagraha* as an *absolute* creed, though eventually they were resolved by the ghastly spectacle of communal violence on the eve and in the immediate aftermath of Independence twenty-five years later. And even at this stage, faith in Gandhi's wisdom was such that Jawaharlal was prepared to trust his judgement, despite grave reservations. 'After all, he was the author and originator of it, and who could be a better judge of what it was and what it was not? And without him where was our movement?'[1] Moreover, Nehru's feelings were soothed by an explanatory letter from Gandhi which he received in jail. 'I assure you', wrote the Mahatma, 'that if the thing had not been suspended we would have been leading not a non-violent struggle but essentially a violent struggle. . . . The cause will prosper by this retreat. The movement had unconsciously drifted from the right path. We have come back to our moorings. . . .'[2]

Gandhi's action seemed all the more regrettable to his followers because it occurred when optimism reigned supreme and when the campaign was advancing throughout the country. On the eve of this irrevocable decision, the Viceroy cabled the following appreciation report to the Secretary of State for India:

The lower classes in the towns have been seriously affected by the non-co-operation movement. . . . And although [its] influence . . . has been much smaller in the rural tracts generally, in certain areas the peasantry have been affected, particularly in parts of the Assam Valley, United Provinces, Bihar and Orissa and Bengal. . . . As regards the Punjab, the Akali agitation . . . has penetrated to the rural Sikhs. A large proportion of the Mahommedan population throughout the country are embittered and sullen as a result of the Khilafat agitation. . . . The Army and the great majority of the Police are staunch. . . . Religious and racial feeling at the same time is so bitter that the Government of India are prepared for disorder of a more formidable nature than has in the past occurred, and do

[1] *Toward Freedom*, p. 82.   [2] Tendulkar, *Mahatma*, vol. 2, p. 118.

not seek to minimise in any way the fact that great anxiety is caused by the situation. *It has not been possible to ignore the fact that the non-co-operation movement has to a large extent been engendered and sustained by nationalist aspirations,* and, so far as Mahommedans are concerned, by religious feelings which have a strong appeal to those also who have not adopted its programme . . .[1]

The Governor of Bombay at the time, Lord Lloyd, summed up the reaction of British officials more pungently: 'He gave us a scare. Gandhi's was the most colossal experiment in world history, and it came within an inch of succeeding.'[2]

Thus, when Jawaharlal emerged from the Lucknow District Jail on 3 March 1922, he was forlorn and depressed. He also had guilt feelings about leaving his father and many colleagues behind the prison walls. The separation was to be short-lived, for within six weeks he was back in jail.

After his initial release, Nehru hastened to Ahmedabad where Gandhi was on trial for sedition—the Government had finally moved against him when it became apparent that the civil disobedience campaign was no longer a serious threat. His faith in the Mahatma restored by Gandhi's magnetism, he returned to Allahabad and turned his attention to the boycott of foreign cloth, one of the few items of the non-co-operation programme still in effect. Under his direction the cloth merchants formed an association which decided to boycott all foreign cloth until the end of the year and to impose fines on violators of the pledge. When it was discovered that some of the larger dealers had reneged on their promise, their shops were picketed. It was this campaign which led to Nehru's second imprisonment. He was charged with criminal intimidation and the abetment of extortion, for which he received a sentence of eighteen months' rigorous imprisonment.

In a lengthy statement before the court, Jawaharlal enunciated his principles unequivocally. He refused to plead guilty or not guilty, he said, for he did not recognize the court as one in which justice would be administered. He remarked on his British outlook when he returned to India ten years earlier and

[1] Telegram dated 9 February 1922 in *Telegraphic Correspondence regarding the Situation in India.* Cmd. 1586, 1922, paras. 7–8. (Emphasis added.)

[2] As quoted in Andrews, C. F., 'Heart Beats in India' in *Asia,* vol. xxx, No. 3, March 1930, p. 198.

the contrast at present, when sedition had become his creed. 'I shall go to jail again most willingly and joyfully', he added. 'Jail has, indeed, become a haven for us, a place of pilgrimage. . . . One feels almost lonely outside. . . .' And then, in a burst of youthful emotionalism, he affirmed his devotion to Gandhi and the nationalist ideal: 'I marvel at my good fortune. To serve India in the battle of freedom is honour enough. To serve her under a leader like Mahatma Gandhi is doubly fortunate. But to suffer for the dear country! What greater fortune could befall an Indian unless it be death for the cause or the full realization of our glorious dream.'[1]

His uncompromising hostility to the *Raj* and his faith in Gandhi were also conveyed in a private letter to Dr. Syed Mahmud at this time: 'We are laying sound foundations. . . . God willing, our next march forward will end in victory. Rest assured that there will be no relaxation . . . and above all there will be no false compromise with Government. We stand for the truth. How can we tamper with anything which has been soiled by the touch of falsehood?'[2]

*   *   *   *

To court imprisonment deliberately and openly was the supreme obligation of those who followed the creed of *satyagraha*. To be sent to jail was a mark of distinction and success. But the reality of life in prison was completely unknown to Nehru in 1921. It was shrouded in mystery and associated with social degradation and isolation. With the passage of time it was to become a second home, for he returned nine times, some of them for short terms. Altogether, he spent about nine years away from family, home, friends and work.[3]

As he approached the Lucknow Jail the first time he was gripped with a strange sensation, a natural feeling of tension. Fortunately he was not alone. His father and two cousins were there as well, along with many colleagues and friends from the Congress. Nor were conditions unduly harsh for political prisoners under the British *Raj*, though they were far from

---

[1] The text of this Statement before the Allahabad Court on 17 May 1922 is in Dwivedi, op. cit., pp. 3-16.
[2] Unpublished Nehru-Mahmud Correspondence, 4 April 1922.
[3] See facing page.

pleasant. Especially was this true in 1921, when the first great wave of Indian nationalists descended upon the bewildered jail officials. The sheer number confounded them, but even more, the type of convict, which was utterly foreign to their experience —respectable middle- or upper-class professional men, many of them distinguished leaders in community life, proud of their violation of the law.

The political prisoners comprised a separate class. They were kept apart from the ordinary convicts and received special amenities, unthinkable in the normal prisons of the West, let alone the concentration camps for political prisoners that have grown up under totalitarian régimes. And among the politicals, sub-castes developed.

During his first stay at the Lucknow Jail, Jawaharlal, his father, and two cousins, Mohenlal and Shyamlal, lived alone in a small shed, 16 ft. by 20 ft., with a large enclosure. Free contact with other barracks was provided, as were ample books, newspapers, interviews with relatives, and the right to supplement prison food from beyond the walls. Much time was spent in political discussions, for the campaign was then raging all over India; and they waited for daily news with eager anticipation. The routine was rather simple: the morning was spent cleaning the shed and washing his own and his father's clothes, and spinning; for a few weeks there were literacy classes conducted for uneducated political prisoners; the afternoon was occupied

3 NEHRU IN PRISON

Sentence	Dates of Imprisonment	Days	Place
1. Six months	6 December 1921–3 March 1922	87	Lucknow District Jail
2. Eighteen months	11 May 1922–31 January 1923	265	Lucknow District Jail
3. Two years (suspended)	22 September 1923–4 October 1923	12	Nabha Jail (Nabha State)
4. Six months	14 April 1930–11 October 1930	180	Naini Central Prison, Allahabad
5. Two years and four months	19 October 1930–26 January 1931	99	Naini Central Prison
6. Two years	26 December 1931–30 August 1933	612	Naini Central Prison Bareilly District Jail, Punjab Dehra Dun Jail, U.P.
7. Two years	12 February 1934–4 September 1935	569	Presidency Jail, Calcutta Alipore Central Jail, Calcutta Dehra Dun Jail Naini Central Prison Almora District Jail, U.P.
8. Four years	31 October 1940–3 December 1941	398	Gorakhpur Prison, U.P.
9. Indefinite detention	9 August 1942–15 June 1945	1040	Ahmadnagar Fort, Bombay Province
	Total:	3262	(Nine years less twenty-three days)

Source: Based on various published materials.

with volleyball and occasional reading. Prison life lacked the luxury of *Anand Bhawan*, but did not involve serious privation.

When he returned to the Lucknow Jail after six weeks of liberty, Nehru found that conditions had deteriorated. His father had been transferred to another prison, the splendid isolation of his first stay had been terminated, and all politicals were now crowded together in the inner jail. Interviews were reduced in frequency, but reading and writing materials remained.

The most disconcerting aspect of life at this time was the almost complete absence of privacy, which Nehru prized very highly. Prison existence 'was the dull side of family life, magnified a hundredfold, with few of its graces and compensations. . . . It was a great nervous strain for all of us, and often I yearned for solitude.'[1] To his relief he was later transferred with a few friends to a remote section of the prison where he had time and peace of mind for serious reading. He read everything in sight and many books sent from home. In a sense, this enforced rest was a welcome respite from the hectic pace of political life during the months of non-co-operation. Years later, in the solitude of prison, Nehru was to compose the famous trilogy which narrates his discovery of the world, himself and his native land.[2] But this life was monotonous, dreary and cold. Finally it came to an end: on 31 January 1923 he walked through the prison gates to freedom.

Only four years had passed since Gandhi had unfurled the banner of *satyagraha*. But in Jawaharlal Nehru's life this was a crucial period. Above all, it was a phase of mental and emotional growth. The young Brahmin had become an eager and devoted political worker, fired by the goal of Indian freedom and the example of Gandhi. For this was the period in which he discovered the Mahatma and came under his influence, a relationship which profoundly shaped his future as a man and a statesman. He had also discovered the peasants and had seen their miserable conditions of life. He had overcome his aversion to public speaking and had established the basis of communion with the masses, from which he later derived spiritual strength and political power. This period also provided his

---

[1] *Toward Freedom*, p. 88.

[2] *Glimpses of World History* (1934), *The Autobiography* (*Toward Freedom*) (1936) and *The Discovery of India* (1946), respectively.

first experience of political responsibility, though of a modest character. And he had tasted the bitter fruit of prison life. No longer was he the dilettante aloof from the problems of India and his people. His future was now clearly charted, a life of politics in the quest for national freedom.

CHAPTER IV

In the Doldrums

OUT of the sands, out of lethargy and fear, Gandhi had fashioned a mighty movement in India based on the creed of non-violence. The magic word of *swaraj*, self-rule, had fired the imagination of millions. A new era in Hindu-Muslim friendship seemed at hand. Muslim divines addressed Hindu audiences in temples, Brahmin priests reciprocated in mosques. Hindus and Muslims dined together and drank water from the same cup, symbol of mutual affection and trust. The bane of Indian politics seemed on the verge of disappearance. There was confidence in the air during 1921–2 and hope—hope in a resounding victory.

But what had they achieved? The first wave of civil disobedience had broken on the rock of Gandhi's insistence on pure non-violence. The movement had disintegrated almost immediately after he had sounded the call to retreat. So too had the communal alliance, fragile and artificial as it was. By the end of 1922, Muslim frustration deepened with the news that the secular-minded Kemal Ataturk had taken control of Istanbul and that the Sultan-Khalif of Turkey, spiritual head of Islam, had been forced to flee. The purpose of Muslim agitation had vanished. The reaction was swift and sharp. Hindu-Muslim tension reappeared, and serious communal disturbances broke out in 1923. It was an inevitable reaction to the false hopes which had been generated by their leaders.

Among Jawaharlal's friends and colleagues, exuberance had given way to passivity. They felt cheated. To what purpose, they asked, had thousands faced the hardships of prison life? Why had the campaign been suspended so abruptly, when victory seemed within their grasp? From the height of optimism they had swung to the depths of despair. Their reaction was expressed in renewed doubt about the value of civil disobedience and in intra-party friction.

Such was the atmosphere that greeted Nehru upon his release

from prison at the beginning of 1923. It did not really come as a surprise, for he had followed the disquieting turn of events during the eight long months in Lucknow District Jail. Like so many of his generation and class at the end of the first world war, he had placed his faith in Gandhi and had indulged in wishful thinking about the prospects of civil disobedience. Now, in the face of defeat, he too became despondent.

His elation of 1920–1 gave way to depression, and with good reason. Civil disobedience had withered away, at least temporarily. Everywhere there was gloom. The Mahatma was in prison. The alliance between the Congress and the *Khilafat* movement was rapidly disintegrating, with the unfortunate reversion to Hindu-Muslim tension. Within the Congress there were petty squabbles and intrigues. India had withdrawn to its submissive shell, and the future was dim and foreboding. The *élan* had died, and a feeling of hopelessness pervaded the land. The years of disenchantment were upon him.

* * * *

Factional strife began soon after Gandhi's imprisonment in the middle of March 1922. Shorn of its leader and unity of purpose, the Congress turned in upon itself and indulged in agonizing self-criticism. After the initial shock had worn off, the party appointed a Civil Disobedience Inquiry Committee to tour the country, to take stock of the prevalent moods and to recommend policies for the future. It was apparent that a revival of mass civil disobedience in the immediate future was impracticable—the rank and file were exhausted and, in any event, no one but Gandhi could command the necessary allegiance. The crucial question was the proper attitude to the forthcoming general elections under the provisions of the 1919 Government of India Act. On this the Committee divided, setting the stage for an acrimonious debate within the Congress during the next two years.

One group, led by C. R. Das and the elder Nehru, the two outstanding constitutionalists in the party, favoured entry into the Legislative Councils. The *pro-changers*, they came to be called, for they deviated from Gandhi's programme of complete non-co-operation. They recommended that the Congress contest the elections and use its influence in the legislatures to paralyse the experiment in semi-constitutional government. Strongly opposed were the *no-changers*, the pure Gandhians, who advocated total boycott of the elections and concentration on the Mahatma's Constructive Programme—spinning, communal harmony, abolition of untouchability, etc. Their leaders were C. Rajagopalacharia (C.R. or Rajaji), the first and last Governor-General of the Dominion of India, and Rajendra Prasad, first President of the Union of India.

Rajagopalacharia is probably the most astute intellectual among the élite of Indian nationalists. He is also the only south Indian to achieve nation-wide prominence as a Congress leader. A Madrassi Brahmin of fair complexion, Rajaji's delicate appearance belies his intellectual vigour. Short, slim and completely bald, he walks with a slight stoop. Perhaps the most striking physical characteristics are his protruding chin, an impassive expression on his long, thin face, and the ever-present dark, horn-rimmed glasses which conceal his eyes from the viewer. There is a cold, almost icy reserve about him, a pronounced aloofness and stern composure. Precise in thought and speech, he is also capable of biting satire. His is a quick, razor-sharp mind, less given to emotion than that of any of his colleagues in the nationalist movement. Now in his late seventies, he is India's Elder Statesman, having served with distinction as Chief Minister of Madras and Governor of Bengal, as well as Governor-General of India and Home Minister in New Delhi.

By contrast, Prasad is a kindly, gentle-looking man. He is sturdy and tall, heavy, slow-moving, with a ruddy complexion and an impressive, bushy moustache. Simple in dress and manner, never without his Gandhi cap, he looks very much like the father figure which he is to many Indians today. An orthodox Hindu and a devout believer in pure non-violence, Prasad was, among all of Gandhi's leading political disciples, the most spiritually akin to the Mahatma.

Twenty years later Rajaji was to clash with Gandhi over the issues of Pakistan and active co-operation with the Allies in the war. Prasad has been loyal to his mentor throughout his public life. On this occasion they were united in support of the Mahatma's policy of total non-co-operation. Theirs was a negative attitude, abstention from politics until conditions were ripe for a renewed campaign of civil disobedience.

Gradually the Congress split into these two factions. It was, indeed, a house divided, sick in mind and body, floundering in a morass of tactical disagreement. The first test of strength came at the end of 1922 when the Congress met in annual session at Gaya, the site of the Buddha's attainment of Enlightenment. Das, leader of the pro-changers, presided, but the no-changers triumphed; Gandhi's original non-co-operation programme was reaffirmed in its entirety, including the boycott of the legislatures. It was a pyrrhic victory. The split widened. Das submitted his resignation as Congress President and announced his intention to form the Swaraj Party to contest the elections. The elder Nehru supported him. Through intensive lobbying, Das was persuaded to postpone his decision for a few months.

At that point the younger Nehru entered the stage. He had just been released from prison. With Maulana Azad, later the dean of Congress Muslims, he was able to effect a temporary reconciliation in February 1923: both factions were to suspend all propaganda regarding the vexed issue of Council-entry for two months. But the factions were too emotionally involved and the truce collapsed. The battle of words continued unabated during most of 1923 and was only terminated by a face-saving formula at a special Congress session in Delhi in the autumn. To satisfy the pro-changers or Swarajists, those who had no 'religious or other conscientious objections' were given *carte blanche* to stand for election and to participate in the legislatures. As a sop to the Gandhians or no-changers, Congressmen were urged to intensify their support of the Mahatma's Constructive Programme.[1]

Jawaharlal played a key role in working out the compromise solution. His sympathies lay with Gandhi and the no-changers. He doubted the wisdom, as well as the propriety, of his father's policy of limited co-operation. It was not the first time the two Nehrus had clashed on political tactics, nor was it the last. In fact, rarely did they agree on the proper course of action, on objectives or on political philosophy, except for the broad goal

---

[1] The texts of the various resolutions pertaining to the controversy between no-changers and pro-changers are to be found in *The Indian National Congress 1920–1923, Being a collection of the resolutions of the Congress and of the A.I.C.C. and of the Working Committee of the Congress from September 1920 to December 1923* (Allahabad, 1924).

of self-determination. But on this occasion, on the issue of boy-
cotting the elections, the younger Nehru did not hold strong
views. His primary concern was to reconcile the warring factions and thereby to restore unity to the shattered party organization. This led him to join a middle-of-the-road group which
was formed in the midst of the debate on Council-entry; the
Centre Party it was called, for want of a better term. Its leader
was a highly respected Congress Muslim and an intimate friend
of the Nehru family, Dr. Ansari. Among its other well-known
figures were Jawaharlal, Maulana Azad and Dr. Syed Mahmud. Largely through their efforts a semblance of unity was
restored to the party.

The controversy between no-changers and pro-changers
marks Nehru's *entrée* into the inner politics of the party. Until
then he was merely one of the Mahatma's bright young disciples and the son of Pandit Motilal Nehru, entirely overshadowed by his elders. Now, for the first time, he showed
initiative and dexterity in weaving his way through the intrica-
cies of factional dissension. Far more important, this episode
witnessed Nehru's earliest performance as a mediator, a role
which he was to play with increasing skill in the struggle for
national freedom, in independent India, and in world affairs
after 1947. Frequently during the 'thirties and 'forties he was
to provide a formula which reflected the consensus within the
Congress High Command; so too on the stage of international
politics. This penchant for honourable compromise, derived
from the Mahatma, and his talent for mediation found their
earliest expression during the party squabbles of 1922 and
1923.

The petty bickering and degeneration of the Congress were
extremely distasteful to Nehru, as reflected in his presidential
address to the United Provinces Provincial Conference in the
autumn of 1923, his first major speech to a party organization:
'All our energy [during the past year] was diverted to combating
and checkmating our erstwhile comrades in the rival camp. . . .
[This is] a critical period in our national history, when rival
theories and principles are at war with each other and the
foundations of our great movement for freedom . . . have been
shaken, when senseless and communal bigotry struts about in
the name of religion.' He admitted that the compromise on

elections and the legislatures was contrary to Gandhi's principles but justified it on the grounds that retreat from principle
was necessary at that stage, that both methods, no-change and
pro-change, were honourable, and that it 'put an end to this
long agony'. Independence was the only proper goal of the
Congress, he said, but he did not favour altering the party
creed because 'this would give rise to unnecessary debate and
controversy and might narrow the Congress and exclude some
people'. Above everything else, unity was the watchword of
Nehru's political programme, then as later. Indeed, with the
passage of time there developed an almost pathological stress
on party unity, the absolute prerequisite to victory in the struggle
for independence. Here was the motive force for his role as
mediator—to prevent fragmentation of the Congress, which he
saw as the only vehicle for the attainment of India's freedom.

Ideologically, Jawaharlal was a Gandhian *par excellence*
during this period: 'I believe that the salvation of India and,
indeed, of the whole world will come through non-violence.
Violence has had a long career in the world. It has been
weighed repeatedly and has been found wanting.' Although he
deviated from his allegiance to non-violence in later years, this
undoubtedly remains an accurate statement of his outlook at
the present time.[1]

*   *   *   *

Soon after the Delhi session of the Congress Nehru had a
curious and unpleasant adventure in the Sikh State of Nabha.
It culminated in his third, short-lived imprisonment and influenced his maturing political outlook.

Gandhi's non-co-operation programme had infected one segment of the Sikh community, the *Akalis*, who sought fundamental reform in the control and operation of the Sikh temples, the
gurdwaras. Serious clashes occurred in 1921, especially at the
birthplace of Guru Nanak, the founder of Sikhism. The *Akalis*
proclaimed *satyagraha* against the Government and merged their
movement in the Congress. Tension was high, and friction continued during 1922 and 1923. In the middle of 1923 the
Maharaja of Nabha abdicated under British pressure after a protracted quarrel with the Maharaja of Patiala, largest of the Sikh

---

[1] For the text of this speech see Dwivedi, op. cit., pp. 17–36.

princely States. The *Akalis* resented this deposition and launched a campaign to restore the fallen ruler to his throne. The agitation took the form of sending *jathas* (groups) of men to Jaito, the capital of Nabha, where protest meetings were held. Many were imprisoned, but the 'invasion' of unarmed *Akalis* continued.

At the end of September 1923 Jawaharlal and two colleagues from the Akali Committee of the Congress were invited to observe one of these *jathas* in action. When he arrived at Jaito Nehru was ordered to leave the State at once. He demurred, explaining that he was not participating in the agitation, that no transport was available for some hours, and that he was not violating any law. However, the princely States were autonomous in their internal affairs and could impose any regulations they deemed fit. Nehru, Gidwani and Santhanam were arrested and were paraded down the main street of the town, handcuffed and chained to a policeman. For Jawaharlal this was a severe shock, since his previous encounters with the police had been relatively civilized. 'To be handcuffed to another person for a whole night and part of a day is not an experience I should like to repeat.'[1] To make matters worse they were kept in a foul, insanitary cell, with rats for companions; some of them, to his horror, scampered across his face.

After a few days the 'trial' began. None of the defendants participated in the proceedings, though Nehru submitted a lengthy written statement narrating the events leading up to his arrest. The judge appeared to be illiterate; no witnesses were produced; and the case dragged on for a week. Suddenly, one evening, the accused were taken to another room in the jail where they were informed that they were now being tried on the additional charge of conspiracy. Nehru sought a lawyer from outside the State but was informed that this was not permitted under Nabha law. In the midst of the second trial they were approached by the (British) Administrator, who offered to free them if they expressed apologies and agreed to leave at once. The Congressmen refused. Finally, after two weeks, the trials ended. On the first count, refusal to obey the order to leave the State, they were given a six months' sentence; on the charge of conspiracy, eighteen months. The sentences were suspended, however, and they were allowed to leave.

[1] *Toward Freedom*, p. 98.

The Nabha experience was of great educational value for Nehru. Although he was, of course, aware of the sharp distinction between British and princely India, this was his first direct contact with the methods of administration in these enclaves of medievalism. From this 'discovery' dates his genuine interest in the conditions of the States' subjects. Later, he was to play a crucial role in the All-India States Peoples' Conference, the Congress affiliate in the princely domains.

The price of this education was high. Along with his colleagues, Nehru contracted typhoid in the Nabha jail. For a month he lay seriously ill at home, rare for one who has been strengthened by a robust health throughout his adult life. And yet there were compensations. '. . . I felt a strange detachment from my surroundings', he wrote of this period many years later. 'I felt as if I had extricated myself from the trees and could see the wood as a whole; my mind seemed clearer and more peaceful than it had previously been . . . it was in the nature of a spiritual experience . . . and it influenced me considerably. I felt lifted out of the emotional atmosphere of our politics and could view the objectives and the springs that had moved me to action more clearly . . . more and more I moved away from the religious outlook on life and politics . . . for the next two years or more I went about my work with something of that air of detachment.' Thus, the 'Interlude at Nabha', as Nehru terms it in his autobiography, 'had a lasting effect on me and my way of thinking'.[1]

*   *   *   *

When the Congress assembled for its annual session in the last week of December 1923, the no-changer–pro-changer controversy was still far from settled. The Gandhian wing (no-changers) opposed the Delhi compromise vigorously, in a final effort to undo what it considered to be an unforgivable deviation from the Mahatma's principles. In the meantime, however, the pro-changers (Swarajists) had strengthened their bargaining position immensely, as a result of the elections in the autumn. They had emerged the largest and best disciplined group in the central Legislative Assembly, with forty-five members out of a total of 145. (Thirty-seven M.L.A.s were

[1] Ibid., p. 112.

appointed directly by the Viceroy.) Although short of a working majority, the Swarajists were able to hinder the smooth flow of Government-inspired legislation, in co-operation with the Nationalist Party and some Independents. In the provincial elections the Swarajists' success was less spectacular; but they won a clear majority in the Central Provinces and were the largest party in Bengal. In both they succeeded in wrecking the experiment in dyarchy, semi-responsible government, by refusing to form ministries and by using their power to nullify the efforts of other groups to create stable majorities in the legislatures. Thus, the no-changers were compelled to yield, to accept the reaffirmation of the compromise settlement which permitted Congress entry into the legislative councils. To make the pill more palatable, the original non-co-operation programme of boycott was also reaffirmed.

It was, of course, a contradiction in terms, revealing the split personality of the Congress in the early 'twenties. But it was necessary to placate the Gandhian wing and to restore the façade of unity. In reality the Congress was now divided into two distinct parties tenuously linked by ties of the past. The schism was to continue for five years, until external pressures and the failure of the Swarajist policy created conditions for a return to non-co-operation. During the lean years of the middle 'twenties the constitutionalists led by Das and the elder Nehru held the stage. The Mahatma was content to remain in the background, concentrating on his Constructive Programme, especially on spinning as an instrument of economic and social regeneration.

The younger Nehru was present at the Congress session in 1923 but he remained silent during the major debate on Council-entry. His role in the final reconciliation does not appear to have been significant, though he undoubtedly pressed for compromise in behind-the-scenes discussions, along with Mohammed Ali, Congress President for the year, Ansari, and others of the Centre Party's persuasion. His only public act at the session was to move a resolution calling for the creation of an All-India Volunteer Organization, on the grounds that a cadre of disciplined workers was required to implement all aspects of the Congress programme. The proposal was accepted, and Jawaharlal was appointed President of the All-India Board. In time the Volunteers were to play an important role in mobilizing Congress strength, notably during the civil disobedience campaign of 1930.

One aspect of Nehru's outlook at the time was reflected in his presidential address to the first conference of Volunteers, held as a side-show to the Congress session. 'Most of our weaknesses', he stressed, 'can be traced to our lack of discipline.'[1] For Jawaharlal this was not the elucidation of the obvious, but an important political truth. Frequently during the freedom struggle he witnessed the adverse effects of indiscipline on the Congress organization. Again and again, he was to reiterate what was to him a pre-condition of victory in the struggle for independence—party discipline. And during the transitional period of free India many of his speeches were to focus on this theme.

After 1947, however, the need for discipline applied to the nation at large. In town and village, party conclave and Parliament, Nehru has brought the full weight of his prestige to bear on the virtues of individual and collective discipline. Unity and discipline—these have been the twin pillars of Nehru's one-man educational campaign to ease India's transition to a modern, progressive society. The early 1920's provided him with dramatic evidence of their importance. Later crises were to strengthen his belief that they were imperative.

At the behest of Congress President Mohammed Ali, one of the towering Muslim figures in recent Indian history, Nehru was appointed General Secretary for 1924; along with him were G. Deshpande and Saif-ud-din Kitchlew, a Cambridge contemporary who had achieved prominence during the days of the Amritsar Tragedy.[2] Nehru was reluctant to accept the post, partly because of doubts about future policy and partly because of his sensitivity to the apparent opposition within the High Command. But Mohammed Ali persisted, and Nehru yielded. 'I . . . must "protest most indignantly" once more against your

---

[1] The text of his presidential address is to be found in *Indian Annual Register*, vol. ii, 1923, Supplement, pp. 215–18.

[2] Dr. Kitchlew was one of the two persons whose arrest in Amritsar early in April 1919 set off the chain reaction which culminated in the massacre at *Jallianwalla Bagh*. For a long time thereafter he was a prominent Muslim Congress leader in the Punjab. In 1950, however, without breaking from the Congress officially, he became the President of the All-India Peace Council, and in 1952 he was awarded the Stalin Peace Prize.

misplaced modesty', wrote the Muslim divine to the uncertain Jawaharlal on 15 January 1924. 'My dear Jawahar! It is just because some members of the Working Committee distrust and dislike your presence as Secretary that *I like it*. . . . So do be cheerful and let us start work.'[1]

The two men got on very well together, despite Mohammed Ali's 'most irrationally religious' attitude, as Nehru termed it in his memoirs of the period. There was a strong bond of mutual affection and trust, and Nehru was drawn to the elder man's dedication, his enthusiasm, his keen intelligence and sharp wit. They clashed on minor points, invariably related to religion. The most noteworthy was Nehru's unilateral instruction to Congress organizations to delete honorary titles in referring to members, such as Pandit, meaning 'learned man', Maulana (Mohammed Ali himself was one of this select group of Muslim scholars), Mahatma, used only for Gandhi, and others. The President was annoyed at what he considered to be insulting behaviour, and the General Secretary relented. In recounting this episode Nehru commented upon the remarkable hold of Hinduism over its children, professed believers and atheists alike. As for his own feelings, he wrote: 'A Brahman I was born, and a Brahman I seem to remain whatever I might say or do in regard to religion or social custom.'[2]

Soon after he returned to Allahabad, at the beginning of January 1924, Nehru inadvertently became involved in a strange incident with highly religious overtones. It was the time of the *Kumbh mela*, the great annual festival in Allahabad when thousands of pilgrims gathered to bathe at the confluence of the Ganges and Jumna rivers in a collective emission of sins. Because of the dangerous Ganges current that year, the provincial authorities issued instructions prohibiting bathing at the holy junction. Orthodox Hindus were incensed. Under the leadership of the venerable Pandit Malaviya, one of the grand old men of Indian nationalism and a close friend of the Nehrus, they announced their intention to violate the order. Tension rose as the dissidents, two hundred strong, marched towards the river-bank. Police reinforcements were hastily called to the scene.

Nehru himself was wholly indifferent to the *mela* and its religious significance. But his interest was roused by news of the

---

[1] Unpublished Nehru Letters.   [2] *Toward Freedom*, p. 105.

satyagraha. He raced to the river and took his position among the civil resisters. There was a romantic touch to the episode, and this aspect of politics has always appealed to India's Prime Minister, especially in his youth, when boyish enthusiasm and an adventurous spirit were given free rein. At one point, when the cavalry appeared to be about to charge, Jawaharlal led a group over the barrier erected at the river and raised the Congress flag as a symbol of defiance. This was typical of the romantic streak in his personality. 'Faint memories of revolutionary barricades came to me', he recalled with glee in his autobiography.[1]

A few days later came news which electrified the nation. Gandhi suffered an acute attack of appendicitis while in prison at Poona. The emotional impact on Nehru and millions of Indians was akin to a personal tragedy. 'India was numbed with anxiety', he wrote without exaggeration. 'We held our breaths almost and waited, full of fear.'[2] Fortunately for Indians and the Government alike, Gandhi's life was spared: an emergency operation performed by an English doctor was successful. As so often in the future, the Government decided to release the Mahatma lest he die while in prison, with incalculable consequences for the political stability of India.

The two Nehrus rushed to Poona to visit Gandhi and then followed him to Juhu, a seaside resort near Bombay, where he had gone to recuperate from the ordeal. For Jawaharlal it was in the nature of a holiday, his first since the hectic days of civil disobedience. While the younger Nehru frolicked on the beach and satisfied his craving for swimming and riding, his father and Das engaged in serious talks with Gandhi.

The Mahatma listened sympathetically to their case for the Swaraj Party but would not be moved. Without denying its utility, he was adamant on the issue of principle: entry into the legislative councils was a deviation from the programme of non-co-operation and could not receive his blessing. They agreed only to disagree. Both parties issued 'communiqués' about the 'Juhu Conversations', and the cleavage remained. However, a *modus vivendi* was reached. Gandhi called on his followers, the no-changers, to respect the Swarajists' sincerity and their right to continue their activities in the legislatures,

[1] Ibid., p. 107. [2] Ibid., p. 108.

suggesting at the same time that those in the Councils should focus their work on assisting the Constructive Programme.[1] Congress was still a house divided.

Jawaharlal had serious doubts about the value of a constitutional approach to politics and never fully endorsed his father's views. Yet he found Gandhi's leadership wanting at this stage, particularly the Mahatma's preoccupation with spinning. In the summer of 1924 Gandhi moved a resolution before the All-India Congress Committee limiting membership in the Congress to persons who submitted 2,000 yards of self-spun yarn every month. The elder Nehru and Das correctly saw this as undermining the Swaraj Party and, along with their followers, they walked out of the meeting. The younger Nehru was also opposed, though on different grounds; the scope of the Congress would have been narrowed to the purist Gandhians. He submitted his resignation as General Secretary.

Gandhi's resolution was carried but was eventually withdrawn, as he became aware that it had failed to infuse the party with a new spirit. On the contrary, it had widened the fissures. Before the year was out the Mahatma retreated, in the form of an understanding with the elder Nehru which recognized the Swaraj Party as the constitutional arm of the Congress, entitled to full support by all Congressmen. The agreement was formally approved at the Belgaum session of the Congress in December 1924, the only one ever presided over by Gandhi.

At the Mahatma's request, Jawaharlal agreed to stay on as General Secretary another year, though there was comparatively little work in the circumstances. During the next four years the Swarajists dominated nationalist politics. And Nehru was unwilling to succumb to the temptations of the limelight offered by a leading role in the legislature. To Motilal Nehru's credit, he never pressed his son to accept the Swarajist creed.

*   *   *   *

What disturbed the younger Nehru even more than the Mahatma's seeming withdrawal from politics was the sharp deterioration in Hindu-Muslim relations. During 1924 communal

---

[1] The texts of the Gandhi and Das-Motilal Nehru statements after the Juhu Conversations are to be found in Sitaramayya, P., *History of the Indian National Congress*, vol. i, pp. 269–74.

'Nehru Abhinandan Granth: A Birthday Book'

3. At Harrow, 1906

'*Nehru Abhinandan Granth: A Birthday Book*'

4. At Cambridge, 1908

violence spread over the land in ever-increasing frequency and intensity. Riots broke out in Delhi, Nagpur, Lucknow, Shahjahanpur, Allahabad and Jubbulpore, most of them over petty matters such as the playing of music before mosques or cow-slaughter on the Muslim festival of *Bakr-id*. These had always been sources of friction. But to them was now added the frustration resulting from the abortive civil disobedience campaign and the collapse of the *Khilafat* agitation. The climax was reached at Kohat in the North West Frontier Province. More than 100 persons were killed on September 9th and 10th, and 4,000 Hindus were evacuated from the town.

The prelude to this resurgence of communal tension was the tragic Moplah Rebellion of 1921, perhaps the bloodiest communal clash prior to the catastrophic riots which were to accompany the partition of India. It was, indeed, a tragic episode, fanning the flames of Hindu-Muslim friction. Little is known of the Moplah Rebellion, for strict military censorship was clamped on the entire area of disturbance, the Malabar district of Kerala, at the south-western tip of India. The Moplahs are poor Muslim peasants and petty traders descended from Arab invaders many centuries ago. Like tenants in many parts of India they suffered from the oppression of absentee landlordism. But in their case the situation was complicated by the fact that most of the landlords were Hindus. Fanatically religious, they had a reputation for periodic outbursts of violence.

Early in 1921 the message of civil disobedience was carried to the Moplahs by Congress and *Khilafat* spokesmen. When some of their local leaders were arrested, tension among the Moplahs rose. Then martial law was proclaimed in the two sub-districts where the Moplahs are concentrated. Thus far the agitation had been non-violent. The spark to the uprising was alleged insults to their religious leaders. Although the Moplahs had few guns at their disposal, they were expert guerrilla fighters and used their swords to good effect. At first the rebellion was directed against the Government. As it spread, however, it took the form of a peasant uprising against Hindu landlords. The provincial government moved thousands of troops into the area, and a full-scale military operation followed.

Official figures on the casualties suggest its magnitude: 2,339 killed, 1,652 wounded, 5,955 captured and 39,348 'prisoners',

E

of whom 24,167 were convicted of rebellion or lesser crimes.[1] The communal twist to the uprising inevitably affected Hindu-Muslim relations elsewhere in India. And when the Congress-*Khilafat* alliance disintegrated, the Moplah tragedy was still fresh in many Indian minds. In 1924 it was to bear bitter fruit. The communal danger was now becoming ominous. News of the Kohat incident in September 1924 reverberated throughout the country. In an effort to prevent the plague from spreading, Gandhi embarked on a dramatic and perilous twenty-one-day fast. As always, the danger to his life galvanized the protagonists into action. A Unity Conference of leaders of all communities was hastily called in Delhi, and the tension receded. But communal peace was short-lived. As long as the Congress was stagnant and engaged in intra-party strife, as long as it failed to rally people of all communities by an inspiring goal, as was the case from 1922 to 1928, extremists from both major communities had a free hand. And so the much-vaunted Hindu-Muslim friendship was transformed into continuous communal conflict.

Nehru was no less appalled than the Mahatma by this upsurge of violence. Indeed, one of the most attractive features of the non-co-operation movement was the remarkable unity that it created between Hindu and Muslim. Nehru was incapable of thinking in terms of communalism, which he viewed as basically a struggle for jobs and prestige among opportunistic politicians using religious symbols and loyalties to further their own aims. Then as later he was of the firm belief that the Hindu and Muslim peasant masses resort to communal violence only because they are misled by anti-social politicians, indifferent to the welfare of the nation.

As he surveyed the tension of the mid-'twenties from home and abroad, his hostility to orthodox religion crystallized. Writing to Syed Mahmud on 24 May 1926, Nehru gave vent to his feelings about the state of affairs in India at the time: 'I do not attach very much importance to political squabbles, but the communal frenzy is awful to contemplate. We seem to have

---

[1] Figures given by the Hon. Sir Malcolm Hailey in reply to the question of Khan Bahadur Sarfaraz Hussain Khan regarding the number of casualties during the Moplah rebellion, in the Legislative Assembly, 1923. H.O.R. No. 1749, made available by the National Archives of India.

been caught in a whirlpool of mutual hatred and we go round and round and down and down this abyss. . . . For months or even a year or more we have thought that the situation was so bad that it could not become worse. . . . But it does go worse and heaven knows where it will end.'[1]

About religion itself Nehru was even more critical; along with dogma of any kind it was a curse to be eradicated. In other letters to his friend, Dr. Mahmud, he declared: 'No country or people who are slaves to dogma . . . can progress, and unhappily our country and people have become extraordinarily dogmatic and little-minded. . . . Religion as practised in India has become the old man of the sea for us, and it has not only broken our backs but stultified and almost killed all originality of thought and mind. Like Sinbad the sailor we must get rid of this terrible burden before we can aspire to breathe freely or do anything useful. . . . I have no patience left with the legitimate and illegitimate offspring of religion.'[2]

* * * *

These were, in truth, lean years for Jawaharlal Nehru. The Congress was at a low ebb, ridden with jealousy and petty squabbles; communal tension was on the rise; independence seemed more remote than ever; the scope for fruitful activity on the national plane was restricted to the negative tactics of the Swarajists in the legislatures. Revulsion against these developments led Nehru to the one area of public affairs where constructive work seemed possible—municipal politics.

Soon after the Nabha adventure, in the autumn of 1923, Jawaharlal was elected Chairman of the Allahabad Municipality. There was nothing unique about this. Many Congressmen, especially the rabid no-changers, favoured the capture of municipal corporations in order to retain a link with the masses. Thus it was that a host of leading Congressmen migrated to the municipal field: C. R. Das in Calcutta, Vithalbhai Patel in Bombay, Vallabhbhai Patel in Ahmedabad, Rajendra Prasad in Patna, Sri Prakasa in Benares, and Jawaharlal in his home town.

As in every other field of endeavour, Nehru plunged into his

[1] Unpublished Nehru-Mahmud Correspondence.
[2] Ibid., 12 June 1926 and 12 January 1927.

work with vigour and enthusiasm. Here was an outlet for frustrated energy. And there was much to do—enlarging the scope of social services, reducing taxes, infusing a moribund organization with efficiency and *élan*. By his own admission he worked hard and was attracted to the challenge of municipal reform. Being a perfectionist by nature, he concentrated authority in his own hands, as he was to do in the Congress secretariat during his lengthy tenure as General Secretary, from 1923 to 1925 and from 1927 to 1929, and in the Government of India after 1947. Memoranda flowed from his pen on issues great and small—education, sanitation, prostitution, the removing of billboards which disfigured the city, and the like.

His tenure of office was three years, but by the beginning of the second he was anxious to resign. At every turn his reform programme came up against serious obstacles. Nepotism and corruption were rampant in the permanent ranks of the service. His proposals for a tax on land and a general reorganization of the municipal tax structure were rejected as beyond the jurisdiction of the local government. The bureaucracy moved slowly, far too slowly for his mercurial temperament. The municipality was utterly dependent on the provincial treasury. It was not, he admitted, deliberate obstruction in most cases. Rather, it was the very nature of the division of functions and powers between provincial and local governments which was the root of the problem. 'Politics' were excluded from the latter, but politics in his terms meant the Constructive Programme of Gandhi as well as his own reform schemes. No fundamental changes were possible. And Nehru has rarely been satisfied with palliatives, on the local, national or international planes. Gradually he came to the conclusion that his energy was being dissipated in a hopeless cause.

Yet the experience was highly instructive: it brought the intellectual down to earth, into the realm of day-to-day administration with its many unsavoury features. For the first time he was subjected to the rigours of detail, which he has never fully mastered. Undoubtedly this apprenticeship influenced his attitude to the civil service and machine politics in later years.

By all accounts his venture into the arena of local politics was successful, within the limits imposed by scanty funds and the legal framework of municipal administration. The provincial government commended his services. The machinery of local government was toned up. Corruption was reduced, though it could not be eradicated, probably the main reason for his dissatisfaction. And his colleagues were impressed. One bitter political opponent was reported to have said: 'Whatever we may think of young Nehru's socialistic doctrines and his Bolshevist ideas, the efficient way in which he handled the Allahabad Municipality was beyond all praise.'[1]

While Nehru was busily engaged in local politics, along with the then uninspiring functions of Congress General Secretary, his father was at the pinnacle of his career, as the Swarajist leader in the Legislative Assembly. Motilal Nehru had no objections to his son's interest in the affairs of Allahabad but he could not appreciate Jawaharlal's devotion to what seemed a secondary matter. In particular, the suave, polished aristocrat was unimpressed by his son's persistent efforts to come into closer touch with the masses.

One incident illustrates the difference in their temperament and outlook. During this period the younger Nehru was in the habit of dressing simply and of using a bullock cart to get around the city. One evening, while Motilal was holding court on the veranda of the palatial *Anand Bhawan*, his son arrived. As he turned up the driveway his father yelled out, 'If you want to come up to the house, leave that monstrosity at the gate.' The elder Nehru's sensibilities were hurt by this seeming reversion to the primitive.

Despite such friction and their disagreements on national politics—Jawaharlal was much closer to Gandhi's views—the personal relations between father and son were essentially unimpaired. Nehru admired his father's strength of character and his devotion to principles, his generosity and his deep, patriarchal concern for the family. Motilal Nehru was proud of his beloved Jawahar, a rising star in the firmament of nationalist politics. During this period the younger Nehru found much solace and comfort in his family, compensations for his frustration with the dismal political scene. He drew closer to his wife who had shown sympathy and understanding during the period of travail after 1920.

[1] Quoted by Mitra, Sunilkumar, in Brown, Ermine A. (ed.), *Eminent Indians*, p. 45.

One source of dissatisfaction, however, was his continuing financial dependence on his father. Jawaharlal was then in his mid-thirties but had no regular source of income. He had abandoned his law practice, and the idea of remuneration for public service was alien to the Congress, largely because of its upper middle-class composition until 1920. He was unhappy with this state of affairs but he found the alternatives equally unattractive. A return to the law was 'out of the question', emotionally repellent. Lucrative offers from business organizations he rejected because of his antipathy to such an association. In 1924 a way out of his dilemma presented itself, a proposal to pay full-time officials of the Congress. Alas, Motilal Nehru was strongly opposed, for public work was *noblesse oblige*. The son yielded. On one occasion Jawaharlal broached the issue of dependence to his father. Motilal explained that he could earn enough for his son's annual needs in a few days at the Bar —which was not exaggerated—while Jawaharlal would be compelled to spend most of his time earning a living. Although he remained dissatisfied, Nehru yielded once again to his father's persuasion.

During 1925 Jawaharlal began to notice a tendency to baldness. He was anxious to stay the inevitable and consulted a friend, who recommended a special hair tonic. Nehru was appalled by the odour. 'It is a most evil-smelling concoction,' he wrote, 'and if offensiveness in smell is a measure of its efficacy, then I should have a thick crop of hair in the future!'[1] Alas, there was no correlation.

Some insight into Nehru's character was provided by two other letters in 1925, both concerning Syed Mahmud's decision to name a son after his idol. 'For heaven's sake don't call your son Jawahar Lal', he admonished his friend. 'Jawahar by itself might pass but the addition of Lal makes it odious. . . . I cannot congratulate you on your aesthetic taste. I dislike my name intensely.'[2] The streak of vanity in Nehru's character was already evident in this early, trivial episode.

This relatively uneventful period in Nehru's life was brought to an end abruptly by the news in the autumn of 1925 that his wife's tubercular infection had become much worse. For months

---

[1] Unpublished Nehru-Mahmud Correspondence, 3 September 1925.
[2] Ibid., 24 May 1925 and 3 June 1925.

she lay seriously ill in a Lucknow hospital. It was a hectic period for Jawaharlal. As General Secretary he carried the heavy burden of organizing the annual Congress session scheduled for Kanpur, as well as directing the office of the All-India Congress Committee in Allahabad. His old friend, Dr. Ansari, recommended medical attention in Switzerland to try to arrest the spreading disease. And so Nehru made preparations for what he mistakenly believed would be a brief stay in Europe.

Aside from the urgent need to take his wife abroad for health reasons, Nehru welcomed the opportunity to get away from the depressing atmosphere of Indian politics. Conditions were ripe for a change. His mind was clouded, there seemed no way out of the impasse, and he felt that a trip abroad would give him a new perspective. In this he was remarkably prescient, for his European sojourn in 1926–7 proved to be a turning-point in his intellectual growth.

CHAPTER V

Sojourn in the West

IT was early in March 1926 that Jawaharlal, Kamala and their eight-year-old daughter sailed from Bombay for Venice *en route* to Switzerland. Accompanying them were his sister, Vijaya Lakshmi, Nan as she was known to family and friends, and her husband, Ranjit Pandit, a handsome, wealthy north Indian Brahmin with a deep interest in India's past. Although Nehru never developed an intimate friendship with his brother-in-law, his awakened interest in the history and traditions of his native land owed much to conversations with the studious Ranjit who achieved some prominence among scholars by his translation of a famous chronicle of early Kashmiri history, the *Rajatarangini*. Sensitive and fragile, and ill-suited to the hurly-burly of nationalist politics, Ranjit participated actively in Congress civil disobedience campaigns. Weakened by the experience, he died in prison in 1944.[1]

The Nehrus intended to stay abroad six or seven months, but Kamala's disease responded to treatment less quickly than anticipated. In the summer of 1926 Jawaharlal's younger sister, Krishna, arrived, to keep house and tour Europe with her brother. Then, in the autumn of 1927, when they were on the verge of returning to India, their father joined them. Thus it was that the sojourn stretched to twenty-one months.

Much had changed since the younger Nehru last said farewell to the West, in the summer of 1912. A world war had unleashed new social forces everywhere. Conflicting ideologies vied for supremacy amidst the ruins of nineteenth-century Europe. In

---

[1] The highly respected Pandit family was originally from the village of Bambuli on the Ratnagir coast of Maharashtra. Ranjit's father moved to the princely State of Rajkot in the Kathiawar peninsula, north of Bombay. It was there, in a feudal, carefree atmosphere that Jawaharlal's brother-in-law spent his formative years. His record at Christ Church, Oxford, and the Middle Temple, was a brilliant one, and he also gained higher degrees at the Sorbonne and Heidelberg. For a touching portrait of Ranjit Pandit see Sahgal Nayantara (his daughter), *Prison and Chocolate Cake*, especially pp. 42–48.

the vast domain of the Czars the old order had been swept away by Communist revolution. The Hapsburg empire had disintegrated. The Ottoman dynasty had collapsed. With several notable exceptions, the map of Europe had been redrawn to conform with Wilsonian idealism. Nationalism had triumphed, and socialism was not far behind. America had emerged temporarily from isolationism. And in Asia the colonial peoples had begun to demand a larger measure of self-government, a demand which became increasingly vocal until, at the end of the second world war, the European withdrawal could no longer be stayed.

The tragedy of war had penetrated deeply into the consciousness of European peoples—though, alas, not deeply enough to prevent another holocaust twenty years later. The hatreds of the past had not yet subsided. The victors, notably France, sought to retain the spoils of war and to ensure their security. The vanquished, especially Germany, brooded over their defeat and the *diktat*, the Versailles Treaty, which many swore to cast aside at the first opportunity. Soviet Russia was outlawed from the family of nations, and concerted efforts were made to destroy the new régime by direct military intervention. Disastrous inflation in Germany during the early 'twenties had cast a dark shadow over the Weimar Republic and was to contribute to its undoing. America retreated behind the Atlantic moat, and Europe struggled for some semblance of stability. Revolutions and *coups d'état* were frequent occurrences in the aftermath of war. Socialism and trade union federations grew in strength, attracting millions of urban workers to their cause.

Gradually a measure of pacification came to the Continent. The League of Nations, that slim hope of international order, was at the height of its prestige. Just before the Nehrus arrived, political tensions in western Europe were eased with the signing of the Locarno Pacts. The passions of war and revolution had temporarily exhausted themselves, and a period of tranquillity seemed to be at hand.

Nehru himself had undergone a radical change during the fourteen years separating his visits to Europe. He had emerged from the sheltered life of *Anand Bhawan*. He had experienced the thrill and pain of political strife, the sense of fulfilment during the civil disobedience campaign of 1921–2 and the disillusionment of its aftermath. Three times had he been behind the prison walls. No longer was he the priggish, rich man's son, a typical product of Harrow and Cambridge. He had ventured out of his class and surroundings to feel the pulse of India's peasants and urban workers. He had seen at first hand the squalid reality of Indian poverty. The effect on his sensitive spirit was electrifying.

He had come under the influence of Gandhi and had abandoned the life of leisure which greeted him on his return. The great stage of politics had beckoned, and he was drawn to its drama and its pathos. He had risen rapidly in the ranks of the Congress, an acknowledged 'protégé' of the Mahatma. Although Nehru was still a Westerner in thought, Gandhi's views and his own experiences had infused a distinctively Indian flavour. He was a convert to *satyagraha*, though not all of his questions or yearnings were satisfied by his mentor's teachings. He had experienced the frustrations of municipal administration and the petty politics of his colleagues in the gloomy days of 1923 to 1925. He was still in search of a faith when he arrived in Europe the following year.

*   *   *   *

On the whole Nehru's sojourn in the West was a quiet, peaceful interlude, a period for reflection and serious reading. Of necessity most of the time was spent in Switzerland, either in Geneva or at a nearby mountain sanatorium in Montana. But as Kamala's health improved, Jawaharlal was able to pay brief visits to neighbouring countries. Before they returned to India he managed to pause in France, England, Belgium, Holland, Germany and the Soviet Union. Two of these excursions were to leave a marked imprint on Nehru's outlook, namely Brussels, the site of an anti-imperialist congress in February 1927, and Moscow in November of that year.

While in Geneva Nehru lived modestly, in a three-room flat, cared for by his sister, Krishna. From afar, he anxiously watched developments at home. It was a depressing sight, for the Congress sank ever-deeper into the morass of factionalism; and communal strife continued unabated. Yet he was in high spirits and did not long to return to India, certainly not until the end of 1926. In reply to a friend's inquiry about his mood and health, he wrote on 11 August of that year: 'The outlook in

India is dark enough, but somehow I do not feel as pessimistic as the news would warrant. Do not get downhearted. We shall still see swaraj. . . . As for me, I am flourishing like the proverbial green bay tree!'[1] A few months later Sarojini Naidu, the poetess-laureate of the Congress, shed some light on his mood, in her typically florid style. 'I hear all sorts of nice rumours about you,' she wrote to Nehru, 'things that please me —of your restored *joie de vivre*. I am so glad that you have had such a prolonged vacation from the torpid horrors of Indian life. . . . How I rejoice that you are out of India and that your soul has found its chance to renew its youth and glory.'[2]

Towards the end of 1926, however, his impulse to action asserted itself. In a letter to Dr. Syed Mahmud he wrote,

I am beginning to feel a bit restive and I wish I could hurl myself into the whirlpool of Indian politics. The suppressed energy of some months wants an outlet. I should have liked to be at the Gauhati Congress [the annual session held at the end of December]. Not that I think I would have done any good to anybody, but I would feel better for a little aggressiveness. And there seem to be so many people about in India whom I should like to go for! There is nothing to be downhearted about. . . . We are passing through an inevitable phase and we shall be the better for it. So cheer up and give it hot to everybody at Gauhati. And more power to your elbow if you do so.[3]

The early months of Nehru's stay in Europe were among the most uneventful of his adult life. As always during his periods of inaction, in prison and elsewhere, he read voraciously. He also observed with interest the changing moods of Europe in transition, the flow of ideas, the intellectual debates of the time and the struggles waged by the Powers. The experiments in world organization, both the League of Nations and the I.L.O., attracted him but did not seem to leave any noticeable influence; his internationalism was yet to emerge under the impact of the ideological and political conflicts of the 1930's.

Ever in search of more satisfying answers to the basic problems of ethics and politics, he went on various 'pilgrimages' to Villa Olga, the home of Romain Rolland in nearby Villeneuve.

---

[1] Unpublished Nehru-Mahmud Correspondence, 11 August 1926. (From Geneva.)

[2] Unpublished Nehru Letters, 15 October 1926.

[3] Unpublished Nehru-Mahmud Correspondence. 1 December 1926. (From Montana.)

Towards the end of his life Rolland became an admirer of
Gandhi and tried to bring the Mahatma's message before the
European public. Although Nehru was impressed by the great
French novelist, the highly spiritual tone of Rolland's social
philosophy was too remote and abstract to inspire him, either
emotionally or intellectually. By contrast Nehru was immediately drawn to the sensitive, morose, passionate young German
poet, Ernst Toller, whom he met at the anti-imperialist Congress in Brussels. There was a natural affinity in their temperament and ideas, though Toller expressed them in words and
Nehru in deeds. Thereafter they maintained an irregular
correspondence. When Toller committed suicide, on the eve of
the second world war, Jawaharlal wrote a moving eulogy on his
friend, victim of Nazi racialism, broken in spirit by a sense of
impending disaster. Nehru also met Frank Buchman and was
appalled by the ideas of Moral Rearmament.

In Geneva itself the Nehrus had few friends or acquaintances.
Jawaharlal and his sister, Krishna, recall only two from this
period: Roger Baldwin, later prominent in the Union of Civil
Liberties; and Dhan Gopal Mukerji, an Indian expatriate in
America, who showed some promise as a writer, notably for his
controversial *My Brother's Face*. Like Toller, Mukerji took his
own life.

In the mountain resort where Kamala was undergoing treatment time moved even more slowly. There was no sense of
urgency, no rigorous schedule, no commitments of any kind.
Thus, with the approach of winter Jawaharlal indulged in
sports—skiing, ice-skating and tobogganing, and climbing
among the lofty peaks which reminded him of his beloved
Himalayas. 'I succumbed to its fascination', he wrote later of
his initial effort at skiing. 'It was a painful experience for a
long time, but I persisted bravely, in spite of innumerable falls,
and I came to enjoy it.'[1]

On one of these outings he narrowly escaped death. It was
on the Col de Voza. Nehru was tobogganing with some friends
and was oblivious to the world about him. One of them pushed
him forward when he was unprepared. Down the slope he went
towards a sharp precipice less than a hundred feet away. But
the gods were kind—he was able to swerve away from the cliff

[1] *Toward Freedom*, p. 122.

and escaped with only minor injuries.[1] It was not the first time that he had cheated death while holidaying in the hills. Many years before, in the summer of 1909, a similar incident occurred while he was on vacation in Norway. And in 1916, soon after his marriage, he barely escaped death in Kashmir while trekking north of the Zoji-la Pass towards the holy cave of Amarnath. Nor was it his last encounter with death. But in the future the dangers were man-made—attempts at assassination.

* * * *

During a brief visit to Berlin towards the end of 1926 Nehru learned about a proposed Congress of Oppressed Nationalities at Brussels in February 1927. The idea immediately attracted him and, at his suggestion, the Indian National Congress decided to participate. Being on the scene, Jawaharlal was appointed Congress representative to this unusual gathering of radical spokesmen for colonial peoples and their sympathizers in Latin America and Europe.

The Brussels Congress proved to be a milestone in the development of Nehru's political thought, notably his espousal of socialism and a broad international outlook. It was there that he first came into contact with orthodox communists, left-wing socialists and radical nationalists from Asia and Africa. It was there that the goals of national independence and social reform became linked inextricably in his conception of future political strategy. It was there, too, that the notion of an Afro-Asian group of nations co-operating with one another was conceived. Indeed, the Bandung Conference in 1955 may be seen as the fruition of an idea which first found emotional expression at Brussels almost thirty years earlier.

Nehru himself sees Bandung in this perspective. In talking about the Bandung Conference he remarked, 'I will tell you an old story. Perhaps you have come across the fact that I attended a conference in Brussels in 1927.' The Asian delegates wanted to meet regularly thereafter but 'found that it was not possible for us to meet anywhere except in some country of Western Europe'. When I interjected, 'the world has changed since then', his face glowed and, in slow, measured words, he said, 'the world has changed and of course we meet'.[2]

[1] Hutheesingh, *With No Regrets*, pp. 41–42.
[2] To the author in New Delhi on 13 June 1956.

The idea for an anti-imperialist conference came from a small group of revolutionaries in Berlin, then the European centre of political exiles from the colonial world. It had strong moral support from Moscow which welcomed such a gathering as a device for infiltration into nationalist circles throughout Asia. Diverse European intellectuals and leftist trade union leaders were drawn by sympathy for the underdog and, possibly, by a sense of guilt over the unsavoury aspects of European domination. Many delegates had strong communist sympathies, though the ideologies of those present varied considerably, from left-Centre to orthodox Marxism. Among the most prominent figures were George Lansbury, the arch-pacifist, Albert Einstein and Romain Rolland, both of whom sent messages of sympathy. The principal sources of funds were the Mexican Government, which viewed the conference as a symbol of protest against American intervention in the affairs of Latin America, and the Kuomintang, the Chinese Nationalist Party, which hoped to rouse Western public opinion against British intervention in China. The response was impressive, with representatives from the Middle and Far East, North Africa, Central and South America, and from Britain, France and Italy. Among them were persons who were to play important roles in the struggles for national independence in Asia.

For Nehru this was an informal début on the international stage. Yet even at Brussels his role was far from unimportant. As a mark of honour to the movement he represented he was elected to the presidium of the conference and later served on the nine-man Executive Committee of the newly formed League against Imperialism, along with George Lansbury, Albert Einstein, Romain Rolland and Mme. Sun Yat-sen.

Words are often the clue to a man's thought. Nehru's speeches at Brussels throw much light on his prevailing outlook, as well as on the priority of his loyalties and political objectives. On the eve of the conference he issued a statement to the press, a forthright attack on Imperialism bristling with Marxist terminology—though he was not yet deeply read in Marxist literature. There was, too, a broad world perspective, which was to be refined and developed in the mid-'thirties. The Indian National Congress, he said, 'is based on the most intense internationalism'. It was the wish giving rise to the thought, for no one else in the Congress thought seriously in these terms at the time; indeed, most Indian nationalists never rose above their limited national horizon. He attacked England bitterly for sending troops from one Asian colony (India) to suppress a nationalist movement in another Asian country (China) and appealed to subject peoples everywhere to co-operate in a world-wide struggle against foreign rule.

At the plenary session of the conference he delivered an impassioned address on 'India's exploitation—how India is maltreated, repressed and plundered'. In tone and language it was typical of the radical socialist pronouncements then in vogue, an angry critique of Imperialism and all its misdeeds. The early history of British rule in India was denounced in a flourish of rhetoric: 'An epoch of predatory war—a period in which freebooters prowled about and committed plunders and robberies in an unbridled manner.' He accused the British of fostering and aggravating communal discord, of destroying India's traditional economy at the cost of human misery, and of uprooting India's ancient educational system, replacing it with something 'which is ridiculously meagre'. He predicted that when India became independent 'it is certain that the British world-empire will cease to exist'. Ironically, it was Nehru's decision to remain in the Commonwealth which helped to preserve the empire twenty-two years later. He was acutely aware of India's pivotal role in the Afro-Asian world, politically and strategically, noting that many countries in the area would achieve their freedom only when India itself were independent. There was evidence, too, of a marked socialist outlook. The resolution on India, drafted and moved by Nehru, declared that 'this Congress further trusts that the Indian national movement will base its programme on the full emancipation of the peasants and workers of India, without which there can be no real freedom'.[1]

In his report to the All-India Congress Committee, written on his return to Switzerland, Nehru referred to 'the rising imperialism of the United States' which was acquiring a stranglehold in Central and South America. Looking to the future, he

---

[1] The texts of Nehru's statement to the press, his address to the Brussels Congress, and the resolution moved by him in the Plenary Session are to be found in the *Indian Quarterly Register*, vol. i, 1927, pp. 204–5, 209–11 and 207 respectively.

anticipated orthodox Marxists in viewing American expansion as a graver danger than existing British imperialism unless the two unite in an Anglo-Saxon bloc to dominate the world. His account of the conference was most favourable and he urged the Congress to maintain a link with the newly established League against Imperialism. It was, he wrote, a useful channel for propaganda and it offered facilities for closer contact with other Asian nationalist movements. '. . . Regarded from any point of view, [it] was an event of first-class importance and it is likely to have far-reaching results.'[1]

There was a large element of wishful thinking in this prognosis. Nehru could not have anticipated the degree to which Asia and Africa would be altered politically during the next three decades. Yet when the Afro-Asian conference met at Bandung in the spring of 1955, the Brussels Congress had already become a legend. President Sukarno of Indonesia, in his opening address, paid tribute to the Brussels conclave as the earliest expression of a desire for stronger links among Eastern peoples.[2] For Nehru Bandung was the fulfilment of a dream—Asia reborn, proud and free, playing an important role in the world community. At Brussels this goal was proclaimed by a handful of nationalist leaders. At Bandung it was realized in some measure by official spokesmen for governments representing well over a billion people.

Nehru's attraction to Marxism was perhaps the most striking feature of his role at the Brussels Congress. Nor was he unaware of the communist bias of its creation, the League against Imperialism. But at this stage of his political outlook, and indeed for the next fifteen years, collaboration between nationalism and communism seemed to him natural and desirable. It was not Marxist theory that attracted him at the outset; rather, it was an emotional aversion to the social democrats and faith in the Soviet experiment. Recalling this period in his autobiography, he wrote: 'As between the labour worlds of the Second International and the Third International, my sympathies were with the latter. The whole record of the Second

---

[1] The text of this report is to be found in *Indian Quarterly Register*, vol. ii, 1927, pp. 152–9.
[2] The text of Sukarno's address is in Kahin, George McT., *The Asian-African Conference*, pp. 39–51.

International from the war onward filled me with distaste, and we in India had had sufficient personal experience of the methods of one of its strongest supports—the British Labour party. So I turned inevitably with good will towards communism, for, whatever its faults, it was at least not hypocritical and not imperialistic. . . . These attracted me, as also the tremendous changes taking place in Russia.' And yet, even at this time, Nehru had serious reservations about his communist colleagues. 'But communists often irritated me by their dictatorial ways, their aggressive and rather vulgar methods, their habit of denouncing everybody who did not agree with them.'[1]

As early as 1927, then, the dichotomy in Nehru's attitude to communism was already visible. He was emotionally attracted to the vision of a classless society but he was emotionally repelled by the communist militant; 'their aggressive and rather vulgar methods' went against the grain of the cultivated aristocrat. From that time onwards this split mentality is evident in his attitude to communism both at home and abroad.

Nehru's doubts went far beyond these emotional sources of friction. Then as later his primary loyalty was to Indian national interests. In case of conflict his attachment to socialism and internationalism was invariably expendable. While this priority is normal for a responsible statesman, it was also true of Nehru twenty years before he assumed power. He has always been the nationalist *par excellence*.

This oft-disputed aspect of Nehru's political outlook emerges clearly from a supplementary report on the Brussels Congress marked 'confidential and not for publication' which he prepared for the High Command of his party. 'The disadvantages [of affiliation with the League against Imperialism]', he wrote, 'might be *the socialist character of the League and the possibility that Russian foreign policy might influence it.* [Moreover] Mr. Saklatwala [a prominent Indian communist, resident in London] . . . has been criticizing the boycott of Lancashire goods in India on the ground that it injures their comrades in Lancashire. This is an example of a possible conflict between *our nationalistic interests* and the interests of the workers outside.'[2]

[1] *Toward Freedom*, p. 126.
[2] Extracts from Nehru's confidential report on the Brussels Congress to the Working Committee are in the files of the History of the Freedom Movement

Nehru's relations with the League against Imperialism were excellent during the first two years of its existence. He was its principal contact in India and its staunchest supporter within the Indian National Congress, as well as a member of its Executive Committee. At his behest the Congress was formally affiliated to the League in 1927 and reaffirmed its support of the League's aims the following year. By the middle of 1929, however, dissension became apparent. At the second session of the League, held in Frankfurt in July 1929, a resolution was passed, without the knowledge of the Congress delegate, criticizing Gandhi and his supporters for compromising with the British and for allegedly suppressing the revolutionary urge of Indian workers. Later in the year the clash came into the open. Nehru had signed the 'Delhi Manifesto', a Gandhi-inspired compromise to render civil disobedience unnecessary if Dominion status were granted immediately.

The League against Imperialism was appalled. In vain it urged him to withdraw his approval. Virendranath Chattopadhyaya, General Secretary of the League, wrote to Nehru: 'Internationally your position will be quite untenable unless you do what great leaders have often done, namely publicly admit a mistake and take *the right line*. . . . Your signature of the Delhi Manifesto was a betrayal of the Indian masses in the struggle for Independence.'[1] A similar 'order' to recant was issued by Reginald Bridgeman, secretary of the British branch of the League.

Nehru's response was typical of the man. His pride revolted against the slightest hint of dictation. 'I have not done any such thing', he replied to Bridgeman. Moreover, he was not prepared to brook any interference in the internal affairs of the Congress from an international organization. 'Good advice is always welcome, but . . . people have a tendency to jump to conclusions without sufficient data', was his rebuke to the League. What incensed Nehru even more was a circular sent by Chattopadhyaya to workers' and peasants' organizations and 'sincere anti-imperialist elements' in India criticizing Gandhi for 'chronic reformism and betrayal of the cause of

Project in New Delhi, File 1 (B.19). These were made available by the Government of India. (Emphasis added.)
[1] Unpublished Nehru Letters, 4 December 1929. (Emphasis added.)

workers and peasants'. This sealed the issue for Nehru—it was reprehensible interference. His loyalty to Gandhi and the Congress came first. Only so long as the League's anti-imperialist goal and its tactics did not come into conflict with the Congress was the alliance maintained. For his 'deviationism' Nehru was expelled from the League. He in turn severed all relations with the League. On 15 April 1930 he issued a directive to the All-India Congress Committee secretariat: 'No further communications are to be sent to the League against Imperialism from this office.'[1] In 1930, as in the 1950's, Nehru placed the interests of India ahead of extra-national considerations.

* * * *

Nehru's initial exposure to communist views at Brussels was widened by a brief visit to Moscow early in November 1927. The Nehrus were invited to attend the tenth anniversary celebration of the Bolshevik Revolution. Motilal was reluctant to accept, partly because of his indifference to the communist experiment, partly because of their impending departure for India. But 'Jawahar was keen to go and so father gave in.'[2]

With Kamala and Krishna they went by train from Berlin across the desolate Polish plain. It was a tedious and uncomfortable journey, unrelieved by the monotonous landscape of the surrounding countryside. After twenty-eight hours they arrived at the Soviet frontier town of Niegeroloje, their first contact with 'the new society'. The whole town, according to Nehru, was seized with a mood of gay abandon and was bedecked with red flags and pictures of Lenin. He felt that they were simple people, politically unsophisticated but jovial and friendly. Everywhere there was evidence of a personality cult— hero-worship of Lenin.

As honoured guests of the Kremlin the Nehrus were given an enthusiastic reception, a makeshift banquet and an appropriate speech by a local dignitary, which was translated into something that resembled French—to which the younger Nehru made a brief reply. Its apparent spontaneity made the desired impression. Actually the spectacle was far from alien to their

[1] History of the Freedom Movement Project, File 2 (B.21).
[2] Hutheesingh, *With No Regrets*, p. 51.

experience; as Motilal remarked to his son, it seemed no different from the response of Indian villagers to leading Congressmen during the civil disobedience campaign.

In contrast to the journey across Poland the Russian part of their trip to Moscow was not unpleasant. Special sleeping accommodation, ample food, and a festive atmosphere along the route compensated for fatigue and boredom on the slow-moving train. They were greeted in the capital by officials of the reception committee and by some young Indian communists, notably S. J. Saklatwala, a member of the British House of Commons whom Jawaharlal had met at Brussels. To their regret they arrived too late to witness the customary mammoth parade in Red Square.

The Nehrus' visit to Russia in 1927 was confined to Moscow and lasted only four days. Yet these few days helped to shape Jawaharlal Nehru's political outlook—his attitude to communism, to the Soviet Union, to the relationship between socialism and nationalism, to Indo-Soviet relations, to Soviet foreign policy in the 'thirties and beyond, and to Indian communists in the Congress until the middle of the second world war. Not that his earliest impressions were rigidly maintained throughout the subsequent thirty years. Nevertheless, his initial direct contact with the Soviets created a basic sympathy which influenced his future outlook. Particularly is this true because they were, in 1927, emotional reactions. And Nehru's approach to most political issues has a strong emotional content.

Genuine sympathy for Soviet society is the dominant theme of his 'random sketches and impressions' which were published in the Indian press in 1928.[1] Read in the 1950's they appear incredibly naïve, an almost unquestioning assumption that the idealistic pronouncements of the Soviet leaders would be translated into reality without blemish. Occasional reservations creep into his 'discovery of Russia', but on the whole he accepted what he saw and heard as indices of 'the good society'. In this he was not alone. And undoubtedly those impressions reflected his receptive mood at the time, a will to believe, and perhaps to find answers to some of the questions still troubling

---

[1] Nehru's articles were published in book form in 1929—*Soviet Russia*. (The Inter-Continental Library.) The following quotations relating to his visit to Russia in 1927 are taken from this book. (Emphasis added.)

him, questions to which Gandhi's answers were not entirely acceptable.

Moscow itself struck a responsive chord. He was drawn to its blend of the Orient and the Occident, its collection of 'strange peoples from the east and the west', its sheer variety of dress so different from that of other European capitals. All this appealed to his pride as an Asian. '. . . In Moscow Asia peeps out from every corner, not tropical Asia but the Asia of the wide steppes and the cold regions of the north and east and centre.'

Its apparent equalitarianism was also a source of attraction: '. . . The real change one notices in Moscow, and which grows on one with every day's stay, is in the atmosphere and the very air of the place. The contrasts between extreme luxury and poverty are not visible, nor does one notice the hierarchy of class or caste.' He was impressed, too, by the seeming simplicity of the life of Soviet officials and members of the Communist Party, as contrasted with the large salaries, the material comforts and the ostentation of British officials in Delhi. In describing his visit to Mikhail Kalinin, then president of the Soviet Union, he noted that the Russian leader lived in three small rooms in the Kremlin.

On a visit to the State Opera House he was surprised by the casual dress of the audience, consisting mostly of ordinary workers. How different they were from the elegant ladies and gentlemen in the opera houses of the West. The beauty of the Moscow ballet amply satisfied his aesthetic taste and might have become synonymous in his mind with the culture of the new Soviet world. Only two features of life in the capital marred his favourable impression—the failure to stamp out begging on the streets and the ubiquity of the *droshky*, the archaic horse-drawn carriage which was widely used in the absence of automobiles.

As an 'expert' on the Indian penal system his curiosity was aroused by prison life in the Soviet Union. A brief tour of a prison just outside Moscow added to his admiration of communism. It contrasted sharply, he believed, with conditions in Indian jails. From his account it must have appeared an idyllic system. The warders carried no weapons; *he was told* that handcuffs were never used—they were kept in museums, said the

Governor; prisoners were allowed to smoke whenever they wished; trade union rules applied to their working conditions wherever possible; physical punishment had been eliminated. He met a Czech political prisoner who was a professional musician and was told that he had been made director of music in the prison.

All this 'created a most favourable impression on our minds'. So too did the declared emphasis on rehabilitation of prisoners to facilitate their reabsorption into normal society. Yet Nehru was cautious in his assessment of prison life and expressed certain reservations. The fact that he was asked to select any cell for inspection suggested to him that 'the whole prison was more or less of a show place, specially meant for the edification of visitors'. Moreover, '*if* this account is correct, and *if* what we saw ourselves truly represents the state of prisons . . . it can be said without a shadow of a doubt that to be in a Russian prison is far preferable than to be a worker in an Indian factory'.

With all this he felt that he had seen 'desirable and radical improvements over the old system prevailing even now in most countries' and that the mentality of prison officials was an ideal approach to the problem. In later years his articles on prison reform drew much from this experience.

Nehru's impressions of other aspects of Soviet society, based on a brief visit and considerable reading, were also very favourable, though doubts protruded from his panegyric now and then. Being acutely conscious of the minority problem in India he was naturally drawn to a study of Soviet policy in this field. His assessment was one of guarded optimism. 'It is difficult to draw any final conclusions about anything Russian at this stage, but it would certainly appear from the progress made in the last five years that the problem of minorities has been largely solved there. This does not mean that complete equality has been established and there are no evils left.' His view of the Soviet record in education was similar. '. . . Although they failed to liquidate illiteracy they have shown remarkable results within these ten years.' In particular he noted its social orientation and the stress on education for the masses which, in his view, provided some guidance for education in a predominantly illiterate India. Basing his judgement on official statistics, he also found peasant conditions improved. 'The progress is remarkable when the manifold difficulties and the lack of aid from outside are considered.' He was impressed, too, by the efforts to establish equality between the sexes, though he recognized that much of the revolutionary legislation in this sphere had not yet been fully implemented.

Among his reflections on Russia at that time was a laudatory portrait of Lenin. His indomitable will, realism, flexibility, and perseverance in the face of overwhelming odds struck Nehru as the hallmarks of political greatness. After a visit to Lenin's mausoleum, he wrote, 'In life they say he was not beautiful to look at. . . . But in death there is a strange beauty and his brow is peaceful and unclouded. On his lips there hovers a smile and there is a suggestion of pugnacity, of work done and success achieved. He has a uniform on and one of his hands is tightly clenched. Even in death he is the dictator.' Nehru called on his readers to learn from Lenin's realism and concluded with a tribute to the Bolshevik leader which resembles his estimate of Gandhi's achievement years later: 'By amazing power of will he hypnotised a nation and filled a disunited and demoralised people with energy and determination and the strength to endure and suffer for a cause.'

Apart from his emotional attraction to the Soviet experiment, Nehru was acutely conscious, even at this early stage, of its practical significance for India. His idealism was not divorced from reality, for he remarked, 'even our self-interest compels us to understand the vast forces which have upset the old order of things. . . . *Russia again cannot be ignored by us, because she is our neighbour, a powerful neighbour, which may be friendly to us and co-operate with us, or may be a thorn in our side. In either event we have to know her and understand her and shape our policy accordingly.*' Although written thirty years ago, here is a lucid statement of one of the core elements in Nehru's foreign policy since Independence.

As he surveyed the international scene in the late 'twenties, Nehru was disturbed by the sharp antagonism between Great Britain and Russia and its implications for subject India. The villain in the piece, he believed, was the former, for 'to every student of recent history it is clear that Russia does not want war'. He lashed out at the British, charged them with perpetuating the *cordon sanitaire*, with sabotaging the Kellogg-Briand

Pact renouncing war as an instrument of national policy, and with pursuing a policy aimed at the destruction of the Soviet régime. As for Russo-Indian relations, he saw no danger from the north. Indeed, he enunciated a thesis which is identical with his later view of India's relations with communist China. 'It is inconceivable that Russia, in her present condition at least, and for a long time to come, will threaten India. . . . The two counties are today too similar to be exploited by each other, and there can be no economic motive for Russia to covet India.' The continuity of thought and policy suggests that the roots of Nehru's foreign policy may be traced to his outlook in the late 1920's.

This hostility to British foreign policy and his personal conflict with British rule in India would seem to explain, at least in part, his sympathy for the Soviets at that time. Not only did communism offer a path to the solution of some of India's basic problems—education, agrarian reform and the problem of minorities—but Russia and Indian nationalism shared a common antipathy to Britain. This community of interests provided an additional support for his view that national independence was bound up with far-reaching social reform.

Nehru's infatuation with the Soviets later gave way to a more sober and mature attitude. This is not to suggest that his attraction was ephemeral. On the contrary, it lingered on for at least twenty years and influenced his thought and action. However, he became increasingly aware of its unsavoury qualities. Misgivings are already evident in his laudatory account of 1928. Although his impressions were favourable on the whole, 'there is much that I do not understand and much that I do not like or admire'. As revealed more fully in subsequent writings, his individualism and liberal philosophy rebelled against the ruthless methods of communism.

*   *   *   *

Nehru's visit to Moscow was the last noteworthy event of his European tour. There was nothing else to keep him in the West. Kamala's health was much improved. His own physical and mental condition was excellent after the prolonged holiday. The sense of inner conflict which plagued him on the eve of his arrival had been overcome. Through reading and visual experience, personal contacts and discussion, he had acquired a wider perspective and a clearer picture of the tasks ahead. There was a self-confidence which had wilted during the period of quiescence in the mid-'twenties.

Perhaps the most far-reaching effect of Nehru's sojourn in the West was to convince him that political freedom was too narrow a goal for the Indian nationalist movement. A socialist society now became the ultimate objective, though he realized that the Congress was primarily concerned with the purely political struggle. And in that respect his European experience strengthened his determination to press for complete independence, not merely Dominion status. This battle was to dominate Congress politics for the next two years.

Not only was Nehru's return to India timely, in terms of his own personal and family problems. The political situation at home was showing signs of emerging from the doldrums. And he was anxious to attend the annual Congress session in Madras at the end of December 1927. Thus, early that month he sailed from Marseilles with Kamala, Krishna, and his daughter Indira. The elder Nehru remained on the Continent a few months longer.

Although he had derived considerable benefit from his stay in Europe, and though it was necessary because of Kamala's health, Jawaharlal had qualms of conscience about his lengthy absence from the Indian political scene. This he admitted to party stalwarts and friends in his home town soon after his return: 'For a soldier to desert from the field of battle and while away his time in leisurely repose far from the scenes of conflict is not usually considered a very praiseworthy act.'[1] There is no evidence that his colleagues begrudged him the holiday.

[1] Reply to the Address of Welcome by the Allahabad District Board, in Dwivedi, op. cit., p. 67.

CHAPTER VI

Nehru comes of Age

FRESH from his European tour, Nehru plunged into Congress politics with renewed vigour at the Madras session in 1927. Many of his proposals dealt with 'foreign policy'. Although these were without practical importance at the time, they heralded Nehru's new role as Congress spokesman on international affairs, a position which he has held without interruption for the past thirty years. One of these resolutions, on the War Danger, was to be recalled in the autumn of 1939, for it spelled out the Congress determination not to participate in an 'Imperialist War'.

The most striking feature of Nehru's return to the political wars, however, was a sharp clash with Gandhi, the first of a series during the next two decades. The precipitating cause was a resolution on the political objective which Jawaharlal moved at the Madras session: 'The Congress declares the goal of the Indian people to be complete national independence.' Though it did not alter the party's official creed which, under Gandhi's influence in 1920, had been defined merely as *swaraj* (self-rule), Nehru's formulation reflected the rumblings of discontent among impatient nationalist youth. A similar proposal had been raised at every Congress session from 1921 to 1925, but Gandhi's firm opposition had thwarted its sponsors.[1]

The Mahatma was absent from the proceedings on this occasion. But when he learned that Nehru's 'complete independence' resolution had been approved, he exclaimed: 'The Congress stultifies itself by repeating year after year resolutions of this character when it knows that it is not capable of carrying them into effect. By passing such resolutions we make an exhibition of our impotence. . . . We have almost sunk to the level of a schoolboys' debating society.'[2] The opening bell had

---

[1] The texts of Nehru's resolutions at the Madras session are to be found in the *Report of the Forty-Second Indian National Congress, Madras, 1927.*

[2] Tendulkar, *Mahatma*, vol. 2, p. 402.

sounded for the great debate of the next two years—the debate over complete independence versus Dominion status. For Nehru it was to be a major test of political courage. Though he ultimately triumphed, he was not to emerge unscathed.

What disturbed Gandhi more than anything else at Madras was the tone of Nehru's speeches, his surge to radicalism, and his apparent abandonment of non-violence. It was as if a son had gone astray. The Mahatma rebuked the younger man but not in the spirit of anger. On the contrary, there is evidence here of that deep affection which was to forge an unbreakable bond between the two, despite their many disagreements in the future. 'I feel that you love me too well to resent what I am about to write', began the Mahatma in his letter of 4 January 1928. 'In any case, I love you too well to restrain my pen when I feel I must write. You are going too fast. You should have taken time to think and become acclimatized. Most of the resolutions you framed and got carried could have been delayed for one year. Your plunging into the "republican army" was a hasty step. [Nehru had presided over a Republican Congress, a one-day sideshow at the Madras session.] But I do not mind these acts of yours so much as I mind your encouraging mischief-makers and hooligans. . . . If after careful observation of the country in the light of your European experiences you are convinced of the error of the current ways and means, by all means enforce your own views, but do please form a disciplined party.' Finally, he advised Nehru to concentrate on the party unity resolution which 'requires the use of all your great gifts of organization and persuasion'.[1]

A few weeks later Gandhi wrote again, stressing the differences which had come into the open. 'I see quite clearly that you must carry on open warfare against me and my views. For, if I am wrong . . . it is your duty . . . to rise in revolt against me.' The sense of an imminent break pained the Mahatma. 'The differences between you and me appear to be so vast and so radical that there seems to be no meeting ground between us. I cannot conceal from you my grief that I should lose a comrade so valiant, so faithful, so able and so honest, as you have always been; but in serving a cause, comradeships have got to be sacrificed.' To soften the blow Gandhi assured him that their

[1] Tendulkar, ibid., vol. 8, Appendix on Gandhi-Nehru Letters, p. 349.

personal relationship would not be impaired: 'But this dissolution of comradeship—if dissolution must come—in no way
affects our personal intimacy.' With his flair for the dramatic
the Mahatma proposed that Nehru write to him at length, setting out their differences. He would then publish their correspondence in his weekly newspaper, *Young India*, thereby
announcing the split 'to the nation'. Jawaharlal did not accept
the challenge.[1]

Despite the tone of Gandhi's letters to Nehru at this time,
an open break was not seriously entertained by either. The
Mahatma had an uncanny insight into the mainsprings of his
protégé's character and outlook. It was as if he were testing
Nehru's loyalty. This play would be re-enacted often in the
future. Gandhi would give him *carte blanche* to form his own
party and go his own way. Invariably Nehru would remain
loyal to the master, partly because of a powerful emotional
bond, partly because of his conviction that Gandhi's leadership
was indispensable during the freedom struggle and that to leave
him meant to go into the political wilderness, a fate which
Nehru did not relish.

The cleavage of 1928 was not unreal, however. On the contrary, the gap widened during the year, reaching its climax at
the Calcutta session of the Congress in December. But the disagreement centred on tactics, not on strategy. Nehru believed
that they would have to launch another campaign of mass civil
disobedience, even without the support of the wealthy and
educated groups in the party. Gandhi agreed but he felt that
conditions were not yet suitable. In general, Gandhi was more
cautious, more moderate, more restrained. Nehru was impetuous, exuberant and romantic in his approach to politics,
with a strong will to action. It was, however, a healthy difference of opinion, almost always kept within bounds by a mutual
recognition of their roles in the freedom struggle. Gandhi's
ideas often came under fire, but their alliance remained un-
broken to the very end.

*   *   *   *

Nehru had now emerged from the shadow of his elders. His
talents were openly recognized by Gandhi. He was becoming

[1] Tendulkar, op. cit., vol. 8, letter of 17 January 1928, pp. 350–1.

a leader of the younger generation of nationalists. He was a young man in a hurry, a man of energy and charm, with ideas transcending the outlook of the Old Guard. Encouraged by his victory at Madras, he pressed forward with his 'mission' of educating colleagues and the rank and file. As General Secretary of the party and spokesman for the new radicalism he was in great demand as a public speaker. In 1928 he presided over five provincial party conferences, was elected president of the All-India Trade Union Congress, and addressed various gatherings of nationalist youth. His fear of public speaking was a thing of the past. In this sense, too, he was coming of age.

Everywhere Nehru hammered on one basic theme—the twin goals of the nationalist movement must be complete independence and socialism. As a corollary he emphasized the key role of the peasantry and the working class. Caution was thrown to the winds. 'Two things are very dear to me,' he told the Allahabad District Board, 'independence for this country of ours and equality between man and man. . . . The future of India lies with the peasantry.'[1] 'The world is in a ferment,' he said, 'and strange forces are at work. . . . The world has become internationalized . . . but our ideas continue in the old rut.' Action was essential; even wrong action was better than no action at all. He called on his audiences to refashion their views, to appreciate the new world forces and their impact on the Indian freedom struggle. Industrialization was inevitable but its evils must be opposed. Capitalism and Imperialism must be eradicated. The struggle against British rule must be waged on both the political and economic fronts, and all connections with the Empire must be severed. Yet he clung to Gandhian teachings in that he denounced violence as counter-revolutionary. As for communalism, it was a giant with feet of clay which would soon disappear. He urged his listeners to boycott all foreign cloth and defended *khaddar* (home-spun cloth) as a boon to the peasantry and as an aid to the drive for self-sufficiency. Reformism was rejected as inadequate to the needs of India.[2]

[1] Dwivedi, op. cit., pp. 69, 71. The texts of Nehru's principal speeches from 1922 to 1929 are to be found in Dwivedi and in Ram Mohan Lal, L., *Jawaharlal Nehru, Statements, Speeches and Writings, With an Appreciation by Mahatma Gandhi*, Allahabad, 1929.

[2] Presidential Address to the Punjab Provincial Conference on 13 April 1928. Dwivedi, op. cit., pp. 73–102. The quotations are on pp. 74 and 79 respectively.

To India's young men he held up the ideals of Internationalism and Socialism. At the Bengal Students' Conference in 1928
he praised Russia as 'the greatest opponent of imperialism' and
reaffirmed his belief in communism 'as an *ideal* of society. For
essentially it is socialism, and socialism . . . is the only way if the
world is to escape disaster.'[1]

Yet Nehru's outlook was far from a well-digested Marxism.
For one thing, he rejected the *methods* of communism. For
another, he espoused a cyclical rather than a dialectical theory
of history: 'Society . . . must alternate between revolution and
consolidation', he told the Bombay Youth Conference. 'It is
the function of youth to supply this dynamic element.'[2] Thirdly,
his attitude to Imperialism was based on emotional antipathy to
colonial rule, not on orthodox Marxism. And while he favoured
a total break with Britain, he left open the road to friendship, a
road which, to the surprise of many, he was to follow twenty
years later. 'The day England sheds her imperialism we shall
gladly co-operate with her.'[3] On political tactics, he followed
Gandhi's lead, rejecting secrecy in negotiations and organization. He subscribed to the Marxist dictum that religion is an
opiate of the people, terming it 'the fountainhead of authoritarianism'. But he was equivocal on the question of compensation for expropriated property, favouring partial compensation
for hardship cases. Perhaps the most significant feature of his
outlook in the late 'twenties was his preference for a powerful
central government, a view which found concrete expression
in the Constitution of India in 1950 and in the policies of
the Nehru régime after the Partition. From his speeches in
1928 it is evident that Jawaharlal had not yet worked out a
coherent ideology. It is questionable whether he has ever
done so.[4]

As Nehru travelled throughout the land he detected a new
spirit among the people, in town and village alike. Trade
unions were mushrooming in the large industrial centres, youth
groups were springing up in the major provincial capitals,
notably in Bombay and Calcutta, and the peasantry were be-

[1] 22 September 1928. Dwivedi, op. cit., p. 135. (Emphasis added.)
[2] 12 December 1928. Ibid., p. 166.
[3] Presidential Address to the United Provinces Provincial Conference on 27 October 1928. Ibid., p. 146.
[4] Nehru's philosophy will be elaborated in Chapter XX.

ginning to show signs of discontent. The years of passivity were drawing to a close.

As so often in the history of the Indian freedom movement the new mood of defiance was sparked by a minor incident in a remote corner of the country. The place was Bardoli, a sub-district of Gujarat (Gandhi's homeland) in the northern part of Bombay Province. The issue was a revised land tax, an increase of 22 per cent., which was greeted with dismay and anger by the small landlords of the area. To their rescue came a man who was later to be honoured as one of the three heroes of the Indian revolution, Vallabhbhai Patel. A lawyer by profession and a native of Gujarat, a brilliant organizer and a man of decision, Patel brought the Mahatma's message to the sullen but fearful peasants of Bardoli. With Gandhi's blessing he organized a small-scale *satyagraha* against the government decree. Under his leadership they stood fast and refused to pay the tax.

The Government retaliated with wholesale arrests and confiscation of property. Patel refused to yield. Gradually the story of Bardoli spread to other parts of India, a symbol of hope for the peasant everywhere, an example of Gandhian non-violence at its best. For in the face of Patel's determination, the Bombay Government gave way and reduced the proposed tax increase to 7 per cent. In appreciation of his services, the peasants of Bardoli gave Patel the honorary title *Sardar* (leader), and Indian nationalists applauded. His fame spread throughout the sub-continent and the Sardar became a prominent figure in the Congress élite.[1]

It was not only Bardoli, however, that served as a catalyst to the revival of nationalist fervour. The beginning of 1928 saw the arrival of the Simon Commission to study the working of the 1919 Government of India Act and to propose another instalment of constitutional reform. Indian political opinion was outraged by the exclusion of Indians from the seven-man commission, and an ideal focus for agitation was given to the Congress. At the Madras session the party had called for a complete boycott of the Commission and the organization of *hartals* in every major city when it arrived. The setting was

[1] For an account of the Bardoli episode see Parikh, Narhari D., *Sardar Vallabhbhai Patel*, vol. i, ch. xxvi.

provided for Nehru's first real experience as a civil resister 'at the barricades'.

Wherever the Simon Commission travelled it was greeted with black-flag processions. Occasionally there were clashes between demonstrators and the police. In the autumn of 1928 Indian nationalists were stunned by the death of Lala Lajpat Rai, Congress leader of the Punjab, a few weeks after he was severely beaten while leading a demonstration against the Commission in Lahore. Then, at the end of November, the Commission came to Lucknow. It was Nehru's turn to feel the physical pain of *lathi* blows.

On the 28th Jawaharlal led a column of *satyagrahis* towards the central meeting-ground—though all processions were prohibited. He was promised safe conduct if he requested it in writing. He refused. Suddenly, mounted police descended upon the group swinging their clubs in all directions. Nehru's reaction sheds much light on his character. His instinct bade him to seek safety and he began to move away, 'but . . . I stopped and had a little argument with myself, and decided that it would be unbecoming. . . . The decision, prompted by my pride, I suppose . . . could not tolerate the idea of my behaving like a coward. Yet the line between cowardice and courage was a thin one. . . .' The pain was severe, but he was compensated by the satisfaction that he could endure it.

The following day this scene was re-enacted on a larger scale. A huge crowd marched towards the railway station to 'greet' Simon and his colleagues who, ironically, included Clement Attlee, the man who was to preside over the transfer of power from Britain to India almost twenty years later. The demonstrators were forcibly prevented from reaching their destination. Then came the charge of mounted police, wreaking havoc among the *satyagrahis*, including Nehru. 'It was a tremendous hammering and the clearness of vision that I had had the evening before left me. . . . I felt half blinded with the blows, and sometimes a dull anger seized me and a desire to hit out . . . but long training and discipline held, and I did not raise a hand, except to protect my face from a blow.' What remained in his memory was not so much the sensation of pain as the physical appearance of his attackers, 'those faces, full of hate and blood-lust, almost mad, with no trace of sympathy or touch of

humanity!' There was also a feeling of despair, perhaps the
return of doubt about the efficacy of non-violence: 'To what
end was all this? To what end?'[1] And yet it strengthened his
will to persevere in the struggle for independence, for it added
direct personal experience to intellectual conviction.

*   *   *   *

At the level of high politics the year 1928 was dominated by
the search for a constitution acceptable to all communities and
political parties. The result was the 'Nehru Report', drafted
by Jawaharlal's father and adopted by the All-Parties Conference in August of that year, only the Muslim League dissenting. Given the state of communal tension and distrust in the
late 'twenties, it was a major achievement, representing the
maximum agreement on highly-charged issues, notably communal representation and safeguards for the minorities. It also
restored a large measure of harmony among the warring groups,
except for the Muslim League, then an insignificant minority
organization on the Indian political scene.

One feature of the 'Nehru Report', however, caused a sharp
division within the Congress. The elder Nehru, supported by
Gandhi and a majority of the Old Guard, called for Dominion
status, partly as a concession to other groups who saw added
protection in continued Commonwealth membership. Against
them were ranged the radicals led by Jawaharlal and Subhas
Bose, then a fiery young man of thirty and already the hero of
Bengali youth. It was an awkward position for the younger
Nehru. His father was adamant on Dominion status and considered it an integral part of the constitutional settlement. The
son was equally stubborn. In his speech before the All-Parties
Conference he endorsed the communal agreement but rejected
the Dominion status formula. The Empire, he said, 'stands for
one part domineering over and exploiting the other', and Dominion status was merely a promotion from the exploited to the
exploiting section. He ridiculed the idea of co-operation with the
British, particularly with 'the sanctimonious and canting hum-
bugs who lead the Labour Party'.[2] No wonder that many were
surprised in 1947 when Nehru accepted Dominion status and

---

[1] *Toward Freedom*, pp. 135, 137 and 138.
[2] 29 August 1928. Dwivedi, op. cit., pp. 115 and 119.

F

expressed his gratitude to the Labour Party. Immediately after the session the 'young Turks' issued a statement approving the 'Nehru Report' as such but disassociating themselves from the commitment to Dominion status. They also announced their intention to form an Independence for India League.[1]

The League was established early in November 1928 with the sole aim of persuading the Congress to accept complete independence as its immediate and fundamental goal. As Secretary of the All-India Council, Jawaharlal was the dominant figure in this short-lived organization. He virtually created the League and did most of the work, drafting its communications and preparing its constitution. Indeed, but for his interest the organization would have been stillborn.

Further light is shed on Nehru's political outlook at the time by the unpublished Draft Programme of the United Provinces branch: '. . . The League aims at a Social Democratic State . . . and State control of the means of production and distribution.' More specifically, it called for steeply graduated income and inheritance taxes; universal, free, and compulsory primary education; adult suffrage; a minimum living wage; excess profits taxes; support for trade unions; unemployment insurance; an eight-hour work-day; the abolition of untouchability; equal status for the sexes; and far-reaching land reform—removal of intermediaries, partial annulment of debts, creation of small-holdings. Two years later some of these goals were officially endorsed by the Congress in the Karachi Resolution on Fundamental Rights.[2]

The Independence League was merely a pressure group within the Congress: membership was confined to Congressmen; its avowed goal was to influence the Congress programme; and it invariably met at the time of A.I.C.C. or annual sessions of the parent body. Although it lingered on for more than a year, it never achieved organizational unity or any real sense of purpose.

From the very outset Nehru was disturbed by the indifference of its members. 'Our League is at present a little chaotic', he wrote to a friend at the end of January 1929. '[It] cannot con-

---

[1] The following account of the Independence for India League, except where specific references are cited, is based upon a hitherto unpublished file on the League in the archives of the All-India Congress Committee, New Delhi. It is used with the permission of the Congress President, in 1956, U. N. Dhebar.

[2] See pp. 175–77, below.

tinue in a state of coma.' The various committees failed to submit reports. Nehru himself had to prepare the Draft Programme—and he received little response to his proposals. Even
membership dues were not paid.

The cause of this dismal state of affairs was a dearth of
intellectuals with a genuine desire for radical economic change.
As Narendra Dev, one of the founders of the Congress Socialist
Party in the mid-'thirties, wrote to Nehru, 'We lack in our midst
a body of earnest men of deep convictions who have a living
faith in some economic programme. . . . Up to now we have
done almost nothing to justify our existence. . . . We cannot
hope to prosper if we do not mend matters.'[1] The League
never did emerge from this rut, as Nehru himself admitted in
the middle of November 1929: '. . . our League has hardly
functioned this year. . . . [It] has lain in a dormant condition.'
Only in the United Provinces was there any sign of interest, and
this was due entirely to Nehru's personal efforts. Finally, with
the Congress acceptance of the goal of complete independence at
the end of 1929, the League disappeared. It is doubtful whether
it exerted any major influence on the outcome of the debate,
except in so far as a few enthusiasts like Nehru pressed their case
within the Congress.

And yet, despite its atrophy, British officials were disturbed by
the League's propaganda effect. Such concern is evident in a
secret minute on the political situation in India during the
summer of 1929 prepared by David Petrie, head of the Home
Department's Intelligence Bureau: 'By the end of 1928, Jawahir
Lal Nehru had established his Independence League, and the
ideal of independence could command such a following that
amongst the younger and more ardent spirits it completely
swept away the more prudent counsels of the advocates of
Dominion Status.'[2]

*   *   *   *

The pace quickened as the annual Congress session drew
near. The debate over Dominion status versus complete independence had caused a split within the party. The protagonists

---

[1] Unpublished Nehru Letters, 9 February 1929.
[2] Submitted 19 June 1929. Used with the permission of the Ministry of Home
Affairs, Government of India.

were prepared for a showdown. And everyone knew that this issue would dominate the proceedings at Calcutta during Christmas week of 1928. The elder Nehru, president-elect for the session, had the support of Gandhi and the Old Guard, and was prepared to stake his political life on the 'Nehru Report'. The young rebels, led by Jawaharlal and Subhas Bose, seemed equally determined.

The setting for the drama was provided by a resolution of the All-India Congress Committee early in November 1928, re-iterating the party's adherence to the Madras Resolution on complete independence and accepting the recommendations of the 'Nehru Report' as a great step forward in the solution of the communal problem. It was a compromise, but Motilal Nehru was unhappy that Dominion status had been shelved. During the next seven weeks he and Gandhi used their influence to win the support of the Working Committee, the party's High Command. Then, on 27 December, the Mahatma pressed their view before a closed meeting of delegates at Calcutta. While paying lip service to the goal of complete independence, Gandhi praised the 'Nehru Report' as a 'great contribution' and moved that the Congress adopt its proposals in their entirety, i.e., including the Dominion status formula, if the British Parliament accepted the Report as a constitution for India before the end of 1930. In the absence of such acceptance he proposed another mass civil disobedience campaign.

The atmosphere was tense as Jawaharlal took the floor and urged civil disobedience if complete independence were not granted by the end of 1929, i.e., only one year of grace. In an impassioned speech he condemned the acceptance of Dominion status as 'an extremely wrong and foolish act' which would amount to the acceptance of the 'psychology of imperialism'. In a tone of mild censure of his father and Gandhi he noted that his amendment was merely a restatement of the resolution adopted by the All-India Congress Committee less than two months earlier.

After a lengthy, heated debate, the party leaders held an emergency session in the evening. Although records of this meeting are unavailable, it is almost certain, in view of subsequent developments, that Nehru yielded to the persuasion of Gandhi and his father who played on the theme of party unity.

At the same time the Mahatma gave way to the pressure of the radicals.

The following day, 28 December, Gandhi withdrew his original resolution and proposed another giving London only one year to accept the Dominion status formula. Despite this concession, Nehru was still unhappy. In an attempt to escape from the dilemma—displeasing Gandhi and his father or retreating from principle—he absented himself from the proceedings. Many were surprised, and the Mahatma made a special point of explaining his absence. Nehru was opposed to the amended resolution, Gandhi informed the delegates, but 'he is a high-souled man. He does not want to create unnecessary bitterness of words. He seeks deliverance out of it by putting a self-imposed silence upon himself.' To many of the younger men this action seemed political cowardice. Bose, too, withdrew, and in the closed meeting of A.I.C.C. delegates Gandhi's motion was carried by 118 to 45. Bose even went so far as to issue a press statement to the effect that he would not vote against the resolution in the open session.

However, between 28 and 31 December a revolt must have occurred in the rank and file. For when Gandhi moved his resolution before the full assembly, Bose followed with an amendment explicitly rejecting Dominion status. Nehru reasserted himself and supported Bose, 'though I did so halfheartedly'.[1]

The Mahatma was annoyed and hurt by this unexpected turn of events. He lashed out at his critics 'who were in honour bound to support it [Gandhi's resolution]'. If they felt that a blunder had been committed, said Gandhi, 'it is their bounden duty to swallow that blunder and to abide by that compromise'. He shamed the opposition mercilessly: 'When we have no sense of honour, when we cannot allow our words to remain unaltered for twenty-four hours, do not talk of independence.' The appeal proved effective; Bose's amendment was rejected by 1,350 to 973. And yet the strength of the Left

[1] *Toward Freedom*, p. 141. Bose later explained to a friend the tactical reasons for not pressing his case before the A.I.C.C.: firstly, so as not to embarrass Jawaharlal; secondly, if the A.I.C.C. rejected his views, an appeal to the open session would have been very awkward; and thirdly, he was convinced that Nehru would come round at the open session. The source of this story, the person to whom Bose conveyed his tactics at Calcutta, wishes to remain anonymous.

opposition was very considerable, despite the Mahatma's magnetism and his appeal to emotion.[1]

In perspective, the controversy over Dominion status and complete independence was over a straw man, for there is no substantive difference between them. The elder Nehru was correct in identifying the two formulae. Why then the depth of feeling on this issue? Until the very end of the freedom struggle, Dominion status was genuinely misunderstood by many Indian nationalists, including the younger Nehru, who viewed it as a symbol of dependence on Britain and the Empire. Especially in 1928–9—before the Statute of Westminster had altered the meaning of Dominion status—the radical nationalists insisted on a total break with London as the visible expression as well as the reality of political freedom. Ironically, Nehru's attitude to this question in 1947–8 was identical with that of his father in 1928.

The Calcutta episode was forgotten after the Congress adopted the goal of complete independence the following year. Yet it revealed a number of Nehru's characteristics: his vacillation when confronted with the problem of unpleasant choice; his devotion to Gandhi and his father, even at the expense of yielding on principle; and his profound conviction that party unity had the highest political priority. This incident also witnessed the emergence of an alliance between Nehru and Subhas Bose—though at heart Bose never trusted Nehru fully again—and their acceptance as the two leaders of nationalist youth. But along with that was evidence of the precarious nature of the alliance and the tendency of Nehru to swing between his loyalty to Gandhi and his agreement on principle with Bose. With the passage of time this led to more mistrust on the part of Bose, a feeling which was accentuated by the unstated but very real rivalry between the two men. Finally, they parted company during another Congress crisis, on the eve of the second world war.

Between the two Nehrus the debate of 1928 caused much emotional strain. As Krishna Nehru noted in her autobiographical memoir: 'The mental conflict between father and son

---

[1] This account of the 1928 Calcutta session is based upon *Indian Quarterly Register*, vol. ii, 1928, pp. 19–48, and the *Report of the Forty-Third Indian National Congress, Calcutta, 1928*.

continued and the atmosphere at home as well as outside became more and more tense.'[1] They were both proud and stubborn men, yet devoted to each other. Helplessly, Jawaharlal's wife watched the breach, not wanting to upset her father-in-law but standing loyally beside her husband. The younger Nehru finally conceded, and the breach was healed.

* * * *

The Calcutta compromise set the stage for a year of uneasy quiet, a lull before the storm of civil disobedience broke over the land. While the Congress élite was debating its political aims, individual terrorism reappeared. In Delhi, the decorum of the Legislative Assembly was shattered by the explosion of two bombs on the floor of the House. The perpetrators of the crime, Bhagat Singh, later to become a legendary hero of militant nationalists, and B. K. Dutt were sentenced to life imprisonment. In Lahore, a senior British police officer was killed—in the mistaken assumption that it was he who had struck Lajpat Rai. And in Bengal, the seat of revolutionary terrorism, arson and assassination increased in frequency. But there were other, more basic symptoms of unrest. Over 100,000 textile workers went on strike in Bombay Province and remained off the job for six months. A quarter of a million jute workers in Bengal followed suit. So too did the employees of the South Indian Railways and the tinplate workers. Hunger strikes among political prisoners raised the tension; the death of Jatindra Nath Das in prison after sixty-one days without food added fuel to the flames.

The Government of India retaliated swiftly, notably by arresting thirty-two prominent trade unionists, among them the leaders of the All-India Trade Union Congress (A.I.T.U.C.) and the Communist Party. In the meantime Nehru had been elected president of the A.I.T.U.C. for the coming year and was directly involved in the prolonged Meerut trial which followed. Largely on his initiative a Meerut Prisoners Defence Committee was hastily created, under the chairmanship of his father, and included a number of prominent nationalists, some of them moderate in their outlook. Nehru himself sought to raise funds for the accused and used his international connections to secure

[1] Hutheesingh, *With No Regrets*, p. 60.

outside sympathy and support. The fact that most of the defendants were Communists did not disturb him for, in his opinion, 'the Meerut Trial . . . is a blow against the whole working class'.[1] To this view the Government itself apparently subscribed: '. . . The removal of the thirty leading Communist agitators from the political arena was immediately followed by a marked improvement in the industrial situation. There can be no doubt whatsoever that the arrests . . . placed the authorities in a commanding position and created a vacuum in the leadership of the [trade union] movement which was filled by very inferior material.'[2]

The Meerut case did have this effect. The trial lasted for three and a half years, the principal charge being the attempt to deprive the King-Emperor of his sovereignty over India, i.e., treason. Almost all were sentenced to prison, ranging from a life term to three years' rigorous imprisonment. The sentences were reduced later, under the pressure of the British Trades Union Congress and others.

This renewal of a hard policy by the authorities was prompted by a growing concern about the scope and intensity of unrest in the country at large, as revealed in a 'strictly secret' assessment prepared in the summer of 1929 by the Director of the Intelligence Bureau. 'I regard the situation now confronting the Government of India as the gravest I have known in the course of some twenty years' contact with the revolutionary movements in this country. . . . [The dangers are due to] the increase in the number of its members and adherents [and] the encouragement and support the revolutionaries have found . . . in the utterances of Indian nationalist leaders. . . . The chief ingredient in that excitement is racial hate. . . . The feeling against the Government among the educated who belong to such movements as the Congress, the Swarajist Party or the Independence Party, is most intense . . . The only safe guiding principle I can see is that violence must *at all costs* be repressed . . ., must be dealt with with exemplary severity.' Finally, lest his readers suspect an alarmist view, 'I have

[1] History of the Freedom Movement Project. File on the League against Imperialism.
[2] Government of India, India and Communism (1935), p. 72. The official view of the Meerut Conspiracy Case is treated exhaustively in chs. 15 and 16 of this confidential and unpublished report.

throughout endeavoured to refrain from using too lurid colours and from laying them on too thickly.'[1]

Amidst this turmoil Congressmen became engrossed in the election of a president for the crucial year 1930. Because civil disobedience was considered inevitable, the majority turned to Gandhi for guidance. Of the eighteen Provincial Congress Committees (P.C.C.s), ten proposed the Mahatma, five nominated Patel and three Nehru. Gandhi declined and remained adamant, despite considerable pressure from his colleagues and the rank and file. It was a curious election, indeed. To the surprise of many, the Mahatma threw his weight behind Nehru, then only thirty-nine. Patel was persuaded to withdraw, though in terms of seniority and support by the P.C.C.s he was the logical second choice. But Gandhi had an instinct for the right political decision.

On 6 July 1929 he informed the press of his support for Nehru and, with typical candour, provided a glimpse into his rationale. 'The battle of the future has to be fought by younger men and women', he remarked. 'And it is but meet that they are led by one of themselves', i.e., the 'Young Turks' would be rallied to the cause. Further, 'responsibility will mellow and sober the youth, and prepare them for the burden they must discharge'. Thirdly, 'those who know the relations that subsist between Jawaharlal and me know that his being in the chair is as good as my being in it', a remarkably frank statement intended to assuage the feelings of those opposed to Nehru's radicalism. By way of further assurance, 'a President of the Congress is not an autocrat. . . . He can no more impose his views on the people than the English King.'[2]

The consensus among prominent Congressmen interviewed on this point was that Gandhi saw in Nehru the ideal instrument to achieve two basic objectives: namely to divert the radical youth away from Communism and to secure their allegiance to the Congress; and to wean Nehru himself from the drift to the far Left. Nehru was then in his extremist phase, a visionary, critical of the moderate policies of the Congress and strongly attracted to the Marxist ideal. As formal head of the

---

[1] Submitted 19 June 1929. Used with the permission of the Ministry of Home Affairs, Government of India. (Emphasis added.)

[2] Tendulkar, op. cit., vol. 2, pp. 488–9.

party, he would become aware of the necessity of compromise in order to reconcile the various factions in his polyglot movement. This would take the edge off his extreme leftism. In any event the potential risk was minimal, for Gandhi would be at his side.

So it was done. Gandhi's refusal to assume direct control necessitated a special session of the All-India Congress Committee which was held in Lucknow at the end of September 1929. The Mahatma again resisted the pressure, Patel withdrew and Nehru was elected. The proceedings were distasteful to the proud Brahmin. 'I have seldom felt quite so annoyed and humiliated as I did at that election', he wrote five years later. 'It was not that I was not sensible of the honour, for it was a great honour, and I would have rejoiced if I had been elected in the ordinary way. But I did not come to it by the main entrance or even a side entrance; I appeared suddenly by a trap door and bewildered the audience into acceptance. . . . My pride was hurt, and I almost felt like handing back the honour.'[1]

To placate the Old Guard and to justify his choice to the rank and file, Gandhi wrote a moving panegyric to his protégé: 'Some fear in this transference of power [sic] from the old to the young the doom of the Congress. I do not. . . . In bravery he [Nehru] is not to be surpassed. Who can excel him in the love of the country? "He is rash and impetuous" say some. This quality is an additional qualification at the present moment. And if he has the dash and the rashness of a warrior, he has also the prudence of a statesman. He is undoubtedly an extremist, thinking far ahead of his surroundings. But he is humble enough and practical enough not to force the pace to the breaking point. He is pure as crystal, he is truthful beyond suspicion. He is a knight *sans peur et sans reproche*. The nation is safe in his hands.'[2]

*   *   *   *

A mood of sombre anticipation gripped the Indian political scene in the autumn of 1929. In an effort to stave off the impending clash, Lord Irwin (later Halifax), the much-respected

---

[1] *Toward Freedom*, p. 145.
[2] Mohan Lal, op. cit., p. ii.

Viceroy at the time, succeeded in persuading London to re-affirm the goal of Dominion status. '. . . I am authorised on behalf of His Majesty's Government', he announced on 31 October, 'to state clearly that in their judgment it is implicit in the declaration of 1917 [the Montagu Declaration] that the natural issue of India's constitutional progress, as there contemplated, is the attainment of Dominion status.' He also proposed a conference between the British Government and representatives of all shades of Indian political opinion to con-sider the recommendations of the Simon Commission before their submission to Parliament.[1]

The Liberals, the Muslim League, the Princes and even the Old Guard of the Congress were most impressed. Gandhi him-self welcomed the concession and was prepared to put his trust in the Viceroy. The following day a conference of political leaders was summoned in Delhi to study its implications— 'almost with indecent haste, so it seemed', thought Jawaharlal. Before another day was out, spokesmen for the Congress, the Hindu Mahasabha and the Liberals issued a joint manifesto accepting the Viceroy's declaration and indicating their willing-ness to participate in a Round Table Conference. There were, however, four conditions—or recommendations—inserted largely at the insistence of the younger Nehru: that the Con-ference be empowered to draw up a constitution granting im-mediate Dominion status; that the Congress have a majority of the Indian representatives; that all political prisoners be released immediately; and that in the interim the Government of India be conducted along the lines of a Dominion government, in so far as possible.

Despite these 'conditions', Nehru was dissatisfied with the manifesto, for it fell short of complete independence. At first he was adamant. But under the pressure of Gandhi and his father he succumbed. '. . . As was not unusual with me,' he noted in his autobiography, 'I allowed myself to be talked into signing.' No more revealing vignette of self-analysis is to be found in his voluminous writings. And yet he continued to be troubled by this 'retreat from principle'. As so often in the past and in the

---

[1] The text of the Viceroy's declaration is to be found in H.M.S.O., *Statement exhibiting the moral and material progress and condition of India during the year 1929–30*, Appendix II, pp. 466–8.

future, he conveyed his misgivings to the Mahatma and even offered to resign from the Congress Presidency. 'A soothing letter from Gandhiji and three days of reflection calmed me.'[1] How accurate was the Mahatma's appraisal, '. . . he is humble enough and practical enough not to force the pace to the breaking point'.

It was this compromise on the 'Delhi Manifesto' which led to the attack on Nehru by the League against Imperialism.[2] Within India his action offended some radical nationalists, like Subhas Bose and Dr. Kitchlew, neither of whom was torn by conflicting loyalties to Gandhi and leftism, as was Nehru during most of his public life. Yet circumstances came to the rescue and restored his position among the extremists of the Congress.

During a British parliamentary debate on India in November, Irwin's pledge was seriously undermined by an array of Conservative spokesmen. Lord Birkenhead, a former Secretary of State for India, called on the Simon Commission 'to treat that which the Government have instructed or authorized the Viceroy to do as irrelevance'. Baldwin reversed his support of the commitment to Dominion status. Simon himself was neutral. And the Labour Prime Minister, Ramsay Mac-Donald, made no effort to reassure Indian political opinion.[3]

The feeling of distrust hardened in India. At a special All-Party Conference in Allahabad, on 16 November 1929, Nehru retrieved his position when, along with Bose, he criticized the assembled leaders for being taken in by an 'empty statement'. Both resigned from the Congress Working Committee. The moderates, however, were not so easily disillusioned; and Sapru, the Liberal spokesman, arranged a special conference with the Viceroy to seek clarification. It was to be the last attempt to prevent open conflict with the *Raj*.

At this juncture Nehru made a brief appearance on the stage of trade union politics, as President of the All-India Trades Union

---

[1] *Toward Freedom*, p. 147. The letter referred to was written by Gandhi on 4 November 1929. The Mahatma justified Nehru's action in signing the 'Delhi Manifesto' on the grounds that it did not conflict with Nehru's goal of independence. Furthermore, he argued that as President-elect of the Congress Nehru was bound to go along with his colleagues. 'In my opinion, your signature was logical, wise and otherwise correct.' Tendulkar, op. cit., vol. 8, Appendix on Gandhi-Nehru Letters, p. 355.

[2] See pp. 114–15 above.

[3] Campbell-Johnson, Alan, *Viscount Halifax*, pp. 227–30.

Congress for 1929–30. The labour movement was then in the throes of sharp growing pains. Many of its leaders had been removed by the Meerut Conspiracy Case; its spirit was shattered; and its ranks were rent by factional strife. On the eve of the annual session a split occurred between moderates and extremists over the proposal to affiliate with the Pan-Pacific Secretariat, the Asian branch of the Comintern. The Right-wing leaders decided to boycott the open session.

It was not an enviable situation for Nehru, a newcomer to the trade union field whose role was that of sympathizer rather than active participant. His address was filled with socialist jargon. He commended the growth of militant class consciousness among Indian workers, called for a new socio-economic system of equal opportunity and fair conditions for labour, attacked the record of the British Labour Party, and called for the eradication of Imperialism and Capitalism.

On the vital issue of the moment, the cleavage between Left and Right, he adopted a typical middle-of-the-road position. Stand aloof from both Internationals, he advised, the Second International because it has become the exponent of a new form of Imperialism, and the Third because it would only be a gesture and would mean the adoption of communist methods in their entirety—something that Nehru opposed. In this area of public affairs, too, he revealed a desire for mediation and unity. He expressed regret for the split but considered it inevitable. He criticized both factions for causing the break and censured them for not waiting until the Congress session at Lahore which might have made it unnecessary. Finally, he had no doubt, he said, that unity would be restored. It was an appropriate plea for moderation by an outsider more interested at the moment in rallying the trade unions to the impending civil disobedience campaign.[1]

Tension was heightened by an attempt to assassinate the Viceroy on 22 December 1929, as his train approached New Delhi. The conference with Indian leaders was held as scheduled the following day, but to no avail. Jinnah, the Liberals, the Mahasabha and some moderate Congressmen were prepared to

---

[1] A partial text of Nehru's Presidential Address to the All-India Trade Union Congress on 30 November 1929 is to be found in *Indian Quarterly Register*, vol. ii, 1929, pp. 425–8.

take Lord Irwin at his word. But Gandhi, under strong pressure
from Nehru and Bose, and troubled by the revelations of the
British parliamentary debate, insisted on more definite assurances of immediate Dominion status. The Viceroy acknowledged that he could not promise anything beyond his initial
declaration, and so the conference ended in failure.

*   *   *   *

There was now nothing to prevent the Congress from proceeding with its avowed objectives. Within a week some
300,000 persons gathered on the banks of the Ravi River
on the outskirts of Lahore where the Congress camp had
been pitched. It was a dramatic affair by all accounts, and
Nehru held the limelight. On the opening day he rode through
the streets on a white charger, surrounded by a detachment of
the Youth League and followed by a herd of elephants. It was
his crowning moment thus far, as vast crowds acclaimed him.
He was then barely forty, one of the youngest Presidents in
Congress history.

No one was more moved than Jawaharlal's parents, particularly his mother who 'was in a sort of ecstasy' because father
and son in succession had received the highest honour of the
Congress, the only case in the party's history. Some who were
present recall the scene when Motilal handed over the chair to
his son; it was, they said, like a king passing on the sceptre of the
throne to his logical successor—very much in keeping with
Motilal's majestic bearing and outlook. He predicted that his
son would accomplish what he himself had failed to achieve
but he did not see this proud hope come to pass. In little more
than a year the elder Nehru was dead.

The issue at Lahore was war or peace. Despite appearances
to the contrary, the party was divided as it approached the
crossroads. Pleading for caution was a powerful section of the
Old Guard led by Pandit Malaviya, Sarojini Naidu and Dr.
Ansari. In the centre was Gandhi, supported by the elder
Nehru, and determined to fulfil the pledge taken at Calcutta
one year earlier. Jawaharlal urged the Mahatma on and stood
somewhere between his mentor and the radicals led by Subhas
Bose who were anxious for a complete break.

The clash between Gandhi and Bose, already apparent the

year before, now came into the open. Steering a middle course, the Mahatma offered congratulations to the Viceroy and his party on their narrow escape from death. The Left wing was in no mood for gracious words and forced the issue to a vote in the open session. Despite Gandhi's plea for unanimity, it passed by the narrow margin of 935 to 897. As Edward Thompson remarked, 'Let us be sure that Lord Irwin's sense of humour will value the knowledge that 897 of the Congress gentlemen think it a pity he was not blown to bits, while 935 think otherwise.'[1]

The key resolution was moved by Gandhi. 'In the existing circumstances', he declared, there was no purpose in attending the Round Table Conference. In accordance with the pledge taken at Calcutta, the Congress goal of *swaraj* should henceforth be interpreted to mean complete independence. The first step towards the attainment of this goal should be a boycott of the legislatures. Most important, the party was called upon to authorize the All-India Congress Committee, 'whenever it deems fit, to launch upon a programme of civil disobedience, including non-payment of taxes'.

The Right wing pressed for delay until another all-party conference considered the matter again—and showed surprising strength; the amendment was rejected in the Subjects Committee by 114 to 77. Then came the challenge from the Left, in the form of an 'amendment' by Bose. Actually it was an alternative resolution, far more radical in tone and containing a more positive programme of action. There was no reference to the Round Table Conference; in no circumstances should the Congress negotiate, declared the Bengali leader. While the change in the party's creed was welcomed, he proposed the addition of a rider to complete independence—'implying thereby complete severance of the British connexion'. Similarly, civil disobedience should be accompanied by the establishment of parallel governments based on local Congress committees and the effective organization of workers, peasants and youth for direct action.

Gandhi insisted that his resolution be accepted or rejected *in toto*. The idea of parallel governments was criticized as impracticable, for '... the Congress flag does not at present fly even

[1] *The Reconstruction of India*, p. 169.

in one thousand villages', a revealing disclosure. His own resolution, he added, was 'the longest step we can take today'. Finally, he justified the open-door policy to negotiation, on the grounds that 'some day or other we shall have to meet in conference with the enemy for the establishment of independence'. It was typical of Gandhi's realism. His words were persuasive and his resolution was carried. But the fissures remained. The Bose group expressed its displeasure by forming a Congress Democratic faction—within the party.[1]

Nehru was silent throughout this momentous debate. Emotionally he was sympathetic to the Bose position. But intellectually he was drawn to Gandhi's resolution, particularly since it accepted the twin demands of complete independence and direct action. And it did so without shattering party unity. Moreover, his position as President made it awkward to differ openly with the Mahatma and the Working Committee. Yet he did speak his mind, in a moving presidential address.

'I must frankly confess that I am a Socialist and a republican and am no believer in kings and princes or in the order which produces the modern kings of industry, who have greater power over the lives and fortunes of men than even the kings of old, and whose methods are as predatory as those of old.' Having shocked the more conservative elements, he acknowledged that the Congress could not adopt a full socialist programme now. But 'India will have to go that way . . . if she seeks to end her poverty.' Once again he was demonstrating Gandhi's dictum that he would not force the pace.

As was his habit then and now, he rambled over the universe of political problems. The age of faith, he said, was giving way to general scepticism from which a new order would emerge. Europe's traditional mastery was rapidly coming to an end, and 'the future lies with America and Asia'. Although India desires independence, it was not narrow nationalism which animated the Congress. Indeed, once freedom is attained, India 'will even agree to give up part of her own independence to a larger group . . .' Throughout this address the influence of Marxism and his world perspective is evident. 'Out of imperialism and capitalism peace can never come', he said, using the

---

[1] This account of the Lahore Congress is based upon *Indian National Congress: Report of the Forty-Fourth Annual Session, Lahore, 1929.*

simple Leninist dictum about the cause of war. He reiterated his hostility to Dominion status but again left the door open to friendship with Britain: 'India could never be an equal member of the commonwealth *unless* imperialism and all it implies is discarded.' Unlike Bose he was not irrevocably committed to a total break under any conditions.

Turning to the Indian scene, Nehru stressed three problems—the minorities, the princely States, and the peasants and workers. Real communal differences have largely gone, he argued naïvely, but the legacy of fear and distrust had to be removed. It was incumbent on the Hindus, the majority, to take the initiative. As for the States, they are 'the products of a vicious system that will ultimately have to go'. Twenty years later this seed of opposition to the Princes bore fruit.

Speaking as a champion of the peasants and urban workers he called for basic economic and social change. Taking issue with Gandhi, he criticized the theory of trusteeship (of wealth) and paternalism as 'equally barren. . . . The sole trusteeship that can be fair is the trusteeship of the nation. . . .' He also differed with the Mahatma on the question of violence. 'The great majority of us, I take it, judge the issue not on moral but on practical grounds, and if we reject the way of violence, it is because it promises no substantive results. But if the Congress . . . comes to the conclusion that methods of violence will rid us of slavery, then I have no doubt that it will adopt them. Violence is bad, but slavery is worse.' Perhaps the most significant comment was on his priority of goals—independence first, socialism thereafter: 'All these are pious hopes till we gain power, and the real problem, therefore, before us is the conquest of power.' Viewed in these terms it is not difficult to understand why Nehru *always* acted to maintain party unity, sometimes at the apparent expense of his socialist convictions. Finally, the call to action: 'We cannot command success. But success often comes to those who dare and act; it seldom goes to the timid who are ever afraid of the consequences.'[1]

Here was Nehru's first major triumph in national politics—though it occurred by chance. He had reached the front-rank of Congress leaders. He was acclaimed by radicals and youth.

[1] The text of Nehru's Presidential Address at Lahore is to be found in *Indian Quarterly Register*, vol. ii, 1929, pp. 288–97. (Emphasis added.)

He had delivered a forthright address openly proclaiming his ideals, the flowering of his European 'education'. He had presided over an historic Congress session when the long-sought goal of *purna swaraj*, complete independence, had become the official creed of the party. And the declaration of war had been issued—his will to action was about to be satisfied. The period of apprenticeship had come to an end. At the relatively young age of forty he became the rising star of India. The young Brahmin had arrived.

Yet he had no illusions about the real centre of power in the Congress or about the likely course of events. On 1 January 1930 the A.I.C.C. met to select a Working Committee. Gandhi proposed ten names *en bloc*; amendments were submitted by the Left opposition, the Congress Democratic faction headed by Bose. As President, Nehru ruled the amendments out of order and claimed that it would be unwise to select persons who had voted against Gandhi's resolution—because this might cause a deadlock and paralyse the imminent campaign. To Bose this tended to confirm his view that Nehru had become a captive of the Mahatma.[1]

Looking to the future, Nehru was unperturbed. 'We have got a stiff time ahead of us here,' he wrote to an English friend, 'Probably the Labour Government will have the honour of sending some of us to prison before long.'[2] The shouting was over. The war was soon to begin.

---

[1] Bose, Subhas Chandra, *The Indian Struggle*, p. 38.

[2] To Reginald Bridgeman, Secretary of the British Section of the League against Imperialism. (Unpublished.) History of the Freedom Movement Project. File on the League against Imperialism.

CHAPTER VII

Congress goes to War

An air of uncertainty hung over the Indian political scene as the Lahore Congress drew to a close on New Year's Day of 1930. The declaration of war had been issued with much fanfare; *purna swaraj* (complete independence) had been proclaimed the party's goal; civil disobedience had been authorized; and all power had been vested in Gandhi. But beyond this nothing was clear. What form should the campaign take? When and where should it begin? Was the mood of the country ripe for non-violent struggle? No one had given serious thought to these crucial questions. Gandhi himself relied on his 'inner voice' to point the way. Nehru was 'vague about the future . . . [and] full of doubt about our program . . . [for] we had burned our boats and could not go back, but the country ahead of us was an almost strange and uncharted land'.[1] Everyone waited for the Mahatma's lead. But Gandhi was never disposed to hasty action. The strategy of *satyagraha* had a marked Fabian strain.

To pave the way for mass civil disobedience it was first necessary to gauge the mood of his followers, élite and mass alike. Almost immediately after Lahore all Congress legislators were urged to resign their seats. The response suggested discipline of a high order, for within a few weeks 172 heeded the call, including thirty members of the central Legislative Assembly and the Council of State. Even more encouraging was the enthusiasm of the rank and file at 'Independence Day' gatherings fixed for 26 January. All over the country thousands adopted a pledge to *swaraj* after hearing Congress spokesmen on the evils of British rule. 'We believe that it is the inalienable right of the Indian people, as of any other people, to have freedom and to enjoy the fruits of their toil. . . . We believe also that if any government deprives a people of these rights and oppresses them the people have a further right to alter it or abolish it.'

---

[1] *Toward Freedom*, p. 150.

The shades of the American Declaration of Independence are evident in this hallowed document of Indian nationalism. 'India has been ruined economically. . . . Village industries . . . have been destroyed. . . . Politically, India's status has never been so reduced as under the British régime. . . . Culturally, the system of education has torn us from our moorings. . . . Spiritually, compulsory disarmament has made us unmanly. . . . We hold it to be a crime against man and God to submit any longer to a rule that has caused this fourfold disaster to our country. We recognize, however, that the most effective way of gaining our freedom is not through violence.' Then came the pledge to prepare for civil disobedience, including non-payment of taxes, and the resolution to implement Congress directives 'for the purpose of establishing *Purna Swaraj*'.[1] From that time onward the Congress observed 26 January as 'Independence Day'. And twenty years later a free India paid tribute to this landmark by formally inaugurating the Constitution of the Republic on that day.

In the light of widespread enthusiasm, Congress activists, and Nehru among them, expected a positive move from their leader. But Gandhi bided his time. Indeed, he seemed prepared to retreat. At the end of January he actually offered to desist from civil disobedience—if the Viceroy would concede eleven points which for Gandhi formed the 'substance of *purna swaraj*': total prohibition; reduction of the sterling-rupee ratio from 1*s*. 6*d*. to 1*s*. 4*d*.; decrease of land revenue by at least 50 per cent.; abolition of the salt tax; reduction of military expenditure by 50 per cent.; reduction of all civil servants' salaries by at least one half; protective tariffs on foreign cloth; passage of a bill in favour of Indian coastal shipping; release of all political prisoners, except those charged with violent crimes, and withdrawal of all repressive ordinances; abolition of the C.I.D.; and the right of Indians to carry arms.[2]

Lord Irwin took no notice, but many Congressmen were disconcerted. As Nehru wrote a few years later, 'what was the point of making a list of some political and social reforms—good in themselves, no doubt—when we were talking in terms

---

[1] The text of this 'Declaration of Independence' is in Sitaramayya, P., *History of the Indian National Congress*, vol. i, pp. 363-4.

[2] Ibid., p. 366.

of independence? Did Gandhiji mean the same thing when he used this term as we did, or did we speak a different language?'[1] Few understood the Mahatma's tactics at the time, but it proved to be a shrewd manœuvre. By offering co-operation in the proposed Round Table Conference for Constitutional Reform he was placing the onus for civil disobedience on the Government. At the same time, there was not the remotest possibility of acceptance of his Eleven Points; hence the 'danger' of abandoning civil disobedience was unreal. Moreover, these demands satisfied diverse sections of the Indian people, thereby widening the basis of support for the coming campaign.

Another month passed while Gandhi waited for inspiration before announcing the proper course of action. His colleagues grew steadily more impatient. At last the Mahatma divulged his plan. He would disobey the salt tax, he said, for here was the most iniquitous of all laws in India, a burden on millions which taxed even the poorest peasants. This he would do by marching from his *ashram* (spiritual retreat) near Ahmedabad to the Arabian Sea, a distance of 241 miles, and there openly violate the law by taking salt from the sea. To ensure complete non-violence he would confine this initial act of civil disobedience to a group of hand-picked disciples from his *ashram*. Mass civil disobedience against the salt tax would follow.

Many like Nehru were stunned by this novel approach to political warfare. But time and experience proved the Mahatma's unerring instinct for tactics attuned to the temper of the Indian masses. A campaign of civil disobedience to achieve *purna swaraj* would not arouse the peasantry, for it was too vague to inspire self-sacrifice. But salt, an absolute necessity for everyday life, touched the very core of resentment against the *Raj*. Here was something tangible, on which there were no divided opinions. The very simplicity of the issue was its greatest strength as a focus for political action. And with his flair for the dramatic—for Gandhi was a superb political artist —the Mahatma chose the technique of a long march from village to village, the only means of transport for millions of peasants in India. It was, too, an ideal method for attracting attention to the campaign throughout the country.

[1] *Toward Freedom*, p. 157.

In accordance with the *satyagrahi's* (civil resister's) firm conviction that all action must be 'in the public view', Gandhi informed the Viceroy of his plans and reiterated his offer of co-operation on the basis of the Eleven Points. Lord Irwin was unimpressed. The way was now open to non-violent war.

As the sun rose on 12 March 1930 Gandhi and seventy-eight disciples set out for the sea. Day by day the tension mounted, as all India followed the elderly Mahatma—he was then sixty-one—plodding through the countryside on his crusade. Along the route Gandhi preached the message of non-violence, an article of absolute faith throughout his life. Everywhere he was greeted as a saint. Three hundred village officials resigned their posts to register their support for civil disobedience. Anxiously both Congressmen and Government officials awaited his arrival at Dandi on the sea.

In the meantime the Congress made preparations for the anticipated widespread arrests once mass civil disobedience got under way. The All-India Congress Committee delegated special powers to its President, the younger Nehru, to act for the Committee if necessary and to nominate replacements to the Working Committee, as well as a successor in case of arrest; similar powers were vested in the lower levels of the party organization. Before returning to their home in Allahabad, Nehru and his father joined Gandhi briefly at the village of Jambusar, for final conversations before the storm broke.

When the 'Salt March' began Nehru had waxed eloquent about its significance: 'Today the pilgrim marches onward on his long trek. . . . The fire of a great resolve is in him and surpassing love of his miserable countrymen. And love of truth that scorches and love of freedom that inspires. And none that passes him can escape the spell, and men of common clay feel the spark of life.' Now he enjoined the youth of India: 'The field of battle lies before you, the flag of India beckons to you, and freedom herself awaits your coming. . . . Will you be mere lookers-on in this glorious struggle? . . . Who lives if India dies? Who dies if India lives?'[1] Recalling this episode in his autobiography, Nehru wrote: 'That was my last glimpse of him then as I saw him, staff in hand, marching along at the head of his followers, with firm step and a peaceful but undaunted look.

[1] Tendulkar, op. cit., vol. 3, pp. 31 and 34.

It was a moving sight.'[1] It was during this brief rendezvous that the elder Nehru decided to donate his palatial home, *Anand Bhawan*, to the Congress. Henceforth it was to be known as *Swaraj Bhawan*—Abode of Freedom.

Gandhi reached the sea on the morning of 5 April. He paused for prayers and then proceeded to break the law by picking up salt lying on the shore. The spark having been ignited in a dramatic fashion, the explosion followed with devastating effect. The pent-up emotions of thousands burst forth, and a nation-wide violation of the Salt Law followed. Giant public meetings were held in the major cities, with Congress leaders preaching the immorality of the state monopoly over the production of salt, symbolic of the evil character of the British *Raj* generally. The word salt had acquired a magic power. An amusing feature of the mass response was the practice of purchasing salt themselves and then, in defiance of the law, boiling it in a public place for the police to see. The operations extended to an effective boycott of British cloth—avidly supported by Indian cotton manufacturers—and picketing of liquor shops. The campaign rapidly gathered momentum and by early summer the 'revolt' had assumed mammoth proportions.

Nehru, however, was prevented from playing more than a token role in the struggle. During the first week he directed operations from Congress headquarters in Allahabad, issuing a stream of circulars to local organs on day-to-day tactics. Typical was the directive on 'Defence in Political Cases' which fell into the hands of the Government of the North West Frontier Province, soon to become the scene of the Congress's greatest victory. 'If volunteers are arrested for civil disobedience, it is clear that there can be no question of offering defence. . . . [They] should take up a dignified attitude in court . . . [and] give no information. . . . Our very creed at present is sedition and there can be no denial of this . . .'[2] But his freedom of action was short-lived. As Congress President he was the most exposed person in the party—Gandhi being a special case. On 14 April Nehru was arrested in Allahabad as

---

[1] *Toward Freedom*, p. 159.
[2] All-India Congress Committee: No. P. 1/1784, Circular No. 32, Allahabad, 4 April 1930. In the National Archives of India, New Delhi.

he was about to leave for Raipur in Madhya Bharat to address a conference. For violating the Salt Law he was sentenced to six months in Naini Central Prison, just across the river from his home town.

In all logic Gandhi should have been the first to be taken into custody. But as in the past—and in the future—the authorities hesitated to do so for fear of dangerous repercussions. Not that the Government of India lacked the power or, indeed, the support of London. As early as 17 January 1930, even before Gandhi had shown his hand, the Labour Secretary of State, Wedgwood Benn, cabled Lord Irwin: 'If, as we both hope may not prove to be the case, you find it necessary to make use of extraordinary powers, I need not tell you I have every confidence in your judgment and will support you fully.' The Labour Prime Minister, Ramsay MacDonald, added a pesonal message of unqualified support: 'Keep up moral authority of Government and rally round it those who respect law and order and whose political instincts will defend India from revolutionary movement whilst pursuing evolutionary politics. Maintain policy of reform whilst handling with firm determination revolutionary leaders. . . . Go ahead with calm assurance. I add my sympathies to my pledge of confidence.'[1] Despite this free hand Delhi was reluctant to risk the danger of arresting the Mahatma. Only after he wrote to the Viceroy of his intention to demand possession of the Salt Works at Dharsana—which would have given added impetus to the campaign—was he taken into preventive detention, under Regulation III of 1818. To avoid undue publicity he was whisked away in a car to Yeravda Prison near Poona at one o'clock in the morning of 5 May. No trial was held.

As expected by nationalists and Government officials alike, Gandhi's arrest led to demonstrations in every major Indian city. In Bombay especially the reaction was swift and sharp. Some 50,000 textile workers walked off the job and Hindu cloth merchants proclaimed a six-day *hartal* (suspension of business). The boycott of foreign cloth was complete. From the specific attack on the Salt Law the campaign developed into a general onslaught on British rule. The Government responded with

[1] Telegram P., 17 January 1930, Private and Personal. Important. No. 202. In the National Archives of India, New Delhi.

mass arrests, estimated at 60,000 (official) to 90,000 (Congress) before the year was out. There was also rigid press censorship on any news about the campaign and lavish use of the Viceroy's and provincial Governors' reserve powers, in the form of special ordinances which, in time, covered almost every conceivable type of civil disobedience. 'Between the middle of April and the end of December [1930]', wrote Lord Irwin's sympathetic biographer, 'Irwin had powers through no less than ten Ordinances—an unprecedented number representing a sum total of arbitrary rule which had been wielded by no previous Viceroy.'[1] Yet the campaign attracted a steady flow of recruits during the spring and summer of 1930.

Official quarters in Delhi showed supreme confidence and attempted to minimize its scope and intensity—in their public pronouncements. But in their confidential reports they expressed concern about the dangers inherent in the situation.[2] As early as 26 March, while Gandhi was still trekking to the sea, the Special Branch in Bombay wired a secret assessment to the Home Department in Simla, the summer capital of the Government of India: 'The hope that was entertained in many quarters that the movement will be discredited must be abandoned. On the contrary day by day individuals and bodies of men hitherto regarded as sane and reasonable are joining the movement . . . because among the educated Hindus . . . the belief that the British connexion is morally indefensible and economically intolerable is gaining strength. [The] . . . movement has therefore developed beyond [the] point at which even [the] arrest of Gandhi will break it down . . .'

Early in June the Viceroy informed the Secretary of State in London: 'All thinking Indians deeply resent racial inferiority with which they consider we regard them, and they passionately want substantial advance which will give them power to manage their own affairs. . . . I think every European and Indian would tell you that he was surprised at the dimensions the movement had assumed. I certainly am myself—and we should delude ourselves if we sought to underrate it.' As for the

---

[1] Campbell-Johnson, op. cit., p. 268.

[2] The following extracts were made available by the National Archives of India, New Delhi, and are used with the permission of the Ministry of Home Affairs, Government of India.

breakdown by groups, Lord Irwin divided the support as follows: Communist and Revolutionary—5 per cent.; Gandhi and
sincere Congress adherents—30 per cent.; General nationalist
sympathizers—50 per cent.; and Commercial and economic discontent—15 per cent. '[The] broad appreciation therefore is
that the movement is serious and has permeated many strata
of Hindu society. It has caught their imagination and swept
them off their feet and obviously has dangerous potentialities.
Among these must be reckoned [the] question whether [the]
Police and [the] Indian Army will stand indefinitely the strain
of intrigue, abuse and persuasion to which they are necessarily
subjected.' After proposing certain measures to alleviate the
situation, he added that 'measures of repression . . . are not
likely to provide [an] ultimate remedy for what undoubtedly
under much froth and unreality is a national movement. If you
circulate this telegram to Cabinet,' concluded the Viceroy, 'I
hope you will impress upon them the necessity of utter secrecy.
The damage of any disclosure cannot be exaggerated.'

    In his *Weekly Report* on 10 July 1930, the Director of the
Intelligence Bureau of the Government of India noted: 'The
"awakening" among women is something that I am told has
taken Congressmen themselves by surprise. . . . Furthermore it
is useless to suppose that the campaign is now confined to the
towns.' The following week he showed greater concern: '. . . It
is impossible to discount . . . the self-sacrificing attitude of
many business-men towards the boycott movement, the unend-
ing supply of volunteers for picketing, the participation of large
numbers of women, and, above all, the abundance of funds for
every branch of Congress activity. There are signs that the
position may be further complicated by the addition of large
numbers of the labouring classes to the forces of disorder.'

    The military were even more pungent in their appraisal. In
a letter to the Chief of the General Staff on 14 June 1930 the
G.O.C. Eastern Command, General Shea, wrote: 'The general
results have been a serious dislocation of trade . . ., a most
highly organized attack by a gang of revolutionary terrorists,
open rebellion in certain urban areas, the inflammation of
the Frontier tribes, and systematic attempts to undermine the
loyalty of the Army. . . . I am deeply concerned about the
effect which is being produced in the minds of Indian soldiers

by current events . . . they are being subjected to an insidious strain which is bound in time to have a far-reaching effect.' It was these varied considerations which influenced Lord Irwin to make a conciliatory speech on 9 July renewing his plea for Congress co-operation in formulating plans for constitutional reform. But the gesture was premature.

On the whole the campaign of 1930 was non-violent in character, a testimony to Gandhi's remarkable hold on his followers. But in a movement of that size and intensity deviations from the norm were inevitable. Clashes between demonstrators and police were frequent, particularly during the large public meetings immediately after Gandhi violated the Salt Law at Dandi and again after his arrest. It is impossible to apportion responsibility for resort to violence during these highly-charged incidents.

There were three outstanding events in the campaign. The first was a daring raid on the police armouries of Chittagong, a small port city of East Bengal, during which six officials were killed and substantial quantities of small arms were seized by a non-Congress terrorist group. This *coup* occurred after three days of demonstrations and was followed by reprisals in which dozens of people were killed by police fire. The second incident took place in the town of Sholapur in Bombay Province early in May, when *satyagrahis* secured effective control for a few days and then clashed with the military. Twelve demonstrators were killed, twenty-eight wounded and a number sentenced to long terms of imprisonment. Immediately thereafter martial law was clamped on the town.

By far the most dramatic event of 1930 took place in Peshawar, capital of the North West Frontier Province, homeland of the warlike Pathan tribesmen. Government and Congress accounts of the cause of violence are diametrically opposed, but both agree that for five days, from 23 to 28 April, this strategic gateway to the Khyber Pass was in complete control of the local Congress organization, more particularly of the *Khudai Khidmatgars* (Servants of God) or 'Redshirts' led by Khan Abdul Ghaffar Khan, a devoted follower of Gandhi. The principal clash occurred on the evening of 23 April when a procession was organized in the main street of the town to protest against the Government's decision to prohibit the entry of an All-India

Congress Committee deputation. In the police firing that followed thirty were killed and thirty-three were wounded, according to official estimates. Congress estimates place the figures at about 200 killed.

The Peshawar episode caused grave concern among senior officials, for it witnessed Congress power in the area, the historic invasion route from central Asia. Even more dangerous was the refusal of two platoons of the Second Battalion, 18th Royal Garhwali Rifles, to fire on the unarmed crowd. Although an isolated incident, it revived faint memories of the Rebellion of 1857. Nor was it lost on Delhi that the ultimate base of British power in India was the Army's loyalty.

Frantic cables between Simla and Peshawar reveal the state of alarm.[1] On 24 April the Home Department of the Government of India sent the following instructions: 'Please put strict censorship on all news from Peshawar and in particular do not allow any news to be transmitted about the Garhwali regiment ...' Two days later the divide-and-rule tactics were invoked: 'It is of the utmost importance to maintain the attitude of opposition on part of Mahommedans to the Civil Disobedience Movement.' However, the Frontier Government informed Simla that 'support of great majority of inhabitants of Peshawar City and of considerable numbers in villages has been secured by Congress'. In effect it meant that the Muslims had joined the campaign, for over 90 per cent. of the people in the Frontier Province are devout Muslims. No better evidence of the divide-and-rule policy in 1930 is to be found than the reply of the central Government: 'At present vital need is to find some means of winning back Muslim intelligentsia of this Province from Congress to Central Muslim Party.'

The scare was short-lived. Order was restored on 28 April, the mutinous soldiers were discharged or sentenced to prison, and the Congress leaders were arrested. For the Congress, however, the Peshawar incident was a source of pride, particularly because it revealed the degree to which the precepts of non-violence had permeated the normally warlike Pathans. From that point on the Congress was firmly established in this

---

[1] The following extracts were made available by the National Archives of India, New Delhi, and are used with the permission of the Ministry of Home Affairs, Government of India.

most Muslim of all Indian provinces. Not without reason was Abdul Ghaffar Khan henceforth referred to as 'the Frontier Gandhi'.

*   *   *   *

All this Nehru followed with eager interest from his prison cell at Naini. Seven years had elapsed since his last enforced residence in this huge fortress-like jail. The majority of its inmates were criminal offenders, but in times of political stress, notably during civil disobedience campaigns, there was a stream or a flood of 'politicals'.

To prevent 'contamination' of non-political prisoners the two groups were kept apart wherever possible. Moreover, so deep was caste consciousness embedded in Indian society that the prison community was divided into three categories, 'A', 'B', and 'C'. Important 'politicals' were placed in the first group and were given special privileges, such as books and writing materials, prison service and, most important, the right to have food sent from home. And even within the 'A' category, a measure of caste distinction was often maintained. Because of their all-India prominence and their social prestige, the Nehrus, especially the father, were treated with respect.

When he returned to Naini, on 14 April 1930, Jawaharlal was the only important political prisoner there. Whether out of deference or the desire to prevent contact with criminal inmates, he was kept in isolation, in a small circular enclosure about one hundred feet in diameter, separated from the main prison compound by a fifteen-foot wall. 'The Doghouse' it was called, having been originally designed for dangerous criminals. Now it was used for distinguished nationalist politicians. For a month he had no companions of any kind, except a guard, a prison cook and a 'sweeper'. As long as he was alone the accommodation was not unbearable, two cells in a four-cell barrack. Yet it was a frustrating experience, especially after the sense of fulfilment in the early days of civil disobedience.

Time passed slowly in this confining atmosphere. Ever a believer in routine, particularly during the long years in prison, Nehru managed to fill out the day. Early to rise, about four in the morning, he spent about three hours a day spinning and another few hours weaving. He read voraciously, busied himself with household chores and tried to calm his restless mind. It was a rigorous schedule, self-imposed because of a self-created guilt complex: 'The thought that I was having a relatively easy time in prison . . . began to oppress me. I longed to go out; and, as I could not do that, I made my life in prison a hard one, full of work.'[1]

He derived some compensation from news of his wife's active participation in the struggle. Fragile though she was, Kamala took the lead, along with Jawaharlal's elder sister, in organizing the women of Allahabad and surrounding villages, particularly in the boycott of liquor shops and foreign cloth. As the campaign progressed she was appointed a substitute member of the Working Committee and helped to draw thousands of women from behind the *purdah* or the security of their homes. Nehru was usually reticent about Kamala in his writings, but in this connection he paid tribute to her self-sacrifice.[2] It was as if she had replaced him in the front lines. For her part, though motives are always difficult to determine, it would seem that this provided an opportunity to reveal herself in a new role, that of political companion. A new dimension was added to their relationship.

For a month Jawaharlal remained in virtually solitary confinement. Relief came with the arrival of a colleague, Narmada Prasad Singh. And then, on 30 June, they were joined by his father and an intimate friend, Dr. Syed Mahmud. The elder Nehru had succeeded his son as acting Congress President, after Gandhi had declined the appointment, and had thrown himself into the campaign with vigour, despite his failing health. He had recently returned from an organizing tour of Bombay when he was arrested and sentenced to six months.

The reunion with his father was a source of much joy. But the discomforts of prison life and the extreme heat of the plains led to a rapid deterioration in Motilal's health. Now seventy, he was beginning to show symptoms of the disease which caused his death seven months later. Jawaharlal ministered to his father's needs with love and devotion. But the elder Nehru's condition grew steadily worse. Finally, on the advice of doctors, he was released early in September 1930. By way of partial compensation for his father's departure, Jawaharlal was joined within a few days by his brother-in-law, Ranjit Pandit.

---

[1] *Toward Freedom*, p. 170.   [2] Ibid.

The normally placid existence behind the prison walls was enlivened by one episode in which both Nehrus were involved, an attempt to mediate in the war between the Congress and the *Raj* by two well-known Indian Liberals, Dr. (later Sir) Tej Bahadur Sapru and M. R. Jayakar. The Viceroy gave his blessing to the enterprise, and the two 'peacemakers' hastened to Yeravda Prison near Poona in an effort to win Gandhi to their view—essentially to trust Lord Irwin's good intentions and to participate in the Round Table Conference (R.T.C.). The conversation was inconclusive. Gandhi remained adamant on his Eleven Points and urged that the R.T.C. should be confined to the discussion of safeguards in the transition period, with Dominion status assured immediately. Moreover, he did not think the time was ripe for negotiations and insisted that he could not act on his own. As Congress President, 'Jawaharlal's must be the final voice'.

All this the Mahatma conveyed to the Nehrus in a letter which was transmitted by the 'peacemakers' to Naini Prison on 27 July. For two days they engaged in fruitless discussions, their basic lines of argument being irreconcilable. The younger Nehru, in particular, was disturbed by the very idea of a compromise settlement. In the midst of these conversations he wrote to the Mahatma, questioning the propriety of participating in the R.T.C. even if, as Gandhi insisted, the issue of independence could be raised at the Conference. Moreover, he argued that Gandhi's Eleven Points were not an adequate substitute for *purna swaraj*. 'For myself,' he added, 'I delight in warfare. It makes me feel that I am alive.'[1]

To the 'peacemakers' the Nehrus declared that they would not make any suggestions without first meeting Gandhi and the Working Committee. Lord Irwin agreed to the meeting with the Mahatma, and so, on 10 August, Sapru and Jayakar, along with the Nehrus, sped across the country in a special train to Yeravda Prison. In the joint talks that followed the 'peacemakers' pressed for Congress concessions, but to no avail. If anything the price of peace had risen, largely at the insistence of Jawaharlal. It now comprised the right of India to secede

---

[1] Letter of 28 July 1930, in *Indian Annual Register*, vol. ii, 1930, p. 87. A comprehensive survey of the Sapru-Jayakar 'Peace Negotiations', including the text of all relevant letters and documents, is to be found on pp. 83–96.

from the Empire at will; a complete 'national government' responsible to the Indian people, including control over armed forces and economic affairs; the fulfilment of Gandhi's Eleven Points; and the right to refer to an independent tribunal such British claims regarding concessions and the public debt of India as seemed unjust. As might have been expected, the Viceroy refused to negotiate on these terms except to offer the release of prisoners on a generous scale. The Nehrus were equally adamant and the peace talks collapsed. They returned to Naini Jail.

One lighter moment intruded into the serious atmosphere of the Yeravda talks. When asked by the prison superintendent what food he desired, the elder Nehru mentioned that he was accustomed to simple fare and then proceeded to enumerate his typical meals—based, of course, on his *Anand Bhawan* habits. He was apparently oblivious to the incongruity of the list, in the atmosphere of Yeravda Prison. His colleagues were amused, as Jawaharlal recounts in his autobiography, but according to one of those present the younger Nehru was also annoyed. 'What is this nonsense', he is reported to have said, half in jest. 'This is not a hotel, but a prison.'

Soon after the peace talks Motilal was released. On 11 October his son followed, having completed the six months' sentence. But he was to remain at liberty only eight days. For though civil disobedience had by this time settled down to a war of attrition, Jawaharlal was too important and too dangerous to be allowed to roam unhindered throughout the country. Indeed, even before his release, the Government of India was determined to make his freedom short-lived. In the last week of September 1930 the Director of the Intelligence Bureau penned the following note: 'I suggest that the Home Department should at once consult the U.P. [United Provinces, where Nehru lived] as to the desirability of allowing *this irreconcilable* at large to stir up mischief all over again.' The Secretary of the Home Department agreed to suggest that a letter be written to the Governor of the U.P., 'expressing the hope that the first opportunity will be taken *to put Jawahar Lal out of harm's way*'.[1]

Nehru was probably unaware of this plan. In any event, he was indifferent to such machinations, for the creed of *satyagraha*

[1] In the files of the National Archives of India, New Delhi. (Emphasis added.)

5. Barrister-at-Law, 1912

6. Jawaharlal and Kamala Nehru at the time of their wedding, 1916

impelled him to court arrest. The day after his release he provided the desired 'opportunity' by addressing a meeting of 8,000 in Purshottam Das Park in Allahabad, urging his audience to violate the Salt Law and, more important, advising non-payment of taxes. While still in prison he had come to the conclusion that conditions were ripe for a large-scale no-tax campaign, partly because the Great Depression had caused a severe drop in agricultural income—never really adequate for the downtrodden U.P. peasants—and partly because of the need to infuse the civil disobedience movement with a new, dramatic issue. Thus, while in Allahabad on 12 October 1930, he summoned a meeting of the Provincial Congress Committee and prepared the ground for a no-tax campaign by convening a peasants' conference for Allahabad District the following week.

In the interim he and Kamala went to Mussourie where the elder Nehru was convalescing. It was a delightful holiday, the last one with his father. Always fond of children, Jawaharlal romped about with his daughter Indira and the three girls of his sister Nan in the serene and beautiful surroundings of the queen of India's hill stations. His father's apparent improvement added to the gaiety. After three days Jawaharlal returned to Allahabad to be on hand for the peasant conference on non-payment of taxes. Motilal decided to return a day later in order to spend more time with his son, but the police and arrest intervened. The conference took place as scheduled on 19 October and gave the signal for a district-wide no-tax campaign. Jawaharlal and Kamala then went to the railway station to meet the family but had to rush off immediately to a large public meeting. He was aware of his imminent arrest, for while they were on the way from Mussourie to Allahabad three orders for detention had been issued, though not officially served. Then, on the evening of 19 October, as he and Kamala were returning to *Anand Bhawan* from the meeting, their car was stopped near his home and Jawaharlal was taken into custody. The authorities had made good their threat 'to put him out of harm's way', and he returned to Naini Prison. The trial was brief, for *satyagrahis* did not offer a defence in court. Altogether he was sentenced to two years and four months—eighteen months for sedition, six months for abetting violation of the Salt Act of 1882, six months under the Instigation Ordinance of 1930, these two to

G

run concurrently, and four months in default of payment of fines.

Once again among familiar faces, Nehru settled down to his normal prison routine—spinning, reading and the like. There were, however, some additions, made possible by his brother-in-law's versatile talents. Ranjit's flair for gardening brightened the atmosphere considerably. Moreover, with skill and imagination he succeeded in creating the facsimile of a tiny golf course. How utterly incongruous it must have seemed for four political revolutionaries to be playing golf in 'The Doghouse' of Naini Jail! They were also able to benefit from the veranda which the prison authorities had built off their barrack to ease Motilal Nehru's confinement some months earlier. And the autumn had come, with its cool breezes and blue skies, a relief from the torpid heat of Indian summer.

The reimprisonment of Jawaharlal so soon after his release angered his father and infused the flagging civil disobedience campaign with new vigour. Despite his grave illness, Motilal rose from his sick-bed, determined to 'avenge' this action of the *Raj*. Aside from providing leadership to his colleagues, he organized 'Jawahar Day' on 14 November, the date of his son's forty-first birthday. All over India the Congress held public meetings at which were read those portions of his original speech which had caused his rearrest. To Nehru it was a 'unique birthday celebration', for about 5,000 persons were arrested on the occasion. Another source of pride was the news of Kamala's arrest on 1 January 1931. 'It was a pleasant New Year's gift for me', he wrote to his daughter.[1] Although concerned about his wife's health, he was delighted that Kamala had attained the goal of all *satyagrahis*—imprisonment. He was especially touched by her parting message to nationalist women: 'I am happy beyond measure and proud to follow in the footsteps of my husband. I hope the people will keep the flag flying.'[2]

*   *   *   *

It was during this, his fifth term in prison, that Nehru began a series of letters to his daughter, later published as *Glimpses of World History*. The solitude of life behind the prison walls provided the leisure for reading and reflection. A sense of parental

---

[1] *Glimpses of World History*, p. 5.   [2] Quoted in *Toward Freedom*, p. 181.

obligation to Indira, whose normal upbringing had suffered from his preoccupation with politics and his frequent 'visits' to prison, supplied the initiative for this informal survey of world history. Nehru is not a trained historian, but his feel for the flow of human history, his sensitivity to the many facets of social evolution, his capacity to weave together a wide range of knowledge in a meaningful pattern give to this book qualities of a high order. Perhaps its most impressive feature is the creative selection of significant data from the array of facts on the many cultures of East and West and their orderly presentation in a simple style making it intelligible to a girl in her early 'teens. Moreover, it was written in prison at varying periods during three years, without the assistance of the source materials, except for Wells's *Outline of History* and chance books that came his way. What makes it original and unique, a marked departure from the standard universal histories, is its Asian-centred orientation. The lack of balance in historical writing is redressed, Europe and America are placed in the perspective of 'world history', and the reader is made aware of the fact that the history of non-European peoples is not merely an extension of European culture overseas.

This is no scholar's work, nor was it intended to be. Indeed, it is not a book in the proper sense. Rather, it is a series of thinly connected sketches of the story of mankind. It is rambling and repetitious, introspective and 'romantic'. There are errors of fact and dubious interpretations. It lacks 'objectivity', for Nehru cannot and does not wish to remove himself completely from his subject-matter. It also reveals his shifting moods; and his assessment of a particular epoch or situation shows the influence of his momentary reflections. It is, then, uneven in quality and perspective.

Written during the height of what he considered to be a life-and-death struggle with British rule, the sections dealing with British history are marked by an aggressive tone. Those on Indian culture are marked by deep sympathy and understanding, though he was not averse to sharp criticism of India's social and political ills, notably caste, the deadening effects of orthodox religion and near-perpetual fragmentation. Similarly with Chinese culture, for which he has much admiration, and those of South-east Asia.

The French Revolution is for him, as for many others, the decisive force in modern European history, the great divide, liberating peoples from foreign domination, a process which was uppermost in his mind at the time of writing. Strong men called forth much praise, and the hero-worship of Napoleon is striking. So too is the respect for persons like Kemal Ataturk who were revolutionizing the fossilized societies of Asia. The Russian Revolution evokes some of his most emotional observations. To him it was the harbinger of a new age, an ideal worthy of emulation—for this was the period when Marxism exercised a profound influence on his thought and action. But it is in his many letters on nationalism, Indian and other, that Nehru reveals his basic outlook. For him it is the force of the century, the carrier of the ideas of political independence, social regeneration and cultural renaissance, the key to a new age.

Despite its polemical character in many sections and its shortcomings as an 'impartial' history, the *Glimpses* is a work of great artistic value, a worthy precursor of his noble and magnanimous Autobiography. The canvas is as large as the record of man itself, the strokes are sweeping and multi-coloured. There is a sure grasp of detail, yet a breadth of outlook which distinguishes it from the standard 'history'. This is no dry, scholastic tome. The author is deeply involved in his story, freely contributing personal judgements viewed from his own world outlook. It can best be described as cultural history, though there is no dearth of political events. It is, too, a human document, a projection of Nehru the man and seeker of truth on to the stage of societies in motion.

There is much light on Nehru himself in these glimpses of history.[1] There is evidence of humility—'the real reason . . . why I put off writing was another one. I am beginning to doubt if I know enough to teach you!' There is, as well, some indication of his devotion to his family and to Gandhi, for whom respect and admiration merge with affection, indeed love. Nehru has long prided himself on his impulse to action and the priority of deed over word. This, too, finds expression in his opening letter: 'To read history is good, but even more interesting and fascinating is to help in making history. . . . I am

---

[1] The following quotations are taken from the *Glimpses of World History*.

too full of the present and the future to think of the past . . .'
Nehru is a sensitive and moody man, though basically optimistic in his world outlook. These traits are also amply revealed in
the *Glimpses*.

His theory of history, as expressed in these letters, combines
three strands: the classical nineteenth-century belief in perpetual progress; a stress on the role of 'the great man'; and
sociological analysis of groups or societies in motion, with a
strong infusion of Marxist method. '. . . A study of history',
wrote Nehru, 'should teach us how the world has slowly but
surely progressed, how the first simple animals gave place to
more complicated and advanced animals, how last of all came
the master animal—Man, and how by force of his intellect he
triumphed over the others.' His letters also abound in descrip-
tions of the 'great men', whether political or spiritual—Ashoka
and Alexander, Akbar, Genghis and Napoleon, Lenin and
Gandhi, Jesus and Mohammed, Buddha and Confucius. As
Nehru approaches the modern world, the nineteenth century
and beyond, there is a Marxist tinge in his appraisal of events.
More than twenty-five years have passed since he completed his
survey. Yet it is likely that these three elements still influence
his approach to historical change.

The *leitmotif* of Nehru's thought and action in this period of
his life was the global struggle for freedom, indeed, the primacy
of international over national goals. In this sense the *Glimpses
of World History* is a milestone in his developing political outlook, embodying in its purest form his international idealism.
As he wrote to Indira, 'to-day we are trying to free India.
That is a great thing. But an even greater is the cause of
humanity itself. And because we feel that our struggle is a part
of the great human struggle to end suffering and misery, we can
rejoice that we are doing our little bit to help the progress of the
world.'

Nehru's analysis of the rise of Fascism and Nazism, the cause
of the Great Depression, the growing disunity among the Western Powers, and the approach of war bears a marked resemblance to Strachey's *The Coming Struggle for Power*, though not
quite as outspoken in its Marxism. Typical of his revolutionary
fervour is the following passage: 'The reformer who is afraid of
radical change or of overthrowing an oppressive regime and

seeks merely to eliminate some of its abuses becomes in reality one of its defenders. We must therefore cultivate a revolutionary outlook.' No less pointed was his comment on war and social revolution: 'The costs of social revolution, however great they might be, are less than those evils and the cost of war which come to us from time to time under our present political and social system.' Over the years his attitude to these questions has changed drastically.[1]

Two of his characteristics revealed in these letters to his daughter have not changed—optimism and the attraction of struggle: 'We have the surety that success awaits us', he wrote on 1 January 1933, at the lowest ebb of the civil disobedience campaign. In the same letter he remarked, 'Life would be dull and colourless but for the obstacles that we have to overcome and the fights that we have to win.'

A strange feature of Nehru's outlook in the early 'thirties is the combination of revolutionary goals with purist Gandhian methods: 'Never do anything in secret or anything that you would wish to hide. For the desire to hide anything means that you are afraid, and fear is a bad thing and unworthy of you. Be brave, and all the rest follows.' It is no surprise, therefore, that orthodox communists considered Nehru 'unreliable' and 'petty bourgeois' at the time.

Typical of the Indian Communists' attitude to Nehru until 1936 are the following comments: 'Why do you bother so much about what Mr. Jawaharlal Nehru had told you', wrote M. Ahmad to P. C. Joshi, Secretary-General of the Communist Party of India, on 9 March 1929. 'What more can one expect from a timid reformist like him?'[2]

The following year the *Platform of Action of the Communist Party of India* stated the party's view of Nehru more pungently: 'The most harmful and dangerous obstacle to victory of the Indian revolution is the agitation carried on by the "left" elements of the National Congress led by Jawaharlal Nehru, Bose . . . and others. . . . The exposure of the "left" Congress leaders . . . is the *primary* task of our Party.'[3]

---

[1] This point will be elaborated in a more comprehensive analysis of Nehru's political philosophy in Chapter XX.

[2] Prosecution Exhibit No. 304, *Meerut Conspiracy Case, Official Records* (1929).

[3] Originally published in *International Press Correspondence* (Inprecor), December 1930, as quoted in Limaye, Madhu, *Communist Party: Facts and Fiction*, pp. 18–19.

While Nehru was engrossed in reflections on history, the Round Table Conference opened in London. There were 89 delegates, 16 representing the three major parties in England, 57 from British India and 16 from the princely States. At first no progress was made, particularly on the vexed issue of communal representation, as the Hindu Mahasabha and Muslim parties clung to their fixed positions. It seemed as if the search for a suitable basis of constitutional reform was doomed to failure. However, at the beginning of January 1931, the deadlock was broken by Sir Tej Bahadur Sapru's proposal for responsible self-government in an All-India Federation with appropriate safeguards in the transition period. To the surprise of most, the Princes indicated a willingness to join such a federation, and British Liberal and Labour spokesmen approved the scheme.

The communal representation issue had not been resolved, but enough progress had been made to adjourn the proceedings —in the hope that the Congress could be induced to abandon civil disobedience and co-operate in the plan. Thus, on 19 January 1931, Prime Minister Ramsay MacDonald declared that the British Government was prepared to recognize the all-important principle of Executive responsibility to the Legislature, except for the safeguards, notably defence, external affairs, the maintenance of tranquillity in the realm, and the guarantee of financial stability. Exactly one week later, ironically on the first anniversary of the Congress 'Independence Day', the Viceroy passed the burden of decision to the Congress by releasing Gandhi and nineteen members of the Working Committee.

Among them were Jawaharlal and Kamala. Actually Nehru was released a few hours before the others because his father's condition had taken a sharp turn for the worse. When the message arrived, he was writing a letter to his daughter, and since this was 'Independence Day', he was thinking 'with pride and joy and anguish' of the tumultuous events during the preceding year.

The last days of Motilal Nehru were among the most trying his son has ever experienced. There had always been a deep attachment between father and son, which surmounted their disagreements in public affairs. The scene of their reunion was recorded by his younger sister, Krishna: 'As Jawahar withdrew from father's embrace ... his eyes were dimmed with tears which he vainly tried to suppress. I do not think I shall ever forget the light that shone in father's eyes or the joyousness of his expression as he greeted Jawahar. Nor shall I ever forget the agony in Jawahar's eyes as he approached the sickbed of the father he loved so deeply.'[1] 'There he sat,' wrote Nehru of his father during the last ten days, 'like an old lion mortally wounded and with his physical strength almost gone, but still very leonine and kingly.'[2] Next door, at *Swaraj Bhawan*, the home which Motilal had donated to the Congress, friends and colleagues were debating the next step. They came at intervals to pay their respects, and though Motilal could hardly speak, he greeted them all in the traditional *namaste* salutation. Gandhi, too, hurried to the bedside of his dear friend and right hand in politics.

On 4 February Motilal showed signs of improvement and so was moved to Lucknow for deep X-ray treatment, in a last effort to halt the disease; but in vain. He died on the morning of the 6th. His son mistook the serene expression for sleep. His wife knew better. The end had come. When he realized this, 'Jawahar sat behind him, his hand on father's head as though he were stroking it, his eyes full of tears unshed. . . . Suddenly [he] seemed to have aged overnight.'[3]

The news of Motilal Nehru's death spread quickly. Huge crowds gathered in Lucknow to pay homage to the nationalist leader. So too along the route, as the procession moved towards Allahabad, with Jawaharlal, Ranjit Pandit, and Hari, his faithful personal servant, accompanying the body on the last journey. Within a few hours of their arrival, while thousands watched, the cremation ceremony was performed on the banks of the holy Ganges.

Nehru's feelings were perhaps best expressed in a letter to his daughter:

Millions have sorrowed for him; but what of us, children of his, flesh of his flesh and bone of his bone! And what of the new Anand Bhawan, child of his also, even as we are, fashioned by him so lovingly and carefully. It is lonely and deserted and its spirit seems to have gone; and we walk along its verandahs with light steps, lest

---

[1] Hutheesingh, *With No Regrets*, p.. 68.   [2] *Toward Freedom*, p. 184.
[3] Hutheesingh, op. cit., pp. 71, 72

we disturb, thinking ever of him who made it. We sorrow for him and miss him at every step. And as the days go by the sorrow does not seem to grow less or his absence more tolerable. But, then, I think that he would not have us so. . . . He would like us to go on with the work he left unfinished. . . . For that cause he died. For that cause we will live and strive and, if necessary, die. After all, we are his children and have something of his fire and strength and determination in us.[1]

Nehru eulogized Gandhi in almost identical words after his assassination by a Hindu fanatic seventeen years later.[2] This is not surprising because Gandhi succeeded Motilal as his mentor. The younger Nehru's respect for and dependence on the Mahatma now became almost filial. He had been an avid disciple of Gandhi since his emergence on the Indian political stage in 1919; indeed, he had been much closer to Gandhi's outlook than to his father's. These two men were the dominant personal influences on Jawaharlal's actions throughout this early period. And Motilal, as we have seen, was a strong father. His death left a deep void in Jawaharlal's personal life. Imperceptibly, but very naturally, it was filled by Gandhi. Henceforth his function of political leader merged with that of father figure, with a resultant attachment between Gandhi and Nehru that could not be destroyed by conflict on political strategy and tactics.

Such conflicts were, indeed, frequent. And their social, economic and political philosophies differed in certain fundamental respects. Yet they were tied to each other by personal bonds, as well as the realization, perhaps not entirely conscious, that theirs were complementary roles of leadership in the struggle for independence. Gandhi was the symbol of traditional India, capable of galvanizing the masses into action as no other man in Indian history, and few men in any country. Nehru was the spokesman of the radical, Westernized intelligentsia, bringing to the Indian scene the ideas of liberalism and socialism, the faith in science, and the vision of a new society. As such, he was capable of attracting the urban middle and working classes to the nationalist movement. Through his association with Gandhi and his programme of agrarian reform he appealed to the masses as well.

[1] 21 April 1931. *Glimpses of World History*, p. 54.   [2] See pp. 386–8, below.

It was this combination, along with the organizational genius of Sardar Patel—who brought the industrial and merchant groups with him—that carried the Congress to eventual victory. The main strands of Indian society and the various aspirations —some contradictory—which animated them were embodied in the philosophies of these three men. The result was that as long as Gandhi and Patel lived there were severe limits to the degree of radicalism that Nehru could impose upon his col- leagues in the party. Like Motilal before them, Gandhi and Patel acted as brakes on Nehru's socialism in economic affairs. It is in these terms that Nehru's concessions to Gandhi and his apparent retreats from principle during the 'thirties and 'forties may acquire a proper perspective. It may well be that both Nehru and Gandhi understood their historic roles: the Mahatma was the only conceivable leader as long as the struggle for free- dom continued; and Nehru would succeed him once indepen- dence was attained. It is doubtful whether Gandhi, with his archaic ideas about economic policy, could have carried through the transformation of India into a modern state. This Nehru was pre-eminently fitted to do.

*   *   *   *

The passing of Motilal Nehru coincided with a crucial deci- sion of the Congress—the abandonment of civil disobedience in favour of a truce with the *Raj*. For his son it was as if salt had been added to the wound; the personal loss was deepened by what he considered to be a political defeat of the first magnitude.

It began the very day the elder Nehru died, with the return of the Indian delegation to the first Round Table Conference, headed by the three distinguished Liberals, Sapru, Jayakar and Shastri. Upon their arrival in Bombay they wired Gandhi and the Congress Working Committee which was then deliberating future policy in Allahabad, to plead for a delay in decisions until the results of the London talks could be conveyed person- ally. Ever willing to compromise, Gandhi consented. Indeed, upon his release from prison at the end of January 1931 he had said: 'I have come out of gaol with an absolutely open mind, unfettered by enmity and unbiased in argument. I am pre- pared to study the whole situation from every point of view . . .'[1]

---

[1] Campbell-Johnson, op. cit., p. 286.

Long conversations followed with the 'peacemakers'. Gandhi then made his first tactical move—a letter to the Viceroy seeking an inquiry into reports of police atrocities, especially into the alleged assault on women in the town of Borsad. Lord Irwin refused, for this would have unsettled one of the pillars of British rule in India, a loyal police force. At the insistence of the Liberals, supported by the Nawab of Bhopal, a friend of Gandhi, and such Congress moderates as Mrs. Naidu, the Mahatma asked for a 'heart-to-heart' talk with the Viceroy— without agenda. The gesture was immediately accepted and negotiations began forthwith, on 17 February 1931. They met six times at the Viceregal House until at last, on the morning of 5 March, agreement was reached.

There was much opposition on both sides. Many British Tories were aghast at what Churchill, the supreme diehard on Indian affairs, termed 'the nauseating and humiliating spectacle of this one-time Inner Temple lawyer, now seditious fakir, striding half-naked up the steps of the Viceroy's Palace, there to negotiate and to parley on equal terms with the representa- tive of the King-Emperor'.[1] Left-wing Congressmen like Nehru questioned the practical value of such a personal meet- ing on the grounds that Lord Irwin was not a free agent. But Gandhi, with his complete trust in the 'enemy', saw the possi- bility of converting his opponents by persuasion.

Only in one respect did the Mahatma score a victory, how- ever intangible it was. The Viceroy's willingness to negotiate was an implied recognition of the Congress as *the* representative of the Indian people. On specific issues, however, it was an unmitigated Congress defeat. The Viceroy stood fast on the crucial question of a police inquiry and Gandhi gave up his initial demand. The Congress agreed to stop civil disobedience and to participate in the next Round Table Conference. (Gandhi argued for the word 'suspends'; the Viceroy preferred 'terminates'; they compromised on 'discontinues'.) In return it received concessions from the *Raj*: the withdrawal of special Ordinances; the release of political prisoners, but not those convicted of violent acts or the soldiers who refused to fire in Peshawar; the remission of certain fines imposed on recalcitrant villages and not yet collected, but not the return of fines already

[1] Ibid, p. 294.

paid. The Government refused to abolish the Salt Tax, the precipitating cause of the war, though to save the Mahatma's face it agreed to allow certain villages to manufacture salt for their own use. Picketing was to be allowed 'but only within the limits permitted by the ordinary law', and discrimination against British goods was to cease. The land and immovable property seized by the Government during the Bardoli agitation of 1928 would be returned to their original owners—except where they had been sold to third parties. But by far the most significant concession made by Gandhi was on the basic constitutional issue: he agreed that in the future scheme of Indian government 'Federation is an essential part; so also are Indian responsibility and reservations or safeguards in the interests of India, for such matters as, for instance, defence; external affairs; the position of minorities; the financial credit of India, and the discharge of obligations' (Clause 2).[1]

It appears that Gandhi made this concession entirely on his own. His normal practice was to consult the Working Committee, which was in almost permanent session at the home of Dr. Ansari in Delhi, and to act as its spokesman in the negotiations. He added to the drama by walking to and from the Viceroy's Palace for each meeting, a distance of five miles. On this occasion, however, he took his colleagues by surprise. As Nehru later wrote, the Mahatma returned early in the morning of 4 March with news of an agreement. 'I knew most of the clauses, for they had been often discussed, but, at the very top, Clause 2 with its reference to safeguards, etc., gave me a tremendous shock. I was wholly unprepared for it. I said nothing then, and we all retired.' What a shattering anti-climax, he thought. 'Was it for this that our people had behaved so gallantly for a year? Were all our brave words and deeds to end in this?'[2] Even Gandhi's Eleven Points remained unfulfilled.

Until the very end Nehru pressed for rejection of the truce terms; and even after Gandhi signed the agreement he was opposed. According to one member of the Working Committee at the time, all of them had agreed reluctantly to accept the

[1] The text of the Gandhi-Irwin Agreement, also known as the 'Delhi Pact', is to be found in Sitaramayya, op. cit., vol. i, pp. 437–42.
[2] *Toward Freedom*, pp. 192, 193.

truce. But while Gandhi was at the Viceroy's Palace, Nehru started to bemoan the retreat. When the Mahatma returned and found his favourite son distraught, he asked what the trouble was. ' "We shouldn't have agreed," cried Nehru. "It will demoralize our Movement." "What would you have me do?" asked Gandhi. "If you wish I will phone the Viceroy and ask him to nullify my acceptance." "If Motilalji [his father] were here it wouldn't have happened," Nehru continued. But on Gandhi's crucial question, he replied, "No, we can't do that." '[1]

It was, indeed, a heart-breaking decision for Nehru. His presidency of the Congress had begun on a militant and optimistic note. Under his formal leadership the party had gone to war. Now, at the end of the year, it suffered a severe defeat. ' . . . Not without great mental conflict and physical distress' did he finally give way—after a soothing talk with Gandhi who claimed that no principle had been abandoned. In any event, thought Nehru, by way of rationalization, nothing could be served by holding out. Once it were known that Gandhi had signed the agreement, civil disobedience would collapse. It had already come to a virtual halt in the expectation of peace.

Neither Gandhi nor Lord Irwin divulged all the nuances of their discussions at the time. Their reticence was a logical corollary of the 'man-to-man' character of their conversations and a testimony of their mutual trust. In his memoirs, however, written long after the Mahatma's death, Lord Halifax referred to this crisis during his tenure as Viceroy. His reflections shed much light on the immense value which Gandhi placed on morality in the pursuit of political objectives, so much so that it was more important than the goals themselves.

The key stumbling-block to agreement was Gandhi's request for an inquiry into police activities. The Viceroy refused, on the grounds that nothing would be achieved except to aggravate feelings on both sides. 'This did not satisfy him [Gandhi] at all, and we argued the point for two or three days. Finally, I said that I would tell him the main reason why I could not give him what he wanted. I had no guarantee that he might not start civil disobedience again, and if and when he did, I wanted

---

[1] A paraphrase of their conversation as related to the author in India in 1956 by a person who wishes to remain anonymous.

the police to have their tails up and not down. Whereupon his face lit up and he said, "Ah, now Your Excellency treats me like General Smuts treated me in South Africa. You do not deny that I have an equitable claim, but you advance unanswerable reasons from the point of view of Government why you cannot meet it. I drop the demand." [1]

The informal atmosphere of the talks is illustrated by the following anecdote. Churchill's remark about the 'half-naked fakir' had caused a sensation. At the end of one of their conversations, when the Mahatma was about to leave without his shawl, the Viceroy picked it up and said, 'Gandhi, you haven't so much on, you know, that you can afford to leave this behind!' [2]

Soon after the 'Delhi Pact', as the truce came to be known, Gandhi held a press conference to clarify his views. One comment, in particular, seems to merit rescue from obscurity. When referring to the British and *purna swaraj*, he remarked, 'I know, if the time comes to concede the equality I want for India, they will say that that is what they have all along desired. The British people have a faculty of self-delusion as no other people have.' [3]

It remained only for the Congress as a whole to ratify the truce. This was done at the end of March 1931 at the annual session in Karachi, under the presidency of Sardar Patel, but under the domination of the Mahatma. A tense atmosphere surrounded the session as a result of the execution a few days earlier of Bhagat Singh, the legendary terrorist hero of the Punjab, despite Gandhi's plea to the Viceroy. Indignation ran high. Nehru expressed the prevalent mood when he said: 'The corpse of Bhagat Singh shall stand between us and England.' [4] March 24, the day following the hanging, witnessed demonstrations in all major cities and the walk-out of some members of

---

[1] The Earl of Halifax, *Fulness of Days*, pp. 148–9. Lord Halifax related two other incidents during this crisis and paid the following tribute to Gandhi: '. . . I can think of no person whose undertaking to respect a confidence I should ever have been more ready to accept than his. Measured by human standards, the abrupt cutting short of his life was a tragic deprivation for the country that he loved' (pp. 150–1).

[2] Campbell-Johnson, op. cit., p. 308. Chapter XXI of this book is a valuable source on the events leading up to the 'Delhi Pact'.

[3] Sitaramayya, op. cit., vol. i, p. 452.

[4] Tendulkar, op. cit., vol. 3, p. 92.

the central Legislative Assembly. To make matters worse, the *hartal* in Cawnpore (Kanpur) led to severe Hindu-Muslim riots, with 166 killed and 480 wounded.

Despite these circumstances, there was no real threat to the truce at that time. Patel and the Right wing were firmly committed. So too was Nehru, though he was still unhappy with the turn of events. In a shrewd political manœuvre, Gandhi persuaded him to move the resolution on the 'Delhi Pact' in the open session, thereby stifling any real opposition. Jawaharlal refused at first but again he rationalized—if he accepted the truce, he must do so in public. And so, at the very last moment, he acceded to the Mahatma's request.

As a sop to the dissidents, the resolution reiterated the goal of *purna swaraj* and spelled this out to mean 'control over the Defence forces, External Affairs, finance, fiscal and economic policy', as well as the right to secede from the Empire and an impartial scrutiny of all British financial claims on India, i.e., a reaffirmation of the original demands at Lahore in 1929. To maintain a semblance of faith with the 'Delhi Pact', it added that the Congress delegation to the Round Table Conference 'will be free to accept such adjustments as may be demonstrably necessary in the interests of India'. Gandhi was given *carte blanche* to interpret this, as the sole Congress representative to the Conference.[1] Little was to come of this defiant resolution or of the Round Table Conference itself.

Far more important, in the perspective of free India's welfare goals, was the Resolution on Fundamental Rights and Economic and Social Changes. Although secondary at the time, and somewhat unexpected, it proved to be the point of departure for all future decisions in these areas of public policy. There is still some doubt as to who really drafted this resolution, but it is generally agreed that Nehru played the decisive role.

According to a confidential (British) Government of India study, M. N. Roy, India's most famous communits, who had recently been expelled from the executive of the Comintern, was in Karachi incognito 'at Jawaharlal Nehru's invitation'. Further, that the Karachi Resolution 'is, in some respects, the minimum programme which Roy had advocated in Bombay a

[1] The text of this resolution is to be found in Sitaramayya, op. cit., vol. i, p. 459.

few weeks previously'.[1] This may well be, for Nehru was considerably influenced by Roy's views in the early 'thirties. But there is no evidence that Roy actually drafted this resolution. According to Nehru, it began to take shape during one of his early morning talks with Gandhi in the midst of the negotiations leading to the truce. The Mahatma asked him to prepare a draft, which he did. Gandhi then proposed various changes, and Nehru made several drafts before it was submitted, with their joint approval, to the Working Committee and later to the open session.[2]

In essence, the Karachi Resolution on Fundamental Rights laid down a programme of reform which the Congress was henceforth pledged to include in a constitution for independent India. Among them were the liberal freedoms of expression, religion, thought and assembly 'for purposes not opposed to law or morality'; equality before the law, regardless of caste, creed or sex; protection of regional languages and cultures; 'a living wage' for industrial workers, limited hours of labour, unemployment and old age insurance; the abolition of untouchability; the right to form unions; reduction of land revenue and rent; a system of progressive income taxes and graduated inheritance taxes; universal adult suffrage; free primary education; total prohibition; severe limitations on salaries of civil servants; a secular state; state protection of *khaddar* (hand-spun cloth), etc. The most important provision read: 'The State shall own or control key industries and services, mineral resources, railways, waterways, shipping and other means of public transport.'[3]

Viewed in the late 1950's, this was a moderate programme embodying various principles now enforced in many parts of the

[1] *India and Communism*. Extracts from this report in the files of the History of the Freedom Movement Project, p. 82.

[2] Tendulkar, op. cit., vol. 3, p. 111.

[3] The text of the Resolution on Fundamental Rights as passed at Karachi is to be found in *Report of the 45th Indian National Congress, at Karachi, 1931*, pp. 139–41. The All-India Congress Committee, under pressure from the right wing, was authorized to revise the resolution on the basis of suggestions from the Provincial Congress Committees and did so. There was no fundamental revision; but the original resolution was spelled out in greater detail and clarity, with the prime objective of reassuring landlords that wholesale expropriation of property was not intended by the Congress—though Nehru's views were more extreme than his colleagues'. The text of the amended resolution is to be found in *Congress Bulletin*, No. 4, 21 August 1931, pp. 31–34.

non-socialist world. Yet at the time it was considered a pioneering act, a broadening of the Congress programme beyond the purely political goal of complete self-government. And rightly so, for despite earlier attempts in this direction, notably the socialist programme of the U.P. Provincial Congress in 1924, also inspired by Nehru, the Karachi Resolution was the first official Congress pledge in favour of socialism. As such, it was one of Nehru's major contributions during the struggle for independence. He knew that little could be done in this sphere until political freedom was attained. As it happened, positive action was delayed until the death of Sardar Patel, an extreme conservative in economic, as in other matters. But thereafter nothing stood in Nehru's way. The inauguration of national planning in 1951 and, more particularly, the Avadi Resolution on a 'socialist pattern of society' in 1955 may be traced to the Karachi Resolution of 1931.

Civil disobedience had suffered a setback. But the principle of farr-eaching social and economic reform had now penetrated the ranks of the Congress. Within a few years Nehru's initiative was to reap rich rewards—in the elections of 1937.

CHAPTER VIII

Prison Becomes a Habit

THE 'Delhi Pact' provided a respite to both parties in the long-drawn-out struggle of the early 'thirties. A truce had been proclaimed, but tension and distrust remained—the conflict had been too bitter and the stakes too high.

No one felt defeat more deeply than Nehru. What made it so distressing was the emotional strain he was under at the time. There were ten anxious days at his father's bedside and a wrenching sense of loss when his father died. Then came weeks of negotiations with the Viceroy. Finally, there was the truce itself, symbol of retreat. All this, superimposed on his indifferent health during the final months in prison, produced exhaustion and irritability. His doctor advised prolonged rest. The truce made this possible.

For seven weeks Nehru escaped from the political wars in India. With his wife he went to Ceylon. There, amidst the lush tropical beauty of the highlands, he overcame the weariness of recent months. It was his first holiday since the European sojourn in 1926-7 and the last with Kamala. Writing many years later of their visit to Ceylon, Nehru recalled, 'we seemed to have discovered each other anew. All the past years that we had passed together had been but a preparation for this new and more intimate relationship. We came back all too soon and work claimed me and, later, prison. There was to be no more holidaying, no working together, except for a brief while . . .'[1]

Two weeks they spent at the lovely resort of Nuwara Eliya. For another fortnight they toured the island, pausing at some Buddhist monuments and historical landmarks of early Ceylonese culture. Then to the southern tip of India and a leisurely return to Allahabad, via the princely States of Travancore, Cochin, Mysore and Hyderabad, where they visited old family friends, Sarojini Naidu and her daughters.

[1] *The Discovery of India*, p. 33.

In the interim the truce showed signs of cracking under the pressures of Government and Congress. The principal source of tension was Bardoli, where officials insisted on the immediate payment of all taxes, both current and those in arrears, despite the peasant plea of inability to pay. There were also continuing disputes over the restoration of confiscated lands provided for in the 'Delhi Pact'. In Bengal thousands of political prisoners remained in jail, and sporadic acts of terrorism led to repression. Prohibition of peaceful picketing in Bombay was also charged by the Congress, as well as unprovoked arrests in the United Provinces and elsewhere. And in the Frontier Province the 'Redshirts' continued their agitation against the special ordinances still in force.

Some Congress leaders, notably Nehru, doubted the wisdom of attending the Second Round Table Conference. As increasing reports of truce violations came to the fore even Gandhi had second thoughts. In the middle of July 1931 he presented the Congress charges to the Viceroy in Simla and requested the establishment of an impartial tribunal. Lord Willingdon, who had succeeded Lord Irwin soon after the truce came into being, refused. The deadlock became serious in mid-August when the Mahatma announced that he would not attend the Conference. A second interview was hastily arranged and a face-saving formula was devised. The Government refused the request for general arbitration but agreed to inquire into the Bardoli claims. Gandhi, for his part, reserved for the Congress the right of 'defensive direct action' in case of future grievances. It was an eleventh-hour agreement to save the Round Table Conference from stillbirth.[1] Nehru accompanied the Mahatma from Simla to Bombay. Two years were to pass before they would meet again, years of resumed civil disobedience, imprisonment and a growing cleavage of ideas.

Much has been written about Gandhi's stay in London and the course of the Second Round Table Conference in the autumn of 1931. The details need not detain us. Suffice it to say that it was a complete fiasco. The basic task, in theory, was to formulate the essentials of a constitution for an All-India

---

[1] The correspondence between Gandhi and the Government of India, and the agreement reached with the Viceroy are to be found in Sitaramayya, op. cit., vol. i, pp. 472–9 and 487–91.

Federation. Almost immediately, however, the discussion became bogged down in the quicksand of communal representation. Delegates of the minorities—Muslims, Sikhs, Untouchables, Parsis, Indian Christians, Anglo-Indians and Europeans —banded together and presented a memorandum calling for heavily-weighted minority representation in the proposed federal and provincial legislatures. Gandhi reiterated the Congress's willingness to accept any solution agreeable to Hindus, Sikhs and Muslims, who comprised well over 90 per cent. of the population, but he rejected the idea of separate electorates for any other group. In particular, he vehemently opposed reserved seats for the Untouchables on the grounds that they were an integral part of the Hindu community. He argued that the communal issue should be tackled later, after the basic issues had been resolved and that, in fact, the emphasis being given to it at that stage was hindering progress in constitution-making. His pleas were in vain. At one point he offered to accept the demands of the minority delegates, headed by the Aga Khan, if they would support the Congress's demand for independence. The reply was that a recognition of communal claims was a precondition of everything else.

The Conference floundered on this issue and finally adjourned in total deadlock, on 1 December 1931. At the closing session the Mahatma expressed regret that a parting of the ways had come. To the press he indicated that a resumption of mass civil disobedience was unlikely.

During his absence, however, political conditions at home deteriorated, and everything pointed to an early renewal of political warfare. In Bengal things were kept at the boil by individual terrorism and police excesses, notably at Chittagong and the Hijli Detention Camp near Calcutta. In the Frontier Province the steady growth of the 'Redshirt' Movement alarmed the authorities. Agitation led to clashes with the police, to police firing on unarmed demonstrators, and to frequent arrests. Towards the end of December 1931 the Frontier Government declared the 'Redshirts' illegal and imprisoned their leaders, Khan Abdul Ghaffar Khan, the 'Frontier Gandhi', and his brother, Dr. Khan Saheb.[1]

[1] The Khan brothers have had stormy political careers, especially since 1947. On the eve of Indian independence Dr. Khan Saheb was Chief Minister (Premier)

The most critical area of tension was the United Provinces, where Congress politics had long been dominated by the Nehrus, father and son. Friction arose from agrarian discontent, almost endemic in that part of India. The Great Depression had dealt the peasants a shattering blow. But the land revenue had to be paid. A no-tax campaign in 1930 had been suspended as part of the truce terms. Now the peasants pleaded their inability to pay. Gandhi had interceded before his departure for London and had advised them to pay half the taxes. The provincial Government recognized the special circumstances and remitted a portion of the land revenue. The peasants claimed the reduction was inadequate and requested Congress support. Negotiations followed, with Nehru and Pandit Pant taking the lead, but to no avail.[1]

The crisis reached a head in November 1931. The U.P. Government insisted that taxes be paid pending negotiations. The peasants proposed a moratorium until agreement was reached. Gandhi's advice was sought in London, but the reply came back: 'Do as you think fit.' Finally, under pressure from the *Kisan Sabha* (Peasant League), and with Nehru's wholehearted approval, the Congress advised a no-tax campaign. The Government refused to negotiate on these terms. It was this highly-charged issue which led to Nehru's sixth imprisonment.

*　　*　　*　　*

Events moved swiftly after this open break on the question of land taxes. The U.P. Government responded to the challenge

of the North West Frontier Province, and Abdul Ghaffar Khan was the most popular leader of the Pathans. Both opposed the Partition, for which they paid a heavy price when Pakistan came into being. Dr. Khan Saheb was under strict surveillance for about three years and Abdul Ghaffar spent six years in Pakistani jails. Dr. Khan Saheb emerged from the political limbo in the autumn of 1954 when he was appointed to the central Cabinet of Pakistan. One year later, after the provinces, princely States and tribal areas of the western half of Pakistan had been integrated into one unit, he became Chief Minister of West Pakistan as well as leader of the newly formed Republican Party. Abdul Ghaffar was the most vociferous opponent of the 'One Unit' scheme and remains one of the outstanding opposition leaders in Pakistan. Dr. Khan Saheb was assassinated in May 1958. For further details on the unification of West Pakistan, see Callard, K., *Pakistan, A Political Study*, pp. 183-93.

[1] Pandit Pant was a prominent figure in the U.P. Congress for many years. He was Chief Minister of the United Provinces from 1937 to 1939 and again from 1947 to the beginning of 1955. Thereafter he moved to the Centre as Home Minister and became Nehru's right-hand man in domestic politics.

in mid-December 1931 with a sweeping ordinance against all agrarian agitation. Nehru was in Bombay at the time, arranging medical treatment for Kamala who was ailing once more. He proceeded to the Karnatak, in south-west India, to fulfil a long-standing political obligation and returned to Bombay on 21 December. As Gandhi was expected a week later, he was urged by friends to remain. But spurred on by news of arrests at home, Nehru returned to Allahabad—and almost certain imprisonment, for the authorities held him primarily responsible for the no-tax campaign.[1]

By the time he reached *Anand Bhawan* no fewer than three orders had been served upon him under the newly issued decree confining him to the city limits of Allahabad and prohibiting his participation in public affairs. But Nehru was never one to accept such decrees. He informed the District Magistrate that he would carry on his normal routine and that he planned to return to Bombay to meet Gandhi. He was not permitted to fulfil this defiant threat. On 26 December he left for Bombay by train, along with T. A. K. Sherwani, President of the U.P. Provincial Congress Committee. Within an hour the game was up: the train came to an unexpected halt at Iradatganj and they were whisked away to Naini Prison.

Such was the atmosphere which greeted Gandhi upon his return to India two days later—ordinances in Bengal, the Frontier and the U.P., as well as the arrest of senior colleagues. More hurt than angry at what he took to be an unprovoked violation of the truce, he wired the Viceroy, seeking a personal interview. The Government of India was in no mood to repeat the spectacle of a summit conference with the 'rebels', probably because it was in a much stronger position than at the beginning of 1931, when Lord Irwin was at the helm.

The Viceroy, Lord Willingdon, replied that he would not discuss the emergency measures imposed on Bengal, the U.P. and the Frontier. The Congress Working Committee then hurriedly drafted an equivocal rejoinder on New Year's Day 1932, offering co-operation if the Viceroy reconsidered his

---

[1] The confidential, unpublished Government of India report, India and Communism (1935), refers to Nehru's decision 'to launch his "no tax" campaign at the end of November, 1931'. On page 83 of the extracts from this report in the files of the History of the Freedom Movement Project.

response to Gandhi, provided 'adequate relief' in regard to the ordinances, and left the Congress 'free scope' to pursue its goal of complete independence in future consultations. Otherwise, it would call for a resumption of civil disobedience. The Viceroy refused to grant an interview 'under threat' and Gandhi reminded him that civil disobedience had only been 'suspended' under the terms of the 'Delhi Pact'.[1]

The following day, 4 January, the Government of India struck and struck hard. Gandhi and Sardar Patel, the Congress President, were taken into custody. At the same time four new ordinances were issued: an Emergency Powers Ordinance; an Unlawful Instigation Ordinance; an Unlawful Association Ordinance, and a Prevention of Molestation and Boycott Ordinance. Together they gave the Government of India powers even more far-reaching than those of 1930 which Lord Irwin's biographer had termed 'this catalogue of absolutism'.[2] As the Secretary of State for India, Sir Samuel Hoare, told the House of Commons, 'I admit that the Ordinances that we have approved are very drastic and severe. They cover almost every activity of Indian life.'[3]

The most striking features of the Government's onslaught were its precision, its thoroughness, and its scope, all of which strongly suggested premeditated action. The ordinances were obviously prepared in advance. Moreover, unlike 1930, when emergency measures were taken piecemeal, New Delhi now promulgated sweeping decrees covering all of India at one time.

The Congress was unprepared for all-out warfare at this stage. The truce was theoretically still in force when the Mahatma returned from the Round Table Conference; Gandhi himself had openly expressed doubt about the likelihood of civil disobedience; and many believed he would be able to restore the *status quo* after a 'man-to-man' talk with the Viceroy. No plans are evident in Congress actions at the time except for the conditional threat to resume non-violent war. No orders had been issued to local organs and no provision had been made for substitute members of its High Command.

---

[1] The correspondence between Gandhi and Lord Willingdon, and the Working Committee's resolution, are to be found in Sitaramayya, op. cit., vol. i, pp. 510–19.

[2] Campbell-Johnson, op. cit., p. 269.

[3] 24 March 1932. Gt. Brit. H.C., *Debates*, 1931–2, vol. 263, col. 1226.

In any event the Government's campaign was devastating. Within a week almost everybody of any consequence in the Congress was in prison. The party was outlawed, its records destroyed, its funds confiscated and its buildings seized. Moreover, some eighty affiliated or sympathetic organizations were declared illegal—youth leagues, *kisan sabhas*, Congress-supported schools, economic enterprises, student clubs. Even the Congress-run hospital in *Swaraj Bhawan* was closed. Political meetings and processions were prohibited. The Congress press was gagged. Severe fines and imprisonment were meted out to those guilty of aiding the Congress or hiding *satyagrahis*. Land and property were confiscated in cases of failure to pay taxes. Civil liberties were suspended. It was nothing short of martial law.

Government policy differed from the 1930 campaign in one respect. A calculated attempt was made to wean the moneyed interests away from 'sedition' by imposing severe fines and other economic penalties on middle-class offenders. The principal difference, however, was the efficiency of the Government's repressive measures; it was a smooth, well-integrated programme, using the key element of surprise.

The Congress never recovered from the initial assault. However, it fought back with the traditional weapons of civil disobedience: picketing of liquor and foreign cloth shops, with women taking the lead; violation of the salt law; illegal publication of propaganda sheets; organization of *hartals* and processions; and in some parts of the countryside, peasant resistance to punitive measures of the local authorities. For eight months the semblance of mass civil disobedience was maintained. But it was a desultory campaign and there was never any doubt as to the outcome. Bereft of leadership, funds and organization, the rank and file were compelled to fall back on their own resources. There was no lack of enthusiasm. Many courted arrest and many were arrested. According to the Congress, no fewer than 80,000 were imprisoned in the first four months of 1932.[1]

Despite the ban on public meetings, the annual session of the party was held, after a fashion, in Old Delhi, on 24 April. The President-elect, Pandit Malaviya, was arrested on his way to the capital, but the conference took place nonetheless. While

---

[1] An estimate by Congress President Pandit Malaviya, in a public statement on 2 May 1932. *The Statesman* (Calcutta), 3 May 1932.

the police were engaged in a thorough search of New Delhi about 500 delegates met under the clock tower in Chandni Chowk, the main bazaar of the old city, and there passed a series of resolutions, reaffirming *purna swaraj* as the nationalist goal, endorsing (!) the resumption of civil disobedience and the like. Other efforts were made to maintain the *élan* of the masses, such as the celebration of *Swadeshi* Day at the end of May, to focus attention on Indian-made goods, and Prisoners' Day early in July. Yet the decline in intensity became obvious with the approach of summer, and a serious setback was registered in May with the outbreak of Hindu-Muslim riots in Bombay. It was only a question of time before nationalist ardour would be extinguished.

*   *   *   *

All this Nehru observed from prison, with mixed emotions, sometimes with anger at the news of police brutalities, at other times with detachment. As in 1930 and again in 1942 he was denied the satisfaction of direct involvement in the struggle. On 4 January, the day the Government struck, he was tried in Naini Prison. He refused to say anything in defence of his action but he began to read a fiery statement on peasant discontent. The Magistrate threatened to clear the Court if he continued in this vein. Nehru 'then stopped with a curse on the Government' and handed his statement to the judge. Found guilty under section 13 of the United Provinces Emergency Ordinance, he was sentenced to two years' rigorous imprisonment and a fine of Rs. 500.[1] Sherwani, who was arrested with him and was tried for the same offence, received a sentence of only six months.

One incident in particular stirred Nehru to a point of bitter hatred of the *Raj*. It was 8 April 1932, the second day of the Congress's National Week, commemorating the tragic events of 1919. As everywhere in India Allahabad was the scene of a large demonstration; his elderly mother was in the front line there. The advancing procession was stopped by the police. At that point, in deference to her age, one of her friends provided a chair for Mrs. Swarup Rani Nehru in the middle of the road, at the head of the procession. Suddenly the police

[1] Based on the report of the trial and judgement in the Home Department (Political Section), confidential reports. In the National Archives of India.

charged, and among those seriously injured was Nehru's mother. In the midst of the mêlée she lay in the road unnoticed until the demonstration was dispersed.

According to the medical officer who attended her, she had received severe blows from a wooden cane and was bleeding badly. There were even rumours of her death, causing retaliation that evening by an angry crowd. When news of this episode reached Nehru in Bareilly District Jail, whence he had been transferred from Naini, he was beside himself with rage. As he wrote some time later, 'the thought of my frail old mother lying bleeding on the dusty road obsessed me, and I wondered how I would have behaved if I had been there. How far would my non-violence have carried me? Not very far, I fear, for that sight would have made me forget the long lesson I had tried to learn for more than a dozen years . . .'[1]

He remained at Bareilly District Jail from mid-February to mid-June 1932. The change from Naini was distasteful, partly because it meant leaving friends and familiar surroundings, partly because his new 'home' was surrounded by a twenty-five-foot wall. Aside from the feeling of claustrophobia which it produced, the 'Great Wall', as he termed it, interfered with his work, reducing the hours of sunlight for reading and writing.

What disturbed Nehru even more was an unusual deterioration in health, both at Bareilly and at Dehra Dun Jail, in the United Provinces, where he spent the last fourteen months of this imprisonment, from June 1932 until August 1933. An unexplained daily rise in temperature plagued him for some months. It made him moodier than he is wont to be and temporarily reduced his interest in the struggle going on beyond the walls. But the illness passed and with it the mood of despair.

With time Nehru's attitude to prison life mellowed. Writing to his sister Krishna in the autumn of 1933, he said: 'Those who have had the advantage of prison experience know at least the value of patience, and if they have profited by their experience they have learned adaptability, and that is a great thing.'[2] On another occasion he wrote to her: 'Going to jail is a trivial matter. . . . As a mere routine I think it has some value . . . but that value is not very great unless there is an inner urge to do it. . . . That represents something vital.'[3] Nehru possessed this

[1] *Toward Freedom*, p. 223.   [2] Hutheesingh, *With No Regrets*, p. 109.   [3] Ibid., p. 146.

urge in abundance, and this undoubtedly eased the problem of adjustment.

His prison routine during 1932–3 was essentially the same as in earlier periods, with a heavy concentration on reading and writing. In Bareilly District Jail he resumed the letters to his daughter, and by the time he was released from Dehra Dun Jail at the conclusion of his two-year term his reflections on world history were complete. But with the coming of spring 1933 his mind turned to the world crisis as he saw it from prison.

Hitler had come to power. Japan had completed its conquest of Manchuria. The Great Depression continued to wreak havoc the world over. The Western democracies appeared to him to be entering a stage of decadence. Only Soviet Russia seemed to offer a ray of hope.

The sources of attraction to the Soviet experiment, at that time, were both negative and positive. On the one hand were the shattering effects of the lengthy economic crisis and the human misery it entailed; the storm clouds of new wars more devastating than the old; and his conviction that violence and inequality were inherent in the existing capitalist order. On the other hand, he was impressed with the achievements of the Soviet régime in the face of severe obstacles. In particular he was influenced by the reports of progress in Soviet Central Asia, whose problems were so similar to those of India, and the appearance of rapid economic development in Russia contrasting with the stagnation of the Western world. He continued to be repelled by the harsh methods employed in Russia—the regimentation, the violence, the ruthlessness and the intolerance. But like so many sympathizers then and now, Nehru rationalized these ills as necessities of the 'transition period'. 'I do not approve of many things that have taken place in Russia,' he wrote at the end of 1933, 'nor am I a Communist in the accepted sense of the word. But taking everything together, I have been greatly impressed by the Russian experiment.'[1]

This is not the response of an unquestioning follower of Marxism-Leninism, and Nehru was *never* a true believer. From the very outset of his flirtation with Communism he was

---

[1] From a letter to a correspondent in the United Kingdom published in the *Manchester Guardian*, 15 December 1933. Also in Nehru, *Recent Essays and Writings*, p. 123.

sceptical, especially on the question of means. The Gandhian influence, as well as a streak of individualism and non-conformism, prevented him from embracing the creed completely. To term Nehru a Communist is to ignore the record of his speeches and writings on the subject—and his deeds. Even at this period, when the Communist appeal was at its height, Nehru did not go beyond emotional attraction to its goals. He never overcame his distaste for the authoritarian aspects of the Soviet régime. The Marxist world-view appealed to him intellectually, his reaction to Russia was mixed though generally favourable, and he disdained all dogmatism on the subject.

What made Nehru sympathetic to Communism in the early 'thirties was the apparent polarization of ideologies. He saw the world entering a titanic struggle between Communism and Fascism and he found himself condoning the former's excesses. His most considered thoughts on this question were conveyed to the Indian press on 18 December 1933: 'I do believe that fundamentally the choice before the world today is between *some form* of Communism and some form of Fascism, and I am all for the former, i.e. Communism. . . . There is no *middle road* . . . and I choose the Communist *ideal*. In regard to the methods and approach to this ideal I may not agree with everything that orthodox Communists have done. *I think that these methods will have to adapt themselves to changing conditions and may vary in different countries. But I do think that the basic ideology of Communism and its scientific interpretation of history is sound.*'[1]

Not only are there serious reservations about means and a tendency to stress the ideal of Communism rather than the reality of Russia. There is, too, a striking flexibility in approach to social and economic change. In fact, Nehru's remarks anticipate the great debate which dominated the Communist world in the late 'fifties, epitomized in the phrase, 'many roads to socialism'. In other writings of the period he also revealed an affinity with Mao Tse-tung's basic revision of Marxism, a firm belief that the peasantry, not the industrial working class, was the primary social force for change and that the future of India lay in the solution of the agrarian problem.

*   *   *   *

[1] *Recent Essays and Writings*, p. 126. (Emphasis added.)

While Nehru was engaged in reflections on universal history and the crisis of the contemporary world, the struggle within India took a dramatic turn. On 13 September 1932 Gandhi announced that he would 'fast unto death' because of the 'Communal Award' of British Prime Minister Ramsay Mac-Donald. Among other things it provided for separate electorates for the Untouchables, a scheme which the Mahatma considered immoral.[1]

Alarm and anxiety greeted the news of Gandhi's gesture. Nehru himself was tormented by the thought of Gandhi's possible death, all the more because the issue seemed peripheral to the struggle for independence, although important in its own right. His immediate reaction was expressed in a letter to his daughter just after he learned of the proposed fast: 'I am shaken up completely and I know not what to do. . . . My little world, in which he has occupied such a big place, shakes and totters, and there seems to be darkness and emptiness everywhere. His picture comes before my eyes again and again. . . . Shall I not see him again? And whom shall I go to when I am in doubt and require wise counsel, or am afflicted and in sorrow and need loving comfort? What shall we all do when our beloved chief who inspired us and led us has gone?'[2] Though this was written under emotional strain, it illuminates the inner attachment of Nehru to Gandhi. Jawaharlal was over forty when he penned these words.

The fast began on 18 September 1932, despite the pleas of friends, colleagues and even critics. The Government, concerned lest Gandhi die in prison, offered to release him under certain conditions. The Mahatma refused. The following day a conference of Hindu leaders was hurriedly convened, at first in Bombay and then at Gandhi's bedside in Yeravda Prison, near Poona. Three more days passed in tense discussion. Gandhi's condition deteriorated rapidly. Dr. Ambedkar, a leader of the Untouchables, was adamant on the issue of separate electorates. However, on the fifth day of the fast, with Gandhi's life hanging by a thread, Ambedkar gave way and an agreement was reached.

Under the terms of the 'Poona Pact' the Untouchables

---

[1] The text of the 'Communal Award' is in Cmd. 4147, 1932.
[2] On 15 September 1932. *Glimpses of World History*, p. 327.

abandoned separate electorates. To safeguard their interests, however, they were guaranteed a number of reserved seats from those assigned to the Hindu community in the British 'Communal Award', in fact, twice as many as originally assured the Untouchables by that Award. In short, the façade of an integrated Hindu community was maintained along with the substance of reserved seats—for a period of ten years. The 'Poona Pact' was accepted by the British Government, thereby nullifying the 'Communal Award' of MacDonald, much to Gandhi's satisfaction. Gandhi called off the fast, and the crisis ended.

The most astonishing result of Gandhi's 'epic fast' was the widespread sympathy it evoked in favour of the fifty million Untouchables. By focusing attention on the *Harijans*, the Sons of God, as he termed the Untouchables, the Mahatma set in motion a massive attack on this unmitigated evil of Hindu society. Temples of worship, hitherto held sacrosanct by caste Hindus, were thrown open to Untouchables all over the country. The right to use the village water supply, considered unthinkable in the past, was now granted the *Harijans* as a pledge of faith in the Mahatma. The cause of the Untouchables took on the character of a holy crusade. Unfortunately, the initial enthusiasm was soon dissipated. But Gandhi's action and his subsequent efforts on behalf of the Untouchables ultimately bore fruit. Since Independence, Nehru has sought to obliterate the inequalities of caste. It is a slow process, for these are rooted in more than three thousand years of Hindu culture but progress is being made. This attack on untouchability can properly be dated to Gandhi's fast in 1932.[1]

In the short run, however, Gandhi's gesture had an adverse effect. Nationalist attention was diverted from the political issue of independence, and civil disobedience received a severe blow. Formally it continued another eight months, but decay set in at once. Many who were weary of imprisonment and separation from their families seized upon the opportunity to abandon *satyagraha*. For Nehru and others it was a painful sight.

The months in prison dragged on. Nehru was now at the small district jail in Dehra Dun, in the foothills of the Himalayas, seat of the new India's military academy, its most exclusive

[1] The most complete account of Gandhi's fast is to be found in Pyarelal, U. N., *The Epic Fast*, 1933.

public school, and its forestry institute. He had been moved from Bareilly in the dead of night early in June 1932, and was driven by car some fifty miles to a wayside station to forestall any demonstrations. After months of close confinement 'it was delightful to feel the cool night air and to see the phantom trees and men and animals rush by in the semi-darkness . . .'[1]

This joyful contact with nature was brief. The following morning he was in prison once more. Yet Dehra Dun was a welcome change from Bareilly, where the temperature rose to 110 degrees and above. And the walls were lower. The nearby trees soothed him, and beyond were the mountains. Although hidden from sight, their proximity fed his imagination and provided vicarious pleasure. Nehru has always been enamoured of the panoramic beauty of the hills of northern India.

In the stillness and isolation of his surroundings he had almost forgotten the world outside. But suddenly another rude shock was administered by Gandhi. On 8 May 1933, when civil disobedience was at its lowest ebb, the Mahatma began a twenty-one-day fast for 'self-purification'. Nehru was appalled by this seeming reversion to the primitive. His rational mind rebelled at the master's strange tactics. Nor has Nehru's attitude to the political fast changed these many years. In 1956 he remarked, 'Gandhi would go on a fast. I didn't understand it then—and I don't understand it now.'[2]

Knowing of Nehru's disapproval of the fasting technique, Gandhi wrote him a soothing letter: 'As I was struggling against the coming fast, you were before me as it were in flesh and blood. But it was no use. How I wish I could feel that you had understood the absolute necessity of it [to stress the importance of eradicating untouchability and to restore his own faith]. . . . But I won't convince you by argument, if you did not see the truth intuitively. I know that . . . I shall retain your precious love during all those days of ordeal . . .'[3]

Nehru's opposition was somewhat tempered by these words of affection. Confused and disturbed, he replied: 'What can I say about matters I do not understand? I feel lost in strange

[1] Letter to his daughter, 10 June 1932. *Glimpses of World History*, p. 171.
[2] To the author in New Delhi on 6 June 1956.
[3] On 2 May 1933, from Yeravda Central Prison. Tendulkar, op. cit., vol. 8, Appendix on Gandhi-Nehru Letters, p. 356.

country where you are the only familiar landmark and I try to
grope my way in the dark but I stumble. Whatever happens
my love and thoughts will be with you.'[1] Later, concerned
about the possible untoward effects of his reaction, he sent
another more reassuring wire.

The first day of the fast, 8 May 1933, marks the *de facto* end of
the lengthy civil disobedience campaign. On the grounds that
the fast was in no sense a political act the Government released
Gandhi unconditionally. He reciprocated by recommending
(ordering) that the campaign be suspended for six weeks and
called for the release of all remaining civil disobedience prisoners, estimated at about 9,000, including a few leaders like
Nehru and Prasad. The Government was adamant and insisted
on complete termination of civil disobedience. Total surrender
was now inevitable, for the Congress was exhausted after three
years of struggle.

In the middle of June the suspension was extended another
six weeks, and in July at a conference of prominent Congressmen, held under Gandhi's leadership, *mass* civil disobedience
was formally abandoned. The façade of struggle was retained
a little longer. Gandhi sought an interview with the Viceroy.
His request refused, he offered individual *satyagraha* at the
beginning of August. He was imprisoned and went on another
fast over some trivial issue. When the danger to his life became
serious, he was released. The end had come. To save face, the
Mahatma announced that he would abjure civil disobedience
of any kind until the conclusion of his one-year sentence, i.e
August 1934. By that time the Congress was at its lowest
fortunes in a decade.

*   *   *   *

These events coincided with Nehru's release from prison. He
was moved from Dehra Dun to Naini in the latter part of August
1933, and was due to be discharged in mid-September. But on
30 August news came that his mother was critically ill. As a
humanitarian gesture the authorities allowed him to leave immediately.

After a brief stay at his mother's bedside in Lucknow he hurried to Poona for the long-awaited reunion with the Mahatma.

[1] *Toward Freedom*, p. 239.

Mrs. Krishna Hutheesingh, 'With No Regrets'

7. Kamala Nehru

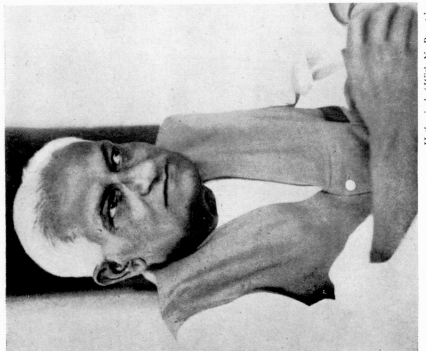

Hutheesingh, 'With No Regrets'

Hutheesingh, 'With No Regrets'

Much had happened in the intervening two years, much that was distressing to Nehru: civil disobedience had collapsed; Gandhi had virtually withdrawn from the political arena; and most disquieting of all, no serious thought was being given to the social and economic ideals which should animate independent India. Nehru was also aware that Gandhi was not favourably disposed to his socialist views. The time was more than ripe for serious conversation.

Their intimate talks were followed by an exchange of letters which brought into bold relief the temperamental and substantive differences between the two men, as well as the many things they had in common. In theory they seemed agreed on ultimate objectives. But their divergence on means laid bare the gap in social and economic philosophy. Nehru stressed anew the goal of complete independence and strongly urged that freedom should entail the abolition of vested economic interests. Gandhi agreed in principle but insisted that this be done by conversion not coercion. Here was the core issue of disagreement. Moreover, Gandhi, on principle, abhorred secrecy in political tactics while Nehru was pragmatic, arguing that it was permissible in special circumstances. Similarly, the Mahatma emphasized the 'constructive activities' of the Congress, notably spinning, the removal of untouchability and communal unity, while Nehru did not even mention them in his programme.

Beyond the specific sources of cleavage was the striking difference in their ways of thought. Nehru was a rationalist who felt the necessity of a clear statement of goals and the ideology from which they emerged. Gandhi, by contrast, arrived at decisions intuitively, relying on his 'inner voice', and was repelled by the notion of a systematic ideology. Nehru's was the Western mind, thinking in terms of the long-run, a plan of action; Gandhi refused to be pressed beyond the immediate aim. Finally, there was the Mahatma's categorical belief that ends were subservient to means. 'I feel', he wrote at the time, 'that our progress towards the goal will be in the exact proportion to the purity of our means.' In recent years Nehru has shown a growing acceptance of this view, but at the time he considered ends of prior value.

It would be wrong, however, to think of Nehru in the early

H

'thirties as a fiery revolutionary in the Western meaning of the term. Clarifying his intent on the elimination of entrenched interests, he remarked: 'We do not wish to injure any class or group and the divesting should be done as gently as possible.'[1] It was this Fabian approach, rather than his intellectual attraction to Marxism in the 'thirties, which later found expression in the Indian Constitution and in Nehru's economic policy.

For many Congressmen there was an air of unreality about the 'Poona Talks', a preoccupation with doctrinal matters without any practical relevance to the burning issue of the day, namely, 'Where do we go from here?' Such was the charge levelled by Subhas Bose, who still looked to Nehru as his guide. Bose went further. 'With a popularity only second to that of the Mahatma, with unbounded prestige among his countrymen, with a clear brain possessing the finest ideas, with an up-to-date knowledge of modern world movements—that he [Nehru] should be found wanting in the essential quality of leadership, namely the capacity to make decisions and face unpopularity if need be, was a great disappointment.'[2] This is not the place to evaluate such a sweeping allegation.[3] Suffice it to note that in the context of 1933 Bose's criticism was unfair, for Nehru had just emerged from a lengthy stay in prison and was completely cut off from the currents of thought in the party.

In a sense Nehru did provide leadership during this period, but it was in the sphere of ideas. He had returned to Lucknow from Poona in the middle of September 1933, to spend a few weeks with his ailing mother. There he set down his thoughts on 'Whither India', a provocative series of articles on 'what do we want and why'.[4] Their justification, he wrote, was that 'right action cannot come out of nothing; it must be preceded by thought . . . action which is not based on thought is chaos and confusion'. The indirect rebuke to Gandhi was not lost on his readers.

He criticized Indian nationalists for their excessive concern with trivia and personalities and for their failure to think deeply about basic principles. Politics, he said, must be based either on

---

[1] The text of the Gandhi-Nehru correspondence in September 1933 is in *Indian Annual Register*, vol. ii, 1933, pp. 356–60.

[2] *The Indian Struggle*, p. 366.

[3] See Chapter XX, below.

[4] Reprinted in Nehru, *Recent Essays and Writings*, pp. 1–24.

magic or science. 'Personally I have no faith in or use for the ways of magic and religion.' The basic goal is freedom, he continued, but freedom itself is only a *means* to desirable social ends —well-being for the masses, the eradication of poverty, disease and suffering, the opportunity to live the 'good life'.

The influence of Marxist theory is evident in these essays, notably in his sweeping survey of the rise of capitalism in the West; India's role in the industrial revolution; the impact of British rule on the sub-continent; the emergence of imperialism; his theory of war; his explanation of fascism, and the analysis of the Great Depression. The purpose of this survey was to persuade his readers that the Indian freedom struggle must be viewed in a global perspective.

Asia, he wrote, is the main theatre of conflict between nationalism and imperialism. Nationalism is still the strongest force, but economic objectives are inextricably bound up with the political. Hence the twin goals of independence and socialism. By independence he meant total severance of the British connection, though he left the door ajar for co-operation with England after a transfer of power. The economic goal was the termination of all special class privileges and vested interests. Ultimately, he predicted, India would become part of a socialist world federation.

'Whither India' summed up Nehru's socialist philosophy in the 'thirties. In Western terms, he emerged as a left-socialist of the classical Austrian variety, Marxist in theory, democratic in practice.

These essays aroused considerable interest among people of all political persuasions. Communists accepted his main line of argument but said it did not go far enough. Conservatives attacked his premisses and angrily rejected his conclusions. Nehru replied to the Left that his views and actions were consistent since 1920, though he admitted that he had been compelled to make some compromises over the years. As for the Right wing, he denied that he had said anything new and scorned its 'ignorant jumble of crude ideas and prejudices'. Equality in a socialist sense, he added, meant for him equality of opportunity—hardly the Communist view. But as if to reassure the Left, 'I have no doubt that coercion or pressure is necessary to bring about political and social change in India. . . .

Non-violence is no infallible creed with me, and although I greatly prefer it to violence, I prefer freedom with violence to subjection with non-violence.' After Independence he came closer to Gandhi's position.[1]

Although 'Whither India' did not have any immediate con-crete effect on the party, it provided food for thought among some younger leftist Congressmen who in the following year were to form the Congress Socialist Party, a faction within the Congress, with Nehru as the acknowledged spiritual godfather. More than that, it provided a focus and a leader for all radical elements within the Congress. As such it was a milestone in Nehru's emergence as the hero of the Left in the middle and late 'thirties.

Nehru's role as the ideologue of left-nationalism received further expression in his assault on the still-powerful force of communalism, an ideology and system of values deriving from membership of a religious group. On 12 November 1933 he delivered a scathing attack on the Hindu Mahasabha in an address at the Hindu University of Benares, the very citadel of Hindu communal thought. He denounced communalism as a reactionary movement threatening the unity of India and hindering the struggle for independence. His hosts were ap-palled, as were orthodox Hindus everywhere. Jawaharlal was taken to task, particularly because he made no reference to Muslim communalism. This he rectified in a reply to the critics. The key problem regarding communal actions, he wrote, is fear. 'Honest communalism is fear; false communal-ism is political reaction.' There is no basic difference between Hindu and Muslim forms of communal mentality, but a special responsibility for concessions rests with the Hindus because they are more numerous and more advanced, educationally and economically. Both movements, he insisted, were essentially struggles for power, prestige and jobs on the part of their upper-class leaders, without any social and economic programme for the masses worthy of the name.[2]

Sir Mohammed Iqbal, the great Urdu poet and one of the spiritual founders of Pakistan, claimed that it was impossible to

---

[1] 'Some Criticisms Considered' relating to 'Whither India', in *Recent Essays and Writings*, pp. 34, 35.

[2] A summary of his address is to be found in ibid., pp. 43–44.

fuse the various Indian communities. Nehru dissented, arguing that there is no racial or cultural difference between the Hindu and Muslim masses, and that an Indian nation exists at present despite superficial differences. He agreed that because of the prevalent fear, aggravated in his view by British machinations, safeguards for the minorities were essential. But who is to make the decisions? Surely not the British, he replied. Nor, indeed, the Muslim League, which was a microscopic minority at the time. The proper authority, said Nehru, was a Constituent Assembly elected by adult or near-adult franchise, with separate electorates for the minorities if they so desired. He offered to accept any demands for safeguards put forward by the Muslim representatives to such a Constituent Assembly.[1]

The Congress adopted his proposal for a Constituent Assembly at its annual session in 1934. The Muslim League under Mohammed Ali Jinnah was less impressed. Much time and energy were to be expended in correspondence and negotiations between Nehru and Jinnah during subsequent years. And ultimately much blood was to flow before the communal problem was 'settled' by the partition of India in 1947.

*   *   *   *

These were trying months for Nehru, a period of uneasy freedom between his two lengthy imprisonments in the early 'thirties. The danger of rearrest was ever-present, and he felt an obligation to settle his family affairs. His mother's slow recovery was a source of continuing concern, and he was anxious to ease her burden by providing financial security for the remaining years of her life. There was the problem of arranging his daughter's university education which, he felt, would be incomplete without a stay in the West. There were also renewed fears for Kamala's health as the year 1933 drew to a close. Finally, his younger sister, Krishna, became engaged soon after his release. Fortunately, he was still at liberty when the wedding, a quiet and unostentatious affair, was held at *Anand Bhawan* in the latter part of October.

Nehru has never attached much importance to money, probably because his father had long ensured the family's economic security. But as his obligations mounted in the autumn of 1933

[1] 'A Reply to Sir Mohammed Iqbal' in ibid., pp. 60–69.

he felt the need for retrenchment. The position was improved, in the short-run, by the sale of family heirlooms, silverware and his wife's jewellery, along with sundry articles which were of no functional value. Later his income was enhanced by the very considerable royalties from his books. To this day, they supplement his paltry salary of Rs. 2,250 (approximately $475) per month as Prime Minister of India.[1]

Early in the new year, 1934, Nehru and his wife went to Calcutta, partly to secure medical advice and partly because Jawaharlal was anxious to pay tribute to the Bengali role in the freedom struggle. His public activities since his release had been negligible thus far. The Congress organization had been temporarily dismantled at Gandhi's behest. Nehru refused to be bound by the directive, but there was little he could do under the circumstances beyond the occasional informal meeting with the Mahatma and his colleagues in the High Command and a few public speeches. The only issue being debated was the merits of continuing the façade of civil disobedience. It was also apparent to Nehru that his preaching of socialist ideas annoyed most senior Congress leaders who were concerned about its effect on their middle-class supporters. He in turn was increasingly hostile to Gandhi's defence of the *status quo* in economic affairs as expressed in the 'theory of trusteeship', according to which the privileged classes held their wealth as 'trustees' of the nation at large. Whatever hopes Nehru had that the Mahatma would ultimately embrace his socialist ideas were rapidly being dissipated in the face of reality.

Calcutta proved to be the beginning of the end of Jawaharlal's short-lived freedom. He was there only a few days, but during that time he delivered three provocative speeches against the current policies of the *Raj*. He was not apprehended immediately, for much time was required to determine whether or not his speeches were seditious. He had made an outspoken anti-British speech in Delhi a month earlier. Local officials were hesitant to take legal action because the outcome was uncertain. Then, on 23 December 1933, Nehru made a sharp

[1] Up to 13 June 1957 all members of the Indian Cabinet received a monthly salary equivalent to $472.50 (after taxes $336), an allowance of $105 and a free furnished house. On that day the Prime Minister announced that he and his Cabinet colleagues agreed to a 10 per cent. cut in their salary and allowances. *New York Times*, 14 June 1957.

attack on the *Raj* before the All-India Trades Union Congress in Kanpur. The machinery was set in motion to prosecute him. But in the meantime there were the speeches in Calcutta which offered a stronger case. Word was passed from the Home Department in New Delhi to the Government of the United Provinces: 'The Government of India regard him [Nehru] as by far the most dangerous element at large in India and . . . are definitely of the opinion that the opportunity afforded by this speech [in Calcutta] should not be lost and that it is desirable to institute a prosecution at once.'[1] It was merely a matter of time.

Just before the Nehrus left Allahabad for Calcutta there occurred one of the most devastating natural disasters in the long history of India—the Bihar earthquake. Within a few minutes the face of the area was changed beyond all recognition. Accurate statistics were impossible to secure, but the estimates are staggering: the area affected was about 30,000 square miles, with a population of 10–15,000,000; at least 20,000 are known to have died, and well over 1,000,000 homes were destroyed. Cities like Muzaffarpur and Monghyr lay in utter ruin. Patna, the provincial capital, though far removed from the centre of the 'quake, also had the appearance of death and destruction. Shock gave way to panic and then gradually to the herculean task of rehabilitation.

Nehru's first intimation of the earthquake came a few hours before his departure for Calcutta, while he was addressing a group of peasants from the veranda of his home. Since geological disturbances are fairly common in that part of India he was not unduly alarmed. Within a few days, however, news of the disaster spread through Calcutta. It was difficult at first to distinguish rumour from fact.

On their return journey to Allahabad the Nehrus paused briefly to visit Rabindranath Tagore and to arrange for Indira's entry into Santiniketan, that unique university founded by the great Indian poet to blend the cultures of East and West. Then they went to Patna and Muzaffarpur where they saw the catastrophe at first hand. Upon returning home Nehru threw himself into the task of raising funds for the victims of the earthquake. Later he returned to the area for ten days. Gruesome sights

---

[1] D.O. No. S-282/34-Poll./19 January 1934, in the Home Department (Political Section) files. Used with the permission of the Government of India.

greeted him everywhere—smashed buildings, torn-up roads, flooded fields, corpses by the thousand. It was a veritable graveyard. He was the first Congress leader to visit the country-side. Some of those who survived the ordeal still recall his tire-less efforts on their behalf and his words of sympathy to numbed peasants of the area.

The earthquake was bad enough. But when Gandhi termed it a punishment for the sin of untouchability, Nehru was hurt and angry. This mystical outlook widened still more the intel-lectual gap between them. Exhausted by the gruelling pace of the tour and saddened by the sight of human misery, he re-turned to Allahabad on 11 February. The following day his time had come. He was taken into custody and returned to Calcutta to stand trial for sedition.

Normally Jawaharlal and Kamala took these separations stoically. This time it was different, perhaps because Kamala sensed the approaching end. Describing the scene many years later, Nehru wrote, '. . . Kamala went to our rooms to collect some clothes for me. I followed her to say goodbye to her. Suddenly she clung to me and, fainting, collapsed.'[1] The next time they met she was caught once more in the grip of her relentless disease.

*   *   *   *

And so it began again, the long nights in prison, the loneli-ness, the constant search for the 'right path'. In fact his life behind the walls was beginning to seem endless. During a period of almost four years, from the end of 1931 to early September 1935, he was free only six months.

The first few days he spent in Presidency Jail, Calcutta, pending his trial. He offered no defence, only the usual state-ment of defiance: 'Individuals sometimes misbehave; officials also sometimes misbehave; crowds and mobs get excited and misbehave; all that is very regrettable. But it is a terrible thing when brutality becomes a method of behaviour.' At that point he was silenced by the Court and was sentenced to two years simple imprisonment. It was Nehru's seventh term.[2]

---

[1] *The Discovery of India*, p. 34.

[2] As reported in the account of the proceedings of the trial in the Home Depart-ment (Political Section) files. Used with the permission of the Government of India.

His next 'home' was a ten- by nine-foot cell in Alipore Central Jail, located within the city limits of Calcutta. There was the usual veranda and open yard, this time surrounded by a seven-foot wall. But the view beyond was of the unprepossessing wings of this giant prison, and close by were the kitchen chimneys which frequently wafted disagreeable smells into his enclosure. The regimen was no different from Nehru's normal prison experience: confinement to the cell from early evening to early morning; permission to walk about the open yard and to have reading and writing materials; occasional interviews with relatives. Much of his time was spent poring over books he received from home and the *Manchester Guardian Weekly* which enabled him to keep in touch with events in the outside world. They were disquieting events on the whole during the spring of 1934—the Dollfuss *putsch* in Austria, the *Croix de Feu* riots in Paris, the consolidation of Nazi power in Germany, and the decline of Liberalism in Spain.

Indian news was hard to come by, for he was not permitted a local paper. But early in April 1934 he learned of Gandhi's decision to terminate all forms of civil disobedience—primarily because 'a valued companion of long standing [not Nehru] was found reluctant to perform the full prison task, preferring his private studies to the allotted task'. Jawaharlal was appalled, not because it impugned his own standards of conduct indirectly, but because of the implications of Gandhi's reasoning: 'was a vast national movement . . . to be thrown out of gear because an individual had erred', he wrote of this episode. 'This seemed to me a monstrous proposition and an immoral one. . . . The whole statement frightened me and oppressed me tremendously. . . . A vast distance seemed to separate him [Gandhi] from me. With a stab of pain I felt that the cords of allegiance that had bound me to him for many years had snapped.' And in this context Nehru penned one of the most revealing disclosures about his personality: 'Of the many hard lessons that I had learned, the hardest and the most painful now faced me: that *it is not possible in any vital matter to rely on anyone. One must journey through life alone; to rely on others is to invite heartbreak.*'[1]

Nehru is by nature an individualist. His power in the

---

[1] *Toward Freedom*, p. 312. (Emphasis added.)

Congress, both before and after Independence, rested largely on his personality, the adoration of the masses, and his acknowledged position as Gandhi's heir-apparent, never on the organization itself. On the contrary, he wielded power in spite of the machine, which was long controlled by Sardar Patel. And as Prime Minister he has concentrated authority and decisions in his own hands. This is not because of a love of power, though like all men who have tasted power he wishes to preserve it, but because of a conviction that he alone can ensure the realization of his social, political and economic goals. It would be wrong, of course, to suggest that Gandhi's action in 1934 is alone responsible for his tendency to 'go it alone'. But there can be no doubt that it owes much to periodic shocks of this kind, especially those administered by the Mahatma.

What made the experience even more wrenching was the Congress's decision to revive the Swaraj Party and the return to parliamentary methods of political struggle. Just as in the early 'twenties when civil disobedience had collapsed, so now the moderates appeared on the centre of the stage. The wheel had turned full circle. Nehru's attack of depression lasted longer than usual. But Kamala, sick though she was, visited him one day and eased his sense of loneliness.

Another source of concern was a swing to the Right in Congress economic policy. In mid-June 1934 the Working Committee condemned confiscation of private property and class war as contrary to the creed of non-violence. Nehru interpreted it as a retreat from the Karachi Resolution on Fundamental Rights and a direct rebuke to his socialist views.

By that time he had been transferred from Alipore to Dehra Dun Jail. His health had suffered from the Calcutta climate and he had lost a good deal of weight. Thus, on 7 May 1934, he was moved to the hills. It was a welcome change on the whole. His old cell, vacated nine months earlier, was now occupied, and so he was lodged in a refurbished cattle-shed with an attached yard some fifty feet long. But the surrounding wall was too high to allow him to gaze upon the nearby mountains. Nor was he allowed to take occasional walks outside his enclosure.

The long months in prison made him irritable and lonely. Relief came with the monsoon, but the restrictions on his movements and contacts remained. Occasionally his appetite for a view of the lovely countryside was whetted when a jailer came into his yard. It was only a fleeting glimpse and he felt cheated. His depression was deepened as Kamala's health deteriorated rapidly. Then, too, the political situation showed no signs of improvement. Although the ban on the Congress had been lifted, many affiliated bodies remained illegal, such as the 'Redshirts' of the Frontier, peasant leagues and the like.

Under these pressures Nehru turned for solace to the past and began the searching self-analysis which emerged as one of the memorable autobiographies of his generation. Though not its primary aim, *Toward Freedom* brought the Indian struggle for freedom to the attention of hundreds of thousands in the West. Indeed it became the crucial link between Indian nationalism and the outside world. It also revealed Nehru to himself and to others—the mainsprings of his thought and action, the influences moulding his character and personality, the development of his ideas, the constant struggle within himself for answers to questions both personal and political.[1] Suddenly came news that Kamala's condition had taken a turn for the worse. On the advice of Government doctors he was rushed from Dehra Dun Jail to Allahabad and there released temporarily to be with his wife.

*   *   *   *

The reunion was short-lived. Kamala was in the very painful grip of advanced pulmonary tuberculosis. As he sat by her

---

[1] First published in 1936 under the title *The Autobiography of Jawaharlal Nehru* (John Lane, London). It was immediately acclaimed by many people in India and the West, including such British Conservatives as Lord Halifax, formerly Lord Irwin, who pronounced it indispensable reading for an understanding of modern India. Among the numerous comments are two extracts from Nehru's correspondence which are noteworthy, one from Rabindranath Tagore, the other from the distinguished British historian Charles Trevelyan. Tagore wrote: 'I have just finished reading your great book and I feel intensely impressed and proud of your achievement. Through all its details there runs a deep current of humanity which overpasses the tangles of facts and leads us to the person who is greater than his deeds and truer than his surroundings.' Trevelyan wrote: 'You and I both began at Harrow where we were not taught to be champions of the underdog. But the oppression and poverty of your people taught you, and the war and the slums taught me. We think pretty much alike.' Unpublished Nehru Letters, 31 May and 12 June 1936.

bedside hour after hour, Nehru thought back over the eighteen years of their married life. In his reminiscences of Kamala, he reprimanded himself for his 'semi-forgetful, casual attitude' during the first years of their marriage. Now time was running out. 'Surely she was not going to leave me now when I needed her most', he wrote upon his return to prison. 'Why, we had just begun to know and understand each other, really; our joint life was only now properly beginning. We relied so much on each other; we had so much to do together.'[1]

The parole lasted only eleven days. As soon as Kamala's health showed a slight improvement, Jawaharlal was returned to prison. This time he was sent to Naini so that he would be close by in case of emergency. During his stay at home Nehru had refrained from all public activities, a gentleman's response to the Government's humane gesture. But he did seize the opportunity to write a lengthy letter to Gandhi, in the form of a general commentary on the state of the nation. Incidentally, it shed much light on the state of Nehru's mind as well.

All the pent-up emotions of years in prison came to the fore in this letter. Its main themes are dismay and anger at Gandhi's reasons for terminating civil disobedience; his feeling of loneliness and despair; the effects of prison; criticism of the Congress and of its attack on socialism; and hurt feelings about an alleged insult to the memory of his father.

When I heard that you had called off the CD [civil disobedience] movement I felt unhappy [he began]. Much later I read your statement and this gave me one of the biggest shocks I have ever had. I was prepared to reconcile myself to the withdrawal of CD. But the reasons you gave for doing so and the suggestions you made for future work astounded me. I had a sudden and intense feeling, that something broke inside me, a bond that I had valued very greatly had snapped. I felt terribly lonely in this wide world.

I have always felt a little lonely almost from childhood up. That loneliness never went, but it was lessened . . . now I felt absolutely alone, left high and dry on a desert island. . . .

The keenness of my feelings on the subject, which amounted almost to physical pain, passed off; the edge was dulled. But shock after shock, a succession of events sharpened that edge to a fine point, and allowed my mind or feelings no peace or rest. Again I felt that sensation of spiritual isolation, of being a perfect stranger

[1] *Toward Freedom*, p. 334.

out of harmony, not only with the crowds that passed me, but also with those whom I valued as dear and close comrades.

My stay in prison this time became a greater ordeal for my nerves than any previous visit had been. . . . Physically I kept fairly well. I always do in prison. My body has served me well and can stand a great deal of ill-treatment and strain.

Then came the criticism of the party, particularly of the constitutionalists who had opposed civil disobedience. 'They became the high priests in our temple of freedom' and those who had struggled 'had become untouchables' or were even called traitors for opposing the Swaraj Party. Its policies he termed 'a pitiful hotch-potch, avoiding real issues', toning down the political goal of the Congress, 'expressing a tender solicitude for every vested interest', bowing to the enemy. 'The Congress from top to bottom is a caucus and opportunism triumphs.' While the Working Committee was not directly responsible, it was indirectly to blame, for it 'had deliberately encouraged vagueness in the definition of our ideals and objectives and this was bound to lead not only to confusion but to demoralisation during periods of reaction. . . . [And] it is the leaders and their policy that shape the activities of their followers. . . . I feel that the time is overdue for the Congress to think clearly on social and economic issues.'

As for socialism, 'those views may be right or wrong but they deserve at least some understanding before the Working Committee sets out to denounce them. It is hardly becoming for a reasoned argument to be answered by sentimental appeals or by the cheap remark that the conditions in India are different and the economic laws that apply elsewhere do not function here. . . . It seemed that the overmastering desire of the committee was somehow to assure vested interests even at the risk of talking nonsense.'

Finally there was an outburst at the Working Committee's proposal to rent part of *Swaraj Bhawan* because the maintenance costs were allegedly too high. 'The very idea of the wishes of my father being flouted in this way is intolerable to me. The trust represented not only his wishes, but was also in a small way a memorial to him . . . and his memory is dearer to me than a hundred rupees a month.' He offered to provide the necessary funds himself. 'I would also beg the trustees to respect my feelings in this matter.' 'Perhaps some parts of this letter might pain you', he concluded. 'But you would not have me hide my heart from you.'[1]

Gandhi's reply was firm but gentle. 'I understand your deep sorrow. You were quite right in giving full and free expression to your feelings.' But he reassured Nehru that he had not changed. 'I am the same as you knew me in 1917 and after. . . . I want complete independence for the country in the full English sense of the term.' All the party resolutions which upset Nehru, he said, were framed with independence in view, and Gandhi took full responsibility for them. By way of justification, 'I fancy that I have the knack for knowing the need of the time.' As for the resolution on socialism, he denied that there had been any criticism, but 'I cannot march as quick'. He reiterated his interest and asked Nehru for some books on the subject. Finally, he chided Nehru for his harsh remarks about the Working Committee and his anger about *Swaraj Bhawan*. He promised to look into the matter of the house, but requested Jawaharlal not to take it as a personal affront.[2]

The Mahatma's attachment to Nehru was revealed once more in a letter to Patel the following month explaining why he had decided to resign from the Congress—though he did, of course, remain the dominant figure in the party's decisions. 'I miss at this juncture the association and advice of Jawaharlal who is bound to be the rightful helmsman of the organisation in the near future.' (This was the first indication that Gandhi favoured Nehru for the presidency upon his release from prison, a preference that came to fruition at the Lucknow session in 1936.) 'I feel that I am in no sense deserting one who is much more than a comrade and whom no amount of political differences will ever separate from me. . . . He is courage personified. . . . He has an indomitable faith in his mission . . .' The reasons for Gandhi's formal resignation were his feeling that 'I am a dead weight in the Congress now', that there was a growing and vital difference between him and the intelligentsia, and that the socialists, recently organized into the Congress Socialist Party, must have free right to expression.[3]

---

[1] The text of this letter, dated 13 August 1934, is in Tendulkar, op. cit., vol. 3, Appendix on Gandhi-Nehru Letters, pp. 379–84.
[2] Letter of 17 August 1934, ibid., pp. 384–5.   [3] Ibid., pp. 386–8.

Gandhi's withdrawal from 'active' politics coincided with the 'annual' session of the Congress, held in Bombay in the latter part of October 1934, the first in three years. Rajendra Prasad, spokesman for Gandhi and the Right wing, presided. An attempt by the Socialists to introduce a radical economic programme was soundly defeated—with the Mahatma's full backing. Even though he was now 'outside' the organization, the party reaffirmed its confidence in his leadership. His Constructive Programme again became the centre of attention and the moderates were in control.

The following month elections were held for the central Legislative Assembly. The Congress scored a notable victory, winning 44 of the 49 'General', i.e. Hindu, seats.[1] Its success was all the more striking because of powerful Government opposition. As early as seven months before the elections, a senior British official in Delhi indicated the Government's attitude in a confidential memorandum: '... for the Congress Party to achieve power at the outset of the new constitution would be dangerous. ... As ... our policy is to prevent any marked accession of strength to Congress, we should be deaf to the siren voice of the conciliators [Congress moderates]. We should recognise that the Congress are, and for a long time will remain, our enemies. We should treat them not vindictively, but coldly, keeping them at arm's length, and we should encourage the political forces that are naturally opposed to them.'[2]

* * * *

While these events were taking place Nehru remained in prison. In other less trying circumstances he had managed to adjust. As he wrote to his daughter, 'here all is different; everything is quiet, and there is little movement, and I sit for long intervals, and for long hours I am silent. The days and the weeks and the months pass by, one after the other, merging into each other, and there is little to distinguish one from the other. ... It is the life of a vegetable rooted to one place, growing there

[1] The composition of the central Legislative Assembly as a result of the elections at the end of 1934 was as follows: 41 officials and nominated members; 30 Muslims; 8 Europeans; 11 Landholders and other special interests; 49 General of whom 44 were Congressmen, and 6 others.

[2] Dated 8 April 1934. Taken from the Home Department (Political Section) files of 1934 and used with the permission of the Government of India.

without comment or argument, silent, motionless. And sometimes the activities of the outside world appear strange and a
little bewildering to one in prison . . . [but] one gets used to
everything in time, even to the routine and sameness of gaol.
And rest is good for the body; and quiet is good for the mind;
it makes one think.'[1]

Now, however, the habit was becoming a drain on his health.
He had lost ten pounds in a few months and was down to 130.
He had some difficulty in breathing; his personal doctor suspected pleurisy. A thorough examination at Naini by three
physicians showed this to be a false alarm and found his condition reasonably sound. But it was far below Nehru's norm of
vigorous good health. Waiting for news about Kamala—he
received a daily bulletin for a short while—was an ordeal,
made even more trying by his feeling of helplessness in the face
of personal tragedy. He was allowed to visit her a month after
his re-imprisonment and again early in October 1934. But
there was no improvement.

Nehru was also upset by the thought that his wife might be
suffering needlessly because of his stubborn adherence to principles. The authorities were apparently prepared to release him
on the condition that he refrain from all political activity until
the end of his term. The thought of it stuck in his throat.
'. . . To give an assurance! And to be disloyal to my pledges, to
the cause, to my colleagues, to myself! It was an impossible
condition. . . . To do so meant inflicting mortal injuries on the
roots of my being, on almost everything I held sacred.'[2] His
dilemma was resolved when Kamala stood by his refusal.

Soon thereafter Kamala was moved to the hills, to the town
of Bhowali in the eastern United Provinces. A few weeks later,
largely in response to pressure both in India and in England,
he was transferred to the Almora District Jail close by her
sanatorium.[3] His new 'home' was spacious by comparison with

---

[1] Letter of 1 January 1933, in *Glimpses of World History*, p. 475.

[2] *Toward Freedom*, p. 337.

[3] In India, people like Tagore and the Liberal leader, Sir Tej Bahadur Sapru,
pleaded for his release. In England, leaders of the Labour Party, notably Lansbury
and Attlee, sought his release in interviews with the Secretary of State for India.
The Viceroy expressed concern to the Secretary of State that Nehru's release would
strengthen the Socialist movement. Taken from the Home Department (Political
Section) files of 1935 and used with the permission of the Government of India.

his cell at Naini—a large hall, fifty-one feet by seventeen, with ample room to stroll about and fresh breezes penetrating the many openings in the walls. Yet it was lonelier than the normal prison cell, and with the approach of winter the 'mansion' became less attractive. Much of his time was spent completing his autobiography and waiting anxiously for news of his wife.

The highlights of his stay at Almora were his visits to Kamala. Every few weeks he was taken along the mountain road to Bhowali for the long-awaited reunion. But the hours passed swiftly and then weeks of loneliness once more. In the middle of January 1935 came more disconcerting news. His mother suffered a paralytic stroke. Her condition improved but another source of concern had been added.

Kamala grew worse, and in May of that year it was decided to send her to Europe for special treatment. Jawaharlal came to Bhowali to bid her farewell. Life returned to its dismal routine with the added worry, now an obsession, that he might never see Kamala again. A few months later came news that her condition had become critical once more. In a humane gesture, mixed with concern lest Indian feelings be alienated, the Government released him early in September.[1] He hastened to Allahabad and from there by air to Basle; then to Badenweiler in the Black Forest of Germany.

There was little he could do at this stage, for her disease was now beyond cure. To it was added angina pectoris. She was too weak for lengthy conversations now. Twice a day Nehru walked from his *pension* in town to visit her. Occasionally he read to her. At other times they reminisced about the past and old friends. For a very brief period there were signs of improvement, enough for Jawaharlal and his daughter, then studying in Switzerland, to visit England for a fortnight.

On the whole he managed to keep his mind occupied during these trying months in Europe. As he wrote to Dr. Mahmud towards the end of 1935, 'most of my days were spent with Kamala in the sanatorium and then till very late at night I worked at various things. A revision of a book I wrote in prison

[1] The amount of time and correspondence devoted to the pros and cons of Nehru's release by officials of the Government of India is astonishing. Political pressure, both in India and in England, in the form of questions in Parliament and the Indian Legislative Assembly undoubtedly hastened his release, as revealed in the Home Department (Political Section) files of 1935.

[his autobiography] took up much of my time. It was heavy work. And then there are so many people in Europe and India who are continually writing to me that it is difficult to keep up the correspondence. . . . My visits to London and Paris were a terrible rush which exhausted me though they were refreshing in a way.'[1]

Just before Christmas 1935 a new crisis appeared. 'Kamala, we thought, was making progress though this was slow', wrote Nehru to Mahmud. 'But we were deluding ourselves and she has grown progressively weaker. Last week there was a sudden crisis which brought matters to a head. For two days her life hung by a thread and it hardly seemed possible that she would survive it. . . . The immediate crisis has passed. . . . But the future outlook is dark. She is terribly thin and emaciated and unless she can gain strength she can hardly resist the disease.'[2]

When the crisis passed Nehru went briefly to Paris and again to London, where he learned of his election to the Congress presidency for 1936. The pressure of friends to return, a callous pressure indeed, was growing. At the end of January the Nehrus left Badenweiler for Switzerland. Kamala seemed to be holding her own. After lengthy consultations, and with the doctors' approval, Jawaharlal decided to return to India for a few months. All was prepared; he was to leave by air on 28 February. A few days before his scheduled departure, however, the doctors advised a postponement for a week or more. The change in Kamala became marked. The end came in the early morning of 28 February 1936. And soon thereafter, 'that fair body and that lovely face, which used to smile so often and so well, were reduced to ashes'.[3]

Nehru set out for home, his thoughts engrossed by Kamala and the days gone by. Yet even at this moment of grief he could not entirely escape the limelight. It was a curious and irritating incident, but one which endeared him to many in Europe and India alike. Some weeks earlier, while his wife lay dying, he had been informed that Mussolini was anxious to meet him. Nehru had declined because of his strong antipathy to Fascism. But when his plane landed in Rome he was informed that the Italian dictator was expecting him in the evening. It was merely

[1] Unpublished Nehru-Mahmud Correspondence, 26 December 1935.
[2] Ibid., 25 December 1935.   [3] *The Discovery of India*, p. 38.

to convey condolences, he was assured. But Nehru persisted and the meeting was never held. When he reached Baghdad a touching memorial to his wife came to mind. To his publishers in London he cabled the dedication for his autobiography: 'To Kamala who is no more.' And then to Allahabad.

CHAPTER IX

Hero of the Left

THE anxious days at Kamala's bedside were over. But the ordeal had left its mark. Many who saw Jawaharlal on his return to India perceived his sense of loss. 'His face, which a few months ago had looked so youthful,' wrote his younger sister, 'was aged and lined with sorrow. He looked desperately tired and worn out. Though he tried hard to hide the anguish of his heart, his sad, expressive eyes held a world of agony.'[1] Nehru himself expressed his grief to the Indian people at large: 'I am weary and I have come back like a tired child yearning for solace in the bosom of our common mother, India. That solace has come to me in overflowing measure. . . . How can I thank you, men and women of India? How can I express in words feelings that are too deep for utterance?'[2]

In moments of despair Nehru has always found consolation in his life work—the struggle for Indian freedom and the creation of a 'good society'. On this occasion, in the spring of 1936, India was astir. Far-reaching events were on the horizon, and Nehru was to play the leading role. The setting was far from propitious. The Congress was in the doldrums once more, its spirit shattered by long years of struggle against the *Raj*, its enrolled membership thinned to less than half a million. The prevailing atmosphere was reminiscent of the mid-'twenties: Gandhi had withdrawn from 'active politics', but the Old Guard remained in control, impervious to new ideas and fearful of alienating its middle-class support. There was also a sharp ideological cleavage between the conservatives, led by Patel and Prasad, and the recently formed Congress Socialists led by Jaya Prakash Narayan and Narendra Dev, who looked to Nehru for leadership. It was the old pro-changer–no-changer controversy in a different guise.

---

[1] Hutheesingh, *With No Regrets*, p. 120.

[2] Presidential Address to the Lucknow session of the Indian National Congress on 19 April 1936. Nehru, *India and the World*, p. 65.

No wonder that some of Jawaharlal's friends had misgivings about his election as Congress President for the year 1936. 'To tell you frankly,' wrote Dr. Ansari, while Nehru was still in Europe, 'I have felt all along that all those who are responsible for your election this year are very thoughtless and unkind to you. . . . I do not think that in the present condition of things even your dynamic personality would be able to do much during your year of Presidentship.'[1]

A more ominous indication of the obstacles awaiting him was contained in a private letter from Dr. Rajendra Prasad, later President of India, on 19 December 1935: 'I know that there is a certain difference between your outlook and that of men like Vallabhbhai [Patel], Jamnalalji [Bajaj] and myself and it is even of a fundamental character. . . . I believe that *unless a radical change comes to be made in the programme and methods of our work it will be still possible for all of us to continue to work together*. . . . The difficulties [facing the party] are inherent in the situation and it seems to us it is not possible to force the pace or cause any wholesale change.' Nehru was assured he would have a free hand to form a Working Committee of his own choice and 'to shape things as you would like'; 'none of us will create any difficulty'.[2] But the implied warning could not have been lost on Nehru—do not attempt any fundamental revision of the *status quo*, or else . . . And he was aware of the fact that the Old Guard controlled the party organization. Prasad's letter is noteworthy because it foreshadowed the constant friction between Nehru and the right-wing Congress leaders during the next few years and, in particular, because it gave advance notice of the major crisis to follow in the summer of 1936.

It was Gandhi who had pressed Nehru to accept 'the crown of thorns'. 'If you are elected [a foregone conclusion because of Gandhi's support], you will be elected for the policy and principles you stand for', the Mahatma assured him.

However, he was gently reminded that 'in the huge organisation the Congress has become, no one man can hope to run the show'. And Gandhi's ultimate control of the party was reaffirmed: 'As to the present policy of the Congress, whilst I can in no way be responsible for the detailed working of it, it is in

[1] Unpublished Nehru Letters, 11 February 1936.
[2] Ibid. (Emphasis added.)

the main of my shaping.' About the likely response of the Old
Guard, he was far from encouraging: 'So far as I know they will
not resist you, even though they may not be able to follow you.'[1]

Why then was Gandhi anxious to have Nehru as formal head
of the Congress at that stage? There were various reasons, both
personal and political. For one thing, the Mahatma admired
him much more than any other party leader. For another, he
wanted to offer a token of sympathy for the loss of Kamala.
Moreover, Gandhi realized that apart from himself Nehru was
the only nationalist leader with genuine mass appeal. He was
also concerned about his protégé's drift to the Left. As in 1929,
when Nehru showed signs of discontent, Gandhi hoped that
responsibility would moderate his views.

The basic motive, however, arose from the rift between conservatives and radicals which threatened to wreck the party.
Gandhi knew that Nehru was the one person who could bridge
the growing gap between Socialism and Gandhism. As the
godfather of the Congress Socialist Party Nehru was entirely
acceptable to the Left. As Gandhi's favourite son he was tolerated by the Old Guard, most of whom were colleagues of at
least fifteen years' standing. Thus he was uniquely suited to the
task of reconciliation.

Nehru himself frankly admitted this special quality and
seemed to relish the role of mediation—then as later. 'In a way
I represented a link between various sets of ideas and so I
helped somewhat in toning down the differences and emphasi-
zing the essential unity of our struggle against imperialism.'[2]
Indeed, this was one of the main reasons why he succumbed to
the temptation of party leadership.

He had just returned from Europe troubled by the growing
crisis in world affairs. Italy was then engaged in the rape of
Ethiopia and the League of Nations stood idly by, paralysed by
the indifference of Britain and France. Nazi Germany had
openly repudiated the Treaty of Versailles and had begun to
re-establish its naval power under the generous terms of the

---

[1] Written to Nehru on 22 September 1935, a fortnight after his release from prison
to join his wife in Germany. The letter was intercepted by the Government of
India and was found by the author in the Home Department (Political Section)
files, in the National Archives of India. It is being used with the permission of the
Government of India.

[2] *Eighteen Months in India*, p. 64.

Anglo-German Naval Treaty. Democracy in Spain was totter-ing. Fascism was on the march while liberalism everywhere seemed on the defensive. And the war clouds were gathering once more.

Nehru was alarmed by the prospects. England, he thought, might well be at war in the near future, probably against the Soviet Union. Fascism might emerge triumphant and British imperialism might thereby become impregnable. An attempt would undoubtedly be made to drag India into the conflict. The only weapon at his disposal to forestall this development was the Congress. Hence the need to rebuild the party, now dissipating its energy in factional strife.

This sense of urgency was strengthened by disquieting con-ditions at home. Communal tension showed no signs of abating. The will to direct action had gone out of the Congress. But most important from Nehru's point of view was the challenge posed by the latest instalment of constitutional reform, em-bodied in the 1935 Government of India Act. In essence it provided virtually complete responsible government in the provinces of British India and the framework for a loose All-India Federation of the provinces and as many of the six hundred-odd princely States as wished to join.

It had taken eight years to produce the Act, from the Simon Commission through the three Round Table Conferences, the White Paper, the Report of the Joint Select Committee of the British Parliament, to the final document itself. Much care had been taken to ensure the ultimate authority of Great Britain in the affairs of India, through an array of special powers vested in the Viceroy and, to a lesser extent, in the Governors of the provinces. Over ninety articles conferred 'discretionary powers' on the Viceroy. There were, as well, 'reserve powers' which gave him exclusive control over defence, external affairs, ecclesiastical affairs and certain frontier areas. Finally came the 'safeguards' or 'special responsibilities' which were all-em-bracing, for example 'the prevention of any grave menace to the peace or tranquillity of India or any part thereof', the preven-tion of discrimination against British imports, corporations or individuals, protection of the rights of Princes, etc. Moreover, representation in the federal legislature was to be heavily weighted in favour of the Princes—40 per cent. in the Council of

States and 33⅓ per cent. in the Federal Assembly, whereas the population of the princely States was only 24 per cent. of the total population of India at the time. The States' representatives were to be *appointed* by the Princes.

This Act, suitably amended, served as the constitution of the Dominion of India from 1947 to 1950 (and of Pakistan from 1947 to 1956). It is in fact the basis of India's present constitution. But in its original form the *federal* part of the Act was hedged by so many 'safeguards' as to deny complete self-government to *India as a whole*. Such was the view of most Indian politicians and of many Englishmen. According to Professor A. B. Keith, one of Britain's leading authorities on the constitutional history of India, 'it is difficult to resist the impression that either responsible government should have been frankly declared impossible or the reality conceded. . . . For the federal scheme it is difficult to feel any satisfaction . . . it is too obvious that on the British side the scheme is favoured in order to provide an element of pure conservatism in order to combat any dangerous elements of democracy contributed by British India. . . . It is difficult to deny the justice of the contention in India that federation was largely evoked by the desire to evade the issue of extending responsible government to the central government of British India. Moreover, the withholding of defence and external affairs from federal control, inevitable as the course is, renders the alleged concession of responsibility all but meaningless.'[1]

By contrast, the *provincial* part of the Act was a far-reaching concession to self-government. Apart from some general safeguards, which were not intended to be used except in rare circumstances, daily administration was to be entrusted to a Cabinet selected from the legislature, all of whose members were to be elected by a much larger proportion of the population than at any time previously.

It was this temptation of power, however limited it might be, which attracted many Congress moderates. For Nehru it was precisely this possibility of 'co-operation' with the *Raj* which had to be severely condemned as a grave danger to the nationalist movement. He had no strong objections in principle to contesting the elections but he was vehemently opposed to the idea

---

[1] *A Constitutional History of India 1600–1935*, pp. 473–4.

of taking office under what he termed the 'slave' constitution. If he refused Gandhi's offer of the presidency, the Congress would certainly adopt this 'reformist' line. (It ultimately did so anyway.) And if the Congress were determined to wage an electoral campaign, unity was an absolute precondition to success. Nehru's actions in earlier party crises, notably in 1922-3 and 1928-9, revealed his emphasis on unity. Now, in the shadow of international tension and Congress strife, this concern asserted itself once more.

Beyond these specific factors was his desire to push the Congress to the Left. Conditions, he felt, were ripe for an injection of socialism into the party programme. In this he proved to be prescient, for beneath the surface of Indian politics new social forces were fermenting. The peasants had been galvanized into action during the civil disobedience campaign of the early 'thirties and were becoming aware of their power for the first time. The economic hardships imposed by the Great Depression had made them susceptible to socialist propaganda, spread in many parts of the country by radical young nationalists and individual Communists. (The Communist Party had been outlawed in 1934.) Under the leadership of Professor Ranga and others they began to organize *Kisan sabhas* (peasant leagues). The cry of land reform had now become too loud to be ignored. Similarly, urban workers began to demand greater recognition from the nationalist movement. And even that oft-forgotten segment of Indian society, the women, had been aroused by the years of political struggle.

Much of this ferment found expression in the Congress Socialist Party (C.S.P.), created in the spring of 1934 by a group of left-nationalists headed by Jaya Prakash Narayan. Nehru was in prison at the time, but his influence among them was great. His clear enunciation of socialist ideas in 'Whither India' was a model for many of them. Politically, he was their main hope to 'capture' the Congress machine. He had come to their defence in August 1934, with a blunt attack on the Old Guard's contemptuous attitude to socialism.[1] At the Bombay session of the Congress a few months later, the C.S.P. controlled one-third of the delegates to the All-India Congress Committee. Only Gandhi's opposition at the time prevented a change in

[1] See p. 205, above.

the party's economic and social programme. Now Nehru was at the helm and a move to the Left seemed possible.

Even though he acted as the C.S.P.'s godfather and continued to give it his blessing, Nehru never associated himself officially with this group, a source of disappointment to his admirers. The reasons are not entirely clear, but his action conformed to pattern. He agreed fully with its basic objective of converting the Congress to socialism. He felt, however, that the C.S.P. had rigidly adopted the language of Western socialism which was little understood by the rank and file and which therefore created a barrier for the majority of nationalists. This difference of approach he noted in a friendly message to the C.S.P. at the end of 1936: '. . . Two aspects of this question [socialism] fill my mind. One is how to apply this approach [socialism] to Indian conditions. The other is how to speak of Socialism in the language of India. . . . I am not merely referring to the various languages of India. I am referring much more to the language which grows from a complex of associations of past history and culture and present environment. . . . Merely to use words and phrases, which may have meaning for us but which are not current coin among the masses of India, is often wasted effort. . . . That is a question which I should like a socialist to consider well.'[1]

There were other reasons, both political and personal. Nehru has always shown antipathy to factions of any kind, and the C.S.P. was clearly that type of organization; its membership was confined to Congressmen and it subscribed to the Congress programme and constitution. Furthermore, he wished to avoid being classified as a sectarian. By remaining outside the group he retained his status as Congress mediator and the power flowing from his friendly links with all sections of the party. Concerned as he was with party unity, he may have felt that by joining the socialist faction he would widen the fissures. He was also probably convinced that the cause of socialism itself could be pushed further within the Congress if he maintained his identity as a 'national' leader. Another likely factor was concern lest official membership of the C.S.P. alienate Gandhi. As the Mahatma's leading lieutenant his own position was assured. In opposition to Gandhi the struggle for freedom would

---

[1] Quoted in Sitaramayya, op. cit., vol. ii, p. 15.

suffer, as would his own political future. Finally Nehru is a staunch individualist.

Despite his aloofness the Congress Socialists continued to look to Jawaharlal for leadership and provided the main source of his support in the battles to follow. His role at this time was to give direction to the growing body of leftist opinion within the Congress, to channel the new social forces into the nationalist movement, and to act as the supreme spokesman of radical ideas in the late 'thirties. With this background and in this frame of mind Nehru took up the reins of office at Lucknow.

*   *   *   *

From the outset a clash with the Old Guard seemed inevitable. Nehru realized that his election to the presidency did not mean the party's conversion to socialism. But he did assume that it reflected a growing desire for change among sections of the rank and file. Acting on this belief he sponsored a number of radical resolutions at a meeting of the Working Committee on the eve of the Lucknow session. The right-wing leaders played their cards skilfully. They did not object at that stage, partly because, in theory at least, they were about to make way for a new Working Committee of the President's own choosing, and partly because it was more convenient to place the onus of rejection on the Congress organization as a whole. His proposals were approved by the High Command. But when they came before the All-India Congress Committee some of the controversial ones were either rejected or drastically modified. At the open session the changes were confirmed.

On the peripheral issue of 'foreign policy', so dear to Nehru's heart, the Old Guard could afford to be generous. His request for a Foreign Department to act as a liaison with the outside world was granted. There were expressions of sympathy for Ethiopia and for Indians abroad. And the Congress reaffirmed its refusal to participate in an 'Imperialist War'. But on the key resolutions of substance the Right wing triumphed.

Nehru's proposal to permit the collective affiliation of trade unions and peasant leagues with the Congress was rejected, almost certainly because it would have shifted the balance of power in favour of the Left wing. Instead, a Mass Contacts Committee was formed, leaving control over this crucial sphere of activity in the hands of the High Command. Similarly Nehru's attempt to associate the Congress more directly with the struggle for political reform in the princely States was turned down and Gandhi's policy of passive support was reiterated. The resolution on agrarian reform was as moderate as conditions permitted; there was no frontal attack on the land problem. On the vital issue of the moment, the party's attitude to the 1935 Government of India Act, Nehru also suffered a defeat. The Congress rejected the Act 'in its entirety' and renewed the demand for a Constituent Assembly. But at the same time it agreed to contest the elections and, most important, it shelved the question of 'office acceptance'. Critics on the Left endorsed Nehru's views and called for an unequivocal rejection of office in advance, but the lure of power and prestige was too great for the majority.[1]

Nehru was bitterly disappointed by this turn of events. Confronted with formidable opposition to his views, despite the assurance of a 'free hand' by Prasad, he decided to resign, the first of three such 'decisions' in the next few months. 'After much mental conflict' he changed his mind because 'our whole organization might have been shaken up by it'.[2] The fixation on party unity had come to the fore again.

If Nehru could not overcome the power of the Old Guard he could nevertheless give expression to his radical views. This he did in his presidential address to the Lucknow session on 14 April 1936. It was a speech worthy of the occasion, refreshingly free from the hackneyed phrases and narrow vision of so many of its predecessors. It had literary grace and a tone of passionate sincerity. It was sentimental but forceful, with a majestic sweep which none of his colleagues could match.[3]

He began on a note of humility and affection: 'Comrades, after many years I face you again from this tribune—many weary years of strife and turmoil and common suffering.... Many a dear comrade and friend has left us. . . . But what of us who remain behind with a heavier burden to carry? There is no rest for us or for those who languish in prison or in detention

---

[1] This summary is based upon the *Report of the 49th Session of the Indian National Congress held at Lucknow in April, 1936.*

[2] 'Where Are We?', reprinted in Nehru, *The Unity of India*, p. 99.

[3] The text is to be found in *India and the World*, pp. 64–107, and in *Toward Freedom*, Appendix B, pp. 389–416. (Emphasis added.)

camp. We cannot rest, for rest is betrayal of those who have gone. . . . it is betrayal of the millions who never rest.'

As always the substantive part of his speech began with a survey of the international scene. Ranging far and wide, in terms made familiar by his writings of the early 'thirties, he stressed the 'organic connection' of India's struggle for independence with the world-wide urge for change. Capitalism was denounced for its policy of colonial expansion and linked with the onward march of Fascism. It was a bi-polar world for Nehru—Imperialism and Fascism versus Nationalism and Socialism, though some overlapping was admitted between the two. 'Inevitably we take our stand with the progressive forces of the world . . .' His most scathing words were levelled at British rule, especially at the curtailment of civil liberties. A government resorting to such acts as have been committed in recent years 'has ceased to have even a shadow of a justification for its existence'.

Turning to domestic affairs, he acknowledged the spirit of disunity in the Congress, which he ascribed to the gradual divorce of its middle-class leadership from the masses—a direct snub to the Old Guard. That leadership was still essential, he declared, 'but [it] must look more and more toward the masses and draw strength and inspiration from them. The Congress must be not only *for* the masses, as it claims to be, but *of* the masses.' Another source of weakness was the existing constitution, which 'lost its roots in the soil and became a matter of small committees functioning in the air. . . . It became a prey to authoritarianism and a battle ground for rival cliques fighting for control, and, in doing so, stooping to the lowest and most objectionable of tactics.' He deplored the Old Guard's refusal to broaden the bases of representation. Then came the core of the address, the proposal for a 'joint anti-imperialist front' which would link the mass organizations to the nationalist movement. 'The essence of a joint popular front must be un-compromising opposition to imperialism, and *the strength of it must inevitably come from the active participation of the peasantry and workers.*'

Nehru offered his listeners a candid restatement of his socialist ideals. Yet 'I have no desire to force the issue in the Congress and thereby create difficulties in the way of our struggle for independence.' Once more his flexible approach was revealed: 'I imagine that every country will fashion it [socialism] after its own way and fit it in with its national genius.'

About the 1935 Government of India Act he was merciless— 'this new charter of slavery to strengthen the bonds of imperialist domination and to intensify the exploitation of our masses'. He claimed that all Congressmen were agreed on the desirability of combating the Act, but there were marked differences on method. His own view was that the elections should be contested—to bring the Congress message to the masses—but that government office should be spurned. The basic goal of independence would be lost in a series of petty compromises, he said. The federal part of the Act was its worst feature and must be nullified. The communal provisions were also condemned, as were the Princes; 'they have long survived their day, propped up by an alien Power', and will have to go.

Nehru paid tribute to Gandhi who was ill at the time and unable to attend the session. Then came the epilogue, in strikingly Western terms: 'The promised land may yet be far from us, and we may have to march wearily through the deserts, but . . . who will dare to crush the spirit of India which has found rebirth again and again after so many crucifixions?'

This speech revealed the touch of the universal in Nehru's intellectual make-up which made him so attractive to the modernists in India. Yet it was precisely this quality which explains the hesitant response of the average Congressman. As for Nehru himself, he was cast in an unenviable role at Lucknow— to apply methods he disliked, with associates who misunderstood him, for purposes which were not fully shared.

The Left wing was thrilled by his address, but the Old Guard felt betrayed by his caustic attack. Gandhi himself was disturbed lest his protégé's bold proclamation of socialist ideas at that juncture cause an irrevocable split within the party.[1]

---

[1] 'My life work is ruined', the Mahatma was alleged to have said. 'Not even the firmness and repression of the British government have harmed my work as much as the new policy outlined by Pandit Jawaharlal Nehru. Still, in two or three years' time, this excitable and enthusiastic young leader will return to me and once again invite me to lead India to freedom. He is facing a rude setback by persisting in his present policy.' As quoted in Anup Singh, 'Is Gandhi's Life Work Ruined?' in *Asia*, October 1936, p. 627. Gandhi denied categorically that he had ever

Political friction between them continued for some time, but there was no real danger of a complete break.

Despite his fiery words, Nehru was not prepared to force the issue with the Old Guard. Such an opportunity arose immediately after the Lucknow session, when a new Working Committee had to be formed. As President of the Congress Nehru had the right to pack the Committee with his own supporters, but he felt it would be 'improper' to act contrary to the express wishes of the delegates to the session, as reflected in the various resolutions. Hence ten Right-wing leaders were invited to join the Committee and only four from the Left.[1]

The reaction among his followers was dismay and incredulity. Typical were the feelings expressed by Rafi Ahmad Kidwai, one of Nehru's oldest friends. 'I have passed the last few days in agony', he wrote on 20 April 1936. 'Apparently you were our only hope, but are you going to prove an illusory one? Some people had their doubts as to how far you will be able to withstand the combined opposition and influence of Gandhism. You were given an opportunity of reshuffling the W.C. [Working Committee]. They have manœuvred to isolate you from the middlemen. We have been weakened both in the A.I.C.C. and the delegates. And the Working Committee you have formed is bound to prove more reactionary than the one it has replaced. It may be my vision is narrow. I rely more on the number of heads than on ideological discourses.'[2]

Kidwai's fears were soon to be realized. At the first meeting of the new Working Committee no questions of high policy were discussed. Yet, Nehru confided to a friend, 'I was completely isolated and there was not a single member to support me.'[3] During the next two months he spent much of his time on tour spreading the Congress gospel as laid down at Lucknow but with a powerful injection of socialist ideas. Everywhere he found a 'bubbling vitality' among the masses. His conservative

uttered these words, in an article entitled 'Are We Rivals?' in *Harijan* (Ahmedabad), 25 July 1936. 'No doubt there are differences of opinion between us', wrote the Mahatma. 'But they do not affect our personal relations in any way whatsoever. . . . I cannot think of myself as a rival to Jawaharlal or him to me.'

[1] Nehru's rationale for this decision was expressed in an article entitled 'Working Committee 1936', reprinted in *Eighteen Months in India*, pp. 6–8.

[2] Unpublished Nehru Letters.

[3] Unpublished Nehru-Mahmud Correspondence, 5 May 1936.

colleagues in the High Command became alarmed. The clash could not be averted much longer.

It came at the end of June 1936, when six members of the Working Committee, headed by Prasad, Patel and Rajagopala-charia, submitted their resignations. The cleavage takes on added significance in the light of the prominent positions held by these right-wing leaders in the years since Independence.[1] 'We feel', wrote Prasad on behalf of the six dissidents, 'that the preaching and emphasising of socialism particularly at this stage by the President and other socialist members of the Working Committee while the Congress has not adopted it is prejudicial to the best interests of the country and to the success of the national struggle for freedom which we all hold to be the first and paramount concern of the country. You also appear to feel and have even expressed that the Working Committee as it is constituted is not of your choice but forced on you and that you accepted it against your better judgment. Our own impression of events at Lucknow is contrary to yours. . . . The effect of your propaganda on the political work immediately before the nation, particularly the programme for election, has been very harmful . . .'

Gandhi intervened and the resignations were withdrawn. The six leaders apologized for having hurt Nehru's feelings but did not retract their charges. How hurt Nehru really was becomes clear from his letter to Gandhi on 5 July: 'I read again Rajendra Babu's [Prasad's] letter to me and his formidable indictment of me. . . . The main thing is that my activities are harmful to the Congress cause. . . . However tenderly the fact may be stated, it amounts to this: that I am an intolerable nuisance and the very qualities that I possess—a measure of ability, energy, earnestness, some personality which has a vague appeal—become dangerous for they are harnessed to a wrong chariot. . . . Perhaps the fault may lie with me . . . but

[1] Dr. Rajendra Prasad was President of the Indian Constituent Assembly from the end of 1946—when it began its labours—until January 1950, when the Constitution was inaugurated. Since 1950 he has been President of India. Sardar Patel was Deputy Prime Minister, Minister of States and Minister of Information and Broadcasting from 1947 until his death in December 1950. C. Rajagopalacharia was the last Governor General of India, from the middle of 1948 until January 1950. Thereafter he held many important posts including those of Chief Minister of Madras and Home Minister of the Government of India.

the fact remains that today there is no loyalty of the spirit which binds our group together. It is a mechanical group and on either side there is a dull resentment and a sense of suppression. . . . Because I attached importance to a larger unity I tried to express [my ideas] in the mildest way possible and more as an invitation to thought than as fixed conclusions. . . . But my approach, mild and vague as it was, is considered dangerous and harmful by my colleagues.' Because of this basic conflict Nehru decided to resign, the second such 'decision', and he recommended that the matter be brought before the All-India Congress Committee.[1]

In the same letter Nehru thanked Gandhi for smoothing over the crisis, underlining once more the Mahatma's supreme arbitral position within the party. He also remarked that his health had suffered as a result of the crisis: 'Since my return from Europe I have found that meetings of the Working Committee exhaust me greatly; they have a devitalizing effect on me, and I have almost the feeling of being much older in years after every fresh experience.' He agreed that an open split would have had serious consequences. 'And yet, and yet, where are we now and what does the future hold for us?'[2]

Gandhi replied ten days later: 'The fact is that your colleagues have lacked your courage and your frankness. The result has been disastrous. I have always pleaded with them to speak out to you freely and fearlessly. But having lacked the courage, whenever they have spoken, they have done it clumsily and you have felt irritated. . . . They have chafed under your rebukes and magisterial manner and above all your arrogation of what to them has appeared your infallibility and superior knowledge. They feel that you have treated them with scant courtesy and have never defended them from the socialists' ridicule and even misrepresentation.' To soothe Nehru's hurt pride the Mahatma added, 'they know that you cannot be dispensed with'. He tried to pass the crisis off lightly —'I look upon the whole affair as a tragicomedy'—and requested Nehru not to wash the 'family linen' before the A.I.C.C., compelling it to choose between him and his colleagues. Most

---

[1] Unpublished Nehru Letters. Prasad's letter to Nehru is dated 29 June 1936 and was written from Gandhi's *ashram* at Wardha.
[2] Quoted in 'Where Are We?', reprinted in *The Unity of India*, p. 101.

I

significant, perhaps, was Gandhi's gentle reminder, 'You are in office by their unanimous choice but you are not in power yet.'[1]

Nehru agreed to withdraw his resignation, but the reason was entirely unrelated to the intra-party squabble. While on tour in the latter part of July he learned of the outbreak of the Spanish Civil War. 'I saw this . . . developing into a European or even a world conflict. . . . Was I going to weaken our organisation and create an internal crisis by resigning just when it was essential for us to pull together? My mind became tense with expectation and all thought of resignation left it.'[2] It was a typical example of the influence which international affairs have always exerted on Nehru's decisions at home.

*   *   *   *

As the date of provincial elections drew near, Congress leaders closed ranks. With Gandhi's backing Nehru was able to secure approval for a left-of-centre election manifesto.[3] There were pledges to remove all social, economic and political discrimination against women; to encourage *khaddar* (home-spun cloth); to secure better treatment for political prisoners; to combat the 1935 Government of India Act; to give industrial workers improved conditions; and to struggle for the oft-stated Congress goals—complete independence, the abolition of un-touchability, etc. The most striking feature of the manifesto was its special appeal to the peasantry in the form of a pledge to sponsor substantial agrarian reforms: immediate relief to the poorer peasants by a reduction of rent and land taxes; exemption of uneconomic holdings from all rent and taxes; a moratorium on debts; the scaling down of rural indebtedness; and the provision of cheap credit facilities. There was something for all groups, but its primary emphasis was on improved conditions for the rural masses.

On the eve of the election campaign there arose the question of choosing a Congress President for the year 1937. Nehru stated that he would welcome the election of any of his colleagues and

---

[1] Tendulkar, op. cit., vol. 8, Appendix on Gandhi-Nehru Letters, pp. 359–60. The letter is dated 15 July 1936.

[2] 'Where Are We?', in *The Unity of India*, p. 102.

[3] The text of the Congress Election Manifesto, adopted by the A.I.C.C. on 22 August 1936, is to be found in *The Unity of India*, Appendix A, pp. 401–5.

would extend his complete co-operation. 'Should, however, the choice of my countrymen fall on me, I dare not say "no" to it. . . . But before they so decide they must realize fully what I stand for . . .' The leading contender was Patel. But as in 1929 and again in 1946 he was persuaded to withdraw by Gandhi, this time probably because of the recognition that Nehru alone had a mass appeal. Lest his decision be misunderstood, the Sardar stressed that it should not be taken to mean that he endorsed all of Nehru's views. 'Indeed, Congressmen know that on some vital matters my views are in conflict with those held by Jawaharlalji.' Moreover, he served notice that the Old Guard was not ready to abandon control of the party machine: 'The Congress President has no dictatorial powers. He is the chairman of our well-built organization. He regulates the proceedings and carries out the decisions of the Congress. . . . The Congress does not part with its ample powers by electing any individual—no matter who he is.' Hence he asked the delegates to elect Nehru as 'the best person to . . . guide in the right channel the different forces that are at work in the country'.[1]

And so it was done. Nehru was re-elected and led the Congress to a sweeping victory at the polls. In his presidential address to the Faizpur session, held at the end of December 1936, he set the tone for the election campaign by re-enacting his Lucknow performance—as the tribune of left-socialism and a 'popular front'.[2]

His election campaign can only be described as a fury of activity. Like an arrow he shot through the country, carrying the Congress message to remote hamlets in the hills and on the plains. He covered some 50,000 miles in less than five months, using every conceivable means of transport. Most of the time he travelled by car, train or aeroplane, occasionally by horse, camel, steamer, bicycle or canoe, and where necessary, on foot through the trackless dusty plains. Even the elephant was harnessed into service. All told, about 10,000,000 persons attended his meetings, and millions more lined the route to catch a glimpse of the Congress's crown prince. Many of the gatherings exceeded 20,000, some attracted 100,000, mostly peasant

[1] Sitaramayya, op. cit., vol. ii, pp. 31–32.
[2] The text of this address is to be found in *Indian Annual Register*, vol. ii, 1936, pp. 222–30, and in *Toward Freedom*, Appendix C, pp. 416–31.

men and women who walked from distant villages to see and to hear their much-loved 'Panditji'. His average working day ranged from twelve to eighteen hours, and on one occasion he dragged his weary body through engagements for twenty-three hours without rest. It was a prodigious feat, a worthy model for the campaign he was to conduct during the general elections of 1951–2.

Then as later he enjoyed the sense of communion with large masses of people. He was exhilarated, indeed intoxicated, by the 'surging crowds, [with] an enthusiasm bordering on frenzy, and shining eyes with unspoken pledges looking through them'.[1] He had come into contact with the village as early as 1920 and had often gone back to renew his association. But it was not until the prolonged tour of 1936–7 that he was able to penetrate the mass mind, to acquire the kind of insight that Gandhi seemed to have intuitively. From this experience dates his genuine discovery of India. And from that time onwards he possessed, in only slightly less measure than Gandhi, a capacity to feel the pulse of the Indian masses, their fears and hopes, their changing moods, their dreams of a better life. As with Gandhi, herein lay the key to Nehru's power. Although their appeal differed, they were the only two men in modern India who could evoke unquestioning devotion from the peasant millions, Gandhi because he was the incarnation of traditional India, Nehru because he was the symbol and hope of future regeneration.

Nehru's approach to the predominantly illiterate electors was ideological in the main, with very few references to individual candidates. The Congress election manifesto was explained in simple, straightforward terms, and a few core themes were stated *ad infinitum*: 'fight for Indian freedom; build the Congress into a mighty army of the Indian people; organize to remove poverty, unemployment and social and cultural degradation'. 'Let every voter, man or woman, do his or her duty by the country and vote for the Congress', was his constant refrain. 'Thus we shall write in millions of hands our flaming re-loves to be free.'[2] The technique of hammering on a few key

---

[1] *Eighteen Months in India*, p. 58. For Nehru's account of the election campaign, see *The Discovery of India*, pp. 58–65.

[2] Tendulkar, op. cit., vol. 4, p. 165.

objectives is one which Nehru still uses in order to rouse his people from lethargy and to prop up a decaying Congress Party.

In 1937 this approach made a signal contribution to the party's victory at the polls. Of the 1,585 seats the Congress won 711, a particularly striking success since it had contested only 1,161 seats. To its regret in later years it had run candidates in only 58 of the 482 separate Muslim constituencies. The Congress sweep is all the more impressive when it is borne in mind that of the 1,585 seats less than half, 657, were 'General' or open, i.e., not allotted to a separate, closed electoral group. The balance was fragmented among Muslims, Sikhs, Christians, Europeans, Landholders and others. Of the eleven provinces in British India, the Congress won an absolute majority in five and was the largest party in three others. By contrast, the Muslim League, which was to attain the separate State of Pakistan only ten years later, secured only 4·8 per cent. of the total *Muslim* vote. Nor did it win a majority of seats in *any* of the four Muslim-majority provinces.[1]

There were two fundamental reasons for the Congress victory: a broadly based organizational network throughout the country and the mass appeal of its election manifesto, especially its pledge of agrarian reform. As *The Times* of London remarked on 9 March 1937, 'the party has won its victories . . . on issues which interested millions of Indian rural voters and scores of millions who had no votes.' To Nehru goes most of the credit for the Congress stress on land reform. And it was he who carried the message so effectively to the Indian countryside.

[1] Detailed results of the 1937 elections are to be found in Cmd. 5589, 1937.

CHAPTER X

Days of Ferment

To accept or not to accept office—this was the question which confronted the Congress. A decision had become imperative, for the provincial part of the 1935 Government of India Act was due to go into effect on 1 April 1937. Nehru and the Left wing strongly urged rejection. But the majority of Congressmen hungered for power after many years in the wilderness. A compromise formula was finally evolved by Gandhi: the Congress would agree to form a Cabinet in those provinces where the party leader in the legislature could state publicly that the Governor would not use his 'special powers' and would act on the advice of his ministers in all matters under provincial jurisdiction. The Governors refused to give these assurances, on the ground that they would violate the provisions of the Act, and the Congress refused to take office. Thus interim ministries were formed in those provinces where the Congress held a majority. After three months of negotiations a face-saving device was found: the Viceroy issued a statement to the effect that the spirit of the 1935 Act called for co-operation between Governors and their Ministers. The Working Committee accepted this 'assurance', and Congress governments were formed in seven provinces followed by an eighth a year later. The experiment in constitutionalism lasted two and a half years, until October 1939, when all Congress governments resigned because of the way India was brought into the war.[1]

Nehru was unhappy with the decision, but he had no choice; the pressure among his colleagues and the rank and file was too great. Faced with reality, he tried to rationalize the 'retreat': 'Acceptance of office does not mean by an iota acceptance of the slave Constitution.[!] It means a fight against the coming of the Federation by all means in our power. . . . We have taken a new step involving new responsibilities and some risks.

[1] See pp. 262, 264, below.

But if we are true to our objectives and are ever vigilant, we shall overcome these risks and gain strength and power . . .'[1]

The immediate and most far-reaching effect of the Congress victory at the polls was a widening of the breach with the Muslim League. Flushed with success the Congress adopted an imperious attitude to all other political parties, a 'Himalayan blunder', for which it was to pay dearly in the years to come. Nehru himself set the tone with his haughty remark in March 1937: 'There are only two forces in India today, British imperialism, and Indian nationalism as represented by the Congress.' Jinnah was quick to retort: 'No, there is a third party, the Mussulmans.' History was to bear him out.

The Congress went beyond contemptuous words. During the election campaign the two parties had co-operated to some extent, notably in the United Provinces where there developed a tacit understanding that a coalition government would be formed. However, this was before the elections, when the Congress did not expect a clear majority. It was no longer necessary to make concessions. The League offer of co-operation was now treated with disdain. It was not rejected outright, but a series of incredible conditions was laid down by the Congress: League members of the provincial Cabinet should join the Congress; the League group in the Assembly should disband and its members follow Congress orders; and the League should no longer contest by-elections in the United Provinces. It was nothing short of an ultimatum for the League's self-destruction.

Jinnah took the Congress demand as a declaration of war and replied in kind. At the end of July he called upon the Muslims to consolidate their strength for the coming struggle. Then, at its annual session in October, the League decided to frame a comprehensive social, economic and educational programme to win the support of the Muslim masses. Alarmed by the election results and the Congress arrogation of total power, Jinnah embarked on a country-wide tour to rally the hitherto-ignored Muslim peasants. 'Islam is in danger', he cried, and Muslims began to respond. The opening shots had been fired in the calamitous Congress-League war which was to envelop north India in flames and ultimately result in partition.

In historical perspective Nehru's attitude to the League in

[1] *The Unity of India*, pp. 61, 62.

1937 was a grave error of judgement. But neither he nor Jinnah could possibly foresee the consequences. And his views seemed justified by existing conditions. The League was still a small, upper- and middle-class organization which had little contact with, or interest in, the Muslim masses. Its primary goals were to safeguard the interests of Muslim landlords and Princes and to secure greater opportunities in government service for the growing Muslim intelligentsia. It had fared badly at the polls; indeed, it had fewer Muslim supporters than the Congress, which had the additional backing of various nationalist Muslim parties. At most it had nuisance value, a potential alternative attraction for some of the 90,000,000 Muslims. Moreover, Nehru's attitude was a consistent extension of his general political ideology. He had often expressed hostility to the communalist approach to politics, with particular reference to the Muslim League and the Hindu Mahasabha. For him the main struggle was against British rule; in that sense the League was merely a hindrance to the marshalling of complete national support in an 'anti-imperialist front'. 'All third parties', he wrote at the time, 'have no real importance in this historic sense.'[1] This view was belied by subsequent events, but in 1937 he thought the League could be safely ignored.

Nehru was not among the most rabid foes of the League. Though denying its claim to act as the authoritative representative of *all* Indian Muslims, a pretentious claim at the time, he was prepared to meet the League half-way in an effort to reduce the growing friction after the elections. This becomes evident from a significant exchange of letters with Jinnah during the early months of 1938.

The correspondence began with Nehru's request for clarification of the points in dispute and an expression of eagerness to end the League's fears. Jinnah was suspicious and retorted, 'surely you know what the points are'. The League leader indicated a willingness to meet. Nehru was agreeable, 'but what about? The issues must first be defined and there is nothing wrong with doing this by correspondence.' Jinnah then reiterated the 'Fourteen Points', a series of League demands first raised in 1929, along with some recent claims he had put forward in the press. Nehru termed the 'Fourteen

[1]. *Eighteen Months in India*, p. 146.

Points' out of date but was conciliatory on some of them. While the Congress still opposed the 'Communal Award', he said, there would be no alteration without the consent of all communities. He agreed that the minorities must have a just share of jobs in the Services. As for Muslim cultural and religious rights, the Congress Karachi Resolution of 1931 was emphatic. Redistribution of provincial boundaries was certainly in order if the interested parties consented. Jinnah had also demanded that Urdu be made the national language. While Nehru was opposed, his views on the language question were closer to Jinnah's than to most Congressmen's. He rejected the League claim to represent 90,000,000 Muslims, along with the criticism of the use of the Congress flag on public buildings. On the whole it was a conciliatory response, accompanied by an invitation to Jinnah to meet in Allahabad. Jinnah replied that this letter was 'painful reading', that it misrepresented the League's views and that it displayed Congress's assumption of total power. Unless the League were recognized as an equal, he concluded, a trial of strength was inevitable. And so it was. Nehru conveyed his regret at having caused Jinnah pain, pleaded sincerity and a desire to reach agreement, but declined Jinnah's counter-invitation for a meeting in Bombay, on the grounds that he was about to sail for Europe.

Many exchanges were to follow in the years to come but this one set the pattern. It accomplished nothing and laid bare the basic difference in approach to the Indian problem. It also revealed that there was no meeting of minds though both men were essentially Western in their outlook: Nehru thought and acted in terms of Indian unity; Jinnah was concerned only with the position of Indian Muslims. Here were two explosive personalities engaged in verbal combat. Perhaps the most revealing disclosure of this correspondence is that, in theory at least, Jinnah considered himself an *Indian* nationalist as late as 1938. 'It is the duty of every true nationalist', he wrote on 17 March, 'to whichever party or community he may belong' to help achieve a united front.[1] Two years later, in the Lahore ('Pakistan') resolution, he 'discovered' a separate nation of

[1] The text of the Nehru-Jinnah correspondence is to be found in *Indian Annual Register*, vol. i, 1938, pp. 363–76.

Muslims in India. With the enunciation of the two-nation theory the conflict was to enter a crucial phase.

Just as the Nehru-Jinnah correspondence drew to a close the League established a Committee of Inquiry into alleged Congress persecution of Muslims. The *Pirpur Report* added fuel to the flames. Some of the grievances were picayune, such as the decision of various Congress governments to permit the singing of the nationalist anthem, *Bande Mataram*, previously banned by the British, and the use of the Congress flag on public buildings. Others, more serious, alleged Congress discrimination against Muslims in the Services and partiality to Hindus during communal riots; inadequate subsidies to Muslim schools; official support to the propagation of Hindi; and in general an onslaught on Muslim culture. The overall conclusion of the Report was that the Muslim community was much better off under the British than under Congress rule.[1]

How much truth there was in these charges was never verified. The Congress offered to submit them to the (British) Chief Justice of India, but the League refused. Jinnah urged an inquiry by a Royal Commission of judges under the chairmanship of a Law Lord of the Privy Council. The Congress was agreeable, 'but at the instance of the Viceroy the matter was dropped. . . . The Viceroy felt that, while specific instances might admit of being proved in particular provinces, it would be most difficult for Jinnah to prove any general anti-Muslim action on the part of the Congress governments . . .' Furthermore, 'the [provincial] Governors . . . were satisfied that there was no basis for the allegations'.[2]

In any event, Congress haughtiness and undoubted acts of favouritism to the Hindus caused widespread fear among Muslims. When at last the Congress provincial governments resigned, Jinnah dramatized the event for millions of Muslims by proclaiming a 'Day of Deliverance'. According to Professor Coupland, 'Hindu-Moslem discord became so bitter that, at the time the Ministries resigned (1939) it seemed, in the United Provinces and Bihar at any rate, that, without a drastic change

---

[1] *Report of the Inquiry Committee appointed by the All-India Muslim League to inquire into Muslim grievances in Congress Provinces* (1938). The Committee was headed by the Nawab of Pirpur.

[2] Menon, V. P., *The Transfer of Power in India*, p. 71.

of policy [on communal relations], constitutional government might soon become impossible.'[1]

*   *   *   *

Among the sources of Muslim discontent was a fear for the future of Urdu, a product of the Moghul period and the *lingua franca* of northern India and the Muslims in particular. Fanatical Hindus were beginning to press the claims of Hindi which shares a common vocabulary with Urdu but is derived from Sanskrit and is written in *Devanagri* script, whereas Urdu uses the Persian script.

The character of the debate annoyed Nehru. 'It is curious how many things in our country take a communal tinge', he wrote to a nationalist Muslim friend. 'For some mysterious reasons, Urdu is supposed to be the hallmark of the Muslims. With all due deference, I am not prepared to admit this. I consider Urdu as my language which I have spoken from childhood up. . . . Why is it that whenever such so-called cultural and similar questions are pushed to the front, political reactionaries take the lead in them? . . .'[2]

Desirous of rescuing this controversial issue from the bigots, Nehru set down his reflections and proposals in a comprehensive analysis of 'the language question'.[3] 'A living language', he wrote, 'is a throbbing, vital thing, ever changing, ever growing and mirroring the people who speak and write it. It has its roots in the masses, though its superstructure may represent the culture of the few. How, then, can we change it or shape it to our liking by resolutions or orders from above?'

Turning to a language policy for free India, he attempted to reassure the Muslims and regional linguistic interests. The national or all-India language should be Hindustani, a fusion of Hindi and Urdu, which was the common language of about 150 million people in north, north-west and central India; and *Devanagri* and Persian scripts should have equal status. However, state education and all public activities should be carried out in the dominant language of each linguistic area, with

---

[1] *Indian Politics 1936–1942*, p. 157.

[2] Unpublished Nehru-Mahmud Correspondence, 24 September 1936.

[3] 'The Question of Language', reprinted in *Eighteen Months in India*, pp. 245–72, and in *The Unity of India*, pp. 241–61.

suitable provisions for minority language groups. The languages recognized for these purposes should be Hindustani (both Hindi and Urdu), Bengali, Gujarati, Marathi, Tamil, Telugu, Kannada, Malayalam, Oriya, Assamese, Sindhi, and to some extent Pushtu and Punjabi. In the Hindustani area all public notifications should be issued in both scripts and students should be allowed to choose either. An attempt should be made to unify the scripts of all north Indian languages deriving from Sanskrit and using the *Devanagri* script. Similarly, an effort should be made to approximate *Devanagri* to the scripts of the four southern languages—Tamil, Telugu, Kannada and Malayalam; if this were not feasible, a composite script for the southern languages should be devised. Thus there would be two scripts in the north and one in the south.

Basic Hindustani, a complete language of about one thousand words, should be developed as an aid to mass education—a proposal which has great merit for India today. Technical, political, and commercial words should be standardized wherever possible, and foreign languages should be drawn on where necessary. University education should be imparted in the regional language, but a foreign language should be compulsory. Provision should also be made for the teaching of foreign and Indian languages in secondary schools. Anticipating the sweeping reorganization of boundaries in 1956, he added that all this 'necessitates that provincial units should correspond with such language areas'.

The partition of India 'solved' the Hindi-Urdu squabble, with Hindi now the 'official language' of India and Urdu one of the two 'official languages' of Pakistan. At the time they were made, however, these proposals aroused considerable interest. In a letter to Nehru, Sarojini Naidu remarked: 'Your language pamphlet is a miracle worker. You should see the radiant satisfaction it has produced among the most disgruntled. Old Maulvi Abul Hakk, whose opinion counts for so much in Urdu literary circles, to whom I sent a copy, has returned [from a conference] glowing with satisfaction.'[1] Gandhi, too, gave it his blessing, but he urged a revised form of *Devanagri* as the script for the four southern languages and expressed the hope that speakers of Hindustani would eventually adopt one script.

[1] Unpublished Nehru Letters, 7 September 1937.

Nehru continued to act as the 'guardian' of Urdu and the southern languages. In response to the growing pressure aroused by Nehru's views, the All-India Congress Committee reaffirmed in September 1938 that Hindustani in both scripts would be the national language. Had India remained united Nehru's proposals would probably have been incorporated with little or no change. As it is, many of them found their way into the Indian Constitution of 1950 and the reorganization of states six years later.

* * * *

Nehru's thoughts at this time were not confined to the language problem and the larger question of Hindu-Muslim relations. His primary interest remained in the realm of politics proper. As early as the summer of 1936 he was responsible for the creation of a Civil Liberties Union with the distinguished poet, Rabindranath Tagore, as Honorary President. Many critics in recent years have taken Nehru to task for the Preventive Detention Acts which have been in force in India since 1950. It is interesting to note, in this connection, his 'realistic' caution twenty years ago on the limits of civil liberties. 'It is clear that, in spite of every desire to avoid it, coercive action may become necessary in particular cases. . . . Violence or dangerous incitement to violence and communal strife cannot . . . be tolerated by any State.'[1]

Another problem that occupied his attention was the proper relationship of the Congress to mass functional organizations, notably *kisan sabhas* (peasant leagues) and trade unions. The election campaign of 1936–7 and the 'mass contacts campaign' had reaped rich dividends for the Congress, though almost entirely among the Hindus. From a membership of 457,000 in the spring of 1936 it leapt to over 3,000,000 at the beginning of 1938. A year later it approached 5,000,000. The *kisan sabhas* had also grown rapidly and were adopting a militant attitude to agrarian reform. Indeed, to some extent they were beginning to rival the local Congress committees in the countryside, causing alarm among the more orthodox sections of the party.

Ever the mediator, Nehru undertook to 'reconcile the irreconcilables'. He welcomed the growth of labour and peasant

[1] *Indian Annual Register*, vol. ii, 1937, p. 335.

movements but emphasized the need to avoid rivalry with the Congress. Since the party constitution did not permit collective affiliation of these organizations, the only way to achieve harmony was by mass individual membership of the Congress. He also recommended that peasant leagues be organized only in those areas where the party was weak. While he recognized the primacy of the land problem, he called upon the *kisan sabhas* to co-operate with the Lucknow resolution on agrarian reform rather than embark on a 'Left deviation' of their own. Fundamental land reform, he reminded them, had to await political freedom. In short, follow the Congress lead and concentrate on the struggle for independence by joining ranks in an 'anti-imperialist front'.[1] By and large they accepted his advice.

It was at this period, too, that Nehru laid the foundations for the structure and philosophy of economic planning which plays so important a role in India today. At his suggestion the Congress Working Committee called on the new Congress governments in the summer of 1937 to appoint committees of experts to devise machinery for planning. From this emerged the National Planning Committee of the Congress.

The original Committee consisted of eleven members but was later enlarged to thirty-three, with Nehru as Chairman and Professor K. T. Shah as Honorary Secretary. Shah was the central figure, collating the mass of information collected from various sources. The Committee met only eight times from 1938 to 1946, and little of concrete value was accomplished. However, the National Planning Committee did make an important contribution. It made the Congress plan-conscious and thereby paved the way for the introduction of All-India economic planning in 1950. Most of the credit for this achievement was undoubtedly Nehru's (as was the 1950 decision).[2]

Among the political problems of the late 1930's none caused more concern than the record of the Congress ministries and their relationship to the party organization. Nehru had yielded to the pressure for 'office acceptance' with serious misgivings. It was doubtful, he thought, whether many substantive benefits

---

[1] The text of Nehru's statement is to be found in *Indian Annual Register*, vol. ii, 1937, pp. 362–6.

[2] This point will be elaborated in Chapter XVIII.

would accrue to the Indian masses because of the limits imposed by finance, the constitution of 1935 and the possible hostility of the civil service. There was, too, the danger of conflict between Congressmen in and out of power.

In an effort to minimize these dangers, he issued a presidential call for 'the right perspective' soon after the experiment in constitutionalism got under way. To those about to assume power he stressed the basic Congress objectives—independence and the eradication of poverty. The immediate goal, he added, should be alleviation of the most glaring ills besetting the Indian people, notably by changes in agrarian legislation and the release of political prisoners, some of whom had languished in jail since the civil disobedience campaign of 1921–2.

On the vital question of party–ministry relations he tried to steer a middle course. 'It is manifest that the Congress is more important than any Ministry. Ministries may come or go, but the Congress goes on till it fulfils its historic mission of achieving national independence for India.' While asserting the supremacy of the party as a whole, i.e. of the Working Committee, he trod more cautiously on the horizontal relationship, namely, provincial government and Provincial Congress Committee. 'It is patent that for a Congress Committee to condemn a Congress Ministry is both improper and absurd. . . . On the other hand, for Congress Committees and Congressmen to become silent and tongue-tied spectators of the doings of Congress Governments would be equally absurd. . . . Friendly criticism or suggestion should always be welcome. . . . [But] any attempt to embarrass the Congress Ministries and put difficulties in their way will end in embarrassing ourselves.'[1]

This plea proved unequal to the task. As in the years following Independence, personal and factional rivalries, the corrupting influence of power, and ideological conflict, particularly on the agrarian problem, led to constant friction between ministers and local party officials. It became necessary to demarcate the lines more rigidly. This Nehru did in a directive of 4 November 1937. What made the position of the ministries embarrassing, he said, was that they were responsible to a diverse group of bodies—the electorate, the Congress Party in the legislature, the Provincial Congress Committees and their executives, the

[1] *The Unity of India*, pp. 65–77. The quotations are from pp. 75–76.

A.I.C.C. and the Working Committee. Their primary responsibility, he emphasized, was to the Congress and only indirectly to the electorate. 'We have thus to strike a mean—to keep the control of *policy* in the hands of the A.I.C.C., and not to interfere too much in *administrative* matters.' Nor were all Congress organs equipped for the task of supervision. 'Where such intervention is considered desirable, the Working Committee should make inquiries and, if necessary, report to the A.I.C.C.' There remained the basic question of criticism. Nehru renewed his plea for friendly suggestions but no usurpation of administrative functions.[1]

In this complicated hierarchy final authority lay with the Working Committee and its Parliamentary Board, consisting of Patel, Prasad and Maulana Azad. It was this concentration of power that gave rise to a charge of Congress 'totalitarianism' and the obstruction of parliamentary government.[2] Nehru ridiculed this on the grounds that office acceptance did not imply abandonment of the basic goal—Indian independence—and that participation in provincial government was merely one front in a continuing struggle. On this point a British writer has recently commented: 'To these charges there is really no reply—except the adequate one that it is not reasonable to expect nationalist movements to behave as parliamentary parties.'[3]

The problem of party–government relations has not been solved to the present day. At the Centre the Cabinet is supreme, primarily because of Nehru's commanding position. In the States, however, there are many examples of Congress Committees exceeding the bounds of 'friendly criticism'. And the Congress High Command continues to exercise great power over state governments and state Congress organizations alike.

On the whole the record of the Congress ministries was not unattractive. Provincial legislatures functioned with relative efficiency. Relations with the Governors were smooth except for brief ministerial crises in Bihar and the United Provinces over the release of political prisoners early in 1938, both of

---

[1] *The Unity of India*, pp. 78–85. The quotations are from p. 78. (Emphasis added.)

[2] For this allegation, see Coupland, op. cit., ch. x, and Griffiths, Sir P., *The British Impact on India*, p. 340.

[3] Morris-Jones, W. H., *Parliament in India*, p. 67.

which were resolved by a compromise formula.[1] During their two years in office almost all remaining political prisoners were freed. Their social and economic programme, though limited in scope, was in line with the party's pledge for reform. A moratorium on debts was imposed in Bombay and the U.P.; some of the existing debts in Madras were cancelled; tenancy legislation was passed in various provinces; land revenue was remitted in some areas; trade unions received encouragement, though the Bombay Trades Disputes Act was received with mixed feelings because of the four months' mandatory delay in the right to strike; a 'Basic Education' scheme was introduced; and social legislation was enacted within the limits set by finance.

In a more intangible sense, this experiment gave the Indian people pride in governing themselves, a psychological boost to national morale. By far the most important benefit was the valuable experience in administration for a number of Congress politicians. '. . . the men who began to learn governmental and parliamentary politics during 1937-9 were to a great extent the men who took over the total responsibility in 1947'.[2]

Nehru was not unaware of these attainments: 'true that they had done good work, their record of achievement was impressive, the Ministers were working terribly hard. . . . Theirs was a thankless job. Still, I felt that progress was slow and their outlook was not what it should be.' The machinery of government was working in much the same way, especially in Madras where it was 'perilously like the old Government'. He was also disturbed by the lack of co-operation between Congress committees and the ministries, the growth of ideological conflict and, most of all, by the tendency of provincial governments to shrink from advanced social legislation.[3]

In a letter to Pandit Pant, Premier of the United Provinces, he expressed his views more bluntly. 'I am greatly distressed at the turn events are taking all over India, in so far as the Congress Ministries are concerned. . . . If I may put it in technical language, the Congress Ministries are tending to become

[1] For the details, see *Congress Bulletin*, No. 1, 12 March 1938, pp. 27-37.
[2] Morris-Jones, op. cit., p. 71. For assessments of the Congress provincial ministries, see Coupland, R., *Indian Politics 1936-1942*, ch. XI-XIV, and Nehru, *The Discovery of India*, pp. 436-55.
[3] 'Where Are We?', in *The Unity of India*, pp. 108, 103.

counter-revolutionary. This is, of course, not a conscious development. . . . Apart from this the general attitude is static. I am quite sure that the advent of the Congress Ministries has resulted in a great accession of strength to us . . . very largely the change was psychological. . . . But we cannot live on psychology or on the reputation of a few good deeds. . . . I am quite clear that we are better out [of office] than in unless we can go ahead much faster than we have been doing.'[1]

To Gandhi he expressed similar views. 'They are trying to adapt themselves far too much to the old order and trying to justify it. . . . What is far worse is that we are losing the high position that we have built up, with so much labour, in the hearts of the people. We are sinking to the level of ordinary politicians . . .'[2]   Hence he welcomed their resignations—though for very different reasons from Jinnah. 'I can assure you with all earnestness', he wrote to Dr. Mahmud, 'that I am exceedingly pleased that the Congress governments have resigned. I am pleased from every possible point of view and for the last six months or more I had been wanting them to resign.'[3]

*   *   *   *

By the spring of 1938 Nehru felt the need for a change and decided to make another 'pilgrimage' to the West. It was not only the record of the Congress ministries, though this weighed heavily on his mind. Congress–League tension was growing ominously, and his correspondence with Jinnah had come to nought. Factional strife within the party showed no signs of abating. And only a few months before he had come into conflict with Gandhi over a seemingly innocuous resolution of the A.I.C.C. which condemned the repressive policies of the Maharaja of Mysore. The Mahatma had criticized the resolution severely, on the grounds that it violated the Congress policy of non-intervention in the affairs of the princely States. Nehru insisted that there was nothing to prevent the A.I.C.C. from discussing any issue, but Gandhi was adamant. So disturbed was Nehru by this attack that he 'decided' to withdraw from

---

[1] Unpublished Nehru Letters, 25 November 1937.
[2] Quoted in 'Where Are We?' in *The Unity of India*, p. 106.
[3] Unpublished Nehru-Mahmud Correspondence, 12 December 1939.

the Working Committee at the next Congress session. It was only in deference to Subhas Bose, the President-elect, that he changed his mind.

The friction with Gandhi at this time found expression in a private letter to Mahadev Desai, the Mahatma's private secretary, on 26 December 1937: 'I feel that it is not very profitable for us to discuss such matters [politics with Gandhi]. I have not expressed my opinion on many vital matters which have occurred during the past two months. But I have felt about them very deeply. . . .'[1] As always the friction passed, but not the mood. 'I have felt out of place and a misfit', he wrote to Gandhi in April 1938, conveying his decision to go abroad. In Europe 'I would freshen up my tired and puzzled mind.'[2]

There was also disquieting news on the international scene. Fascism was moving from one victory to another, both in Asia and the West, and the danger of war grew ominous. Indeed, the precipitating cause of his decision to visit Europe at that time was Hitler's occupation of Austria in March 1938. It happened while Nehru was at Khali, in the Kumaun Hills of the U.P., close by the mountains he loved so well. He had gone there after the annual Congress session in Haripura, seeking escape from 'political life [which] was an exhausting business'. For two weeks he 'drank deep of the mountain air and took my fill of the sight of the snows and the valleys'.

The days passed and with them his feeling of despair. But the escape was short-lived. 'Suddenly there came a rude shock. Hitler was marching into Austria, and I heard the tramp of barbarian feet over the pleasant gardens of Vienna. Was this the prelude to that world catastrophe which had hung over us for so long? Was this war? I forgot Khali and the snows and the mountains, and my body became taut and my mind tense. . . . There was no peace for me then even in Khali, no escape.'[3]

He returned to the plains, his mind made up. Early in June he sailed for Europe. At Suez he paused to meet Nahas Pasha, leader of the Egyptian Wafd Party. It was Nehru's first direct

[1] Unpublished Nehru Letters.
[2] Quoted in 'Where Are We?' in *The Unity of India*, p. 106.
[3] 'Escape', reprinted in *The Unity of India*, pp. 200-4.

contact with Arab nationalism, whose goals he has since supported with striking consistency. Then to Genoa and Marseilles where he was joined by Krishna Menon, head of the India League in London and already an admirer of Nehru.

After a brief delay in connection with their Spanish visa, they hurried to Barcelona for a five-day visit. Much of the time was spent 'at the barricades', in the front lines on the outskirts of the city, where the International Brigade stood fast against overwhelming odds. Later he wrote a sensitive ode to Barcelona and the courage of the Loyalist Army, singling out two of its officers, Lister and Modero, who were amateurs in the arts of war, but had risen to the challenge. Among those who impressed him was 'La Passionara', the Spanish Communist leader, with whom he later shared a platform in Paris in support of the Loyalist cause.

Nehru's stay in the embattled capital of the Republic remains vivid in his memory. All the values of European civilization which he held dear seemed to him to be at stake in the Spanish Civil War—democracy, socialism, human dignity, self-determination, individual freedom. When the Republic was destroyed Nehru's faith in the West was severely shaken. The depth of his feelings is evident in his own writings at the time. The Republic, he wrote, was not killed by rebels or traitors or even by the Fascist States. 'Britain and France must be held responsible for this, as for the betrayal of Czechoslovakia, and history long ages hence will remember this infamy and will not forgive them.' 'For Spain was not Spain only, but the new world locked in a death struggle with the barbarian hordes of reaction and brutal violence.' ' . . . they [Spain and Czechoslovakia] represented to me precious values in life. . . . If I deserted them, what would I cherish in India; for what kind of freedom do we struggle here?'[1]

Much of his stay in Europe during the summer and autumn of 1938 was devoted to pleading the causes of anti-fascism and Indian freedom. He divided his time between London and Paris, addressing gatherings on the iniquities of British rule in his native land, on the horrors of bombing open cities, on the Fascist menace in Europe, on the false security of appeasement. At the same time he served notice that the Indian National

---

[1] *China, Spain and the War*, pp. 20, 92 and 17.

Congress would not accept meekly a British decision to drag India into a world war.[1]

He watched with dismay the events leading to the dismemberment of Czechoslovakia. To the *National Herald* in Lucknow, of which he was Board Chairman and the moving spirit, he conveyed the mood of a disillusioned Western idealist observing the end of an epoch. His most scathing words were directed at Chamberlain and the French appeasers, as much for their folly and cowardice as for their complicity in the 'murder of another nation'. And when Munich came he knew that the evil day had only been postponed.

* * * *

Nehru returned to India in November 1938, only to find himself in the midst of another Congress crisis, one of the gravest in the party's history. The 'Tripuri Crisis' provides a dramatic example of his role as 'the mediator' in the nationalist movement. More important, it throws considerable light on Nehru's relations with Subhas Bose, the proud, ambitious, fiery hero of Bengal, his most serious rival for Indian political leadership once Gandhi passed from the scene. By the time the crisis was over, Bose's power within the Congress was broken. Neither Nehru nor Bose could have been aware of the consequences while the conflict took its course. Nor is there any evidence that either was conscious of the possible effects on their rivalry— which, in any event, remained unstated. On the contrary, though they disagreed, they acted with a desire to resolve the cleavage in the best interests of the party as a whole. Of all the participants only Gandhi had a clear and consistent objective —to oust Bose. This he did in the end.

It was a complex affair in that the ideological lines were blurred by a clash of temperaments and personal ambition. By the late 1930's the Congress was divided into two vague bodies of opinion, Gandhians and Modernists. Conservatives and the Old Guard fell into the category of Gandhians, and Socialists among the Modernists, but the division was not rigid. All were united by the goal of independence and all followed the Mahatma's lead, except for the relatively small

[1] Letter to the *Manchester Guardian* on 8 September 1938, reprinted in *The Unity of India*, pp. 284-7.

Communist element in the party. Indeed, Gandhi's paramount position made Western-type ideological terms inapplicable to the Congress at that time. Nor was there any real clash on policy in 1939; at most it was a difference of emphasis.

There was, however, deep dissatisfaction with the Old Guard, particularly among the powerful Bengali group led by Subhas Bose. Moreover, Bose and some right-wing leaders, notably Patel, disliked each other intensely. In the true Bengali tradition, Bose was an 'activist' who disdained the caution of the Old Guard and of Gandhi himself. Of all the Congress leaders Bose was the least devoted to the Mahatma.[1] There was also tension arising from the Bengali feeling that though they were the pioneers of Indian nationalism, the Congress was dominated by 'north Indians', notably Gujarat (Gandhi and Patel) and the United Provinces (Nehru). Finally, as Bose was to reveal more clearly during the second world war, he was strongly attracted to the *Führer Prinzip*; in 1939 he was anxious to 'lead' the Congress to victory in a final struggle. It was this militancy that disturbed Gandhi who was convinced conditions were not ripe for civil disobedience. Had the clash of 1939 been along clear ideological lines, it would not have left such a bitter taste among the protagonists. The strong injection of personal factors explains much of what follows.

When Nehru returned from Europe he was asked by Gandhi to assume the presidency for the coming year. He declined and recommended Maulana Azad as the person acceptable to all factions. Azad accepted at first but changed his mind when it became apparent that there would be a contest; Bose decided to run for re-election despite advice to the contrary by Gandhi and Nehru. Nehru's opposition was largely due to the belief that it would hinder a united 'anti-imperialist' front which was uppermost in his mind. A radical change in policy at that juncture, he felt, should be avoided at all costs.

The election was scheduled for 29 January 1939. During the preceding nine days the clash came into the open. Azad withdrew his candidacy on the 20th, pleading ill health, and recommended Sitaramayya, best known in later years for his unofficial history of the Congress. The following day Bose threw his hat into the ring, on the grounds that new ideas, problems, and

---

[1] See in this connection Bose, *The Indian Struggle*, ch. 16.

programmes had emerged and with them a feeling among the rank and file that the elections should be contested. On the 24th the Old Guard counter-attacked. Led by Patel and Prasad, seven members of the Working Committee issued a statement dissenting from Bose's views. They claimed that preceding elections had been unanimous and that, while Bose had a right to contest it, party unity would be jeopardized. They backed Sitaramayya, stating that this decision 'was taken with much deliberation'. They doubted the wisdom of one person succeeding himself except under special circumstances and added that, in any event, the President was only first among equals. Hence they called upon Bose to withdraw. Patel later revealed in a private letter to Nehru that this statement had been drafted at Gandhi's urging.[1]

Bose replied vigorously the next day. It was wrong for Working Committee members to support one candidate against another, he declared. He had no knowledge of the 'deliberation' on Sitaramayya's candidacy, implying a conspiracy. He noted, correctly, that presidents had been re-elected in the past, and urged that the President should be likened to a Prime Minister rather than a constitutional monarch. Policy questions are not irrelevant, said Bose; the only reason they had not been raised before was that Leftists (Nehru and himself) had been in the presidential chair since 1936. Now, however, there was a widespread belief that the Right wing was prepared to compromise on the crucial issue of an All-India Federation, as embodied in the 1935 Government of India Act. He was prepared to withdraw in favour of a genuine anti-federationist like Narendra Dev, the Socialist.

The Old Guard was unwilling to compromise. Patel countered on the 25th that no principles were involved and that it had been agreed in informal conversations that if Azad withdrew, Sitaramayya was 'the only choice left'. The next day Bose declared that he would go ahead. Nehru entered the picture on the 27th with a conciliatory statement. The controversy had taken a wrong turn and had raised the wrong issues. There was no conflict over the Federation, he said. 'Personally, I do

---

[1] 'The joint statement was also issued at his [Gandhi's] instance. In fact I told him that this will be one more pretext to hurl abuses against me but he insisted and I obeyed him.' Patel to Nehru, 8 February 1939. Unpublished Nehru Letters.

not see what principles or programmes are at stake', he added, in a rebuke to Bose. But he also turned on the Old Guard: 'The Congress President is not, in my opinion, merely a speaker.' Gandhi took no direct part in the controversy during this early phase. But on 28 January, the day before the election, he published an article in *Harijan* entitled 'Internal Decay'. 'Out of the present condition of the Congress', he wrote, 'I see nothing but anarchy and red ruin in front of the country.' The advice was clear.

To the consternation of the Old Guard, Bose was re-elected, by 1,580 to 1,375. Gandhi took it as a personal snub and declared, 'I rejoice in this defeat.' He made it known that he had opposed Bose but called on the minority to co-operate with the President. Bose expressed grief at the Mahatma's attitude, as well as the hope that he would win Gandhi's confidence. So ended round one. The real struggle was about to begin.

In the middle of February Bose consulted Gandhi at his *ashram* in Wardha, but no decisions were reached. A meeting of the (old) Working Committee was scheduled for the 22nd. Bose, lying ill in Calcutta, issued a statement renewing the charge that some members of the Working Committee were prepared to compromise on the Federation issue. To make matters worse he sent a telegram prohibiting the Committee from transacting any business, even of a procedural nature. Taking this as a vote of no-confidence, and perhaps as an ideal pretext to nullify Bose's election victory, twelve of the fifteen members of the Working Committee resigned; their letter was 'believed to have been drafted by Gandhi'.[1] The three exceptions were Bose himself, his brother, Sarat, and Nehru.

Nehru tried to mediate by asking Bose to retract the charge against the Old Guard, but without success. They had no choice in the circumstances, he said. And yet he refused to follow their lead or that of anyone else. He did not resign officially, but he did issue a separate statement that he would not serve on the new Working Committee. The press interpreted it as resignation; 'not quite correct,' remarked Nehru later, 'and yet . . . correct enough'.[2] Thus he appeared to have aligned himself with the Old Guard. In reality he was closer to Bose—'my

[1] Tendulkar, *Mahatma*, vol. 5, p. 56.
[2] 'Where Are We?' in *The Unity of India*, p. 87.

parting was more with them than with others [Bose]'. Actually he was in isolation once more, trying desperately to maintain party unity.

The substantive point of conflict, if there was one, concerned the composition of the Working Committee. The Old Guard and Gandhi desired a 'homogeneous' High Command whereas Bose urged a composite Committee to represent various groups in the party. Nehru adopted a typical middle-of-the-road approach which reflected his role throughout the crisis. The urgent need of the day was a united front; and this must be under the leadership of Gandhi and the Old Guard, for 'the Left *today* can destroy; it cannot build. . . . To over-reach the mark now might mean reaction tomorrow.' But this did not justify a sectarian 'homogeneity' in the Working Committee; elements of the Left should be included.[1]

The struggle for power shifted to the larger stage of the Congress annual session which opened in the village of Tripuri on 7 March. During the intervening weeks the Old Guard had marshalled their forces in the A.I.C.C. for a showdown with the 'upstart' President who had flouted Gandhi's wishes. The drama was heightened by the Mahatma's decision to begin a fast a few days before the session, over a relatively trivial issue in the princely State of Rajkot. The fast ended as the Subjects Committee (the All-India Congress Committee when it meets at annual sessions) began its deliberations.

Bose arrived from Calcutta in critical health and was able to attend only the two sessions of the Subjects Committee, on the 8th and 9th. The Old Guard moved to the attack. On the 8th Pandit Pant tabled a resolution backed by 160 delegates which called for firm adherence to the fundamental policies of the past under Gandhi's leadership, expressed confidence in the old Working Committee and deep regret at the aspersions cast upon it by Bose, and, most important, 'requests [!] the President to appoint the Working Committee in accordance with the wishes of Gandhiji'. There was a tumultuous uproar. For two days the battle raged in the Subjects Committee. Bose's supporters claimed that it was a vote of censure, but the Right wing was unmoved. The resolution passed.

The following day Bose was carried to the open session where

[1] Ibid., pp. 124–5. (Emphasis added.)

his presidential address was read. He proposed a threefold radical programme: an ultimatum to the *Raj* with a specific time limit, and if this were rejected, the launching of mass civil disobedience; positive guidance to the freedom movement in the princely States; and close co-operation with all other 'anti-imperialist' organizations, especially peasant leagues and trade unions.

Bose was too ill to appear on the second day of the open session, and so Azad, the most senior ex-Congress President, took the chair. Fearing Bose's strength among the delegates at large, the Old Guard proposed that the censure resolution be referred to the A.I.C.C. for disposal later, ostensibly because of the President's illness. A tremendous demonstration by Bose's supporters followed. Nehru rose to speak but he was repeatedly interrupted. For half an hour he waited patiently. Then he turned on his hecklers: 'It is time to be united and disciplined. It is a grievous sight, a painful sight. . . . During the last twenty-six years, I have attended the Indian National Congress year after year; I have never seen such a scene, though I have seen many strange things.'[1] Turning to Bose's brother, Sarat, he lashed out at 'this hooliganism and fascist behaviour', but his words were carried on the microphone, adding to the uproar. Yet in the course of his remarks he tried to mediate again, by assuring his audience that Gandhi was preparing for another non-violent struggle. In the face of strong opposition the Old Guard's proposal to shelve the censure resolution was withdrawn.

A more moderate 'National Demand' was put forward by Narayan, leader of the Congress Socialists, who followed Gandhi's lead. It reaffirmed the party's goals but without an ultimatum. Sarat Bose expressed the mood of the 'rebels' when he attacked it as 'merely words, words, words, ineffective words, soulless words. . . . [They] do not lay down any plan of action.'[2] Nehru supported the 'official' resolution, which was carried in the open session. The victory of the Old Guard was complete. Not only was Gandhi's policy accepted, but the censure resolution was passed, after a fiery debate. The key to Bose's defeat was the abstention of the Congress Socialists. Nehru's vote is unknown. The climax was still to come.

[1] Tendulkar, op. cit., vol. 5, pp. 78–9.
[2] *Report of the Fifty-Second Indian National Congress, Tripuri, 1939*, p. 93.

Throughout the 'Tripuri Crisis' Nehru and Bose carried on a spirited correspondence which reveals much about their relationship, their political differences and their frustrating roles—Bose in his inability to break down Gandhi's opposition, Nehru in his failure to mediate in the conflict. Just after Bose's election Nehru asked him to clarify his views on a wide range of problems. Bose replied at very great length a few weeks after the Tripuri session and levelled a series of charges against his 'elder brother'. Nehru's response on 3 April 1939 is an illuminating document.

'Your letter is essentially an indictment of my conduct and an investigation into my failings. . . . So far as the failings are concerned . . . I have little to say. I plead guilty to them. May I also say that I entirely appreciate the truth of your remark that ever since you came out of internment in 1937 you treated me with the utmost regard and consideration. . . . Personally, I have always had and still have, regard and affection for you, though sometimes I did not like at all what you did or how you did it. To some extent, I suppose, we are temperamentally different and our approach to life and its problems is not the same.'

As for challenging Gandhi: 'It is of course absurd to say that there should be unity at any cost. . . . It all depends on the circumstances . . . and I was convinced at the time [before the election] that the pushing out, or the attempt to push out Gandhi and his group would weaken us greatly at a critical moment. I was not prepared to face that contingency. . . . We might have to face a big struggle in the course of a few months. That struggle, without Gandhiji's active participation and leadership, was not likely to be an effective one.'

Regarding the resignation of the Old Guard and Bose's allegations: 'It is obviously not good enough for . . . the Congress President to repeat press rumours or bazaar statements. . . . It was a fantastic statement and it hurt to the quick. . . . [It] was an effective barrier to any further co-operation between you and Gandhiji. . . . I pressed you therefore to clear this barrier and have a frank talk with Gandhiji [but you did not] . . . . It made me realise how difficult it was to work together with you . . .'

As for Nehru's handling of party affairs: 'You say that "in

the habit of interfering from the top, no Congress President can beat" me. I realise that I am an interfering sort of person but . . . I do not recollect having interfered with the work of the office of the A.I.C.C. though I sought to influence it frequently . . .'

About his 'resignation' Nehru wrote: 'I felt strongly that under the circumstances I could not offer you my co-operation, but I felt equally strongly that I was in a sense breaking with the others. In fact the latter feeling was the stronger. . . . I had been pressed hard to join the others in their resignation. I had refused.'

Bose's re-election was opposed partly because it would have meant a break with Gandhi and partly because it would have been,

I thought, a set-back for the real Left. . . . There were so many disruptive tendencies already existing in the country and instead of controlling them, we would add to them. I saw also that you were closely associated with a number of odd individuals who were apparently influencing you considerably. . . . The fact that . . . you . . . did not wholly approve our condemnation of Nazi Germany or Fascist Italy added to my discomfort, and looking at the picture as a whole, I did not at all fancy the direction in which you apparently wanted us to go.

One personal aspect. . . . I felt all along that you were too keen on re-election. . . . it did distress me for I felt that you had a big enough position to be above that kind of thing.

Regarding the censure resolution, Nehru related that he had tried to tone it down and did not like the final draft. Further, he had told the Old Guard: 'I would take no part in the discussion.' Just before it was moved in the Subjects Committee he had tried again to tone it down but was told 'it was a question of honour'. 'I made one more strenuous effort to get the resolution varied on the eve of the open session when you were lying very ill.'

In one of his more significant passages Nehru remarked: 'To my misfortune, I am affected by international happenings more than I should be. . . . I felt that we should not passively await events.'

About Nehru's traits as administrator and draftsman: 'You are right in saying that as President I functioned often as a secretary or a glorified clerk. I have long developed the habit of being my own secretary and clerk and I fear I encroach in this way on others' preserves. It is also true that because of me Congress resolutions have tended to become long and verbose and rather like theses. In the Working Committee, I fear, I talked too much and did not always behave as I should.'

About the overall effect of his role in the crisis up to that point: 'You refer to my "clients". . . . I have succeeded in becoming very unpopular with them. Quite a remarkable feat— to displease almost everybody concerned.'

Perhaps the most illuminating passage relates to Nehru's political philosophy: 'Am I a Socialist or an individualist? Is there a necessary contradiction in the two terms?. . . . I suppose I am temperamentally and by training an individualist, and intellectually a socialist. . . . I hope that socialism does not kill or suppress individuality; indeed I am attracted to it because it will release innumerable individuals from economic and cultural bondage.'[1]

During the six weeks following the Tripuri session Nehru made strenuous efforts to heal the breach between Gandhi and Bose. Bose was markedly conciliatory and he relied heavily on Nehru's advice. But Gandhi seemed determined to oust him.

Despite Nehru's candid criticism of Bose (as well as of himself), Bose wrote soon after this letter, 'I would very much like to have your reaction as well as your advice as to how I should proceed next.' Referring to his letter to Gandhi, Bose remarked: 'I have ended by saying that failing everything, he [Gandhi] should accept the responsibility of forming the Working Committee.' And to Nehru, 'I feel that if no settlement is effected through correspondence, I should make a last effort at settlement through a personal talk with Gandhiji. . . . Will it be possible for you to run up here for a few hours? We could then have a talk . . .' Although Bose was often at odds with Gandhi, more so in 1939 than at any other time, he too was under the Mahatma's spell. To Nehru he added, 'I am rather worried about Gandhiji's fever. I do hope that it will pass off soon. If however it persists—which God forbid—what shall we do?'[2]

Nehru's attempt at mediation and his opposition to Gandhi's attitude to Bose are evident in his letter to the Mahatma on

[1] Unpublished Nehru Letters. [2] Ibid., 15 and 20 April 1939.

17 April: 'I think now, as I thought in Delhi, that you should accept Subhas [Bose] as President. To try to push him out seems to me to be an exceedingly wrong step. As for the Working Committee, it is for you to decide. . . . I would beg of you, therefore, to make up your mind to settle this matter, even though that way of settlement may not be to the liking of all of us.'[1]

The belief that Bose was determined to have his way is brought into serious question by his letter to Gandhi on 20 April: 'From all accounts it should be clear beyond a shadow of doubt that we are approaching a crisis of unprecedented magnitude. We can hope to cope with it only if we sink our differences at once and do our very best to restore unity and discipline within our ranks. This task can be achieved only if you come forward and take the lead. In that event you will find that all of us will do our very best to co-operate with and follow you.'[2]

The climax of the 'Tripuri Crisis' was at hand. Bose and Gandhi held prolonged conversations in Calcutta on the eve of the A.I.C.C. meeting beginning on 29 April. The Mahatma's advice was to form a Working Committee of Bose's own choice. Bose refused on the grounds that it was contrary to the Tripuri directive and that in time of crisis the Congress needed a composite High Command. Gandhi replied that if he (Gandhi) formed the Committee it would be an imposition on Bose as President and suggested consultations with members of the old Committee. The talks ended in failure.

Having exhausted all avenues of conciliation, Bose submitted his resignation. Nehru made a final effort at compromise by asking him to withdraw his resignation and to reappoint the old Working Committee. As for 'new blood', there would be two vacancies shortly, he added. Bose refused, terming Nehru's proposal essentially the same as that of Gandhi and others. A final appeal by Sarojini Naidu was ineffective, too, and so the A.I.C.C. proceeded to elect a new president, Dr. Rajendra Prasad, one of the most prominent of the Old Guard. Bose's supporters claimed it was unconstitutional but were overruled. The old Working Committee remained in office, except for Bose, his brother and Nehru. But Nehru pledged his co-operation. The Bose faction walked out and soon after Bose formed the Forward Bloc—theoretically within the Congress.

[1] Unpublished Nehru Letters.   [2] Ibid.

The epilogue came a few months later. At the end of June 1939 the A.I.C.C. passed two resolutions aimed at any attempt to usurp the powers of the High Command: an order to all Provincial Congress Committees to cease any form of interference with the Congress governments and a directive that non-co-operation should not be resorted to without the sanction of the A.I.C.C. Early in July Bose organized demonstrations against the two directives, providing an opportunity to destroy the last vestige of his power within the party. This was done on 12 August. Bose was removed as President of the Bengal Provincial Congress Committee for indiscipline, and was disqualified from any elective office in the party for three years. The 'rebellion' had been crushed. Early in 1941 Bose was to leave India, never to return.[1]

* * * *

Nehru was unhappy about this unsavoury affair. By that time, too, the twenty years' armistice in the world war was drawing to a close. He was able to escape temporarily, in a manner often resorted to in the past. The Indian National Congress had a standing invitation to send a representative to China to strengthen the bonds between the nationalist movements of the two largest Asian states. What better time than now, when China was in the midst of a death struggle with a foreign invader and India was tottering towards war? The obvious choice was Nehru, the party's acknowledged spokesman on foreign affairs. He had already served as 'ambassador to the east' on two occasions. In 1937 he visited Burma and Malaya for six weeks, primarily to bring greetings to the large Indian communities in those countries. And in the summer of 1939 he went to Ceylon in an effort to reduce the friction between Indian settlers and the Sinhalese. Twenty years later this problem remains unsolved.

Nehru left India on 20 August 1939 to spend four weeks in Nationalist-held China, but the war intervened. He remained only twelve days. Most of his visit was spent in Chungking,

[1] For the details of the final acts in the Tripuri story see *Congress Bulletin*, No. 2, 19 May 1939, pp. 2–13, and No. 4, 7 September 1939, pp. 19–22. Bose was killed in an aeroplane crash in 1945. For an account of his war-time activities in South-East Asia, see pp. 305–6, below.

where few visitors were greeted with such enthusiasm and
respect, a symbol of the hoped-for alliance between India and
China in the 'brave new world'. As usual he was brimming
over with vitality. With boyish enthusiasm he insisted on walking, at times running, up the three hundred steps leading to the
city. After this invigorating experience he wrote that he realized
that he was no longer a young man: he was then just short of
fifty. Meetings with Chinese leaders from all walks of life
occupied him around the clock. Nightly air-raids added a touch
of realism to his stay in the Chinese capital.

Nehru's diary of this 'voyage of discovery' reveals a deep
interest in Chinese civilization, admiration for Chinese courage
against formidable odds, and perception of the dramatic
changes to take place a decade later: 'A new China is rising,
rooted in her culture, but shedding the lethargy and weakness
of ages, strong and united . . .'[1] Fifteen years after this 'personal visit', he returned to China as India's Prime Minister, to
find, not without some concern, how accurate was this observation.[2]

[1] Nehru's account of his visit to China in 1939 is to be found in *China, Spain and
the War*, pp. 11–53.

[2] See pp. 529–30, and 591–2 below.

CHAPTER XI

The War and Inner Torment

'MUNICH' had come and gone, but the illusion of peace was soon to be dispelled. In the spring of 1939 the German army marched into Prague and occupied the remnants of Czechoslovakia, despite the solemn pledge of the Great Powers. The world was drifting rapidly towards war.

Jawaharlal Nehru had long been sensitive to the changing currents of the international situation and their impact on India's freedom struggle. This was apparent in his writings and speeches, notably in the *Glimpses of World History* and the *Autobiography*, and in his presidential addresses to the Congress in 1929, 1936 and 1937. His observation of the realities of war in Spain had added emotional depth to intellectual conviction. Now, as the world approached its gravest crisis for twenty-five years, Nehru pondered the implications for his native land, especially for the Indian nationalist movement.

In the West, he wrote a few months before the war, nationalism had been a source of good in the nineteenth century, the inspiration of unity, democracy and the flowering of culture. By the 1930's, however, it had become the parent of aggressiveness, intolerance and racial discrimination, serving as a camouflage for the most reactionary features of European life. By contrast, nationalism in the East at the present time produced unity, vitality, strength and a cultural renaissance.

He agreed that nationalism ultimately becomes identified with reaction and that even in its liberating phase it is a narrow creed. India was no exception. But with added strength, he argued, movements for national freedom develop a broader horizon, as India had done in the 'thirties, and recognize their own struggle as part of a world phenomenon.

Turning to the domestic arena, Nehru anticipated the tragic controversy over India's role in the war. If Britain recognized its claim to freedom, India would be prepared to make trade and financial concessions, and 'would be a friend and colleague

in world affairs . . .' But if Britain chose the path of continued
domination, it was absurd to think that Indian nationalists
would support London's lead in foreign policy. India in the
spring of 1939 looked anxiously at the world, he concluded.
And within, it posed a picture of tension between nationalism
and British rule.[1]

Later in the summer Nehru expressed the mood of millions
of people in all lands: 'The world is in a tragic mess; tragic to
those who are sensitive, heartbreaking to those who feel.'[2] Less
than a fortnight before the Germans marched into Poland, he
wrote, 'We sit on the edge of a sword, balancing precariously,
and waiting for the succession of events.'[3]

On 3 September the uncertainty came to an end: the Viceroy
proclaimed India a belligerent state. The legality of the act
was beyond dispute, but it was done without as much as a
gesture of consulting India's political leaders. To Lord Linlithgow and British officials generally it was axiomatic that 'the
crown jewel of the Empire' would automatically come to the
assistance of Great Britain in time of need. To Nehru and most
Indian nationalists, however, the issue appeared in an entirely
different light. Surveying the world scene in the autumn of
1939, they termed it an 'imperialist' war, a struggle between
'aggressive' Fascism, seeking further power, prestige and
wealth, and 'reactionary' Britain and France, clinging to the
spoils of empire. A subject India, they had often declared,
would not participate in such a conflict unless its right to
freedom were acknowledged.

As early as 1927, at the Madras session of the Congress,
Nehru had stated this view in his 'Resolution on the War
Danger': 'The Congress declares that the people of India have
no quarrel with their neighbours. . . . [In the event of Britain
entering an 'imperialist' war] it will be the duty of the people
of India to refuse to take part in such a war or to co-operate
with them in any way whatsoever.'[4] Nor was this a whim of the
moment. At Lucknow in 1936, at Faizpur in 1937, at Haripura
in 1938, and most recently at the Tripuri session in March

---

[1] 'Anxious India' in *Asia*, May 1939.
[2] Quoted in Anup Singh, *Nehru*, p. 147.
[3] On 18 August 1939. *China, Spain and the War*, p. 17.
[4] *Report of the Forty-Second Indian National Congress at Madras, 1927*, p. 5.

1939, the Congress had reaffirmed this policy. The Viceroy's decree could not but arouse indignation among Indian nationalists. In particular, they resented the technique of *force majeure*.

Many British liberals were also perturbed by this episode. As Edward Thompson, the distinguished novelist and critic, wrote to Nehru, 'at any rate, one or two points have sunk deeply and widely. Everyone now knows that we made a gross error when we declared India a belligerent without consulting her.'[1] The decree was, indeed, a political blunder which set in motion the protracted negotiations between the Congress and the British *Raj* from 1939 to 1942, culminating in the 'August Rebellion'.

For Nehru the war crisis was an agonizing quest for an honourable political settlement with Britain which would permit active Congress participation in the war on the Allies' side. On the one hand he was emotionally and intellectually hostile to the Axis powers. At the same time he was devoted to the cause of Indian freedom. For most of his colleagues the dilemma was easily resolved. Their vision was narrow, the war in Europe was remote, and their energies were channelled into the struggle for independence. But Nehru was an internationalist who felt deeply the challenge of Fascism. As a result, his was a constant torment between these two highly-charged political currents. The polar attractions of anti-fascism and Indian freedom were never reconciled, for the forces ranged against him proved to be insurmountable.

From the outbreak of war Nehru favoured active support to the Allies—if freedom were granted to India. He never wavered from this policy, but in vain. The British Government consistently rejected his condition. And within the Congress he was confronted with Gandhi's powerful opposition to the use of violence under any circumstances. Ultimately, Nehru's allegiance to nationalism triumphed.

Nehru's role during the war may best be sketched within the framework of a five-act drama, for such was the character of the Indian war crisis. The cast includes many prominent statesmen of the age—Gandhi, Nehru, Jinnah, Linlithgow, Cripps, Churchill, Roosevelt and others. There were various sub-plots

[1] Unpublished Nehru Letters, 28 April 1940.

to the main theme. The climax was rebellion and mass imprisonments. For Nehru it meant frustrated isolation while the fate of the world was being decided.

*   *   *   *

The first act opened with the Viceroy's proclamation of belligerency on 3 September. Five days later the Congress Working Committee met at Wardha in emergency session. Nehru cut short his goodwill mission to China and hurried back on the 10th. Then, on 14 September, the Congress issued the first of many statements on the 'War Crisis and India'. The Viceroy's slight was ignored and the Congress view clearly stated: 'If the war is to defend the status quo, imperialist possessions, colonies, vested interests and privilege, then India can have nothing to do with it. If, however, the issue is democracy and a world order based on democracy, then India is intensely interested in it. . . . A free democratic India will gladly associate herself with other free nations for mutual defence against aggression and for economic co-operation . . . [but] co-operation must be between equals and by mutual consent.' The Congress then passed the burden of decision to the Viceroy: 'The Working Committee therefore invite the British Government to declare in unequivocal terms what their war aims are in regard to democracy and imperialism and the new order that is envisaged; in particular, how these aims are going to apply to India and to be given effect to in the present. . . . The real test of any declaration is its application in the present . . .'[1]

Nehru's vital role in shaping the 'war aims resolution' was confirmed by Gandhi.[2] In doing so the Mahatma also provided an illuminating commentary on his political heir: 'The author of the statement is an artist. Though he cannot be surpassed in his implacable opposition to imperialism in any shape or form,

---

[1] The text is in *Congress Bulletin*, No. 5, 25 September 1939, pp. 8–14.

[2] According to V. P. Menon, a senior Indian civil servant at the time, Gandhi told the Viceroy a few weeks later 'that, had he been ten or fifteen years younger he would probably have taken the responsibility for drafting the resolution, in which event it might have emerged in a very different form. But he thought that the burden was more than he could carry by himself at his age and he had felt bound to take Nehru with him, even though their views might not coincide.' *The Transfer of Power in India*, p. 63.

he is a friend of the English people. Indeed, *he is more English than Indian in his thoughts and make-up.* He is often more at home with Englishmen than with his own countrymen. And he is a humanitarian in the sense that he reacts to every wrong, no matter where perpetrated . . . his nationalism is enriched by his fine internationalism. Hence the statement is a manifesto addressed not only to his own countrymen, not only to the British Government and the British people, but is addressed also to the nations of the world including those that are exploited like India. He has compelled India, through the Working Committee, to think not merely of her own freedom but of the freedom of all the exploited nations of the world.'[1] This, indeed, was one of Nehru's contributions to Indian nationalism.

Yet all was not well within the Congress High Command. With typical candour the Mahatma revealed that he was alone in thinking that if support were given to the British it should be unconditional. He was also dissatisfied with the policy of active co-operation in the war, including the use of violence, of which Nehru was the leading advocate. Writing to Nehru on 10 October 1939 he stressed this disagreement, one of the main subplots in the war drama. 'Differences in outlook between us are becoming most marked. I hold very strong views on the most important questions. . . . I know you too hold strong views on them but different from mine. . . . I feel that I must not lead, if I cannot carry you all with me. . . . I feel that you should take full charge and lead the country, leaving me free to voice me own opinion' or to remain silent if the Working Committee thinks it desirable.[2]

The breach widened during the following months, and a temporary split ultimately occurred. At this time, however, an open break was avoided, probably because Gandhi's leadership was still considered indispensable; partly, no doubt, because of the Viceroy's vague response to the Congress 'war aims' resolution. For the duration of the war Linlithgow offered to include more Indians in his Executive Council, the supreme advisory and administrative body for the Viceroys of British India until 1947. The Congress demand for an immediate transfer of substantial power was dismissed as impracticable. But as a sop to nationalist

---

[1] Tendulkar, op. cit., vol. 5, pp. 204–5. (Emphasis added.)
[2] Ibid., vol. 8, Appendix on Gandhi-Nehru Letters, p. 363.

aspirations, the British Government would be willing to consult with the communities, political parties and Princes—at the end of the war—in order to consider modifications in the 1935 India Act, so that 'India may attain her due place among the great Dominions'.[1]

The gap was too great to permit mutual trust and compromise. Instead of an unequivocal assurance of Indian freedom, the Congress was promised only 'consultation' at some future date, with the ultimate goal of Dominion status, which had been rejected as early as 1929. Thus the Working Committee rejected Linlithgow's invitation and called on the eight Congress provincial governments to resign before the end of October. And yet the door to co-operation was left open. '*In the circumstances*', it declared, 'the Committee cannot possibly give any support to Great Britain for it would amount to an endorsement of the imperialist policy . . .'[2] Twice more before the end of the year the Congress reiterated its offer of conditional co-operation, but in vain.

Throughout the autumn negotiations Nehru performed a dual political function; he was chief draftsman of party resolutions and the principal Congress publicist. In a series of articles at the time he pleaded the nationalist case with supreme passion. Over and over again a few themes were cogently stated: India's sympathies lie with the Allies, as testified by Congress policy declarations in the 'thirties; only a free India can play a meaningful role in a war for democracy; England must demonstrate its sincerity by stating its war aims boldly, and these must include freedom for India; friendship is possible between India and England but only on equal terms.

The immediate cause of the war, he wrote, 'is the growth and aggression of Fascism and Nazism. . . . It is clear, therefore, that we must oppose Fascism. . . . [But] we cannot serve a victory over Fascism by surrendering our freedom and the struggle to achieve it.' Here, in essence, was Nehru's view throughout the war. It would be a lengthy war, he predicted at this early stage, and would develop into a world conflict. In the long run the advantages would lie with the Allies because of their superiority in resources. Germany would break with the

---

[1] Cmd. 6121, *India and the War*, 17 October 1939.
[2] *Congress Bulletin*, No. 7, 9 December 1939, p. 3. (Emphasis added.)

Soviet Union, and America would become a fully-fledged member of the anti-fascist coalition.[1]

There was an air of unreality about the Congress–British negotiations in the autumn of 1939. The Congress attached the stigma of colonialism to Dominion status and wanted tangible evidence of real power immediately, however limited it might be for the duration of the war. The British were extremely rigid in their approach. The mentality of the white *sahib* remained unchanged, the sense of 'white man's burden' was too deeply rooted in the minds of British policy-makers. Imagination and vision were sadly lacking, both in London and Delhi. They acted as if this were still the age of Kipling, not of Hitler.

The Viceroy throughout this crucial period was Lord Linlithgow, of whom Nehru wrote with brutal candour:

Heavy of body and slow of mind, solid as a rock and with almost a rock's lack of awareness, possessing the qualities and failings of an old-fashioned British aristocrat, he sought with integrity and honesty of purpose to find a way out of the tangle. But his limitations were too many; his mind worked in the old groove and shrank back from any innovations; his vision was limited by the traditions of the ruling class out of which he came; he saw and heard through the eyes and ears of the Civil Service and others who surrounded him; he distrusted people who talked of fundamental political and social changes; he disliked those who did not show a becoming appreciation of the high mission of the British Empire and its chief representative in India.[2]

More important than Linlithgow's failings was the fact that this was the period of the 'phoney war', when the armies of France and Germany faced each other across the Maginot Line in a spectacle of armed truce. The threat to Britain was still remote, its Asian empire relatively secure. As long as these conditions prevailed neither the India Office nor the Viceroy was prepared to make any real concessions. Only in the face of imminent catastrophe, more than two years later, did they attempt to break the deadlock. By that time it was too late.

Amidst these fruitless negotiations on the main front an

---

[1] *China, Spain and the War*, pp. 159–233. The quotation is from pp. 160–1.

[2] *The Discovery of India* (Signet Press, Calcutta), p. 528.

attempt was made to heal the breach between the Congress and the Muslim League, the second important sub-plot of the war drama. As so often in the past Nehru was appointed Congress delegate to the renewed talks with Jinnah which had proved abortive the preceding year. The League was in a more receptive mood. Nehru was so informed by Raghunandan Saran, a prominent Congress lawyer who paved the way by conversations with Jinnah and Liaquat Ali Khan. After a meeting with Liaquat he wrote: 'Very feelingly he began his conversation with the remark that if only our Leaders would rise to the Great Occasion we could successfully exploit this great opportunity to win our freedom. After all, the communal differences were not insuperable.' Jinnah, too, seemed friendly. 'Talking about you,' wrote Saran to Nehru, 'he said that he had affection for you coupled with high regard for your character and integrity. . . . It is a tragedy that the matter [the Hindu–Muslim problem] could not be settled in a friendly spirit, said he. He went on to say that we were not poles asunder; we were very much closer than we thought we were.'[1]

The talks were never held. Jinnah changed his mind and proclaimed a 'Day of Deliverance' from the 'tyranny, oppression and injustice' of Congress rule, referring to the resignation of the Congress ministries. He also repeated the charges of Congress oppression of Muslims contained in the *Pirpur Report* of 1938. Gandhi appealed to him to call off the 'Day of Deliverance', but to no avail. Nehru expressed his annoyance to Mahadev Desai, Gandhi's private secretary: 'You must have seen Jinnah's new statement. There is a limit even to political falsehood and indecency but all limits have been passed. I do not see how I can even meet Jinnah now.'[2]

The change in Jinnah's attitude is difficult to explain, but most well-informed persons are agreed that the Viceroy sought to weaken the Congress at this time and to strengthen the League. 'When . . . the Congress resigned [provincial] office,' wrote V. P. Menon, 'Lord Linlithgow's attitude automatically changed. . . . [He] began to lean more on the support of the Muslim League. . . . For all practical purposes Jinnah was given a veto on further constitutional progress. . . . The

---

[1] Unpublished Nehru Letters, 14 and 17 October 1939.
[2] Ibid., 9 December 1939.

Viceroy even discouraged the efforts of certain well-wishers to bridge the gulf between the Congress and the Government.'[1]

An uneasy quiet descended upon the Indian political scene after the hectic autumn days, the counterpart of military stalemate in western Europe. In both cases it was a lull before the storm. In both it gave rise to a tendency to seek a compromise. Not all Congressmen favoured the resignation of the Congress governments, especially those who had tasted the fruits of power. Some pressed for a return to office. Nehru's fears in this regard were conveyed to Gandhi early in February 1940, on the eve of one of the Mahatma's meetings with the Viceroy. 'An atmosphere of approaching compromise pervades the country', he warned,

when, in effect, there is no ground for it. It is enervating and depressing because it does not come out of strength but, in the case of many individuals, from the excessive desire to avoid conflict at all costs and to get back to the shreds of power which we had previously [i.e. the Congress provincial ministries]. . . . It seems to me that while we cannot and must not precipitate a conflict and, while we need not bang the door to a possible and honourable compromise . . . still we must make it crystal clear that there can be or will be no compromise except on conditions stated by us previously.[2]

Nehru's concern lest Gandhi concede too much to the Viceroy proved to be unfounded. The talk failed to resolve the deadlock.[3] The stage was now set for the climax to Act I of the war crisis. The place—Ramgarh, a small town in the province of Bihar; the time—17 March to 20 March 1940; the occasion— the annual session of the Congress; the mood—frustration, mixed with a determination to break out of the impasse by some form of action, very much like the mood at Lahore in 1929. On both occasions the deadlock in negotiations led to civil disobedience.

The policy of direct conflict with the *Raj* heralded Gandhi's return to the centre of the political stage. Whenever the opportunity for negotiation arose during the war Nehru came to the fore. But in time of open struggle, as always in the past, the Congress turned to its mentor. Thus, in this phase of the war

[1] *The Transfer of Power in India*, pp. 69–72.
[2] Unpublished Nehru Letters, 4 February 1940.
[3] For an account of this conversation, see Menon, op. cit., pp. 74–7.

drama Nehru's role receded into the background. His only contribution at Ramgarh was a superb translation of Maulana Azad's presidential address from literary Urdu to intelligible English.[1]

Although the Mahatma was not even a formal member of the party—he had resigned from the Congress in 1934—his power was absolute at this time. It was he who pressed for civil disobedience as the way out. All his conditions were accepted, including a period of delay until the organization was, in his view, ready for non-violent war. Gandhi was in complete control; the Congress awaited his word of command. In his own blunt words to the delegates, 'as soldiers we have got to take orders from the General and obey them implicitly. His word must be law. I am your General.'

Among the critics, M. N. Roy, the defeated candidate for Congress President and semi-legendary ex-Communist, called for the establishment of parallel governments by primary Congress committees. The Communists dissented because of the implication that the war was 'imperialist' only because nationalist India's demands had not been conceded. A few called for the immediate drafting of a 'national' constitution by the Congress, and others, impatient for action, pleaded for immediate civil disobedience. But these were voices in the wilderness. At the open session all six proposed amendments were rejected and the original (Gandhi) resolution was passed by a vote of 2,500 to 16. Once again the Gandhian touch seemed to restore unity and hope to the party.

In reply to those who criticized his dilatory tactics, Gandhi declared: 'You must know that compromise is in my very being. I will go to the Viceroy fifty times if there is need for it.' A

---

[1] Most Indians deplore Nehru's alleged inadequacy in his native language. It is surprising, therefore, to find the following tribute from Azad, an acknowledged peer among Indian Urdu scholars: 'The impression it has created upon me compels me to shake off my usual reserve for the moment and offer my sincere tribute to your first-rate intellect and exceptional talents. . . . What particularly strikes me in your translation is the fact that no feature of the original has suffered through it and you have conveyed my Urdu literary style so successfully in English that I should not be surprised if it occurs to the reader that the original was English and not Urdu! An equally impressive feature is your remarkable grasp of the architectonic imagination from which the details flow. You have perfectly visualised my imagination. . . . Surely, it was a stupendous task. . . .' Unpublished Nehru Letters, 27 March 1940.

striking fact was the lack of any concrete plan of action, typical of Gandhi's methods. Acharya Kripalani, then General-Secretary of the Congress, tried to rationalize this by informing his colleagues, 'the struggle is inherent in the situation. Nay, it has already commenced.' But in reality the Congress had merely transferred all power to the Mahatma, with complete discretion to act when and as he saw fit.[1]

*   *   *   *

While Congressmen waited for Gandhi's call to action, events moved swiftly in the West. In May 1940 the German blitzkrieg gathered momentum. First the Scandinavian countries, then Holland and Belgium, and finally France, fell before the *panzer* onslaught. Hitler's armies were poised at the Channel, and England stood alone, open to invasion. This rapid sweep of events caused second thoughts among the Congress élite, especially in Nehru, the leader most sensitive to the general world situation. The collapse of France, the retreat at Dunkirk and the heroic defence of Britain against massive aerial bombardment evoked considerable sympathy in nationalist circles, though a few like Subhas Bose viewed England's peril as India's opportunity.

Nehru strongly opposed civil disobedience at this crucial juncture. The idea of using England's distress for political advantage was utterly repugnant. 'Satyagraha [non-co-operation] is not immediately indicated even if we were ready for it', he wrote to Prasad. 'I think it would be wrong for us at this particular moment, when Britain is in peril, to take advantage of her distress and rush at her throat.' Gandhi shared this view, but Azad dissented. 'I fail absolutely to grasp this mode of thinking', he wrote to Nehru. 'We gave Britain fullest opportunity to take us with her, but she stubbornly refused to do so. We were forced to decide not to participate in this Imperialist War. If our present stand is such that it "embarrasses" her . . . we are not responsible for it; it lies with the imprudent vanity of the British Government.'[2]

---

[1] *Report of the Indian National Congress at Ramgarh 1940* and *Congress Bulletin,* No. 1, 12 April 1940, pp. 2–16. The quotations from Gandhi's speeches are on pp. 89 and 90 of the *Annual Report*; the extract from Kripalani's circular is on p. 22 of the *Bulletin.*

[2] Unpublished Nehru Letters, 25 May 1940.

Despite Azad's criticism, Nehru reflected the fundamental change in mood as a result of the French débâcle. The tide of battle in Europe was a turning-point in the Congress attitude to the war and provided the setting for the second, brief act in the drama.

The Working Committee met in emergency session in mid-June and reopened the door to negotiation, offering its complete co-operation in the war effort—if two conditions were met. These were an unequivocal declaration of Indian independence and the immediate formation of an all-party national government. The armed forces would remain under the control of the British Commander-in-Chief; the Viceroy's constitutional position would remain unchanged, though it was assumed his veto would not be exercised abnormally; and the civil administration would continue unhindered by the change at the executive level.

The purpose, stated Nehru and others, was to provide an incentive to India's millions to contribute to the common cause, by giving them concrete evidence of British willingness to transfer all power at the end of the war. In effect it would have been nothing more than a promissory note. Yet Nehru's expectation may well have been the product of wishful thinking. The Indian masses had little interest in the war as such. Theirs was the more mundane problem of eking out a living with archaic implements of production, a task made more difficult by inflation and shortages of consumer goods. Fascism, democracy, the war were meaningless to the poverty-stricken millions of Indian peasants.

Of the Congress leaders' sincerity there can be no doubt. So powerful was their urge to align themselves with the Allies that for the first time since 1920 Nehru, Rajagopalacharia, Azad and others defied Gandhi on the crucial issue of violence. The Working Committee reaffirmed its faith in non-violence for the freedom struggle within India but felt compelled to abandon Gandhi's method for national defence. It was a heart-rending break between the master and his disciples.

The cleavage had been in the making a long time. Gandhi had first raised the question during the Munich crisis; he wanted the Congress to go on record that a free India would eschew all violence and armed forces. The majority of the Working Committee disagreed, but the issue was shelved as the threat of war receded. Just after the outbreak of war Gandhi had asked to be relieved of the leadership in order that he might 'go it alone', as noted earlier in his letter to Nehru. The Working Committee persuaded him to postpone the decision. The third occasion was at Ramgarh when the Mahatma wanted to forsake the leadership. Azad again secured a postponement. Finally, in the summer of 1940, the parting of the ways occurred, though only for a brief period.

The sharp dissent was not confined to Gandhi. At the Poona session of the A.I.C.C. in July, the vote was 95 to 47 in favour of conditional co-operation. Four members of the Working Committee abstained—Prasad, Kripalani, P. C. Ghose and Shankerrao Deo—while Khan Abdul Ghaffar Khan, the 'Frontier Gandhi', resigned in protest against the sanction to violence.[1]

The moving spirit behind the 'Poona Offer' was Rajagopalacharia (C.R. or Rajaji) the brilliant, haughty and silver-tongued Madrassi Brahmin. Leftists attacked it as 'the surrender to Imperialism', but without success. 'Rajaji has stabbed us in the back', wrote Jaya Prakash Narayan to Nehru. 'All of us here [in prison] expect you and beseech you to lead the opposition in the A.I.C.C. and the country. You should resign your seat in the [Working] Committee. . . . Will you hesitate to fulfil your obvious historic task?'[2] Nehru supported Rajagopalacharia, but not without misgivings. As he reflected upon these events from prison Nehru referred to 'much difficult and anxious thinking' before he did so. International considerations shaped his decision, as well as his genuine desire to participate in the struggle against fascism.[3]

He tried to minimize the significance of the split. 'The difference between Gandhiji's approach and that of the Working Committee must be understood and must not lead the people to think that there is a break between him and the Congress. The Congress of the past twenty years is his creation and child and nothing can break the bond.'[4] Gandhi was deeply moved by this expression of loyalty. 'His [Nehru's] love for and confidence in me peep out of every sentence referring to me', wrote

[1] *Congress Bulletin*, No. 4, 7 September 1940.
[2] Unpublished Nehru Letters, 20 July 1940.
[3] *The Discovery of India*, p. 527.   [4] Tendulkar, op. cit., vol. 5, pp. 355-6.

the Mahatma. 'Good must come out of this separation.'[1] To the British Nehru stressed that there was a brief time limit to the offer.

The Viceroy's response was rigid and uninspired, a very slight modification of his initial statement in October 1939. The only innovation was an offer to create a War Advisory Council.[2] Here was an opportunity for honourable compromise which would have galvanized the Indian National Congress into positive action. The Viceroy made no effort to remove its deep-rooted mistrust of British intentions. Indeed, he aggravated the situation by reassuring the Muslims and other minorities that Britain would not sanction a constitutional settlement for India to which they were firmly opposed.

Congress reaction to the 'August Offer' was summed up in Nehru's pithy remark that the conception of Dominion status for India was 'as dead as a doornail'.[3] (Yet seven years later India attained independence as a Dominion.) The Working Committee rejected the Viceroy's proposals as totally inadequate. The impasse was complete. There seemed nothing left but Gandhi's ultimate weapon—though the Congress might have gained in the long run by joining the Viceroy's Executive Council and by resuming power in the provinces.

When the A.I.C.C. assembled in Bombay on 15 September 1940 the prevalent mood was sombre and depressing. With the failure of conciliatory diplomacy Nehru receded into the background once more. Gandhi returned to the leadership and dominated the proceedings. 'The language of this resolution [calling for civil disobedience] is in the main mine', he informed the delegates. 'It appealed to Pandit Jawaharlal Nehru. . . . He saw it was inevitable, if we were to be true to non-violent resistance to the extent to which we wanted to go.' Nehru's function was that of draftsman. 'I used to be the Congress draftsman', Gandhi added. 'Now he has taken my place.'[4]

*　　*　　*　　*

The opening scene of the third act was slow-moving, as in the case of its predecessors. Gandhi declared that the issue was one

---

[1] *Harijan* (Ahmedabad), 24 June 1940.   [2] The text is in Cmd. 6219, 1940.
[3] Tendulkar, op. cit., vol. 5, p. 394.
[4] *Congress Bulletin*, No. 5, 24 October 1940, p. 14.

of moral principle, that if the Congress were allowed to preach non-co-operation with the war effort there would be no need for civil disobedience. He therefore proposed to approach the Viceroy. Conferences were held at the end of September 1940, but Linlithgow rejected the demand for unlimited freedom of speech on the grounds that the war effort would be seriously impaired. It was only then that the Mahatma launched his campaign.

The most striking characteristic of Act III was Gandhi's moderation. Despite the free hand given him by the Congress, he restricted himself to the least effective weapon in his armoury —*individual* civil disobedience. His primary objectives were to symbolize the Congress protest against 'participation without consultation' and to establish the right of free speech, even in time of war, but not to embarrass the war effort as such. It was a strange campaign indeed. Selected individuals were to recite in public a set formula of an anti-war slogan: 'It is wrong to help the British war effort with men or money. The only worthy effort is to resist all war with non-violent resistance.' No other action was prescribed.

Yet Nehru's torment remained, for his dual loyalties could not be reconciled. Gandhi was aware of his dilemma. 'I know what strain you are bearing in giving me your loyalty', wrote the Mahatma at this time. 'I prize it beyond measure. I hope it will be found to have been well-placed.'[1] Once again discipline and devotion to the master had triumphed over intellectual conviction.

The first *satyagrahi* was Vinoba Bhave, one of Gandhi's most devoted spiritual disciples. He was little known then, though highly respected in the 'inner circle'. His learning was impressive, including a dozen languages and the basic teachings of the great religions. A gaunt, spare man in his early forties at the time, Vinoba had renounced material comfort, in the tradition of India's sages, and had followed in the footsteps of his *guru*. Many years later, with the passing of Gandhi, he emerged from obscurity and achieved international recognition as the founder of the *Bhoodan* (land gift) movement, applying the Mahatma's message to India's unsolved problem of land reform. When

---

[1] 24 October 1940. Tendulkar, op. cit., vol. 8, Appendix on Gandhi-Nehru Letters, p. 364.

Vinoba was selected for this honour, most Indians did not know who he was. He repeated the symbolic protest against the war in a number of villages and was arrested for sedition. His sentence—three months.

Nehru was to follow Vinoba after giving notice to the authorities. But before he could offer *satyagraha* he was arrested—at the Cheokhi railway station in the United Provinces while returning from a visit to Gandhi on the evening of 31 October. He was tried in Gorakhpur prison for a series of speeches delivered earlier in the month and was sentenced to four years' rigorous imprisonment. The nation was stunned by this severe sentence. So too was Churchill. Indeed, the British Prime Minister 'had to be assured that Nehru would . . . receive specially considerate treatment'.[1]

As the news of his arrest was flashed around the country, the reaction was widespread shock and anger. All over India protest meetings were held. The pattern was the same everywhere, though the reaction was spontaneous. There was deep resentment at the harsh treatment of their idol. Speakers railed against the Government, praised Jawaharlal's virtues, and called for a redress of grievances. These were then formalized in resolutions expressing their dismay, their attachment to Indian freedom and their admiration for 'Panditji'. Nor was the indignation confined to Congress followers. Many who disagreed with Nehru's political creed, like Sir Tej Bahadur Sapru, the Liberal leader, were also appalled by this seemingly vindictive action of the authorities.

The Government's motive and the consequences of Nehru's imprisonment were clearly indicated in a confidential British account of the 1940 civil disobedience campaign: 'The immediate and local effect was good; it put an end to the sort of agrarian discontent that Nehru had been endeavouring to stir up. . . . On the other hand, it gave a handle to those, both in India, and also in England and the U.S.A. who desired to accuse Government of repression and vindictiveness. . . . It therefore caused some embarrassment in dealing with the less important people who followed in Nehru's footsteps.'[2]

---

[1] Menon, op. cit., p. 101.

[2] Government of India: *History of the Civil Disobedience Movement 1940–41* (unpublished), p. 5.

In the course of his trial Nehru delivered a stirring defence of his political faith and a condemnation of the *Raj*. 'It is not me that you are seeking to judge and condemn', he declared, 'but rather the hundreds of millions of the people of India, and that is a large task even for a proud Empire. Perhaps it may be that, though I am standing before you on trial, it is the British Empire itself that is on trial before the bar of the world. . . . It is a small matter to me what happens to me in this trial or subsequently. Individuals count for little; they come and go, as I shall go when my time is up. Seven times I have been tried and convicted by British authority in India, and many years of my life lie buried within prison walls. . . . But it is no small matter what happens to India and her millions of sons and daughters. That is the issue before me, and that ultimately is the issue before you, sir.'[1] To Indians who supported the Government he said: 'Let those who seek the favour and protection of this imperialism go their way. We go ours. The parting of the ways has come.'[2]

Gandhi's original intention was to fast after the arrest of the third *satyagrahi*, the completely unknown Brahmo Dutt, but he was dissuaded by his colleagues.[3] Early in November 1940 the Mahatma informed the Viceroy of his new plan of action: this was to extend civil disobedience to individuals from three groups in the Congress. The first consisted of about 1,200 members of the Working Committee, the All-India Congress Committee and the legislatures, who were to offer *satyagraha* before the end of the year. About 700 did so, including all the leaders, except Prasad and Kripalani who were given an exemption by Gandhi. 'Comparatively little excitement was caused by these arrests, although there were the usual *hartals* and other devices for inflaming public opinion.' Congress members of the central legislature encouraged the campaign. The British retaliated with military censorship of correspondence, as well as a press decree prohibiting the publication of any matter connected with the movement.

In a typically Gandhian gesture, a truce was proclaimed at

[1] The text is in *Indian Annual Register*, vol. ii, 1941, pp. 198–200.
[2] 'Parting of the Ways' in *Asia*, November 1940.
[3] The following account is based upon Government of India, *History of the Civil Disobedience Movement 1940–41*.

Christmas to allow British officials to enjoy their holidays! The next phase began in January 1941, with volunteers from the provincial, district, *tehsil* and primary committees of the Congress, and was to last three months. By mid-April 13,300 of the 15,000 potential *satyagrahis* from these groups had been convicted. The second and third stages overlapped and by early summer the campaign had petered out, though it continued officially until December 1941. The end came a few days before Pearl Harbour with the release of all remaining C.D. prisoners whose offences had been symbolic in character, including Nehru and Azad who had been convicted for seditious speeches. On the whole civil disobedience in 1940–1 was a tame affair with little public enthusiasm compared with the campaigns of 1930 and 1942.

*   *   *   *

As the fall of France had caused a reshaping of Congress policy in the summer of 1940, so Pearl Harbour marked the beginning of another act in the war drama. On both occasions the current of anti-fascism asserted itself. Nehru came to the forefront, and a split with Gandhi occurred over the issue of non-violence against aggression.

'There is no doubt', said Nehru the day of his release, 'that the progressive forces of the world are aligned with the group represented by the United States, Britain, Russia and China', but the Congress could not participate actively until its freedom was acknowledged. The day following Pearl Harbour he expressed the reaction of many Indian nationalists by retreating from pure non-violence: 'I have been unable in the past to accept all the implications of the doctrine so far as their practicable application is concerned. But I had held that this is an ideal worth striving for, with all our might.'[1] By the middle of January 1942 he had gone even further: 'When we face the enemy, as in the case of Assam, which may be bombed, it would be preposterous indeed to advise the people to offer passive resistance against the war.'[2]

With the pendulum shifting rapidly towards active co-operation, Gandhi asked to be relieved of the leadership. This was

---

[1] Bright, J. S. (ed.), *Before and After Independence*, pp. 204–5.
[2] Quoted in publisher's foreword to *Toward Freedom*, p. viii.

done on 16 January 1942, when the A.I.C.C. made another offer of conditional co-operation. But it was not without much soul-searching that the Congress High Command adopted this policy. For the second time during the war a sharp rift occurred in the Working Committee. According to Gandhi the original draft was prepared by Nehru. It then went to a sub-committee which 'opened a tiny window for [C.R.] to squeeze in'. The adherents of non-violence could support it because active co-operation in the war was still hypothetical. In short, 'the resolution is a mirror in which all groups can see themselves'. Prasad and Patel were on the verge of resigning. Only Gandhi's influence dissuaded them. Indeed, he pleaded with all those who shared his views on non-violence to support the resolution. Nehru himself did not have much faith in a favourable British response.[1]

In the life of Nehru this was an historic Congress session—because the Mahatma publicly designated him his successor. Rumours were rife at the time of a fundamental split between them. Nehru denied this categorically: 'There has been none and there can be no break with him [Gandhi] for he represents the mind and heart of our people as no one else can.'[2] Gandhi responded in a similar vein: 'It will require much more than differences of opinion to estrange us. We have had differences from the moment we became co-workers, and yet I have said for some years and say now that not Rajaji [Rajagopalacharia] but Jawaharlal will be my successor. He says he does not understand my language, and that he speaks a language foreign to me. This may or may not be true. But language is no bar to a union of hearts. And *I know this, that when I am gone he will speak my language.*'[3] It was a prophetic statement which even Nehru must have doubted at the time. Although many persons considered Nehru the logical successor long before 1942, Gandhi's statement put an end to lingering doubts in the country at large.

While the Congress re-examined its attitude to the war, the danger to India grew ominous. In rapid succession, Japanese armies overran Hong Kong, the Philippines and Malaya. Indo-China and Thailand were firmly under their control. Then, on 15 February 1942, the unbelievable happened—the

[1] *Congress Bulletin*, No. 1, 5 February 1942, pp. 17 ff. [2] Bright (ed.), op. cit., p. 209.
[3] *Indian Annual Register*, vol. i, 1942, pp. 282–3. (Emphasis added.)

great bastion of Singapore fell. In Burma, too, the British were retreating. India lay open to invasion.

Indian reaction was a mixture of vicarious pleasure, surprise, suppressed fear and inertia. Many derived satisfaction from the collapse of Western colonial empires all over South-east Asia, especially from the spectacle of a triumphant Asian state, though few had any positive liking for Japan. On the contrary, the majority of thinking Indians were horrified by Japanese atrocities in China. All who observed these events were amazed at the rapidity of the Japanese conquest and wondered whether the colonial empires were really flimsy structures based on pillars of clay. The followers of Subhas Bose and some Congressmen viewed it as an opportunity to press the demand for Indian freedom and to expel the British from the sub-continent. A few, like Nehru, were aghast at the prospect of a Japanese 'Co-prosperity sphere', the real danger to India, and the broader implications for the world struggle against the Axis powers. The masses on the whole were indifferent, preoccupied as they were with the perennial struggle for economic survival.

The war was brought home to Indians in one respect. The conquest of Malaya and Burma led to a flight of Indians from those countries. As they returned to their homeland they carried to town and village stories of their suffering during the long trek to safety. They also told of the special treatment given to white refugees. All this created deep resentment and a growing awareness of the meaning of war.

In the midst of this turmoil Chiang Kai-shek made a brief appearance on the Indian political stage. During a goodwill visit to India towards the end of February, he called for the immediate transfer of 'real political power' to the Indian people so that they would rally against the invader. Nehru reciprocated by paying tribute to Chiang as 'a remarkable man [who] has proved himself a very great leader and captain in war'.[1] The turning-point came on 8 March 1942, when Rangoon was occupied by the Japanese.

It was only in the face of this imminent threat that London responded to the Congress offer.[2] Until that time the danger to

---

[1] Bright (ed.), op. cit., p. 216.

[2] This was confirmed by Churchill in his war memoirs: 'On March 8 the Japanese Army had entered Rangoon. If the effective defence of India was to be organised

its Indian Empire had been remote, and so the British Government had been indifferent to the attitude of Indian nationalists. Now the Japanese were at the gates, and pressure was being exerted by Chiang and Roosevelt.[1] It could delay no longer. Thus, on 11 March, Churchill announced in the Commons that Sir Stafford Cripps was being dispatched to Delhi with new proposals in an effort to break the deadlock.

The negotiations began hopefully on 25 March. They ended in complete failure eighteen days later, amidst mutual recriminations. The Congress was represented by Nehru and Azad, though Gandhi was to play the decisive role in its rejection of the proposals. Jinnah spoke for the Muslim League, Savarkar for the Hindu Mahasabha, Ambedkar and M. C. Rajah for the Untouchables, and Sapru and Jayakar for the Liberals. Other minorities and the Princes were also represented in the talks. In reality, however, the negotiations were confined almost entirely to the Congress.

Cripps offered full Dominion status after the war with the right of secession from the Commonwealth. To achieve this goal he promised the establishment of a constituent assembly immediately after the conclusion of hostilities; the delegates from British India were to be elected by the lower houses of the provincial legislatures, those from the States were to be appointed by the Princes. Cripps also pledged British acceptance of a constitution so framed, subject to the right of any province to remain outside the Dominion. Such non-acceding units would receive a status comparable to that of the projected Indian Union. For the duration of the war no constitutional changes were proposed. But Cripps expressed the hope that the principal political parties would co-operate in a 'National Government'. Defence would remain the prerogative of the British Commander-in-Chief.[2]

it seemed to most of my colleagues important to make every effort to break the political deadlock.' *The Hinge of Fate*, p. 214.

[1] Roosevelt's initial intervention took the form of a suggestion to Churchill on 10 March to establish a temporary Dominion Government for India along the lines of the American Articles of Confederation. He reiterated this proposal on the eve of the collapse of the Cripps Mission. But Churchill was wholly unimpressed. Years later Churchill recorded his horrified reaction in these words: 'I was thankful that events had already made such an act of madness impossible.' *The Hinge of Fate*, p. 219. The texts of the cable correspondence at the time are in ibid., pp. 212–214, 218–19, 220–1.　　[2] Cmd. 6350, 1942.

Although few realized it at the time, the right of non-accession for the provinces was of great importance, for it implied British acceptance of the Pakistan demand which had been formally enunciated by the Muslim League at Lahore in 1940. It posed as well the grave danger of Balkanization in the sub-continent. In another five years it was to culminate in the partition of India.

Both the Congress and the Muslim League finally rejected the offer but for almost diametrically opposed reasons. The Working Committee balked at 'the uncertain future' surrounding the commitment to self-determination, the 'novel principle of non-accession for a province', which encouraged separation, and 'the introduction of non-representative elements', namely the Princes, in the Constituent Assembly. The short-run proposals were also criticized because no real change was contemplated. Nehru himself was 'profoundly depressed' by the proposals, for he had anticipated greater vision from Sir Stafford, particularly in view of the crisis at hand. He was especially troubled by the apparent acceptance of the League demand for Pakistan and the danger of widespread fragmentation of the sub-continent. Yet he did not reject the offer outright. Indeed, the evidence suggests that he made a sincere effort to find a compromise solution for an interim government and persuaded his colleagues to leave the post-war proposals in abeyance.

The League welcomed the implied recognition of Pakistan—the reference to one or more unions—but criticized the vague procedure for its achievement and the rigid character of the offer, a package deal that could not be modified. Like the Congress it termed the interim arrangements vague and refused to express an opinion until the whole picture was clarified. Other Indian parties and groups were also dissatisfied with the Cripps proposals: the Hindu Mahasabha because of the implied danger of partition; the Sikhs because of fear that a Muslim majority in the Punjab would opt out of the Indian Union; and the Untouchables on the ground that they would be at the mercy of caste Hindus. Gandhi himself termed the offer a 'post-dated cheque on a failing bank'.

Long after the Cripps Offer had been forgotten, one section of the Congress resolution was recalled, to the dismay of its leaders. While criticizing the right of provinces and States to remain outside the Union, it apparently felt the need to demonstrate its faith in democracy: 'Nevertheless, the Committee cannot think in terms of compelling the people of any territorial unit to remain in an Indian union against their declared and established will.' Here was a trump card for Jinnah—and the British—which was to be used with devastating effect in the last stage leading to Partition.

Sir Stafford Cripps was probably the ideal choice for this delicate task of mediation. As a leader of the Labour Party's left wing he was free from the stigma attaching to Whitehall, the India Office and the Viceroy's Palace. On the contrary, he had earned the respect and goodwill of many Indians for his sympathy with their aspirations for freedom. A brilliant advocate and a serious student of the 'Indian problem' for many years, he was aware of the legal complexities and psychological subtleties of the case. He was a friend of Nehru, he shared with Gandhi a deeply religious outlook and the practice of vegetarianism, and he was acquainted with most prominent Indian politicians of the day. But his task was a formidable one. It was made more difficult by the oppressive political atmosphere in Delhi in the spring of 1942. Indeed, the suspicions were so intense that the gradualist, constitutional approach seemed doomed to failure. And yet, the parties were very close to agreement on the eve of collapse.

According to Nehru the chances of agreement were excellent, about 75 per cent., before his last interview with Cripps. At that meeting, however, 'a big change had occurred'.[1] It was obvious, said Nehru, that there was trouble between Cripps and others, the implication being that Churchill recalled Cripps because he had gone beyond his terms of reference. (This view was confirmed by Churchill himself in a speech before the House of Commons more than four years later.)[2] By shifting his ground from a 'Cabinet' and a 'National Government' to the Viceroy's Executive Council, said Nehru, Cripps had retreated to the August Offer of 1940, i.e., merely an invitation to join the

---

[1] This view was also held by Roosevelt who cabled Churchill on 12 April: 'According to my reading, an agreement appeared very near last Thursday night.' *The Hinge of Fate*, p. 218.

[2] Menon, op. cit., p. 136. Churchill's speech was made on 12 December 1946.

existing government.[1] As for Britain's refusal to budge on
the issue of constitutional change during the war, Nehru noted
Churchill's dramatic offer of union with France in the summer
of 1940 and asked why it was not possible to enact a bill agreeing
to India's self-government with the details to be arranged
later.

The negotiations ended on a note of bitterness. On the eve
of his departure Cripps mentioned the danger of 'tyrannical
rule of the [Congress] majority'. Nehru chided the distinguished lawyer for even thinking in these terms. Cripps had
also accused the Congress of seeking the assistance of Louis
Johnson, Roosevelt's personal representative in Delhi. Nehru
denied this categorically and reprimanded Cripps for dragging
Roosevelt's name into the dispute.[2] 'For the first time in these
twenty-two years', he concluded his commentary on the Cripps
Mission, 'I swallowed many a bitter pill . . . because I did want
to throw all my sympathy and . . . energy . . . into the organization of the defence of India.'[3]

Cripps's fundamental error was his assumption that Nehru
held the power of final decision in the Congress. In the dying
moments of the talks he addressed a stirring appeal to Nehru.
'Let me make a final appeal to you,' he wrote, 'upon whom rests
the great burden of decision. . . . We can and must carry our
people through to friendship and co-operation—I in my sphere,
you in yours. The chance which now offers cannot recur. . . .

[1] This view was shared by the semi-official historian of the Cripps Mission. 'The
Draft Declaration [Cripps Offer]', wrote Sir Reginald Coupland, 'did not represent
a drastic change of policy. . . . In principle, in fact, the Draft Declaration went no
further than the "August Offer" . . .' *The Cripps Mission*, pp. 45–46.

[2] This criticism of Cripps was also voiced by Harry Hopkins who was then in
London discussing the Cripps Mission, among other things, with Churchill.
Considerable light on the last days of the Cripps negotiations, especially on the role
of Roosevelt, Johnson, the Viceroy and the British Cabinet was shed by Hopkins's
diary entry on 9 April 1942 after a lengthy conversation with Churchill. Sherwood,
Robert E., *Roosevelt and Hopkins*, p. 524. According to V. P. Menon, Johnson was
actively involved in the search for a compromise formula on the defence question—
'with Sir Stafford Cripps' permission'. For the details of the 'Johnson formula' see
Menon, op. cit., pp. 128–9.

[3] The texts of the Cripps Offer, the Working Committee Resolution, correspondence between Cripps and the Congress, Cripps's press statement and Nehru's press
statement of 12 April 1942, are in *Congress Bulletin*, No. 2, 22 April 1942, pp. 3–53.
For Nehru's reflections on the Cripps Mission two and a half years later see *The
Discovery of India*, pp. 548–62. A comprehensive summary of the Cripps Mission is
to be found in Menon, op. cit., ch. v.

Leadership—the sort of leadership you have—can alone accomplish the result. It is the moment for the supreme courage of a great leader to face all the risks and the difficulties—and I know they are there—to drive through to the desired end. I know your qualities, and your capacity and I beg you to make use of them now.'[1]

Nehru's reply is unknown but his candid assessment of the Cripps Mission was conveyed to an English friend a few months after the talks broke down: 'Cripps surprised me greatly. I have liked Cripps as a man. . . . But on this occasion I was surprised at his woodenness and insensitiveness, in spite of his public smiles. He was all the time the formal representative of the War Cabinet, in fact he was the War Cabinet speaking to us with a take it or leave it attitude. Always he seemed to impress on us that he knew the Indian problem in and out and he had found the only solution for it. Anyone who did not agree with it was, to say the least of it, utterly misguided. Indeed, I made it perfectly plain to him that there were limits beyond which I could not carry the Congress and there were limits beyond which the Congress could not carry the people. But he thought that all this was totally beside the point.'[2]

Cripps could not have been unaware of Gandhi's firm opposition. He seemed to be trying to inspire Nehru to reject the Mahatma's recommendation. Four years later, during the Cabinet Mission talks in Delhi, Cripps told his private secretary, Woodrow Wyatt, that the Congress had been on the verge of acceptance in 1942. 'Gandhi then rang up the Working Committee from Wardha and recommended rejection.'[3]

There is no doubt that Gandhi tipped the Congress scales against the Cripps offer. But the responsibility for deadlock was shared by other prominent figures, notably Cripps, Churchill and Linlithgow. Cripps was unduly optimistic about his ability to win Congress approval of his short-run proposals and underestimated Gandhi's crucial role. Churchill did not extend full support to his envoy; in fact, there was no clear understanding between Cripps and the British Cabinet or between Cripps and the Viceroy. Lord Linlithgow opposed Cripps's efforts to find

---

[1] Unpublished Nehru Letters, 12 April 1942.
[2] To Evelyn Wood on 5 June 1942. Unpublished Nehru Letters.
[3] Related to the author in London in October 1955.

a compromise defence formula and it was largely at his initiative that Churchill intervened.

Beyond these individual roles was a climate of opinion which virtually assured deadlock. The Congress approach was legalistic, almost sectarian, but it had become so distrustful of Churchill's representative bearing gifts, after two and a half years of frustrating negotiations, that concrete evidence of British sincerity was required there and then, not at some time in the future. Had not Churchill explicitly excluded India from the sweeping principle of the Atlantic Charter—'the right of all peoples to choose the form of government under which they will live'? And did he not throw out a clear challenge to Indian nationalists in the summer of 1941: 'I have not become His Majesty's first minister to preside over the liquidation of the British Empire'? Cripps and his superiors failed to cut through the clouds of suspicion with a bold gesture to demonstrate their sincerity beyond any shadow of doubt. If the British were going to part with total power at the end of the war a limited transfer could have taken place during the conflict, including the creation of a substantive Indian-controlled Defence Ministry, one of the technical bones of contention. The other was the transformation of the Viceroy's Executive Council into a 'National Government'.

Ironically, the wheel had turned full circle, for the Congress had acted exactly as Cripps himself had urged at the beginning of the war: 'I am quite convinced', he wrote to Nehru, 'that for the good of the British as well as the Indian people, Congress should now stand as firm as a rock upon its demands.' In the same letter Cripps anticipated the basic cause of the collapse of his mission in the spring of 1942: 'The trouble is that, as always, it [a sympathetic British offer] is likely to come too late to save the situation.'[1] Thus ended Act IV of the drama.

*   *   *   *

From the moment the deadlock was announced bitterness mounted swiftly in the Congress. There seemed only one way out—the ultimate weapon of civil disobedience. But this course of action was fraught with danger, for the Japanese were poised to strike against eastern India. Should nationalists swallow their

[1] Unpublished Nehru Letters, 11 October 1939.

pride and support the war effort? Doubt and anxiety filled the minds of many. The High Command sought desperately to resolve the dilemma. Unfortunately the circle could not be squared.

For Nehru, more so than any other nationalist leader, the spring and summer of 1942 were months of emotional turmoil. He knew that civil disobedience could play havoc with the defence of India and loathed the idea of Japanese conquest. He felt deeply the misery of those who had come under Nazi, Fascist or Japanese domination. He admired the Chinese and the Russians for their defence against the invader. He never doubted the righteousness of the Allied cause and longed to identify himself with it. Intellectually his course was clear, for Allied victory was a precondition to Indian freedom. But the issue was blurred in Nehru's mind by the cause of independence and his distrust of British intentions. In vain had he tried for two and a half years to reach a compromise which would strengthen the Indian war effort and, at the same time, ensure the cherished goal. Where to go from here? How could the impasse be broken? Passionately and earnestly he sought the answers. Alas, there were none.

The atmosphere was gloomy, the future dark. But of one thing Nehru was certain: the situation could not be allowed to drift. Total inaction was suicidal, both for the war effort and the struggle for independence. Sullen passivity reigned among the masses. Amongst the intelligentsia pro-Japanese propaganda was beginning to take effect. Nehru threw the full weight of his influence against this defeatist mentality. 'We are not going to surrender to the invader', he declared on the morrow of Cripps's departure. 'In spite of all that has happened, we are not going to embarrass the British war effort. . . . The problem for us is how to organize our own.'[1] But how? Nehru pressed for guerrilla war against the Japanese, in an effort to rouse the bewildered millions of his countrymen. Gandhi was opposed but did not attach much importance to this deviation. 'I am sorry that he has developed a fancy for guerrilla warfare', the Mahatma commented at the time. 'But I have no doubt that it will be a nine days' wonder. It will take no effect. . . . They [Nehru and Rajagopalacharia] will return to non-violence with

[1] Quoted in Churchill, *The Hinge of Fate*, p. 221.

renewed zest, strengthened by the failure of their effort.'[1] The events proved him right about his successor but entirely wrong about Rajaji.

The issue came to a head at the end of April when the A.I.C.C. met in Allahabad to chart its future course. From all accounts it was a stormy session. Rajaji challenged the Mahatma by moving a resolution on 'the way out'—acceptance of the Muslim League demand for Pakistan, if the League still wanted it when the time came to frame a constitution, and on this basis the immediate formation of a coalition government to prosecute the war.[2] The Congress was not yet ready to contemplate partition. It rejected this 'treasonable suggestion' by 120 to 15 and passed a Gandhi-inspired resolution for non-violent resistance to the Japanese. 'In case an invasion takes place, it must be resisted. Such resistance can only take the form of non-violent non-co-operation, as the British Government has prevented the organization of national defence by the people in any other way. . . . We may not bend the knee to the aggressor nor obey any of his orders. We may not look to him for favours nor fall to his bribes. . . . We will refuse to give them up [homes and property] even if we have to die in the effort . . .'[3]

The draft was prepared by Nehru, but the ideas were Gandhi's. It was a strange directive. The Government's war effort was not to be hindered—nor assisted; the Congress was to pursue a programme of parallel resistance to the Japanese by means of a scorched-earth policy. Nehru had surrendered to the Mahatma once again. Weary from the political struggle and troubled by the turn of events, he sought escape in the solitude of nature. Early in May he spent a fortnight in the beautiful Kulu valley in the foothills of the Himalayas. It was to be his last holiday until after the war.

During Nehru's absence Gandhi injected a new element into the highly-charged political atmosphere. Sensing the need for some form of action or dramatic gesture, the Mahatma invoked the slogan 'Quit India' and issued a provocative challenge to the *Raj*. Leave India at once, he urged, so that a free India

[1] *Harijan* (Ahmedabad), 26 April 1942.

[2] This theme was later developed by Rajagopalacharia in his pamphlet, *The Way Out* (1944).

[3] The text of the Allahabad Resolution is to be found in *Indian Annual Register* vol. i, 1942, pp. 293–4.

could mobilize its full strength against the Japanese menace. Beyond this slogan nothing was spelled out, though Gandhi was certainly thinking of mass civil disobedience if the British did not heed his call. The effect was electrifying. Throughout the country thousands rallied to the cry, 'Quit India', an ingenious symbol of the freedom struggle in crisis. Some like Nehru were disconcerted by the prospect of civil disobedience at this critical period in the war. On the one hand, he felt that a Japanese invasion would stir millions from 'the peace of the grave' that had been imposed by India's foreign rulers. But far more important would be the effect of civil disobedience on India's war effort and the battlefields beyond its borders. As a result he fought a strong rearguard action against the Mahatma's plan until the very last moment, when he gave way to Gandhian persuasion. Secret reports of the Intelligence Bureau's Special Branch confirm the basic clash between the two men from May to August 1942. So do the comments of many who observed the events of this period at close range.

Nehru capitulated but not without a struggle. In lengthy talks at Gandhi's *ashram* in Wardha, he tried to delay the decision by stressing the international consequences of direct action against the Government. He succeeded to some extent, in that Gandhi later offered to accept the stationing of Allied forces in India for the duration of the war without any interference from a free Indian government. But on the core issue Gandhi stood firm. At a tense meeting of the Working Committee early in July, Nehru made a supreme effort to dissuade the Mahatma from his hazardous course of action. The discussions lasted a week, and Gandhi was hard-pressed to impose his will. According to one member of the Working Committee in 1942, half the Committee opposed him at the outset. Another told the author that Gandhi finally threatened to leave the Congress and 'out of the sands of India create a movement which would be larger than the Congress itself'. At that point his colleagues surrendered.

The 'National Demand', formulated at Wardha, called on the British to 'Quit India' and transfer power to Indian hands. It was made clear that the intent was not to embarrass the war effort of Britain and the Allies nor to encourage the Japanese. As a gesture of its sincerity, the Congress offered the Allies bases in India. If these proposals were rejected, 'the Congress will then be reluctantly compelled to utilize all the non-violent strength it might have gathered since 1920'. To pass judgement on this policy, the A.I.C.C. was summoned to Bombay on 7 August.[1]

While the Congress moved hesitantly towards direct action, the Chinese were attempting to prevent a collision. On 26 June 1942 Mme. Chiang Kai-shek wrote to Nehru: 'When the Generalissimo received Gandhi's letter [saying that he approved of armed Indian resistance to the Japanese] he at once telegraphed to Washington, urging that America and China should take concerted action. The Generalissimo . . . wants me to impress upon you that nothing whatever should be done until the result of his negotiations with Washington is definitely known . . . we may be able to take advantage of Mr. Churchill's presence in Washington. . . . I know how hard you must have worked on Gandhiji to make him commit himself to the extent he has written.'[2] But Churchill was in no mood to compromise.

Until the very eve of the Bombay session Nehru persisted in expounding the idea of armed resistance to Japan. This was revealed by Gandhi to a correspondent of the *Manchester Guardian* as late as 6 August.[3] According to one Congress leader Nehru was so distraught by the impending clash that, at one point between the Wardha and Bombay meetings, he berated Gandhi for pursuing a policy which might destroy all that had been created over the years. But the outburst passed, as did the opposition.

Nehru's dilemma in the summer of 1942 was described by Gandhi in a letter to the Viceroy: 'In that misery [fear of impending ruin of China and Russia] he [Nehru] tried to forget his old quarrel with imperialism. . . . I have argued with him for days together. He fought against my position with a passion which I have no words to describe. But the logic of facts overwhelmed him. He yielded when he saw clearly that without the freedom of India that of the other two was in great jeopardy. Surely you are wrong in having imprisoned such a powerful friend and ally.'[4]

[1] The text of the Wardha Resolution is in *Congress Bulletin*, No. 1, 1 November 1945, Part I, pp. 5–8.
[2] Unpublished Nehru Letters.   [3] Tendulkar, op. cit., vol. 6, p. 181.
[4] On 14 August 1942. Government of India, *Correspondence with Mr. Gandhi, August 1942–April 1944.*

Having succumbed to Gandhi's logic, Nehru closed ranks with his mentor and made a show of unity before the delegates of the A.I.C.C. It was he who moved the resolution on 7 August calling on the British to quit India at once. The resolution does not flow from narrow nationalism, he began; rather, it provides the basis for effective co-operation in the war. 'As for the so-called National War Front, there is neither the nation nor the war nor any front to it.' Thus, 'whatever change comes about would be for the better'.

A strong Asian consciousness and sensitivity to the racial question, two features of Indian foreign policy after 1947, are evident in his criticism of the Anglo-Saxon powers. 'You have considered yourself, with your inventions of the Machine Age, to be infinitely better than us and that we are a benighted backward people. But the people of Asia do not propose to be treated in that manner any longer.' As for the British, 'my grievance is that they have made Indians miserable, poverty-stricken wrecks of humanity'. Nor was the Muslim League spared his caustic remarks. Comparing its demand for Pakistan with the Sudeten German agitation, he declared that the Congress was not prepared to be 'kicked about by men who have made no sacrifice for the freedom of India', a charge that he was to level at Pakistani leaders on more than one occasion. [1]

The 'Quit India' resolution contained an offer and a challenge. 'On the declaration of India's independence a Provisional Government will be formed and a *Free India will become an ally of the United Nations* . . .' As a concession to the Muslim League it proposed the framing of a constitution 'with the largest measure of autonomy for the federating units, and with the residuary powers vesting in these units'. The Congress renewed its appeal to Britain and the United Nations but felt 'that it is no longer justified in holding the nation back from endeavouring to assert its will against an imperialist and authoritarian government. . . . The Committee resolves, therefore, *to sanction* . . . the starting of a mass struggle on non-violent lines on the widest possible scale. . . . Such a struggle must inevitably be under the leadership of Gandhiji. . . .' [2]

[1] The texts of Nehru's speeches on 7 and 8 August 1942 are in *Indian Annual Register*, vol. ii, 1942, pp. 239–41 and 252–4.
[2] The text is in *Congress Bulletin*, No. 1, 1 November 1945, Part I, pp. 10–13. (Emphasis added.)

The Government of India reacted within a few hours. On the morning of 9 August 1942 Gandhi and all members of the Working Committee were arrested. Nehru was then staying at the home of his younger sister, Mrs. Krishna Hutheesingh. He returned late in the evening of the 8th, exhausted and still uncertain about the wisdom of the 'Quit India' decision. There was an air of suppressed excitement as family and friends sat late into the night discussing the historic session. Nehru had no illusions about his impending arrest. But he did not expect to be awakened at 5 a.m. and to be informed that the police were waiting to take him into custody. The High Command were bundled into a special train for the journey to prison. Gandhi was detained at the Aga Khan's palace in Poona, while the Committee members were taken to Ahmadnagar Fort, a Moghul relic in a remote corner of Bombay Province. There they were to remain until 15 June 1945. It was Nehru's last and longest period behind the walls.

*   *   *   *

The arrest of the Congress leaders set off a nation-wide political explosion, the climax to the war drama. As the news spread over the land, the rank and file rose in fury against the Government. There was no need for directives and planning. Congressmen and their sympathizers were galvanized into immediate and spontaneous action. For more than a week business life was paralysed in Ahmedabad, Bombay, Delhi, Madras, Bangalore and Amritsar. In almost every major city mass demonstrations mushroomed from the bazaars. Students and workers, shopkeepers and housewives marched through the streets, singing nationalist songs and demanding the release of Gandhi and the Working Committee. They were peaceful at first. But tension was great and the authorities were nervous. In Delhi the police fired on forty-seven separate occasions during 11 and 12 August. In the United Provinces they fired twenty-nine times between 9 and 21 August, killing seventy-six persons and severely injuring 114. 'Many more were more or less severely injured.' In Calcutta serious demonstrations began on 13 August. In the Central Provinces the police killed sixty-four, wounded 102 and arrested 1,088 in the first three weeks.

The pattern was the same everywhere—protest meetings, police violence and arrests.

Students were in the vanguard. They walked out of the universities and started a campaign of sabotage—derailing trains, cutting telephone wires, instigating peasants to withhold payment of taxes. Later, cases of arson and bomb-throwing became common. At the large, spacious, modern University of Benares, the faculty and students joined hands. They closed the campus gates to all officials, proclaimed the University 'Free India' and, in an emotional outburst, mobilized the University Training Corps to fight against the *Raj*!

Violence bred violence. In the United Provinces three police stations were burned, four post offices razed to the ground and seventy-nine village records totally destroyed. In the princely State of Mysore 32,000 workers remained on strike for two weeks, while 80 per cent. of all university students walked out. According to the Congress account of the 'August Movement', about 600 persons were killed by police fire during the first few days. In the Sikh State of Patiala eight students were killed while trying to raise the national flag over public buildings; 100 were shot in a Mysore procession. The most brutal police atrocity was reported in Chimur, a tiny village in the Chanda district of Bengal. Four officials were killed there. By way of retaliation, said the Congress account, sixty women were raped, collective fines were imposed, twenty villagers were sentenced to death and twenty-six to life imprisonment. Under public pressure they were later released. In the Ballesore district of Orissa 200 were reported killed. Perhaps the most dramatic episode of the campaign occurred in the Midnapore district of Bengal, well known for radicalism in earlier campaigns. Two *tehsils* succeeded in expelling all officials, declared themselves part of 'Free India' and maintained their 'independence' for four months.

Everywhere government repression was harsh, for this was the gravest threat to British rule since the Rebellion of 1857. No quarter was given. None was asked. In addition to frequent police firing on unarmed crowds, there were mass arrests and extensive use of *lathi* charges to break up demonstrations. In short, it was the establishment of a police state or, as the Congress termed it, 'Ordinance *Raj*'. Rigid control of the press

L

throughout the revolt prevented one part of the country from knowing what was happening elsewhere. Indeed, the whole story has not yet been made public. But the confidential *Fortnightly Reports*, sent from the provincial governments to the Home Department in Delhi, bear out, in general, the magnitude of the upheaval. During the last five months of 1942 India was fired by the spirit of revolt.[1]

One of the most striking features of the campaign was the 'general conspiracy of silence'. 'The public as a whole is either apathetic or tacitly sympathetic [to the Congress]', wrote the Chief Secretary of Bombay at the end of October. 'The reasons are purely political in character and will continue as long as the present political impasse continues. . . . There is still general distrust of the British Government.' From all over India came similar reports, suggesting very wide support for the aims, though not necessarily the techniques, of the movement.

Not all groups were sympathetic. The League was jubilant about the arrest of the Congress leaders and continued its policy of passive support to the war effort. The Communists openly opposed civil disobedience on the grounds that the Allies' precarious position in East Asia would be further impaired. They blamed the Government for the revolt but criticized the nationalist response. The Hindu Mahasabha favoured the 'Quit India' demand but was not prepared to court jail for its goal.

The campaign was short-lived but intensive. By the end of August the rebellion was broken, though incidents continued for months. According to the Secretary of State for India, the casualties from 9 August to 30 November 1942 were 1,028 killed and 3,215 seriously injured.[2] These figures are almost certainly an underestimate. In any event, the far more significant fact is that within a few months about 100,000 nationalists were imprisoned, many of them for the duration of the war. And as the Chief Secretary of Bengal reported on 2 September, 'all sections of Indian opinion may be said to be at one in support of the demand for the immediate transference of power

---

[1] The Congress account is taken from All-India Satyagraha Council, Report of the August Struggle (unpublished). The following quotations from the official Mo*tnightly Reports* are taken from extracts in the files of the History of the Freedom For,vement Project in the National Archives of India.

[2] Gt. Brit. H.C. *Debates*, 1942–3, vol. 386, col. 1941.

and the establishment of a national government'. The campaign failed, inevitable in the face of overwhelming armed strength, but the feelings of politically conscious India had been expressed. The tragedy was that it assumed violent forms, against the will of Gandhi and at a delicate stage in the war. In time the 'August Movement' became a legend, the last open challenge to British rule. Five years later Independence came—without the need for another round of civil disobedience.

* * * *

Apologists for the British campaign of mass arrests and punitive police measures in the late summer and autumn of 1942 contend that the 'Quit India' Resolution clearly envisaged a mass rebellion. Further, that it threatened the Allied war effort in South-east Asia when Japanese armies were poised to strike at the sub-continent. Finally, they argue, the events following the resolution proved that it was a violent and planned rebellion. For all these reasons decisive preventive action was necessary.

Indian nationalists put their case this way. The resolution stated emphatically that it was to be a non-violent struggle. Furthermore, Gandhi made it perfectly clear in his closing remarks to the Bombay session that he would not take hasty action. 'Our struggle is now to start', he told the A.I.C.C. 'But before launching the movement, I will address a letter to the Viceroy and wait for his reply.'[1] As for the outbreak of violence, this followed the arrest of the Congress leaders. Finally, neither Gandhi nor the Working Committee had any plan of action beyond the slogan, 'Quit India'. Hence the Government of India precipitated the revolt and must bear responsibility for everything that followed.

What does the evidence suggest? There can be no doubt, from the text of the resolution and from the speeches of Nehru and Gandhi, that the Congress intended to launch a civil disobedience campaign if its final offer of co-operation were rejected. There is no less doubt that it was to be non-violent, for this was the pattern established by Gandhi during the three earlier campaigns. Moreover, neither the Mahatma nor the resolution indicated any specific date for the inauguration of

[1] Tendulkar, op. cit., vol. 6, p. 199.

civil disobedience. If historical experience is any guide it would have been delayed for some time: in 1921 it began five months after the Congress approved of civil disobedience; in 1930, three months after; and in 1940 there was a delay of seven months. The 'Quit India' Resolution only *sanctioned* non-co-operation. The decision as to when and how it was to be translated into reality was left entirely to Gandhi's discretion. On all previous occasions he had informed the Viceroy of his plans in advance. From his statement noted above it is evident that he intended to follow the same procedure.

The Government of India claimed at the time that a raid on A.I.C.C. headquarters in Allahabad had uncovered evidence of a planned rebellion—material which served as the basis of the 'Puckle Circular' in July 1942, calling for more vigorous propaganda against the Congress. The evidence is dubious for it contradicts the secret reports of the Special Branch of the Intelligence Bureau which the author was given an opportunity to study. On the contrary, Gandhi had no plan of action at any time. Between the Wardha and Bombay meetings, 14 July to 7 August 1942, he proposed nothing more concrete to his followers than support for his Constructive Programme—spinning, abolition of untouchability, communal harmony and the like. One section of the Congress did work out a programme in advance—'the Andhra Congress Circular'—which set down a twelve-point plan of action to begin after Gandhi gave the signal for civil disobedience. However, there is no evidence that it was drafted at the instigation or with the support of the Congress High Command.

Both the Government and the Congress were guilty of large-scale violence, but it began after the arrest of the Congress leaders. From that point onwards it gave rise to a chain reaction for which the two parties shared responsibility. Most Congressmen were sincere in abjuring violence for political objectives, no one more so than Gandhi. One group, the Congress Socialists led by Jaya Prakash Narayan, had no such inhibitions. On the nationalist side it was they and some middle-rank leaders of the party who openly called for retaliation after the early days of police action.

The Viceroy charged that Gandhi was partly responsible for the violence because of his 'Do or Die' statement on 8 August.

In his closing remarks at the Bombay session Gandhi had said: 'Here is a *mantra* [dictum], a short one, that I give you. You may imprint it on your hearts and let every breath of yours give expression to it. The *mantra* is "Do or Die". We shall either free India or die in the attempt; we shall not live to see the perpetuation of our slavery. . . . Let that be your pledge.'[1]

Gandhi's words were '*karo* [do] *ya* [or] *maro* [die]', but *maro* has been translated by some as strike or kill also. The British charged that this was incitement to violence. Gandhi denied this categorically, saying that it was within the context of non-violence. Since non-violence was the governing passion of his life, there is no reason to doubt his intent, though some of his more militant followers seized upon it as a pretext for violent action. Moreover, Gandhi's last instructions to his followers, just before his arrest, were unambiguous: 'Let every non-violent soldier of freedom write out the slogan "Do or Die" on a piece of paper or cloth and stick it on his clothes, so that in case he died in the course of offering *satyagraha*, he might be distinguished by that sign from other elements who do not subscribe to non-violence.'[2]

Seen in historical perspective, the 'August Movement' was the outcome of persistent British intransigence during the preceding three years. This created such frustration among Indian nationalists that the only, though unwise, course of action was civil disobedience, as a symbolic act of defiance. If, instead, violence ensued, it was precipitated by the Government of India's abrupt and repressive action on 9 August which decapitated the Indian National Congress of its entire leadership. Thereafter the clash could not be averted.

It is difficult to gauge the effects of the revolt on the Indian war effort. According to General Sir Francis Tuker, then G.O.C. in eastern India, the riots accompanying the struggle 'nearly brought our armies to a standstill, fighting the Japanese on the Assam border'.[3] The Home Member of the Viceroy's Executive Council, Sir Reginald Maxwell, expressed a similar view to a special session of the central legislature in September 1942.

The long-range political consequences were even more significant. For almost three years the Congress was outlawed, its

---

[1] Tendulkar, op. cit., vol. 6, p. 216. [2] Ibid. Conveyed through his private secretary, Pyarelal. [3] *While Memory Serves*, p. 154.

leaders in prison, its funds seized and its organization virtually
destroyed. In the political vacuum thus created the Muslim
League was able to build a mass party, by appealing successfully to religious emotions and genuine Muslim fears. Between
1942 and 1945 the League increased its membership to two
million with the result that by the end of the war it was able to
put forward a strong claim to Pakistan. It could no longer be
said that there were only two political forces in India, the British
and the Congress. The Muslim League, too, was now a serious
contender for power. The Congress was to pay dearly for its
'Quit India' Resolution. Unwittingly it helped to pave the way
for Partition.[1]

In recalling the 'August Struggle' fourteen years later, Nehru
remarked: 'I don't think that the action we took in 1942 could
have been avoided or ought to have been avoided. It might
have been in slightly different terms; that is a different matter.
Circumstances drove us into a particular direction. If we had
been passive then, I think we would have lost all our strength.'
As for the Muslim League, he suggested that its growth was due
to two factors: 'the encouragement given to it by the British
Government . . . [and] a vague mass following on the religious
ground'.[2]

In retrospect, the Congress committed another blunder in
September 1944, when Gandhi was persuaded by Rajagopalacharia to meet Jinnah in a further effort to break the deadlock.
The talks proved futile: Jinnah insisted on Congress acceptance
of the principle of a sovereign, independent Pakistan as a basis
for agreement; Gandhi was prepared to accept an autonomous
Muslim state(s) within a loose all-India federation, the central
government of which would continue to administer foreign
affairs, defence, communications and related subjects. For Jinnah this was a 'maimed, mutilated and moth-eaten Pakistan'.
But the talks strengthened the League; they enhanced Jinnah's
prestige and gave him a status of virtual equality with Gandhi.[3]

*   *   *   *

[1] Some writers, notably V. P. Menon, trace the League's rise to prominence to
the resignation of the Congress provincial governments in 1939. However, the
marked expansion of League strength is evident only after the outlawry of the
Congress in 1942.   [2] To the author in New Delhi on 6 June 1956.
[3] The text of their accompanying correspondence is in *Gandhi-Jinnah Talks*
Hindustan Times Press, New Delhi), 1944.

While the 'August Revolt' raged over British India and the world war continued unabated Nehru remained in prison with his eleven colleagues of the Working Committee. The oldest of this unique band was the doughty, earthy Sardar Patel, organizing genius of the Congress. In appearance and dress the Sardar resembled a wise old Roman senator. He was a robust man, then in his late sixties, one of those Indians whose native male dress, the *dhoti*, gave dignity and nobility, an impression strengthened by his massive, strikingly bald head. His face was usually expressionless. But this mask concealed a clear, rational mind, forceful and determined. His piercing eyes and the hard lines around his mouth denoted strength of character and decisiveness, the dominant characteristics of modern India's most astute party politician. Yet he was not without a caustic wit which he exercised on occasion during the thousand days and nights at the Fort.

The most stimulating of Nehru's companions were: Maulana Azad, dean of the nationalist Muslims, a renowned Islamic scholar and a political comrade for twenty years; and Acharya Narendra Dev, gentle scholar and humanist, steeped in India's cultural traditions, a founder of the Socialist Party and a friend since pre-Gandhi days. There was Asaf Ali, later India's first Ambassador to the United States, fastidious to a fault, with an alert mind and a lawyer's outlook. Another Muslim companion was Dr. Syed Mahmud, a close associate since the early 1920's whom Nehru had befriended on many occasions.

Two members of the group were to bolt from the Congress and become prominent figures in the Praja-Socialist Party: Acharya Kripalani, in appearance the prototype of India's ascetics among the politicians, a man of strong and often divergent views; and Dr. Profullah Ghose, chemist by profession, a staunch Gandhian pacifist during the war-time cleavages within the High Command. An imposing figure was Pandit Pant, long-time leader of the United Provinces, with his massive frame and walrus moustache; though slow of movement, he was articulate and verbose. Later, he became Nehru's right hand at the Centre as Home Minister. From Maharashtra in Western India came Shankerrao Deo, devoted Gandhian, who was unique among Congress leaders in that he never occupied a position in government. A storehouse of information and an

engaging raconteur was Dr. Pattabhi Sitaramayya, historian of
the Congress, who served as party President and Governor of
Madhya Pradesh after Independence. The youngest was Hare-
krishna Mahtab, later Chief Minister of Orissa, Minister of
Commerce at the Centre and Governor of Bombay, who added
a touch of lightheartedness to the discussions. It was an odd
assortment. All shared a devotion to the cause of Indian freedom and, to a greater or lesser extent, an allegiance to Gandhi
and his ideals. Their temperaments varied, as did their cultural
interests, their habits of living, and their sensitivity to immediate
surroundings.

In one respect it was a novel experience, for though all were
veterans of prison life they had never been detained together,
nor for so long a period. It was a mild imprisonment on the
whole. The accommodation was adequate. They had a series
of adjoining rooms in a large quadrangle set apart from the main
prison and leading on to a long-neglected garden. They were
given a private kitchen, with service performed by convict
warders. The greatest punishment was a confining atmosphere;
for almost three years they were removed from the public stage
most of them loved so well.

From all accounts Nehru was, as usual, a model prisoner and
companion. According to Kripalani, he adjusted very well to
his surroundings. His presence brightened the gloomy atmosphere, and his varied interests and vitality were sources of
strength in the enforced communal environment. Though a
voracious reader, he participated in most of the humdrum activities carried on by his colleagues and took a leading interest in
gardening. In short, he was 'the soul of our party'.[1]

His routine was severely regulated. Early to rise, he began
the day with yoga exercises. After breakfast he settled down to
work—careful reading and painstaking notes. This lasted until
3 p.m. with only a short break for lunch. Then, after a brief
nap, there was discussion on politics and culture with his fellow
prisoners and a spell of gardening. In the evening he strolled in
the prison compound or played badminton. From nine to
eleven at night he returned to his books.

According to Narendra Dev, he was utterly devoted to his
companions and nursed his sick comrades with scrupulous

_____
[1] *Tribune* (Ambala), 15 November 1949.

attention. He had a passion for order and cleanliness, meticulous in the extreme, and was a model of tolerance in political discussions. He was full of energy, boyish in his exuberance and vitality. Despite his periodic outbursts and fiery temperament, he always made an effort to see the other person's viewpoint and was open to persuasion.[1]

For three weeks Nehru and his companions were completely isolated from the world. Thereafter news gradually seeped in through the government censors. They were also permitted a wide assortment of books and occasional letters from relatives, but no interviews. Thus, it was only after their release in the summer of 1945 that the full impact of events during these momentous years was brought home to the Congress leaders. In that sense these were utterly barren years, a period of unreality, when sweeping and dramatic changes were taking place throughout the world. Time stood still in the deadening atmosphere of prison. Had it been twenty years earlier, this might well have become a school for greatness, a training-ground for ideas, political tactics and plans for free India, for the creation of an *esprit* among the future moulders of a nation's destiny. But it was too late for that now. They were middle-aged men, whose formative political years were long since past.

Nevertheless, this period of inaction was productive for Nehru personally. As so often in the past, prison provided leisure for contemplation and writing. Now free from the daily political strife, he read voraciously and pondered with a fresh, inquisitive mind the problems which had long troubled him. It was another 'voyage of discovery', part of his endless quest for knowledge on the meaning of his life and the universe around him. From it emerged the last of his trilogy, *The Discovery of India*, written at the Fort between April and September 1944.

During the early 'thirties Nehru had explored the panorama of history on a grand scale, in his letters to his daughter, later published as *Glimpses of World History*. From this broad canvas he turned to self-analysis and related his own experience to India's struggle for freedom, in the celebrated *Autobiography*. Now he examined his cultural heritage, in the form of a rambling and discursive history of his native land, social, philosophical, economic, political and cultural. Largely under the

---

[1] *Nehru Abhinandan Granth: A Birthday Book*, pp. 111–12.

influence of Azad and Narendra Dev, with whom he spent
many hours in leisurely conversation, Nehru acquired a deep
appreciation of the various strands which make up the cultural
tradition of India and of their influence on his own thought and
action. He now sought and found the mainsprings of India's
struggle for independence within the context of India's historical
experience.

The Discovery of India is not especially profound or original.
Indeed, scholars question the accuracy of some of the facts and
his interpretation of many controversial issues. Yet it is important for the light it throws on Nehru's new awareness of the
specifically Indian influences on his character and outlook. Like
most of his writings it is partly autobiographical in form. In
essence it unfolds Nehru's discovery of his Indian antecedents,
the flow of Indian history seen through the eyes of a person who
had described himself earlier as 'out of place everywhere, at
home nowhere'.

CHAPTER XII

India at the Crossroads

AMIDST Nehru's reflections on Indian history the war entered its decisive stage. By the beginning of 1945 the outcome was no longer in doubt. The armies of the Grand Alliance were advancing towards the heart of Nazi Europe. Within India discontent was rampant, though partly concealed by an air of resignation. The political stalemate was complete. The continued imprisonment of Congress leaders was resented. And the Viceroy's silence about India's status after the war deepened the suspicion about London's intentions.

Dissatisfaction was increased by rapid economic deterioration. The priorities of war, bureaucratic mismanagement, and selfishness of Indian merchants had created a serious shortage of consumer goods with resultant inflation. Famine soon followed. In Bengal man and nature conspired to produce the most disastrous famine of the century. By official estimate $1\frac{1}{2}$ million persons perished and $4\frac{1}{2}$ million more suffered greatly during 1943 and 1944.[1] Towards the end of the war the food crisis spread ominously to other parts of the country.

Nehru observed this spectacle of death from afar, and recorded his anguish in prison: 'Famine came, ghastly, staggering, horrible beyond words. In Malabar, in Bijapur, in Orissa and, above all, in the rich and fertile province of Bengal, men and women and little children died in their thousands daily for lack of food. They dropped down dead before the palaces of Calcutta, their corpses lay in the mud-huts of Bengal's innumerable villages and covered the roads and fields of its rural areas. Men were dying all over the world and killing each other in battle; usually a quick death, often a brave death, death for a cause, death with a purpose, death which seemed in this mad world of ours an inexorable logic of events, a sudden end to the life we could not mould or control. Death was common enough everywhere. But here death had no purpose, no logic, no necessity;

[1] See Government of India, *Famine Inquiry Commission, Report on Bengal*, ch. XI.

it was the result of man's incompetence and callousness, man-made, a slow creeping thing of horror with nothing to redeem it, life merging and fading into death, with death looking out of the shrunken eyes and withered frame while life still lingered for a while. . . . Something was done at last. Some relief was given. But a million had died, or two millions, or three; no one knows how many starved to death or died of disease during these months of horror. No one knows of the many millions of emaciated boys and girls and little children who just escaped death then, but are stunted and broken in body and spirit.'[1]

The British *Raj* was generally slow to respond to pressures for change. In 1945, however, a new factor weighed heavily with the Viceroy. The consensus of military opinion was that the war against Japan would last a year or two after the end of hostilities in Europe—and India was expected to be the prin-cipal base of allied operations in East Asia. As a professional soldier, Lord Wavell appreciated the crucial role assigned to India. He was also aware of the temper of the country. Hence the necessity of finding a way out of the political impasse.

The Viceroy placed these considerations before the British Government in the spring of 1945. After ten weeks of consulta-tions in London, he returned to Delhi. In the interval much had happened. The war in Europe had ended. Churchill had re-signed and new elections were pending. The atom. bomb had not yet been tested. And a protracted struggle against Japan was anticipated. The time was ripe for concessions. Thus, on 14 June proposals were announced for Indian constitutional change 'within the framework of the 1935 Government of India Act'.

The Viceroy's Executive Council would be reconstituted, with only Indian members except for the Viceroy and the Commander-in-Chief. The Congress was assured that while the Viceroy's reserve powers could not be formally abandoned they would not be exercised unreasonably. The League was offered an even greater prize—'equal proportions of Caste Hindus and Moslems' in the Council. It was a novel twist to the concept of parity. Equal representation of the Congress and the League in a provisional national Government had served as the basis of the abortive 'Liaquat Ali–Bhulabhbhai Desai Pact' in January

[1] *The Discovery of India*, pp. 2–4.

1945.[1] By a slight change of terminology, *political parity*, which the Congress never officially accepted, was transformed into *communal parity*, a tactical objective of the League, and was incorporated into an official statement of British policy. These proposals, which were 'not an attempt to obtain or impose a constitutional settlement', would be discussed at a conference of representative political leaders in Simla on 25 June. To ease Congress acceptance of the invitation, all members of the Working Committee (but no other Congress prisoners) were to be released immediately.[2]

Nehru was released on 15 June at Almora, an exquisite but remote hill station in the United Provinces, in the foothills of the Himalayas. His first act was to visit the home of Ranjit Pandit at nearby Khali, as a mark of respect to his brother-in-law who had died in prison early in 1944. It was difficult to absorb the reality of freedom after more than a thousand days of close confinement. But there was no time for a leisurely adjustment. He hurried to Allahabad for a one-day reunion with the family and then to Bombay where the Congress Working Committee was meeting to consider the Wavell–Amery (Secretary of State) proposals. The invitation to Simla was accepted. But the League claim to the right to appoint *all* Muslim members of the Executive Council was emphatically rejected in advance.

Twenty-one persons were invited to Simla: the eleven provincial Premiers, most of whom were appointees of the Viceroy because of the resignation of the Congress ministries in 1939; the Congress and League leaders in the Central Assembly and the Council of State; the leaders of the insignificant Nationalist Party and the European Group in the Assembly; one delegate each for the Untouchables and the Sikhs; and Gandhi and Jinnah, 'as the recognized leaders of the two main political parties'. Conspicuously missing was an invitation to the (Muslim) President of the Congress, Maulana Azad. Gandhi declined on the ground that this was an official conference and he was not even a member of the Congress. However, he agreed

---

[1] For a discussion of this Pact see *Indian Annual Register*, vol. i, 1945, pp. 130–2, and vol. ii, 1945, pp. 124–7.

[2] The text is in Cmd. 6652, 1945. See also Gt. Brit. H.C. *Debates*, 1944–5, vol. 411, cols. 1831, 1834–40.

to go to Simla as an observer, in response to the Viceroy's persistent request. He also gently reminded Wavell that Azad was the official Congress spokesman and the 'error' was duly rectified.[1]

Optimism prevailed at the outset of the Conference, but this rapidly gave way to frustration. Stripped of the façade of multi-party and communal representation—for it was really a contest between the Congress and the League—the fate of the 1945 Simla Conference hung on one issue. The League insisted on the right to appoint *all* Muslims to the Executive Council and the Congress refused to abdicate its status as a national organization. Conversations took place between Jinnah and Pandit Pant (for the League President refused to meet the Muslim President of the Congress) but the deadlock remained. Wavell then tried to mediate. He requested both parties to submit lists of persons for the proposed Executive Council from which he would make the final selection. Jinnah sought a prior assurance that the five Muslims nominated by the League would be accepted *en bloc* (which would have eliminated the possibility of a Congress Muslim being appointed) but Wavell was non-committal. By 7 July all groups except the League had complied. For another week the Viceroy tried to win Jinnah's co-operation, but in vain. Finally, on the 14th, he terminated the Conference.

The manner in which this was done indicates the pattern to follow in the next two years. Confronted with Jinnah's intransigence, Wavell prepared his own list for an Executive Council, including non-League Muslims. 'When I explained my solution to Mr. Jinnah, he told me that it was not acceptable to the Muslim League and he was so decided that I felt it would be useless to continue the discussion. In the circumstances, I did not show my selections as a whole to Mr. Jinnah and there was no object in showing them to the other leaders. The conference has therefore failed.'[2]

The Viceroy's explanation reveals the twin sources of collapse. Jinnah threatened to boycott the Executive Council

[1] *Congress Bulletin*, No. 1, 1 November 1945, Part II, pp. 50–55.
[2] *The Statesman* (Calcutta), 26 July 1945. A detailed account of the Simla Conference along with texts of important speeches and correspondence is to be found in *The Statesman*, 26 June–15 July 1945; in Menon, op. cit., ch. VIII, and in *Congress Bulletin*, No. 1, 1 November 1945, Part II, pp. 43–63.

unless his demands were met; and Wavell acquiesced. The Conference failed because Wavell allowed Jinnah to veto its decisions, a precedent that strengthened Jinnah's hand in the crucial battles to follow. The League claim to represent all Muslims *at that time* was dubious: of the four Muslim-majority provinces, the North-West Frontier was under Congress control, the Punjab was governed by the Unionists, and Sind was dependent on Congress support for a stable ministry.

Nehru attended the Conference, but his role was of no importance. From Simla he went to Kashmir for a post-imprisonment holiday. His attachment springs not only from his family's ancestral roots there but also from his fondness for its exquisite natural beauty. Some years earlier, on a visit to the Vale, he had written: 'The loveliness of the land enthralled me and cast an enchantment all about me. I wandered about like one possessed and drunk with beauty, and the intoxication of it filled my mind. Like some supremely beautiful woman, whose beauty is almost impersonal and above human desire, such was Kashmir in all its feminine beauty of river and valley and lake and graceful trees. And then another aspect of this magic beauty would come to view, a masculine one, of hard mountains and precipices, and snow-capped peaks and glaciers, and cruel and fierce torrents rushing down to the valleys below.'[1]

*   *   *   *

While Nehru was in Kashmir a new chapter in Anglo-Indian relations began. On 26 July 1945 the British Labour Party took office. Time was not wasted. On 21 August the Viceroy was summoned to London for a fresh examination of the entire 'Indian problem'. It was announced simultaneously that general elections to the central and provincial legislatures, the first since 1937, would be held in the winter. Before another month had passed, Wavell returned to Delhi and a new policy statement appeared: provincial autonomy would be restored immediately after the elections; a constitution-making body for India would be established as soon as possible; and the Viceroy's Executive Council would be reconstituted in consultation with the principal Indian parties.[2]

[1] *The Unity of India*, p. 223.

[2] The text of Lord Wavell's statement on 19 September is to be found in *The Times* (London), 20 September 1945.

The Congress agreed to participate in the elections, though with some misgivings: 'There is little difference between Conservative Churchill and Laborite Attlee', wrote the party's General-Secretary. 'The present elections were devised merely to gain time.'[1] Like all such policy declarations, the Congress election manifesto was a catch-all.[2] It promised equal rights and opportunities for all men and women and a 'free democratic state with fundamental rights guaranteed in the Constitution'. These combined the freedoms of the liberal West with party commitments dating from the Karachi Resolution on Fundamental Rights in 1931: the abolition of untouchability; free and compulsory basic education; special safeguards for the Scheduled (Backward) Tribes; and neutrality in religious matters, i.e., secularism. Also deriving from the Karachi Resolution was the stress on the eradication of poverty and the raising of living standards through planning; state control or ownership of key industries; and regulation of banking and insurance. The provision about land reform attempted to satisfy both peasants and landlords; the removal of intermediaries by 'equitable compensation'; the scaling down of rural indebtedness; and encouragement to co-operative farming and cottage industries. Urban labour was promised a minimum wage and the right to form unions. To allay Muslim fears about their status in a united India the Congress called for a federal constitution 'with autonomy for its constituent parts [and] a minimum list of common and essential federal subjects'. Finally, it reaffirmed the principles enunciated in the 'Quit India' Resolution.

The Muslim League fought the elections on the issue of Hindu domination in a united India and the consequent need of a separate Muslim homeland, i.e., Pakistan. The results were astonishing. The League won all 30 Muslim seats in the Central Assembly, with 86 per cent. of the Muslim vote, and 427 of the 507 Muslim seats in the provincial legislatures, with 74 per cent. of the Muslim vote. Its only setback was in the North-West Frontier Province where the Congress-supported 'Redshirt

---

[1] Kripalani's circular of 25 October 1945. *Congress Bulletin*, No. 2, 24 January 1946, p. 9.

[2] Actually two manifestos were issued, one for the Central Assembly elections, the other for the provincial elections. For the texts see respectively Rosinger, L., *Restless India*, pp. 121–5, and *What Congress Fights For* (Central Election Board, Congress House, Bombay), 1945.

Movement' of the Khan brothers captured a clear majority. Most of the remaining seats were won by the Congress, 56 in the Central Assembly, with 91 per cent. of the 'General' vote, and 930 in the provinces. The trend to polarization was now evident; the Congress had paid a high price for the 'August Revolt'. All other groups faded into insignificance.[1]

The Congress formed provincial ministries in eight of the eleven provinces, the League in Bengal and Sind, and the Unionists, with Congress support, in the Punjab. The stage was now set for the reconstitution of the Viceroy's Executive Council and the convening of a Constituent Assembly. To achieve these goals the Labour Government dispatched a three-man Cabinet Delegation consisting of Lord Pethick-Lawrence, Sir Stafford Cripps and A. V. Alexander. Another frustrating bargaining session was soon to begin.

*   *   *   *

Two dramatic issues dominated Indian politics in the winter of 1945–6: the trial of members of the Indian National Army (I.N.A.) and the naval mutiny in Bombay. The first became a symbol of national pride. The second heralded the decline of British prestige.

Much has been written about the I.N.A.[2] Its origins lay with the 60,000 Indian prisoners-of-war in Malaya. Japanese soldiers were instructed to be lenient to the Indian community in Malaya and Singapore, and prisoners were given inducements to transfer their allegiance. Almost immediately after the conquest of the peninsula in February 1942 the Japanese created Indian Independence Leagues with prominent Indian residents as figureheads. Those prisoners who were prepared to take an oath to Japan were released and given special amenities. The movement was clearly Japanese-sponsored.

It was not until the arrival of Subhas Bose in the summer of

---

[1] For a detailed picture of the election results see *Indian Annual Register*, vol. i, 1946, pp. 229–31.

[2] For a representative British view see Tuker, op. cit., ch. iv. For a semi-official I.N.A. view see Shah Nawaz Khan, *I.N.A. and its Netaji* (1946), and Dhillon, G. S., *The Indian National Army in East Asia* (1946). The only objective account known to the author is to be found in Chin Kee Onn, *Malaya Upside Down* (1946) (published in Chinese). An English translation of the chapter on the I.N.A. is available in the files of the History of the Freedom Movement Project.

1943 that the Independence Leagues acquired mass popularity. Under his fiery leadership about 20,000 prisoners joined the newly-formed Indian National Army, many lured by the prospects of power and prestige in the 'Free India' that Bose promised his followers. On 21 October 1943 he proclaimed the Provisional Government of Free India with himself as Head of State, Commander-in-Chief of the I.N.A., War Minister and Foreign Minister. Three days later he declared war on the U.S. and Britain.

The I.N.A.'s performance on the battlefield sowed the seeds of its rapid disintegration. The Japanese held it in reserve until the threat to their own armies became acute. In April 1944 it was thrown into the battle of Imphal and suffered a savage defeat from which it never recovered. Bose reverted to propaganda war, but enthusiasm faded rapidly. Only the inspiring leadership of the *Netaji*—the Leader—as Bose was called by his followers, kept the movement alive. With his death in an aeroplane accident in August 1945 the I.N.A. collapsed.

All nationalist movements distort the role and significance of their aberrations. The I.N.A. was the most attractive deviation from the principles of non-violence which guided Indian nationalism during its Gandhian era, from 1920 to 1947. Thus, when the Government of India made known its intention of punishing some I.N.A. officers, nationalists rallied to their defence. Nehru was no exception. 'Whatever their failing and mistakes . . . they are a fine body of young men . . . and their dominating motive was love for India's freedom.'[1] Pleading for generous treatment, he claimed that they 'functioned as a regular, organized, disciplined and uniformed combatant force' and were therefore entitled to treatment as prisoners-of-war. They only allied themselves with Japan to facilitate Indian freedom. He rejected the charge that Bose was a war criminal, defended the levy of taxes by the Bose Government, and stated that he never doubted Bose's passion for Indian freedom. He welcomed the trial of alleged war criminals but added, 'in my list there will be many officials sitting in Delhi'.[2]

Nehru's attitude to the I.N.A. expressed the Congress mood just after V-J Day. Nor was his support confined to words. The Congress set up an I.N.A. Defence Committee consisting of

[1] Bright, J. S., *The Great Nehrus*, p. 115.   [2] Ibid., p. 118.

some of the ablest lawyers in the country—Bhulabhbhai Desai, Congress Leader in the Central Assembly, Sir Tej Bahadur Sapru, the aged Liberal leader, Dr. Katju, Asaf Ali, Raghunandan Saran—and Nehru. For the first time in almost thirty years he donned his legal robes and attended court. It was only a symbolic act, but thousands were roused by the sight of Nehru, Bhulabhbhai and Sapru approaching the Red Fort where the trials were held. The Congress also appointed an I.N.A. Relief and Inquiry Committee of twelve members, including Nehru.

By the time the trials began in November 1945 all eyes were on the I.N.A. The drama was heightened by the fact that the legal battle took place at the Red Fort in Delhi, the enduring expression of Moghul power in the sub-continent, which called forth visions of a united India without the British. It was intensified by the inter-communal character of the first and most important trial. Major-General Shah Nawaz, a Muslim, Colonel Dhillon, a Sikh, and Major Sahgal, a Hindu, were put on trial together for waging war against the King-Emperor, i.e., for rebellion, with the additional charge of abetment to murder in Shah Nawaz's case. All were convicted, but under pressure from Nehru, Gandhi and others the sentences were suspended. The I.N.A. officers were lionized throughout the country, to the horror of British (and some Indian) officers. History abounds with examples of the impact of the declining prestige of the armed forces on the stability of a régime. By conceding to the demand for leniency, the Government of India weakened the *élan* of the army. In the opinion of one senior British officer at the time, General Sir Francis Tuker, this concession was a monumental blunder.

Nehru's motives in defending the I.N.A. are not entirely clear. Political necessity may have been one. National pride was certainly involved, as revealed in his foreword to Shah Nawaz's book, *The I.N.A. and its Netaji*: 'My friend and colleague Major-General Shah Nawaz Khan of the I.N.A. has presented these facts in sober fashion, and thus provided an important record of an important undertaking. . . . I recommend it, therefore, to others and I hope that a reading of it will bring enlightenment about many aspects of this brave adventure.' This affectionate comment was dated 10 October 1946, when Nehru was Vice-President of the Viceroy's Executive Council.

And yet he was not uncritically devoted to the I.N.A. When a Muslim member of the Central Assembly urged the release of all I.N.A. personnel convicted of specific crimes, Nehru objected forcefully, saying that it consisted of morally good, bad and indifferent men.[1]

During the winter of 1945–6 disaffection penetrated the military services, further undermining British prestige. Ironically, it began in the R.A.F. which mutinied at Dum Dum airport near Calcutta and other stations in India and the Middle East. These were followed by hunger strikes in the R.I.A.F. (Royal Indian Air Force) and minor cases of indiscipline in the R.I.N. (Royal Indian Navy). The explosion occurred on 18 February 1946 in the form of a mutiny of naval ratings at Bombay. For the next five days the leading base of the R.I.N. and the city itself presented the appearance of a minor battlefield, though there was little bloodshed.

There were strong political overtones to the mutiny. Congress and Muslim League flags were flown from the 'captured' ships and shore establishments. Left-wing parties called for a 'union of Hindus and Muslims at the barricades'. Communist influence was evident in the Sailors' Central Strike Committee. Congress leaders sympathized with the sailors' grievances but opposed their reliance on the Communists and the talk of violence. Patel hurried to Bombay, condemned the mutiny and persuaded the ratings to surrender unconditionally—by promising Congress aid against victimization and support for their legitimate demands. Nehru adopted a similar attitude. The mutiny spread to other naval bases, notably Karachi on 20 February, but these incidents were short-lived and less dramatic.

Genuine grievances were at the root of the mutinies, along with the restlessness common to all servicemen at the end of a war. However, there can be little doubt that the loss of 'face' by the Government of India as a result of the I.N.A. affair contributed to the belief in the armed forces generally that mutiny was not a serious offence. The political significance of the events in Bombay cannot be gauged accurately, but it seems more than a mere coincidence that the announcement about the British

---

[1] Campbell-Johnson, A., *Mission with Mountbatten*, p. 53. The incident occurred in the Central Assembly on 2 April 1947.

Cabinet Mission was made on 19 February 1946, one day after the outbreak of the mutiny. And General Tuker noted that 'as late as June 1946 the ripples of the R.I.N. mutinies were still disturbing the surface of India'.[1]

*   *   *   *

The initial announcement about the Cabinet Mission was obscure on the approach to a settlement. Attlee filled in the gaps in a statement before the House of Commons on 15 March 1946. It was the turn of the Congress to be reassured. On the core issue of independence the British Prime Minister declared: 'India herself must choose what will be her future Constitution. I hope that the Indian people may elect to remain within the British Commonwealth. . . . But if she does so elect, it must be by her own free will. . . . If, on the other hand, she elects for independence, in our view she has a right to do so.' As for the Muslim League's goal of Pakistan, he said: 'We are very mindful of the rights of minorities and minorities should be able to live free from fear. On the other hand, *we cannot allow a minority to place a veto on the advance of the majority.*'[2] The Congress was jubilant, the League dismayed by this unexpected shift of policy. Both marshalled their forces for a showdown.

Cripps was the dominant figure in the Cabinet Mission, the person who produced the complex plans which attempted to please every shade of political opinion but satisfied no one. The Mission's goals were twofold—to reconstitute the Viceroy's Executive Council as a coalition Interim Government and to secure agreement on a constitution-making body. The 'three wise men' arrived in Delhi on 24 March and began a round of interviews with representatives of all political parties. After a brief adjournment to Kashmir Pethick-Lawrence, the senior member of the Mission, conveyed the bases of a compromise settlement to the Congress and League Presidents.

The 'fundamental principles' of the scheme were deceptively simple. There was to be 'a Union Government dealing with . . . Foreign Affairs, Defence and Communications . . . [and]

---

[1] Tuker, op. cit., p. 92. A British account of the R.I.N. mutiny is to be found in ch. VI of Tuker's book. For a Congress account see Pyarelal, *Mahatma Gandhi, The Last Phase*, vol. i, pp. 168–70, 172–5. For a Communist view see Dutt, R. P., *India To-day* (Indian edition 1947), pp. 471–5.

[2] Gt. Brit. H.C. *Debates*, 1946, vol. 420, cols. 1421 1422. (Emphasis added.)

two groups of Provinces, the one of the predominantly Hindu Provinces and the other of the predominantly Muslim Provinces, dealing with all other subjects which the Provinces in the respective groups desire to be dealt with in common. The Provincial Governments will deal with all other subjects and will have all the residuary Sovereign rights. It is contemplated that the Indian [princely] States will take their appropriate place in this structure on terms to be negotiated with them.'[1] This three-tier plan was drafted by Cripps at breakfast one morning in Delhi just after his return from Kashmir.[2]

For the next few months a battle of interpretation raged fiercely in the Indian capital, reflecting the complexity of the scheme, the intensity of feelings and the depth of disagreement between the Congress and the League. The Mission itself was to add to the confusion by its successive 'clarifications'.

The negotiations began with a cautious, qualified acceptance by both parties of the invitation to discuss these 'fundamental principles' at Simla. From the outset the lines of division were clearly drawn by the Congress and the League. Their spokesmen moved to Simla early in May, with Nehru, Azad, Patel and Abdul Ghaffar Khan acting for the Congress, Jinnah, Liaquat Ali, Nishtar and Mohammed Ismail representing the League. Gandhi attended at the Mission's request because Cripps was determined to avoid a repetition of the 1942 fiasco. Minor concessions were made in an effort to secure agreement, but to no avail. On fundamental issues the impasse was complete. The Congress insisted that the Union Constitution be framed first, the League, after the Group Constitutions were drafted. The Congress insisted on the optional character of the Groups, the League demanded that they be compulsory. The Congress insisted on the right of the Union to raise revenue by taxation, the League refused. After a week of fruitless negotiations the second Simla Conference came to an end.

The Cabinet Mission now offered its own recommendations, in two instalments: on 16 May it announced a long-range plan, i.e., proposals for a constitutional settlement; and on 16 June it outlined a procedure for the formation of an Interim Govern-

---

[1] Cmd. 6829, 1946, p. 3.
[2] Related to the author in London in October 1955, by the Private Secretary to Cripps during the Cabinet Mission.

ment. The long-range plan followed the 'fundamental principles' of Pethick-Lawrence, noted earlier. Theoretically, all the warring parties could have been satisfied. There were to be three Sections for British India: B, consisting of the Muslim-majority provinces in the north-west, namely, the Punjab, Sind, the North-West Frontier Province and Baluchistan; C, consisting of Bengal and Assam; and A, the rest of British India. The Sections would meet to form Groups and to draft the provincial and group constitutions. Each province would have the right to opt out of a Group by a simple majority of its legislature *after* the first elections under the new provincial constitutions. Thus the League was offered a *de facto* Pakistan. The Congress could find in the scheme a united India, though somewhat emasculated, and an assurance of provincial autonomy. The plan also provided for the lapse of Paramountcy, thereby granting freedom of action to the Princes.

The Mission tried to find an acceptable compromise on many controversial issues by drawing an imaginary line half-way between the demands of the Congress and the League. This procedure reached absurd heights on the grouping scheme, the hardest bone of contention. There were two clauses which appeared to contradict each other directly. In Paragraph 15, clause 5, it was stated that '*Provinces should be free* to form groups, with executives and legislatures, and each *group could* determine the provincial subjects to be taken in common.' In laying down the procedure, however, Paragraph 19, sub-clauses (iv) and (v), stipulated that 'the *provincial representatives will divide up* into three sections. . . . These sections *shall* proceed to settle provincial constitutions . . . and *shall also decide* whether any group constitution shall be set up for those provinces . . .'[1] The first provision made grouping voluntary, the second compulsory. The battle of interpretation was concentrated on this point.

The League accepted the plan 'inasmuch as the basis and the foundation of Pakistan are inherent in the Mission's plan by virtue of compulsory grouping of the six Muslim Provinces . . .' —which included the Hindu-majority province of Assam.[2] The Congress played for time. On 24 May the Working Committee

[1] The text of the Cabinet Mission Statement on 16 May 1946 is in Cmd. 6821, 1946. (Emphasis added.)
[2] Lumby, E. W. R., *The Transfer of Power in India*, p. 94.

made its decision dependent on the short-run plan for an Interim Government which was still under discussion. It stated further that it read Paragraph 15 to mean that provinces could decide to opt out of the Groups from the very beginning. The Mission replied the following day that this 'does not accord with the Delegation's [Mission's] intentions'.[1]

At that point the verbal battle shifted to the problem of an Interim Government. Once again the protagonists disagreed sharply. Nehru sought the Viceroy's assurance that in fact, if not in law, the Interim Government would function like a Dominion Cabinet. Wavell avoided iron-clad guarantees but pledged wide latitude to the Interim Government. Jinnah clung to the letter of the law and argued that the Interim Government would be simply a reconstituted Executive Council with advisory powers, under the terms of the 1919 Government of India Act.

In the face of deadlock the Cabinet Mission put forward its own recommendations. On 16 June 1946 it proposed the formation of an Interim Government consisting of six Hindu members of the Congress, one being an Untouchable, five Muslims of the League and three representatives of the minorities—one Sikh, one Christian, and one Parsi. Jinnah had scored another victory, despite the Viceroy's assurance to the Congress President two days before that the Congress would have the right to appoint a nationalist Muslim.[2] Furthermore, all five League nominees were approved, but three Congress nominees were replaced by the Viceroy without consulting the party. Despite these developments, the Congress was on the verge of accepting the proposed Interim Government—on the 18th of June.

At that crucial point Nehru rushed to Kashmir in order to assist in the defence of his protégé at the time, Sheikh Abdullah, then on trial for treason. He was prohibited entry and was detained when he violated the Maharaja's order. In Nehru's absence Jinnah won further concessions from the Viceroy. When Azad, the Congress President, raised these matters with Wavell, the Viceroy replied: 'For reasons of which you are

---

[1] The Working Committee Resolution and the Cabinet Mission Statement on 25 May are in Cmd. 6835, 1946.

[2] Letter of 14 June 1946. Sitaramayya, op. cit., vol. ii, p. ccix.

already aware, it is not possible for the Cabinet Delegation or myself to accept this request', i.e., the right to appoint a Congress Muslim to the Interim Government.[1] Gandhi threatened to leave Delhi and, by inference, the Congress if his colleagues acquiesced.

Nehru was urged by Azad to return at once, and the Viceroy intervened through the British Resident in Kashmir to expedite it. Nehru did so, 'though not without misgivings', and only after Azad assured him, with the consent of Gandhi and the Working Committee, 'that the Congress would make his cause in Kashmir their own' and that, if necessary, Gandhi himself would go to Kashmir.[2] To many Nehru's behaviour seemed immature. Although it showed commendable loyalty to a friend the political battle in Delhi was far more important.

The climax was approaching. From 20 to 25 June the Congress Working Committee met in almost permanent session.[3] Gandhi's position hardened and he advised rejection of both plans. His colleagues, however, were not completely persuaded. The Working Committee rejected the plan for an Interim Government but accepted the long-term plan—with its own interpretation of the disputed clauses. The Cabinet Mission, instead of recognizing the harsh reality of continued deadlock, interpreted the Congress resolution as 'acceptance' of its constitutional proposals and shelved its recommendations for an Interim Government. It left for England at the end of June, having accomplished virtually nothing. Indeed, the heightened tension augured ill for the future. The gap was as wide as ever.

*   *   *   *

In the midst of these negotiations the Congress held a presidential election, the first since 1940. Normally it was an annual affair, but special circumstances had resulted in postponement for six years: the civil disobedience campaign in 1940–1; the imprisonment of Congress leaders from 1942 to 1945; the general elections of 1945–6, and the Cabinet Mission. Normally, too, the choice of president was secondary because Gandhi remained the dominant figure in the party until 1947. Indeed, the office

[1] Letter of 22 June 1946. Sitaramayya, op. cit., vol. ii, p. ccxix.
[2] *Congress Bulletin*, No. 7, 15 October 1946, p. 3.
[3] For an illuminating account of the proceedings see Pyarelal, op. cit., pp. 233–9.

of president conferred more status than power, a position of first among equals with the Mahatma as super-president. Contests were rare, the most noteworthy being the bitter campaign of 1939 when Bose defeated Sitaramayya, the candidate of Gandhi and the Old Guard. In 1946, however, the choice assumed greater importance because of the impending formation of an Interim Government. The circumstances attending the election in that year throw considerable light on the relations between Nehru, Gandhi and Patel and on decision-making in the Congress High Command.

Officially there were three candidates—Patel, Nehru and Kripalani, Congress General-Secretary at the time. Bose and Narayan were also nominated but were ruled ineligible, the former because he was not a member of the party—he was in fact dead—and the latter because he was not among the delegates—he was still in prison. The election was scheduled for 16 May, the day the Cabinet Mission published its long-term plan. Before that date, however, Patel and Kripalani 'informed the A.I.C.C. office of their intention to withdraw their candidature. . . . Nehru remained the only candidate.'[1]

The real story behind the 1946 election was very different. In accordance with the time-honoured practice of rotating the presidency, Patel was in line for the post. Fifteen years had elapsed since he presided over the Karachi session whereas Nehru had presided at Lucknow and Faizpur in 1936 and 1937. Moreover, Patel was the overwhelming choice of the Provincial Congress Committees; according to one source twelve of fifteen P.C.C.s favoured him, the balance supporting Nehru. Nehru's 'election' was due to Gandhi's intervention. Patel was persuaded to step down. The Mahatma's decisive influence was confirmed by his own remarks to the A.I.C.C. on 6 July: 'I told Jawaharlal that he must wear the crown of thorns for the sake of the nation and he has agreed.'[2] The following day while taking over the chair from Azad, Nehru declared: 'I was for a long time unable to make up my mind. . . . But the day before yesterday I persuaded myself to shoulder the responsibility on the advice of Mahatmaji and also my colleagues in the Working Committee.'[3]

---

[1] *Congress Bulletin*, No. 5, 3 August 1946, p. 28.
[2] Tendulkar, op. cit., vol. 7, p. 176. [3] *Indian Annual Register*, vol. ii, 1946, p. 131.

The general consensus is that the Mahatma preferred Nehru because of his greater international prestige. Gandhi himself strengthened this belief by his remarks to a prayer meeting on the eve of Partition: 'Jawaharlal cannot be replaced today, whilst the charge is being taken from Englishmen. He, a Harrow boy, a Cambridge graduate and a barrister, is wanted to carry on the negotiations with Englishmen.'[1] A close colleague of Patel minimized this factor and stressed the point that Nehru could speak with greater authority for a united Congress than Patel, who allegedly disliked Azad and was inclined to distrust nationalist Muslims in general. On another occasion Patel was reported to have said, 'there is only one genuinely nationalist Muslim in India—Jawaharlal', presumably because of Nehru's secularism and sympathy for Muslims.[2]

One month after the election the Viceroy invited Nehru, as Congress President, to form an Interim Government. If Gandhi had not intervened, Patel would have been the first de facto Premier of India, in 1946–7. Gandhi certainly knew of the impending creation of the Interim Government. One must infer, therefore, that he preferred Nehru as the first Prime Minister of free India. The Sardar was 'robbed of the prize' and 'it rankled deeply'.[3] He was then seventy-one while Nehru was fifty-six; in traditionalist Indian terms the elder statesman should have been the first premier, some suggested; and Patel knew that because of his advanced age another opportunity would probably not arise.

There is a striking parallel with the Congress election of 1929; on both occasions Gandhi threw his weight behind Nehru at the expense of Patel. It may well be that he showed foresight both times, for it was easier to moderate the radicalism of the Congress Left than to liberalize the Right.

* * * *

The next stage in the tangled story of the Cabinet Mission began early in July 1946, when the A.I.C.C. met in Bombay to consider the Mission's plans. The debate was spirited, but the

---

[1] On 1 June 1947. Tendulkar, op. cit., vol. 8, p. 3.
[2] Related to the author in India in 1956 by a person who wishes to remain anonymous.
[3] Ibid.

outcome was never in doubt. The policy enunciated by the Working Committee was approved by 204 to 51. Yet the Congress was unhappy about the plans, as evident in Nehru's speech on 10 July, one of the most fiery and provocative statements in his forty years of public life.

The Congress was committed to participate in the Constituent Assembly, he said, but nothing else. And the Assembly would be a sovereign body, regardless of policy statements from London. Of course, protection of the minorities had to be assured, as Congress had always pledged, but this would be done by the Constituent Assembly alone. As for a treaty with Britain, this would depend on the British attitude. If they tried to delay the transfer of power, he said, there would be a direct clash. If they treated Indians as equals there would be a treaty, but any attempt to impose it would be resisted. About the grouping scheme Nehru was brutally candid. It would probably never come to fruition, he declared, because section A, the Hindu-majority provinces, would be opposed, the Frontier Province would oppose it in section B as would Assam in section C, and provincial jealousies would thwart it. He also stressed the likelihood of a much stronger central government than that envisaged by the Cabinet Mission. While its jurisdiction would be confined to foreign affairs, defence and communications, he said, each of these would be broadly interpreted and would probably include defence industries, foreign trade policy, loans, and taxing power for the Centre, 'because it couldn't live on doles. . . . The scope of the Centre, even though limited, inevitably grows, because it cannot exist otherwise.'[1]

There was much political insight in Nehru's speech. Few would deny that the Frontier and Assam, both Congress provinces at the time, would opt out of their Groups if given an opportunity to do so in 1946. His reference to provincial jealousies found ample support in the post-partition history of West Pakistan and India. So too did his observations on a strong Centre; both India and Pakistan have had frequent recourse to emergency powers since Independence.

Whether it was wise to utter such views in the political atmosphere of 1946 is another question. Nehru's remarks certainly cleared the air of confusion and hypocrisy. At the same time

---

[1] *Indian Annual Register*, vol. ii, 1946, pp. 145–7.

they destroyed the façade of agreement which the Cabinet Mission tried to maintain. In fact, his speech sparked the collapse of the Mission. There was nothing fundamentally new in his speech, but it was a serious tactical error: Jinnah was given an incomparable wedge to press more openly for Pakistan on the grounds of Congress 'tyranny'. This was done on 27 July when the League withdrew its acceptance of the Mission's long-run plan and called for 'Direct Action' to achieve the goal of Pakistan. The 'Direct Action' decision was ominous, for it set in motion the disastrous civil war which was to engulf the sub-continent for the next eighteen months. August 16 was proclaimed 'Direct Action Day'. To the Council of the League Jinnah announced: 'Today we bid goodbye to constitutional methods.' The die was cast. The death knell to the Cabinet Mission's long-run plan had been sounded, though it was to linger on for another seven months.[1]

Many persons regret that this plan never came to fruition. But it satisfied neither party and was unworkable in the tension of 1946–7. Neither the Congress nor the League ever really accepted the plan, though both placed their formal approval on record for bargaining purposes. It suffered from other disabilities as well. The Labour Government and its three envoys were sincere in wanting to transfer power, but none seemed to know how to accomplish it. By contrast, the India Office and some permanent officials in India opposed the transfer, especially as long as the Congress was committed to secession from the Commonwealth, as it then was.

The basic drawback of the plan was its complexity and cumbersome procedure. Cripps approached the highly-charged problem of a constitutional settlement as if it were an intellectual exercise. The three-tier scheme (Centre, Groups, provinces) was an intellectual *tour de force* but it was impracticable in the environment of a deadly struggle for power. It would have led to endless friction between the Centre, the Groups and the provinces, and between the Congress and the League, making normal administration impossible. Cripps apparently never thought out the consequences. He was riding two horses at the same time, trying to find a solution on paper which both parties

[1] A comprehensive account of the Cabinet Mission is to be found in Menon, op. cit., ch. x and xi and pp. 280–4.

would accept. His proposal, in effect, would have brought Pakistan in through the back door, by the group scheme, and would have maintained the façade of a united India. As long as the two Indian parties disagreed on fundamentals any plan was doomed, until the communal riots weakened the Congress will to persist in the demand for a united India. Such a disaster had yet to run its course.

In the meantime the efforts to form an Interim Government continued. Towards the end of July the Viceroy approached Nehru and Jinnah with a fresh assurance that it would be treated with the same consideration as a Dominion Cabinet. Nehru declined the invitation unless its status and powers were clarified in unambiguous terms so as to avoid another battle of interpretation. Jinnah replied with the 'Direct Action' Resolution. The threat backfired, for Wavell then called on Nehru alone to submit proposals for an Interim Government.

At that point Nehru approached Jinnah directly in an effort to cut the Gordian knot of suspicion. The two leaders met at Jinnah's home in Bombay on 15 August, but their goals could not be reconciled. (Little did either realize that exactly one year later the impasse would be broken in the cataclysm of Partition and communal war.) The parties resumed their propaganda war with renewed vigour. Wavell was distressed by the turn of events and persisted in his attempt to square a circle. So matters stood on 2 September 1946 when the Interim Government was formally installed. The League continued its boycott. Nehru became Vice-President of the Viceroy's Executive Council (*de facto* Prime Minister) and Member for External Affairs and Commonwealth Relations.[1]

*   *   *   *

Amidst these 'summit talks' the poison of communalism penetrated deeper into the body politic of India. Restlessness, frustration and the contest for power heightened the tension to boiling point. All that was required was leadership and organization. The 'War of Succession' was ready to begin.[2] Its spark

---

[1] For the details see Menon, op. cit., pp. 285–305, and Pyarelal, op. cit., pp. 264–71.

[2] This term was coined by Sir Evan Jenkins, the last Governor of the undivided Punjab, to designate the communal riots in the Punjab during the spring and

was Jinnah's proclamation of 'Direct Action Day' at the end of July. The initial result was the 'Great Calcutta Killing'.

There is no evidence to suggest that Jinnah himself planned or even desired the holocaust, though he had no compunction about resorting to violence. Whether orders were dispatched to the Muslim League Ministry in Bengal is unknown. In any event they were unnecessary. The Bengal Government declared a public holiday on 16 August which enabled thousands of civil servants to attend a mammoth League rally in Calcutta. Reports of what followed vary in details. But there can be no reasonable doubt that the tragedy was a direct by-product of the incitement to violence by the Muslim League in general and the Bengal League Ministry in particular.

The British-owned *Statesman* of Calcutta, one of the most reputable newspapers in Asia, placed the blame squarely on the League: 'The origin of the appalling carnage and loss in the capital of a great Province—we believe the worst communal riot in India's history—was a political demonstration by the Muslim League,' it wrote on 20 August when the killing had subsided. 'The bloody shambles to which this country's largest city has been reduced is an abounding disgrace, which . . . has inevitably tarnished seriously the all-India reputation of the League itself.' Of the hell that was Calcutta from 16 August to 19 August 1946, the senior British military officer in the area wrote: 'February's killings had shocked us all but this was different: it was unbridled savagery with homicidal maniacs let loose to kill and kill and to maim and burn. The underworld of Calcutta was taking charge of the city.'[1] Only after four days of lunacy, in which 4,000 were killed and thousands more wounded, did the city return to relative sanity.

General Tuker's eyewitness account sheds no light on who 'let loose' the 'homicidal maniacs'. On this and other points the *Statesman* was pungent. 'This is not a riot', it wrote on 20 August. 'It needs a word found in medieval history, a fury. Yet "fury" sounds spontaneous and there must have been some deliberation and organization to set this fury on the way. Hordes who ran about battering and killing with eight-foot

summer of 1947. In this context it is used to describe the Hindu–Muslim and Congress–League conflict in India as a whole during the last year before Partition.
[1] Tuker, op. cit., p. 160.

lathis may have found them lying about or bought them out of their own pockets, but that is hard to believe. We have already commented on the bands who found it easy to get petrol and vehicles when no others were permitted on the streets. It is not mere supposition that men were imported into Calcutta to help in making an impression.' To make matters worse the police acted slowly. According to General Tuker, the extent of the slaughter in the Calcutta slums became known to the police only on the afternoon of the 17th with the result that the army was called in long after the disorders had begun. Others claim that Suhrawardy, the Premier of Bengal, had prepared for the 'Killing' by placing Muslims in charge of the majority of police posts and that they were in no hurry to report the riots—until the Hindus retaliated with equal vehemence.

Nothing comparable to the 'Great Calcutta Killing' had occurred in the annals of British rule. But this was only the beginning of a tidal wave of communal madness which was to sweep over India during the next year. As with all mass up-heavals an irrevocable chain reaction was set in motion. Early in October 1946 the scene shifted to the Noakhali District of eastern Bengal where Muslim gangs went on the rampage, killing, looting, converting Hindus by force, and destroying Hindu temples and property indiscriminately. The official esti-mate was 300 killed and thousands made homeless; the Congress press kindled the flames with exaggerated reports of casualties. These spread like wildfire to the neighbouring province of Bihar where from 27 October to 6 November the Hindu majority wreaked vengeance with equal savagery. The estimates varied again, but not less than 7,000 Muslims were killed.[1] Nehru arrived on 3 November with Patel, Liaquat Ali Khan and Nishtar, all members of the Interim Government.

The difference in approach of Gandhi and Nehru was brought into sharp relief during the 1946 riots. The Mahatma went on a prolonged walking tour of Noakhali, addressing small groups at every village, bringing the message of communal harmony and appealing to their sanity. His soothing words were directed to the hearts of each individual; there was no recrimination. To

---

[1] For accounts of the autumn 1946 riots see Tuker, op. cit., ch. XII, XIV, XV and XVII; Khosla, G. D., *Stern Reckoning*, ch. II; and *Indian Annual Register*, vol. ii, 1946, pp. 182–4, 194–9 and 200–14.

some extent Nehru did the same in Bihar, though there was less of the personal touch in his passionate words to the crowds who gathered in thousands to hear him. He scolded the Hindus mercilessly for their brutal behaviour towards those with whom they had lived in peace for centuries. He appealed for a return to sanity but also threatened harsh punishment unless the killing ceased. Both had a quieting effect on the people of Bengal and Bihar, but their methods were basically different.

Nehru's reaction to the riots was typical of the man: deep sympathy for the victims of both communities; stern rebukes to the perpetrators of the ghastly crimes, regardless of the source; courageous tours of the worst affected areas disregarding his personal safety; appeals for communal peace supplemented by threats of military retaliation. Nehru was appalled by the crazed resort to mass murder among normally placid peasants. With the long-sought prize of independence so near, the riots struck him as a dastardly blow to his hopes for a free India. 'There appears to be a competition in murder and brutality', he said in the course of a moving report on the riots to the Central Assembly.[1] The shock waves were to recur time and time again, leaving indelible marks on Nehru's outlook for the future.

* * * *

While the early battles of the 'War of Succession' raged in Bengal and Bihar the Interim Government entered on a stormy course in Delhi. Initially the experiment went well, for the League boycott permitted joint responsibility in the Congress-dominated Executive Council. In his inaugural broadcast as *de facto* Prime Minister, on 7 September 1946, Nehru outlined 'his government's' broad policy objectives, both domestic and foreign. The statement followed the Congress election manifesto in its stress on relief and higher standards of living for the 'common and forgotten man in India', communal harmony, the struggle against untouchability, special aid for backward tribes, etc. A striking feature was the clear indication of the essentials of his foreign policy: non-alignment with power blocs; the emancipation of colonial and dependent peoples; the repudiation of racialism; co-operative relations with the U.K. and

---

[1] A summary of his speech on 14 November 1946 is to be found in *Indian Annual Register*, vol. ii, 1946, pp. 212–14.

M

the Commonwealth; friendship with the U.S. and the U.S.S.R.; specially close ties with the countries of Asia, notably with South-east Asia and China, and the long-range goal of a world commonwealth. He concluded with an appeal for co-operation by all parties and left the door open to the League to enter the Interim Government.[1]

During the next month the political atmosphere in Delhi was relatively placid, though undercurrents of friction between permanent officials and Congress ministers broke through the surface on various occasions. Members of the Interim Government were directed to notify the Political Department (the liaison between the Government of India and the Princes) before visiting any princely State and to abstain from political speeches in the States. Nehru was annoyed and wrote to the Viceroy: 'I do not quite understand why we should function . . . under the tutelage of the Political Department. . . . It will be more fitting if the Political Department brought itself in line with the present Government.'[2]

At the beginning of October the Viceroy entered into separate negotiations with Jinnah who presented nine 'demands' as a basis for League entry into the Government. These were brought to the attention of Nehru and another fruitless correspondence followed. There was nothing essentially new in Jinnah's demands: that the Viceroy's Executive Council be strictly limited to fourteen members—six Hindu Congressmen, including one Untouchable, five League Muslims and three representatives of the minorities—with the explicit denial of the Congress right to appoint a nationalist Muslim; that vacancies be filled by the Viceroy in consultation with both parties; that the League be given a veto over all Council decisions on communal questions; that the Vice-Presidency of the Council rotate between Congress and League Members; that the major portfolios be distributed equally; and that no changes be made in their allocation without the agreement of both parties.

Nehru made only minor concessions. Along with Wavell he offered the League the Vice-Chairmanship of the Co-ordinating Committee of the Executive Council instead of a rotating Vice-Presidency. Vacancies, he said, should be decided by the

---

[1] The text is in Nehru, *Independence and After*, pp. 339–43.
[2] Letter of 4 September 1946. Quoted in Pyarelal, op. cit., pp. 273–4.

Council, not by the Viceroy, and disagreements on communal issues could be submitted to the Federal Court. He also offered the leadership of the Central Assembly to a League Minister. Jinnah yielded on most points.[1]

The Interim Government was reconstituted on 15 October with the inclusion of five Muslim League nominees, among them an Untouchable.[2] Almost immediately it became another battle-front of the 'War of Succession'. That the League had no intention of working in co-operation with the Congress became crystal clear in a speech by Ghazanfar Ali Khan, one of the League nominees: 'We are going into the Interim Government to get a foothold to fight for our cherished goal of Pakistan. . . . The Interim Government is one of the fronts of the Direct Action Campaign.'[3] Jinnah's motives for joining the Government, even though few of his demands had been met, appear to have been twofold. From the negative standpoint, continued League boycott would perpetuate the Congress monopoly of power at the Centre and would jeopardize the goal of Pakistan. Added to this was a desire to demonstrate that the two communities could not function in harmony and that Pakistan was the only way out of the impasse.

Nehru was aware of the danger in such a coalition but he was powerless to alter the course of events. On the very day the League joined the Government he conveyed his misgivings to the Viceroy: 'I think I owe it to you to tell you privately and personally that I regret deeply the choice [of candidates] which the Muslim League has made. That choice itself indicates a desire to have conflict rather than to work in co-operation. . . . Our past experience does not encourage us to rely on vague and ambiguous phrases. . . . It is desirable . . . to be precise . . . and to know exactly where we stand.'[4] A week later, when the question of allocating portfolios arose, Nehru sought clarification on two points: prior League approval of the Cabinet

[1] The texts of the Nehru-Jinnah correspondence and the Jinnah-Wavell correspondence in early October 1946 are to be found in *Indian Annual Register*, vol. ii, 1946, pp. 265–9 and 273–5 respectively.

[2] Jogendranath Mandal, a leader of the Bengal Scheduled Castes (Untouchables) Federation, who later served in the Pakistani Cabinet from 1947 to 1950, when he fled to India, charging Pakistani maltreatment of the minorities.

[3] *Indian Annual Register*, vol. ii, 1946, p. 270.

[4] Letter of 15 October 1946. Quoted partly in Pyarelal, op. cit., p. 283, and partly in *Indian Annual Register*, vol. ii, 1946, p. 280.

Mission's long-run plan and an indication whether its official policy was that reflected in the remarks of Ghazanfar Ali Khan. The Viceroy replied that he had told Jinnah of the necessity of formal League approval of the Cabinet Mission plan and that Jinnah had assured him of his intention to co-operate. Nehru was far from satisfied: 'While you have made this clear to Mr. Jinnah', he wrote to Wavell, 'it is not equally clear what the Muslim League's view is on this subject.'[1]

It was Nehru's turn to adopt an uncompromising attitude. The Viceroy urged that one of the three senior portfolios —External Affairs, Defence and Home Affairs—be transferred to the League. Nehru refused, on the specious grounds that this would have an unsettling effect all over the country. In the face of Wavell's persistence he threatened to resign. 'I have consulted my colleagues', he wrote the Viceroy on 24 October. 'We cannot continue in the Government if a decision is imposed on us against our will. . . . A crisis has arisen which is leading to our resignation and termination of this Government.'[2] The Viceroy and the League yielded, but the incident revealed the depth of mistrust. The coalition was doomed from the beginning.

If there was any doubt about the incompatibility of the partners or about the League's motives in joining the Government, Jinnah set these at rest in mid-November: 'We shall resist anything that militates against the Pakistan demand', he said. League ministers were instructed to oppose any Government action of substance which prejudiced this goal. Then, as if to taunt the Congress, he denied the existence of a species called Indian; 4,000 years of history evaporated in a sentence.[3] He pressed for an indefinite postponement of the Constituent Assembly and, on 21 November, he delivered the death blow to the Cabinet Mission plan by ordering all League members to boycott the Assembly.

Nehru replied the same day. 'Our patience is fast reaching the limit', he told the Meerut session of the Congress. 'If these things continue, a struggle on a large scale is inevitable.' He lashed out at the League's tactics and charged that 'there is a mental alliance between the League and senior British officials'.

---

[1] Letter of 23 October 1946. Quoted in Pyarelal, op. cit., p. 285.
[2] Quoted in Pyarelal, op. cit., p. 286.
[3] Statement of 14 November 1946. *Indian Annual Register*, vol. ii, 1946, pp. 275-7.

Hector Bolitho, 'Jinnah: Creator of Pakistan'

9. With Jinnah at Simla, 1946

10. With Mahatma Gandhi and Maulana Azad

As for Jinnah's boycott decree, he declared 'whether they come in or keep out, we will go on'. Nor was the Viceroy spared. He was accused of having discarded some of the conventions which had been built up during the first month of the Interim Government and of having deviated from the spirit in which the Government was originally formed. Nehru intimated that the Congress Members had threatened to resign twice and concluded, 'I cannot say how long we will remain in the Interim Government.'[1]

Jinnah responded in a caustic vein: 'If he [Nehru] can only come down to earth and think coolly and calmly, he must understand that he is neither the Prime Minister nor is it a Nehru Government; he is only the Member for the External Affairs and Commonwealth Department.' As for Nehru's insistence that the Viceroy's Executive Council be termed a Cabinet, he remarked: 'Little things please little minds and you cannot turn a donkey into an elephant by calling it an elephant.'[2] This verbal fencing showed up the crux of the disagreement: the Congress and the League read different meanings into the same words. The Viceroy could and should have made the position absolutely clear.

*   *   *   *

There seemed to be no way out. At that point Attlee intervened with an invitation to the Viceroy, two representatives of the Congress, two from the League and one Sikh to confer in London in an effort to reconcile the warring parties. Nehru and the Working Committee sensed a trap. At first he declined, on the grounds that such a conference would appear to reopen the whole constitutional question which the Cabinet Mission plan had terminated and that this would make a bad impression on the public; further, that a brief visit would be fruitless and that there was little time to prepare for the Constituent Assembly scheduled to convene on 9 December. As an alternative he proposed a conference in Delhi. Attlee persisted and Nehru finally accepted, but only after the British Prime Minister assured him that there was no intention to alter the Cabinet Mission plan or the date set for the opening of the Assembly. On the contrary, the purpose of the conference was 'to see that the [Mission's

[1] *Indian Annual Register*, vol. ii, 1946, p. 279.
[2] Statement of 25 November 1946. Ibid., p. 297.

plan] was implemented'. Jinnah also declined at first because the conference would presumably be confined to minor problems. He too gave way in the face of Attlee's assurance that 'there was nothing to prejudice a full consideration of all points of view'. The British Prime Minister's pledges to Nehru and Jinnah seemed to contradict each other, but neither was aware of this at the time.[1]

The talks lasted four days but the deadlock remained. At their conclusion the British Cabinet issued a statement which pointed the way to the final solution. The declaration of 6 December 1946 contained two closely related provisions. On the procedure for Groups it supported the League's view unequivocally. The Cabinet announced that it had sought legal advice which had confirmed the Cabinet Mission's interpretation of the disputed clauses and that this 'must therefore be considered an essential part of the Scheme of May 16'. Thus, provinces would be *compelled* to meet in Groups; they could still opt out of the Groups but only *after* the first elections under the new Group constitutions. The Congress was urged to accept this interpretation as an inducement to the League to participate in the Constituent Assembly. As a sop to the Congress, the Assembly was given the right to submit this and other disputed issues to the Federal Court. However, this right was nullified within two weeks. The Congress indicated its intention of submitting the grouping scheme to the Federal Court. On 16 December Pethick-Lawrence announced in the House of Lords that the British Government would 'by no means depart from [its interpretation of the grouping scheme] even if the Federal Court should be appealed to'.[2]

The significance of the 6 December declaration was evident in its concluding paragraph: 'There has never been any prospect of success for the Constituent Assembly except upon the basis of an agreed procedure. Should a constitution come to be framed by a Constituent Assembly in which a large section of the Indian population had not been represented [i.e., the Muslim League], His Majesty's Government could not of course contemplate—as the Congress have stated they would not con-

---

[1] The texts of Attlee's correspondence with Nehru and Jinnah are in *Indian Annual Register*, vol. ii, 1946, pp. 299–300.

[2] Gt. Brit. H.L. *Debates*, 1946–7, vol. 144, col. 945.

template—forcing such a Constitution upon any unwilling parts of the country.'[1] This was nothing less than a Pakistan Award.

Only ten months earlier Attlee had declared in the House of Commons that the minorities would not be allowed to veto the advance of the majority. Moreover, the Cabinet Mission plan, still the official basis of a constitutional settlement, had explicitly ruled out Pakistan as a solution. And in his appeal to Nehru to attend the London Conference Attlee had assured him that the Mission's plan would not be abandoned. It is true that the 6 December declaration did not formally shelve the plan. But in reality it provided a green light to the League to persist in the demand for Pakistan. The stated purpose of the London Conference was to smooth the path of the Constituent Assembly and the Cabinet Mission plan, but the declaration killed the plan, invited Jinnah to stand fast, and spelled the doom of a united India. Ironically, this policy was partly justified by the oft-stated Congress view that it would not force a Union on any unwilling sections of the population. The British Government had yielded to Nehru in constitutional *discussion* (by assuring him that the Cabinet Mission plan would not be altered by the London Conference) and had yielded to Jinnah in the matter of constitutional *decision* (by virtually assuring him Pakistan).

Nehru was stunned by this turn of events. The London declaration was 'a blow to me', he told the Constituent Assembly. 'Obstructions were placed in our way, new limitations were mentioned', there was 'no imagination in the understanding of the Indian problem'.[2] Why then did he accept Attlee's invitation? The principal reason was to protect the Constituent Assembly. 'By accepting . . . we would leave the door open for the League to enter [the Assembly]. Rejection of the invitation would give an opportunity to the British Government to change or withdraw . . . their Statement of May 16th [Cabinet Mission plan], with the result that the Constituent Assembly may be changed radically'—precisely what happened even though he attended the Conference. The Congress was tempted 'to accept the challenge', he continued, but reason overruled emotions. There were the additional desires not to 'add to our

[1] The text of the 6 December declaration is to be found in *The Times* (London), December 1946.
[2] On 13 December 1946. *Independence and After*, p. 352.

enemies' and not to give anyone the opportunity to accuse the Congress of rejecting the British plan to transfer power.[1] Actually Nehru had little choice. Had he refused to negotiate he would have been saddled with the responsibility for the League's continued boycott. His intentions were sound but he had been outmanœuvred.

*   *   *   *

Three days after the London Conference the Constituent Assembly was formally convened. The League was absent, but the Sikhs, initially opposed, had been persuaded by Nehru and Patel to attend. The Congress had an overwhelming majority —205 of the 296 seats allotted to British India. A number of distinguished Liberals and scholars had been elected with Congress support. The Princes were still to join the proceedings. And Gandhi remained in Bengal, trying to heal the wounds caused by communal riots. After a few meetings on procedural questions Nehru moved the historic Objectives Resolution, the Assembly's basic frame of reference until the new Indian Constitution came into force on 26 January 1950.

It was a memorable event, a realization of the dreams of years gone by. Since the late 'twenties Nehru had been the principal advocate of a Constituent Assembly to express the national will. With the passage of time the Assembly had become an article of faith, a symbol of independence. The dream had now come to pass. It was a moment of personal and national pride. It was also a time for reflection, at a turning-point in India's chequered history. Nehru rose to the occasion with an eloquent address.

'We are at the end of an era . . . and my mind goes back . . . to the 5,000 years of India's history. . . . All that past crowds upon me and exhilarates me and, at the same time, somewhat oppresses me. Am I worthy of that past? When I think also of the future . . . standing on this sword's edge of the present between the mighty past and the mightier future, I tremble a little and feel overwhelmed by this mighty task. . . . Because of all this I find a little difficulty in addressing this House and putting

[1] Speech to the A.I.C.C. on 5 January 1947. Bose, D. R., *New India Speaks*, pp. 118–23.

all my ideas before it. . . . And now we stand on the verge of this passing age, trying, labouring, to usher in the new.' Here was a typical example of Nehru's stream-of-consciousness approach to public speaking. The mood was all-important.

He paid tribute to Gandhi, 'the Father of our Nation'. He acknowledged, as well, the inspiration of the American, French and Russian Revolutions. The new India would be a democracy, he declared emphatically, but 'what form of democracy, what shape it may take is another matter. . . .' He pleaded with the League to abandon its boycott and invoked national symbols in an effort to achieve the long-sought reconciliation. As an inducement to the Princes he pledged the right of the people of the States to retain the monarchical institution. To the resolution proper he attached the aura of the general will duly proclaimed: 'It is a Resolution and yet it is something much more than a resolution. It is a Declaration. It is a firm resolve. It is a pledge and an undertaking and it is for all of us, I hope, a dedication.'

Along with humility and conciliation there was a spirit of defiance. After relating his shock at the London declaration of 6 December, he declared: 'India, as she is constituted today, wants no one's advice and no one's imposition upon her. . . . Any attempt at imposition, the slightest trace of patronage, is resented and will be resented.' He concluded with a challenge to his people: 'We have just come out of a world war and people talk vaguely and rather wildly of new wars to come. At such a moment is this New India taking birth—renascent, vital, fearless. Perhaps it is a suitable moment. . . . But we have to be clear-eyed at this moment. . . . We have to think of this tremendous prospect . . . and not get lost in seeking small gains for this group or that . . .'

The objectives laid down in the resolution were general in character as befitted the occasion. The Assembly was called upon to declare its 'firm and solemn resolve to proclaim India as an Independent Sovereign Republic' and to draw up a constitution for a union consisting of British India and the princely States. These 'autonomous Units' would retain all existing and residuary powers 'save and except such powers and functions as are vested in or assigned to the Union, or as are inherent or implied in the Union. . . '. The classical Western freedoms would be guaranteed in such a constitution 'subject to law and public morality', and safeguards would be provided for minorities and backward tribes and castes.[1]

It is generally believed that Nehru played a key role in shaping the Objectives Resolution. The emphasis on fundamental rights, federalism and, most important, the goal of an independent republic owe much to his political outlook. But by 1946 these ideas had become part of the Congress programme. Some people were surprised by the omission of any reference to socialism. Nehru himself seemed embarrassed by this gap, but 'we wanted this Resolution not to be controversial in regard to such matters'. Perhaps Patel was opposed to its inclusion. Others viewed it as an indication of the extent to which Nehru was prepared to compromise as an inducement to the League. Both pressures were probably at work. Congress unity was absolutely essential in this period of crisis, and there was still hope of reconciliation with the League. In any event, Nehru's contribution was vital. He expressed the mood of nationalist India on the eve of Independence and set the tone for future Assembly debates, as well as providing the basic frame of reference for the new constitution.

His conciliatory approach to the League was in sharp contrast to his defiance of the British. In reply to Churchill's statement that London would not be bound by the decisions of the Constituent Assembly, he declared: 'Whatever form of Constitution we may decide in the Constituent Assembly will become the Constitution of free India—whether Britain accepts it or not. . . . We have now altogether stopped looking towards London. . . . We cannot and will not tolerate any outside interference . . .'[2]

Further debate on the Objectives Resolution was postponed until mid-January 1947 in an effort to placate the League. But the gesture was in vain. Jinnah's attention remained focused on the grouping scheme. On 21 December he demanded unequivocal Congress endorsement of the British Cabinet's interpretation as a precondition of the League's entry into the Assembly. The Congress refused.

---

[1] The text of the Objectives Resolution and Nehru's speech to the Constituent Assembly, delivered on 13 December 1946, are in *Independence and After*, pp. 344–53.

[2] On 15 December 1946. Quoted in Bolitho, H., *Jinnah, Creator of Pakistan*, p. 171.

Gandhi was still on his pilgrimage of faith. In the face of his refusal to return to Delhi, Nehru went to consult him in the heart of Bengal. More than anything Nehru needed solace. As so often in the past and in the future he seemed rejuvenated after a meeting with the Mahatma. 'It is always a pleasure and inspiration to meet this young man of seventy-seven', he remarked on his return to the capital. 'We always feel a little younger and stronger after meeting him and the burdens we carry seem a little lighter.'[1] But there was more than the Constituent Assembly to discuss.

A cleavage between Nehru and Patel had come into the open. 'I heard many complaints against you,' wrote Gandhi to Patel. 'Your speeches are inflammatory. . . . There is not that unison in the Working Committee that there should be.' The core issue was revealed in Patel's reply: 'The charge that I want to stick to office is a pure concoction. Only, I was opposed to Jawaharlal's hurling idle threats of resigning from the Interim Government. They damage the prestige of the Congress and have a demoralising effect on the services. We should take a firm decision to resign first. Repetition of empty threats has lost us the Viceroy's respect and now he regards our threats of resignation as nothing but bluff. . . . If there are divisions in the Working Committee, they are not today's growth. They have been there for a long time.'[2]

This exchange demonstrates Gandhi's continuing role of arbitrator between the two leading figures in the Congress as Independence approached. It also reveals a fundamental difference between the Congress and the League during the period 1945–7. The League spoke with one voice and its policy was determined by Jinnah alone. The Congress spoke with three or more voices and was subject to the strains of a more heterogeneous organization. Moreover, the Congress was inclined to negotiate in public, with a variety of statements which perforce could not follow a standard line. These factors strengthened the League's bargaining power in the last stages of the constitutional battle.

When the All-India Congress Committee assembled early in January 1947 its decision on the grouping scheme could be de-

---

[1] *Hindustan Times* (New Delhi), 31 December 1946.
[2] Quoted in Pyarelal, op. cit., pp. 488–9.

layed no longer. Following Gandhi's advice, conveyed to Nehru in Bengal, it adopted an ambivalent resolution—nominal acceptance of the British Cabinet ruling, along with *carte blanche* to the affected parties, the Sikhs, Assam, and the Frontier Province, to act as they saw fit. Yet even this formal concession was considered appeasement by many members of the A.I.C.C., notably the Congress Socialists. The resolution was passed by 99 to 52 with 80 abstentions; despite its sponsorship by the High Command only 40 per cent. gave their consent.[1]

When the Constituent Assembly reconvened on 20 January it was clear that the League did not intend to lift the boycott. Hence the Assembly proceeded to pass the Objectives Resolution, unanimously, after Nehru's closing speech. He renewed his invitation to the League but added that 'No work will be held up in the future, whether anyone comes or not. There has been waiting enough. . . .' The only novel feature of his address was a hint that India's continued membership in the Commonwealth was not unthinkable: 'At no time have we ever thought in terms of isolating ourselves . . . or of being hostile to countries which have dominated over us. . . . We want to be friendly with the British people and the British Commonwealth of Nations.'[2]

The League took up Nehru's challenge at the end of January. It dismissed the latest Congress resolution as a 'dishonest trick and jugglery of words'. The proceedings of the Constituent Assembly were severely criticized, especially the Objectives Resolution which it claimed was beyond the Assembly's competence. The British Government was called upon to pronounce the Cabinet Mission plan a failure and to dismiss the Assembly. The mood was defiant; there was no conciliatory gesture to the Congress provinces or the Sikhs who would be swamped by a Muslim majority in the Groups assigned the Muslims under the Mission's plan. Nothing less than Pakistan was acceptable.[3] The Congress responded in the middle of February with a

---

[1] Resolution of 6 January 1947. The text is in *Congress Bulletin*, No. 2, 8 February 1947, pp. 6–7.

[2] The text of Nehru's speech, delivered on 22 January 1947, is in *Independence and After*, pp. 354–61. The quotation is from p. 358. For a discussion of India's decision to remain in the Commonwealth see pp. 413–18 below.

[3] The text of the League's resolution, on 31 January 1947, is to be found in *Indian Annual Register*, vol. i, 1947, pp. 147–51.

demand that League Ministers be removed from the Interim Government unless the League participated in the Assembly. At that critical juncture London intervened with an historic proclamation about the transfer of power. The year of decision was about to begin.

CHAPTER XIII

1947: Triumph

NINETEEN FORTY-SEVEN was a fateful year in the life of Nehru and in the turbulent history of India. For both it was a year of mixed fortunes. For both it marked the end of an era and a venture into the unknown. The quest for freedom was finally crowned with success, but the pride of achievement was marred by much pain and suffering. Nehru's accession to power and responsibility was accompanied by a savage communal war in which half a million people died and millions more were uprooted from their ancestral homes. Neither he nor the sub-continent at large has recovered fully from that experience. For Nehru and the Congress generally, the joy of Independence was tempered by the sadness of Partition. The moment of their greatest triumph was also the moment of their greatest defeat. A few months after the transfer of power the successor states were at war in Kashmir. And then there occurred the death of Gandhi, the beloved and revered master.[1] For the first time in his political life Nehru was alone, leading his country through its greatest crisis. The Gandhi era in Indian politics had come to an end. The Nehru era was about to begin. But no one could anticipate this sequence of events.

The year of decision began with an historic declaration in the House of Commons on 20 February 1947. Prime Minister Attlee announced the British Government's 'definite intention to take the necessary steps to effect the transfer of power into responsible Indian hands by a date not later than June 1948'. However, if a constitution could not be drafted by a 'fully representative Constituent Assembly before that time', he continued, 'His Majesty's Government will have to consider to whom the powers of the central Government of British India should be handed over, on the due date, whether as a whole to some form of central Government for British India,

---

[1] Mahatma Gandhi was assassinated on 30 January 1948. In a political sense, however, this was the climactic event of the year 1947.

or in some areas to the existing Provincial Governments, or in such other way as may seem most reasonable and in the best interests of the Indian People'. Wavell's 'war-time' appointment was terminated and Lord Louis Mountbatten was named his successor to effect the transfer.[1] As for the princely States, Paramountcy would end with the transfer of power in British India and would *not* devolve upon the successor Government(s).[2]

Nehru's immediate reaction was unqualified approval. Speaking on behalf of the Congress members of the Interim Government, he hailed Attlee's statement as 'a wise and courageous' decision. 'The clear and definite declaration [about the transfer of power] removes all misconceptions and suspicions. . . . [It] also brings reality and a certain dynamic quality to the present situation. . . . It is a challenge to all of us.' As a conciliatory gesture, he added that India looked forward to the establishment of friendly relations with the British people.[3] In a private letter to Gandhi he was less exuberant but still favourably disposed: 'Mr. Attlee's statement contains much that is indefinite and likely to give trouble. But I am convinced that it is in the final analysis a brave and definite statement. It meets our oft-repeated demand for quitting India.'[4]

There is only a hint here about the dangerous implications of the statement of 20 February, from the Congress point of view. Of all the Congress leaders only Gandhi clearly perceived its meaning. 'This may lead to Pakistan for those Provinces or portions which may want it', he cautioned Nehru. 'No one will be forced one way or the other.'[5]

London's motives remain somewhat obscure. Cripps told the House of Commons that the British Government was reluctant to take sides in the controversies over the Interim Government and the Constituent Assembly. To support the Congress demand for the expulsion of the League 'Ministers' would have

---

[1] There is evidence to suggest that the British Government had decided to recall Wavell some months earlier. Prime Minister Attlee first broached this matter to Mountbatten on 18 December 1946, and invited him to succeed Wavell as Viceroy of India. Campbell-Johnson, A., *Mission with Mountbatten*, p. 17. All references to this book are taken from the English edition (Robert Hale Ltd., 1951).

[2] The text of Attlee's statement on 20 February 1947 is to be found in Cmd. 7047, 1947, and in Gt. Brit. H.C. *Debates*, 1946–7, vol. 433, cols. 1395–9.

[3] *The Hindu* (Madras), 24 February 1947.

[4] Letter of 24 February 1947. Quoted in Pyarelal, op. cit., p. 566.

[5] Ibid., p. 565.

wrecked all possibility—if indeed any remained—of League entry into the Assembly. To dismiss the Constituent Assembly would have made it an illegal and revolutionary body. The object of Attlee's statement, he declared, was to bring about a reconciliation by shock treatment.[1] If this were the case it proved to be a grave miscalculation.

It was now clearly stated that power would be transferred by a specific date and that if the League refused to join the Constituent Assembly power would be transferred to the central Government or the provincial Governments or in some other suitable way—which obviously meant partition. The first alternative had been virtually ruled out by the Cabinet declaration of 6 December 1946, which stated emphatically that an all-India constitution would not be forced upon any unwilling parts of the country. Why then should Jinnah suddenly agree to co-operate with the Congress and remove his boycott of the Assembly when he was assured his goal by remaining adamant? The statement of 20 February was a logical continuation of the declaration of 6 December. Whether or not so intended, it paved the way for partition. It remained for Mountbatten to execute the withdrawal of British power from India.

The inference that Attlee's statement of 20 February paved the way for partition and even represented an indirect concession to the League demand for Pakistan is shared by various English officials prominently connected with the last stage of British rule.[2] It would appear that Cripps's stated objective of a Congress-League reconciliation via shock treatment was, at best, an eleventh-hour attempt which would almost certainly fail. The prevalent feeling in London by February 1947 seemed to be that Pakistan was the only way out of the impasse.

Tory spokesmen led by Churchill and Sir John Anderson attempted to stay the inevitable by calling for a return to the Cripps Offer of 1942. Churchill himself had no illusions about the meaning of Attlee's statement: 'India is to be subjected not merely to partition, but to fragmentation, and to haphazard fragmentation', he declared, referring to the freedom of action

---

[1] For Cripps's speech on 5 March 1947, see Gt. Brit. H.C. *Debates*, 1946–7, vol. 434, cols. 494–512.

[2] With whom the author held conversations in England in the summer and autumn of 1955.

granted the princely States. His attitude to Indian politicians was reaffirmed in words which Nehru and others have probably never forgotten: 'In handing over the Government of India to these so-called political classes we are handing over to men of straw, of whom, in a few years, no trace will remain.' And in a passionate outburst he appealed to the House, '. . . let us not add—by shameful flight, by a premature, hurried scuttle—at least, let us not add, to the pangs of sorrow so many of us feel, the taint and smear of shame'.[1] The Labour benches were unmoved.

One aspect of Attlee's statement which puzzled his audience was the summary dismissal of Wavell with the specious explanation that it was a 'war-time' appointment. Labour spokesmen refused to elaborate and Wavell himself never commented on the issue in public. However, it is known that the Viceroy had prepared a two-stage military evacuation plan.[2] The territory now comprising the Republic of India was to be given its independence and British troops were to be withdrawn. However, troops were to remain indefinitely in what is now West Pakistan to maintain law and order. The justification for the two stages was Wavell's belief that much blood would be spilled if power were transferred simultaneously to the sub-continent as a whole. It was this plan which led to his recall. Relations between Wavell and the Labour Government were severely strained. Attlee allegedly informed the Viceroy that the plan was politically unfeasible and would require revision; Wavell refused. Attlee then requested his resignation, but Wavell remained adamant. Hence the conspicuous reference to his appointment being 'terminated'.[3]

There were rumours in the Indian press that Nehru was pleased by the news of Wavell's dismissal. While acknowledging their differences of opinion, he remarked, 'I have never doubted Lord Wavell's sincerity and desire to serve India's interests. He has carried a heavy burden and has worked hard. I have a high regard for him and shall be sorry in many ways to part from him.'[4]

[1] Gt. Brit. H.C. *Debates*, 1946–7, vol. 434, cols. 673, 674 and 678.
[2] Campbell-Johnson, op. cit., p. 17.
[3] Based on conversations with former British officials in 1955.
[4] *Leader* (Allahabad), 23 February 1947.

More than a month passed between Mountbatten's appointment and his arrival in India. It was a crucial interregnum. Events moved so swiftly that by the time he began his first round of conversations in Delhi the political situation had changed radically. The struggle for power had moved from the conference room to the streets.

Attlee's historic declaration introduced two new elements into the turmoil of Indian politics. By indicating a specific date for the transfer of power, the British Prime Minister added a sense of urgency to the struggle for the succession. By remaining vague about the successor(s) and by mentioning the provincial Governments as possible recipients of legal authority, he galvanized the parties into vigorous action. The Muslim League was especially vulnerable because it controlled only two of the six provinces claimed for Pakistan, namely Bengal and Sind. Congress Governments were in office in Assam and the North West Frontier Province while a Unionist-Congress-Sikh coalition held power in the Punjab. Baluchistan, a Chief Commissioner's Province, was of little consequence and could be expected to support the League.

*   *   *   *

The kingpin of the Pakistan demand was the Punjab, the largest, most populous and wealthiest province in northern India. On communal grounds the claim was valid, for the Muslims comprised about 56 per cent. of the total population of 29 million. On political grounds the League claim was less persuasive but powerful none the less. It had swept the polls in the 1946 elections, winning 79 of the 86 seats reserved for Muslims and was the largest party in the Punjab legislature. But it lacked a clear majority. Khizr Hayat Khan, the incumbent Premier and Unionist leader, succeeded in forming a government in coalition with the Congress and the Sikhs. The League bitterly resented its exclusion from office. Constitutional government was virtually at a standstill because the coalition was uneasy and had a majority of only three; the legislature met only when it was essential to pass the budget.

Throughout 1946 tension mounted in the Punjab even though it remained comparatively free from communal disturbances, then raging in Bengal, Bihar, and the U.P. The most disturbing

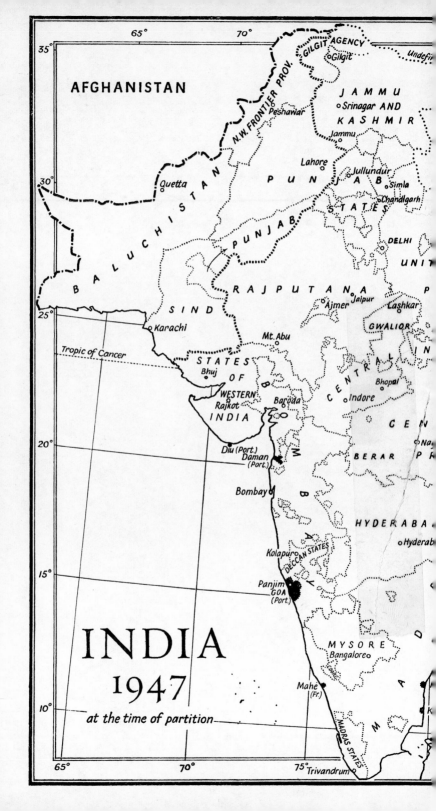

INDIA
1947
at the time of partition

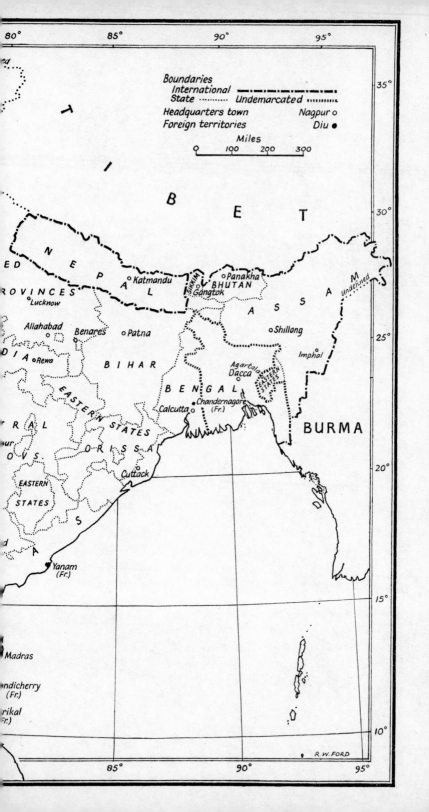

feature of Punjabi politics was the formation of private armies by the three communities. The Governor, Sir Evan Jenkins, strongly urged Khizr to declare them unlawful but the latter procrastinated until it was too late. In January 1947 the League resorted to 'direct action'. Stealing a leaf from Gandhi's book, it launched a campaign of mass civil disobedience against the Punjab Government's belated ban on private armies, announced on 24 January. The agitation continued for more than a month. Then came Attlee's statement of 20 February which strengthened the League determination to capture power. Khizr faltered and then compromised by removing the ban on public meetings and by releasing League political prisoners in return for the end of civil disobedience. The coalition, never stable, was subjected to intense pressure, and the Congress and the Sikhs were making preparations for the inevitable struggle. Seizing the pretext that Attlee's statement had altered the political situation, Khizr submitted his resignation on 2 March, on the eve of the Budget session.

The following day Jenkins called on the Khan of Mamdot, the League leader in the legislature, to form a ministry. The Sikhs responded the same evening with a mass rally at which their fiery leader, Master Tara Singh, added fuel to the flames with an exuberant call to action: 'O Hindus and Sikhs! Be ready for self-destruction. . . . If we can snatch the Government from the Britishers no one can stop us from snatching the Government from the Muslims. . . . Disperse from here on the solemn affirmation that we shall not allow the League to exist . . .. We shall rule over them and will get the Government, fighting. I have sounded the bugle. Finish the Muslim League.'[1] It was a dangerous boast and an idle threat, for the National Guards of the League were much better organized at the time.

The next day, 4 March, the struggle for the Punjab shifted to the streets; and on the 5th Jenkins was compelled to take over direct administration of the province. Serious rioting broke out in Lahore, Amritsar, Multan, Rawalpindi, Sialkot and Jullundur, and for the first time in the Punjab's history in rural areas as well. The initial wave of communal killings lasted about a fortnight; because of its superior organization the League 'army' scored a major 'victory'. But the 'War of

[1] Quoted in Khosla, op. cit., p. 100.

Succession' had just begun. Before it ended, all three communities were to pay a fantastic price in killed, wounded, missing and prisoners. Of its ferocious character, even in the early stages, Nehru remarked after a tour of Lahore, 'I have seen ghastly sights and I have heard of behaviour by human beings which would disgrace brutes.'[1]

During the next two months there was a lull in the Punjab War, though daily incidents and frequent cases of arson occurred in the two main theatres of operation, Lahore and Amritsar. Large-scale violence flared anew early in May. No quarter was offered. By the time the transfer of power took place on 15 August one-twentieth of Lahore had been destroyed by fire and many villages had murdered every member of the minority community. Yet, by comparison with the slaughter after the Partition, the Punjab disturbances in the spring of 1947 were mere skirmishes of a massive civil war.

It was against this background that the Congress Working Committee met early in March. The pressure for a compromise settlement with the League was growing. Hindus and Sikhs in eastern Punjab and Hindus in western Bengal, reading the Attlee statement as a Pakistan Award, feared being swallowed in a Muslim state and urged the Congress leaders to seek a partition of these two provinces to protect the minorities. There was also a growing feeling within the Congress leadership that the alternative to partition was chaos. Their will to persevere for a united India was being undermined. Thus, on 8 March, the Working Committee finally acknowledged the essence of the British Government's policy declarations: 'It has been made clear that the constitution framed by the Constituent Assembly will apply *only to those areas which accept it.*' However, in an effort to salvage the non-Muslim majority areas of the Punjab and Bengal, 'it must also be understood that any Province or part of a Province which accepts the constitution and desires to join the Union cannot be prevented from doing so'. To remove any doubt of its intention, the Congress proposed partition of the Punjab into two provinces and invited the League to a joint conference for this purpose.[2] Ostensibly this was suggested to lessen communal friction. But in perspective

---

[1] Bose, D. R., op. cit., p. 133.
[2] *Congress Bulletin*, No. 3, 26 March 1947, pp. 3–5. (Emphasis added.)

the Congress had taken a very long step towards partition of the entire country. And this was three months before the Mount-batten Plan was formally approved. Indeed, it occurred even before the new Viceroy arrived in Delhi.

*　　*　　*　　*

Amidst the upsurge of communal violence, Nehru made his formal début on the stage of international politics. The place was the Red Fort in Old Delhi; the time—23 March 1947; the occasion—the first Asian Relations Conference. It was an impressive gathering, symbolizing the political renaissance of Asia. Arabs and Jews from the Middle East, Uzbeks and Kazakhs from Soviet Central Asia, Burmese, Indonesians, Indo-Chinese and others from South-east Asia, Chinese and Koreans from East Asia, more than a score of nations, cultures and languages with little in common except the urge to assert Asia's place in the world political community. For some the Conference was the fulfilment of a vow taken almost twenty years earlier at the Brussels Anti-Imperialist Congress. For Nehru it was also a source of personal and national pride. Many had favoured an exchange of ideas and an affirmation of solidarity among the peoples of Asia but it was he who took the initiative in translating this into reality.

Perhaps more than any other statesman of the age, Nehru responds to the mood of his immediate surroundings. On this occasion he was conscious of the drama of a gathering of Asian peoples after centuries of political subjection. The deep-rooted urge for recognition and equality of status provided the main theme for his inaugural address.

'Asia, after a long period of quiescence, has suddenly become important again in world affairs', he began. 'We live in a tremendous age of transition and already the next stage takes shape when Asia takes her rightful place with other continents.' He decried the long period of isolation among the countries of Asia as a result of European domination. But 'as that domination goes, the walls that surround us fall down and we . . . meet as old friends long parted'. He denied the charge that a pan-Asian movement was being formed but asserted Asia's right to be heard: 'Far too long have we of Asia been petitioners in western courts and chancelleries. That story must now belong to the past . . . . We do not intend to be the playthings of others.' He reaffirmed the ideal of World Government and saw the new Asia as a powerful influence for peace. With obvious pride he referred to India's pivotal role in Asia: 'It is fitting that India should play her part in this new phase of Asian development. . . . She is the natural centre and focal point of the many forces at work in Asia. Geography is a compelling factor, and geographically she is so situated as to be the meeting point of Western and Northern and Eastern and South-East Asia. . . . [Moreover] streams of culture have come to India from the west and east and been absorbed in India. . . . At the same time, streams of culture have flowed from India to distant parts of Asia.' Lest these remarks be misunderstood, he pointedly denied any claim to Asian leadership. As for the Conference, 'the mere fact of its taking place is itself of historic significance. . . . This event may well stand out as a land-mark which divides the past of Asia from the future.' He served notice of Asia's 'special responsibility' for Africa and concluded with a plea for faith in the human spirit.[1]

According to eyewitness accounts the Conference was dominated by India's delegation, particularly by Nehru. Almost all his colleagues were too engrossed in the deadly struggle for power within India to concern themselves with its deliberations. Typical of the indifference was Patel's alleged comment when asked if the Conference would take any formal stand on the Indonesian demand for independence: 'Indonesia, Indonesia, let me see—where is Indonesia? You better ask Jawaharlal about that.'[2] Gandhi appeared briefly to plead his philosophy of non-violence. The League leaders ignored the Conference completely; they, too, were obsessed with the great issues within India.

The Conference lasted twelve days. Nothing concrete was achieved, except the creation of a pro-forma organization of Asian states. Nehru became the President of the Provisional Council of the Asian Relations Organization. There was much talk of cultural exchanges and co-operation among universities and governments, but the conditions for any meaningful Asian unity were absent. Nevertheless, Nehru and others had given

---

[1] The text is in *Independence and After*, pp. 295–301.
[2] Related to the author by an eyewitness who wishes to remain anonymous.

expression to one of the most significant phenomena of the century, the re-entry of Asia into world politics. Moreover, Nehru's initiative was to reap for India the reward of international prestige. Two years later Delhi again played host to Asian countries on the Indonesian crisis; and in 1955 Bandung took up the threads of the earlier conferences on an even larger scale.

*   *   *   *

While the spokesmen of Asia discussed the advantages of unity and pledged their peoples to co-operation, the leaders of India were emphatically proclaiming their disunity and were preparing for mortal combat. The struggle for power was intensified with the coming of Mountbatten on 22 March 1947. The range of problems bequeathed to the new Viceroy was formidable indeed: communal frenzy in the Punjab; League agitation in the Frontier and Assam; virtual paralysis of the Interim Government where tension had been heightened by Liaquat Ali's budget which proposed heavy taxes—25 per cent. on business profits of more than Rs. 100,000 ($33,000)—thereby threatening to split the industrialist and socialist wings of the Congress; a sharp decline in the efficiency of the Administration and the loss of *élan* among civil servants; a series of British Government pronouncements which could not be reconciled— the Cabinet Mission Statement of 16 May 1946 providing for a united India, still the official terms of reference for Mountbatten, the declaration of 6 December 1946 which opened a wedge for Pakistan, and Attlee's statement of 20 February 1947 which added more confusion by its vagueness about the successor authorities; a Congress demand for a united India, with the added complication of a sovereign, independent republic; a League demand for Pakistan; evidence that the Sikhs would resist partition; and potential Balkanization of the country because of the freedom of action given the six hundred princely States.

The new Viceroy plunged into a round of intensive interviews with the Big Five of Indian politics—Gandhi, Jinnah, Nehru, Liaquat Ali Khan and Patel. From the outset he was drawn to Nehru whom he had met in Malaya a year before. Both possessed charm, vanity, boundless energy, a patrician bearing and background. From this flowed mutual trust and candour. In time it developed into a warm and lasting friendship.[1]

This rapport was evident at their first meeting in Delhi. Nehru was in an expansive mood and Mountbatten considered his account of the major developments during the preceding eight months 'substantially accurate'. The Viceroy sought Nehru's opinions on a variety of pressing issues and even asked for his estimate of Jinnah. The degree of frankness was revealed by Nehru's proposal, astonishing at the time, for 'an Anglo-Indian union involving nothing less than common citizenship— in effect, a far closer bond than Commonwealth status, which Nehru felt was psychologically and emotionally unacceptable'. At the end of their conversation there was a touching exchange. ' "Mr. Nehru," said Mountbatten, "I want you to regard me not as the last Viceroy winding up the British Raj, but as the first to lead the way to the new India." Nehru turned, looked intensely moved, smiled and then said, "Now I know what they mean when they speak of your charm being so dangerous." '[2]

With none of the other leaders did Mountbatten establish such an intimate relationship. Jinnah was too cold and aloof; Liaquat Ali was overshadowed by Jinnah in the negotiations; Patel was a man of few words and, for the most part, maintained contact with the Viceroy through his Constitutional Adviser, V. P. Menon. For Gandhi, he had much respect but their outlooks were fundamentally different and the Mahatma remained on the periphery during the last stage of the negotiations.

The most striking feature of Mountbatten's diplomacy was the rapidity with which he arrived at decisions. A series of interviews with Jinnah and Nehru persuaded him that the League leader would persevere to the end, that the Congress leaders were more amenable to compromise, that the Indian situation was rapidly deteriorating into chaos, and that the Cabinet Mission plan for a united India would have to be scrapped in favour of partition. Gandhi had made the startling proposal that the Interim Government be handed over to the League— in a novel attempt to avoid partition—but no one was impressed. At that point he transferred all responsibility for the negotiations to the Congress Working Committee.

---

[1] For a discussion of the Nehru-Mountbatten relationship see pp. 410–13 below.
[2] Campbell-Johnson, op. cit., p. 45.

From the very beginning Mountbatten was concerned lest the friction give way to total disintegration on the Chinese pattern. Thus, as early as mid-April the basic principles of what later emerged as the Mountbatten Plan were already worked out. It had become obvious soon after his arrival, he suggested some years later, that a united India could not be imposed except at the cost of a major civil war, for events had moved too far and too fast since the Cabinet Mission. The riots had indicated what could happen but a civil war would have been infinitely more costly.[1] It remained only to persuade all the protagonists.

Nehru seemed to be resigned to the necessity of partition very early in the negotiations. In a speech to the All-India States People's Conference on 18 April he declared: 'The Congress . . . have recently on practical considerations passed a resolution accepting the division of the country', presumably referring to the Working Committee Resolution of 8 March.[2] Later in the month he asserted: 'The Muslim League can have Pakistan if they want it but on the condition that they do not take away other parts of India which do not wish to join Pakistan.'[3]

Early in May, Mountbatten's Chief of Staff, Lord Ismay, flew to London to secure Cabinet approval of the partition scheme. On 10 May it was announced that a conference would be held on the 17th at which Mountbatten would present the Plan to the Congress, the League and the Sikhs. However, the date was altered to 2 June because of certain objections raised by Nehru. The compromise was finally hammered out at Simla on 10–11 May where, for a while, the issue hung on the thread of trust. As a precaution the Viceroy had shown the London revision of his draft plan to Nehru in advance of the scheduled round-table conference. It proved to be a shrewd action, though hardly conforming to protocol, for Nehru emphatically rejected the revision on the grounds that it was a marked departure from Mountbatten's original draft.

The bone of contention was not the principle of partition, which Nehru had already accepted, but a number of technicalities relating to the transfer of power. The most important was the issue of constitutional continuity. Nehru was determined

---

[1] To the author in London in October 1955.
[2] Bose, op. cit., p. 154.   [3] Lumby, op. cit., p. 155.

to establish the claim that the proposed Union of India was the rightful successor to the British *Raj* and that Pakistan was merely the secession of a few provinces from British India. This proved to be of some importance for the subsequent international status of the Indian Union: the U.N. recognized this claim. Moreover, Nehru saw in the London revision a real danger of Balkanization of the sub-continent. The way out was the Dominion status formula.

In this connection (i.e., the Dominion status formula) the role of V. P. Menon was crucial. Indeed, without his help and advice the Partition Plan might have fallen through. Menon approached Patel even before the coming of Mountbatten with his own scheme for a solution. Division was the only way out of the impasse, he argued. The alternative was civil war, a logical by-product of the communal riots and the dangerous friction within the Interim Government. As long as the Congress held out for a united India and complete separation from the Commonwealth, he declared, the Viceroy, then Lord Wavell, the civil and military services and London would support the League. Partition, with both India and Pakistan as Dominions, would eliminate the League's preferred status with the British, would facilitate parliamentary approval of the transfer of power and would restore the Congress to the good graces of Delhi. And the Congress would achieve its goal of independence. Patel was impressed and indicated his approval. There the matter ended. Menon submitted his proposal to the India Office in London, but no one took any notice.

When Mountbatten appeared on the scene he was committed to the Cabinet Mission Plan (Cripps's three-tier scheme) but soon decided that a united India was impossible. His next plan was to transfer power to the provinces. Menon proposed it to Nehru and met a blank wall. Finally, Menon persuaded the Viceroy to try his own scheme. The die was cast at Simla where Menon succeeded in winning Nehru's approval. Nehru was unaware of Patel's prior consent. With their acceptance the Congress stood committed. Getting the Plan through the Working Committee and the A.I.C.C. was a formality. Thus Menon emerges as one of the key figures in the momentous last days.[1]

To meet Nehru's objections further revision was necessary.

[1] For Menon's own account see his *The Transfer of Power in India*, pp. 358–65.

The Viceroy made a hurried visit to London after showing his final plan to the Big Four—Gandhi was out of the picture. By 2 June all was ready for the historic conference. In the interim, however, Jinnah added a further complication by demanding an 800-mile corridor to link East and West Pakistan. The Congress was aghast and the tension mounted. Nehru termed the demand 'fantastic and absurd'. His position was hardening once more. 'We stand for a union of India', he told an American correspondent on 24 May, 'with the right to particular areas to opt out. We envisage no compulsion. If there is no proper settlement on this basis without further claims being advanced, then we shall proceed with making and implementing the constitution for the union of India.'[1] In the face of firm Congress opposition, Jinnah did not press the issue.

Another disturbing note was contributed by Gandhi who informed his prayer-meeting audience on 31 May: 'Even if the whole of India burns, we shall not concede Pakistan, even if the Muslims demanded it at the point of the sword.'[2] But these were mere words, for power in the Congress now lay with Nehru and Patel. Still a third problem arose. The Congress requested that Kripalani, the Congress President, be invited to the conference. Jinnah refused. The issue was resolved by adding Kripalani and another Muslim Leaguer, Sardar Abdur Rab Nishtar, to the group. Finally, a bizarre element intruded. Jinnah notified Mountbatten that he could not give his formal approval at the conference for it was necessary to consult his colleagues and the people. However, he did agree to nod in approval when the Viceroy announced that Jinnah had given him acceptable assurances on the League attitude.

The Conference of 2 June was, in a sense, an anti-climax, for the protagonists had already given their verbal consent to the Viceroy. Mountbatten went through the motions of calling on the assembled leaders to accept the Cabinet Mission plan and then proposed his own plan for partition. Its principal merits were clarity, brevity and simplicity, and the critical fact that it embodied the maximum agreement of the parties.

In essence the Mountbatten Plan provided a procedure to ascertain the will of the people living in those areas claimed for

[1] Quoted in Campbell-Johnson, op. cit., p. 96.
[2] Quoted in Lumby, op. cit., p. 161.

Pakistan. In Bengal, Sind and the Punjab the issue was to be determined by the provincial legislatures. But in Bengal and the Punjab the Assemblies would divide into two sections, representing the Muslim-majority and non-Muslim-majority districts respectively. If either section favoured partition of the province this would be an irrevocable verdict; if both decided to remain united, the legislature would vote on which Constituent Assembly it wished to join. In the Frontier there was to be a referendum because of the obvious shift in popular allegiance since the last elections. Similarly, the Muslim-majority Sylhet district of Assam would hold a referendum in the likely event that Bengal favoured partition and would be tacked on to east Bengal if it favoured Pakistan. The Plan also indicated a willingness to transfer power before the specified final date of June 1948. (Indeed, at Mountbatten's prodding, the British Government had agreed to rush the legislation through the current session of Parliament.) This would be on a Dominion status basis and the successor(s) could decide through their Constituent Assembly (Assemblies) whether or not to stay in the Commonwealth.[1]

On the evening of 3 June the leaders announced their agreement to the Indian people. Nehru's mood combined sadness, resignation, reflection, almost detachment. 'It is with no joy in my heart that I commend these proposals though I have no doubt in my mind that this is the right course.' There was humility, too. At the climax of a thirty-year struggle for independence he minimized his own role: 'We are little men serving great causes, but because the cause is great something of that greatness falls upon us also.'[2] Jinnah was non-committal, but it was clear that he supported the 'compromise'. He paid tribute to Mountbatten's impartiality and offered his co-operation. He also called for an end to League agitation in the Frontier Province and appealed to all communities to abandon violence. Baldev Singh, speaking for the Sikhs, for whom partition meant disaster, succeeded in concealing the bitterness of his co-religionists.

[1] The Statement of 3 June was first announced in the House of Commons by Prime Minister Attlee. See Cmd. 7136, 1947, or Gt. Brit. H.C. *Debates*, 1946-7, vol. 438, cols. 35-40.

[2] Quoted in Lord Birdwood, *A Continent Decides*, p. 34, and Campbell-Johnson, op. cit., p. 107.

11. Nehru votes for the resolution to accept the Mountbatten Plan calling for the partition of India, 15 June, 1947. In the background, Pandit Pant and Dr. Rajendra Prasad

Seven days later the League Council granted Jinnah complete authority to accept the Plan, by a vote of 400 to 8, though it rejected the principle of partition of the Punjab and Bengal. Nehru was annoyed by this hedging and was concerned lest the League make further demands in the future. Mountbatten assuaged his fears in this regard.

Formal Congress approval was more emphatic and unequivocal, though there was substantial opposition, primarily from the nationalist Muslims, Hindu communalists and Congress Socialists. Gandhi was present at the historic A.I.C.C. session on 14–15 June but he refused to challenge the decision arrived at by his two senior lieutenants, even though he remained firmly opposed to partition. Nehru spoke briefly, as did Pant, Azad, the Mahatma and Kripalani, but it was Patel who delivered the keynote address. He used the analogy of a diseased body and argued that if one limb was poisoned it must be removed quickly lest the entire organism suffer irreparably. The speech was typical of the man—pointed, brutally frank, unemotional. After two days of debate the Mountbatten Plan was approved by 153 to 29 with 36 abstentions. The most crestfallen was the small but dedicated band of nationalist Muslims who felt betrayed. A rare photograph portrays Nehru's anguish as he pondered the meaning of partition.

*   *   *   *

Although the parties had signified their acceptance, the situation remained very tense during the two months preceding the formal transfer of power, now scheduled for 15 August. The slightest incident seemed capable of upsetting the precarious equilibrium created by the Mountbatten Plan. Less than a week after the Plan was informally approved by the leaders a crisis arose in the Interim Government, one of many that bedevilled its fortunes. The issue was rather trivial, the proposed appointment of an ambassador to Moscow. Liaquat Ali was vehemently opposed; Nehru insisted. To complicate matters the nominee was Mrs. Pandit, Nehru's sister. The Viceroy succeeded in deferring the decision.

To implement the enormous administrative tasks in connection with the transfer, a complex machinery was created. At the apex of the pyramid was the Partition Committee of the

Interim Government, later the Partition Council. This consisted of Patel and Prasad for the Congress, Liaquat Ali and Nishtar, later replaced by Jinnah, for the Muslim League, and Mountbatten as Chairman. Below this decision-making body was a Steering Committee of two senior civil servants, H. M. Patel and Chaudhuri Mahomed Ali (later Prime Minister of Pakistan), which co-ordinated the work of expert committees and sub-committees, each charged with a specific facet of the Partition. Among the most important were those dealing with the armed forces, the civil service, economic relations, especially cash balances, and communications. Though not described as such, this administrative structure was a parallel caretaker government; the Interim Government remained but it lost its *raison d'être* with the decision to divide the country.

The most delicate task was the division of the armed forces. British officers generally were opposed but in the flush of nationalist victory neither Congress nor League was prepared to accept anything which seemed a slight on complete sovereignty. Because of the technical difficulties they agreed to maintain joint administrative control under Field-Marshal Auchinleck, then Commander-in-Chief, until April 1948. However, they insisted on operational control of their respective armies on the day of the transfer of power. To co-ordinate the division, Auchinleck was made responsible to a Joint Defence Council consisting of Lord Mountbatten and the Defence Ministers of the successor states, as well as the Commander-in-Chief, now styled Supreme Commander. To its credit the Council carried through the operation with efficiency and speed, despite the complexities involved in ascertaining the choice of every soldier, sailor, and airman.

With the acceptance of the Mountbatten Plan events moved swiftly. By the middle of July all the disputed areas had made their choice. The results were a foregone conclusion except for the Frontier Province. Bengal and the Punjab decided in favour of partition, Sind, the Sylhet District of Assam, and Baluchistan decided to join Pakistan. Attention was focused on the Frontier Province which, despite a Muslim majority of 92 per cent., was governed by the Congress-orientated 'Redshirt' Party of Dr. Khan Saheb and Khan Abdul Ghaffar Khan.

Geographically the Frontier was now isolated from the

Indian Dominion. The Khan brothers complicated matters by proposing a third alternative—Pathanistan (Pakhtoonistan), a separate state to comprise the Frontier Province and contiguous tribal areas. The League castigated it as a Congress-inspired plot to wean the Frontier from Pakistan. There was also a serious constitutional obstacle. The Mountbatten Plan provided for a referendum to choose between India or Pakistan; there was no third choice; the agreement of all parties was necessary for any change in the Plan and the League was firmly opposed. Thus the 'Redshirts' boycotted the referendum early in July. The result was 289,244 to 2,874 in favour of Pakistan. The consensus of opinion was that a majority would have favoured Pakistan even if the 'Redshirts' had contested the issue.[1] The cry of 'Islam in danger' had penetrated deeply by the summer of 1947.

Amidst these developments the constitutional formalities were hastily completed in London. On 4 July the Indian Independence Bill was introduced in the Commons. In a fortnight it secured the approval of both Houses of Parliament. It was brief, only twenty clauses, but symbolic of the end of an epoch.

In accordance with the Mountbatten Plan, the Act provided for the creation of two new Dominions on 15 August 1947. All powers previously exercised by the British Parliament and Government in British India were to be transferred to the Governments of India and Pakistan on the due date. As for the princely States, Paramountcy would lapse with the transfer of power, by inference granting them freedom of action to accede to India or Pakistan—or to proclaim their independence. The territories of the Dominions were defined, with appropriate qualifications for the areas about to determine their choice by referendum or by vote of their legislature. Each Dominion was to be headed by a Governor-General, but it was expressly stipulated that one person might serve in a dual capacity, in the hope that Mountbatten would be acceptable to both. The absence of a legally constituted Parliament in either of the proposed Dominions was overcome by giving both Constituent Assemblies the dual status and function of legislature and constitution-making body. The 1935 Government of India Act and its accompanying Orders-in-Council would remain in force

---

[1] This view was conveyed to the author by prominent *Indian* politicians in 1956.

(pending alteration or the drafting of new constitutions by the successor authorities), subject to the removal of the reserved and special powers vested in the Governor-General and the provincial Governors. All laws in force in British India on 15 August 1947 would remain in force until amended by the new Dominion legislatures. There was also a provision for continuity in the terms of employment of members of the Services. Indeed, the Indian Independence Act was remarkable for the degree to which it assured continuity in political institutions, the legal and judicial system and the constitutional fabric of British India.[1]

*   *   *   *

Two provisions of the Act gave rise to vigorous controversy, even before the formal transfer of power: the Governor-Generalship and the constitutional future of the princely States. The Congress proposed Mountbatten as Governor-General of the Dominion of India, undoubtedly on the assumption that the League would do likewise. To the consternation of many, Jinnah decided to occupy that post in Pakistan. In reality it made little difference to the power pyramid in Pakistan during the first year, for Jinnah remained the dominant personality until his death in September 1948. However, this schism and Mountbatten's decision to accept the Congress invitation created widespread Pakistani distrust.

To the present day it is alleged that the Viceroy was offended by Jinnah's action and that he used his authority during the transition period to strengthen India's claims in the many disputes that arose. Among others, Mountbatten was accused of collusion with Sir Cyril (later Lord) Radcliffe in the crucial task of demarcating the boundaries of Bengal and the Punjab, and of playing a nefarious role in the early stages of the Kashmir dispute. That the outward animosity lingered on long after Mountbatten's departure from the sub-continent became evident in March 1956, when he was forbidden passage over Pakistani territory *en route* to India for a visit to naval establishments, in his capacity as First Sea Lord of the Royal Navy.

The reasons for Jinnah's choice of the Governor-Generalship

---

[1] Indian Independence Act 1947, 10–11 George VI C.30. *Law Reports–Statutes,* 1947, vol. 1, pp. 236–55. For Nehru's comments on the draft Bill see Menon, op. cit., Appendix XII.

have never been adequately clarified. In part it was probably due to the factor of prestige, namely, Jinnah's urge to enhance his own status and to outdo the Congress in the eyes of his people. There may also have been the desire to eliminate all vestiges of unity with the Hindu-majority Dominion of India. A novel explanation was suggested by one of Jinnah's biographers. According to Hector Bolitho, the Muslim League President was critically ill at the time of Partition, indeed, knew that he was dying; he therefore preferred the less onerous office of Governor-General, leaving the daily tasks of administration to the younger and devoted Liaquat Ali Khan.[1]

It is known that Jinnah was in indifferent health at the very inception of Pakistan and that he died thirteen months later. But there is no evidence to support the view that he was aware of his impending death. If this were the case it was a well-kept secret of major significance. Most commentators on the Partition are convinced that Jinnah's role was crucial and that the unity of India would probably have been maintained but for his perseverance in the quest for Pakistan. If, indeed, Jinnah were critically ill, and the Congress leaders could have learned of this fact, they could have procrastinated a year or two, having waited thirty years already, and could have attained the goal of a united independent India.

The uncertain constitutional position of the princely States posed a problem of greater immediate significance. Paramountcy was to end on 15 August 1947, but the Indian Independence Act was silent about the status of the Princes after the transfer of power. By default the Act appeared to grant them freedom of action to accede to India, to accede to Pakistan or to assert their independence. The result of this vagueness was a formidable challenge to the stability of the two Dominions— a challenge created by the possible fragmentation of the subcontinent. The threat was especially grave for India because all but a dozen of the six hundred-odd princely States were contiguous to Indian territory. Uncertainty also contributed to the dangerous tension between the two Dominions from the very day of their formation. In particular it was partly responsible for the tragic conflict over Kashmir which has poisoned Indo-Pakistani relations since the Partition.

[1] Op. cit., p. 193.

N

The Muslim League accepted the implied doctrine of freedom of action for the Princes, probably because the few States on the Pakistani side of the border would have no real choice. Moreover, the exercise of such freedom by some of the large princely States in India, notably Hyderabad, would imperil the territorial integrity and stability of Pakistan's more powerful neighbour. For precisely opposite reasons the Congress rejected the British Government's interpretation of Paramountcy and declared that it would resist territorial fragmentation. In his speech to the A.I.C.C. on 15 June 1947, when the Mountbatten Plan was formally approved, Nehru asserted: 'There is a certain inherent paramountcy in the Government of India which cannot lapse . . . which must remain because of the very reasons of Geography, History, Defence, etc. . . .' The States cannot remain in a void, he continued; if they do not join the Union, there must be a suzerain relationship. To make his position unmistakably clear, he added that the Congress would not permit any act jeopardizing Indian security and he warned foreign states, i.e., Pakistan and the United Kingdom, that the recognition of any princely State as independent 'will be considered an unfriendly act'.[1] The A.I.C.C. approved this strong line by stating that it 'cannot admit the right of any State in India to declare its independence and to live in isolation from the rest of India'.[2]

The Viceroy, too, was acutely conscious of the constitutional vacuum created by the Indian Independence Act and the danger of Balkanization. He readily agreed to the establishment of a Ministry of States early in July. On 25 July he addressed the Princes in an effort to persuade them to accede to one or the other Dominion, depending upon their geographical position and the communal composition of their population. His speech was a resounding success. By the time power was formally transferred all but three princely States had signified their intention of doing so. Yet the three holding out—Kashmir, Hyderabad and Junagadh—were to cause bitterness and dislocation of such a magnitude that the achievement was overlooked.

Within the Interim Government tension continued. The

[1] Bose, D. R., op. cit., pp. 167–70.
[2] *Congress Bulletin*, No. 4, 10 July 1947, pp. 7–8.

Congress members insisted on the necessity of maintaining the normal administrative functions of a central government; the League members blocked every decision of substance. Early in July Nehru was on the verge of resignation over this issue. As soon as the Independence Act received royal assent, on 18 July, Mountbatten solved the problem by splitting the Interim Government into two provisional administrations for the successor states. In the Punjab communal conflict increased as the day of Partition approached, particularly in the key cities of Lahore and Amritsar. Friction was further intensified by uncertainty over the boundaries, pending the report of the Radcliffe Commission.

Sir Cyril Radcliffe, a noted English barrister, had been appointed Chairman of the Boundary Commissions for both Bengal and the Punjab. Associated with him were two High Court Judges nominated by the Congress and two by the League. As might have been expected in the tense atmosphere then prevailing all over India, the party nominees cancelled each others' votes with the result that the most controversial decisions were awards by Radcliffe himself. Apparently the reports of the Commissions were ready on 9 August, but Mountbatten decided to delay their publication for a week in order not to mar the celebration of Independence. This postponement and a curious set of circumstances were to produce Pakistani animosity towards both Radcliffe and Mountbatten.

*   *   *   *

At last the 'Appointed Day' arrived, the day of triumph and dedication. On the evening of 14 August huge, cheering crowds lined the main streets of New Delhi as Nehru, Prasad, Patel and others made their way to Parliament for the solemn ceremony of dedication to a free India. Nehru rose to the occasion with an eloquent address to the Constituent Assembly. 'Long years ago', he declared,

we made a tryst with destiny, and now the time comes when we shall redeem our pledge, not wholly or in full measure, but very substantially. At the stroke of the midnight hour, when the world sleeps, India will awake to life and freedom. A moment comes, which comes but rarely in history, when we step out from the old to the new, when an age ends, and when the soul of a nation, long suppressed, finds utterance. It is fitting that at this solemn moment we take the pledge of dedication to the service of India and her people and to the still larger cause of humanity. . . . We end today a period of ill fortune and India discovers herself again. The achievement we celebrate today is but a step, an opening of opportunity, to the greater triumphs and achievements that await us. . . . That future is not one of ease or resting but of incessant striving so that we may fulfil the pledges we have so often taken. . . . Peace has been said to be indivisible. So is freedom, so is prosperity now, and so also is disaster in this One World that can no longer be split into isolated fragments.

He concluded with an appeal for unity and magnanimity: 'This is no time for petty and destructive criticism, no time for ill-will or blaming others. We have to build the noble mansion of free India where all her children may dwell.'[1]

After a moving ceremony, in which each member of the Assembly recited a pledge of service to India, Nehru and Prasad went to the Viceroy's Palace to invite Mountbatten to become the first Governor-General of the Dominion of India. Nehru handed him an envelope containing a list of members of the Cabinet to be sworn in the following morning. The excitement of the day was, indeed, overwhelming—the envelope was empty!

All over India the coming of Independence was celebrated with unrestrained enthusiasm. In a hundred towns and in thousands of villages people gathered to welcome the dawn of a new age. It was a great *tamasha* (celebration) and the pent-up emotions of millions gave way to gay abandon. To mark the occasion a general amnesty of political prisoners was proclaimed and all death sentences were commuted to life imprisonment. Parades and firework displays were everywhere, mass meetings with speech-making dotted the land. Gandhi was honoured as the Father of the Nation, Nehru and Patel were hailed as indomitable leaders in the freedom struggle and, in the exuberance of the moment, tribute was paid to Mountbatten as the bearer of Indian freedom. It was a day of national rejoicing.

For Nehru 15 August symbolized the rebirth of a nation after a long and painful struggle for self-determination. It was an achievement of which he could be proud. Yet his joy was tempered by sadness at the impending partition of the country, an act which he had opposed these many years. He could point

[1] The text is in *Independence and After*, pp. 3–4.

12. With Albert Einstein at Princeton, N.J., 1948

13. At Srinagar, Kashmir, on 20 November, 1948

with pride to the peaceful transfer of power, but the accompanying violence and communal hatred marred the occasion and
augured ill for the future. Nor was he unaware of the magnitude
of the problems confronting free India.

August 15 marked the great divide in his public life. Behind
him were three decades of opposition to foreign rule and the
elaboration of theories about social change, economic development, democracy, and India's proper place in the family of
nations. Ahead was the unknown, a challenge to his political
maturity in a period fraught with great danger, an opportunity
to translate ideals into reality, a test of statesmanship. It was a
time for leadership, for the 'War of Succession' was about to
enter its most disastrous phase.

Independence Day itself provided a respite from the nerve-
racking events of the preceding fifteen months. But it was a
day of ceaseless activity, of ceremony and speech-making. In
the morning the official swearing-in of Cabinet Ministers took
place at the Viceroy's House amid the pomp and splendour of
Durbar Hall, followed by the unfurling of the national flag at
the Council of States. Then he attended a gathering of school-
children, another flag-raising ceremony at the war memorial
and a traditional 'crowning' by Hindu Pandits. It is customary
in India to derive authority from the Brahmins. Nehru, the
agnostic, agreed to receive religious blessing for the new dispensation, thereby satisfying the demands of tradition. In the
evening the new era was ushered in at a state banquet at which
Nehru paid tribute to Mountbatten and reflected on the
significance of the occasion.

To his people Nehru addressed two messages, one through the
press, the other on All-India Radio. 'The Appointed Day has
come,' he said, 'the day appointed by destiny, and India stands
forth again after long slumber and struggle, awake, vital, free
and independent. . . . It is a fateful moment for us in India, for
all Asia and for the world. A new star rises, the star of freedom
in the East, a new hope comes into being, a vision long cherished
materializes. May the star never set and that hope never be
betrayed!' He paid tribute to Gandhi as the architect of freedom, as well as to those who had sacrificed wealth, leisure and
life for the Cause. He also expressed the sadness of many
Indians for 'our brothers and sisters who have been cut off from

us by political boundaries and who unhappily cannot share at present in the freedom that has come'. The reality of Partition could not penetrate so soon.[1]

In his broadcast to the nation Nehru concentrated on the critical problems facing free India at its birth. The first objective was the termination of violence and internal strife, a precondition to progress. 'Production is the first priority', he said. But equitable distribution was also essential. He also emphasized the necessity for a rapid and radical reform of the archaic land tenure system. To assuage the feelings of the Services and to remove their fears for the future, he remarked, 'the old distinctions and differences are gone. . . . In the difficult days ahead our Services and experts have a vital role to play and we invite them to do so as comrades in the service of India.'[2] It was a far cry from his condemnation of India's civil servants before Independence. He now realized their indispensability in the chaotic transition period and appealed to their conscience and national pride. Before the year was out they succeeded in winning his trust, even admiration.

The celebrations were brought to a close with an impressive flag-hoisting ceremony at the Red Fort, the majestic symbol of Moghul power and splendour in Old Delhi. A crowd estimated at half a million gathered for the occasion and a deafening roar greeted the unfurling of the Congress flag. They listened attentively as Nehru recounted the highlights of the freedom struggle and posed the challenge of the future, appealing for a closing of ranks and a herculean effort to solve India's problems on the threshold of a new stage in its history. The time of rejoicing was brief, however. Even before the cheers had died down, the rumblings of communal war could be heard in the distance. Independence Day was not only a day of triumph. It was also the prelude to a spectacle of barbaric cruelty, mass murder and wholesale migration.

[1] *Independence and After*, pp. 5–6.   [2] Ibid., pp. 7–9.

—and Anguish

T HE 'War of Succession' was resumed with increased fero-
city on the morrow of jubilation. The catalyst was the
publication of the Radcliffe Awards on 16 August. There were
two great danger spots—Bengal and the Punjab. Largely due to
Gandhi's presence and his remarkable healing powers, communal passions in Bengal were kept within manageable bounds,
though Hindus were incensed by the award of the Chittagong
Hill Tracts to East Pakistan. In the Punjab, however, the accumulated tensions unleashed a full-scale civil war.

The principal bone of contention was Gurdaspur District, an
area with a small Muslim majority situated at the narrowest
point between the Ravi and Beas Rivers. The Radcliffe Commission had been instructed to determine the boundary on the
criteria of communal composition 'and other factors'. Although unstated, these were acknowledged to be economic
considerations, particularly the effect of the demarcation on
canal irrigation systems and rail and road communication. In
this instance Radcliffe adjudged these 'other factors' compelling,
and awarded Gurdaspur to East Punjab, i.e., India. Muslim
League leaders were dismayed, for Gurdaspur was of vital significance; it was then the only usable land link between India
and the princely State of Jammu and Kashmir. A few months
later, when the conflict over Kashmir arose, Pakistani leaders
blamed what they considered to be the manifestly unjust decision on Gurdaspur. Without it, they argued, India had no
claim whatsoever to Kashmir. In their frustration they accused
Mountbatten of using his personal influence to alter the Punjab
Award in India's favour.

This allegation and the theory of collusion between the Viceroy and the Chairman of the Boundary Commission are
tenaciously maintained by Pakistani spokesmen to the present
day. The evidence cited in support of their theory is a letter
dated 8 August 1947 from Sir George Abell, the Viceroy's

Private Secretary, to Sir Evan Jenkins, then Governor of the undivided Punjab, dealing with the anticipated Radcliffe Award. Conversations with some of the principal persons involved in this affair revealed a strange tale of administrative bungling which may be designated 'The Sketch-Map Story'.

Early in August Jenkins asked for advance information on the probable boundary line in order to make the appropriate disposition of troops and police and to inform officials in the border districts. Abell got in touch with the Secretary of the Radcliffe Commission and, on the basis of a telephone conversation, drew a sketch-map which was sent to Jenkins—along with the comment that the final, official Punjab Award would not be ready for a few days. The sketch-map showed the sub-districts of Ferozepur and Zira on the Pakistani side of the line. In the official Radcliffe Award, however, these two areas were included in India.

Pakistanis assume the sketch-map to have been official and contend that these changes could only have occurred as a result of Mountbatten's intervention. They then project the argument to say that since there is 'evidence' of collusion with respect to these areas, it is reasonable to conclude that the Viceroy's influence was responsible for the decision to allocate Gurdaspur as well to India, thereby giving it a direct connection with Kashmir. Mountbatten's alleged villainy is attributed to resentment at Jinnah's action on the Governor-Generalship of Pakistan. How then did the Pakistanis learn of the sketch-map? On the eve of his departure from Lahore, Jenkins destroyed his confidential papers but left the map in his safe for his successor, Sir Francis Mudie, the Governor-designate of West Punjab. Mudie handed the map to the Pakistani leaders.

There can be no doubt that the incident would never have occurred but for a series of administrative improprieties. In Jenkins's case there were extenuating circumstances; communal violence was increasing steadily and it was certain that the Radcliffe Award would aggravate the conflict in the border districts. It was natural, therefore, to prepare for the inevitable by concentrating his limited forces in key areas, and this could only be done effectively by advance knowledge of the probable line of demarcation. Yet it was administratively wrong to seek information before the Award was published. Abell, too, should not have sought such information from the Commission, nor should he have passed this on to Jenkins. And he left himself open to severe criticism by drawing the sketch-map on the basis of a telephone conversation. The Secretary of the Commission was no less wrong in offering such information to Abell. As for Mudie's action in giving the map to Pakistani leaders, this can perhaps be justified on constitutional grounds.[1]

The theory of collusion between Radcliffe and Mountbatten has never been supported by documentary evidence. The assumption that the sketch-map was official is incorrect; it was, in fact, a rough draft, having been drawn by Abell without even seeing the maps of the Commission. The charge regarding Gurdaspur is only an inference from an unproved allegation. Moreover, it challenges Radcliffe's integrity without the slightest evidence. Finally, it impugns Mountbatten's integrity on the specious grounds that he was offended by Jinnah's decision to occupy the Governor-Generalship of Pakistan, also without evidence of any kind.[2]

In commenting on this strange episode (Abell's sketch-map), Lord Mountbatten declared that he considered it beneath his dignity to issue a formal denial of the charge—he has never done so. He added that Jinnah told a trusted mutual friend that he did not himself believe Mountbatten had done anything wrong or dishonourable; that Mountbatten himself was a big enough man to understand the state of public opinion about India, particularly since the Kashmir crisis; and that accusations such as this were inevitable. Liaquat Ali had also mentioned that he did not doubt Mountbatten's probity.[3] Nevertheless, the sketch-map incident created a lasting Pakistani distrust of Mountbatten's bona fides and injected an additional element of friction into the turbulent course of Indo-Pakistani relations.

---

[1] At the height of the Punjab disorders, on 5 September 1947, Mudie, then Governor of West Punjab, wrote to Jinnah, the Governor-General of Pakistan: 'I am telling everyone that I don't care how the Sikhs get across the border; the great thing is to get rid of them as soon as possible. There is still little sign of 3 lakh [300,000] Sikhs in Lyallpur moving, but in the end they too will have to go.' The full text of this letter is to be found in Khosla, op. cit., Appendix I, pp. 314–16.

[2] The author has been told by various persons that there was no communication between Mountbatten and Radcliffe throughout the labours of the Commission.

[3] To the author in London in October 1955. All subsequent references to Mountbatten's views on the events of 1947 are based upon the author's notes of two interviews in October and November 1955.

The immediate effect of the Radcliffe Awards was to heighten the tension to the breaking-point. Mass hysteria and paralysing fear gripped the Sikhs and Hindus of West Punjab and the Muslims of East Punjab. Hatred was already entrenched as a result of the March riots and the persistent violence in Lahore and Amritsar. All three communities were ready to do battle. Insecurity and the desire for revenge were everywhere. But it was the formal announcement of the boundary lines that galvanized them into renewed action. It was as if the Award had closed the prison doors, trapping millions of frightened and confused Punjabi peasants in two large concentration camps. The alternatives were death or flight. They reacted with blind instinct and set out for the 'Promised Land', Pakistan for the Muslims, India for the Hindus and Sikhs. The leaders had offered assurances of protection to minorities but these were belied by the actions of subordinates and by the atrocities of the communal armies. Moreover, years of inflammatory speeches had roused communal passions; a monster had been created, no longer capable of being controlled by rational persuasion and pledges of fair treatment.

While the rest of the sub-continent celebrated the attainment of Independence, the Punjab entered a period of unmitigated horror. In remote villages members of the minority community were mercilessly killed, for no other reason than the accident of birth. Each atrocity bred an equivalent response and, within days, the 'Land of the Five Rivers' was aflame with bestiality. It is impossible to apportion responsibility for the Punjab catastrophe, nor is it easy to prove who set the chain reaction in motion. All communities share the blame for this black record in Indian history. All contributed to the calamity, though many individual Muslims, Sikhs and Hindus risked their lives to save friends in the minority group.

Rumour, fear and the desire for vengeance maintained the momentum of communal fury. Members of minority communities fled from isolated villages to larger centres in the hope that numbers would provide a measure of security. Some were killed *en route*. Frequently these concentrations of men, women and children were attacked by the 'enemy' army and suffered 'heavy casualties'. No quarter was given—torture, mutilation, assault, conversion by force. It was nothing less than a war of extermination. The more fortunate ones succeeded in reaching a railway station and boarded trains for the journey to safety. Many failed to arrive. The battlefield was everywhere, in village, town, road, temple and mosque. Trains going from Lahore to Amritsar and vice versa were considered fair prey, and eyewitnesses have reported incidents where up to 2,000 were killed in one train between these cities. The less fortunate began a trek by foot in a frenzied search for security. In sheer numbers it was the greatest in history, probably about twelve million, equally divided between Hindus and Sikhs fleeing from West Punjab and Muslims from the East. Before the year was out half a million people died, or were murdered.[1]

Those who survived were gradually absorbed on both sides of the border, but the drain on the limited resources of the successor states, especially Pakistan, was nearly disastrous. Further, the refugees served to raise the already high level of tension at a time when India and Pakistan were on the verge of open warfare over Kashmir. And the legacy of evacuee property, running into billions of dollars, continues to plague all efforts to achieve a *rapprochement* between Delhi and Karachi.

When the enormity of the disorders became clear, Nehru and his colleagues resorted to emergency measures. The crisis reached its peak within India early in September, when thousands of refugees poured into Delhi and wreaked vengeance on local Muslims. To Nehru and others it seemed a cruel turn of fate that communal violence should invade the capital of India less than a month after Independence. Sensing the mood of Nehru and Patel, the duumvirs of the new régime, V. P. Menon telephoned Mountbatten in Simla and asked him to return immediately to help meet the challenge of the riots. The Governor-General's Press Attaché wrote in his diary at the time: 'V.P. said that the view of Nehru, Patel and all the responsible Ministers was that the situation was now so serious that his [Mountbatten's] presence alone could save it.'[2]

Mountbatten returned at once and proposed the formation of an Emergency Committee along the lines of a military head-

---

[1] A vivid eyewitness account of the Punjab migration in 1947 is Bourke-White, Margaret, *Halfway to Freedom*, ch. 1. See also Schechtman, Joseph B., *Population Transfers in Asia*, ch. 1.

[2] Campbell-Johnson, op. cit., p. 177.

quarters command. Nehru and Patel agreed and insisted that he assume the chairmanship. He was greatly impressed by this gesture, in the light of India's long, hard struggle for independence.

The Committee was really a parallel government, superseding the Cabinet during the period of greatest crisis. It consisted of those Cabinet Ministers and other officials whose work impinged on the riots and refugee rehabilitation. The Committee met daily with Mountbatten in the chair. Decisions were taken in the morning and were to be implemented in the afternoon. For the first few days they were not acted upon promptly because Indian nationalist leaders lacked sufficient administrative experience. Gradually, however, the emergency response had the desired effect—to restore law and order, especially in the capital.

Nehru's role during the crisis was vital. Mountbatten organized the administrative machinery but it was Nehru who inspired confidence and led his people back to the road of sanity. Indeed, without his spiritual leadership, the efforts of Mountbatten and the Emergency committee would have been in vain. Moreover, he stood firm against the onslaught of communalism and, by decisive action at crucial moments, ensured the restoration of communal peace. Both contributed to the victory over the riots in the autumn of 1947, their efforts complementing one another effectively.

The immediate task was to extinguish the flames of communal violence in Delhi lest they spread to other parts of the country. From the outset Nehru insisted on the need to ban all weapons, including the Sikh *kirpans*, their religious swords. Patel at first agreed but later dissented on the grounds that this would violate religious freedom. Nehru's view prevailed. The mood of both men was anger and frustration. In a broadcast to the nation about the situation in Delhi and the Punjab, he said: 'My mind is full with horror of the things that I saw and that I heard. During these last few days . . . I have supped my fill of horror. That, indeed, is the only feast that we can have now.' He related that he had just seen Gandhi, on his return to the capital, and 'wondered how low we had fallen from the great ideals that he had placed before us'. The riots had another effect on Nehru, an unqualified acceptance of Gandhi's stress on the interrelationship of means and ends. In numerous speeches at the time he was to reiterate, 'for I do believe that good work must bear good results just as . . . evil must bear evil consequences'.[1]

Unlike many of his colleagues and Pakistani leaders, Nehru never succumbed to the communal mentality; throughout, he was the symbol of tolerance and reason. In his broadcast of 19 August, after a tour of the Punjab, he refused to apportion blame for the holocaust and declared war against 'anti-social elements' of all communities.[2] Exactly one month later he analysed the changing character of the upheaval in purely secular terms: 'If I may draw on my Socialist background, what is happening now is to a large extent an upheaval in the lower middle classes. . . . Undoubtedly there has been a communal trend in what has happened, but the trend now is away from killings and towards increased looting. . . . In a sense this is worse, but in another way it is a hopeful sign. It is something we can deal with by persuasion or force, and that is the way we must deal with it.'[3]

Those who observed Nehru during the September crisis noted that he had aged considerably and looked weary and haggard. Yet the consensus was that he responded to the challenge with a presence of mind that surprised even those who knew him best. To a few intimates he confided his pain, disgust and disillusionment, but to the nation he was more resolute than ever.

Many are the stories of Nehru's personal courage and decisiveness during the riots in Delhi. On one occasion he rescued two Muslim children who had taken refuge on a roof while a mob below was waiting to commit another murder. During the height of the riots he raced to Connaught Circus, the commercial heart of the capital, where Hindus were systematically looting Muslim shops with the police standing by as interested onlookers. Panic was enveloping the city. Without regard for his personal safety, he rushed unarmed into the midst of the angry mob, berated them mercilessly and attempted, single-

[1] Nehru's broadcast on All-India Radio, 9 September 1947. Tendulkar, op. cit., vol. 8, p. 135.

[2] *Independence and After*, pp. 43–46.

[3] Quoted in Campbell-Johnson, op. cit., p. 197.

handed, to bring about a return to sanity. As a last resort he ordered the police to shoot the Hindu looters, an extremely un-popular decision at the time. It was this, perhaps more than anything else, that broke the back of violence in Delhi.

It required much courage, too, to declare repeatedly that as long as he was Prime Minister, India would not become a Hindu state. He also threatened to resign if wholehearted co-operation were denied him in the pursuit of his ideals. Even his bitterest critic in India, D. F. Karaka, was compelled to admit that in the aftermath of Partition it was Nehru alone who held the nation together. 'In that crisis he stood firm', not with any plan but with 'honesty of purpose'. The basis of that honesty was his uncompromising secular approach 'which is almost an instinct with him'.[1] Without his decisive leadership at the time the fate of millions of Indian Muslims would have been infinitely worse. It was an achievement which he could look back upon with pride. Sporadic outbreaks continued in Delhi for some weeks but by the beginning of October the threat had been overcome.[2] In the Punjab, however, the migration con-tinued throughout the autumn; by the end of the year the areas on both sides of the border had been denuded of the over-whelming majority of the minority communities, particularly in West Pakistan. The cost of Partition in human suffering was enormous.

*   *   *   *

Was the response of the authorities adequate to the challenge? Could the loss of life have been reduced? Could the excesses have been minimized? Was the size of the migration inevitable? The crux of the answer to all these questions is that no one fore-saw the magnitude of the Punjab migration. This fact emerged clearly from conversations with some of the principal actors in the Indian drama of 1947. Attlee intimated eight years later that the scale of the Punjab disorders came as a rude shock to the British Cabinet. Some disturbances were anticipated, as well as a limited migration from both parts of the province,

---

[1] *Nehru, The Lotus Eater from Kashmir*, p. 104.
[2] For a detailed account of communal violence in Delhi and the Emergency com-mittee see Menon, op. cit., pp. 419–34.

remarked Mountbatten, but certainly not the movement of millions, driven by a herd instinct to abandon their homes. Furthermore, no one could foresee large-scale peasant migration *before* the outbreak of disturbances in their particular village.

Nor were Indian political leaders more realistic in their evaluation of the Punjabi scene. Typical of the Congress view was Nehru's optimism on 15 June 1947: 'There is no reason why the minorities there [in Pakistan] should be tyrannized and persecuted.' He speculated that there might be *individual* cases of violence but thought it most unlikely that organized attacks by the majority community would take place.[1] In part, this illusion was due to the conviction that once Pakistan was conceded, the *raison d'être* for communal violence would vanish or, in Patel's words, once the cancerous growth was surgically removed, health would be restored to the body politic. It should have been realized that such an operation leaves the body in a weakened condition and susceptible to the slightest infection. There was also a naïve belief that Jinnah's assurance of protection for the minorities, in his inaugural speech as Governor-General, would curb communal passions *per se*. It was as if the torrent of communal riots from the 'Great Calcutta Killing' onwards could be relegated to the past as unfortunate excesses of the struggle for freedom without any legacy to the future. When to this is added the fact that violence was a prominent feature of the Punjab landscape for five continuous months, the assumption of Mountbatten, Nehru, Patel and their colleagues that the transfer of power would be peaceful in the Punjab was a 'Himalayan blunder'.

In Nehru's case the incorrect assessment of the forces at work was also partly due to the assumption that his countrymen shared his faith in communal tolerance. Wish was father to the thought; he appeared to identify his utopia—secular harmony—with Indian reality in the summer of 1947, which was communal hatred on a vast scale. No serious thought was given to a possible exchange of population either by Nehru or by the Pakistani leaders, largely because neither anticipated the 'Great Trek'. It was a tragic misreading of mass psychology. Mountbatten's optimistic view was more understandable because of his

[1] Bose, D. R., op. cit., p. 165.

relative unfamiliarity with Indian conditions and the brevity of his direct contact with India. The failure of Congress and League leaders to gauge the temper of the Punjab suggests either a reluctance to accept the obvious or a dangerous gap between the élite and the masses at a time when understanding was essential.

One of the most painful features of the Punjab catastrophe for Nehru and others was the fact that after almost thirty years of preaching Gandhi's philosophy of non-violence, millions of Indians behaved like brutes. Gandhi himself had the remarkable capacity to restore communal peace wherever he went. But no one else possessed this magic at the time. If there had been two Gandhis, things might have been different. But there was only one and he went to Bengal.

Perhaps the only person to sense disaster in the Punjab was Sir Evan Jenkins. Even before the Mountbatten Plan was submitted to the political leaders, he warned the Viceroy that large-scale violence was inevitable. However, in the civil service tradition, it was cautiously worded. The authorities in Delhi do not appear to have been entirely convinced, as Mountbatten's reflections suggest. Yet they did take certain precautions. The basic question is whether or not these precautions were adequate.

Mountbatten suggested that the actions taken were the maximum possible in the given circumstances. A special Boundary Force of 55,000 men under Major-General Rees was moved into the Punjab during the summer of 1947, all picked units with high-calibre officers. Both Indian and Pakistani spokesmen criticized its performance and forced its disbandment in September 1947. Mountbatten claimed that it assisted in mitigating the effects of the calamity and reduced the loss of life. The main criticism is not to be levelled at the Boundary Force; rather, that the prognosis was wrong, that the assumptions were divorced from reality, and that the precautions, geared to minor disturbances, were woefully inadequate in terms of the needs. This is, of course, hindsight, but none the less pertinent to the discussion of one of the most controversial issues arising out of the Partition.

It may well be that the size of the migration was inevitable, given the haste with which the transfer of power was carried out.

In seventy-three days, from the acceptance of the Mountbatten Plan to Independence Day, a large number of complicated problems had to be solved, with resulting dislocation on a vast scale: the partition of Bengal and the Punjab; referenda in the Frontier Province and the Sylhet District of Assam; the division of the military and civil services, and the assets and liabilities of the Government of India; the creation of a new administration for Pakistan; the provision of security for minorities on both sides of the border; and negotiations with about six hundred princely States for accession to one or the other Dominion. It was a gigantic task which created much confusion and taxed the administrative resources of both states to the breaking-point. It also left many problems unsolved, notably Kashmir, the division of canal waters in the Punjab, and indirectly, compensation for property left behind by millions of refugees.

What then persuaded the Viceroy to push the date of the transfer of power ahead from June 1948 to 15 August 1947? In Mountbatten's view there were two critical factors—the instability of the Interim Government and the decline of administrative efficiency. League and Congress members were constantly at odds. Issues were not decided on their merits, the vote invariably being 9 to 5, along party lines, thereby hampering the functioning of the central government. The longer the transfer of power was delayed, the greater the possibility of disorder in the country, particularly after partition had been accepted in principle. The basic reason for haste was the necessity of maintaining a high level of anticipation, aroused by the expectation of freedom.

Mountbatten implied that the leaders' agreement to the Plan of 3 June, i.e., his plan for partition, was precarious. Jinnah was unhappy with the scheme, especially with the provision for partition of Bengal and the Punjab, and approved only indirectly, by his famous nod at the Leaders' Conference. Gandhi, too, was opposed to partition—in any form. As Mountbatten remarked, 'I heard about it in Karachi, on my return from London at the end of May 1947, and so asked him to come and see me. It happened to be a day of silence for which I was grateful. In retrospect I think he chose to make that a day of silence to save him the embarrassment of accepting the Partition. For he had no other solution.' As for Nehru, throughout he was the man of common sense. Having succeeded in getting acceptance of the Plan of 3 June, which raised tremendous excitement throughout the country, it was important to maintain the momentum, almost, it would seem, to prevent them from changing their minds. Thus the date of the transfer was advanced as far as possible. What would have happened if the date had been set a few months later? The Interim Government might well have broken down, the administrative machine might have suffered serious harm, and the Plan of 3 June might have been abandoned.[1] Moreover, had the transfer of power been delayed, widespread communal violence might have followed.

*   *   *   *

These reflections have an added interest, bearing upon the reasons for the British transfer of power. They suggest that the timing of the withdrawal was dictated by the compulsion of events, by the unique circumstances within India in the spring of 1947. The view that postponement of the transfer was not politically feasible is shared by many observers of the Indian scene in 1947 and after. Typical is the comment of Philip Mason who writes with authority on the attitude of the British members of the I.C.S.: 'There is much to regret in the way the end came. But that the end could not have been longer delayed . . . hardly one of the Guardians [the I.C.S. men] would have denied.'[2] The same thought was expressed more bluntly by William Phillips, an American diplomat in India during the war: 'When the Labour Government came to power in July 1945 it saw the writing on the wall.'[3] By that time it was clear that the termination of the *Raj* could not be delayed much longer, for all Indian parties were agreed on the demand for independence. The only question

---

[1] The Viceroy's view about the Administration was shared by most officials in Delhi and by many observers. Philip Mason, a senior British member of the Indian Civil Service, commented typically: 'Everyone then was thinking of what was to come next. Hardly anyone was giving his heart and soul to the task of the moment.' *The Men Who Ruled India: The Guardians* (vol. ii), pp. 338–9. Mason published this book under the pseudonym, Philip Woodruff.

[2] *The Men Who Ruled India: The Guardians*, p. 20.

[3] *Ventures in Diplomacy*, p. 255.

remaining was whether a free India should be united or partitioned.

It was not only the mounting pressure of Indian public opinion that influenced the decision of the British Government. Far more compelling was the weakened position of England as a result of the war and the enormous drain, economic and military, which continued control over India would have entailed, particularly in conditions of widespread opposition. There was, too, growing pressure from the international community, notably from the United States and the Soviet Union, which made the retention of power increasingly untenable. Both of these factors and the absence of any real choice were emphasized in a candid speech by Sir Stafford Cripps to the House of Commons during the debate on Attlee's historic pledge to transfer power.

There were two conceivable alternatives, he said. 'First, we could attempt to strengthen British control in India on the basis of an expanded personnel in the Secretary of States' services, and a considerable reinforcement of British troops . . .' The second was to make another effort to bring the Indian parties together. 'One thing that was, I think, quite obviously *impossible* was to decide *to continue our responsibility indefinitely*—and, indeed, against our own wishes—*into a period when we had not the power to carry it out. . . .* The first alternative we had no hesitation in putting aside. It would be contrary to all we have said. . . . *It would be politically impracticable, from both a national and an international point of view, and would arouse the most bitter animosity of all parties in India against us.* Even if we had been prepared to make available the extra troops that would be required to deal with opposition by the Indian people over that period of years, it is certain that the people of this country—*short as we are of manpower, as we all know*—*would not have consented to the prolonged stationing of large bodies of British troops in India,* for a purpose which was not consistent with our expressed desire that India should achieve self-government at as early a date as possible. . . . We should, therefore, have had to rule India through the Governor-General and the Governors without any representative Indian Government. We therefore ruled out the first alternative, as both undesirable and impracticable.'[1]

---

[1] Gt. Brit. H.C. *Debates*, 1946–7, vol. 434, cols. 503–5. (Emphasis added.)

The choice, then, was coercion on a large scale or independence—and British resources were inadequate to retain power by force. This factor was also noted by General Sir Francis Tuker in his candid answer to the question, 'Why Did We Quit?': 'Ultimately we found that this garrison commitment was more than the industrial needs of our impoverished country could stand. That was one very strong reason for our leaving India and leaving it quickly.'[1] Like Cripps, he added that the abdication of power was in fulfilment of a long-standing British pledge, that the world at large, especially America and Russia, pressed for the British departure, and that the rancour of educated Indians made it difficult to remain.

Another consideration appeared to have been the growing fear in London that further delay would open the road to greater strife from which Communism might emerge the victor. Labour leaders believed that the Congress was in danger of disintegration which would create a vacuum for Communist influence. As early as 18 December 1946 Attlee was reported to have told Mountbatten that 'the Government was most unfavourably impressed with the political trends affecting both the Congress and the Moslem League. If we were not very careful, we might well find ourselves handing India over not simply to civil war, but to political movements of a definitely totalitarian character. Urgent action was needed to break the deadlock . . .'[2]

There can be little doubt that the transfer of power could not have been postponed much longer, even had the Conservatives been returned to office in 1945. The decline of British power and its inability to sustain the burden of India would have remained unchanged. Yet the fact that it was a Labour Government which carried through the withdrawal certainly hastened the process. More than that, it symbolized a fundamental change in the attitude of British public opinion towards India during the preceding half-century. There were large and powerful segments of British society which had developed a guilt complex about continued British rule in India, a feeling that was strengthened by the experience of the war. There was, too, a growing positive sympathy for the aspirations of Indian

---

[1] *While Memory Serves*, p. 518.
[2] Campbell-Johnson, op. cit., pp. 17–18.

nationalism. It was for many a test case of Britain's capacity, and willingness, to come to terms with the nationalist upsurge all over colonial Asia. But this alone would have been insufficient to cause Britain to part with power. Only a realization that power could not be retained except at an excessive cost ensured the outcome in 1947.

Indian independence was inevitable in another sense. Viewed in the long perspective of history, it was the necessary climax of a lengthy process inherent in the character of British rule. The key to its attainment was the creation of a common purpose. Once that purpose, the quest for freedom, penetrated most strata of Indian society, the demission of power by the United Kingdom was inescapable. How, then, was this common purpose achieved? In part, it was an inadvertent legacy of the *Raj*: administrative integration and a transport system that united India physically for the first time in two thousand years; the penetration of English as a medium of communication for the intelligentsia throughout the sub-continent; and secular education, which broke down age-old barriers and facilitated common modes of thought and action among Indians of different castes and classes. In part it was forged by the nationalist movement and especially by Gandhi who superimposed upon these foundations the symbols of a common purpose, such as the nation-wide *hartals*, constructive work, a flag, an anthem, and most important, mass non-violent non-co-operation. The civil disobedience movements strengthened the common bonds and maintained a continuous focus on the goal of national freedom, welding diverse groups together in the common purpose. The growth of political consciousness among Indian peasants and workers hastened the process. The success of the Russian Revolution also acted as a stimulus. Ultimately, the common purpose spread throughout the country and infected the Services with a sense of guilt and impending doom. It was at that point that the British had no choice but to transfer power. In short, independence was the natural and inevitable outcome of the process of creating national consciousness and a common purpose, accomplished by the *Raj*, unconsciously, and by the Congress, consciously, over an extended period of time. In this sense the British *Raj* contained within itself the seeds of its own destruction.

Upon his return to the United Kingdom in June 1948, Mountbatten claimed that the transition period had been relatively peaceful. In support of this contention he noted that only 3 per cent. of the population were involved in the disturbances. But percentages are often misleading; translated into human terms, it meant 10 million or one out of every 35 persons in the sub-continent. Whether or not further delay would have been more catastrophic is difficult to say, for the clock of history cannot be turned back. Suffice it to note that many Indians and Pakistanis, and Englishmen, are convinced that it could not have been worse had the transfer been postponed.

The price of Partition was exceedingly high, not only in terms of the human suffering attending the 'Great Trek' in the Punjab, the travail of Bengal, and the legacy of mistrust and bitterness between the two successor states, but also in terms of the stated objectives of British policy. Among these were avoidance of loss of life and of dislocation as far as possible, protection of the minorities and preservation of unity to the maximum extent. On all three counts the cost was enormous. When measured against these goals, the Partition unquestionably registered a failure.

*   *   *   *

In a moment of reflection, almost a year after the Partition, Nehru stated: 'We consented because we thought that thereby we were purchasing peace and goodwill, though at a high price. . . . I do not know now, if I had the same choice, how I would decide.'[1] The question arises, did Nehru really have a choice or was Partition, like Independence, inevitable? And if so, when did it become irrevocable? Many persons expressed the view that the Partition was never inescapable, that it was a conscious choice of Indian leaders, notably Nehru and Patel.[2] Almost all are convinced that the outcome was certainly in doubt at least as late as the middle of 1946, only one year before the fateful act occurred.

The event most frequently cited as decisive was the collapse of the Cabinet Mission. Some consider the great divide to be

---

[1] *The Hindu* (Madras), 26 July 1948.
[2] To the author in India in 1956.

Nehru's statement early in July 1946 when he proclaimed the sovereignty of the Constituent Assembly and declared that the three-tier scheme of the Cabinet Mission would probably never come into existence. Others claim that the Partition became 'inevitable' as a result of the paralysis of the Interim Government in the following autumn and winter. A few pointed to Attlee's statement of 20 February 1947 as the irrevocable act leading to division of the country.

Mountbatten indicated that he became convinced of its necessity soon after his arrival in Delhi, at the end of March 1947. Nehru himself reflected in the summer of 1956: 'The partition of India became inevitable, I should say, less than a year before it occurred. I think now, looking back, that partition could have been avoided if the British Government's policy had been different, about a year or eighteen months before.'[1] From the consensus that a united India was within the realm of possibility as late as 1946, and the precarious nature of the parties' agreement to Partition even after their approval of the Mountbatten plan, one must assume that it was a voluntary choice by Nehru, Patel and their colleagues.

Nehru's crucial role in the great decision is confirmed by many who witnessed and participated in the momentous events of the spring and summer of 1947. On the Congress side it was he and Patel who carried the party in favour of Partition, however reluctantly. In a sense Nehru was the decisive member of the triangle of Congress leaders, for while Patel controlled the machine he could never have won a majority in favour of the Mountbatten Plan had Nehru opposed and stood by Gandhi. By supporting Patel, Nehru tilted the Congress balance in favour of division of the country. By that time they were the two dominant figures in the Congress, Gandhi having been pushed to the periphery in terms of decision-making. It was ironic that, having followed him faithfully for almost thirty years, with very few exceptions, Nehru and Patel should have broken with the master on the most significant issue affecting India in modern history.

Gandhi was heartbroken by the decision. However, he did not attempt to challenge his disciples. Apparently the Mahatma favoured a final resort to civil disobedience but felt that his

[1] To the author in New Delhi on 6 June 1956.

advanced age precluded his carrying the burden alone. This would have necessitated, too, his recapturing power within the Congress, but Nehru and Patel were firmly opposed to another mass campaign. Hence he acquiesced in their view. What, then, were the reasons that impelled Nehru to accept Partition.

With typical candour Nehru laid bare his innermost thoughts on this vital issue. Seven distinct but closely related factors emerge from his speeches at the time. Perhaps the most compelling was fear—fear that a tragic civil war would ravage the sub-continent unless the deadlock were broken swiftly. Along with this concern was the belief that acceptance of the League demand would ensure security for the minorities. The use of violence to maintain unity, Nehru declared, would have meant civil war and 'would have checked the progress of India for a long time to come'.[1] On another occasion he stated that the Congress had not surrendered to the riots but 'they are very much disturbed at the prevailing madness. . . . Partition is better than the murder of innocent citizens.'[2] This naïve faith and miscalculated risk were echoed in Patel's alleged comment to an English friend after the Punjab catastrophe: 'We were promised peace if we accepted Partition!'

A third reason was Nehru's conviction that 'the problems before India were of such a serious nature that no delay could be tolerated'.[3] The situation in the country had deteriorated and the Interim Government was paralysed by the antagonism of its League members. Partition seemed to him the only solution to the daily conflicts within the Cabinet. The League policy of obstruction reaped rich rewards.

This concern about the consequences of the existing impasse was strengthened by another source of anxiety, namely, grave doubts about the implications of an artificial and enforced unity. 'If they [the League] are forced to stay in the Union,' he said, 'no progress and planning will be possible.'[4] To his colleagues and followers Nehru added that it was necessary to face reality. A section of the population wanted to secede, and unity could not be achieved by compulsion; nor was it in accordance with democratic procedure or desirable in terms of India's long-run

---

[1] Bose, D. R., op. cit., p. 184.   [2] Ibid., pp. 164, 165.
[3] Ibid., p. 184.   [4] Ibid., p. 163.

interests. Further, he was besieged by urgent pleas from Hindus and Sikhs in the Punjab and Bengal to accept Partition of these provinces in order to safeguard them against permanent discrimination and possible annihilation in a Muslim-majority Pakistan.[1] Finally, the thought that Indian freedom itself might be jeopardized or at least delayed weighed heavily in his decision. The Mountbatten Plan seemed to provide a way out of the tangled web of chaos and frustration; it seemed honourable and effective. Partition, he reiterated time and time again, was the lesser of two evils.

There is a striking consistency in Nehru's stated views on the motivations of his decision. Nine years after the decisive act occurred, he remarked: 'Well, I suppose it was the compulsion of events and the feeling that we couldn't get out of that deadlock or morass by pursuing the way we had done; it became worse and worse. Further, a feeling that even if we got freedom for India, with that background, it would be a very weak India, that is, a federal India with far too much power in the federating units. A larger India would have constant troubles, constant disintegrating pulls. And also the fact that we saw no other way of getting our freedom—in the near future, I mean. And so we accepted and said, let us build up a strong India. And if others do not want to be in it, well, how can we and why should we force them to be in it?'[2]

To this array of factors which shaped Nehru's outlook on Partition may be added four others. In the atmosphere of tension, of fears and of hopes which pervaded India throughout 1947, there was a widespread belief that Partition would be short-lived. Most of the Congress leaders, and Nehru among them, subscribed to the view that Pakistan was not a viable state—politically, economically, geographically or militarily—and that sooner or later the areas which had seceded would be compelled by force of circumstances to return to the fold. Nor was this appraisal confined to the Congress. Most impartial observers, sympathizers with the Pakistani cause and, perhaps, some League leaders themselves, were pessimistic about its future.

[1] This acceptance by Nehru reflects the fact that, in contrast to his earlier view of communalism, he now recognized it to be an abiding and centrifugal force in Indian politics.

[2] To the author in New Delhi on 6 June 1956.

The hope of reuniting India was expressed by Kripalani just after the Congress accepted the Mountbatten Plan. Calling on the party to make India a strong, happy, democratic and socialist state, he declared: 'Such an India can win back the seceding children to its lap . . . for the freedom we have achieved cannot be complete without the unity of India.'[1] Nehru himself did not speak directly in this vein, but a Working Committee resolution, in the drafting of which he was undoubtedly involved, contained the following passage: 'The Committee believe that the destiny of India will yet be realised and that, when passions have cooled, a new and stronger unity based on goodwill and co-operation will emerge.'[2] It is possible that this was merely a rationalization for their acceptance of Partition. But conversations with many Indian politicians strongly suggest that this was a sincere conviction, though utterly misguided and revealing a misreading of the forces at work within India and abroad.

One of the unstated considerations in Nehru's dilemma at the time was the belief that if the Congress rejected the Mountbatten Plan the British Government would impose an award which would have been even more disadvantageous. Having rejected Gandhi's alternative of mass civil disobedience, their bargaining position was weakened. Fear of the British response to Congress intransigence helped to condition their acceptance of Partition.

A more positive inducement was the imminent acquisition of power after a long struggle. The alternatives were to accept a divided but independent India or to follow Gandhi into the political wilderness. '. . . But the Congress leadership', declared Kripalani the Congress President, a few months after Partition, 'found the prospect of an immediate and peaceful transfer of power too tempting and chose the first alternative.'[3]

For those who have been in opposition most of their political

---

[1] *Congress Bulletin*, No. 4, 10 July 1947, p. 11.

[2] Ibid., No. 5, 7 November 1947, pp. 1–2.

[3] Ibid., No. 6, 31 December 1947, p. 3. These words were spoken in a moment of anger and in the course of a resignation speech prompted by the tendency of Nehru, Patel and others in the Government to ignore the party after the transfer of power. They are to be treated, therefore, with some reservation; but they undoubtedly contain an element of truth.

life, the prize of power is tempting. The Congress leaders had already tasted its fruits and were naturally reluctant to part with it at the moment of triumph. This applies to Nehru as well as to his colleagues, for he is not averse to the benefits it confers. But his attitude to the assumption of power in the provincial governments in 1937 and his record in the freedom movement strongly suggest that he sought power primarily to translate his ideals into reality. In any event, the habit of power had not yet been formed, for during the period of the Interim Government, his influence was severely limited by the Viceroy's presence and that of the League members.

The attitude of Nehru and his colleagues to Gandhi's alternative policy was embarrassment coupled with the belief that it was unworkable in the conditions of 1947. 'Today also I feel that he [Gandhi], with his supreme fearlessness is correct and my stand is defective. Why then am I not with him? It is because I feel that he has as yet found no way of tackling the problem on a mass basis.'[1] The words were Kripalani's but the thought was shared by Nehru, Patel and most, if not all, of the Congress High Command in the early summer of 1947. They had followed the Mahatma in civil disobedience four times since 1920. But in the greatest crisis of the nationalist movement they refused to take the plunge lest Gandhi should have miscalculated and the country be overrun by uncontrollable civil war. They chose the way of compromise in the hope that large-scale disorders could be avoided. By the end of the year of decision they had ample cause to question the wisdom of their choice, though none did so in public. It is ironic that in this situation Gandhi, the great compromiser, acted as the pure revolutionary, while Nehru, the acknowledged revolutionary in the Congress, accepted a compromise solution.

It is easy to speculate on what might have been. But in terms of their oft-stated goal of a united India would it not have been wiser for Nehru and his colleagues to reject the Mountbatten Plan which, in any case, was on the verge of collapse? By so doing they would probably have won independence—and unity. Having waited thirty years, should they not have waited a little longer, as Gandhi suggested? Perhaps they did not because

[1] *Congress Bulletin*, No. 4, 10 July 1947, p. 9.

they had been totally demoralized by the events of 1942 and beyond.

*   *   *   *

Despite this breach over Partition, the relations between Nehru and Gandhi remained basically unchanged during the last few months of the Mahatma's life. Although he had no official connection with the new Indian Government, Gandhi continued to fulfil the role of guide, elder statesman and father-figure. He was not, however, a super-Prime Minister, as many have assumed. Rather, the relationship was analogous to that of medieval monarch and saint. Gandhi did not interfere with the daily routine of government. Nor did he hamper Nehru's political leadership or determine policy, except on very special occasions, especially when he felt that a strong ethical issue was involved. It is true that in such instances Nehru and the Cabinet submitted to his wishes. But these were few in number.

In the twilight of Gandhi's life Nehru was drawn closer than ever to his *guru*. He had always been dependent on the Mahatma, but during this period of permanent crisis there emerged an almost compulsive attachment. To many, this seemed an abnormal relationship for a man of Nehru's stature and age—he was then fifty-eight. In reality it was the logical by-product of a pattern which had developed between the two men during the preceding thirty years—Gandhi the father, Nehru the son.

Gandhi's position was unique among the great public figures of this century. He was father as well as leader, a genuine patriarch, a philosopher-king, who provided an inexhaustible source of inspiration and strength for those about him, for Nehru perhaps more than any other Congress leader. All the outstanding personalities of the nationalist movement were moulded by Gandhi after 1920 and came under his spell. They sought his advice, in both personal and political matters, and usually abided by his will. Indeed, there was an ingrained habit of leaving all major decisions to him. Nehru expressed this in a letter to Gandhi early in 1947: 'I know that we must learn to rely upon ourselves and not run to you for help on every occasion. But we have got into this bad habit and we do often feel that if you had been easier of access our difficulties would

14. Chatting with the inmates of the hospital in Jawihar Nagar
in 1949

15. Nehru, Sanjay Gandhi (on horseback), Rajiv Gandhi (in model car) and Mrs. Indira Gandhi (his daughter), 1949

have been less.'[1] As the world seemed to crumble beneath him, it was but natural for Nehru to turn for solace and advice to the person who had exerted the most profound influence on his life.

Gandhi returned to Delhi early in September 1947. Refugees from West Pakistan were pouring into the capital bringing with them a desire for revenge. Riots broke out and the ghastly spectacle of the Punjab seemed about to be re-enacted. Congress unity was threatened by factional strife, especially involving Nehru and Patel, and by the strained relations between the party and the Government. The Cabinet itself was rent by dissension over a variety of crucial issues, notably the treatment of minorities and economic policy. Nehru persisted in his determination to build a secular state. Patel was less inclined to treat Indian Muslims with impartiality at a time when Hindus were being maltreated in Pakistan. Nehru remained firm and Gandhi supported him unreservedly.

The disagreement widened over economic policy, Gandhi in this case siding with Patel and the business community. In mid-November the A.I.C.C. yielded to the pressure for decontrol of prices on essential commodities. The Government later translated this into law, against the advice of noted economists like Professor D. R. Gadgil, with disastrous consequences.

Smouldering discontent within the Congress burst forth at the same time with the resignation of Kripalani from the presidency because his colleagues in the Government did not take him into their confidence. Though head of the premier political organization he was excluded from all major decisions. He was ignored even in invitations to conferences. Gandhi knew of his attitude and sympathized with him. The Socialist wing of the party proposed Narendra Dev or Jaya Prakash Narayan for the post. Gandhi was not averse to either and wanted to bring younger men like Narayan to the top. Nehru, too, was sympathetic but gave way before Patel's firm opposition. The crisis was temporarily overcome by the election of Prasad.

In the midst of these strains open warfare broke out in Kashmir. On 21 October 1947 Pathan tribesmen invaded the former

[1] On 30 January 1947. Quoted in Pyarelal, op. cit., p. 568.

princely State with the connivance and material support of high Pakistani officials. Three days later the Maharaja of Kashmir, whose procrastination contributed immeasurably to the dispute, finally sought Indian military aid and offered to accede to the Dominion of India. The offer was accepted and troops were flown into Srinagar to stem the tide of the advancing tribesmen. The city was saved and most of the Vale of Kashmir was cleared of the invaders. In time fighting gave way to military stalemate, political recriminations and, later, total deadlock, which continues to poison Indo-Pakistani relations.[1] Gandhi supported Nehru wholeheartedly on the dispatch of troops to the Vale, on the grounds that India had a moral obligation to come to the aid of victims of aggression.

Thus it was that in the autumn of 1947 Nehru's hopes for a free India appeared to be crumbling. Communal harmony and a secular state were in grave jeopardy, both from external pressures—the riots and mass migration—and from internal dissension within his own party and Cabinet. In economic affairs he was compelled to give way to Patel's demand for *laissez-faire*, with resulting inflation affecting the precarious livelihood of millions. As one crisis followed another he turned to his mentor for advice. During these anxious months Nehru paid a daily visit to Gandhi. Invariably he returned invigorated. As Nehru's niece later wrote: 'It was as if going to see Bapu [father, as Gandhi was affectionately called] were the solution to his dilemma and his weariness, as if the presence of Bapu would in itself answer questions and heal wounds.'[2] Throughout this period Gandhi himself frequently paid tribute to Nehru's herculean efforts to maintain unity and communal peace.

As the new year dawned, communal tension reared its head once more. Isolated incidents in Delhi revived Muslim fears, and another round of blood-letting seemed possible. Gandhi responded with vigour. On 12 January 1948 he informed an unsuspecting world that he proposed to fast until the atmosphere of communal hate were removed from the capital and Muslims could move about freely in the streets. Nehru started a sympathetic fast but abandoned it in deference to the Mahatma's request. In the midst of Gandhi's fast he told a mass meeting in

[1] See the author's *The Struggle for Kashmir* (1953).
[2] Sahgal, op. cit., p. 213.

Delhi, 'the loss of Mahatma Gandhi's life would mean the loss of India's soul'. He appealed to the people to restore communal harmony and save the master's life.[1]

As always in the past Gandhi's threat of self-sacrifice had the desired effect. All communities promised to abandon violence, and peace returned to the city. Before the fast began, however, a new crisis arose: the Indian Government decided to postpone the payment to Pakistan of 550 million rupees, its unpaid share of the cash balances under the Partition Agreements. Gandhi was stunned by what he considered to be an indefensible and immoral act. He was determined to have a showdown, especially with Patel who had taken the lead in persuading the Cabinet to adopt this policy. Indeed, Gandhi's fast was intended not only to restore communal peace in Delhi but also to strengthen Nehru's hand within the Government and the party. The gulf between the two leaders was widening.

Patel argued that a transfer of this large sum at the time would aid Pakistan in its war against India, then in full swing in Kashmir. The intent was to withhold payment only until the end of the military campaign, not indefinitely. Nehru apparently did not feel strongly on the issue and followed the Sardar's lead. Gandhi heard about the decision in the middle of his fast over communal tension and let it be known that he would fast until death. Thus a four-man Cabinet delegation was sent to explain the rationale directly to the Mahatma, whose condition was now causing grave concern. First Nehru, then Patel, tried to justify the decision. Gandhi lay flat on his back, weak and silent. There was no response. Then Patel began again. After a few minutes Gandhi raised himself slowly, with tears streaming down his cheeks. Turning to Patel, he said in a barely audible whisper: 'You are not the Sardar I once knew', and then fell back. The visit ended abruptly. All were stunned and filed out. 'It was', said one of the participants, 'one of the most moving scenes I have ever witnessed.' That night an emergency Cabinet meeting was held and on the following morning it was announced that the funds would be transferred immediately.[2]

---

[1] Tendulkar, op. cit., vol. 8, p. 311.
[2] Related to the author in India in March 1956 by an eyewitness who wishes to remain anonymous.

Patel had been rebuffed and Nehru's position strengthened, but the friction was not over. It required something even more dramatic. This episode also showed Gandhi's great influence when he was aroused. It is, too, a classic example of his ethical approach to politics. Pakistan had a moral right to the funds, for a solemn agreement had been reached; thus the cash balances had to be transferred forthwith. Similarly, Kashmir had a moral claim to Indian aid because of aggression; therefore, troops should be sent. The fact that in political terms they were not in harmony was of no consequence. Moral considerations dictated both decisions. For Gandhi means were far more important than ends.

*　　　*　　　*　　　*

The climax to the year of decision was approaching. Gandhi's habit was to convey his thoughts to the nation through the medium of his daily prayer meeting, where hundreds gathered to have a *darshan* of (to enter into communion with) the master. In the winter of 1947 these were held on the lawns of the palatial residence of G. D. Birla, a prominent Indian industrialist, where Gandhi held court for colleagues, disciples and people of all communities. On 20 January 1948, two days after he broke his fast, the serenity of his prayer meeting was ominously disturbed by the explosion of a crude bomb in the vicinity. Nehru and Patel pleaded with him to accept police protection, but in vain. If he had to die by an assassin's hand, he said, he must do so without anger or fear. He was in the hands of God. Ten days later the Mahatma was dead.

In the interim the friction between Nehru and Patel was approaching an open break. Patel had aggravated the situation by an outspoken speech in Bombay, calling on all Indian Muslims to proclaim their loyalty to India as a precondition to equality of treatment and trust. On the afternoon of 30 January Patel was closeted with Gandhi who, from most accounts, asked the Sardar for a solemn pledge that he would never forsake Nehru nor cause an open split. It was a heart-to-heart talk and many have speculated that they quarrelled. One close friend of Nehru paraphrased the essence of the conversation in these words: 'Vallabhbhai,' said Gandhi, 'you have been with me for thirty years but you have learned nothing.' To this Patel is

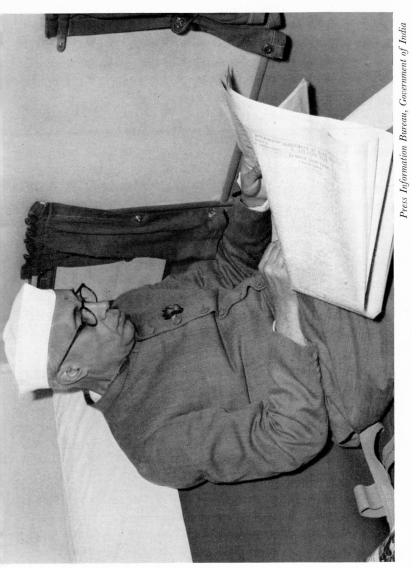

16. On a plane journey in 1949

17. With Patel in April, 1950

alleged to have replied: 'You know nothing about these things [the issues in dispute within the Government] or about what is going on.'[1] It is doubtful that the exact dialogue will ever be revealed, but bluntness was characteristic of both men. Partly because of the growing cleavage between his two leading disciples and partly because of his unhappiness with the chain of events during the last six months of his life, it was generally believed in India that disillusionment entered Gandhi's heart before a bullet entered his body. Nehru and Azad were to see Gandhi in the evening but this was not to be.

Like Nehru, Gandhi was punctual in his appointments. The prayer meeting always began at 5 p.m. On that day he was late. As he strolled towards the meeting, a young man stepped forward from the crowd and greeted Gandhi in the traditional *namaste* salutation, joining his hands palm to palm and bowing slightly. Gandhi reciprocated. At that point the youth pulled out a revolver and fired three shots. Two entered the Mahatma's chest, the third his abdomen. Gandhi fell, with the words *Hé Ram* (Oh God) on his lips. Within a few minutes he was dead.

The news travelled through the city, the country and the world like wildfire. Nehru rushed from his home, overwhelmed with grief. It was for him a personal tragedy as well as a national catastrophe. He could not believe that Gandhi could die so suddenly, wordlessly, when his advice was needed more than ever. Nehru's face was like a white mask and his eyes revealed anguish as he approached the body of his beloved *Bapu*. He knelt beside it for a moment and wept uncontrollably, forgetting himself in his grief. All around him people milled about, too stunned to do anything but to moan and wail at the calamity that had befallen them. 'What is all the snivelling about?' asked Sarojini Naidu. 'Would you rather he had died of decrepit old age or indigestion? This was the only death great enough for him.'[2]

Mountbatten, too, rushed to the scene. As he made his way through the vast throng which had gathered from all over Delhi, someone asked him who did it, a Hindu or a Muslim?

---

[1] To the author in India in March 1956 by a person who wishes to remain anonymous.

[2] Quoted in Sahgal, op. cit., p. 220.

O

Although he himself did not know the communal identity of the assassin, the Governor-General had the presence of mind to reply without hesitation, 'a Hindu'. It was fortunate that he was correct. Had a Muslim been responsible for Gandhi's death a terrible bloodbath might have ensued.

Mountbatten performed another important function. With his flair for the dramatic, he approached Nehru and Patel and related Gandhi's expressed wish for a complete reconciliation. The two men looked at Gandhi's body and then embraced as a gesture of fulfilment of the Mahatma's last request.

After the initial shock Nehru went out to inform the crowd. 'Mahatmaji is gone', he said, in a voice choked with emotion. Later in the evening he addressed the nation. There was no time to prepare his speech but there was no need. Under the stress of this personal loss he rose to the occasion with an eloquent tribute to Gandhi, one of the most moving speeches he has ever made.

Friends and comrades, the light has gone out of our lives and there is darkness everywhere. I do not know what to tell you and how to say it. Our beloved leader, Bapu as we called him, the Father of the Nation, is no more. Perhaps I am wrong to say that. Nevertheless, we will not see him again as we have seen him for these many years. We will not run to him for advice and seek solace from him, and that is a terrible blow, not to me only, but to millions and millions in this country. And it is a little difficult to soften the blow by any other advice I or anyone else can give you.

The light has gone out, I said, and yet I was wrong. For the light that shone in this country was no ordinary light. The light that has illumined this country for these many many years will illumine this country for many more years, and a thousand years later, that light will still be seen in this country and the world will see it and it will give solace to innumerable hearts. For that light represented something more than the immediate present, it represented the living, the eternal truths, reminding us of the right path, drawing us from error, taking this ancient country to freedom.

All this has happened when there was so much more for him to do. We could never think that he was unnecessary or that he had done his task. But now, particularly, when we are faced with so many difficulties, his not being with us is a blow most terrible to bear.

A madman has put an end to his life, for I can only call him mad who did it, and yet there has been enough of poison spread in this country during the past years and months, and this poison has had an effect on people's minds. We must face this poison, we must root out this poison, and we must face all the perils that encompass us, and face them not madly or badly, but rather in the way that our beloved teacher taught us to face them.

The first thing to remember now is that none of us dare misbehave because he is angry. We have to behave like strong and determined people, determined to face all the perils that surround us, determined to carry out the mandate that our great teacher and our great leader has given us, remembering always that if, as I believe, his spirit looks upon us and sees us, nothing would displease his soul so much as to see that we have indulged in any small behaviour or any violence.

So we must not do that. . . . We must hold together and all our petty troubles and difficulties and conflicts must be ended in the face of this great disaster. . . . In his death he has reminded us of the big things of life, that living truth, and if we remember that, then it will be well with India. . . .'[1]

The following day all India mourned the passing of its greatest son since the Buddha. From Birla House to the Jumna River, a distance of six miles, the funeral cortège passed while thousands lined the streets, dumbfounded and sad as they said farewell to the Mahatma. Ironically, he was borne on a gun carrier, not in the traditional Hindu style—on the shoulders of his family and friends. Some were distressed that a prince of peace was being laid to rest with military honours. Over half a million were at the river-bank awaiting the cremation ceremony. In accordance with tradition Nehru paid his last homage by kissing the feet of his *guru*. Gandhi was no more.

Another tribute was paid to Gandhi in the Constituent Assembly by his forlorn successor. '. . . I have a sense of utter shame both as an individual and as the head of the Government of India that we should have failed to protect the greatest treasure that we possessed', began the eulogy.

How shall we praise him and how shall we measure him, because he was not of the common clay that all of us are made of? . . . How can we praise him, how can we who have been children of his . . . for we have all been in some greater or smaller measure the children of his spirit, unworthy as we were? A glory has departed and the sun that warmed and brightened our lives has set and we shiver in the

[1] The text is in *Independence and After*, pp. 17–18.

cold and dark. . . . That man with the divine fire changed us also. . . . He lives in the hearts of millions and he will live for immemorial ages. . . . He was perhaps the greatest symbol of the India of the past, and may I say, of the India of the future, that we could have had. . . . We mourn him; we shall always mourn him, because we are human and cannot forget our beloved Master. But . . . he would chide us if we merely mourn. . . . The only way is . . . to conduct ourselves in a befitting manner and to dedicate ourselves to the great task which he undertook and which he accomplished to such a large extent. . . . Let us be worthy of him.'[1]

Others honoured the passing of a giant. Attlee and Smuts paid moving tributes. The U.N. General Assembly interrupted its session as a mark of respect. Jinnah regretted the passing of a great Hindu. Within India, too, many offered glowing praise. But Nehru's speeches were the best expression of the nation's sorrow. More than a man had passed. An era had come to an end. And Nehru was alone.

[1] *Independence and After*, pp. 20–23.

CHAPTER XV

The Duumvirate

Two men ruled India during the critical transition period from 1947 to 1950—Jawaharlal Nehru and Vallabhbhai Patel, or 'Panditji' and the Sardar as they were known to friends and foes alike. It was a strange alliance in many ways, a striking combination of opposites. Indeed, no two leaders of any Asian nationalist movement in the twentieth century differed more than the duumvirs of the new India—in background, education, temperament, ideology, sources of power, and qualities and defects of leadership.

Nehru is a triple aristocrat, a Brahmin by birth, a gentleman by upbringing and education, and the son of a Westernized lawyer of all-India renown. At an early age he came under the influence of European culture, habits and manners, an influence which is evident throughout his adult life. Patel's origins, by comparison, were plebeian and orthodox, a peasant family from Gujarat which was deeply attached to Hinduism. Like Gandhi he spent his formative years in a traditionalist Indian milieu, though his family was sufficiently modern and comfortable to allow the Sardar and his distinguished brother, Vithalbhai, to complete their studies for the Bar.[1]

Fortune was also kind to Nehru in his early political career. He was twenty-nine when Gandhi appeared on the scene and his rise to prominence in the nationalist movement was assisted by both Gandhi and his father. By contrast, Patel was a relatively unknown lawyer in his early forties when he came under the Mahatma's spell. Nor did he have the benefit of initial support from an elder statesman of the party. These differences

---

[1] Vithalbhai Patel was a prominent figure in the Swaraj Party, the constitutionalist wing of the Congress led by C. R. Das and Motilal Nehru in the 'twenties. From 1925 to 1930 he held the position of President (Speaker) of the central Legislative Assembly 'and did more than any of his successors before 1946 to assert and consolidate the independence of the Chair'. Morris-Jones, op. cit., p. 265. Although he was never intimately associated with the activist wing of the Congress, his is an honoured name in the Indian nationalist movement.

alone were to leave a marked imprint on the future outlook and relationship of the duumvirs. But there were others which set them apart.

Nehru is a man of great charm, generous to a fault, sensitive and aesthetically inclined, impulsive and emotional. Patel was generally dour and ruthless, unimaginative and practical, blunt in speech and action, cool and calculating, never permitting his heart to rule his head. Nehru disliked political intrigue, lobbying and manipulations; he was a lonely and solitary leader, above group loyalties. Patel was a master of machine politics who revelled in political manœuvres. Nehru was the voice of the Congress, Patel its organizer (and Gandhi its inspiration). It is this division of function, the contrasting temperaments, and the sharply conflicting ideologies which provide the keys to the respective sources of power of 'Panditji' and the Sardar.

To the world at large Nehru was, with Gandhi, the symbol of India's struggle for freedom. Patel never attained this stature, not even within India. Nor did he ever capture the imagination of the peasantry as a revolutionary leader, whereas both Gandhi and Nehru did to a remarkable degree, though for different reasons, as noted earlier. Nehru is a master of words and used this technique brilliantly to carry the message of independence and socialism to the far corners of the country, winning the support of millions for the Congress, both at the polls and in civil disobedience campaigns. Patel was utterly lacking in this talent and, in any event, had undisguised contempt for speech-making. He rarely toured the countryside. And except in his native Gujarat he never established a *rapport* with the masses, partly because of his personality, partly because of his economic outlook, and partly because of his disdain for 'the crowd'. The only elements in the countryside who looked to the Sardar for leadership were the landlords and the orthodox Hindus, the one fearing Nehru's threat of far-reaching agrarian reform and the other opposed to Nehru's secularism and his sympathy for the Muslims.

In the cities, too, they commanded the loyalty of different groups—Nehru the radicals and Patel the conservatives. More specifically, Nehru appealed to the working class, the bulk of the Westernized intelligentsia, the young men and the minorities. Patel drew his support from the business community, orthodox Hindus, senior civil servants and most of the party functionaries. As in the rural areas this division was a natural consequence of their conflicting ideologies. Put in schematic terms, Nehru was (and still is) the outstanding idealist of the Congress and its leading exponent of socialism, a broad international outlook, a secular state and a modern approach to social, political, economic, cultural and religious affairs. Patel was the realist *par excellence*, a staunch defender of capitalism, a man whose vision was confined to national interests narrowly conceived, an advocate of Hindu primacy and traditionalism. Both subscribed to the principles of parliamentary government. But while Nehru is devoted to the democratic process, despite his frequent outbursts of anger and imperiousness, Patel revealed a marked streak of authoritarianism.

The ideological cleavage between 'Panditji' and the Sardar was evident long before the coming of Independence, especially on the issue of socialism. By the early 'thirties Nehru had emerged as the leader of the Left and the protector of the Congress Socialists. Patel was hostile from the outset and used his influence to thwart all efforts to commit the Congress to a socialist programme. It was Patel and Prasad who led the 'revolt' against Nehru over the propriety of spreading the socialist gospel, culminating in the collective resignation of the Right wing from the Working Committee in June 1936.[1] Patel also opposed Nehru's proposal of affiliation of the trade unions and peasant leagues. And on the eve of the Faizpur session at the end of 1936, when the Sardar withdrew his candidacy in favour of Nehru, he made it abundantly clear that he did not share many of 'Panditji's' ideas.[2] As long as the primary goal was independence this disagreement was submerged in the interests of unity. It came to the fore again during the period of the duumvirate.

As a party boss with limited vision, Patel was utterly indifferent to world affairs except in so far as he could relate them to the immediate national interests of India. His attitude to other Asian nationalist movements has already been noted in another context. In time he became impatient with Nehru's stress on international politics. Indeed, he seemed to consider it a waste of time and energy. Thus, on the occasion of Nehru's visit to

[1] See pp. 223–6 above.   [2] See p. 227 above.

the United States in the autumn of 1949, the Sardar remarked disdainfully to an English acquaintance, 'We have to get on with the job here. Of what use is the fanfare of a trip through America with speeches and all?'[1]

On the communal problem, too, the duumvirs were temperamentally and intellectually at opposite poles. Nehru is an agnostic and a humanist, a product of a composite Hindu, Muslim and Western liberal environment, and a firm believer in equal rights for all religious communities in India. Patel was a staunch Hindu by upbringing and conviction. He never really trusted the Muslims and shared the extremist Hindu Mahasabha view on the 'natural' right of the Hindus to rule India. For him there was only one true nationalist Muslim—Jawaharlal! The clash on this issue came into the open during the riots of 1947, when Patel openly questioned the loyalty of the Muslims who had remained in India, and Nehru, along with Gandhi, came to their defence. Later this issue almost broke the duumvirate asunder. No wonder, then, that the Muslims turned to Nehru for support during the dark days after Partition and still look upon him as their protector.

Nor did Patel have much respect for the intelligentsia, one of the pillars of Nehru's strength in the party and the country at large. As early as 1931, in his presidential address to the Karachi session of the Congress, the Sardar said with characteristic bluntness: 'The foregoing shows you how uninterested I am in many things that interest the intelligentsia.'[2]

'Jawahar is a thinker, Sardar a doer.' In these words Gandhi summed up the contrast between his two principal lieutenants.[3] There is a large element of truth in this remark. For one thing it portrays with admirable clarity the basic division of function during the final stage of the struggle for independence, Nehru the ideologue, Patel the organizer. For another it points to their fundamental difference of approach to decision-making. Nehru has always been beset by doubt about the wisdom of any decision. Hence his marked tendency to vacillate. Patel was a man of iron will, clear about his objectives and resolute in his actions.

---

[1] Related to the author in 1955 by Horace Alexander, a prominent member of the Society of Friends and a friend of Gandhi and Nehru.

[2] *Report of the 45th Indian National Congress at Karachi, 1931*, p. 25.

[3] To G. D. Birla a few days before Gandhi's death. *Nehru Abhinandan Granth: A Birthday Book*, pp. 177–8.

Herein lay Nehru's greatest political weakness and Patel's greatest strength.

Yet, like all neat formulas for describing the highly complicated, Gandhi's comment is in part misleading. Compared with Patel and, indeed, most political leaders, Nehru must certainly be classified as a 'thinker'. But Jawaharlal has always been a man of action for whom thought is primarily the key to *right action*. While this quality leads to procrastination, it gives him a breadth of outlook which Patel never possessed.

Nor does Gandhi's observation do justice to Nehru's talent as a politician in the technical meaning of that term. As long as the Mahatma and the Sardar were on the scene, there was no need, or inducement, for Nehru to devote much of his attention to organizational matters. In any event Patel was better suited to this task by temperament and skill. The division of function was natural and effective. On a higher level of party organization, however, Nehru had made signal contributions to the Congress in his role as mediator. Patel could command the Right wing only. But Nehru was the indispensable link between Left and Right, Gandhians and modernists. It was he who kept the bulk of the radical youth in the Congress from 1929 onwards. It was he who prevented a rupture between the Congress Socialists and the conservatives. It was he, more than anyone else, who rallied the trade unions and peasant leagues to the support of the Congress. It was he who played the leading role in rebuilding the mass membership of the party from 1936 onwards. And with the passing of Patel at the end of 1950, Nehru was to demonstrate considerable skill as a party tactician in winning control of the party machine. The Sardar himself would have admired his performance.[1]

The contrast between the duumvirs extended to age and appearance. Patel was fifteen years older, but Nehru had primacy of place in the affections of Gandhi and of the nation as a whole.[2]

---

[1] See pp. 432–6 below.

[2] Patel himself was conscious of the Mahatma's special affection for Nehru as revealed in the following private letter to Nehru just before the second world war: 'We were all sorry to find that you were so very angry . . . and we felt that you were less than fair to Bapu [Gandhi]. . . . He feels hurt when your feelings are wounded. I don't think that he loves anybody more than he loves you and when he finds that any action of his has made you unhappy, he broods over it and feels miserable. Since that evening he has been thinking of retiring altogether . . .' Unpublished Nehru Letters, 3 July 1939.

On three occasions—1929, 1937 and 1946—Patel had been 'persuaded' to withdraw his candidacy for Congress President in favour of Nehru, the last time paving the way for Nehru's appointment as *de facto* Prime Minister in the Interim Government.[1] Moreover, Nehru had been designated by Gandhi as his political successor, despite the Sardar's seniority.

Gifted as he was in the art of politics, Patel vastly underestimated the power of the spoken word and the importance of personal contact with the masses. His failure to win nationwide popularity and Nehru's striking success in this regard undoubtedly influenced Gandhi's choice of the younger man. Gandhi also appeared to believe that the loyalty of the Right was assured while Nehru alone could keep the uneasy Left in the coalition. Whatever the reasons, the choice of Nehru and his assumption of the Prime Ministership could not have been accepted by Patel with equanimity, especially because deference to age normally affects every aspect of Indian life, including politics. Yet there was little he could do, even if he were so disposed, for Gandhi decreed it thus. And even after the Mahatma's death, Nehru's status as senior member of the duumvirate was beyond effective challenge; Nehru was Prime Minister, Patel Deputy Prime Minister. The Sardar controlled many levers of power, but it was to Nehru that India's millions looked for guidance and hope in the aftermath of Partition.

The coming of Independence found Nehru in the prime of life. He was fifty-seven then, but his youthful, almost boyish appearance belied his age, as did his seemingly boundless energy. He was strikingly handsome. And in his face were mirrored the changing moods of a complex personality: joy and sadness, anger, petulance, impatience, understanding, sympathy, lightheartedness, thoughtfulness, shock, perplexity and others. Underlying them all was an abiding sense of loneliness.

Patel was seventy-two when the duumvirate came into being. He was short and robust, slow of movement, yet dignified in his ample *dhoti*. Indeed, in appearance and manner he resembled an elder statesmen of ancient Rome. Though he was not devoid of humour, the Sardar's large, oval face generally wore a grave expression. He was impassive, cold, stern, and seemingly aloof and unresponsive. It was difficult for all but a few confidants

[1] See pp. 313–15 above.

to penetrate the mask of calmness which he retained to the end of his life. He rarely revealed his emotions, unlike the mercurial Jawaharlal.

Patel's mental prowess, his strength of character and his political acumen were no less formidable than in his earlier years. But he never possessed Nehru's capacity for work or his physical health. And now the ills of old age were upon him. As a realist the Sardar knew that the future lay with his younger, more dynamic colleague. But in his last years he was to serve his country with the utmost distinction. In fact, Patel's contributions during the 'time of trouble' following Independence were to mark him as one of modern India's men of destiny. The duumvirs had helped Gandhi to make a revolution. Now they carried the heavy burden of rescuing India from the dangers of internal chaos.

The duumvirate was the decisive fact of Indian politics from the Partition until the end of 1950. Even during the last months of 1947, while Gandhi still lived, the reins of power were held by 'Panditji' and the Sardar, except in a few special cases where the Mahatma felt his moral principles were at stake.[1] During the next three years every decision of consequence, as well as many trivial ones, were made by Nehru and/or Patel. On this point there is wide agreement. Cabinet Ministers, prominent officials and senior Congressmen described the arrangement as a super-Cabinet in which Nehru and Patel discussed all matters first and then presented a joint 'recommendation' to the Cabinet as a whole.[2] Though the procedures of Cabinet government were followed, and ministers were at liberty to discuss, even oppose, proposals of the Prime Minister and Deputy Prime Minister, their special position dominated the proceedings. It was the same in Parliament, the Congress and the country at large. The course of events during this period only serves to underline their pre-eminent role.

What is far from obvious, however, is the nature of the duumvirate. Were Nehru and Patel co-equals? Was the division of power and function clearly defined and mutually acceptable? Could either have ousted the other? Did either attempt to do

---

[1] For example, the transfer of cash balances to Pakistan at the beginning of 1948. See pp. 383–4 above.

[2] To the author in India in 1956 by persons who wish to remain anonymous.

so? Did the duumvirs function as a team? What were the consequences of shared power? Most of these questions are difficult to answer with certainty, particularly because informed Indian opinion remains sharply divided on the character of the duumvirate. Patel died years ago, but there remain many persons in the Congress, the Civil Service, the professions and the business community who are devoted to his memory. The task of the impartial chronicler is complicated by the fact that few Indians are capable of viewing Nehru and Patel objectively. Those who admire 'Panditji' generally tend to denigrate the Sardar, and vice versa. And not without reason. Those who were charmed by Nehru were repelled by the brusque manner of Patel. Those who respected the Sardar's decisiveness were critical of Nehru's vacillation. Socialists feared Patel, as many capitalists did Nehru. As a result the duumvirate remains shrouded in bias.

The 'Patelist' view, based upon interviews with some of the Sardar's admirers, may be paraphrased as follows: Patel was unquestionably the senior partner in terms of sheer power, for he controlled the States, the police, propaganda and, most important, the party machine. On any issue requiring party sanction Nehru was compelled to seek Patel's approval. Nehru was allowed to strut the international stage, his control being limited to foreign policy and Kashmir. The two men did not get on well together and the rivalry was genuine. Nehru often felt that Patel was trying to usurp his power; Patel was jealous of Nehru's prestige and popularity. Patel could have ousted Nehru from the Prime Ministership; the party would have backed him. But a severe heart attack in March 1948 ended the possibility of change. Before that he did not attempt to replace Nehru because of the grave threats to Indian unity and stability. It was, then, an uneasy alliance, made necessary by the course of events.

'Nehruites' contend that this view is essentially a figment of imagination: no doubt it was a duumvirate in a sense, but Nehru was the dominant figure from beginning to end. He merely delegated authority to Patel in certain fields. And the Sardar realized the limits of his power. While he was supreme in party and organizational matters, he had to concede to Nehru on such issues as Cabinet appointments, foreign policy, the constitution, a secular state, and Indo-Pakistani relations.

Friction was common and the rivalry deep, but at no time was Nehru's position in jeopardy. Patel was a brilliant tactician but he lacked Nehru's touch with the people. Nehru kept him in the Cabinet despite their disagreements because he was aware of the Sardar's administrative talent, so desperately needed at the time. Moreover, he was unwilling to face the consequences of an open break during a period of crisis. But Nehru would have emerged triumphant had a struggle for power ensued.

Both interpretations seem to this writer to contain elements of fact and fiction. And neither does justice to a subtle, complex relationship at the pyramid of Indian political power. At first glance the division of function appears to have been heavily weighted in favour of Patel. The Sardar held the portfolios of States, Home Affairs and Information and Broadcasting which, along with the party machine, gave him control of the principal levers of power in domestic affairs. Nehru held only the portfolio of External Affairs and Commonwealth Relations. This explains the widely accepted view that Nehru held sway in the international sphere and Patel in the internal.

As a point of departure for an understanding of the duumvirate, this view is not entirely without merit. However, it is a rigid, static and highly simplified formula, whereas the relationship was flexible, dynamic and extremely complicated. For one thing, there were many aspects of domestic politics over which neither Nehru nor Patel had direct supervision, notably economic policy and the constitution. For another, the Sardar never acted on a major policy decision without first securing the agreement or at least acquiescence of Nehru. Herein lies one of the keys to the nature of the duumvirate. The two men were administratively 'sovereign' in different spheres but policy matters were a joint prerogative, except in foreign affairs where Nehru's word was rarely, if ever, challenged. To assert that Nehru was 'allowed' free rein in foreign affairs, as the partisans of Patel do, is thus merely wishful thinking. Patel himself knew better. Similarly, to claim that the Sardar acted as the agent of the all-powerful Nehru is a distortion of reality.

Such conjecture—it is nothing more than that—succeeds only in obscuring a basic truth about the duumvirate. Neither Nehru nor Patel derived his power from the other. Both owed

their position in 1947 and beyond to the Mahatma and, indirectly, to the social forces they represented. It was Gandhi
who created the duumvirate. And in large measure it was he
who kept this unusual combination together. In life he was the
accepted arbiter of all the disputes which arose between
'Panditji' and the Sardar. And in death he forged a bond of
unity which made an open split between them most unlikely.

It is true that the cleavage reached dangerous proportions towards the end of 1947. Patel had impugned the loyalty of all
members of the Muslim League who remained in India, causing
near-panic among the 40,000,000 Muslims who did not opt
for Pakistan. Nehru was furious and made known his intention
of dismissing the Sardar from the Cabinet, a fact often cited by
'Nehruites' to support their 'delegated power' thesis. Yet
Jawaharlal did not carry out his threat. The split was averted,
and with it grave repercussions on the precarious internal
stability of India. The Mahatma had exercised his powers of
mediation once more.

No other episode illuminates with such clarity the essential
character of the duumvirate in the early stage, especially
Gandhi's crucial role. Delhi was aghast at the idea of a break
between Nehru and Patel. When the news first reached the
Mahatma he seemed unperturbed. In fact he stated publicly
that the Prime Minister had a right to select his own colleagues
and could ask Patel to 'retire' if the Sardar's attitude to Muslims violated Cabinet policy.[1] Yet the news did perturb Gandhi,
for unlike the partisans of the duumvirs he knew that both were
essential if internal chaos were to be prevented. Others in high
places were also aware of the implications of a complete break.
V. P. Menon, an admirer of the Sardar and a confidant of the
Viceroy, hurried to Mountbatten and claimed that Nehru was
overreaching himself. The Viceroy himself was disconcerted,
for he viewed the duumvirate as the pillar of Indian stability.
To a prominent Congressman he had described the position as
follows: 'Joint leadership and a happy combination, Nehru
abroad and Patel at home. Thus we are strong abroad and at
home as well.'[2] Acting on this belief he sought Gandhi's inter-

---

[1] Tendulkar, op. cit., vol. 8, p. 306.
[2] N. V. Gadgil, a leading Congressman from Maharashtra (southern part of
Bombay State). Related to the author by Gadgil in 1956.

vention. The Mahatma had satisfied the pride of his favourite son by acknowledging Nehru's right as Prime Minister to dismiss any member of the Cabinet. Having done so, he was able to persuade Jawaharlal to alter his decision on the grounds that the duumvirs complemented each other and that the interests of India at the time demanded unity at the highest level of party and government. This is not to suggest that Nehru could not have fired Patel though the price might have been very heavy; rather, that the duumvirate was kept in being by Gandhi's unique role; he was *Bapu*, father, to both Nehru and Patel.

The immediate crisis of leadership was overcome, but friction between the duumvirs continued. Patel favoured a tough policy towards Pakistan, as evident in the cash-balances incident in January 1948, while Nehru was inclined to moderation. Moreover, Nehru approved the action of Azad in appointing a non-I.C.S. man as Secretary of the Ministry of Education, without reference to a special sub-committee appointed by Patel to arrange all senior appointments to the civil service.[1] There was also disagreement over the status of the Muslim Aligarh University which was located in Indian territory. The growing evidence of tension between Nehru and Patel weighed heavily on the Mahatma and led to his intervention on 30 January 1948, the day he was assassinated. As if anticipating the end, he called Patel to his residence at Birla House and extracted from him a pledge that he would never break with Nehru. A few hours later the shock of Gandhi's death cut through the clouds of suspicion that had gathered in recent months, and the two men became reconciled as a mark of respect to the revered master.

The initial effect of Gandhi's death on the factions that had grown up around the duumvirs was to heighten speculation about an imminent split. So widespread did it become that only a fortnight after the Mahatma's assassination Nehru found it necessary to deny the rumours categorically, in a radio address to the nation: 'Of course, there have been for many years past differences between us, temperamental and other, in regard to many problems. But India at least should know that these differences have been overshadowed by fundamental agreements about the most important aspects of our public life and

[1] Campbell-Johnson, op. cit., p. 254.

that we have co-operated together for a quarter of a century or more in great undertakings. . . . Is it likely that at this crisis in our national destiny either of us should be petty-minded and think of anything but the national good? May I pay my tribute of respect and admiration to Sardar Patel . . .'[1] The following month, on 5 March 1948, Patel suffered a severe heart attack and almost died.

Rivalry between the duumvirs was undoubtedly genuine, but it was highly exaggerated by cliques of civil servants and politicians devoted to one or the other leader. These men sought personal and political advantage by pressing the claims of their respective heroes and thereby caused further suspicion between the leaders themselves. It was a tribute to their statesmanship and patriotism that 'Panditji' and the Sardar were able to overcome these obstacles to fruitful co-operation.

The duumvirate may best be described as a natural and mutually acceptable division of labour with each recognizing the indispensability of the other and Patel possessing substantial power to compensate for Nehru's greater prestige and popularity. Patel was probably crestfallen at not having attained the Prime Ministership but he had no reason to feel disappointed with the distribution of influence, and there is no real evidence that he did. Each knew the limits of his power. In the broadest sense they were equals, with one striking difference. Patel controlled a greater aggregate of power in the short-run, through the party and the key ministries of government, but Nehru commanded the country at large. Theoretically Patel could have ousted Nehru and established a dictatorship but he could not have rallied the Indian people behind such a régime. Moreover, in the existing conditions of 1947–50 Nehru was indispensable to national unity and to the administrative revolution carried out largely by the Sardar—the integration of the princely States. Nehru could have carried the country alone through this period of turmoil, though the attainment of stability would have been delayed. In this sense his leadership was of a higher order.

The Sardar knew that his strength was ebbing and that Jawaharlal was the 'chosen son'. It was these factors, combined with his pledge to Gandhi, his relatively free hand in domestic

[1] *Independence and After*, pp. 31–32.

affairs and a genuine sense of patriotism which probably made the duumvirate acceptable to Patel in its Gandhi-inspired form. What of Nehru? Why was he prepared to share power? There was, of course, less reason to be dissatisfied with the existing state of affairs, for he held the position of Prime Minister. As noted earlier, the factor of national crisis influenced his attitude. But there were other considerations, as he related to an American correspondent.[1] Gandhi had brought them together often, Nehru remarked. 'And now, it's odd, but the memory of Gandhi keeps us together.' Moreover, there was mutual confidence in each other's integrity and a firm belief, shared with Patel, that neither desired power *per se*. Perhaps most important was Nehru's deep loyalty to political comrades: 'When you have been working with a man twenty-eight years, you know all about him and forgive a lot. It's hard to leave people you have struggled with and suffered with that long.' Finally, the habit of compromise between the duumvirs was a legacy of their lengthy association with the Mahatma, a habit which was even stronger than ideologies as such. On the whole the two men adjusted reasonably well to the many stresses, personal and political, which beset the relationship, though towards the end sharp conflict came to the fore, primarily over policy towards Pakistan and social change.

*   *   *   *

The Partition had released torrential forces of disorder which threatened to submerge the new Dominion at its birth: communal riots and mass migration; war in Kashmir; the danger of territorial fragmentation on a scale which few states in modern times have encountered; and economic dislocation. The problem of law and order taxed the Government's limited resources at a time of administrative confusion. A new constitution had to be framed, to embody the Congress pledges of a generation. Relations with the family of nations had to be established on a different footing. The 'Appointed Day', as Nehru had termed the coming of Independence, was a mixed blessing. That chaos was avoided was due primarily to the leadership of Nehru and Patel who carried the full burden of decision affecting the fate of millions and the country at large.

[1] Edgar Snow. *Nehru Abhinandan Granth: A Birthday Book*, p. 91.

The grim story of communal war and mass migration has already been related in some detail. By the end of 1947 the killings had virtually ceased, the flood had subsided and the task of rehabilitating some five million refugees was under way. The bloodshed stopped completely with Gandhi's assassination in January 1948. In the midst of this calamity came the Kashmir War,[1] and the first of many economic crises to plague the new régime.[2]

The gravest danger to Indian unity during the period of the duumvirate was Balkanization, the dispersion of power among hundreds of petty principalities scattered over the sub-continent. The British *Raj* had forged genuine unity in many respects. Constitutionally, however, India under British rule was rigidly divided into two compartments. Approximately two-thirds of the area and three-fourths of the population fell into the category of 'British India', i.e., the eleven Governors' provinces which had achieved a marked degree of responsible government by 1937. Legal sovereignty over the provinces vested in the British Crown and was exercised by Parliament through the Secretary of State for India, the Viceroy and the Governors. The balance, one-third of the area and one-fourth of the population, fell into the category of 'Indian India', about 600 princely States, the vast majority of which were ruled autocratically. They ranged in size and population from Hyderabad, which was about as large as France and had some 16,000,000 people, to tiny estates of a few acres with less than a thousand people. All had one thing in common which differentiated them from 'British India', a constitutional link with England embodied in the doctrine of Paramountcy. In essence the British Government was responsible for their defence, foreign relations and communications, while they remained autonomous in internal affairs. In practice their freedom of action was severely circumscribed by the presence of Residents who were (indirectly) appointed by and responsible to the British Parliament. For administrative convenience the offices of Governor-General and Crown Representative were held by the same person, but their constitutional powers were in no way related. The relationship

---

[1] The Kashmir dispute will be examined in Chapter XIX.

[2] In essence it was a crisis of production and run-away inflation. See pp. 509-10 below.

of the British Crown to the Indian Princes might best be described as suzerainty. Where sovereignty rested was open to debate.

As long as the British held sway over the sub-continent this constitutional distinction was of little or no significance. But with the impending transfer of power it assumed strategic importance. The questions arose—to whom will the Princes owe allegiance once the British have departed, to the Government of India or the Government of Pakistan as the successor authorities, or to no one? Did they have the legal right to proclaim themselves independent? If so, the entire structure of Indian unity built by the British during the preceding two centuries would be destroyed overnight and the sub-continent would return to the political jungle which had been its fate during most of recorded history.

The first hint of possible Balkanization was contained in the Cabinet Mission Memorandum of 12 May 1946. With the transfer of power to 'British India', it noted, the British Government's exercise of Paramountcy over the princely States would lapse. The rights of the States flowing from their relationship to the British Crown would no longer exist and all rights surrendered by the States would return to them. The constitutional vacuum thus created could be filled by a federal relationship between the States and the successor government(s) in 'British India' (partition was not yet certain) or 'particular political arrangements made by the States'.[1] Although a positive doctrine of independence for the princely States was not proclaimed, the lapse of Paramountcy without any *necessary* replacement by the successor government(s) in 'British India' clearly implied this right. If the States chose to interpret the Cabinet Mission Memorandum in these terms and had the power to enforce a claim to independence, Balkanization would be inevitable. The problem would be particularly acute for the Dominion of India because all but ten of the 600 States lay in the territory that ultimately fell within its jurisdiction.

The challenge was met with vision and statesmanship, and within a year of Independence the problem of the princely States had vanished into history. Few believed it possible to reconcile the conflicting claims of the Government of India and

[1] Cmd. 6821, 1946.

hundreds of Princes without bitter strife, certainly in so short a period. Yet, apart from Kashmir and Hyderabad, there was no loss of life. It was a bloodless revolution without parallel in this century, comparable with the unification of Germany and Italy by Bismarck and Cavour.

The story of the integration of the princely States is a fascinating study in the great game of politics. The details need not detain us for they have been related with authority by V. P. Menon.[1] Suffice it to sum up the broad picture and to assess its significance.

The directing genius was Sardar Patel who headed the Ministry of States from its creation on 5 July 1947. The brilliant technician who translated policy into deed and who conducted the bulk of the negotiations was V. P. Menon, one of modern India's most gifted civil servants. Formerly the Constitutional Adviser to the Viceroy, he served as Secretary of the States Ministry and was the Sardar's right-hand man. Together they executed India's bloodless revolution.

The campaign—it may be so called for it was carried out with military efficiency—fell into three stages, accession, democratization and integration. The Instrument of Accession was an ingenious device to fill the void caused by the lapse of British Paramountcy over the States. Through it the Rulers transferred to the Government of India control over the three subjects which had formerly been the care of the Paramount Power, namely, defence, foreign affairs and communications. In all other respects the Princes retained control over their affairs. As a result of a combination of persuasion, cajolery, bribery and the lack of sufficient military power on the part of the Princes to enforce a claim to independence, all but three acceded to the new India before the formal transfer of power on 15 August 1947. The exceptions were Kashmir, which had crucial international implications, Junagadh and Hyderabad.

Junagadh was a tiny State in the Kathiawar peninsula of western India. Ruled by a Muslim, with a Hindu-majority population of 86 per cent., it became a pawn in the Indo-Pakistani struggle over Kashmir. Briefly, the Ruler acceded to Pakistan, despite its predominately Hindu population and the absence of a land link with the Muslim Dominion, the two

[1] *The Story of the Integration of the Indian States* (1956).

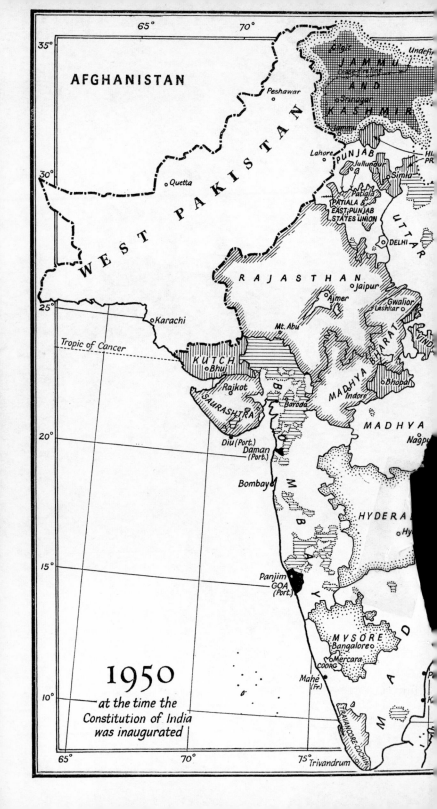

AFGHANISTAN

Peshawar

WEST PAKISTAN

Quetta

JAMMU AND KASHMIR

Undef

Lahore

PUNJAB

Jullundur

Simla

HI. PR.

Patiala

PATIALA & EAST PUNJAB STATES UNION

UTTAR

DELHI

Karachi

Tropic of Cancer

RAJASTHAN

Ajmer

Jaipur

Gwalior Lashkar

Mt. Abu

KUTCH

Bhuj

Rajkot

SAURASHTRA

BHARAT

MADHYA

Baroda

Indore

Bhopal

Diu (Port.)

Daman (Port.)

MADHYA

Nagpur

Bombay

B O M B A Y

HYDERA

Hy

Panjim
GOA
(Port.)

MYSORE

Bangalore

Mercara

COORG

Mahé
(Fr.)

1950

at the time the
Constitution of India
was inaugurated

TRAVANCORE-COCHIN

Trivandrum

AFGHANISTAN

PAKISTAN

RAJASTHAN

MADHYA

MYSORE

BAD
derab

1950

at the time the
Constitution of India
was Inaugurated

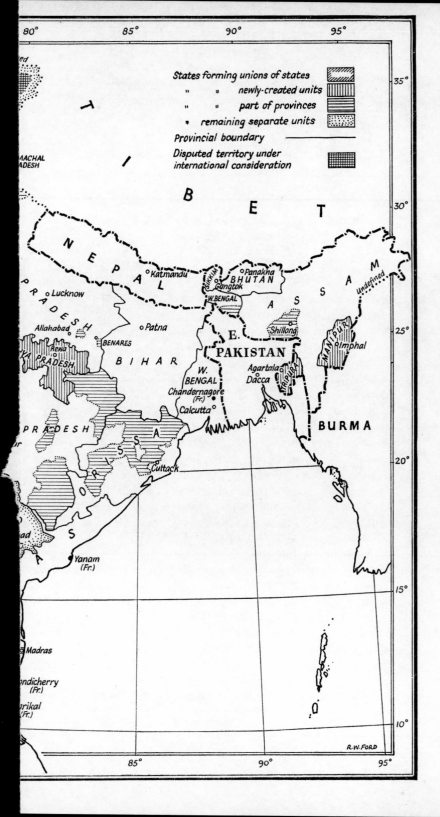

key factors which Lord Mountbatten as Viceroy had urged on the Princes for their decision. The Indian Government objected vehemently. After a brief period of charge and counter-charge between Delhi and Karachi, as well as between Delhi and Junagadh, the Indian Army moved into Junagadh and held a plebiscite. With a declared result of 90 per cent. in favour of India, the State's accession to Pakistan was nullified. Pakistan has never accepted the verdict, but the issue is no longer a serious bone of contention, except in so far as it gives Karachi a debating point over Kashmir.[1]

The case of Hyderabad is much more complex. It was inevitable that Hyderabad should be the most intractable of the princely States. Like Kashmir and Junagadh, it had a fundamental dichotomy in the communal composition of the rulers and the ruled, that is to say, the majority of the population was Hindu, the ruler Muslim. (In Kashmir the position was reversed.) Moreover, its status had long been recognized as somewhat above all other princely States; the Nizam was His Exalted Highness and Faithful Ally of the British Crown. It was large enough to be a viable independent state. And its Muslim aristocracy was determined not to give up its entrenched position without a struggle. Hyderabad also had a substantial fighting force, about 50,000 regulars and an irregular army, the Razakars, estimated at about 200,000. The Nizam and his advisers hoped to maintain a large measure of independence, perhaps with British support, possibly with that of Pakistan which looked upon Hyderabad as a brother Muslim state and an ideal ally against India. Finally, with Delhi's energy concentrated in Kashmir, they hoped that a special arrangement could be made, at least to safeguard the internal autonomy of Hyderabad.

The negotiations were long and tedious. Hyderabad held out against accession; New Delhi was adamant. Finally, on the grounds of atrocities against Hyderabadi Hindus, the imprisonment of 10,000 Congressmen in the State, border incidents imperilling the neighbouring territory of India, and alarming evidence of an alliance between the fanatical Razakars and the Communists, the Government of India moved, in what has been called a 'police action'. The invasion began on 13 September

[1] For a detailed account of the Junagadh story see Menon, *The Story of the Integration of the Indian States*, ch. vi, and Campbell-Johnson, op. cit., ch. 16.

1948 Four days later all resistance collapsed. The Indian Army remained in direct control for a year and was then replaced by a civil administration. After the first general elections in 1951–2 a popular ministry took over the reins of government.[1]

The basic reason for Delhi's concern about the princely States, most especially about the fate of Hyderabad, was cogently stated by Sir Reginald Coupland: 'An India deprived of the States would have lost all coherence. They stand between all four quarters of the country. If no more than the Central Indian States and Hyderabad and Mysore were excluded from the Union, the United Provinces would be almost completely cut off from Bombay, and Bombay completely from Sind. The strategic and economic implications are obvious. India could live if its Moslem limbs in the north-west and north-east were amputated, but could it live without its midriff?'[2]

The process of accession was followed by gradual democratization of the States, with the All-India States Peoples' Conference the principal instrument and major beneficiary. The pace varied from State to State, for some like Mysore had made rapid strides towards responsible government under enlightened Rulers while others like Hyderabad were almost complete autocracies. Civil servants on loan from Delhi assisted the change-over. By the time the new Indian Constitution came into effect (1950), most of the States had representative institutions similar to those of the provinces, though they did not function nearly as well. The structure could be imposed but much time had to elapse before it took root.

Almost immediately after the accession stage was completed, the States Ministry proceeded to the more advanced stage of integration into the Dominion (later the Union) of India. Various techniques were used to reduce the large number of principalities to a dozen viable units. Travancore and Cochin, at the south-western tip of India, were merged. Mysore, Hyderabad and Kashmir remained separate units. The Rajput States were united in the union of Rajasthan, as were Indore and Gwalior in Madhya Bharat, and the Central Indian States

[1] For a detailed account of the Hyderabad story see Menon, *The Story of the Integration of the Indian States*, chs. XVII–XIX; Campbell-Johnson, op. cit., pp. 327–40; 347–50, 359 and 361; and Sir Mirza Ismail, *My Public Life*, chs. IX and X.

[2] *India: A Re-Statement*, p. 278.

in Vindhya Pradesh. In the Kathiawar peninsula some 240 tiny principalities were united in the State of Saurashtra. Many were merged with neighbouring provinces. Some, like Coorg, Manipur, Tripura and Ajmer were placed or retained under direct control of the central Government. From this welter of political entities the Union of India was reduced to twenty-six states—Part A, the former British provinces, Part B, the unions of princely States and those left unchanged, and Part C, those which were centrally administered. The magnitude of the operation is brought into bold relief by the vital statistics: within a year an area of almost half a million square miles, with a population of almost ninety million, was incorporated into the Indian Union. Patel, the master-builder, commented with justifiable pride: 'the great ideal of geographical, political and economic unification of India, an ideal which for centuries remained a distant dream and which appeared as remote and as difficult of attainment as ever even after the advent of Indian independence', had been consummated.[1] Nehru, too, paid tribute to the achievement: 'The historian who looks back will no doubt consider this integration of the States into India as one of the dominant phases of India's history.'[2]

Nehru's role in the execution of this, the greatest triumph of the duumvirate, was negligible. The burden of day-to-day decisions and of the negotiations with the Princes was carried by Patel and Menon. Yet it would be erroneous to disregard, as so many Indians have, Nehru's contribution to the *policy* decisions and, more important, to the shaping of the Congress attitude to the Princes during the fifteen years preceding Independence. Of all the nationalist leaders, Nehru took the most active part in the All-India States Peoples' Conference and the struggle for responsible government in the princely domains. His writings and speeches had stressed the archaic character of the 'relics of medievalism', as he was fond of terming the Princely States. During the tense days before Partition it was he who emphatically stated India's resolve to integrate the States with the Union. During the lengthy negotiations for the entry of the States into the Indian Constituent Assembly, it was he who

---

[1] Quoted in Menon, *The Story of the Integration of the Indian States*, p. 490.
[2] Quoted in ibid., p. 489.

played the decisive role.[1] It was Nehru who tenaciously opposed the official British interpretation of the meaning of the lapse of Paramountcy, arguing that independence was not implicit. As Prime Minister, he delegated responsibility to Mountbatten to 'negotiate' with the Princes, especially with the Nizam of Hyderabad. And it was he who proposed the establishment of the States Ministry to carry through accession and integration.

Menon's account also confirms the view noted earlier that the duumvirs were in constant consultation about any matter of importance. Patel never acted on major issues affecting the States without securing Nehru's approval.[2] On the day-to-day decisions he had free rein. On Kashmir, Nehru alone framed policy. On Junagadh and Hyderabad especially, Nehru played an active part at various stages in the negotiations and his views carried considerable weight—except, according to some Indians, at the very end when Patel made the key decision in favour of military action while Nehru was anxious to delay, especially as Jinnah had died less than two days earlier.[3] The integration of the States was Patel's master achievement, an historic contribution to the consolidation of India. Nehru's role was secondary but none the less important. He set the objectives in general terms. Patel achieved them with consummate skill.

*   *   *   *

As the destruction of the princely order drew to a close another link with the past was severed in New Delhi. On 21 June 1948, with regret on both sides, the last British Governor-General of India set out for home. A century of pomp and pageantry had come to an end.[4]

Lord Mountbatten's tenure as Viceroy was the shortest in the history of the *Raj* but no other representative of the Crown had

---

[1] See *Constituent Assembly Debates, Official Report*, vol. i, pp. 154–5, vol. ii, pp. 304–5, and vol. iii, pp. 350–6. The text of the Report of the Constituent Assembly's Negotiating Committee with the States is to be found in vol. iii, Appendix A, pp. 363–75.

[2] See Menon, op. cit., pp. 97, 99, and the chapters on Junagadh and Hyderabad.

[3] Related to the author in 1956 by Indian politicians who wish to remain anonymous.

[4] Direct British Crown rule over India began in 1858 following the Rebellion. The transfer from the East India Company to the Crown was formally effected through the Government of India Act, 1858. The pomp continues, but with an Indian President occupying the centre of the pageant.

acquired such popularity with the Indian people. He had arrived in the spring of 1947 when India was aflame with communal riots. His mission was to supervise the transfer of power, a task requiring statesmanship of the highest order. The mission was accomplished a few months later, but the price was high—with half a million dead and ten million forced to leave their ancestral homes. Whether any other course of action would have reduced the human suffering, or have magnified it, will long remain a subject of conjecture. The fact remains, however, that the climax of Mountbatten's mission was accompanied by the gravest outbreak of communal violence in the 4,000-year-old history of the sub-continent. And yet he was acclaimed by the leaders and people of India alike. Indeed, few men in any country, certainly no foreign rulers, have been honoured with such affection and respect.

The basic reason must be sought in the peculiar psychological atmosphere of India at the time. The struggle for freedom had been long and arduous. Many Indians doubted British sincerity even as late as the spring of 1947, despite Attlee's unqualified pledge to transfer power. When at last Independence came, Mountbatten was its carrier, the symbol of a promise fulfilled and the personification of the best qualities of the *Raj*. He was likened to a prince in Hindu folklore who had come to the rescue of a people in revolt. He could do no wrong.

His appearance and manner seemed to give visible expression to this idealized portrait. An exceptionally handsome man in his late forties, Mountbatten of Burma was one of the most striking figures in public life anywhere in the world. He was tall and erect, with an impressive, well-proportioned physique and strong, masculine features. His bearing and movement carried the imprint of a lifetime naval career and the pride of a man born to the highest rank of the aristocracy. He was polished, urbane, imperious and completely self-controlled. He could be stern or light-hearted, attentive or indifferent, conciliatory or adamant. To some his gestures and expression were consciously calculated to achieve the maximum effect. To others they were natural and intensely human. All agree, however, that there was a magnetic quality about 'the Admiral' as Lord Mountbatten was known to his devoted subordinates.

In his immaculate white naval uniform Mountbatten looked

every inch the born leader of men. He was a man of many talents—military commander, administrator, statesman. He was, too, a superb showman on the public stage, highly articulate and gifted with a sense of timing. His personality was forceful and dynamic, his energy irrepressible, his capacity for work enormous. Perhaps his greatest asset—and liability—was his habit of making important decisions swiftly, in the opinion of many, too swiftly. Of his capacity for leadership, a former colleague remarked: 'No man could get us out of a mess more quickly, or into one, than Mountbatten.'[1]

He approached the problem of Indian independence as if it were a military campaign. Most revealing in this connection was a calendar hanging on the wall behind his desk; inscribed in large, black print were numbers and below each, 'Days Left to Prepare for the Transfer of Power.' When D-Day arrived the surgical operation was performed. He drove his staff and himself mercilessly, for the deadline had to be met.

Mountbatten was acutely conscious of his own place in history and acted his role with supreme self-confidence. He had a shrewd insight into men and affairs and possessed formidable powers of persuasion. His mind was quick and he was able to remember all manner of detail. In the darkest days he remained calm and serene, immovable in a raging storm. Even when the communal riots swept over northern India and western Pakistan and the 'Great Trek' got under way, he retained his composure.

Unlike most of his predecessors, he was gifted with a common touch. He mingled freely with Indians at all levels, showed a keen interest in their problems and sympathy with their aspirations. And was he not, after all, a prince in fact, cousin to the King. It was this unusual combination of qualities, along with his role as the bearer of Independence, that endeared him to many Indians. By all accounts he was an arresting figure, a man of irresistible charm.

Mountbatten's most notable triumph in the sphere of personal relations was an intimate bond of friendship with Nehru. Other Congress leaders, including Gandhi and Patel, were well-disposed to the Governor-General. But with Nehru there developed a relationship of mutual trust, respect, admiration and

---

[1] Related to the author in London in 1955 by a person who wishes to remain anonymous.

affection which is rare among statesmen and unprecedented in the annals of the British *Raj*. From their first meeting in Malaya in 1946 they were drawn to each other. The friendship blossomed during the tempestuous months leading up to the Partition and beyond.

On the eve of their departure from India in the summer of 1948, Nehru paid an effusive tribute to the Mountbattens. Of their popularity, he remarked: 'this was not connected so much with what had happened, but rather with the good faith, the friendship and the love of India that these two possessed. . . . And so the people of India, realizing that Lord and Lady Mountbatten undoubtedly were friendly to the people of India . . . gave you their affection and love. They could not give very much else.' To Lord Mountbatten he directed the following remarks: 'You came here, Sir, with a high reputation, but many a reputation has foundered in India. You lived here during a period of great difficulty and crisis and yet your reputation has not foundered. This is a remarkable feat. Many of us who came in contact with you from day to day in these days of crisis learnt much from you, we gathered confidence when sometimes we were rather shaken and I have no doubt that the many lessons we have learnt from you will endure . . .'

There were gracious words for young Pamela Mountbatten. And to Lady Mountbatten he said: 'The gods or some fairy gave you beauty and high intelligence, and grace and charm and vitality, great gifts, and she who possesses them is a great lady wherever she goes. But unto those that have, even more shall be given, and they gave you something which was even rarer than these gifts, the human touch, the love of humanity, the urge to serve those who suffer and who are in distress, and this amazing mixture of qualities resulted in a radiant personality and in the healer's touch. Wherever you have gone, you have brought solace. . . . Is it surprising, therefore, that the people of India should love you and look up to you as one of themselves and should grieve that you are going? The bonds that tie the Mountbattens to us are too strong to be broken and we hope to meet here or elsewhere from time to time . . .'[1]

Nehru's friendship with Lord Mountbatten was the product of various factors, some of them highly intangible. First and

[1] The text is in *Independence and After*, pp. 368–71.

foremost was a powerful mutual attraction between very similar personalities. Both men were proud, cultivated, worldly and conscious aristocrats; both possessed great charm and a human touch; both were men of action and masters of the art of public relations; both were vain. They differed, of course, in some respects, but there was no clash of personalities. Nehru was far more sensitive in his responses, an intellectual thrust into the political arena, a lonely man constantly beset by doubt. Mountbatten was more self-assured and decisive. Nehru had a mercurial temperament. Mountbatten was always serene. In the large, Nehru was the more noble man, more human personality, whose vision was broader and sense of morality more pronounced. Where they differed they supplemented each other well.

There was, too, a marked affinity of ideas to strengthen the friendship. Nehru's stress on science, secularism, industrialization and a welfare state found a more sympathetic response in Mountbatten than in most of his nationalist colleagues. It was easy to talk with Mountbatten, for their modes of thought were similar, two aristocrats who had forsaken the ideologies of their class. Moreover, Mountbatten was the first Viceroy to treat him as an equal, to abandon the rigid code of 'ruler' and 'subject'. Cripps realized how much the proud Nehru had been irked by the behaviour of previous Viceroys and had advised Mountbatten to act accordingly. This alone broke down the initial barrier between any Viceroy and a nationalist leader.

Mountbatten's sympathy for Indian freedom undoubtedly cemented the friendship. So too did his behaviour during the fifteen months he served as Viceroy and Governor-General. In particular, his role during the Delhi riots in the autumn of 1947 and his direction of the Emergency committee left a deep impression on Nehru. After years of frustrated struggle and rebuffs by a series of Viceroys, Nehru found in Mountbatten an understanding, sympathetic representative of the Crown who worked in India's interests. It restored his faith in Britain, weakened in the past but never shattered.

As for Lady Mountbatten, it can only be surmised that she helped to fill a void in Nehru's life. He had always suffered from a sense of loneliness. His wife's death at an early age had accentuated this feeling. Especially during the Partition days, when he was more prone to moods of despair, Lady Mountbatten's sympathy was a source of comfort. She, too, was a cultivated Westerner, and a woman of great charm who could understand him as most Indian women whom he knew could not.

In the years that followed, his friendship with the Mountbattens was sustained by fond memories and personal reunions. During his frequent visits to England, usually for the Commonwealth Prime Ministers Conference, Nehru invariably spent a week-end with the Mountbattens at their country estate at Romsey. At the Delhi end there were annual visits by Lady Mountbatten as part of her tour of the East for various welfare agencies; and Lord Mountbatten paid a brief official visit in 1956 as Britain's First Sea Lord. Although friendship cannot be measured precisely, Nehru probably feels closer to the Mountbattens than to anyone in India, except for his daughter and, perhaps, Krishna Menon.

The political consequences of the Nehru-Mountbatten friendship are also difficult to measure, but it would be wrong to discount them as trivial. There can be little doubt that the Mountbattens' persuasive powers helped to ease Nehru's acceptance of partition as the only feasible solution. They also succeeded in dispelling his distrust of British motives. It would be reasonable to infer, therefore, that Nehru was influenced by this relationship in weighing the merits of membership in the Commonwealth. In the broadest sense, Indo-British friendship immediately after Partition must be credited largely to Mountbatten's handling of the transfer of power. India paid an exorbitant price for his military approach. But in terms of British interests it was a brilliant achievement, the skilful execution of a policy of withdrawal. Mountbatten's diplomacy at the time and his continuing friendship with Nehru won rich dividends for Britain.

*   *   *   *

When Nehru accepted the Dominion status formula for the transfer of power many people were startled. Had he not proclaimed his unqualified rejection of anything less than complete independence since the late 'twenties? Had he not written in 1936 that the idea of India becoming a Dominion 'seems to be fantastic'?[1] And again in the same year, 'the whole conception of Dominion status seems to me to be an acceptance of the basic fabric of British imperialism'?[2] Yet the *volte face* in 1947 could easily be rationalized as a temporary expedient to ease the transfer of real power, something which would give way to a republic in the near future.

When India agreed to remain in the Commonwealth, however, Nehru was accused of violating solemn pledges undertaken during the struggle for freedom. No doubt, many extracts from his writings and speeches can be culled to support this criticism. But they represent only a half-truth. The striking feature of Nehru's numerous pronouncements on the subject of Indo-British relations is the sharp distinction he always made between Britain as the ruling power in India and Britain as an equal. Thus in 1936 he said that complete independence means 'the separation of India from England'. But, he hastened to add: 'Personally, I can conceive and welcome the idea of a close association between India and England on terms other than those of imperialism.'[3] The key stumbling-block was British control over India; once that ended friendship was possible. This view was reiterated many times during the next decade.[4] Seen in this light the decision to remain in the Commonwealth should not have occasioned such an outcry of 'betrayal'.

The road to India's membership in the Commonwealth as an independent republic is a fascinating story of diplomacy in action and an illuminating example of Nehru's dominant role in the shaping of India's foreign policy. Many hands helped to pave the way, notably Mountbatten, Krishna Menon and Attlee. There were tortuous legal barriers in the final stage. Its completion was a triumph of fortitude and ingenious construction.

The foundation, hardly noticed at the time, took the form of an equivocal statement by Nehru to the Constituent Assembly on 22 January 1947: 'At no time have we ever thought in terms of isolating ourselves in this part of the world from other countries or of being hostile to countries which have dominated

[1] *India and the World*, p. 204.   [2] *Eighteen Months in India*, p. 20.
[3] To a meeting of the Indian Conciliation Group in London on 4 February 1936, *India and the World*, p. 228.
[4] See, for example, *China, Spain and the War*, p. 125, and 'Anxious India' in *Asia*, May 1939.

over us. . . . We want to be friendly to all. We want to be friendly with the British people and the British Commonwealth of Nations.'[1] The direction of the architect's thoughts was made clearer two months later in the course of his first discussion with Mountbatten. As noted earlier, Nehru actually proposed an Anglo-Indian union involving common citizenship.[2] Krishna Menon entered the picture in April 1947, when he informed Mountbatten that he was searching for a formula which would ensure a close link with Britain![3] During the next ten months activity ceased while India went through the cataclysm of Partition.

At the beginning of 1948 Panikkar informed a member of the Governor-General's staff that Nehru was now more firmly persuaded of the need for an Indo-British understanding. Then, on 25 February 1948, the day before the Indian draft constitution was published, Mountbatten made a signal contribution to the completion of the road. In an *aide-memoire* for the British Secretary of State for Commonwealth Relations, he proposed certain changes in the structure of the association, 'particularly in nomenclature, to allow Asian countries to remain more easily associated with it'. Though he was unhappy with the word republic, he remarked, 'I think there can be no doubt that there is room for a Republic within the Commonwealth.'[4]

The turning-point came at the Commonwealth Prime Ministers Conference in London in October 1948, the first which Nehru attended. There was no formal discussion of the issue, but Nehru and Attlee exchanged views. According to Attlee, 'there was no background. We merely discussed it among ourselves and found the formula satisfactory.' As for Nehru's reaction, 'he realized that membership in the Commonwealth meant independence plus, not independence minus'.[5] Having persuaded himself of its virtues, Nehru had to convince his colleagues and Indian political opinion at large. Upon his return from London he noted that he had not committed India in any sense, for this was a matter to be decided by the Constituent Assembly. However, since the Congress dominated the

---

[1] *Independence and After*, p. 358.   [2] See p. 344 above.
[3] Campbell-Johnson, op. cit., p. 66.   [4] Ibid., pp. 290–1.
[5] To the author in London in October 1955.

Assembly, it became a mere formality. The issue was decided by Nehru with his Cabinet's assent.

The Congress, complying with Nehru's wish, gave its approval at the Jaipur session in December 1948. The formal arrangement was concluded at the Commonwealth Prime Ministers Conference in April, 1949 and was embodied in the Declaration of London. It was a very brief document indeed, only four paragraphs. The first noted the existing position, referred to the *British* Commonwealth of Nations and the common *allegiance* to the *Crown*. The second indicated that India had informed the participants of its decision to establish a sovereign independent republic, of its desire to retain full membership in the Commonwealth, and of its willingness to accept the *King* as *symbol* of the free association of members and as such as *Head* of *the Commonwealth*. The participants accepted India on these terms and affirmed their status as free and equal members.[1]

Despite its simplicity of phrasing, the Declaration of London had many hurdles to overcome. At the Delhi end there was no real problem, for Nehru's views on foreign policy were final, and in any event Patel strongly favoured the idea.[2] According to one prominent person who played a key role in the negotiations, the King supported the novel idea of a Republic in the Commonwealth. The Foreign Office lawyers, however, were strongly opposed. Lengthy negotiations took place, but the lawyers were adamant, saying it was impossible to devise a formula under international law which would make a Republic compatible with a Commonwealth. Initially there were about ten problems to be solved, but these were reduced to three—citizenship, reciprocity and the place of the Crown. A suggestion for Commonwealth citizenship was made. Though it was finally rejected, the substance was later incorporated into the

[1] The text of the Declaration of London is to be found in *Constituent Assembly Debates: Official Report*, vol. viii, p. 2, footnote.

[2] This is not surprising in view of the fact that as early as 1931, in the midst of the great civil disobedience campaign, Patel did not rule out a close association with England. In his presidential address to the Karachi session of the Congress he commented on complete independence as follows: 'This independence does not mean, was not intended to mean, a churlish refusal to associate with Britain or any other power. Independence, therefore, does not preclude the possibility of equal partnership for mutual benefit and dissolvable at the will of either party.' *Report of the 45th Indian National Congress, Karachi, 1931*, pp. 16–17. His attitude was consistent over the years.

Press Information Bureau, Government of India

18. On the Tibet road, Sikkim, in April, 1952

19. At the M.P.s' charity cricket match at the National Stadium, New
Delhi, 1953

citizenship laws of various Commonwealth countries. The core issue was the Crown. The Australians wanted the King to be designated King of the Commonwealth, but South Africa, Canada and India were opposed. There was a proposal to have the President of India formally appointed by the King, but India was opposed. Mountbatten suggested the inclusion of the Crown in the Indian flag; this, too, was rejected. Finally, they devised the formula, 'Head of the Commonwealth.' At the last moment the Pakistanis wanted a more direct monarchical link. To break the impasse the words 'as such' were added, connecting the terms 'Head of the Commonwealth' and 'symbol of the free association of members'.

Churchill's role was insignificant. He was only informed at a late stage and welcomed it as a magnanimous gesture by India. Cripps made his contribution by stressing to his colleagues India's categorical insistence on the Republic; that was the irreducible point of departure. From a strictly formal point of view India took the initiative. Perhaps the most significant facet of the story was that 'absolutely no pressure was exerted by the British on us to remain in the Commonwealth. They wanted us, of course, but Attlee did not lift a finger to intervene.'[1]

Within India criticism of the decision was confined to the Left, which termed it 'the great betrayal', and sections of the right wing Hindu Mahasabha. The debate in the Constituent Assembly was spirited, with thirteen members voicing support of Nehru's action, six opposition. The outcome was a foregone conclusion. The main themes of the critics were that it violated previous pledges; committed India to the West; represented a loss of independence; and was immoral because of racial discrimination in South Africa. In defence of his policy Nehru declared that it did not violate previous pledges, for India's independence was unimpaired; that it was in India's self-interest, for it enabled Delhi to act more effectively in foreign affairs, even with respect to Indians in South Africa; and that it helped to promote international stability and therefore world peace.[2]

[1] To the author in New Delhi in 1956 by a person who wishes to remain anonymous.

[2] The verbatim record of the debate on the Declaration of London is in *Constituent Assembly Debates: Official Report*, vol. viii, pp. 11–65. Nehru's opening speech and his reply to the debate are on pp. 2–10 and 65–71 respectively.

Various considerations influenced Nehru's decision. (In the last analysis it was his decision alone.) At the subconscious level was his affection for Britain dating from his formative years, an attachment which was deepened by his friendship with the Mountbattens. The reservoir of goodwill which America possessed in India at the end of the second world war had evaporated. But by far the most important was the realization that India could not remain isolated in a world of great tension—the 'Cold War' was then a harsh reality—and that the Commonwealth link was the most advantageous. The bulk of India's trade was with the Commonwealth; its foreign exchange reserves were tied up in the Sterling Area; its armed forces depended on British-made weapons. Moreover, membership of the Commonwealth would enable India to render greater assistance to the substantial communities of Indian settlers in South Africa, Malaya, British Guiana and other parts of the Empire. Viewed in the perspective of the duumvirate, it was an act of high statesmanship, for it thwarted the danger of isolation in foreign affairs at a time of grave crisis internally and on the world scene. It marks the first real stabilizing act in India's relations with the outside world.

In the midst of his negotiations with the Commonwealth, Nehru made his formal début on the world stage as Prime Minister of India. Many people in the West knew of him as Gandhi's aide in the struggle for freedom and as an author of renown. But it was not until he addressed the U.N. General Assembly in Paris on 3 November 1948 that he became a name to remember. For on that occasion he emerged as the voice of new Asia.

He praised the principles of the Charter but called for a new approach to peace and stressed the priority of means over ends. In fact, this speech was in the nature of an exposition of Gandhian non-violence. But it was more. While paying tribute to European cultures, he noted that the world was no longer synonymous with Europe. He pleaded for recognition of renascent Asia and the end of colonialism and racial inequality. Economic problems were more vital than the political, he said, in criticism of the U.N.'s preoccupation with the latter. The great plague of the age was fear, fear of war, fear of aggression, fear of a host of evils that beset the world. And all states shared in the guilt for the vicious circle which had led to re-armament and constant preparation for war. In this speech are contained most of the ingredients of Nehru's foreign policy since Independence. They have been repeated *ad infinitum*. But on this occasion his audience was visibly moved, especially by his eloquent appeal for understanding of the Asian revolution.[1]

A year later Nehru made his first 'voyage of discovery' to America. For three weeks he toured the United States and tried to convey the aspirations of Asia's hungry millions to Government leaders and the common man alike. His pride prevented him from begging for aid, though India was in the throes of famine. He sought food—2,000,000 tons of wheat—and capital to help India break out of economic stagnation. The food came—eighteen months later—after thousands had died awaiting an act of mercy. The American Congress sought concessions from India. Nehru refused. More than that, he developed a thinly disguised contempt for American 'materialism'.

This attitude was traceable in part to his English public-school education in the Edwardian age when Americans were looked upon as *nouveaux riches* who lacked both social graces and a distinctive culture, let alone a tradition worthy of the name. As a Brahmin and a product of one of the world's oldest civilizations, Nehru was inclined to accept this view, though he was fully aware of America's great technical achievements, its enormous power and its strong democratic roots, all of which he admired. During World War Two he saw in America a friend of the colonial peoples, as indeed it was. By 1949, however, he had become disillusioned with American policy in Asia. The rebuff to his request for aid without strings deepened his disenchantment.

Nor was he impressed by the boastfulness of some Americans. 'You know, Mr. Prime Minister, around this table are seated leaders of corporations worth twenty billion dollars', he was told by a prominent businessman at a dinner in his honour. To a sensitive socialist from a poverty-stricken land, these words must have seemed graceless and typical of America's set of values. It is generally believed that they annoyed him greatly. By any standards this first visit to America was a failure. Nehru came away empty-handed. American leaders were not

[1] The text is in *Independence and After*, pp. 318–24.

over-impressed with him, primarily because of his refusal to 'stand up and be counted'. And he was decidedly unhappy at his experience. Yet he had succeeded in impressing on his hosts the fact that India was not prepared to be bought—for sums large or small.[1]

*   *   *   *

Nehru's visit to America coincided with another milestone in the story of the duumvirate, the completion of India's new constitution. The drafting process had lasted almost three years. It lacked the dramatic quality of the integration of the States, the rehabilitation of five million refugees and the attainment of international prestige, three major achievements of the transition period. Nor was there a sense of urgency as in the crisis of production, the danger of territorial fragmentation and the communal upheaval in the Punjab. Indeed, at the time of Independence, India had an eminently workable constitution in the 1935 Government of India Act. Thus, in the quest for stability which preoccupied Nehru and Patel, the framing of a constitution was relegated to the background. Yet it was one of the notable accomplishments of the duumvirate. Symbolically it marked the realization of a goal which the Congress had long termed vital to genuine freedom, a republican constitution drafted by Indians alone. Substantively it provided the framework for the operation of democratic political institutions and incorporated many basic principles to which the party had pledged itself over the years.

An exhaustive analysis of the Indian Constitution is beyond the scope of this book. In any event, others have dissected it with care and insight.[2] Nor is this the place for an assessment of the practice of democratic government in India during the past decade.[3] The primary interest is Nehru's role in the shaping of this legal charter. To examine this, however, it is necessary to indicate some of its salient features and to sketch the constitution-making process.

[1] For a collection of Nehru's speeches in America in 1949 see *Visit to America* (John Day, 1950).

[2] See Gledhill, A., *The Republic of India* (1951) and *Fundamental Rights in India* (1955); Jennings, Sir Ivor, *Some Characteristics of the Indian Constitution* (1952); and Basu, D. D., *Commentary on the Constitution of India* (second edition, 1952).

[3] This will be treated in Chapter XVII.

Firstly, as to the vital statistics. The deliberations of the Constituent Assembly extended from 9 December 1946 to 26 November 1949 and were divided into twelve sessions. The first two were devoted to the Objectives Resolution, in the framing of which Nehru played the decisive part. The next four were concerned with the reports of various committees of the Assembly. This stage was completed on the eve of Partition. A few weeks later a Drafting Committee was formed to collate the reports and to prepare a draft for consideration by the Assembly as a whole. The draft was completed in February 1948. For the next eight months it was subjected to public scrutiny. From November 1948 to November 1949 the finished product was hammered out in almost continuous session of the Constituent Assembly.

From these deliberations emerged the Constitution of India, the longest and most comprehensive written constitution in the world. It is, indeed, a forbidding document, with 395 articles (divided into 22 parts) and 8 schedules.[1] The principal reason for its inordinate length is that the drafters included many details normally left to the growth of convention.

One of the striking features of India's 'new' constitution is the continuity with British-Indian practice. Approximately 250 articles were taken either verbatim or with minor changes in phraseology from the 1935 Government of India Act, and the basic principles remain unchanged. Another is the total absence of distinctively Indian ideas. The Constitution of India is a purely Western charter, a *mélange* of ideas and practices drawn from various constitutions in Europe and America. The influence of Great Britain is paramount, not merely as expressed through the 1935 Act, but also through the adoption of the parliamentary form of government. The federal idea owes much to the United States and Australia. From the Irish Free State came the inspiration for Part IV, the Directive Principles of State Policy, an expression of goals which have no legal force but which convey the intent of the 'fathers' of the Indian Constitution. From the United States was derived the idea of a detailed list of fundamental rights which comprise Part III. These two parts alone account for 40 articles.

The new India is defined in the preamble as a Sovereign

---

[1] *The Constitution of India* (Government of India Press, Delhi, 1949).

Democratic Republic and in Article 1 as a Union of States. Although federal in form, it is conspicuously unitary in spirit. This becomes evident from the division of powers among the three lists, Union, States and Concurrent (Part XI and Seventh Schedule); the control over and distribution of finances (Part XII); the organization of administrative services (Part XIV); the appointment and responsibility of State Governors (Part VI, Chapter II); the right of Parliament to form new States or alter existing boundaries (Article 3); and, most important, from the imposing array of emergency powers vested in the central government (Part XVIII). Among the controversial provisions are those pertaining to language—Hindi is to be the official language of the Union within fifteen years, with English retain·ing its existing status in the interim (Part XVII); and compulsory compensation for expropriated property (Article 31).[1]

Many criticisms were levelled at the Constitution. There were those who decried the lack of originality and the absence of Indian influence; some even suggested that it should have been based on the traditional village *panchayats* (councils). On the first point the chief drafter of the Constitution remarked: 'I hold that these village republics have been the ruination of India. . . . What is the village but a sink of localism, a den of ignorance, narrow-mindedness and communalism.'[2] Some argued that the fundamental rights were circumscribed by too many exceptions; the reply was that these rights can never be absolute. Others criticized the fact that the Directive Principles of State Policy had no legal force; in defence it was noted that they have moral sanction. Proponents of States' rights opposed the marked degree of centralization, but the 'fathers' claimed that this was inevitable in the modern world, especially in the conditions of India. Finally, it was claimed that the amendment process was too difficult; time has proved this view erroneous. In the nation at large the only organized group opposition came from the Communists and Socialists, though others felt that the framing of a constitution should have awaited

[1] According to official estimates, 7,635 amendments were tabled and 2,473 were actually moved. Very few of these were accepted by the drafters. *Constituent Assembly Debates: Official Report*, vol. xii, p. 972.

[2] Dr. B. R. Ambedkar, in his speech of 4 November 1948, introducing the draft Constitution to the Constituent Assembly. For the text of Ambedkar's speech see *Constituent Assembly Debates: Official Report*, vol. vii, pp. 31–44.

the election of a new Constituent Assembly on the basis of adult suffrage.

The chief architect or, more correctly, the field general of this campaign was Dr. B. R. Ambedkar, one of recent India's most controversial politicians. An Untouchable by birth, Ambedkar had been an inveterate foe of the treatment of the *Harijans* and had openly supported Jinnah on the partition of the sub-continent.[1] Through good fortune he received a higher education, including a doctorate from Columbia University. As the acknowledged leader of the Untouchables he was appointed to the central Cabinet and served as Minister of Law until his resignation in the autumn of 1951.[2] But it was in his capacity as Chairman of the Drafting Committee of the Constituent Assembly that Ambedkar held the spotlight, steering the draft through the oft-stormy debates.[3] On the purely technical side the burden fell mainly on Sir Benegal Rau, Constitutional Adviser to the Constituent Assembly, S. N. Mukerjee, Chief Draftsman, and H. V. R. Iyengar, Secretary of the Assembly.

Ambedkar played a vital role as the principal Government spokesman, but it is very doubtful whether he shaped policy on controversial questions. Speaking in Parliament in the autumn of 1953, he called for a complete repudiation of the Constitution. When reminded of his role, he said, 'I was a hack. I did what I was asked to do. I only carried out the wishes of the majority.'[4] The disillusioned Ambedkar reiterated this view in the spring of 1956, a few months before his death.[5] By this he meant that decisions were first taken in the Congress party caucus and then translated into constitutional language by the Drafting Committee.

Neither Nehru nor Patel was actively involved in the debates. Yet Nehru's role was far from unimportant. It was he who dominated the early proceedings with his Objectives Resolution.

[1] See his *Pakistan or the Partition of India* (third edition, 1946).

[2] See pp. 454–5 below.

[3] There were six other members of the Drafting Committee. However, one resigned from the Constituent Assembly, one died and was not replaced, one spent much of his time in America, one was engaged in State affairs, and two were ill or away from Delhi!

[4] *The Hindu* (Madras), 3 September 1953.

[5] To the author in New Delhi in May 1956.

Further, this defined the principles which underlay the Constitution. Moreover, Nehru was Chairman of three important committees—States, Union Powers and Union Constitution—from the reports of which the draft was prepared by Ambedkar and his colleagues. (Patel was Chairman of the remaining three vital committees—Fundamental Rights, Provincial Constitutions and Minorities—another reflection of the duumvirate.) While neither held the centre of the stage in the Assembly, both were involved in all basic decisions in the party caucus. It was inconceivable that anything of more than technical importance could be incorporated without their approval.

Nehru spoke infrequently in the Assembly but he did make a few noteworthy interventions which were reflected in the final draft. On a proposal to introduce the principle of proportional representation, he remarked: 'I can think of nothing more conducive to creating a feeble ministry and a feeble government than this . . .'[1] The issue was thereby settled. He was no less emphatic on the method of selecting State Governors. They should be nominated by the central Government, he told the Assembly, because 'we should always view things from the context of preserving the unity, the stability and the security of India . . .', because it would reduce the danger of provincialism and because it would avoid wasteful expenditure of time, energy and money which another election would entail.[2] The nightmare of Balkanization was ever-present in his mind. Thus, in submitting the report of the Union Powers Committee, he made it clear that he was strongly in favour of a powerful central government. The report called for a very broad interpretation of the three subjects placed under the jurisdiction of the Union by the Cabinet Mission plan, i.e., defence, foreign affairs and communications, to include 'powers implied or inherent in or resultant from the express powers of the Union'. This was before the Partition. Once Pakistan came into being there was no longer any need to make concessions to the States.

On the question of language he was the voice of moderation, the defender of English and regional Indian languages against the Hindi fanatics. Largely at his insistence the fifteen-year interim arrangement regarding the use of English was inserted

[1] *Constituent Assembly Debates: Official Report*, vol. iv, p. 915.
[2] Ibid., vol. viii, pp. 455-6.

in the draft.[1] Finally, it was Nehru who defended the clause ensuring compensation for expropriated property, an issue on which Patel was adamant. But in doing so Nehru moved that the amount of compensation should be determined by Parliament, not the Judiciary, a fact which assumed considerable importance in the early 'fifties when constitutional amendments were made at Nehru's insistence on this very point.[2] In its final form this key article followed the lines laid down by Nehru in the Assembly debate.

The Constitution of India was formally inaugurated on 26 January 1950, exactly twenty years after the Congress 'Declaration of Independence' on the eve of civil disobedience.

The new Constitution marks the end of the initial challenge to stability and unity. Only in the sphere of relations with Pakistan was the situation potentially explosive. The duumvirate continued for another year, a year in which the relations between Nehru and Patel deteriorated sharply. For Nehru it was to be a major test of political leadership at the party level.

[1] Nehru's statement on the language problem is to be found in *Constituent Assembly Debates: Official Report*, vol. ix, pp. 1409-16. For a discussion of the language controversy in the late 1950's and Nehru's role, see pp. 489-93 below.

[2] Nehru's statement on the question of compensation and the accompanying debate are to be found in ibid., vol. ix, pp. 1196-1311.

CHAPTER XVI

Victor at the Polls

INDIAN independence meant different things to different people. To the peasantry it provided hope for land reform and a higher standard of living. To the business community it offered prospects of profit and influence on a scale hitherto unknown. To the Westernized intelligentsia it posed the challenge of creative change, the infusion of modern ideas and institutions without destroying the inner fabric of Indian society. To orthodox Hindus it opened the vista of a return to ancient Hindu glory. To the minorities it meant the need to safeguard their rights against the threat of Hindu chauvinism. To pure Gandhians it signified the triumph of right over might and the opportunity to apply the master's teachings. To professional politicians it meant power, the reward for lengthy service in the 'Cause'. All of these aspirations were mirrored in the Congress and found expression in the ideologies of Nehru and Patel.

As long as the Congress was in opposition it was able to weld together these diverse interest groups in a common struggle for freedom. But with the transfer of power in 1947 the deep fissures in this polyglot movement came to the surface as each sought to realize its particular goals. Hence the growing intensity of labour-management strife. Hence the growing clash between secularists and communalists, both widely represented in the party. Hence the rapid increase of corruption, nepotism and favouritism among the politicians. The spoils of power were now disbursed with feverish intensity. The rot had penetrated deeply. Merchants were raising prices and adulterating goods amidst serious shortages of essentials. Bribery was widespread, and so was black marketeering, 'this new disease which has become an epidemic and which threatens to become pandemic'. The abuse of privileges by party stalwarts was scandalous. In the words of the Congress President at the beginning of 1949, 'if the death of India's patriarch is a tragedy, the scant honour done to his memory is a shame'.[1]

That the Congress remained united during this orgy of self-ishness was largely due to the willingness of the duumvirs to bury their differences in the interests of national survival. With respect to the Congress their roles were clearly understood: Nehru was its voice and its liaison with the masses; Patel was the boss of the machine and the spokesman for the Right wing, but he never attempted to use the party to challenge the Prime Minister openly. At the beginning of 1950, however, their relationship was subjected to severe strain.

The catalytic agent was an outburst of communal tension in East and West Bengal. Relations between Delhi and Karachi have never been satisfactory but the degree of hostility has varied over the years. From the autumn of 1947 to the end of 1948 war in Kashmir threatened to engulf the entire sub-continent. A U.N.-sponsored cease-fire eased the tension briefly. Then in December 1949 all economic relations were severed, resulting in extreme hardship for sections of the population in both countries. The economy of East Bengal was threatened with disaster, for a large surplus of jute which had normally been sold in Calcutta was now rotting away without any alternative market. The Calcutta jute industry was also hard hit with consequent unemployment and loss of profits. Partly because of this renewal of economic warfare, partly because of the East Pakistani desire to eject the still-wealthy Hindu professional and commercial classes, a wholesale migration of Hindus from East Bengal (East Pakistan) got under way. Hindu communalists and extremist newspapers in Calcutta fanned the flames with exaggerated reports of atrocities across the border, and a reverse flow of Muslims from West Bengal (India) was set in motion. By March 1950 the stream of refugees had become a flood, a re-enactment of the 1947 Punjab tragedy on a smaller scale. Charge and counter-charge heightened the tension, as did the tales of woe carried by refugees of both communities. Statistics on the Bengal migration of 1950 must be viewed with caution, for both parties were anxious to place the responsibility on their neighbour. There can be little

---

[1] Pattabhi Sitaramayya, *Congress Bulletin*, No. 3, March-May 1949, pp. 15-16 and 14 respectively.

doubt, however, that more than a million persons abandoned their homes before the year was out, though many returned after a measure of tranquillity was restored.

Among those in India who had not become reconciled to partition, and there were many, the clamour for punitive measures became increasingly vocal. Here seemed an ideal opportunity to 'avenge the wrong' of 1947. Within the central Cabinet the extremist view had powerful support, not only from self-proclaimed communalists like Dr. S. P. Mookerjee but also from the Sardar. It was widely known that the duumvirs differed sharply on policy towards their Muslim neighbour. Patel had pressed for delay in the transfer of cash balances accruing to Pakistan under the terms of the Partition Agreements. It is true that he approved Nehru's decision for military action against the Pakistani-supported tribal invasion of Kashmir. But as the struggle for the Vale dragged on, with a heavy drain on India's economic resources, he became annoyed with Nehru's relatively soft, conciliatory, diplomatic approach. As he put it with typical bluntness to one of his Cabinet colleagues: 'If only Jawaharlal would let me handle Kashmir, I could settle it quickly. Instead, he is fumbling all over the place.'[1] Yet the Sardar dared not interfere directly, for Kashmir lay within Nehru's jurisdiction.

In the case of Bengal, however, Patel had no such qualms and he made his position unmistakably clear. He advocated a tough, retaliatory line, the policy of 'ten eyes for an eye', that is to say, the expulsion of ten Muslims from India for every Hindu driven out of East Bengal. Nehru stood fast against this immorality which would have destroyed the secular foundations of the new India and would almost certainly have led to war with Pakistan. From conversations with members of the Indian Cabinet at the time it is apparent that the duumvirs pressed their respective views vigorously. The Sardar's approach undoubtedly had much popular backing. But Nehru remained firmly committed to principle, and Patel ultimately gave way.

The upshot was an agreement reached between Nehru and Liaquat Ali Khan, the Prime Minister of Pakistan, on 8 April 1950, a reasoned attempt to stem the tide of two-way migration.

---

[1] Related to the author in 1956 by the person in question who wishes to remain anonymous.

In essence the latter-day 'Delhi Pact' provided for the right of refugees to return to their place of residence and their protection in transit; the right to transfer all movable property and to dispose of immovable property as desired; the recovery of looted property and abducted women; the non-recognition of all forced conversions in the area during the period of disturbances, and a renewed pledge of equal rights for minorities in both countries. To implement these provisions and to restore normal conditions, Minority Commissions were to be established in the affected areas, a member of the minority community was to be added to the Cabinets of the provinces concerned and a central Government Minister from each State was delegated to remain in the region as long as necessary.[1]

The depth of the cleavage in Delhi is evident from the fact that two senior non-Congress members of the Cabinet resigned and called for stronger measures.[2] Patel was also dissatisfied, but having conceded to Nehru's policy of moderation he acted accordingly. In a major speech before an irate crowd in Calcutta he urged that the Pact be given a fair trial. The Sardar's words and the joint efforts of Nehru and Liaquat Ali had a soothing effect. Within a few months the flood of refugees subsided and many returned to their homes. Correspondingly the tension declined and the danger of war receded. Yet discontent continued to smoulder among the West Bengalis, aided by a steady trickle of Hindu refugees from East Pakistan and propaganda war over the years.

The duumvirate had been subjected to severe stress by the 'Bengal Crisis'. Other sources of disagreement now came into the open. Patel had never been over-fond of Nehru's secularism

[1] The text of the Nehru-Liaquat Ali Agreement is to be found in *Indiagram* (Embassy of India, Washington), 9 April 1950.

[2] Dr. S. P. Mookerjee and K. C. Neogy. Dr. Mookerjee was the most forceful spokesman for Hindu communalism in recent Indian politics. After resigning as Minister of Industry and Supply in 1950, he became the most effective critic of Nehru in the Indian Parliament. In 1951, on the eve of the first Indian general elections, he formed the *Jan Sangh* which emerged as the strongest communalist party in the country. (Earlier he had been associated with the Hindu Mahasabha.) In 1953 he led the agitation in favour of the complete incorporation of Kashmir into the Indian Union. While on one of his visits to Kashmir in 1954 he was taken seriously ill and died before he could be brought to Delhi, causing a wave of indignation among Hindu communalists.

After a period of obscurity following his resignation from the Cabinet, Mr. Neogy served with distinction as a member of the Planning Commission.

and his sympathy for the Muslims. But when Jawaharlal announced his intention of revolutionizing the system of Hindu laws and customs—the Hindu Code Bill—he was firmly opposed. In the economic realm, the Sardar detested socialism and made known his hostility to Nehru's pet project, the Planning Commission, which was set up early in 1950.[1] The breach widened. There was no longer the absolute necessity of submerging their differences as in the aftermath of Partition.

As Nehru and Patel went so went the Congress. An open split was avoided, but the rivalry was now no longer concealed. The contest took place in the full view of the public: the occasion was the Congress presidential election for the Nasik session in September 1950. Each was identified with a particular candidate, though Nehru was less forceful in his partisanship.

Patel's hand-picked candidate was Purshottamdas Tandon, a bearded, venerable orthodox Hindu from the United Provinces who admirably represented the extreme communalist wing of the party. The restoration of Hindu *Raj*, a harsh policy towards Pakistan, the retention of all Hindu customs and traditions, and the subservience of the Cabinet to the Congress High Command—these were the basic ingredients of his programme. Nehru's stress on industrialization was anathema to him, and socialism was decried as an 'alien import from the West'. Tandon's fanatical devotion to Hindu beliefs and practices was reflected in his well-known fads, such as his refusal to wear machine-made shoes because cow-hide was used and his antipathy to the ordinary razor. In appearance he resembled the patriarch of old. Given the opportunity, he would have turned the clock of history back a few thousand years. Yet he was highly respected, even among some of his ideological opponents, for he was free from the taint of corruption, then as later a very live issue in Indian politics.

His election rival was Acharya J. B. Kripalani, a devoted follower of Gandhi since 1917 and a member of the Congress High Command since the mid-'thirties. For twelve years he had served as General Secretary and, in the crucial year of Partition, as Congress President. During the party squabbles before the second world war he had sided with the Old Guard

[1] The planning process and machinery will be discussed in Chapter XVIII.

against Nehru, particularly on the issue of socialism. He was, however, a staunch believer in the secular ideal and, in time, came to embrace the welfare state as well. By comparison with Tandon he was a revolutionary.

Kripalani was assumed to be Nehru's choice, but the Prime Minister did not make his position clear to the party faithful. By contrast the Sardar brought the full weight of the machine into play. The result was a victory for Tandon, i.e., Patel. In prestige terms Nehru suffered a defeat. However, the voting was exceptionally close (Tandon 1,306, Kripalani 1,092 and a third candidate 202) and made Patel aware once more of the cardinal truth regarding Nehru's influence in the country at large. Despite his control of the machine, the Sardar's candidate won a bare majority. And Nehru had refrained from open support for Kripalani.[1] At the Nasik session Patel drew small audiences while vast crowds gathered to hear Nehru. Only he could command the allegiance of the masses.

Having achieved his immediate goal, Patel did not press the contest. As if in the nature of compensation, Nehru's policies were reaffirmed in the party resolutions—on foreign affairs, Indo-Pakistani relations, the secular state and economic reform. An open challenge by the Right wing was confined to the economic programme, in the form of an amendment to abolish existing controls. Although defeated, the proposal showed considerable strength—190 to 117—and served as a warning of the growing cleavage within the party.[2]

The Nasik session ended on 21 September 1950, but the Congress crisis had just begun. It continued with no holds barred for the next year. Although Nehru does not seem to have been aware of the full implications at the outset, he was fighting for his political life. He did not conceal his dissatisfaction with the outcome of the presidential election and hinted that he would not join the new Working Committee unless some of his ideological colleagues were included.[3] In the name of party unity, however, he dropped the condition and agreed to serve on the Committee, partly no doubt because of the renewed tension in

[1] *Congress Bulletin*, No. 5, July–August 1950, p. 210.
[2] The proceedings of the Nasik session are to be found in *Congress Bulletin*, No. 6, September–October 1950, pp. 224–37.
[3] Nehru, *Press Conferences 1950*, pp. 182–7.

Indo-Pakistani relations after one of the many U.N. abortive efforts to mediate in the Kashmir dispute.[1]

Before the year was out the duumvirate came to an end: at the age of seventy-five Sardar Patel was dead. The struggle for mastery of the party entered a new phase, but the contest no longer posed as grave a threat to Nehru's leadership. The Right had lost its most brilliant tactician and was unable to find an adequate replacement. Patel's supporters still occupied key positions in the machine, but they no longer had anyone who could challenge Nehru's stature.

The course of the crisis in 1950–1 reveals how marked was the conflict within India's governing party. Not only was the Right wing intent on asserting its control over Government policy. From the Left came an equally severe challenge. Just before the Sardar's death, Kripalani formed a Democratic Front within the Congress to act as a pressure group against the communalist wing. Another prominent moderate on the Left, Dr. P. C. Ghose of Bengal, abandoned the Congress and formed the Krishak Praja Mazdoor Party. Later the two groups merged into the Kisan Mazdoor Praja Party (Workers and Peasants People's Party) which drew considerable numbers of disgruntled Congressmen to its ranks. Eventually, the K.M.P.P. merged with the Socialists to form the Praja-Socialist Party, India's equivalent of Western Social-Democrats, with a strong infusion of Gandhism.[2]

By the beginning of 1951 factional strife had become alarming. The Right wing was in revolt and the Left was drifting away from the party, leaving Nehru increasingly isolated. At a special session of the All-India Congress Committee in January the leading protagonists made impassioned pleas for unity. Nehru himself was scathing in his denunciation of the party's passive outlook, factionalism and corruption. The Congress was suffering from inner rot, he said, which threatened to destroy a once great movement. Both the majority and the Left dissidents were at fault. The key issue on the agenda, the composition of the Central Election Committee, was left in abeyance while mediation efforts got under way.

---

[1] The report of Sir Owen Dixon was issued on 15 September 1950. For the text see *United Nations Security Council Official Records*, S/1791.

[2] For an analysis of the K.M.P.P. and the Praja-Socialist Party see Weiner, M., *Party Politics in India*, pp. 25–116.

As so often in the past, Nehru took the lead. With the aid of Maulana Azad he persuaded Kripalani to dissolve his Democratic Front on 3 May 1951, in the interests of national unity. This tactical victory was short-lived, however. Nehru had promised to use his influence to secure adequate representation for Kripalani and his followers on the powerful Central Election Committee. But when the A.I.C.C. met three days later Tandon had sufficient strength to refuse the Prime Minister's request. It was the second rebuff to Nehru, but not the last.

Kripalani resigned from the Congress, carrying many Left dissidents with him. The following month he and Ghosh merged their forces in the K.M.P.P. The battle within the Congress was moving in favour of the communalists and reactionaries, the disciples of Patel, now led by Tandon. The next round occurred in mid-July when the A.I.C.C. met in Bangalore to frame a programme for the general elections to be held at the end of the year. It followed Nehru's lead, indeed, was based upon a lengthy report of his stewardship as Prime Minister delivered to the Bangalore meeting. [1] But when he pressed for reconstitution of the Working Committee and the Central Election Committee the Right wing refused. It was at that point that Nehru apparently realized a showdown was inevitable.

The *casus belli* occurred a few days after the Bangalore session. On 18 July two of Nehru's closest colleagues, Rafi Ahmad Kidwai and Ajit Prasad Jain, resigned from the Congress and asked to be relieved of their Cabinet responsibilities. [2] Nehru replied that Congress membership was not an absolute condition of ministerial appointment and persuaded them to remain in the Cabinet. Tandon took this as a direct violation of party discipline and informed Nehru in a curt note that he held the position of Prime Minister at the pleasure of the Congress. To leave no doubt of his intent, he summoned the Working Committee for 12 August to consider the Kidwai-Jain affair. In the meantime Kidwai told Nehru of his decision to join the newly formed K.M.P.P. and offered to resign from the Cabinet once

[1] *Report to the All-India Congress Committee*, 6 July 1951.

[2] It is striking that all the main figures in the party crisis were from the United Provinces—Nehru, Tandon, Kripalani, Kidwai, Jain—an excellent illustration of the dominant influence of the United Provinces in Congress affairs as well as in the Government.

more. This time it was accepted. Jain stayed on in the Government.

As the fateful meeting of the Working Committee drew near Nehru finally took decisive action.[1] On 10 August, after an exchange of letters with Tandon, he took the dramatic step of resigning from the Working Committee and the Central Election Committee. It was a veritable explosion and brought the clash of personalities and ideologies into the open. Tandon offered to resign if Nehru would reconsider. Nehru was adamant, but stated that there was no reason for Tandon to resign.

Maulana Azad followed Nehru's lead on the 11th. The Working Committee began its session in Delhi, but the Prime Minister refused to attend. After two stormy days the High Command pleaded with Nehru and Tandon to confer and to seek a mutually satisfactory solution. The plea was in vain; their meeting on the 14th made no progress. The crux of the matter, later revealed by Tandon, was Nehru's insistence that the entire Working Committee be dissolved and a new one be formed, presumably in accordance with Nehru's wishes. Tandon refused on the grounds that a change was neither constitutional nor proper but he renewed his offer to resign the presidency. There matters stood in mid-August.

Behind the scenes pressure was being brought to bear by those who considered Nehru indispensable. It was not forgotten that the general elections were imminent. On 21 August the Congress Parliamentary Party—234 of the 279 M.P.s—reiterated its full confidence in his leadership. Nehru stood by his demand for a thorough revamping of the Working Committee. By refusing to give way, as he had on three occasions in the preceding year, his victory was assured. For in the last analysis he was indispensable to the Congress at the time, and most Congressmen knew it. On 6 September all remaining members of the Working Committee offered their resignations. Tandon refused to accept them on the grounds that they resulted from pressure. Nor would he accept Nehru's resignation, for 'Nehru represented the nation more than any other individual in India'. Hence he tendered his own resignation to the A.I.C.C. This

---

[1] The following narrative of the last stage of the crisis is based upon *Congress Bulletin*, No. 5, September 1951, pp. 159–62D.

was accepted on 9 September and Nehru was asked to take over the presidency. The triumph was now complete.

In his assertion of supreme power within the party Nehru had re-enacted the drama which had been played out in 1939 when Bose was forced to resign the presidency by the Mahatma. The technique was identical: he established himself as super-President of the party by insisting that the members of the Working Committee be selected with his approval; the argument of his supporters was also the same—indispensability. The only difference was that Nehru himself took over the position. He had learned well from his mentor. Since 1951 he has retained this extraordinary status in the Congress. He was President until 1954 and personally chose his successor, U. N. Dhebar.

What impelled Nehru to resign from the Working Committee and threaten the unity of the party, which he had prized so highly in the past? In a speech to Congress M.P.s he mentioned three reasons: an instinctive reaction to a deplorable trend of affairs; his changed relations with the party since Patel's death; and a desire to produce a salutary shock which would strengthen the Congress on the eve of the general elections.[1] His reasons for the assumption of the presidency were similar. Almost three years later he attributed his decision to 'weaknesses [that] had crept into the Congress in recent years —dissensions, internecine quarrels, petty rivalries and bickerings'. Beyond that was his conviction that if the Congress split into two or more fragments, 'the country would be swept away . . . [for] it is only the Congress which . . . was responsible for keeping India together . . .'[2]

Many doubted this claim of Congress indispensability, certainly after 1950. But few, if any, would have denied that Nehru was indispensable to the Congress. Subsequent events bore out this contention. Yet the immediate reaction to his triumph was not entirely favourable. As one British eyewitness remarked, 'it has left mixed sensations, ranging from tempered approval to condemnation of tactics employed to achieve his objective, and bitter criticism of his supposed motive'.[3]

[1] On 21 August 1956. *The Statesman* (Calcutta), 23 August 1951.
[2] Address to the Delhi State Congress. *The Hindu* (Madras), 19 May 1954.
[3] Correspondent of the London *Times*, 11 September 1951. Press reaction in India was very mixed indeed. *Hitavada* of Nagpur emphasized Nehru's irritation

The consequences of the crisis were far-reaching. For one thing, Nehru's assertion of leadership in party affairs rescued the Congress from a possible catastrophe at the polls. For another the ouster of Tandon eased the path to social reform, notably the enactment of the Hindu Code Bill. While the policy conflict ranged over the whole gamut of public affairs, perhaps the core issue was the speed at which Hinduism was to adjust to the modern world. Nehru's triumph meant a hastening of the process. Thirdly, it affirmed the supremacy of the parliamentary wing over the party apparatus—at least as long as Nehru is at the helm of affairs. Finally, the crisis marks a turning-point in Nehru's political life.

The duumvirate was effectively terminated by the rout of the Patelists; Nehru emerged as the undisputed leader of the party and the country; the Congress was now for the first time his instrument for effecting the programme of reform; and from that date Nehru's decisiveness increased, though not to the degree that many would have welcomed. He had risen to a serious challenge to his leadership and had demonstrated a talent for political in-fighting. He had acted firmly to safeguard his position and with it the plans with which he was identified. No individual remained to act as a brake on his enthusiasm for planning, modernization, social change and a foreign policy of neutralism. Powerful interest groups remained in opposition to some of his policies but they lacked a leader to challenge Nehru as Prime Minister and as super-President of the party. He was now the sole repository of final decisions, master in his own household. He was also alone in the sense that there was no longer any person of stature with the possible

at Tandon's manner (a view shared by Kripalani's weekly *Vigil*) and his distaste for the type of candidate being selected by the Central Election Committee. The *Tribune* of Ambala saw his action as a response to the dominant influence of the business community in party counsels. The *Statesman* of Calcutta and Delhi viewed it as a desire to stave off defeat in the elections. The *Free Press Journal* of Bombay argued that Nehru resigned to preserve Indian foreign policy. As for the ouster of Tandon, the press was disturbed by the implications. Many agreed that in acceding to Nehru's demand the party was largely dominated by the forthcoming elections. Some expressed misgivings about the precedent of one person holding the positions of Prime Minister and Congress President simultaneously. The *Statesman* was the most perspicacious in noting the dangers of excessive dependence on one man, a problem of increasing importance with the passage of time. Socialists decried the precedent of dual office as presaging a totalitarian drift in Congress politics, while Communists dismissed the change as of no real consequence.

exception of Maulana Azad upon whom he could depend for advice.

* * * *

Nehru's triumph within the Congress occurred at the eleventh hour, on the eve of free India's first general elections based upon universal adult suffrage. The concept of representative government was not novel in the sub-continent. As early as 1882 there had been municipal elections in British India. Thereafter, in 1909, 1921, 1937 and 1945, a steadily increasing proportion of the population had been given the franchise. But all these elections were conducted within the framework of limited responsible government; the levers of power and legal authority were still vested in the British Government.

The nation-wide election of 1951–2 was an historic experiment in constitutional democracy. It was the first to be held in a newly freed Asian state, a vital test of the adaptability of Western political processes to non-European peoples. Moreover, it was the first to be conducted under the auspices of a wholly Indian government which had only recently tasted the fruits of power. The electorate was the largest in the world, 173 million people (compared with about 30 million in the 1937 elections). Noteworthy, too, was the fact that over 80 per cent. of the electorate were illiterate and most of them completely unfamiliar with the technique and meaning of the ballot. Finally, unlike its predecessors, the Indian elections of 1951–2 held forth the prize of power and responsibility unqualified by the presence of a foreign ruler. All Asia watched the experiment of 'government by the people' in the largest 'uncommitted' state in the world. And the two super-powers followed its course with no less interest, for to a large extent the political fate of South-east Asia was involved.

The sheer magnitude of the operation commanded attention.[1] More than 3,800 seats had to be filled, 489 in the House of the People, the lower chamber of the Union Parliament, and 3,373 in the States. More than 17,000 candidates contested the elections, representing 59 parties; many thousands ran as Independents. The technical aspects alone merited the appellation

[1] The following statistics are taken from the Election Commission's *Report on the First General Elections in India, 1951–52.*

'gigantic'—over 2½ million ballot boxes, 600 million ballot papers, 133,000 polling stations and 196,000 polling booths. Because of the preponderant rate of illiteracy each party was allotted a symbol, a visible means of identification for the electors. The problem of delimiting constituencies was of formidable dimensions, as was the preparation of electoral rolls. And as a point of departure a new census had to be taken, to incorporate changes since the 1941 census and the major shifts of population after the Partition.

To ensure impartiality, the supervision, direction and control of the election machinery was vested in an independent Election Commission whose members are appointed by the President and whose tenure of office is identical to that of Supreme Court Judges. Assisting the Commission was a veritable army of officials, including Regional Commissioners, Chief Electoral Officers for each State, Electoral Registration Officers, Return- ing Officers, and Presiding and Polling Officers. Altogether, upwards of a million men were harnessed to the task of administering this exercise in political democracy.

On the purely technical level the election of 1951–2 was a striking success: at only seven of the 133,000 polling stations was the voting adjourned because of violence; in 193 other cases a re-vote was necessary; all told, 1,250 offences were recorded, but more than 800 fell into the category of impersonation. The achievement was especially impressive in view of the high rate of illiteracy, the unfamiliarity of many candidates, officials and voters with the electoral procedure, and the relative haste with which the administrative preparations were completed; less than two years had elapsed between the inauguration of the Constitu- tion and the actual polling.

To the credit of the Congress Government the Election Com- mission was given a free hand; virtually no evidence of political interference was reported. Nehru himself took great pains to ensure the Commission's autonomy. Thus, for example, when approached by a party colleague to delay the elections because the Congress had only recently emerged from the ordeal of factional strife, he replied firmly: 'It is not possible to change the date of elections at all now. They have been finally fixed after great trouble. This is a matter entirely in the hands of the Election Commissioner and the Government does not interfere.'[1] This refusal to interfere with the electoral process flowed from his oft-expressed view that 'the coming elections are important, but it is far more important to know exactly what we stand for and how we want to function in the future. It is better to keep our soul and to lose an election than to win that election in the wrong way and with wrong methods.'[2]

This is not to suggest, however, that Nehru was indifferent to the election results. On the contrary, from the moment he assumed the Congress presidency on 9 September 1951 he brought the full weight of his influence to bear directly on the campaign. Indeed, that action itself set the campaign in motion: the Congress became synonymous with Nehru and Nehru was the popular idol of the masses. From that point onwards the outcome was no longer in doubt.

The Congress campaign was a one-man affair—Nehru, Nehru and more Nehru. He was chief of staff, field commander, spokesman and foot-soldier at one and the same time. It was he who drafted the party's election manifesto, embodying the well-known principles of his foreign policy, the stress on secularism, social reform, education and economic development. It was he who set the tone of the party's appeal—selfless service, devotion to basic principles and faith in the Indian people. In the concluding words of his presidential address to the Congress on 18 October 1951, he admonished his followers: 'We have to pull ourselves up from narrow grooves of thought and action, from factions, from mutual recrimination, from tolerance of evil in public life and in our social structure and become again fighters for a cause and upholders of high principles. Let us not attach too much importance to winning or losing an election. If we win a fight within ourselves, then other triumphs will come to us also.'[3] Nehru the incorruptible, Nehru the dedicated public servant, Nehru, the favourite son of the Mahatma, had taken charge of the Congress.

In accordance with his declared aim of cleansing the party, he laid down the criteria for selection of Congress candidates: known integrity; a non-communal outlook; a 'progressive social outlook'; lengthy service in the Congress; and he also urged

[1] Unpublished Nehru-Mahmud Correspondence, 20 November 1951.
[2] *Report to the All-India Congress Committee* (6 July 1951), p. 18.
[3] *Presidential Address, Indian National Congress, Fifty-Seventh Session*, pp. 20–21.

adequate representation of women, minority communities and various groups in the party. But in vain. Nehru could lay down policy objectives and act as the voice of the party, but the machine remained in the hands of the professionals who were solely interested in winning elections and reaping the fruits of power. Although he had ousted Tandon from the presidency, Nehru could not assert his authority in organizational matters. This he admitted in a letter to the Chairmen of the Pradesh (State) Election Committees: 'I want to confess . . . that an examination of the lists sent to us has considerably depressed me. . . . Indeed I find it difficult to justify the inclusion of some names. . . . I am greatly disappointed that, in spite of my efforts, the result is so poor.'[1] He was being used by the party but not followed.

If the party politicians were not prepared to heed his call, the masses were, and they showed their devotion in the tumultuous receptions given him everywhere. Nehru's election tour in 1951 was a prodigious feat of endurance, a re-enactment of the 1937 campaign. He travelled by almost every conceivable means of transport—plane, train, boat, automobile, horse, and even on foot. Official estimates place the number of persons who heard him at 30,000,000. According to one person who accompanied him during his campaign, they covered over 30,000 miles in forty-three days. Often Nehru delivered as many as nine speeches a day, besides brief roadside talks. Despite this blistering pace, with an average of five hours' rest a day, he seemed tireless. (He was sixty-two at the time.)

As in 1937 he fought the campaign on broad issues, not on the qualities of individual candidates, a wise strategy in view of the widespread disillusionment with local Congress officials. He hammered on the historic role of the Congress as the bearer of Indian freedom and on the unfinished character of the national revolution. He exhorted his people to grow more food (India was then in the throes of a critical food shortage); called for renewed efforts at unity; pledged himself to a ceaseless war on poverty; attacked unprincipled alliances of opposition parties; questioned the sincerity of the Princes who were standing for election; defended his government's record at home and abroad —the integration of the States, land reform, economic planning

[1] On 13 October 1951. *Congress Bulletin*, No. 6, October–November 1951, p. 231.

and his foreign policy, and sought a rededication to the ideals which had animated the nationalist movement. He did not deny mistakes or weaknesses in the Congress record. Thus, to a crowd of 100,000 in the capital of Orissa he admitted that corruption still existed in the Government of India. Firm steps had been taken and it had been checked somewhat, he said, but 'we have not been able to wipe it out completely'.[1] It was this willingness to keep faith with the masses, along with other qualities, which endeared him to them and overcame their antipathy to many individual Congressmen.

Among the rival contenders for power he singled out the communal parties for special attack. Theirs was an evil philosophy, he declared over and over again, the gravest threat to Indian unity, progress and stability. One of the variants of this philosophy had already led to the partition of the sub-continent; the other was equally dangerous and must be eradicated from the minds of men. At times his primary objective seemed to be the defeat of communalist candidates rather than the election of Congressmen. With the parties of the Left he was much more moderate. In fact he showed positive sympathy for the Socialists. 'The Socialist Party contains some of my old intimate friends whom I admire and respect', he said in the midst of the campaign. 'I have not criticized a single member . . . by name or otherwise.'[2] On another occasion he referred to the Socialist Party's economic programme as one 'with which I am in substantial agreement'.[3] This lack of campaign orthodoxy extended in some measure to the Communist Party's goals, though he severely criticized its methods, especially resort to violence. But these concessions did not appreciably mar the effect of his campaign. People came in droves to hear and to see him. They listened and many of them believed. It was a *tour de force*.

Despite the large number of political groups and independent candidates, the contest centred on five parties of all-India stature: the Congress, the K.M.P.P., the Socialist Party, the Communist Party and the Jan Sangh, the most powerful of three Hindu communalist parties. Stripped of the mass of verbiage which poured forth day by day, the campaign focused

---

[1] In answer to Kripalani's charge. *Tribune* (Ambala), 17 December 1951.
[2] On 3 November 1951. *Press Conferences 1951*, p. 71.
[3] *Hindusthan Standard* (Calcutta), 19 December 1951.

on one question only—for or against the Congress. This is not to say that the party programmes were devoid of content. Rather, that all opposition parties concentrated their fire on the Congress record—the blunders, the failures, the shortcomings, the unfulfilled promises, real and alleged—much more than on the positive alternatives which a change in government would entail. Nor did any of these parties seriously expect to oust the Congress from power, certainly not at the Centre and in most of the States. Their primary objective seems to have been to whittle down the Congress majorities and to establish themselves as contenders for future power. How did they fare?[1]

The Congress won an overwhelming majority of *seats* in Parliament (362 of 489) and a working majority in all States except Madras, Orissa, PEPSU (Patiala and East Punjab States Union) and Travancore-Cochin, and in these four it had the largest single bloc of seats. Only in Tripura, a centrally administered strategic frontier area close to China, was it defeated—by the Communists who won its two seats in Parliament. However, in terms of *votes* the Congress was a minority government, with 45 per cent. of the total at the Centre and 42 per cent. of the total in the States. The discrepancy between seats and votes is to be explained by the fragmentation of votes among many opposition groups and the use of the single-member constituency. Only in one State, Saurashtra, did the Congress secure an absolute majority of votes. Thus, while it was returned to power everywhere, more than half the ballots expressed discontent with Congress stewardship during the early years of the Indian Republic.

The Socialists were the second largest party in terms of votes (10·6 per cent. at the Centre and just short of 10 per cent. in the States) but they secured very few seats, only twelve in Parliament. Most observers had predicted a much more impressive performance by this moderate Left party. By contrast, the Communists showed surprising strength in the southern part of the country. Although they received only 3·3 per cent of the votes at the Centre and 4·4 per cent in the States, they returned the largest bloc of opposition Members of Parliament (sixteen) and formed the opposition in four State Assemblies—Madras,

[1] The following statistics are taken from the Election Commission's *Report on the First General Elections in India, 1951–52.*

Hyderabad, West Bengal and Travancore-Cochin.[1] The reason for the discrepancy in Socialist and Communist seats and votes is that the Socialists ran many candidates while the Communists concentrated on those areas where they had considerable strength. The K.M.P.P. showed surprising strength in view of the fact that it was formed less than six months before the elections; it won 5·8 per cent. of the votes and nine seats in Parliament, a heavy price for factionalism in the Congress in the year before the elections. The Jan Sangh secured 3·1 per cent. of the votes and three seats in Parliament, and its ideological allies, the Hindu Mahasabha and the Ram Rajya Parishad, fared even worse—largely due to Nehru's merciless attack on communalism.

Apart from the five principal parties, forty other groups secured representation either in Parliament or in a State Assembly. These ranged from the Akali Dal, a militant Sikh party in the Punjab and PEPSU, which won thirty-three seats in the State Assemblies and four seats in Parliament, to the Mao Maram Union representing tribal groups in Manipur. Moreover, approximately 30 per cent. of all votes for the State Assemblies went to Independents, most of whom were well-known only in the particular constituency which they contested. Another striking feature of the elections was the large number of prominent politicians who went down to defeat. Only two leaders of all-India parties were elected—Nehru and Dr. S. P. Mookerjee, the founder of the Jan Sangh. Many leading Socialists were rejected by the voters, as were Kripalani, Dr. P. C. Ghose and Ambedkar.

Perhaps the most encouraging feature of India's experiment in democracy was the response of the electorate. More than 105,000,000 persons or 60 per cent. of the voters cast their ballot, a figure which compares favourably with many well-established democracies in the West. No less important was the lively interest shown by the electorate. Many observers, this writer among them, were struck by the eagerness with which illiterate peasants listened to the army of speakers who scoured the countryside in search for support at the polls. Indeed, one of

[1] The Communist Party was banned in Hyderabad and in Travancore-Cochin (Kerala), but it dominated the People's Democratic Front and the United Front of Leftists which ran candidates in these States respectively.

the noteworthy features of the experiment was the much greater indifference of urban voters. Whereas the illiterate waited patiently for their turn to vote, sometimes many hours, white-collar workers and sophisticated men and women of the cities frequently left the polling station without casting their ballot. The deeply rooted belief in the West that democratic processes are suitable only to highly literate societies was seriously questioned by the Indian elections in 1951–2.

It may well be that uneducated people are less well equipped to make a meaningful choice among alternative candidates, parties and programmes. But a cursory glance at some of the election results in 'advanced' countries of the West during the past twenty-five years casts serious doubt on the claim of a direct correlation between education and political intelligence. It is true that the voting behaviour revealed instances of total misunderstanding of the electoral process. Many women were reluctant to identify themselves by giving their husbands' names to the polling officers. Some villagers interpreted it to mean a *tamasha* and dressed for the occasion as if it marked a new festival. Some women in *purdah* refused to vote because separate booths were not provided. Some villages voted *en masse*. In one case the choice for an entire village was made by a wrestling match between representatives of the candidates! Some voters looked upon the ballot box as a new idol to be worshipped. Others took the party symbols literally and acted as if they were giving their vote to the bullocks, camel, lion or other symbol of a party. However, these episodes were merely amusing deviations from the norm and, in numbers, infinitesimal when set against the total electorate.

More serious, but more difficult to gauge, was the influence of caste, community, language and local loyalties. Undoubtedly these bonds affected the judgement of many voters—and still do. It could not be otherwise, for they are rooted in an ancient social structure and cultural tradition. Personality also played a key role and will continue to do so as long as the bulk of the electorate can acquire knowledge only through the spoken word. Sectional factors diverted attention from purely political issues, more so than in the West. But the cardinal fact remains that the election was held, that the process was free, peaceful and orderly, that more than half the electorate cast their ballot and that an historic precedent was established—the right of the people to determine their government by periodic elections without restriction as to race, sex, education, religion, language, occupation or any other illiberal criterion. The very fact that the Government of India honoured its pledge and that the election took place gives it a unique importance.

The Congress victory at the polls did not occasion surprise. If anything, most observers had predicted much greater popular support for the governing party of India, the party of Gandhi, the party which had borne the brunt of the struggle for freedom, the party which symbolized the achievement of Independence. That it won less than half the total votes was partly due to the crisis of 1950–1 and the defection of the Kripalani group. Beyond this, however, was an inevitable reaction against the governing party because of the glaring gap between promise and fulfilment.

When in opposition the Congress had promised to transform the 'old' India and to eradicate the many ills that beset an economically depressed society—poverty, illiteracy, disease, famine and fear. It is doubtful whether Congress leaders seriously believed that this could be accomplished within their lifetime. But the cumulative effect of these pledges was an unrealistic expectation of plenty. Even had the transfer of power been free from the upheavals which threatened the very survival of the state, even had India remained united, there would not have been any appreciable improvement in the standard of living four years later. As it happened, the transition period strained the resources of the Government to the breaking-point. Indeed, material conditions were probably worse in 1951 than on the eve of the second world war. The Government was not entirely responsible for this state of affairs, but in the eyes of the Indian people it was accountable. Moreover, India in 1951 was in the grip of near-famine conditions. Nor did the Congress implement its long-standing pledge of sweeping land reform. Its positive record seemed to many woefully short of the paradise which nationalists had been led to expect. Hence the large vote of protest.

That the Congress succeeded in returning to power was due to three factors. Firstly, it alone had established roots in the countryside, a powerful machine extending to most villages and direct contact with the masses for a period of thirty years. Gandhi's revolutionary transformation of the Congress from an urban club to a mass organization in 1920 had paid rich dividends. So too did his 'recommendation' in 1936 that future annual sessions of the party be held in a village setting. Secondly none of the opposition parties offered an impressive alternative programme. Nor could they invoke the hallowed name of the Mahatma, so long associated with the Congress. But the decisive reason was Nehru's matchless popularity with India's millions.

As the acknowledged successor of Gandhi he was the visible link with the past greatness of the Congress, the sole surviving hero of the Indian freedom struggle. In his own right he was a popular idol and the voice of the future, of a better world for the common man. It was he who persuaded the electorate that the Congress was still the most potent instrument of national regeneration. In so doing he carried many Congress candidates into the legislatures, for despite the disillusionment with the Congress record, Nehru himself was above reproach. For many, a vote for the Congress was an expression of faith in one man. As some voters put it, 'We want Nehru's box.' This was also the consensus of Indian comment on the 1951–2 elections. In the words of one newspaper editor, 'Nehru and not Congress has been voted to power in the so-called Congress States.'[1] No impartial observer would disagree.

Nehru himself was less sanguine about the implications of the vote than most of his colleagues who basked in the glory of renewed power. As soon as the results were apparent he set down his thoughts in a self-critical letter to the Presidents of the Provincial Congress Committees. It is 'essential for us to make an objective and correct appraisal', he warned them. There was an understandable expression of pride in the Congress victory but no illusions about the 'quite remarkable reverses' in certain areas. Nor did he shrink from the harsh reality of Congress weaknesses: it is 'true to say that the Congress organization as such has not usually played a satisfactory part in many States. . . . Where we have won, this was not always due to the Congress organization. Indeed, the Congress organization, as a whole, rather failed in this test.' As for the party's candidates, 'our

[1] *Pioneer* (Lucknow), 2 February 1952.

choice . . . sometimes was not good'. But 'the important thing . . . was the almost utter lack of discipline, both among Congress candidates and among Congressmen. . . . The success . . . is a matter of good fortune. . . . The defeats . . . are a just punishment. Let us not find excuses and blame others. The fault is ours.' Five years later, after India's second general election, this sober critique was equally valid.

He paid tribute to the political intelligence of the masses, 'truly surprising', he wrote; '. . . even though largely illiterate, they showed a broad understanding of issues. . . . Indeed, oddly enough the so-called illiterate voter has done probably better than many of the literates.' The defeat of communalism was 'significant and heartening. But it is by no means a complete success.' Surveying the party at that juncture he judged it 'a very feeble instrument for carrying out national work'. Moreover, Congress committees 'have often become close preserves'.

Turning to the future, the great problem was 'how to bring in the youth of the country'. The Congress, warned Nehru, must eschew all factions. Discipline was essential, as was renewed personal contact with the masses. And the Congress must function as a compact political party with a well-defined economic programme, not as a heterogeneous movement.[1] This criticism was wholly justified by the election verdict. And the prescription for the party's ills was a model programme for the future. But the advice was ignored, with the result that the Congress has become steadily weaker in recent years. The rot continues to take its toll.

---

[1] The text of this letter is to be found in *Congress Bulletin*, No. 1, January–February 1952, pp. 11–16. An almost identical letter was sent to all Congress candidates. Ibid., pp. 19–26.

CHAPTER XVII

Democracy at Work

THE general election of 1951–2 represents a bridge between India's 'time of troubles' and a period of consolidation and growth. It was, too, the first major test of political democracy in the new Republic. India passed that test with high honours. But how has democracy fared since? And what role has Nehru played in this crucial experiment in politics by consent, an experiment which will influence the course of events all over Asia? It is to these questions that this chapter is directed. Attention will be focused on the political highlights of the past decade: the central Cabinet and decision-making; Parliament in practice; election experience in the States and the country at large; States Reorganization; the language controversy; the Congress malaise; and Nehru's abortive efforts to resign from office.

* * * *

In form, functions and powers, the Indian Cabinet follows the established British model. The executive power of the Union of India is vested in the President who is 'aided and advised' by a Council of Ministers (Cabinet) headed by a Prime Minister. The President appoints the Prime Minister—by convention, the leader of that party which commands a majority in the Lower House of Parliament—and, upon his advice, all other members of the Cabinet. Ministers must hold seats in the legislature within six months of their appointment. They retain office 'during the pleasure of the President', but the Cabinet is responsible to the Lower House. It is expected to function on the principle of joint responsibility and remains in office as long as it maintains the 'confidence' of the legislature. If defeated on a major issue, the Cabinet must either give way to another capable of commanding a majority in Parliament or must dissolve the legislature and call for new elections. As in Cabinet systems of government elsewhere, the Indian Cabinet drafts and

20. Being congratulated on his 65th birthday (14 Nov. 1954) by a villager

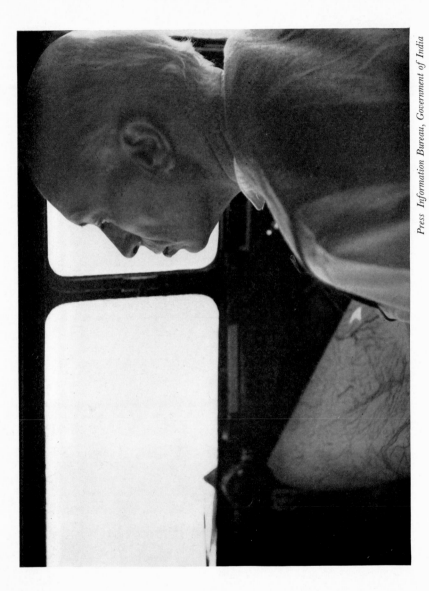

21. In his plane during an aerial survey of the flood-affected areas in Bihar in November, 1953

presents the government's legislative programme and conducts the business of the Union.[1]

There have been four Indian Cabinets since 1947, all headed by Nehru and all composed largely of Congressmen.[2] At no time has the Government been in danger from a vote of 'no confidence', for the Congress has had an overwhelming majority in Parliament thus far.[3] Hence the Cabinet system in India has known a high degree of stability. This has been one of its distinguishing features. Another has been Nehru's pre-eminence.

Only two members of the first Cabinet still held ministerial posts in the summer of 1958—Nehru and Jagjivan Ram, a Congress leader of the Untouchables. A third Cabinet veteran was Maulana Azad, Minister of Education (and later, of Natural Resources and Scientific Research as well) from 1947 until his death early in 1958. Others with lengthy periods of service were Rajkumari Amrit Kaur, the only woman in the Cabinet, who was Minister of Health until 1957; Rafi Ahmad Kidwai, a Muslim leader from the United Provinces, from 1947 until his death in the autumn of 1954; Gopalaswami Ayyangar, a tower of strength from 1947 until his death in the spring of 1953; Baldev Singh, the Sikh leader who participated in the final negotiations leading to the transfer of power, Defence Minister from 1947 to 1952; C. D. Deshmukh, who held the Finance portfolio from 1950 until 1956; and Ajit Prasad Jain, who has held ministerial office since 1950, rising to senior Cabinet status in 1954. Relative newcomers include the three most influential persons after Nehru: Pandit Govind Ballabh Pant, the former Chief Minister of the U.P., Home Minister since the beginning

[1] The constitutional provisions relating to the Cabinet are to be found in Articles 74, 75, 77, and 78 of *The Constitution of India* (1949).

[2] These were formed on 15 August 1947 (Independence Day); 26 January 1950 (Republic Day); 13 May 1952, following the first general election; and on 17 April 1957, after the second general election. The Cabinet was also formally reconstituted on 6 May 1950, soon after the resignation of two senior ministers, Mookerjee and Neogy.

[3] Congress representation in the central legislature is as follows:

(a) The Constituent Assembly (provisional Parliament from 1947 to 1952): 205 of the 296 members from British India.

(b) First Parliament (1952–7): 364 of the 489 elected members to the House of the People.

(c) Second Parliament (1957–): 365 of the 494 elected members to the House of the People.

These figures represent the totals at the time of election.

Q

of 1955; Morarji Desai, the former Chief Minister of Bombay, who entered the Cabinet as Minister of Commerce and Industry in the autumn of 1956 and moved up to the Finance Ministry early in 1958; and V. K. Krishna Menon, who joined the Cabinet at the beginning of 1956 without portfolio and was later given the Defence Ministry.[1]

India is a federal state, in theory at least. It is also a nation of diverse creeds, castes and languages. By convention the principal regions of the country and the major divisions of its population should be represented in the Cabinet. India adheres to this convention by and large—with one notable exception. From the outset a disproportionate share of senior ministerial posts has gone to two States—Uttar Pradesh (the former United Provinces or U.P.) and Bombay. In 1957, for example, they accounted for seven of the thirteen Cabinet Members.[2] In terms of communal representation, there were twenty-three Hindu Members of the Cabinet and Ministers of State, including an Untouchable (Ram), two Muslims (Azad and Kabir), a Sikh (Swaran Singh) and a Jain (Ajit Prasad Jain). Among the Hindus, Brahmins predominated with twelve, headed by Nehru and Pant. As might be expected, Sanskrit-derived languages were spoken by the vast majority (twenty-four out of twenty-seven). Members of the Cabinet on the whole come from cities while Ministers of State are from towns and villages. The majority are from well-to-do families. The educational level is extremely high; almost 90 per cent. of Cabinet Members

---

[1] Since Independence there have been three ministerial ranks in the central Government: Members of the Cabinet, whose number has remained relatively unchanged; Ministers of State, later designated as Ministers of Cabinet Rank; and Deputy Ministers. The last two categories have proliferated over the years. Until the inauguration of the Union at the beginning of 1950 there were fourteen Members of the Cabinet, four Ministers of State and two Deputy Ministers. In the Council of Ministers formed after the 1957 elections there were thirteen Members of the Cabinet, fourteen Ministers of State and twelve Deputy Ministers. All those mentioned above were Members of the Cabinet.

[2] The U.P. contingent consisted of Nehru (Prime Minister and External Affairs, as well as the Department of Atomic Energy); Pant (Home); Shastri (Transport and Communications); and Jain (Food and Agriculture). From Bombay came Morarji Desai (Commerce and Industry); Nanda (Labour and Employment and Planning); and S. K. Patil (Irrigation and Power). No less striking than the preponderance of the U.P. and Bombay was the under-representation of south India —only three: Krishnamachari (Finance); Reddy (Works, Housing and Supply); and Krishna Menon (Defence). The composition of the Council of Ministers formed in 1957 is to be found in *The Hindu Weekly Review* (Madras), 22 April, 1957.

received a university or college education. Many were trained for the law. Perhaps the most noteworthy fact is that sixteen of the twenty-seven (proudly) claim imprisonment under the British *Raj*. No wonder, then, that a prison record—for political activities—has been dubbed 'the union card' for influence in the Congress and, therefore, in the Government. The average age of Cabinet Members was fifty-eight; five of the thirteen were more than sixty and three over sixty-five—Nehru, Pant and Azad.[1]

A curious feature of Indian Cabinets, especially in the early years, was their inclusion of Independents and even representatives of other parties, despite the large Congress majority in Parliament. Of the fourteen Cabinet Members in the first Council of Ministers there were five non-Congressmen.[2] Gradually their number was reduced, as the crisis affecting the nation as a whole diminished. By the summer of 1950 only three non-Congressmen remained; by 1953 there were only two; and by 1958 the senior level of the Council of Ministers was exclusively Congress.

Which persons left a mark on the conduct of affairs during the first eleven years of the experiment in Cabinet government? Or was Nehru's influence and leadership so all-embracing that none came to the fore? Until 1950 the answers are conclusive. Within the Cabinet was a 'super-Cabinet' of two men, Nehru and Patel, who made all the decisions of substance. The only other person whose counsel was regularly sought by the duumvirs, especially Nehru, was Maulana Azad, the dean of India's nationalist Muslims.

With Patel's death at the end of 1950, Nehru's leadership was strengthened—in the Cabinet as elsewhere. During the next four years the Prime Minister relied heavily on three colleagues: Azad, Ayyangar, and Kidwai, protégé of the elder Nehru, an able administrator and political tactician who achieved notable

---

[1] Based upon data furnished by the Cabinet Secretariat in New Delhi and the *Times of India: Directory and Year Book including Who's Who 1957–58* (Bombay, 1958). For a detailed study of the 1956 Council of Ministers see North, Robert C., *The Indian Council of Ministers: A Study of Origins* (paper presented at a seminar on 'Leadership and Political Institutions in India', University of California, Berkeley, 1956).

[2] Dr. John Matthai, a south Indian Christian and prominent financier (Transport, later Finance); Sir R. K. Shanmukham Chetty, a leading south Indian

success as Minister of Food and Agriculture. In financial matters Deshmukh had a relatively free hand. By 1954 Ayyangar and Kidwai were dead. Two years later Deshmukh resigned. By that time the inner Cabinet circle comprised Pant, Desai and Azad in domestic affairs, and Menon in foreign policy. The Maulana's death in 1958 left the domestic field to Pant and Desai.

It is impossible for an outsider to know with certainty how decisions are reached in any Cabinet. Nevertheless, there is substantial evidence that the Indian Cabinet has not always functioned smoothly—there have been eight resignations over policy matters since Independence. Four concerned economic issues, in whole or in part; two arose from Indo-Pakistani relations; one from States Reorganization, and one from the Mundhra Affair, India's 'scandal of the decade'. Only one person was a Congressman of long standing.

The first to go was Sir Shanmukham Chetty, in 1948. A commission of inquiry had been established soon after Independence to examine cases of alleged tax evasion. Various industrialists approached Chetty who, at his own discretion, exempted them from taxes for certain categories in certain years. Although this was apparently within his competence as Finance Minister, he was reticent about his actions. The aura of mystery gave rise to charges of partisanship and the use of his official position to aid friends. The Opposition, and many Congressmen who disliked his appointment initially, were given a political handle which they used to good effect. Chetty resigned. In explaining his decisions before Parliament, he made an able defence, and many felt that had he done so earlier he could have remained in the Cabinet without qualms.

The year 1950 witnessed the resignation of three more non-Congress ministers. Two of them, Mookerjee (Industry and Supply) and K. C. Neogy (Commerce), withdrew in April over the Nehru–Liaquat Ali Pact to ease the tension created by large-scale migration from East to West Bengal. Mookerjee in particular criticized the Pact severely, terming it appeasement of

merchant-banker (Finance); Dr. C. H. Babha, a Parsi (Commerce); Dr. Shyama Prasad Mookerjee, sometime leader of the communalist Hindu Mahasabha (Industry and Supply); and Dr. B. R. Ambedkar, the outstanding political figure among the Untouchables (Law).

Pakistan and a betrayal of Bengali Hindus.[1] As noted earlier, they were not alone in their hostility to the Pact. But the Congress critics in the Cabinet, notably Patel, did not break ranks.

A few months later the highly respected Dr. John Matthai, who had succeeded Chetty in the Finance portfolio, left the Government. According to Matthai himself, the crucial issue was a disagreement with the Prime Minister over the status, functions and scope of the Planning Commission, then under discussion. Nehru proposed senior Cabinet rank and emoluments for all its members; he also favoured a very ambitious national plan. The Finance Minister objected on two grounds. First, the Planning Commission would become a 'super-Cabinet' responsible to no one but itself, a grave infringement of the principles of parliamentary government; the real clash in this context was the relationship of the Finance Ministry to the Commission, and Matthai argued that the Commission would be a favoured body. He also questioned the wisdom of a grandiose plan in 1950, when India's financial position was precarious. There were many specific planning projects drafted by civil servants before the transfer of power; it was preferable to implement these first, he argued, for there would be no need to resort to deficit spending and other unorthodox financial devices.

Closely related was the encroachment on the Finance Minister's authority, dramatized by an incident affecting a ministry under Nehru's direct control—External Affairs—and Krishna Menon. At Menon's request the Finance Committee of the Cabinet agreed to the appointment of an Indian Ambassador to Eire, the position to be held jointly by the High Commissioner to the United Kingdom, who was Menon at the time. This decision was reached, however, on the understanding that there would be no building or staff because of India's financial straits. The Ministry of External Affairs (Nehru) accepted, but Menon insisted on a building and staff. The Cabinet ultimately yielded to Menon's wishes, against the Finance Committee's recommendation. Matthai took this as a direct slap. He also had 'grave misgivings' about the Nehru–Liaquat Ali Pact. His

[1] For the text of Mookerjee's resignation speech see *The Statesman* (Calcutta), overseas edition, 22 April 1950. A summary is to be found in the *New York Times*, 19 April 1950.

resignation was accompanied by harsh words, but the friction passed; and Matthai later served as head of the newly created State Bank.[1] Another unstated factor appears to have been party pressure for a Congress Minister of Finance. In the end a compromise was found in the person of C. D. Deshmukh, a distinguished civil servant who had recently become an Associate Member of the Congress and was in sympathy with its goals.

The sharpest criticism among those who resigned from the Indian Cabinet came from Dr. B. R. Ambedkar, the Untouchable leader. In a lengthy, trenchant statement to Parliament on 11 October 1951, the former Law Minister condemned the Union Government for various sins of omission and commission. Five reasons were given for his resignation. First, he claimed that he was not entrusted with sufficient responsibility in the Cabinet; some of his listeners were surprised, for it was Ambedkar who steered the Draft Constitution through the Constituent Assembly. Of greater substance was his charge of unfair treatment to members of his own community: 'The same old tyranny . . . oppression [and] discrimination which existed before exists now and perhaps in a worse form.' He also dissented from Nehru's foreign policy, arguing that all states wished India well at the time of Independence but that 'to-day . . . we have no friends left'. More specifically, he attacked the policy of friendship with China, on the grounds that it alienated the United States, and the official view on Kashmir. He suggested partition as a way out of the impasse. On decision-making within the Government he was hardly discreet, terming the Cabinet 'merely a recording . . . office of decisions already arrived at by committees' working behind 'an iron curtain'. Nehru himself was not spared. Ambedkar deprecated the shelving of the Hindu Code Bill because of the opposition of orthodox Hindus and remarked, 'I got the impression that the Prime Minister, although sincere, had not the earnestness and determination to get [it] through [Parliament].' Confining legislation to economic measures, he concluded, 'is to make

[1] This account is based largely on conversations with Dr. Matthai and others in India in 1956 and a public exchange between Matthai and Nehru at the time of his resignation. See the *Times of India* (Bombay), 2 June 1950, and Nehru's remarks at a press conference on 7 July 1950, in the *Times of India* (Bombay), 8 July.

a farce of our constitution and to build a palace on a dung heap'.[1]

The Congress never forgot this outburst. In the general election of 1951–2 it opposed Ambedkar in a Bombay constituency—successfully. A year later the Congress again frustrated his effort to secure a seat in Parliament. Ambedkar became increasingly bitter and lavished even harsher criticism on the Government in the spring of 1956.[2] Just before his death a few months later he was converted to Buddhism and called on the Untouchables to follow him. Hundreds of thousands did so.

The next spate of Cabinet dissension occurred in 1954 and early 1955. Altogether there were two threats and one actual resignation. It began at the end of March 1954, with rumours that Deshmukh was on the verge of resignation because of differences with Nehru over financial measures. More specifically, Deshmukh was reported to be aroused by the Chanda Report, which would have limited the authority and control of the Finance Minister; further, that he strongly urged rationalization of the Indian textile industry in order to survive the challenge of Japanese competition. It was also believed that Nehru was impatient with the pace at which appropriations were being made available for Community Development projects. Some observers saw the episode as a symptom of a struggle between the Civil Service and the Congress for direction of affairs. After a flurry of activity Nehru persuaded him to withdraw his resignation by an assurance of unqualified support.[3]

A similar incident occurred in the autumn of 1954, just after Nehru returned from his China tour. Prior to the tour he had agreed to consider a pig-iron and steel project proposed by G. D. Birla, one of India's leading industrialists. After the tour, however, the Government's attitude to private enterprise hardened, and the project was turned down. India was on the eve of moving towards a 'socialist pattern of society'.[4] The Minister

[1] The text of Ambedkar's statement is to be found in *The Statesman* (Calcutta), 12 October 1951. See also the *New York Times*, the *New York Herald Tribune*, and the *Manchester Guardian* of the same date.

[2] During a conversation with the author in New Delhi in May 1956.

[3] See *The Times* (London), 9 April 1954, *The Hindu* (Madras), and the *Manchester Guardian*, 10 April 1954.

[4] See pp. 528–9 below.

of Commerce and Industry, T. T. Krishnamachari, was incensed, claiming that the rejection of Birla's scheme was inconsistent with encouragement to private enterprise. Moreover, he
wanted the abolition of the Production Ministry, one of Nehru's
favourites, and control over raw materials. While the Prime
Minister was in London for a Commonwealth Conference at the
beginning of 1955, Krishnamachari submitted his resignation
and went home to Madras. When Nehru returned he called
T.T.K. to Delhi and found a compromise solution—placing the
iron and steel industry under Krishnamachari's jurisdiction and
retaining the Production Ministry, with the understanding that
it would be concerned only with the 'public sector' while Commerce and Industry would deal with the 'private sector'.
Krishnamachari gave way.[1]

One Cabinet member, however, did not give way. On 30
August 1954 V. V. Giri, the Labour Minister, tendered his
resignation. The issue was the Government's downward revision of an arbitral wage award to bank employees. Giri, a
prominent trade unionist, insisted that the award be accepted
without change for one year, after which another inquiry might
be held. Deshmukh and Krishnamachari opposed the award on
the grounds that it would have adverse economic consequences.
The Cabinet yielded to their pressure and Giri resigned. In an
accompanying letter he indicated that various ministries had
pursued conflicting labour policies during the preceding two and
a half years, and 'each can have its own way'. In a wider sense
he charged that there was a 'certain outlook and a certain philosophy' in the Cabinet which had eroded the authority of the
Labour Ministry. Socialist and Communist leaders applauded
his action.[2]

The most dramatic resignation and one which provides the
greatest insight into the workings of the Indian Cabinet was that
of C. D. Deshmukh, the Finance Minister from 1950 to 1956.
The only I.C.S. man in the Government, he had frequently
come into conflict with his Congress colleagues. But the issue
which culminated in his resignation was totally unrelated to

[1] Based on conversations with members of the Cabinet Secretariat. See also the
Manchester Guardian, 29 November 1954.
[2] The text of Giri's letter of resignation is to be found in *The Hindu* (Madras),
9 September 1954.

financial affairs. It was the highly charged struggle for control of Bombay City, in the nation-wide Reorganization of States.[1]

Briefly, the chain of events to Deshmukh's decision was as follows: The *Report of the States Reorganisation Commission* (SRC) in the autumn of 1955 had proposed a bilingual Greater Bombay State to include all of Maharashtra, all of Gujarat and Bombay City, as well as Saurashtra, Kutch and parts of the former Central Provinces. The Maharashtrians were strongly opposed. Fierce riots caused death and injury in Bombay City in January 1956. In the same month Nehru announced a decision in favour of central administration of the city. The Maharashtrians remained unreconciled and pressed for a separate Maharashtra State including Bombay City during the next four months. Then, early in June, Nehru announced to a Bombay audience a further change in the Government's decision: Bombay City would be administered by the Centre for five years after which, when passions had cooled, a final decision would be made by the people. It was this that led Deshmukh to resign. But in doing so, he gave vent to his dissatisfaction with the decision-making process in the Cabinet.

This he did in a lengthy statement to Parliament on 25 July 1956, parts of which merit attention in Deshmukh's own words. 'I have resigned because I do not wish to share the responsibility for Government's decision to separate the City of Bombay from Maharashtra . . . and because I wish to protest generally against the manner in which this issue, so vitally important . . . has been handled by the Prime Minister.' In particular he protested against the Government's failure to hold an inquiry into the police firings in Bombay and 'to the impropriety of the Prime Minister's announcement in early June in regard to the future of Bombay while the States Reorganization Bill was before the Lok Sabha [Lower House of Parliament] and had been referred to the select committee'.

He noted that he had been on the verge of resigning in January 1956 when Nehru first announced the decision for central administration of Bombay City—'which was not taken in the full Cabinet'—but was persuaded to postpone his decision until the matter was debated in Parliament. He then spelled

[1] The reorganization of States will be analysed more fully on pp. 479–89 below.

out the charge against Nehru's actions and the role of the Cabinet. '. . . discussions [in Parliament] were . . . gravely prejudiced by the extraordinary action of the Prime Minister in making his announcement in Bombay early last June. . . . There was no consideration of the proposal in the Cabinet or even by circulation. There was no individual consultation with members of the Cabinet known to be specially interested, as for instance, myself. There is no record even of a meeting of a committee of the Cabinet, and to this day no authoritative text of the so-called decision is available to the members of the Cabinet. . . . This instance is typical of the cavalier and unconstitutional manner in which decisions have been taken and announced on behalf of the Cabinet by certain unauthorized members of the Cabinet, including the Prime Minister, in matters concerning the reorganisation of the states. [Even] the separation of Andhra from Tamil Nad [Madras State in 1953] was decided upon and announced by the Prime Minister without reference to the Cabinet.' Despite these harsh words, Deshmukh paid tribute to the Prime Minister's 'constant and understanding support in the discharge of my duties, not to speak of his irreproachable courtesy, unlimited patience and unfailing consideration'.[1]

Nehru's initial response was moderate. 'I am reluctant to enter into a controversy which, to some extent, is of a personal character. Since we are ending our close association as members of Government I should like this parting to be with goodwill.' However, he chided Deshmukh for referring to Cabinet proceedings—'it is not usual to do so'—and denied that decisions were taken without proper consultation within the Cabinet. Regarding the propriety of his June announcement at a public meeting in Bombay, 'I am wholly unable to appreciate this argument. What I announced then was Government's policy which had already been included in the draft Bill before Parliament. The only additional statement . . . was that the future of Bombay might be decided five years later by Bombay. . . . [Aside from the need for clarification] it is the business of Government to declare its policy and place it before Parliament. It is open to the select committee to accept it, vary it or reject it. I had in fact stated [this] in Bombay . . .' As for the proposed

[1] *The Statesman* (Calcutta), 26 July 1956.

'udicial inquiry, it was felt that this would exacerbate the existing tension.[1]

A few days later Deshmukh repeated the basic charge that the two key decisions on Bombay City were taken without Cabinet consultation. Nehru's reply this time was blunt. 'I do not know where he got his facts from. I have consulted my papers, my Cabinet papers . . . and I say the two decisions . . . were made absolutely and repeatedly after consultations with every colleague of the Cabinet and with the full consent of the Cabinet. I have no doubt about it. And I say . . . this Bill itself was placed before the Cabinet . . . and the Cabinet adopted the Bill before it came before this House. . . . There was more consultation on this than on any other subject we have had since I have been Prime Minister.' Turning to Deshmukh's charge of animus on the part of certain Congress leaders (excluding Nehru) he deplored the former Finance Minister's unfair allegations 'after six years of functioning together'. Then he took Deshmukh to task on the constitutional issue. 'After all I am the Prime Minister of India and the Prime Minister is the Prime Minister', he said in an emotion-charged voice. 'He can lay down the policy of the Government. I too know something of democratic procedure, about party procedure. I know something of what the Prime Minister's duties are and that in the Constitution the Prime Minister is the linchpin of Government. To say that the Prime Minister cannot make a statement is a monstrous statement itself. I entirely fail to understand where the hon'ble member has got his acquaintance with democracy and the present Constitution of India and the Constitution of England . . .'

While in this angry mood, Nehru questioned Deshmukh's claim to speak for the Maharashtrian peasants, Deshmukh the civil servant of the *Raj*. In so doing there was a mental reflex, a throwback to the days of struggle before Independence: 'I am something more than the Prime Minister of this country, and we are all something more. We are the children of the Indian revolution, and . . . we still have something of the fire of that revolution in us. I venture to say that many of us know a little more about the Indian people and about those poor people and peasants than some others who talk so much about peasants. . . .

[1] *The Statesman* (Calcutta), 26 July 1956.

It does not become anyone to talk of money bags here referring to our party or the Government.'[1]

Deshmukh was succeeded by Krishnamachari who later became the centre of India's *cause célèbre* and the last of the eight ministers to resign from the Indian Cabinet since 1947.[2] This episode began in December 1957, when Feroze Gandhi, journalist, M.P. and Nehru's son-in-law, but no relation of the Mahatma, brought to the public view a strange transaction involving a nationalized corporation. More than a year before, the State-controlled Life Insurance Corporation had purchased 15 million rupees (approximately $3·2 million) worth of poor-risk stock in six corporations controlled by Haridas Mundhra, a young Marwari industrialist and speculator residing in Calcutta. The transaction was common knowledge in 'inside circles' for some time but had not been brought to the surface before. Gandhi asked pointed questions of the Finance Minister, suggesting that there was either a grave error of judgement—or something worse. Krishnamachari tended to minimize its importance, but in the face of a parliamentary uproar, including many Congressmen, he promised an inquiry. According to persons with knowledge of Cabinet affairs in Delhi, the Finance Minister and some of his colleagues hoped to hush up the affair with a *pro forma* inquiry. Feroze Gandhi, however, pressed his case relentlessly and succeeded in persuading the Prime Minister that he had abundant evidence of maladministration, and possibly corruption. Despite some of his colleagues' reluctance, Nehru insisted that a *bona fide* inquiry be held. To leave no doubt of impartiality he appointed a one-man commission consisting of the Chief Justice of Bombay, M. C. Chagla, one of the most highly respected jurists in India.

Hearings were held from 20 January to 3 February 1958, and Indians were astonished by the revelations. There was a parade of star witnesses and much conflicting testimony. The Finance

---

[1] *Times of India* (New Delhi), 31 July 1956.

[2] There were other resignations from the Cabinet, but none arose from specific policy disagreements within the Government and none provides further insight into the working of the Cabinet. Kidwai resigned in July 1951 to join the newly formed K.M.P.P. but returned to the Cabinet soon after. Jain offered to resign for the same reason but did not press the issue. Rajagopalacharia left the Government at the end of 1951 over a variety of unstated points of friction with Nehru and returned to his former post as Chief Minister of Madras.

Minister denied having issued instructions to purchase the shares. The Principal Finance Secretary, H. M. Patel, one of India's most senior civil servants—who rushed back from Europe for the inquiry—stated that the decision had been approved by the Finance Minister. H. V. R. Iyengar, the Governor of the State Bank, was equivocal on this and other aspects of the transaction. The Chairman and Managing Director of the Life Insurance Corporation were no more certain about what had happened. Moreover, the Finance Minister justified the investment on the grounds that it was necessary to stabilize the Calcutta stock market. In Parliament a few months earlier, however, he said that this was not the purpose. Leading financiers dismissed this reason as nonsense or dishonesty, demonstrating that the Calcutta market was in no need of such a large investment. Mundhra himself was revealed as a speculator and manipulator whom a public corporation would not normally be likely to support.

The interested public followed the daily round of hearings as no other political episode since Independence. For the first time in years the press abandoned its self-imposed restraint. Opposition parties were given an opportunity to thunder against Government malpractice. And those who were genuinely interested in 'good government' passed through an anxious period. There were two redeeming features of the Mundhra Affair: Nehru's forthright action in bringing the case to judicial inquiry; and the healthy expression of democracy at work, reminding ministers that they are responsible to Parliament and to the public at large.

The report of the Chagla Commission was awaited with great interest. Chagla questioned the value of the shares and viewed the transaction as an attempt to save the crumbling Mundhra financial empire. Krishnamachari was found responsible in a constitutional sense, in so far as the Life Insurance Corporation was under the jurisdiction of his ministry, and was severely criticized for bad judgement in the use of public funds, though not for corrupt practice. H. M. Patel was also reprimanded. The political outcome was inescapable. Although Nehru paid tribute to Krishnamachari's services to the Government in all other respects, the opposition parties and many Congressmen demanded his resignation. The Government itself was under serious strain in the light of the affair, as was the civil service and the 'public sector' of the economy. The Finance Minister left the Cabinet on 13 February 1958, the fourth person holding that portfolio to do so. Nehru took over the post temporarily and was succeeded by Morarji Desai. Mundhra himself was arrested on a charge of forging share certificates.[1]

Cabinet procedure is similar to British-type Cabinets elsewhere. The agenda is prepared by the Cabinet Secretariat and circulated to all ministries. Members of the Cabinet attend all meetings while Ministers of State are invited when matters relating to their ministry are under consideration. There are a number of Standing Committees, notably on Finance, Defence and External Affairs.

Interviews with former ministers and officials of the Cabinet Secretariat suggest that discussion is frank and free. Nehru is the outstanding figure, as befits his office, and even more, his status in the governing party and the country at large. Each minister is expected to take an active part in discussion of items under his administrative jurisdiction. A few venture beyond. And Nehru's range of interests extends to all questions that come up at Cabinet meetings. The Prime Minister has great skill in winning his colleagues to his viewpoint on most issues by persuasion without offending them. Many testified to his capacity to find a common formula which produced a voluntary consensus.

Where there is disagreement the outcome depends on how strongly Nehru feels about the issue. If he is firm his colleagues give way, not because of fear but because they acknowledge his pre-eminence and respect his leadership. Moreover, he is never dogmatic in presenting his views. For example, in deliberations on the five-year plan some ministers may propose moderate goals. Nehru will make an impassioned plea for more rapid progress on a wider front, adding that if conditions prove them to be too ambitious he will be prepared to modify the targets. In face of this flexible approach the 'opposition' crumbles. However, Nehru does not feel strongly on all questions. There

[1] This account is based upon conversations with many persons in India in January 1958, and on the very extensive press coverage of the Mundhra Affair. See *The Statesman* (New Delhi), the *Times of India* (New Delhi) and the *Hindustan Times* (New Delhi) from 15 January to 20 February 1958. See also the *New York Times* 13, 14, 19 February 1958 and *The Economist* (London), 22 February 1958.

appears to be a gradation with corresponding reactions: first
and foremost the need for social change, notably the eradication
of caste discrimination and the strengthening of secularism;
secondly, socialism, regarding which he is willing to compromise only on marginal points; thirdly, foreign policy, the
sphere in which only Menon and, occasionally, Pant and Azad,
have questioned his specific proposals. On something like prohibition, however, he will concede to the rigidly held views of
Morarji Desai and others, for he considers this secondary and
has no desire to alienate his colleagues.

Since 1957 there appears to be an informal understanding
among the 'Big Three' of the Indian Cabinet—Nehru, Pant
and Desai—as to the permissible limits of disagreement. By
and large they accommodate each other, with Nehru's pre-
eminent position readily acknowledged. Where either of his
colleagues presents a case forcefully he will make concessions in
the interests of harmony—provided they do not undermine
what he considers to be the pillars of his programme.

The cardinal fact remains, however, that all major Cabinet
decisions require Nehru's approval or at least acquiescence.
When Patel lived he acted in the Prime Minister's place during
Nehru's absence from the capital. Since the end of 1950, how-
ever, there has not been a Deputy Prime Minister. Until 1957
Cabinet meetings in Nehru's absence were chaired by Azad,
the senior minister. Since then Pant has occupied this position.
But all decisions are referred to Nehru wherever he may be.

An analysis of the Cabinet in terms of political inclinations
suggests that Nehru tends to surround himself with persons who
do not share his ideology in any marked degree. A precise
designation is difficult, but the following may be considered an
approximation for Members of the Cabinet in the summer of
1958. On the Left is Krishna Menon; centrist with a liberal
orientation are Nanda (the Gandhian spokesman), Shastri, Ram
and Jain; moderate but otherwise not easily categorized—
Ibrahim, Singh and Reddy; and on the Right are Pant, Patil
and Desai. Few may be considered Nehruites in any meaningful sense.

Why then does the Prime Minister retain his conservative
senior colleagues? Several factors probably account for his
behaviour. The heterogeneous character of the Congress must

be reflected in a Congress Government. Moreover, Nehru may be trying to emulate Gandhi, who succeeded in converting his opponents by example and brought them into his inner circle. Thirdly, in the view of some observers, he prefers to keep the potential sources of opposition in the Cabinet, where their activities are less harmful to his programme. There is, too, the need for 'strong administrators' like Pant and Desai and the influence they carry in their home States—the U.P. and Bombay. But most important is an excessive sense of loyalty to old colleagues and an emotional distaste for 'a parting of the ways' with persons who fought side by side for Independence. Recently he railed about the need to bring younger men into positions of responsibility but he shrinks from ruthless action. In 1958, for example, he expressed the desire to stay out of the Congress Working Committee, hoping that his senior colleagues would follow suit. Instead he was persuaded to serve once more. It may be said that, with few exceptions, Nehru has never been in ideological tune with his Cabinet associates.[1]

Majority parties in parliamentary democracies have no inducement to form coalition governments. In India, however, there was one abortive attempt to create a coalition in the Centre and the States, an illuminating incident in the story of Nehru's leadership and in the recent politics of India. It began in the autumn of 1952 when the Prime Minister called in Jaya Prakash Narayan, then leader of the newly merged Praja-Socialist Party,[2] and proposed 'co-operation at all levels'. Narayan seemed favourably disposed. During the next six months a half-dozen meetings were held between Nehru and three Socialist leaders—Narayan, Narendra Dev and Kripalani, the former Congress President. The final talks took place in mid-March 1953. Soon after, the deadlock was announced and the correspondence between Nehru and Narayan was made public.[3]

It was a curious episode, with potential implications of great

[1] Based partly on interviews with persons who wish to remain anonymous.

[2] The K.M.P.P. and the Socialist Party were merged into the Praja-Socialist Party in September 1952. Nehru welcomed the merger. For his sympathetic attitude see his statement of 4 October 1952, in *The Hindu* (Madras), 5 October 1952.

[3] For the text of the Nehru-Narayan correspondence see *The Hindu* (Madras), 20 March 1953. For earlier phases of the negotiations see *The Hindu*, 28 February 1953 ff.

significance. The apparent reason for the impasse in negotiations was Narayan's 'fourteen point' minimum programme for Socialist co-operation: constitutional amendments—to remove obstacles to social change, to abolish second chambers in the central and State legislatures and to abolish guarantees to the Princes and civil servants; administrative reforms at all levels, including decentralization of power and the rooting-out of corruption; reorganization of the States; redistribution of land without compensation and encouragement to co-operative farming; nationalization of banks, insurance companies and the coal industry; development of state trading; etc. This programme was to be achieved in four years. Narayan warned that if India failed to produce something other than an imitation of a Western welfare state all Asia and Africa would turn to China. He also chided Nehru for accepting 'such a drab and conservative Constitution'.

Nehru's reply was a mixture of sympathy and disappointment. No intelligent person could object to the programme, he wrote. 'But surely it is beyond me both as Prime Minister and as President of the Congress to deal with such vital matters and give assurances in regard to them. . . . One can hardly take these things in a bunch.' What, then, were Nehru's motives in initiating the talks? One was certainly the desire to strengthen the left-wing group in the Government and to press forward with more radical reform. As Nehru wrote to Narayan, 'I am not satisfied, if I may say so, with the rate of our progress. . . . I wanted to hasten it and I wanted your help.' Another was to strengthen the moderate left forces in the country against the growing threat from extreme Right and Left, as evident in the rising tide of communalism during the agitation for the complete integration of Kashmir into India and the electoral successes of the Communist Party. A third, though unstated, motive was probably to groom Narayan for the succession by bringing him and a few other socialists into direct contact with administration. This might pave the way for a reintegration of the Congress and the P.S.P., once a united party, and thereby ensure a smooth transition.

Why did the *pourparlers* come to nought? Within the Congress there appears to have been strong opposition from the Right wing, partly because it would have meant sharing power and partly because the socialist elements in the party would have been strengthened in the battle for the succession. Among the Praja-Socialists, too, there was opposition, notably from Dr. Ram Mohan Lohia, who bears a strong personal animus towards Nehru and who later broke from his own party to form the Socialist Party of India. In the later stages the Praja-Socialists were somewhat insincere. According to a senior P.S.P. leader, the publication of the 'fourteen points' was a deliberate act to secure windfall publicity and to clarify the differences between the two party programmes. It was obvious, he added, that Nehru would not—and could not—accept an ultimatum.[1] That Nehru was unhappy at the outcome is evident from the fact that even after the talks broke down he requested informal Praja-Socialist co-operation. More important, in terms of Nehru's leadership, was the revelation that while he was the dominant figure in the Congress he did not control the party machine.

*   *   *   *

The Indian Parliament is 'the one institution of the kind [in Asia] which is working in an exemplary way. . . . Pericles said that Athens was the school of Hellas. Mr. Nehru without boasting may say that Delhi is the school of Asia.' Such was the appraisal of one Western observer.[2] Others have termed it a twentieth-century version of a *darbar*, and still others a façade behind which the Congress and Nehru wield absolute power. The belief that Parliament in India is but a façade, held by many Indians as well as Westerners, must be seen against the background of the British *Raj*, especially in the light of three decades of the central Legislative Assembly which was very much a façade for Viceroy's rule from 1919 to 1947. Underlying this view was the nearly unanimous conviction of British officials that Western parliamentary institutions were not suitable to India—because of the widespread illiteracy, the authoritarian social pattern, the *mélange* of castes and creeds, and the absence of a tradition favourable to constitutional government.

What does the record suggest? At first glance the parliamentary process seems artificial because one party has had a preponderant majority since 1947 and could push through any

---

[1] To the author in New Delhi in February 1956 by a person who wishes to remain anonymous.   [2] *Manchester Guardian*, 5 June 1954.

legislation with ease; the opposition parties have never comprised much more than one-quarter of the membership in the House and were mutually hostile on most issues; in any event they have not thus far provided a potential alternative Government. It is also true that Parliament is not the centre of power and decision-making in India. This function is performed by the Congress caucus and ultimately by Nehru and the party's High Command. And yet it would be misleading to dismiss Parliament as of no consequence or to deny its vital role in Indian politics and Indian society generally.

Despite the Congress majority, debate is often vigorous, as illustrated in the cases of States Reorganization and the Hindu Code Bill. Further, questions raised by members are often forthright and even embarrassing. And the Opposition, though small and fragmented, is keen, able and vociferous. Those who denigrate the Indian legislative process tend to compare it with an idealized version of Westminster at work, a comparison which is likely to lead to grave misjudgement.

One prominent Independent M.P. offered the following reflections:

Gradually precedents are being established and conventions are being recognized. The main difficulty is that the House has too much to do in the time allotted with the result that there are stringent limits on the time available for debate. Nevertheless, debate is often spirited. The committee system does not yet function efficiently, partly because of the size—some are over fifty—and partly because of the lopsided composition. With such a huge Congress majority the work of committees is vitiated somewhat. Yet they do provide ample opportunity for opposition views to be heard. Another drawback is that many Congress M.P.'s are there because of service in the struggle for independence, with few qualifications and little knowledge of the immense range of parliamentary business. An encouraging feature is the attitude of the Prime Minister and, to a lesser extent, his senior colleagues, who are consciously trying to enhance the status of Parliament and to encourage a genuine parliamentary process.[1]

The most authoritative study of the Indian Parliament in its first decade provides an even more sanguine assessment.[2] Professor Morris-Jones sets up four criteria for his overall evaluation:

[1] To the author in New Delhi in June 1956 by a person who wishes to remain anonymous.

[2] Morris-Jones, W. H., *Parliament in India* (1957). The quotation is from p. 332.

the degree to which Parliament provides channels for the ventilation of grievances and the expression of aspirations; the extent
to which it serves as a forum for the debate of public policy; its
capacity to control and sustain the Executive so as to encourage
initiative without permitting arbitrary actions; and its role in
educating public opinion. In all of these respects the evidence
suggests that the parliamentary process is genuine and, on the
whole, effective.

He notes ample opportunity for the ventilation of grievances
—spirited Question Periods, adjournment Motions, Half-an-
Hour Discussions, and debates on Demands for Grants. The
discussion of Bills may not always be thorough but is usually
sufficient to bring the main issues to the fore and to give the
Opposition an opportunity to express their views. Although
Parliament *per se* cannot provide an effective restraint on the
Executive because of the Congress majority, this function is performed in part by the committees and by conflicting viewpoints
within the governing party; the Congress Parliamentary Party
is, in reality, a miniature Parliament. The response of the
public, as evidenced by the attendance at parliamentary debates and the press coverage, suggests that the educational function is also being performed.

Professor Morris-Jones notes various weaknesses. On the
technical side he criticizes the Bill procedure, the still-undefined
role of the Upper House, and methods for controlling public
corporations. He recognizes the adverse effects of a weak
Opposition but argues that these are mitigated by the character
of the Congress. There is, too, the friction arising from the relations between the Congress Party and the Congress Government, the inadequate training of many M.P.s, and the lack of
sufficient private organizations concerned with political affairs.
In the main, however, the Indian Parliament received his
commendation: 'The "experiment" is working and parliamentary institutions are more firmly established in the way of life
of the Indian people than they are in that of many a country in
Europe.'

This achievement must be credited largely to Nehru. He has
frequently declared his faith in the democratic process. Typical
is the following: 'I believe completely in any Government . . ..
having stout critics and having Opposition to face, because

without criticism people become complacent, the Governments become complacent. The whole Parliamentary system of Government is based on this criticism . . .'[1] He has also commended parliamentary democracy to neighbouring governments.[2] Far more important, however, has been his persistent effort to make Parliament the principal forum for the realization of the popular will. He is invariably present in the House every day during the session. He is consulted by the Minister for Parliamentary Affairs before the Business of the Day is decided. And he is an active participant in debate.

He is tolerant and usually courteous to the Opposition, and though often irritated by their use of Points of Order, which tend to slow up the business of the House, he encourages them, for he is genuinely trying to build up conventions of Parliament. Many M.P.s, not all of them politically friendly, noted that he is remarkably attentive to their inquiries and that he often responds within a few hours. Moreover, he has given instructions to civil servants that requests from M.P.s are to have top priority.[3]

That he dominates its proceedings when he is in Parliament is beyond question. His pre-eminence can only be compared with that of Churchill at Westminster during the second world war. His gestures and moods cover a wide range. Sometimes he will sit hunched over, a pensive expression on his face. At other times he will scowl or crease his brow as he listens to a sharp attack from the Opposition. Frequently he will nudge one of his colleagues into silence or leap up to rescue a minister who is feebly answering parliamentary questions and supplementaries. Often he will rise in anger when he feels an insult has been directed at the Government. And at still other times he will make moving and solemn speeches.

In the broadest sense Parliament in India is a symbol and an instrument, a symbol of the method of government which Nehru is trying to establish and an instrument to educate those who will wield power in the future. He uses it as a sounding-board for the enunciation of his views and policies and is trying to

[1] To a public meeting in Madras on 31 January 1957. *The Hindu Weekly Review* (Madras), 4 February 1957.

[2] For example, in a speech to Ceylon's Parliament. *New York Times*, 20 May 1957.

[3] Related to the author by an Indian M.P. who wishes to remain anonymous.

create an attachment to the parliamentary institution among his people. It is also a unifying force, representing different regions, castes, creeds, social and economic groups—the leveller in a country which has not yet fully accepted the notion of equality.

Given time to nurture the seed, he may fashion the habit of looking to Parliament to solve disputes and to reduce the divisions in Indian society. It would be a grave mistake, however, to assume that he has wholly succeeded thus far. Parliament will be respected in India, as elsewhere in Asia, only as long as it can assist the process of radical social and economic change. Should it fail to do so after a trial period it will be swept away or drastically modified. For the crucial fact is that democratic processes are not yet rooted in Indian soil. Economic planning is more important and attracts more widespread enthusiasm. Nehru believes that economic development can be achieved through consent. If India fails to do so, Parliament there, as in Asia generally, will suffer a mortal blow.

*   *   *   *

In the first decade of Independence the Indian experiment in constitutional democracy underwent five tests at the polls: the general elections of 1951–2 and 1957; and three State-wide contests—Travancore-Cochin (later Kerala) in 1954, Patiala and the East Punjab States Union (PEPSU, later integrated with the Punjab) in 1954, and Andhra in 1955. What light do they throw on Indian politics during this transition period?

The elections in Travancore-Cochin and PEPSU may be taken together, for they occurred simultaneously and reveal striking similarities and contrasts. Both States had large and politically significant minorities, PEPSU being one-half Sikh and Travancore-Cochin one-third Christian; in PEPSU the Sikh communalists opposed the Congress whereas the Roman Catholics of Travancore-Cochin were strong supporters of the governing party. Both were politically unstable; in PEPSU direct rule had been imposed by the Centre and in Travancore-Cochin a vote of 'non-confidence' in the Congress régime had forced new elections. The election results were markedly different; in PEPSU the Congress scored a decisive victory but in Travancore-Cochin it suffered defeat. Yet in both the Congress increased its popular vote—to about 45 per cent. of the total. In both the Congress emerged as a genuine conservative party; in PEPSU it was allied with the Princes and landlords and in Travancore-Cochin with the Church. And in both the smaller parties lost heavily; the trend to polarization had begun.

In Travancore-Cochin interest was heightened by the fact that there were really only two contestants, the Congress and a United Front of Leftists consisting of the Communists, the Praja-Socialists (P.S.P.) and the Revolutionary Socialists; these three groups supported each others' candidates and so distributed them that a direct contest with the Congress was held in seventy-three of the 117 constituencies. A parade of national leaders entered the fray; Nehru, Morarji Desai, Rajagopalacharia and S. K. Patil for the Congress; Kripalani and Ashok Mehta for the Praja-Socialists; and Gopalan for the Communists.

Nehru conducted a vigorous five-day campaign. He attacked the United Front of Leftists as a strange alliance and openly termed the Communists followers of an alien creed. The Congress, he said, 'are, for the moment, agents of destiny'. He stressed the need for unity, stable government, hard work, and the goal of a welfare state. He invoked the message of Gandhi and pleaded for a demonstration of support for the governing party. But the voters were not overwhelmed.

The Congress won only 45 seats, a dissident Congress group secured 12, and one pro-Congress Independent was elected, a total of 58. The Communists secured 23 seats, two other Left-socialist parties 17, and the Praja-Socialists 19, giving the Left Front 59. To complicate matters the Governor appointed a pro-Congress Anglo-Indian to fill the remaining vacancy. Neither group had a majority.[1] To some the contest was 'a draw', for the Congress had only two seats less than in the previous assembly and the Communists only six more; the Praja-Socialists gained eight, at the expense of Independents. However, in the light of Nehru's active role, it was more correctly viewed as a Congress defeat.[2]

What factors explain the outcome? For one thing, the

[1] For an analysis of the Travancore-Cochin election in 1954 see Fisher, Margaret W. and Bondurant, Joan V., *The Indian Experience with Democratic Elections*, pp. 63–68.

[2] The *Manchester Guardian*, *The Times* (London), and *The Hindu* (Madras), 4 March 1954, and the *New York Times*, 5 March 1954 (all editorials).

Opposition was united, unlike PEPSU where a split Opposition aided the Congress cause. For another, Travancore-Cochin has the highest literacy rate in India (approximately 50 per cent.) and depressed economic conditions of a special kind. Highly over-populated, with a large army of educated unemployed, it offered attractive conditions for leftist promises of improvement. Finally, the Congress Government in the State was notoriously corrupt and had done little to alleviate the conditions of either plantation or urban workers, or for the educated young men who could not find jobs.

The Praja-Socialists occupied the key position. Despite the electoral alliance with the Communists, their national leaders opposed a coalition government with the far Left. Praja-Socialists in the State, however, had no such qualms. At first the P.S.P. offered to form a government by itself and sought Congress support. It then offered to form a coalition with the Left Front. At that point the Congress extended its support to a P.S.P. government alone. Thus a group with nineteen out of 118 M.L.A.s took over the reins with Congress backing. So it remained until December 1954, when the Congress withdrew its support. The P.S.P. Government fell in February 1955, and was replaced by a Congress Ministry. In the spring of 1956 the Congress Government was brought down in the Assembly. Thereafter President's rule was imposed until the second general election.

The outcome in PEPSU was more encouraging for the Congress. The Left Front was weaker and the Sikh communalists were divided. Moreover, the princelings of the area joined the Congress bandwagon. Nehru spent two days in this strategic border State and concentrated on the theme of stable government which PEPSU had lacked for some years. The electorate responded. Of sixty seats the Congress won thirty-seven, two Sikh groups twelve, the Communists four, and Independents seven.[1]

A striking feature in both elections was the interest shown by the electorate. In Travancore-Cochin 80 per cent. of the voters went to the polls and in PEPSU about 65 per cent., suggesting that the idea of periodic choice of the governors by the governed

[1] For an analysis of the PEPSU election see Fisher and Bondurant, op. cit., pp. 69–79.

had penetrated the minds of the Indian masses. Another was the repudiation of authority; in Travancore-Cochin seven of the eight Congress District leaders were defeated. Most important, perhaps, the Communist gains in Travancore-Cochin indicated that while Nehru was indispensable to the Congress his leadership was not enough to return the party to power; the voters demanded something more.

In Andhra, however, the Congress had its revenge. At the time of its formation in 1953 the Andhra legislature consisted of 140 members who formerly held seats in the Madras Assembly. The three principal groups were Communist (forty-one), Congress (forty) and P.S.P. (twenty-six); a fourth group of some importance was the peasant-based Krishikar Lok Party (K.L.P.) with fifteen members. A Congress-led coalition government held power for little more than a year and was brought down on the issue of prohibition. An election was set for February 1955, the Assembly being enlarged from 140 to 196 seats.

All contestants waged a vigorous campaign, particularly because Andhra posed the first real possibility of a Communist government in India. Nehru himself toured parts of the State. The Congress poured funds and men into the struggle under the able leadership of S. K. Patil, the Bombay party leader. This time it formed an alliance—with the K.L.P. and a splinter of the P.S.P. The only issue was the 'threat of Communism'. The result was a resounding Congress victory—119 of the 196 seats, for the United Congress Front as a whole, 146 seats. The Communists were reduced to fifteen. Yet they had increased their popular vote to over 30 per cent., partly because they contested almost 90 per cent. of the seats.

Various factors explain the Congress triumph: organizational efficiency and ample funds under Patil's skilful direction; election strategy, which gave it the valuable support of the K.L.P.; the appeal of the recently proclaimed goal of a 'socialist pattern of society' which reduced the attraction of the Praja-Socialists; at the same time, a hard-hitting campaign against the Communists who were accused of being agents of a foreign power; unexpected assistance from Moscow in the form of a *Pravda* editorial published a few days before the election which praised the record of the Indian Government; and the revision of constituencies to the Congress's benefit. The triumph in Andhra offset the uninspiring performance in Travancore-Cochin a year earlier and infused new confidence into India's governing party, particularly because it had overcome a formidable challenge from the far Left.[1]

In the spring of 1957 India held its second general election, the largest democratic poll in history. Its dimensions are indicated by a few cold statistics. There were 193 million electors, 20 million more than in 1952, and some 3,400 seats at stake, 494 in the House of the People and 2,908 in the State Assemblies.[2] This time, however, the number of parties was drastically reduced, as a result of a ruling by the Election Commission confining the term 'national parties' to those which had received over 3 per cent. of the popular vote in 1952. Hence there were only four all-India contestants: the Indian National Congress; the Praja-Socialist Party; the Bharatiya Jana Sangh; and the Communist Party of India. Seven other groups were designated 'state parties', such as the Hindu Mahasabha, the Scheduled Castes (Untouchables) Federation and the Forward Bloc. This time, too, the technical aspects were conducted with greater efficiency. Except for a few remote constituencies the poll was completed in three weeks, instead of two months as in 1952. Repolling was necessary in only thirty-nine cases. Perhaps the most encouraging feature was that over 60 per cent. of the electorate actually voted—this in a population of which more than 80 per cent. are illiterate.

The Congress sought a return to power on the basis of its record since Independence, with special emphasis on the Five-Year Plans and Community Development, India's status in the world, and the goal of a Socialist Co-operative Commonwealth.[3] The Praja-Socialists placed before the voters a modi-

[1] On the Andhra election in 1955 see Fisher and Bondurant, op. cit., pp. 79–86, and Windmiller, M., 'The Andhra Election', *Far Eastern Survey*, April 1955, pp. 57–64.

[2] The figure for State Assemblies excludes 194 members of the Andhra legislature elected in 1955. The life of the Andhra Assembly was extended five and a half years from November 1956 by constitutional amendment in order that the next State election would be synchronized with the next general election in 1962. Of the seats in Parliament 74 were reserved for Scheduled Castes (Untouchables) and 29 for Scheduled (backward) Tribes. Of the seats in State Assemblies 470 were reserved for both.

[3] The Congress objective was so defined in Article I of the party constitution as revised at the Indore Session in January 1957.

fied version of Narayan's 'fourteen-point' programme and criticized the Congress for the continued tension with India's neighbours. The Jan Sangh, speaking for Hindu orthodoxy, pledged all things to all people: a ban on cow slaughter; the rapid elimination of English as the official language; the reunion of India and Pakistan; a maximum income of 2,500 rupees per month; a ceiling on land holdings; the restriction of nationalization to basic industries, and 'Indianization' of foreign enterprises; fair treatment of the minorities but no special privileges; in general, the creation of a Hindu *Raj*. The Communists concentrated on economic affairs. While praising the objectives of the second plan, they stressed the need for heavy industry—in the 'public sector'—and criticized the Government's 'soft' attitude to foreign capital. They also recognized the positive role of private enterprise in the development of the Indian economy and pledged special consideration for backward areas of the country.

Apart from the Jan Sangh's criticism of India's policy towards Pakistan and Kashmir, and the Praja-Socialists' mild rebuke, foreign policy was not an issue. There were, however, many local issues: dissatisfaction with the administration of tribal areas in Assam, Bihar and Orissa; unemployment and inflation in Kerala and Bengal; States Reorganization in Bombay, the Punjab, Orissa, Bengal, Bihar, central India, and south India, notably in Madras and Mysore; alleged domination of north India in Madras; and Congress maladministration in Kerala. Indeed, it was these sources of local discontent that explain much about the outcome of the elections.

What was the overall picture of voter preference? The Congress won a very large majority of seats at the Centre and was returned to power in all but one of the thirteen State Assemblies. The Praja-Socialists did better than expected but were ousted by the Communists as the leading opposition party; their popular vote declined at the Centre and in every State Assembly. The Jan Sangh showed some strength among Hindu middle-class voters in the towns of north-central India but did not justify its claim to all-India stature. The Communists won a major prestige victory in Kerala, doubled their popular vote and secured a foothold in every State, penetrating for the first time the Hindi-speaking strongholds of the Congress.

On the surface the Congress victory was impressive. Its popular vote increased from 42 to 45 per cent. in the States and from 45 to 47 per cent. at the Centre. Moreover, it won 75 per cent. of the seats in Parliament and 65 per cent. of all seats in the State Assemblies. In five of the thirteen States it increased its majority of seats. The reasons were essentially the same as in 1952: the diminishing but still potent aura of the 'party of independence'; the association with Gandhi; a nation-wide political machine rooted in the village; ample campaign funds; and the magic name of Nehru. To some extent, too, it was aided by the continued fragmentation of opposition parties.

Its successes seemed all the more striking because of Nehru's relatively inactive role in the campaign. Either because of age or because he wished to see how the party would fare without his personal leadership, or both, the Prime Minister confined his direct participation to a few tours of crucial areas, notably Kerala, where the Communist challenge was known to be strong. The furious pace of 1936–7 and 1951–2 was a thing of the past. Moreover, his approach was somewhat detached. In a 'pep-talk' to Congress M.P.s he remarked: 'We must approach the Indian people absolutely frankly, without inhibitions, frankly confessing what we have not done, what we ought to have done and telling them what we have done.' Further, 'I am not prepared to say that the soul of the Congress is bright and shining at the present moment. . . . It is important . . . that we should not demean ourselves in any way, merely for the sake of some election. . . . With all our strength I am sure we shall win. But I really do not care very much if we win or lose . . .'[1]

Despite its assets, the Congress suffered some noteworthy losses, apart from Kerala. In Bombay, Orissa, Bihar, the Punjab, and the United Provinces its majority and popular vote were reduced. Various factors were responsible. The dramatic defeat in Kerala was due to the same combination of pressures that operated in the State election of 1954—over-population, high unemployment, maladministration by earlier Congress ministries, a powerful Communist trade-union movement and disgruntled educated young men in the towns. The setback in Bombay was due almost entirely to the Government's decision on Bombay City and its failure to hold inquiries into the riots of

[1] *The Hindu Weekly Review* (Madras), 7 January 1957.

1956. In Orissa a group of dispossessed princelings was able to arouse feudal loyalties and almost succeeded in unseating the Congress ministry. The Bihar Congress paid the price for factional strife, which the High Command had tried in vain to terminate. Congress losses in the Punjab resulted largely from the struggle between Hindus and Sikhs which redounded to the benefit of the communalist Jan Sangh. And in the U.P. the dissident Socialists led by Lohia made some inroads into Congress power by playing on economic discontent.

In perspective the real 'defeat' of the Congress lay in the spectacular gains of the Communist Party. Not only did it obtain power in Kerala. Its popular vote was doubled at the Centre (5 to 10 per cent.) and increased even more in the States (4·4 to 10·5 per cent.). Over 12,000,000 Indians cast their ballots for the C.P.I. in a free election, making it the largest opposition party in Parliament and a very close third to the Praja-Socialists in the State Assemblies as a whole. With the exceptions of Andhra and Madras, its proportion of votes rose in every State of the Union; in the key border states of Bengal and the Punjab it rose from 10 to 18 per cent. and from 6 to almost 15 per cent. respectively. What accounts for this swing to the far Left? In part it was due to more effective organization and leadership; in the first general election many Communist leaders had barely been released from detention as a result of the Telengana rebellion. In part it was certainly due to the gap between promise and fulfilment and the lengthy tenure of power by the Congress. To some extent the Communists gained from electoral alliances, as with the Praja-Socialists in Bombay and Bengal. Undoubtedly, they also gained from India's friendly relations with the Soviet Union and the warm reception accorded the Russian leaders on their 1955 tour of India.

Among the major parties the real loser was the P.S.P., whose popular vote declined from 15 to 10 per cent. in the States and from 16·5 to 10·5 per cent. at the Centre. Its percentage of seats, however, rose in seven of the thirteen States. The poor showing of the Praja-Socialists must be attributed to various factors: the lack of popular leadership, especially since the withdrawal of Narayan; the absence of a clear-cut ideology, for Gandhian Socialism and Marxism still vie for supremacy in

the party; the defection of its Left wing, led by Lohia; and the
Congress's adoption of a socialist creed which, along with the
Communist stress on socialism, robbed it of a distinctive character. Indeed, the P.S.P. found itself caught between the two
poles of Indian politics with little to offer as an alternative.

The Jan Sangh doubled its vote at the Centre but showed
itself to be essentially a regional party, attracting orthodox
Hindus only in the United Provinces, the Punjab, Rajasthan
and Madhya Pradesh (Central Provinces). Its once-vaunted
strength in Bengal, home of its founder, Dr. Shyama Prasad
Mookerjee, had been dissipated. Its strength increased in Bombay but only because the Sangh allied itself with disgruntled
Maharashtrian elements over the issue of Bombay City.

The 1957 election witnessed the emergence of strong regional
parties in various States. The right-wing Ganatantra Parishad
won fifty-one seats in Orissa, only five less than the Congress.
The Dravida Munnetra Kazhagam, a virulent anti-north-
Indian group with fascist-like ritual, emerged as the second-
largest party in Madras. Others which strengthened their
electoral position were the Peasants and Workers Party in
Bombay and the Janata and Jharkand Parties in Bihar.

The bonds which tied religious minorities to the Congress
loosened somewhat in the second general election, as evident
in the Muslim and Christian vote, notably in the United
Provinces and Kerala. The pull of language was very powerful, as the Maharashtrian rejection of the Congress revealed.
Feudal loyalties asserted themselves in select areas, especially in
Orissa. The most persistent and one of the most important
forces in Indian electoral behaviour—caste—was evident everywhere, and at all levels of the electoral process: the selection of
candidates; the campaign; voting behaviour; and the formation
of ministries. All parties had to reckon with this core element
in the Hindu social system and cater for its demands.

In the widest sense the elections of 1957 revealed two fundamental trends. The first is the polarization of Indian politics
around the Congress and the Communist Party. The second
is the decline of the Congress, symbolized by the Communist
victory in Kerala. It would be wrong to exaggerate the Communist success at the polls. At the centre they won only twenty-
seven seats compared with 365 for the Congress, and in the States

162 compared with 1,889 for the Congress. Moreover the Communist popular vote was only 10 per cent. while that of the Congress was 47 per cent. Even in Kerala the Communists received only 35 per cent. of the vote. Nevertheless, they moved ahead everywhere and doubled their vote. And they are free of many ills that beset the governing party of India. Finally, their only serious rival as an alternative to the Congress, the Praja-Socialists, suffered setbacks all along the electoral front.[1]

* * * *

A year after the general election Nehru surmised that the Congress had lost 100 seats in the State Assemblies because of resentment arising from the reorganization of States in 1956.[2] The sheer magnitude of this administrative revolution and the turmoil it produced places it in the forefront of Indian politics since Independence. Of special interest is Nehru's role in this tangled story.

The roots of States Reorganization lie deep in the growth of Indian society and in the administrative history of British rule. With rare exceptions India suffered from political fragmentation until comparatively recent times. And its society was always characterized by great diversity. Over the centuries there emerged distinctive regional cultures and languages which came to embrace millions of people, providing a focus of loyalty and attachment which rivalled, sometimes conflicted with, the feeling of belonging to India as a whole. Among them may be mentioned Bengali, Telugu, Tamil, Punjabi, Marathi and Gujarati. By the time the British arrived there were some fourteen such cultures which could be delineated geographically, despite the presence of minority groups among them. The advance of British power, however, was accompanied by the creation of administrative units which cut across these linguistic and cultural patterns. Moreover, expediency dictated a policy of *laissez-faire* towards the Princes after the Rebellion of 1857, with the result that segments of one cultural group were often scattered in different provinces of British India and/or princely

[1] For a detailed analysis of the general election in 1957 see Talbot, P., 'The Second General Elections: Some Impressions' and 'The Second General Elections: Voting in the States' (American Universities Field Staff, 1957).

[2] To *New York Times* correspondent A. M. Rosenthal. *New York Times*, 19 May 1958.

States. A notable example was the Maharashtrians who were divided among Bombay, the Central Provinces, Mysore and Hyderabad.

The desire for administrative union of the members of a linguistic group was already evident in the nineteenth century. Both the Montagu-Chelmsford and Simon Reports (1918 and 1930) recognized the legitimacy of this claim. The Congress favoured reorganization of state (provincial) boundaries along linguistic lines and pledged itself to this goal from 1920 onwards. As evidence of its commitment the party's state (provincial) branches were so organized in 1921, including branches for such non-existent States as Kerala, Andhra and Maharashtra, areas in which Malayalam, Telugu and Marathi were the predominant languages. And as late as the end of 1945, in its election manifesto, the party had renewed this pledge. It was natural, therefore, that on the morrow of Independence linguistic groups pressed the Congress Government to fulfil its promise. In the aftermath of Partition, however, many Congress leaders had second thoughts about the wisdom of adding a nation-wide administrative revolution to the already-dangerous sources of disunity.

The first step was to integrate British and princely India. This was accomplished in 1948–9 by a makeshift division of the constituent units of the federation into Part A, Part B and Part C States. But even during this grave transition period the clamour for linguistic states was heard. To satisfy the demand the Government established a Linguistic Provinces Commission headed by S. K. Dar, a retired High Court jurist, to inquire into the merits of linguistic states in south India. In its report at the end of 1948 the Dar Commission strongly opposed any tampering with the administrative *status quo*. It rejected the 'sub-nation' theory put forward by advocates of linguistic states, claiming that the existing units, the product of almost two centuries of British rule, were firmly established and had taken root in the minds of many. It also urged that linguistic states would be self-defeating since all would contain minorities. The basic objection, however, was that such states and the loyalties they would inevitably create would become major obstacles to the spread of a national language and national consciousness, precisely at a time when Indian unity was under great stress. The

22. London, 1955

23. Nehru and his daughter, Mrs. Indira Gandhi, with colour-smeared faces on the occasion of the Holi Festival in March, 1955

Government (Congress) was called upon to withdraw its support for States Reorganization.[1]

The party responded by appointing its own committee of inquiry. To the surprise of many, the JVP Committee[2] echoed the views of the Dar Commission, though in less blunt terms. The principal reason for the change in outlook was the threat to national unity. As a sop to the disillusioned, however, and perhaps to show good faith with the party's past pledges, the JVP Report suggested that if there were an insistent demand the question should receive further and more detailed examination. This was the opening wedge for the bitter struggle over States Reorganization which was to dominate Indian politics from 1953 to 1956.

The first linguistic group to wage a spirited campaign was the Telugu-speaking community of Madras which sought a separate State of Andhra. The Madras Government was agreeable, as was the Tamilnad Provincial Congress Committee. Even more important, the Congress Working Committee called for the creation of Andhra 'forthwith', as early as November 1949.[3] For some unexplained reasons the Government resisted the pressure—and the policy recommendations of the party's High Command—for three years. The Telugus persisted in their demand. Using the time-honoured technique of Gandhi, one of their most respected leaders, Potti Srimarulu, went on a fast unto death—and he died in the Andhra cause. This act broke the back of Delhi's resistance. A few days later, on 19 December 1952, it yielded to the popular will. The new State was formally inaugurated in October 1953, in Nehru's presence. The gate had been opened and other linguistic groups rushed to the entrance.

The Government could no longer justify delay in a nation-wide reorganization of state boundaries. In any event it had offered to study the problem in the JVP Report four years earlier. By the formation of Andhra the die was cast. But the circumstances attending its birth augured ill for the future,

[1] The report of the Dar Commission is to be found in *Reports of Committees of the Constituent Assembly* (*Third Series*), 1950, pp. 180–239.

[2] The initials are taken from the first names of the three members of the Committee—Jawaharlal (Nehru), Vallabhbhai (Patel) and Pattabhi (Sitaramayya). See Indian National Congress, *Report of the Linguistic Provinces Committee* (1949).

[3] *Congress Bulletin*, No. 7, November–December 1949, p. 3.

R

for they indicated that in the face of mass agitation, including violence, the Government would yield. The Andhra episode was to be re-enacted on an all-India scale.

Nehru tried to slow down the pressure by appeals to rational behaviour. Typical was his stress on 'healthy nationalism . . . to counter these foolish and tribal attitudes, as also provincialism'.[1] India is an indivisible unit, he argued; the States were formed only for administrative purposes.[2] But these were mere words. The glaring fact was that he had yielded to pressure. The interested parties acted accordingly.

The next stage in the drama was the appointment of the States Reorganization Commission (SRC) at the end of 1953, consisting of three men, Sayeed Fazl Ali, then Governor of Orissa (Chairman), Pandit H. N. Kunzru, a distinguished Independent parliamentarian, and Sardar Panikkar, former ambassador to China and Egypt. As Nehru wrote to his colleagues, 'we came to this conclusion because it was not practicable to deal with this problem in an isolated way'.[3] Lest its recommendations strengthen the trend to parochial loyalties, the Commission was instructed to bear in mind the need to preserve and enhance Indian unity; financial and administrative viability; the welfare of the people of each proposed unit, including protection for linguistic minorities; and national security.

The appointment of the Commission provided a respite, but no more. Special interest groups prepared for battle. In the midst of its hearings Nehru expressed concern about the widespread agitation, in which even Congressmen were active. 'The whole past history of our struggle for freedom and of the Congress movement is forgotten. Even our present constitution is ignored', he complained to senior colleagues throughout the country.[4] The worst was yet to come.

The Commission reported in October 1955. In essence it proposed the following changes: the abolition of Part A, Part B and Part C States, along with the institution of *Rajpramukh*, the equivalent position of Governor in the former princely, later

[1] *Indiagram*, No. 309, 13 October 1953.
[2] See *Indiagram*, No. 328, 11 November 1953.
[3] *Congress Bulletin*, No. 10, 11, October–November 1953, pp. 314–15.
[4] Letter to Presidents of the Provincial Congress Committees on 7 July 1954. *Congress Bulletin*, No. 5, June–July 1954, pp. 251–4.

Part B, States; the reduction of the number of States from twenty-seven to sixteen, with three Territories—Delhi, Manipur and the Andaman and Nicobar Islands; the creation of three new linguistic States—Kerala, to be carved out of Travancore-Cochin and Madras; Karnataka, the former Mysore, with territorial adjustments; and Vidarbha, a Marathi-speaking rump of Madhya Pradesh; and the creation of two bilingual States—Bombay, now greatly enlarged by the inclusion of Saurashtra, Kutch and the Marathi-speaking districts of Hyderabad, and the Punjab, enlarged by the inclusion of PEPSU and Himachal Pradesh. There were, as well, a number of border revisions. The residuary State of Hyderabad was to continue at least until 1961 when it could unite with Andhra if a two-thirds majority of its legislature so voted. Of the pre-Commission States, Rajasthan, the United Provinces, Bihar, Bengal, Orissa, Andhra, and Assam were to remain essentially unchanged. The Commission had declared firmly that language was only one, and not the most important, yardstick for boundary revision. In the end, however, this became the effective criterion for the most part.[1]

Almost at once the voices of discontent could be heard. With them came agitation, despite Nehru's plea to the nation that this issue 'be approached with dignity, forbearance and in a spirit of dispassionate consideration'.[2] There were two major areas of discord—Bombay and the Punjab. In addition, two others witnessed agitation and violence—Orissa and Bengal-Bihar. These may be disposed of briefly. The opposition in Orissa was led by disgruntled princely and feudal elements organized in the Ganatantra Parishad over the failure of the Commission to award it a tiny, disputed border area with Bengal. Between Bengal and Bihar, too, friction arose over a border district, but there the agitation was longer and more 'popular'.

Biharis objected strenuously to the proposed transfer of an allegedly valuable Bengali-speaking area to Bengal. The Bengalis responded with equal vehemence. Demonstrations were held in the major cities. In an attempt to solve the wrangle the Chief Minister of Bihar, Sri Krishna Sinha, made a startling

[1] *Report of the States Reorganisation Commission* (1955).
[2] *India News* (London), 15 October 1955.

proposal for the complete union of Bihar and Bengal. His opposite number in Bengal, Dr. B. C. Roy, approved, because of the economic benefits that would accrue to both.[1] Nehru gave it his blessing and the Working Committee applauded this bold gesture. But it was a gesture only. The majority of Bengalis were opposed to the merger, primarily because they were outnumbered by the Biharis and feared a subordinate status in the union, particularly odious because they considered the Biharis culturally inferior. The plan came to nought but it eased the border dispute.

The Bihar-Bengal merger scheme came at an opportune moment, in January 1956, when Bombay was in the midst of great tension. More than any other linguistic group in India, the Maharashtrians accused the Commission of outright discrimination. Why should everyone else (except the Sikhs) get a linguistic state while they remained in a bilingual Bombay? And why were the Marathi-speaking districts of Madhya Pradesh not included? What was the motive for a separate State of Vidarbha? The dismay crossed party lines and found expression in the *Maharashtra Samyuka Samiti* (Organization for Greater Maharashtra). Leading Congressmen joined the chorus of dissent, despite strictures from Delhi. Tension mounted.

The storm broke in January, when riots enveloped Bombay City, which is predominantly Maharashtrian in numbers but is dominated by Gujarati wealth. It is difficult to say who was responsible for what followed. The vital point is that eighty persons were killed and 450 wounded. The Gujarati-controlled Government of Bombay, headed by Morarji Desai, resorted to large-scale police firing. And the demand for an inquiry into police activities was never heeded, the precipitating cause of Deshmukh's resignation, as noted earlier. In the face of pressure the central Government announced that Bombay City would be administered as a separate state, as Nehru related later, because of the expressed preference for a City State on the part of the Maharashtrians.[2] Perhaps the Congressmen in Maharashtra were so disposed but not the majority of Maharashtrians. The agitation continued. New Delhi retreated to the original formula of a bilingual state including the city. The Maharash-

---

[1] Related to the author in Calcutta by Dr. Roy in March 1956.
[2] To Parliament on 30 July 1956. *Times of India* (New Delhi), 31 July 1956.

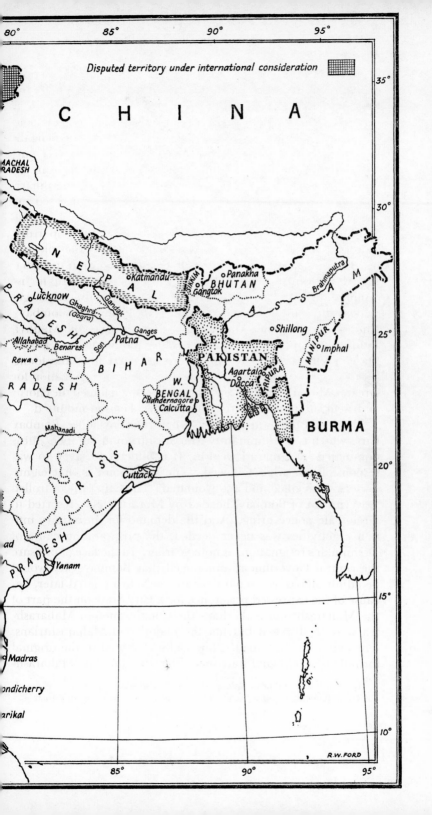

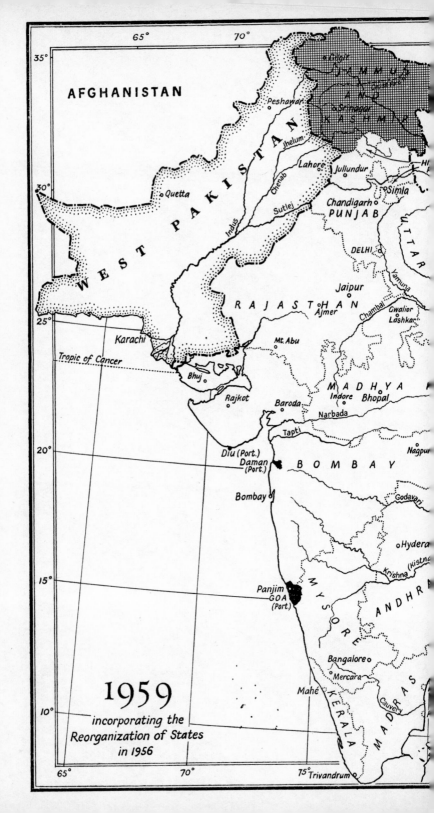

trians insisted on a separate linguistic state with Bombay City as its capital. The Gujaratis—and Parsis—used their influence to frustrate this goal.

In March 1956 another change was made. A bilingual Bombay was abandoned in favour of two separate States of Gujarat and Maharashtra, with Bombay City as a centrally administered territory. To assuage the feelings of Maharashtrians the proposed State of Vidarbha, a Marathi-speaking area, was to be absorbed by Maharashtra. The Maharashtrians remained dissatisfied and made their feelings known. Then came Nehru's statement early in June that after five years the fate of Bombay could be decided by the people of the City. It was this which Deshmukh had termed an 'extraordinary' action by the Prime Minister. By that time many persons were becoming alarmed by the deepening tension. Sentiment shifted rapidly in Parliament in favour of a return to the bilingual state formula including Bombay City, and, within a few days, a petition signed by a majority of Maharashtrian and Gujarati M.P.s proposed the change. The Government was relieved and acceded to the request.

Now it was the turn of the Gujaratis to vent their anger. Riots broke out in Ahmedabad, the proposed capital of a separate Gujarat and the site of Gandhi's *ashram*. The crisis deepened. Morarji Desai rushed to the City, scolded his fellow Gujaratis and went on a Gandhi-type fast. He threatened to continue until calm was restored. In fact, he broke the fast at a mass meeting where rocks were hurled. Ultimately the bilingual formula, the original proposal of the Commission, was accepted. But the bitter feelings remained. The Maharashtrians expressed their disappointment at the polls in 1957; the Congress was severely trounced in the area as a whole.[1]

The other prolonged battle over SRC, in the Punjab, arose from Sikh disappointment at not being given a separate state. Even worse, they resented the inclusion of Himachal Pradesh which increased the proportion of Hindus and Hindi-speaking persons in the enlarged Punjab State. The contending factions prepared for open struggle. The Sikhs, led by the tempestuous

[1] For a detailed analysis of the struggle over Bombay see Windmiller, Marshall, 'The Politics of States Reorganization in India: The Case of Bombay' in *Far Eastern Survey*, September 1956, pp. 129–43.

Master Tara Singh, whose angry words had helped to spark the Punjab riots in the spring of 1947, demanded *Punjabi Subha*, a Punjabi-speaking state, which was really a façade for a truncated Punjab in which the Sikhs would comprise 54 per cent. of the population. The Hindus, led by the Jan Sangh, the Hindu Mahasabha and R.S.S., all communalist organizations, created the Maha (Great) Punjab Front to ensure Hindu and Hindi predominance.

I witnessed one phase of the struggle for power in the Punjab while attending the Congress session in Amritsar in February 1956. On a bright, cool north Indian winter morning the contending groups massed their forces in a show of strength, especially for the benefit of the Congress High Command which was camped closed by. First came the Sikhs in the most impressive—and peaceful—demonstration I have ever seen. Hour after hour and mile after mile they marched, eight abreast, down the main street of Amritsar, a hallowed name in Indian nationalism because of the shootings of 1919. Old and young, men and women, they came in an endless stream, most with an expression of determination and sadness in their eyes, many still remembering the ghastly days of 1947 when their homeland was cut in two and hundreds of thousands fled before the Muslims, and when thousands of their co-religionists died or were maimed. What strength there was in the appearance of the older men who, with their flowing beards, looked like the Hebrew prophets of old! Many carried their traditional sword, the *kirpan*, and many wore blue turbans, symbol of militancy. (The dyers in the city did a handsome business that week.) They had come from the villages and towns of the Punjab and from far-off places as well. Almost without exception they marched in orderly file, portraying their unity of purpose. At intervals came the resounding cry, 'Punjabi Suba Zindabad' ('Long live a Punjabi State') and 'Master Tara Singh Zindabad', with intermittent music to enliven the proceedings. On they came, for five hours. Few who watched them could doubt their genuine fear of being swallowed up in the vice-like embrace of rabid Hinduism. By conservative estimate they numbered over 100,000. To this observer it seemed more like double that figure.

The Maha Punjab Front display was very much smaller, perhaps 50,000. But this was far larger than anticipated. A friend who watched this parade—in a fruitful division of labour—described it as 'nasty and Nazi', no less orderly than the Sikh show but with a militancy resembling pictures of the Hitler Jugend.

The two demonstrations revealed something more than intense feelings on the reorganization of the Punjab. They showed the strength of communalism, both Hindu and Sikh, a grave threat to democratic political institutions and a barrier to social change. They also explained Nehru's continuous onslaught on communalism. This political and social virus is far from being exterminated. It lurks beneath the surface and, in times of stress, rears its head. And it waits for a suitable opportunity to strike for power and Hindu *Raj*. Knowing this, Nehru attacks it mercilessly. Unfortunately, the attack is verbal in the main. And the roots of the disease are not so easily destroyed.

Nehru was sympathetic to Sikh fears but was reported by friends to be under strong pressure from communalist-minded Hindu Congressmen who were not prepared to place the Punjabi Hindus in an inferior political position. A compromise was eventually found. Himachal Pradesh was excluded from the Punjab and placed under central administration; Punjabi was given equal status with Hindi as an official State language; and three regional councils were established, safeguarding the rights of the Sikhs. Yet neither Sikhs nor Hindus were satisfied, and friction continues.

The States Reorganization Bill underwent various changes from the time it was introduced until it was passed by Parliament in November 1956. Ultimately, the sixteen States and three Territories proposed by the Commission were altered to fourteen States and seven Territories, the present administrative structure of India. The basic revisions of the Commission's proposals were: the elimination of Vidarbha and its incorporation into the enlarged bilingual Bombay; the absorption of the residual Hyderabad by neighbouring States, its three linguistic areas, Telugu, Marathi and Hindi, going to Andhra, Bombay and Madhya Pradesh respectively; the name Mysore restored to what was to become Karnataka; and the exclusion of Himachal Pradesh from the Punjab.

The Bill, along with the necessary Constitution Seventh (Amendment) Act, was passed in time to be implemented before the 1957 election. The pledge of States Reorganization along linguistic lines had been honoured in the main. There was comparatively little violence, though enough to cause concern. And communal passions and regional loyalties had been aroused as by no other act since Independence. It is too early to know how this will affect loyalty to India as a whole. But it is certain that the bitter feelings in Bombay and the Punjab will die more slowly than they came to life. For its indecision and concessions to pressure the Congress paid dearly at the polls.

The indecision must be attributed largely to the Prime Minister. Indeed, the story of SRC is one of the most striking illustrations of Nehru's vacillation in public affairs. Interviews with countless persons at the height of the crisis placed the onus for the muddle on weak leadership in the Congress High Command, especially on Nehru. And many of those interviewed were senior colleagues of the Prime Minister. The factual record supports this view. There were five different decisions on Bombay City alone: a bilingual state; a City State for Bombay along with separate states for Gujarat and Maharashtra; central administration for the city; central administration for five years; and a return to the bilingual formula. On the Punjab, too, there was vacillation; and to a lesser extent this was true of some marginal border disputes. Finally, the handling of Hyderabad suggested confusion in the minds of the decision-makers. The core of the difficulty lay in Nehru's attempt to carry everyone with him, a patent impossibility. His penchant for universal consent led to delay and exaggerated tensions. Once it was known that the Prime Minister, in his anxiety for consent, would not take decisive action, all interested groups began to wield pressure with resultant conflict. In trying to please everyone he displeased many.

Nehru underlined this aspect of SRC in a speech to Parliament: 'It might have been much simpler if we had not tried to consult hundreds and thousands of persons in this process and thereby, perhaps, added to the confusion. . . . Our difficulty has been that we have tried, too much perhaps, to balance respective viewpoints and tried to find as large a measure of agreement as possible, and naturally in doing so we have often succeeded in displeasing many people.'[1] The ceaseless quest for consent during SRC demonstrated, even to the sceptics, Nehru's

[1] *Times of India* (New Delhi), 31 July 1956.

devotion to democratic processes. But it also illustrated ineffec-
tual leadership. Had Nehru taken a firm stand from the outset
much of the friction would probably have been avoided.
A commission of inquiry had been appointed in response to
public demand. The commission made far-reaching recommendations on the basis of exhaustive study. Most of them were
acceptable; these could have been endorsed by the Government
forthwith. As for the highly controversial issues, the Prime
Minister could have given the contending parties a specified
time limit to reach an agreed formula. If they were successful
such formulae should have been endorsed by the Government.
If not, the Prime Minister or the Government as a whole should
have issued an award. As an alternative, a body of distinguished
men could have been asked to settle the disputes by arbitration.
Such a procedure would have met the test of democratic process
and would have given a strong lead. There can be little doubt
that Nehru's decisions or those of an arbitration board would
have been accepted without resort to violence, though some
would have been dissatisfied. And the spectacle of disunity and
pressure politics on a nation-wide scale would have been
avoided. It is clear that Nehru was badly jolted by the violence
and bitterness accompanying States Reorganization. It is also
clear that his reputation was not enhanced by the episode. The
price of indecision was high.

* * * *

Even before the dust had settled over SRC, another closely
related source of discord came to the fore. This issue was language, one of the most divisive forces in Indian society. Since
the coming of the Aryans some 3,500 years ago the sub-continent
has known a multitude of languages. With time they were
crystallized into two distinct language groups, apart from hundreds of tribal tongues and dialects: Sanskrit-derived languages,
some of the more noteworthy being Hindi, Bengali, Gujarati,
and Marathi; and Dravidian languages, four in number—
Tamil, Telugu, Kannada and Malayalam. The division was
north–south, the Dravidian languages being spoken in the
southern states of Madras, Andhra, Mysore and Kerala respectively. The intrusion of English in the eighteenth century complicated the situation but it provided a *lingua franca* for the Indian

intelligentsia from every part of the country. In doing so it served as a force for national unity and developing national consciousness, as well as administrative convenience.

Until the arrival of Gandhi, English was the accepted language of the Congress, as of all political parties. Gradually Indian languages appeared in politics, especially as the Congress extended its contacts to the village. But throughout the struggle for independence English remained the prevailing language of the nationalist élite. Attempts were made to create a substitute *lingua franca*, Hindustani, which was essentially a merger of Hindi and Urdu. But at best this could serve for north India only. Language friction aggravated Hindu–Muslim tension and became enmeshed in the conflict over Pakistan. Partition removed that source of discord in the main. But the basic division between north and south Indian languages remains.

During the process of drafting a new constitution much time and energy were devoted to the language question. It was apparent that Hindi was neither sufficiently developed nor sufficiently widespread to be imposed at the outset. It was also apparent that renascent nationalism demanded an Indian 'national' language and that English, associated with the foreign ruler, could not retain this status indefinitely. Yet it served admirably for a transition period, particularly during a period of great stress. Nor did the drafters of the constitution wish to offend the regional-language users. Hence a compromise formula was approved: all major Indian languages (fourteen) were given equal status as 'national languages'; Hindi was made the 'official language' for all-India purposes; and English was to continue as the 'official language' for fifteen years from the date the Constitution took effect; the changeover to Hindi was to occur in 1965.[1]

The compromise was satisfactory for the moment. South Indian fears were mollified by the fifteen-year delay and the continued use of English, as were non-Hindi speakers generally. People were preoccupied with the problems arising from the Partition. Thus for a few years the issue receded into the background—excluding, of course, the demand for linguistic states. By the mid-1950's, however, the language question was revived, partly because of the passions aroused by States Reorganization,

[1] Articles 343, 345–8 of *The Constitution of India*.

partly because the Hindi fanatics were pressing for a more rapid change-over, and partly because the time was approaching when the question would have to be faced directly.

Interest was aroused in the spring of 1955 by the creation of the Official Language Commission to study the progress achieved thus far and to recommend a time-table and methods for the change-over to Hindi. The report was ready by the summer of 1956 but prudence dictated delay in its publication because of the unresolved controversies over States Reorganization. When it finally appeared in the autumn of 1957 the long-smouldering discontent and fears of non-Hindi speakers burst forth. Of the Commission's twenty members only two expressed serious misgivings about the wisdom of replacing English by Hindi. The crucial question remained unanswered by the reports, namely, the time limit for the use of English for official purposes. But the formal change-over in 1965 was assumed by the Commission and specific proposals were made to achieve the goal.[1]

The stage was now set for a re-enactment of the SRC affair. Fortunately some lessons had been learned and the conflict was resolved in a peaceful manner, for the time being. Nehru took the lead in a settlement. Unlike SRC there were only two protagonists, those who favoured adherence to the letter of the Constitution and those who sought delay or outright amendment. The most vociferous critics were south Indians, including prominent Congressmen, educators, scientists and men of letters, led by the venerable Rajagopalacharia. The former Governor-General argued that because India was a federal state the consent of every unit was required before Hindi became the official language, a specious view in the opinion of most because the Constitution stated explicitly that 1965 was the date for the change-over. But Rajaji and others used more persuasive claims, notably that Indian unity would be undermined by an imposition of Hindi throughout the country and that a too rapid change-over would discriminate against south Indians in the Services, a fact which even the Hindi fanatics could not deny.[2] Popular demonstrations and the obliteration

---

[1] *Report of the Official Language Commission* (1957).

[2] For south Indian views on the language question in 1957 see *The Hindu Weekly Review* (Madras), 16 September, 14 October and 21 October 1957.

of Hindi signs at south Indian railway stations gave further evidence of the intense feelings on the subject. Some forty south Indian Congress M.P.s formally petitioned for a delay until 1990. The governing party itself was in danger of a serious split over the issue.

Such was the position when the Congress annual session opened in Gauhati (Assam) at the beginning of 1958. South Indian leaders spoke forcefully about their fears. The Hindi element stood fast. Ironically, of the seventeen participants in the debate nine spoke in English and only six in Hindi. Even Morarji Desai, a staunch advocate of Hindi, addressed the session in English 'because I want to be understood . . . by delegates from the south'.[1] Nehru brought the full weight of his prestige to bear on the side of compromise. He stressed the need for a flexible approach and reprimanded the Hindi enthusiasts for trying to impose a language by decree. He acknowledged the value of English—'I am partial to English. I want the study of English . . . to become even more widespread in the country'—but he categorically rejected the view that it was or could be a national language for India. He also rejected the south Indian request that English and Hindi be given equal status as official languages for another generation. At the same time he stressed the need for gradualism. The contentious issue, he noted, was very narrow, for no one was disputing the 'national' status of India's regional languages and their use for education and public purposes in the States. The question was simply how to ease the change-over to Hindi as the all-India 'official language'. He indicated, too, that he favoured the continued use of English after 1965.[2]

Here lay the essence of the compromise resolution. South Indian Congressmen reconciled themselves to the *formal* introduction of Hindi by 1965 while the Hindi group, at Nehru's prodding, agreed that the change-over would be transitional and would be effected with the support of non-Hindi sections

[1] *Hindustan Times* (New Delhi), 18 January 1958.
[2] For a summary of Nehru's speech on the language question see *The Statesman* (New Delhi), 17 January 1958. For Nehru's earlier views on the language question see pp. 235–7 above; 'The Question of Language' in *Indian Information* (London), 1 March 1949, pp. 248–9; *Constituent Assembly Debates: Official Report*, vol. ix, pp. 1409–16; and his speech to the Congress Parliamentary Party on 7 May 1954, in *Congress Bulletin*, No. 4, May 1954, pp. 164–74.

of the population; further, that English might be used as an 'official language' after 1965.[1] Since the Congress was the governing party, parliamentary endorsement was a foregone conclusion. The breach in Congress ranks was healed and, on the surface at least, the hostile factions seemed satisfied. It is certain, however, that the last act in the language drama has not yet been played. Much will depend on the willingness of the Hindi advocates to tread carefully and to carry the south on each step along the road towards the replacement of English. As a holding action Nehru's role early in 1958 was successful, much more so than his performance during SRC.[2]

* * * *

The reorganization of States and the 1957 election, and to a lesser extent the language controversy, indicated that all was not well with India's governing party. Nehru summed up the prevalent mood at the beginning of 1958 when he wrote: '. . . there can be no doubt that the Congress organisation is suffering from a deep malaise. . . . In a democracy that often happens. But it seems to me that there is something more about it than mere dissatisfaction with a continuing state of affairs.' As for the reasons, 'have we become too stale, too complacent, not having enough touch with realities? Has success itself loosened the fibre which gave strength to the Congress in the past? . . . Our discipline is weakening and without discipline no organisation can function effectively.'[3]

Immediately after the first general election he had written with even greater candour about the ills besetting the party.[4] And in the interim he reiterated this theme in countless speeches to party workers. He railed against the decline in *élan*, the struggle for prestige and power, the emphasis on private gain, the indifference to mass welfare. Frequently he warned his followers, '. . . the moment you lose touch with your people, you are weak. You cannot live on past capital for all time.'[5]

---

[1] *The Statesman* (Calcutta), 19 January 1958.
[2] On the transitional character of the Gauhati language resolution see the *Times of India* (New Delhi), 21 January 1958.
[3] 'A Deep Malaise' in the *Times of India* (New Delhi), 15 January 1958.
[4] See pp. 446–7 above.
[5] Presidential Address to the Tamilnad Political Conference on 3 October 1953. *Congress Bulletin*, No. 10, 11, October–November 1953, pp. 307–13.

More pointedly he had divulged the reason for assuming the Congress presidency in the autumn of 1951: 'I did so because I found that there was no other way out. I felt that several weaknesses had crept into the Congress in recent years—dissensions, internecine quarrels, petty rivalries and bickerings.'[1]

Other party leaders had occasionally indulged in self-criticism.[2] And there was ample evidence of shortcomings long before the 1957 elections. Despite its membership of 8,500,000, the party had only 71,000 active workers in 1954, only a few thousand more than the Communist Party and not nearly as dedicated. By 1958 its membership had been halved and its active workers reduced to 54,000. Most of the 365 Congress M.P.s were content to observe the proceedings as passive spectators and to leave the burden of work to a small group of ministers.[3]

There were other disquieting symptoms of decline. During more than a decade of power the Congress had failed to throw up new leaders. The whole party seemed to depend for its very survival on the health, vigour, popularity and leadership of Nehru. There was, too, a deplorable change in values and ways of living among those who had acquired power after many years of struggle. Most Congress ministers aped their British predecessors in their lavish display of the perquisites of authority: large, luxurious bungalows which are carefully guarded; limousines flying the national flag; private coaches on the railways; clerks and servants in splendid uniforms; and aloofness from the people, along with outward indifference to their needs and wants. They set a bad example to local party officials, the linchpins of Congress power in the countryside. Nehru himself was largely responsible for this retreat from simplicity; soon after he became Prime Minister he gave up his modest home at 17 York Road for the sumptuous estate of British Commanders-in-Chief. It would have been too much to expect his colleagues to do otherwise. Moreover, his towering position in the party and his inability to delegate authority tended to deprive his

---

[1] To the Delhi State Congress. *Free Press Journal* (Bombay), 17 May 1954.

[2] See for example the Report of the Constructive Work Committee. *Congress Bulletin*, No. 9, December 1954, pp. 409–19. The key figures were Katju, Shriman Narayan and Nanda.

[3] This is evident to any observer of Parliamentary proceedings in Delhi, as the author noted on frequent visits in 1951 and 1956.

subordinates of responsibility and offered little inducement to the training of younger men.

Beyond that was the lack of a clear-cut ideology and a disciplined organization. The Congress remained a nationalist movement, a *mélange* of interest groups, often conflicting and ranging the entire spectrum of ideas, from feudal to radical socialist, with capitalists and trade unionists, landlords and peasants, Gandhians and communalists finding shelter under its all-embracing roof. Furthermore, the lure of power attracted the ablest and most ambitious, while the 'constructive workers' were treated as 'second-class members' and were relegated to inferior positions in party committees.

Factional strife was endemic in the States as different groups vied for the favour of the High Command and the power which awaited the victor. In many places the struggle assumed the character of a contest between caste groups. The official party organ, *Congress Bulletin*, reveals how much time and energy were devoted to the quest for at least a show of unity among the warring groups. A special sub-committee of the Working Committee dealt with this problem, and it was very active indeed. In 1957, for example, the contest in Bihar was so fierce that the ballot boxes for the election of the President of the P.C.C. had to be sent to Delhi to ensure a fair count! In a wider sense party squabbles in the States concerned the proper relationship of the ministry to the P.C.C., an issue which has never been resolved. Nehru himself had written at length on this problem in 1937. His advice then was equally valid twenty years later—a division of function with the P.C.C. framing broad policy and the ministry having full control over administration, though encouraging advice from the Congress organization. It was not heeded then. It was also ignored later.

Added to factionalism are two other ills in the State branches: nepotism and corruption on an alarming scale; and disregard of policy decisions arrived at by the party's High Command. Whether on land reform, about which the Congress makes pious resolutions every year, or on the need to eradicate untouchability and a caste mentality, or on fair treatment of the minorities, or on the importance of eliminating corruption, or on the economic plan, the state ministries have often gone their own way, diluting the well-intentioned programme of the central party leadership. In part this is rationalized in terms of the much maligned 'adjustment to local conditions'; in part it is due to the natural desire of those in power to placate the social classes which represent the keys to their power. Ultimately it is due to lack of adequate organizational control and the amorphous character of the Congress creed and programme. Like Hinduism they are all things to all people, and 'socialist pattern of society' is sufficiently vague to permit diverse interpretations by local party leaders. Only in those states where a decisive figure was at the helm, like Bombay (Morarji Desai) and Bengal (Dr. B. C. Roy), has the party been free from constant turmoil.

After a decade in power the Congress is in decline. To many it appears to have alarming similarities to the Kuomintang under Chiang Kai-shek after the second world war. The goal of most Congress leaders is a ministership and the trappings of power and prestige. Few are interested in organizational work. The party controls all governments except one but its organizational base is withering away. The deterioration in morale and sense of mission is understandable, but the Congress shows no sign of remedying the rot that has set in. Little more than lip-service is paid to Nehru's pleas for revitalization of the party. The prevalent attitude seems to be that as long as they can enjoy the fruits of power in their lifetime (which for many of the leaders cannot be very long) why worry about the future. Corruption and factionalism, and the attitude of 'après nous le déluge' also parallels the Kuomintang.

The election results of 1957 jolted the Congress out of its apathy—for a while. Nehru took the lead and warned of the danger of complacency. He stressed the need for new, young leaders and a revolution in attitudes. Others followed suit this time, perhaps because their own positions now seemed in jeopardy. So it went for the month of March 1957. But when the time came for action, the call for reform was stilled in the scramble for power. Of thirteen 'new' State Chief Ministers five were over sixty-five, three were over seventy and one was seventy-seven. Nehru himself failed to set a proper example. In the 'new' central Cabinet there was only one major change, the inclusion of S. K. Patil, the party boss in Bombay—apart from the promotion of Krishna Menon to the Defence Ministry.

Many who had hoped for resolute action were disillusioned. A few vented their concern. One went further. 'The Congress was once a good cause', wrote a young and talented journalist. 'Now it sometimes looks like degenerating into a bad habit.' After dissecting the party's ills, for which Nehru was held largely responsible, he spelled out the belief of a growing section of Indian public opinion: 'The Congress has been given a reprieve for five years. If it cannot rescue itself from itself in good time, it will be swept out of power.'[1]

Perhaps the most striking evidence of the party's decline is the pathetic response to its annual session in recent years. In one sense this is not surprising, for the Congress has had a monopoly of political power for a decade, its leaders are Government leaders, its policies are Government policies—and the annual session has become more than ever a rubber stamp for decisions of the High Command. As the titular head of the Congress remarked sadly in 1950, the President has 'a position of responsibility without authority, expectation without opportunity, prestige without power', a correct appraisal for all presidents since Independence except for Nehru who held that office from 1951 to 1954.[2] And yet, this fact alone does not explain the response to the party conclave, for it is still a *mela* [fair] and *melas* are usually able to attract widespread interest.

Indifference was amply illustrated at the sessions of 1956, 1957 and 1958, at Amritsar, Indore and Gauhati respectively. The first of these, later to be known as the SRC session, was witnessed by this writer who jotted down impressions of people and things. Some extracts follow.

Amritsar, holy city of the Sikhs, just thirty miles from the 'enemy' border, is a typical provincial Indian town, with scattered bungalows for district officials and the local gentry (the former 'civil lines'), and endless rows of hovels that pass for homes in this part of the world. Its fame rests on two shrines, one religious and one national—the great Sikh temple surrounded on three sides by a pool of water, attracting the faithful and tourists alike, and *Jallianwalla Bagh*, site of the 1919 tragedy which sparked the first civil disobedience

---

[1] Verghese, B. G.: 'The Elections and After: II. Reprieve for Congress' in the *Times of India* (New Delhi), 2 May 1957.

[2] Sitaramayya in his parting words to the Nasik session on 18 September 1950. *Congress Bulletin*, No. 6, September–October 1950, p. 217.

campaign. . . . The Congress camp, some five miles from town, is a veritable city in itself, with shops, offices, hastily-constructed corrugated tin-shacks for delegates, pressmen and 'distinguished guests', and a huge *pandal* [enclosed stadium] to seat 200,000 people. . . . At the flag-raising ceremony Nehru and his daughter drove by in an old convertible Buick . . . and many were spellbound as the hood rose and later fell back into place. . . . Even more visitors were fascinated by the telegraph office where husbands explained to wives that 'here messages are sent directly to Madras, there to Calcutta and there to Delhi'.

The first meeting of the Subjects Committee [the A.I.C.C. at annual sessions] was a pallid affair. Delegates and visitors alike could not be less interested—except for a few moments when Nehru proclaimed open war against the proponents of violence. With reference to the Bombay riots, he declared, 'If they think they can gain their objectives in the streets, let me make it clear that we will meet the challenge in the streets.'

Things have livened up considerably [the following day]. The pace is quicker, the speeches longer and less restrained. The moods shift from struggle to acquiescence and back again. . . . Crucial problems came up today, notably economic policy and SRC, the burning issue of the session. Many harsh words were uttered, attempts were made to smooth over troubled waters, but those who feel strongly spoke their minds. . . . First the party brought up its heavy artillery. Pant moved the resolution on SRC which made it clear that violence would not be tolerated but was otherwise vague. Then N. V. Gadgil, highly-respected Congress Maharashtrian leader and former central Cabinet minister, made an impassioned plea for the inclusion of Bombay City in a separate Maharashtra. S. K. Patil responded with no less fervour, and Nehru summed up the official view. Finally, of course, the resolution was passed without amendment.

Gadgil's speech was highly-emotional but moderate in tone, expressing a desire to settle the problem by negotiation and a willingness to accept an award by the Prime Minister. 'This is a matter of life and death to me and my people', he said, with obvious sincerity. Nehru tried to ease the tension by a rambling speech on the virtues of unity and non-violence.

For some strange reason the High Command refuses to accept amendments. A typical example was the Savings resolution. Three amendments were proposed. They were admitted to be excellent but were only 'illustrative' of methods to save and so were 'superfluous'. The movers were asked to withdraw their amendments and obliged. The A.I.C.C. is nothing but a rubber stamp these days . . .

The open session was an anti-climax. The battles had been fought —verbally—in the Subjects Committee. It remained only to repeat the spectacle for the crowd—minus the friction and strong words. The most striking feature was the small crowd gathered to hear the leaders. The *pandal* was less than a quarter full. On the last day even the nominal entrance fee was dropped, but it remained much more than half empty. And many of those present left after Nehru had spoken at length on foreign policy. This time he concentrated on India's interests as the motives of its external policies, with very little moralizing.

The President [Dhebar] minced no words about the state of the party. His key point was that the Congress was living on its past achievements and had nothing left but Nehru. It must therefore embark on a large-scale constructive programme including more mass contact. Otherwise the future was bleak indeed . . .

What of the session as a whole? It seems to me a holding action, an attempt to patch up a family quarrel and to take stock. Of the multitude of speeches only a few were worthwhile, Nehru on the Buddha resolution, Indira Gandhi on the need for savings, and Pant, Gadgil, Patil and Azad on SRC. But most of all I was struck by the small crowds and the passivity of the audience.[1]

Indifference was also evident at the Indore session in 1957 which was dominated by the scramble for seats on the party's ticket. Would-be candidates rushed to and fro in a feverish effort to prove their loyalty and merit. About 40,000 were present at the open session, a very small number indeed. And only 1,100 of the 4,000 delegates considered the session important enough to attend. As for the attitude of the public, 'a large section of the audience rose to depart . . . as soon as Mr. Nehru concluded his unusually brief speech moving for adoption of the Congress election manifesto'.[2]

The story of Gauhati in 1958 is even more dismal. The Congress met under trying circumstances. The shortage of foreign exchange and food deficits had created a serious economic crisis. The country was in the political doldrums. And cynicism was widespread, as the Mundhra Affair was uncovered.

---

[1] Letters to Mrs. Brecher from Amritsar, February 1956.
[2] *The Hindu Weekly Review* (Madras), 14 January 1957.

Finally, the language controversy had reached a critical stage. It was to this that the party devoted most of its attention, as noted earlier. As so often in the past it called for speedy implementation of the land reform programme, implored the Indian people to make new efforts to increase food production and tried to infuse the flagging spirits of the party's supporters with new enthusiasm. It is doubtful whether these appeals made any impact.

Senior Congress leaders termed Gauhati the most dispirited session in living memory. Even fewer delegates attended than at Indore. The audience was estimated at somewhere between 5,000 and 10,000; and on the last day there were only 300— including delegates. In part this was due to the remoteness of the site and the thinly populated surrounding area, in part to the prior announcement that it would be a 'business session'. But to some extent it must be attributed to the growing disenchantment with India's governing party. One disquieting feature was the extraordinarily active role played by Nehru. He delivered no fewer than ten lengthy speeches, drafted every resolution and dominated the pallid proceedings as on no other occasion since Independence. It was, said some leaders, a spectacle of one man trying vainly to reinvigorate a disunited and sluggish organization. His colleagues and the rank and file listened with due respect to 'Panditji's' words but remained unmoved. They had heard these 'pep-talks' more often than they cared to remember and were even less receptive to his ideas than in the past.

The only issue that aroused any interest was the language question. The only remark that left any impression was Nehru's outburst at a foreign press report that he was confronted with the dilemma of abandoning non-alignment or giving up large-scale Western aid. '. . . any intelligent man who understands our basic policy', he thundered, 'knows that this policy will not be changed either because of any temptation of money or threat from any country. . . . I say it with a challenge that even if Jawaharlal Nehru were to go mad, the Congress and the country will not depart from the policy of non-alignment and socialism. . . . So they think we are in such terrible difficulties that we will go to the wall without looking to other countries? . . . We will never change our policy. If somebody does not want to give us aid, well, let him keep his money with him. We will go on without aid.'[1]

One Chief Minister reportedly described the Gauhati session as 'dull, boring, insipid and hungry'.[2] Another prominent Congressman summed it up in these words: 'a dull affair; no one had anything to say, no new ideas to contribute. The language problem caused a little stir but that's all. You didn't miss anything except to see a party in decline.'[3] The press was no less critical. 'The Congress is fast developing a split personality', wrote the *Times of India* on 20 January 1958. 'It picks holes in the Government's policy as if it were an opposition party. And then as the ruling party it persists in the very policies which it continues to criticise. It is in desperate need of a cure for its schizophrenia. . . . The party's leaders are never tired of asking the people to develop a new sense of discipline. It is time they developed a sense of discipline themselves, and while acting in the name of the party, carried out its behests.' Even the staunchly pro-Congress *Hindustan Times* felt constrained to write on 18 January: '. . . one would have expected some reference in the Gauhati resolutions to the progress (or lack of it) in implementing the policies that have been adopted. . . . The ultimate test will be to what extent the newly reorganized Congress [*sic*] will be able to translate these policies into effective action.' Gauhati offered little comfort to Nehru and others who are concerned about the degeneration of the party.

There was, however, one little-publicized development in the Congress during 1957–8 which offers a modicum of hope that the decline can be arrested. A number of middle-grade party leaders, headed by K. D. Malaviya, Minister of State for Mines and Fuel, with members from the U.P., Bengal, Rajasthan, Kerala and Madhya Pradesh, formed a study group to infuse the party with new ideas. The 'Ginger Group' it is called. Of its programme little is known. And an interview with its leader revealed a groping for a coherent set of goals to give the party a new sense of mission. Broadly it may be termed 'modernist', in direct opposition to Gandhism, and socialist in the Western sense. It favours economic development on the Western model

[1] *The Statesman* (Calcutta), 20 January 1958.
[2] Related to the author by persons who wish to remain anonymous.
[3] Ibid.

rather than the 'bullock-cart' and decentralized village approach of Vinoba Bhave and other disciples of the Mahatma. It is convinced that India's economic problems cannot be solved without a concentrated drive to limit population. And it wishes to give the 'socialist pattern of society' a meaningful content, claiming that at the moment it means all things to all people. In that respect it resembles the Congress Socialists of the 'thirties and 'forties. One asset is the sympathy for its aims expressed by Indira Gandhi. Another is Nehru's reported encouragement. Its future will depend largely on Nehru's attitude and the intensity of the economic crisis in the next few years.

*   *   *   *

A few months after the Gauhati session Jawaharlal Nehru expressed the *desire* to relinquish the post of Prime Minister. The place was the great Central Hall of Parliament where M.P.s normally gather during the session to exchange ideas and gossip. The audience was the Congress Parliamentary Party. The time was early evening, a warm, dry Delhi spring evening, the evening of 29 April 1958. They had gathered to hear their leader, without realizing that a political bombshell was about to be exploded in their midst. Some weeks before he had told a press conference that he felt 'stale and flat' and was thinking of ways to remedy the situation. But Nehru had often spoken in this vein. No one denied that he had ample reason to feel tired, mentally and physically; for eleven years he had carried a tremendous burden of responsibility. To his followers, however, 'Panditji' was indestructible and indispensable, the man of destiny whom only death could remove from the centre of the stage.

Many times had Nehru addressed his colleagues in Central Hall, usually in an informal schoolmasterish manner, chiding them for errors and pressing them forward on the mission of creating a 'new' India. On this occasion, however, his manner and his tone were different. He looked more sombre and dejected than usual. He was humble in addressing them. And he had a prepared statement, a very rare practice for India's Prime Minister. 'I feel now that I must have a period when I can free myself from this daily burden and can think of myself as an individual citizen of India and not as Prime Minister', he said. 'There is much to think of. I am greatly concerned at the international situation which hovers on the brink of a precipice, with hydrogen bombs ever ready for discharge and the atmosphere full of hatred and violence and fear and apprehension of some sudden attack. . . . Then there are the problems of India bearing down upon us which require constant attention and fresh thinking. We have to guard against getting into ruts of thought and action. I am anxious to fit myself for the great tasks ahead and I feel that it might help me to do so if I am away from the centre of activity and responsibility. I realise that nothing I may do will lessen that responsibility and, indeed, I have no desire to escape from it, for that comes to me not from the office I hold but from my connection with events in India for forty years.' Before his stunned audience had a chance to react he added that the final decision would be theirs. 'Sir, it is an atom bomb to us', cried one forlorn parliamentarian. 'Panditji, you are leaving us orphans', bewailed another. Nehru calmed his followers and asked them to consider his request.[1]

This they did during the next four days in a desperate effort to stave off what they considered to be disaster. Emergency meetings of the party, hurried conferences among the High Command and the Left wing—together they succeeded in persuading Nehru to yield. The 'Ginger Group' warned that his resignation at that juncture would ensure right-wing control of the party and would jeopardize his reform programme. Conservative colleagues argued that the party would suffer immeasurably by his departure. As so often in his public career Nehru gave way.

On the evening of 3 May he talked to his followers in the same hall. He reminisced about the days of struggle and comradeship and his feeling of attachment to the Congress. He noted that he had thought long before proposing resignation. 'The urge in me [to leave Delhi] became ever more powerful', he remarked. 'Somehow I had to get away from the post even for a while. I had to have an opportunity to think quietly without being pushed or harried.' Pointing to one of the reasons, he added, 'the atmosphere is getting heavier, murkier, more difficult for a sensitive person to breathe easily. What is one to do? I did

---

[1] *New York Times*, 30 April 1958, and *The Hindu Weekly Review* (Madras), 5 May 1958.

not know. I do not know.' However, in the light of advice, 'I shall not proceed to take the step I had suggested.'[1] His audience heaved sighs of relief. But many knew that it was only a respite, that the Prime Minister would try again to leave the Government and to lead his people as Gandhi had done. Those who observed him leaving Central Hall that day saw a disappointed and lonely man, sad at the thought that he had failed to make the break which he so obviously felt was necessary. And few, if any, doubted his sincerity.

What prompted Nehru's dramatic move at that time? He was tired and needed a rest. He was disturbed by the trend of events at home and abroad. Beyond that, however, he did not spell out the sources of his despair. There were many. For one thing the Congress was in the throes of a genuine crisis. A shock was necessary to galvanize the Congress into awareness of its growing plight and, at the same time, to assure greater support for his policies; the analogy of Gandhi's fasting technique comes to mind. Secondly, the controversies over SRC and the language issue revealed deep fissures in Indian society and the alarming growth of 'a certain coarseness, a certain vulgarity' in public life. Third was the increasingly audible concern about 'after Nehru who' and his realization that the succession problem had not been tackled; even more, that he had too long failed to delegate authority. And just a few days before he sought to pass the reins of office to other hands, he had been compelled to make drastic cuts in the Second Five Year Plan.[2] Everything seemed to be going awry.

He was probably not clear in his own mind about long-range plans. For the moment he had a deep 'urge' to 'go to the country', a feeling that he must get away, free from daily administrative routine. In this way he might achieve a number of objectives simultaneously: provide fresh ideas for the future; infuse a much-needed sense of mission into the Congress and the people at large; force the party to move Left by rousing mass demands; undo, at least in part, the damage to Indian unity caused by recent conflicts; inspire his people to make new sacrifices in the interests of economic development; and begin

[1] *New York Times*, 4 May 1958, and *The Hindu Weekly Review* (Madras), 12 May 1958.
[2] See p. 544 below.

the long-overdue experiment in delegation of authority, to ease the transition 'after Nehru'.

Why then did he not follow through? Partly because Nehru has always yielded to pressure, and the pressure in this case was intense; and partly because he was not sure of the wisdom of this act. The results might be contrary to his hopes. Perhaps his direct leadership was more necessary now, in the face of these many problems. There were positive and negative aspects to the proposal and it was difficult to resolve his ambivalence. Hence he turned to his colleagues for advice. It was inevitable that they would beseech him to remain. Their only concession was to 'permit' him a month's vacation. Both they and he hoped that this would be sufficient to restore his strength and give him a fresh perspective. Many also hoped that upon his return he would cast off some of his administrative burdens and concentrate on two much-needed tasks: rejuvenation of the party, and co-ordination of government ministries.

The only possible achievement of this strange episode, strange that is in a Western political context but not in the life of Nehru or in Indian experience, was a shock to the party. And yet Nehru did not seize the opportunity to set in motion drastic changes. He went off to the hills in mid-May leaving his colleagues and his people somewhat bewildered by what had taken place.

This was not the first time Nehru had tried to resign. Three and a half years before, in October 1954, he had also expressed a *desire* to resign. The striking feature of that episode was its similarity—in almost every respect—to the drama of 1958. The fact that he felt tired, he informed the Presidents of the Provincial Congress Committees, 'has no great significance'. He was in good health and felt that there were many tasks still to perform. Why then the talk of resignation? Partly the mood of the moment and partly something deeper, he wrote. He felt 'stale' and wanted to regain his freshness. Further, the question of 'after Nehru what' he found 'somewhat irritating'. No great nation is dependent on one man, he added, and India must accept that challenge. The country had done well and he therefore felt that he could relinquish the Prime Ministership 'at least for some time. . . . I want some leisure to read and think'. He promised to retain a close association with the

Government and felt that he should not continue as Congress President.[1]

As in 1958 observers noted other reasons. One General-Secretary of the party emphasized the prevailing 'lust for power' as the dominant reason.[2] His colleague saw it as 'a shock treatment' for the people at large.[3] Others viewed the gesture as an attempt to build a second line of leaders. Still others claimed that Nehru was trying to strengthen his own position in the party.[4] As one correspondent remarked, 'he is chastened by things that have been left undone rather than inspired by his record of achievement. . . . He is certainly angered by the creeping Hindu superstition which he seems unable to control. . . . He is not tired in the ordinary sense of the word. Perhaps he is looking for another way to tackle the larger tasks ahead.'[5]

Most Congressmen adopted the familiar sycophantic line of Nehru's indispensability. A few blamed him for his weariness and urged him to delegate some of his administrative responsibilities—notably S. K. Patil who later joined the Cabinet.[6] Political opponents commented that if he could not be spared from any posts something must be wrong with the Congress and the Government. The official party view was that a change in the Prime Ministership 'is inconceivable' and appealed to him to relent. This he did, and by the time he returned from China the issue had been settled. As in 1958 the party made one concession; Nehru was relieved of the Congress Presidency, and his hand-picked successor, U. N. Dhebar, was elected. The China tour served as a tonic, as well as a challenge, and Nehru plunged back into his myriad jobs strengthened and more determined than ever. The only difference in 1958 was his deeper 'urge' to give the country a new lead outside the Government, and his greater concern, for time was running out, and the same problems as in 1954 continued to plague the party and the nation.

Nehru had flirted with the idea of resignation on still other occasions: in 1951, in the midst of the struggle with Tandon for

---

[1] The text of this letter is in *The Hindu* (Madras), 13 October 1954.
[2] Shriman Narayan. *The Hindu* (Madras), 20 October 1954.
[3] Balwantrai Mehta. Ibid., 16 October 1954.
[4] *New York Times*, 14 October 1954.
[5] *The Times* (London), 16 October 1954.
[6] *The Hindu* (Madras), 14 October 1954.

control of the party; and in 1957, soon after the general election. The latter was a curious episode and one which sheds light on the machinations of the party's High Command. It was an open secret that Nehru wanted Dr. Radhakrishnan, the Vice-President of India, to succeed Dr. Prasad to the Presidency. The Prime Minister reportedly informed the Vice-President and suggested that it would be a mere formality. But he had not counted on the views of the Right wing. He had told the Congress Parliamentary Party that it was time for older men to retire, a remark that was interpreted to mean the President, among others. He reiterated his remark before the Congress Parliamentary Board, specifically mentioning the President. His senior colleagues agreed—in principle—but urged that Prasad, as an old comrade, should be given the courtesy of making the decision himself. Nehru agreed and arranged to see Prasad the following day. In the interim two members of his Cabinet warned the President of what was afoot and assured him that many opposed Nehru's desire for a change. It was alleged that they were also collecting signatures for Prasad's re-election. When Nehru saw the President, he was informed that Prasad wished to remain and that others had indicated their desire that he do so. Nehru had no choice. The Vice-President was naturally very annoyed by what happened. Nehru was equally upset and thought of resigning, informing the Vice-President of his intention. The Vice-President was asked by a third person to stay on. At first he refused and prepared to leave Delhi—his term as Vice-President since 1952 had ended. Then Maulana Azad and Pant intervened and persuaded him to stand again for the same office. The squall passed.[1] Nehru's gesture was impulsive, hardly comparable with his 'request' the following year.

In the light of these episodes and his awareness that the majority of his colleagues do not share his views on socialism, secularism and radical social change, many persons have wondered why Nehru did not leave the Congress and form a new party. After all, he was the indispensable vote-getter for the Congress and could presumably have carried the country with another group more in sympathy with his goals. Some left-

---

[1] Related to the author in New Delhi in January 1958 by a person who wishes to remain anonymous.

wing Congressmen strongly urged him to do so in 1949. The explanations for his refusal are varied. Some suggested that he was convinced the Congress had not completed its mission and was still the most effective instrument to achieve his objectives. Others claimed that he lacks the administrative capacity to do so. Still others remarked that it would have required much time and energy which would have delayed the initiation of social and economic reform, and that, considering the time at his disposal, Nehru felt it preferable to use the existing machine and to try to change it.[1]

All of these factors probably influenced his decision. The basic reason, however, would seem to be Nehru's deep emotional attachment to the Congress. His whole public life has been bound up with this party, and after thirty years he could not wrench himself away from the party in which he had played a vital role. Nehru himself gave expression to this tie on relinquishing the Congress Presidency at the end of 1954: 'Fifty years ago I attended [the Congress session] as a boy. Forty-two years ago I attended as a delegate. . . . I have thus grown up with the Congress and shared in its wide fold the comradeship of innumerable persons. What I owe to the Congress, I can never repay, for the Congress has made me what I am. . . . I look back with pride and thankfulness to these long years of my association with [it].'[2]

It was primarily due to this association that the Congress retained political power eleven years after Independence. But the age of Congress supremacy appears to be gradually coming to an end. A combination of pressures is at work—the challenge of the Communist Party, the rot in the Congress, the economic problems besetting India, and Nehru's advancing age —which are setting into motion forces that the Congress will not be able to control. Its monopoly of power was broken in 1957. The challenges will grow stronger in the years to come.

---

[1] Related to the author in New Delhi in January 1958, by persons who wish to remain anonymous.

[2] *Express* (Bombay), 17 January 1955.

CHAPTER XVIII

Planning and Welfare

WITH the partition of India the integrated economy of the sub-continent was abruptly torn asunder. The raw jute of eastern Bengal now lay in Pakistan while the jute factories remained in Calcutta, capital of India's West Bengal. The main area of cotton-growing fell to Pakistan whereas the textile centres of Bombay and Ahmedabad were in India. The wheat granary of the sub-continent, the western part of Punjab, went to Pakistan, causing a grave food deficit across the border. Then came the refugees who had to be fed, clothed and housed without delay. The structural dislocation alone was sufficient to produce a major economic crisis.[1] To it was added human folly and selfishness.

The coming of Independence brought to the fore a myriad of sectional economic interests which had long been submerged in the common struggle for freedom. Instead of rallying around a beleaguered government in crisis, various groups pressed their special claims with little thought for the consequences. The principal offender was the business community. Backed by Patel it launched a full-scale attack on the system of price controls over food and other essentials, the only barrier to disastrous inflation—and profits. The battle over controls raged throughout the autumn of 1947. Wisdom decreed their retention until the serious shortage of commodities was overcome. But greed decreed otherwise.[2]

Ironically it was Gandhi who tipped the scales in favour of decontrol. Cabinet Ministers, he declared in mid-November, should not assume greater knowledge than 'those experienced men who do not happen to occupy ministerial chairs, but who hold the view strongly that the sooner the controls are removed

---

[1] See Vakil, C. N., *Economic Consequences of Divided India* (1950).

[2] A strong case for the continuation of controls was made by Professor D. R. Gadgil and Mr. A. D. Gorwala in their *Report* as members of the Commodity Prices Board (1947).

the better'.[1] The Congress complied with his wish, as did the central Government. The result was a tremendous spiral of inflation; within a few months the general price level rose 30 per cent. Only then were controls reimposed, at a heavy cost to millions whose income was rarely sufficient for their needs, even in periods of price stability.

During this period production declined in quantity and quality, and capital moved into ventures which assured a quick profit. It was as if the years of struggle justified an uninhibited quest for personal gain. The business community was not alone in this display of selfishness. Congress officials indulged in corruption and nepotism, especially in the provinces, claiming the rewards of lengthy service. Trade unions joined in the fray with wildcat strikes.

Nehru attempted to stem the tide with words—blunt words, passionate words, angry words. He did not conceal the magnitude of the crisis: '. . . there is a kind of creeping paralysis in our economy and the whole of India', he said in a broadcast to the nation. Neither Capital nor Labour was spared. The right to strike is a 'valued weapon' and 'I am the last man to say that Labour should be denied [this right]. Nevertheless, there are times when strikes are dangerous. . . . This is one of those times.'[2] His most scathing remarks were directed to businessmen. '. . . I hope no one will challenge me when I say that during this last war a certain section of the employer class . . . behaved exceedingly badly, exceedingly egotistically. . . . I have yet to understand how, in spite of the . . . heavy taxation in India, these vast fortunes were made. . . . We have to find some means and machinery to prevent this kind of shameful traffic in human beings and profiting at the expense of the nation.'[3]

A measure of relief came early in 1948, with a tripartite agreement for a three-year truce in industrial warfare. The real problem, however, was a crisis in business confidence, a fear of impending socialism now that Nehru was Prime Minister. Everything pointed to a leftward turn. As late as January 1948

---

[1] Quoted in Karaka, D. F., *Betrayal in India*, p. 220. Gorwala replied with a pungent criticism of this view. *The Statesman* (Calcutta), 16 November 1947.
[2] On 18 January 1948. *Independence and After*, pp. 159, 160.
[3] On 18 December 1947. Ibid., p. 149.

the Economic Programme Committee of the Congress, under Nehru's leadership, had set down the broad lines of policy: nationalization of public utilities and all defence and key industries; public ownership of monopolies; the destruction of the managing agency system as early as possible; and a maximum profit of 5 per cent. on venture capital.[1] Insecurity among businessmen led to a 'strike of capital'; the economy remained at a virtual standstill pending the announcement of the Government's industrial policy.

When it came, on 7 April 1948, Nehru's admirers and critics alike were surprised. Here was no programme of revolutionary change, no real cause for alarm by private investors. Indeed, there was little resemblance to socialism. Public ownership was confined to three industries—munitions, atomic energy and railways. In six others the Government reserved to itself the exclusive right to start *new* ventures—coal, iron and steel, aircraft manufacturing, shipbuilding, telegraphic and telephonic materials, and minerals. *Existing* concerns in these industries were to remain free from government control; nationalization was postponed for at least ten years. 'The rest of the industrial field will normally be left open to private enterprise'.[2]

The business community was jubilant, but radicals were crestfallen at the 'retreat from socialism'. Many recalled Nehru's strong words twenty years earlier: '. . . revolutionary changes cannot be brought about by reformist tactics and methods. The reformer who is afraid of radical change or of overthrowing an oppressive régime and seeks merely to eliminate some of its abuses becomes in reality one of its defenders'.[3] What then impelled him to make these sweeping concessions to private enterprise? For one thing, Patel used his influence to prevent any move to the Left. For another, the crisis of production had reached alarming proportions and had to be surmounted at all costs. Two methods were, theoretically, available—direct government operation of the economy or encouragement to private capital. The first was practically impossible because of staunch opposition in the Congress and the shortage of trained

[1] A summary of the Report of the Economic Programme Committee is to be found in *Charkha* (Bulletin of the A.I.C.C.), vol. 2, No. 4, 1 March 1948, p. 3.

[2] The text of the Resolution on Industrial Policy is to be found in the *Hindustan Times* (New Delhi), 8 April 1948.

[3] To the Punjab Provincial Conference in 1928. Dwivedi, op. cit., p. 90.

personnel. Moreover, Nehru's socialism did not encompass a solution as drastic as 'war communism'. Hence the need to offer inducements to the business community, sufficient to end the strike of capital and to set in motion economic expansion. This was made clear in the Explanatory Memorandum to the Resolution on Industrial Policy: '. . . The expected result of the announcement . . . will be the restoration to their former level of the prices of Government securities . . . and share values are bound to go up.' There was, too, a desire to stimulate the flow of foreign capital and skills into the underdeveloped Indian economy.

Beyond these specific reasons was the shock of the communal riots which dictated a policy of caution. As Nehru told the Constituent Assembly, '. . . after all that has happened in the course of the last seven or eight months, one has to be very careful of the steps one takes so as not to injure the existing structure too much. There has been destruction and injury enough, and certainly I confess to this House that I am not brave and gallant enough to go about destroying any more. I think there is room still for the destruction in India of many things. . . . Nevertheless, it is a matter of approach.'[1] His approach was Fabian. The principle of nationalization was reaffirmed, but gradualism became the keynote. It has remained so ever since.

Caution led Nehru to propound a novel variation of socialist economic planning. For want of a better phrase it may be termed 'socialization of the vacuum', that is to say, the concentration of public investment in those areas of the economy which are totally free from private interests. The line of argument developed in his speeches at the time may be summarized as follows: India is an underdeveloped country with limited capital and skills, both public and private; a steady increase in production is the prime requisite if the basic goal of a higher standard of living for the masses is to be achieved; both public and private capital have important roles to play, even inefficient private enterprise; to use public funds for nationalization of existing industry is both short-sighted and foolhardy; it is a waste of resources, for it does not increase the gross national

[1] On 7 April 1948, while defending the Industrial Policy Resolution. *Independence and After*, p. 173.

24a. Being met at Moscow Airport by Marshal Bulganin on
7 June, 1955

24b. Nehru with Indira Gandhi being shown round the steel-works in
Rustavi, U.S.S.R., in June, 1955

Press Information Bureau, Government of India

25a. On his official visit to the U.S.A., December, 1956

Press Information Bureau, Government of India

25b. Presenting a souvenir to U Nu, former Prime Minister of Burma
at Imphal, 1953

product and diverts capital from much-needed growth in key sectors of the economy; moreover, there are certain fields of development which private capital will not enter because the profit margin is low and the gestation period very long; yet it is precisely in those fields that capital is desperately needed, such as power, irrigation, transport, and agricultural improvement; to nationalize the bulk of private industry is a rigid, formula approach to socialism; it may be appropriate to the highly developed economies of the West but it is singularly unrealistic in India where the key problem is growth, not control over large concentrations of economic power; furthermore, control is possible without nationalization; flourishing private enterprise contributes to the nation's welfare, and the government can impose necessary controls to avoid its evils; the primary function of the State in Indian conditions at this time is to add appreciably to production, not to effect a change in ownership; nationalization is not to be abandoned but it should be applied only in very special circumstances—where it facilitates growth.

In essence, Nehru was subscribing to the principles of a mixed economy, with special emphasis on the historic task of the State to develop the vacuum viewed in realistic economic terms. This approach seemed to him to have political merit as well, because it avoided a clash with private interests, indeed, stimulated expansion in the private sector and, at the same time, eased the way to socialism in areas of the economy hitherto untapped. Few of Nehru's admirers took this long-run view. Critics termed it a 'betrayal' of pledges which he had made during the 'thirties and 'forties. This it was in a formal sense. Yet the deviation served short-run economic and political purposes while the duumvirs created the necessary conditions of stability.[1]

*   *   *   *

Despite this 'retreat', Nehru remained committed to planning and socialism. The Congress, too, had long talked about the need for sweeping economic reform—in the Karachi Resolution on Fundamental Rights (1931), in its election manifestos of 1936 and 1945, and in a series of resolutions during the early years of independence. Just after the transfer of power it had

---

[1] The Industrial Policy Resolution was revised in 1956 as a prelude to the Second Five-Year Plan. The changes will be discussed on pp. 537–8 below.

S

proclaimed the goal of 'a socialist democracy in India'. Frequently it had called for nationalization of basic industries, regulation of banking and insurance, encouragement of cooperatives, progressive taxation and the like. And at the end of 1948 the party had formally recommended the creation of a central planning body.[1]

The idea of economic planning was not unknown in India before Independence. Nehru has preached its virtues since the late 1920's. The Congress Socialists had embraced it wholeheartedly. And the party's National Planning Committee, under Nehru's inspiration, had paved the way for its acceptance through their wide-ranging investigations. During the second world war a spate of national plans appeared in India, the most noteworthy being the 'Bombay Plan' for large-scale industrialization prepared by a group of industrialists.[2] The Government of India's Planning Department did valuable preparatory work in the final years of the *Raj* which continued with little publicity through the Advisory Planning Board of the new régime. Nevertheless, as late as 1949 planning had not yet made a serious dent in the political or economic thinking of the Indian Government.

The inducement to positive action was the steadily deteriorating economic situation. Everything pointed to a deepening long-term crisis: chronic unemployment and under-employment in the village; rising unemployment in the city; the reluctance of private capital to invest in productive enterprise—this despite the moderate Industrial Policy Resolution of 1948; growing inflation; the spread of black-marketeering and corruption; stagnant agriculture; inefficiency in industrial plants, which were further hamstrung by shortages of experienced personnel, raw materials and spare parts; and, at the same time, constantly increasing pressure on resources arising from the growth of population. Discontent was widespread, especially among the intelligentsia, and lethargy was everywhere. Some felt betrayed by the glaring gap between the promise and reality of independence.[3]

[1] For Congress's economic views in the years immediately following Independence see *Congress Bulletin*, No. 5, 7 November 1947, pp. 16–21; No. 6, 31 December 1947, pp. 20–21; and No. 4, June–July 1949, pp. 29–34.
[2] *Plan for the Economic Development of India* (1944).
[3] See for example Karaka, *Betrayal in India* (1950).

An analogy with China in the last years of the Nationalist régime did not seem far-fetched. India in 1949–50 was at the economic crossroads. There was danger that the policy of drift would eventually transform apathy into some form of revolutionary movement which could lead to years of struggle—as in China. What made the crisis even more alarming was the fact that it was due to basic limitations in the Indian economy, not to temporarily unfavourable circumstances such as the dislocation caused by Partition. The choice appeared to be between continued *laissez-faire*, with increased tensions, and a co-ordinated mobilization of resources to meet the challenge.

Various persons impressed this sombre picture upon the Prime Minister. Among them was Dr. Solomon Trone, an American engineer of wide experience who served as Nehru's personal adviser from the autumn of 1949 to the summer of 1950.[1] Arriving in India as the Communists swept to power in China, he conducted an investigation into various aspects of the Indian economy and concluded that conditions were alarmingly similar to those of China at the end of the second world war. Drastic action was required without delay, he argued, the first step being the formation of a central agency to evolve a unified national plan. He was unsparing in his criticism of the existing state of affairs, including what he termed excessive interference from the Secretariat in Delhi.

His report to the Prime Minister was not made public 'simply because it deals rather frankly with some particular industries [and] we feel it might embarrass them'.[2] However, the essence of his proposals was known: the formation of a small expert body which should have authority to prepare and execute a five-year plan under the Prime Minister's supervision, with an array of regional and functional planning groups scattered through the country. Ultimately responsible to the Cabinet, the central agency should have a relatively free hand in implementing the plan. Trone emphasized the need to create capital-goods industries, in particular, additional steel plants, a

[1] Dr. Trone's experience in underdeveloped areas began during the first world war when he was loaned by the General Electric Corporation to the Czarist Government. He stayed on after the Revolution and helped to build the Dneiper Dam. Thereafter he acted as an industrial adviser to the Governments of Japan and Nationalist China.

[2] Nehru at a press conference on 6 January 1950. *Press Conferences 1950*, p. 9.

machine-tool industry and electric-generating equipment on which to build secondary industries. He also urged strong encouragement to agricultural co-operatives of various kinds. Economic development would be financed partly by foreign loans, but would require sacrifices by all sections of the Indian people. Perhaps his most drastic proposal was the mobilization of 'inner reserves', the unfreezing of gold, silver and jewellery which are hoarded in vast quantities.

Powerful groups were alienated by Trone's blunt critique of the shortcomings of existing management and were alarmed by his proposals. A special sub-committee of civil servants termed his conception of planning 'fundamentally totalitarian' and thus inapplicable to Indian conditions. The idea of mobilizing hoarded wealth was considered impracticable and co-operative farming was rejected as a 'Trojan Horse' for collectivization. The notion of a managed mixed economy was approved, but his recommendation of a planning body with wide authority was rejected as an infringement on Cabinet supremacy. Industrialists feared the growth of the public sector and the implied conception of far-reaching government regulation of the economy. Although Trone's proposals were not accepted immediately, they were to reappear in subsequent deliberations over the First and, more particularly, the Second Five-Year Plans. And he strengthened Nehru's determination to create a planning agency at once.

*   *   *   *

The problems confronting India's economic planners can only be described as gargantuan. There is, firstly, the sheer size and diversity of the country and its people, some 360 million (in 1950) inhabiting a sub-continent. Topographical features range from the world's highest mountains to the world's largest alluvial plain and include vast tracts of desert along with areas receiving the world's most concentrated rainfall. United in many respects, India's millions are also divided by language, culture, creed and caste. Planners must cater to the needs and aspirations of these regions and groups and must evoke the co-operation of officials and the people at large in the States and the villages. Operating within a democratic framework, the planners are subject to a myriad of regional and local pressures.

There is, secondly, the novelty of the idea of planning in a predominantly peasant society which does not take easily to change. Indian peasants have, for generations, followed patterns of living and work laid down by their forefathers. Constantly operating on the margin of subsistence, they require evidence of benefits before adopting new methods. Lacking initiative, they must be moved to action by a relative handful of officials struggling against the dead weight of tradition. Apart from lethargy and distrust there is the immobility of the vast majority of Indians, both physical and social. Approximately three out of every four are dependent on the land for their livelihood. The surplus rural population, many millions, lack the funds—and the inducement of jobs—to migrate to the city. Language and cultural barriers confine effective mobility to the linguistic area. And the closely knit family group tends to create self-contained socio-economic units from which individuals can break only with the utmost difficulty.

A powerful hindrance to planned development is the overriding importance of status in Indian society. Inequality is the hallmark of the caste system and caste consciousness continues to pervade Hindu life. Moreover, respect for age and tradition is deeply rooted and neither is conducive to change. All this reduces mobility and hinders the rational process of planning.

These obstacles would be formidable in any country. In India their deterrent effects are increased many-fold by the grim poverty which stalks the land, poverty of such dimensions that its full impact can only be partly conveyed by words and statistics. Hundreds of thousands make their 'homes' on the streets of India's overcrowded cities. Calcutta can lay claim to the dubious distinction of having the foulest slums in the world. Other Indian cities are not far behind. Millions suffer from malnutrition; whereas 2,200 calories per day are the minimum required for health, the average caloric intake in India was less than 1,700 in 1956. The average *per capita* annual income in 1951 was about $53 or 14½ c. a day; and this must cover all expenses—food, clothing, shelter, medicines, education. The 50 million Untouchables and the 40-odd million landless labourers have, perhaps, half that income.

If life in the city is a perpetual struggle for survival, life in the village is devoid of material comfort for all but a few. The typical peasant home is a windowless mud hut with a few cooking utensils and a string cot. It is almost always dark; less than 1 per cent. of India's 500,000 villages had electricity in 1951. At the beginning of the First Plan few village streets were paved and sewage disposal was rare. India in general, and village India in particular, is a land of collective filth and individual cleanliness. Hinduism enjoins personal cleanliness on its followers and most Hindus bathe daily, but most are compelled to wear the same clothes for they lack more than one *dhoti*. Sanitation in the village is abominable. More than half a million die every year from tuberculosis. Famine takes its toll periodically; and malnutrition saps the strength of the majority of Indians. Despite improvements in medical attention there were fewer than 70,000 doctors and 10,000 nurses for a population of 360 million. Most Indians eat only twice a day. Few get meat, fish, eggs or fruit, certainly not in sufficient quantities. The result is a very high death rate and the lowest life expectancy anywhere in the world—twenty-seven years in 1947, raised to thirty-two years in the last decade.

Despite the high death rate, India's population increases by 4 to 5 million a year. In every plan period this means an additional 20 to 25 million mouths to feed and 9 million new jobs to create. At the beginning of the First Plan period there were at least 2 million unemployed in the cities and perhaps 15 million in the villages—this apart from millions who are idle more than half the year. In 1958 it was estimated that 50 million peasant *families* were without work eight months a year, a colossal waste of human energy.[1] This is perhaps the gravest problem of Indian economic development.

The rise in population not only adds to the army of unemployed: it accentuates the grave imbalance between agriculture and industry. The pressure of population on land is already intense. With each passing year it becomes more severe. The possibility of siphoning part of the surplus into the towns depends on the pace of industrialization, housing construction and a steady increase in food production to feed the larger

[1] V. T. Krishnamachari, Deputy Chairman of the Planning Commission, on 12 January 1958. *The Statesman* (Calcutta), 13 January 1958.

urban population. As one senior planner put it, 'we are engaged in a deadly race between economic development, especially industrialization, and the growing pressure on land. Even assuming the achievement of targets set in the first *five* plans this problem cannot be easily solved.'[1]

Another long-run obstacle to development is the dire shortage of trained personnel in all branches of a modern economy. More generally, India is beset by the evil of widespread illiteracy. About 83 per cent. of all Indians are unable to read and write. School facilities in 1951 were available for less than half of the primary school-age children. Over 90 per cent. do not attend high school; and less than 1 per cent. proceed to the university.

Perhaps the most striking economic paradox is that India is a rich country with poor people. The reality is depressing, the potential encouraging. Side by side with poverty, illiteracy and disease are bountiful resources for development: the largest known deposits of high-grade iron ore in the world and adequate reserves of coal for the expansion of the steel industry—which produced less than 2 million tons in 1951; the third-largest reserve of manganese; four-fifths of the world's supply of mica; adequate deposits of bauxite, gypsum, chrome, lime, gold, clay, salt and feldspar. India lacks zinc, copper, tin and lead, but future surveys may unearth some of these minerals. India has always been dependent on the Middle East for oil, but recent discoveries in Assam may well ensure a high degree of self-sufficiency in this vital commodity. Power for electricity is abundant, notably hydro-electric power to be harnessed from India's mighty rivers; only 3 per cent. of the potential was exploited at the time of Independence. The recent discovery of large deposits of thorium provides a basis for atomic power.

Thus the material bases for industrialization are present. There is, too, an almost unlimited supply of labour. But grinding poverty has hindered their utilization thus far. The fundamental problem is that of inadequate capital and know-how. At the same time, India is engaged in a perennial struggle to feed its mounting population. Poverty and its inevitable twins, disease and illiteracy, permeate all aspects of development. The combined effect of these ills is a massive burden on

[1] To the author in New Delhi in February 1956, by a person who wishes to remain anonymous.

all plans for development: pressure on land and the struggle for subsistence; widespread unemployment; a shortage of skilled manpower; the lack of a disciplined labour force for the cities; the absence of entrepreneurial initiative; the preference for speculative activity on the part of businessmen; inefficient production, indeed, the lowest *per capita* productivity in the world; severe limitations on mobility; and archaic methods of agricultural production which cannot be easily altered.

*   *   *   *

Who are India's planners and how did they tackle these awesome problems? What success have they achieved thus far? What role has Nehru played? And what are the prospects? The machinery and method of Indian planning have changed little over the years. The principal agency is the six-member Planning Commission created in March 1950. Of its original members only two still retained membership in 1958—Nehru, the Commission's Chairman since its inception, and G. L. Nanda, who has held the Planning portfolio in the central Government simultaneously since 1951. During most of the First Plan period the other members were V. T. Krishnamachari, a distinguished civil servant who continues to serve as Vice-Chairman; C. D. Deshmukh, the Finance Minister; Dr. J. C. Ghosh; and K. C. Neogy, a former Cabinet Minister. An unofficial member, whose stature and influence have grown with time, is Prof. P. C. Mahalanobis, Director of the Indian Statistical Institute and Honorary Statistical Adviser to the Indian Government. By convention the Finance Minister is an *ex-officio* member of the Commission. Thus, Deshmukh's successor, T. T. Krishnamachari, joined the Commission in the summer of 1956. He, in turn, was followed by Morarji Desai in 1958. Dr. Ghosh was replaced in 1957 by Krishna Menon.

Broad policy decisions are made by the Cabinet, to which the Commission is responsible. Its primary functions are research and the drafting of an all-India programme of development. Apart from Nehru, each member is responsible for certain areas of planning. Thus, during the First Plan period Krishnamachari was in charge of agriculture, irrigation and power, along with overall co-ordination of the plan; Nanda dealt with labour and employment; Ghosh supervised projects for education, social welfare and community development; Neogy directed planning for industry, commerce and transport; and Deshmukh was concerned with the financial aspects. Mahalanobis's sphere was and is ill-defined. He deals with statistical problems and heads a small unit devoted to long-term 'perspective' planning. More generally, he is the Commission's brainstruster, though his views have not always found favour with his colleagues. Within the Commission, under the direction of each member, are various specialized divisions, economic, financial, employment, agricultural, progress, statistical and the like. There are, too, a number of expert advisers attached to the Commission.

In the early years the Commission exerted wide-ranging influence, partly because it was the sole planning agency. Gradually, however, its policy influence has declined. In the summer of 1952 the National Development Council was established as the supreme administrative and advisory body on planning. Consisting of the Prime Minister, all State Chief Ministers and members of the Planning Commission, it meets two or three times a year to consider progress reports and to lay down policy directives, invariably approved by the Cabinet. In it the diverse pressures from the States and the Centre find expression, and compromise solutions, not always desirable on economic grounds, are hammered out. For some time it lacked a sense of unity or direction. To facilitate more purposeful discussion and guidance a Standing Committee of the Council was established in November 1954, with only nine Chief Ministers and a few key Cabinet Members. Since then the National Development Council and its Standing Committee have virtually relegated the Commission to the status of a research arm. Expert advice to the Commission and the Development Council is provided by the Economists Panel. Each State has its own planning agency which feeds the Commission proposals for local projects and constantly lobbies for a 'just' share of appropriations. Once the overall plan is approved, they administer specific programmes within their territory and provide the Commission with a steady flow of progress reports. The Commission itself sends out agents to report on local projects and to stir up interest in the plans. On the basis of its periodic surveys the National Development Council adjusts appropriations and projects.

Indian planning is the product of democratic ways of discussion and decision. The period of time allotted to deliberations, the widespread participation of persons at the State and local levels, the constant search to reconcile different conceptions and goals, the free play given to interest groups—all testify to the democratic planning process in India. The 'Draft Outline' of the First Plan appeared in July 1951, after months of discussion in the States and at the Centre, and was based on proposals 'from below'. The Final Draft was not approved until December 1952. In the interim the Outline was subjected to searching scrutiny by the press, political parties, industry and labour, the intelligentsia and Parliament; the effect is evident in the basic revisions embodied in the Final Draft.

This process was repeated during the preparation of the Second Plan. In April 1954 the Planning Commission asked the State Governments to prepare local plans down to the District and village level and to funnel these to the Centre. At the same time studies for all-India targets and a debate on priorities got under way. The first and most controversial was Professor Mahalanobis's 'plan-frame'. Along with a 'tentative framework' prepared by the Commission and the Finance Ministry, this was discussed by the Economists Panel which produced its own 'Memorandum'. These then went to the National Development Council in May 1955. For the rest of that year detailed consultations took place with State Governments and Union Ministries. From these emerged the Commission's 'Draft Memorandum' at the beginning of 1956, which went before the National Development Council once more and to a Consultative Committee of M.P.s. The 'Draft Outline' was published in February 1956 and, after further public debate, the Final Draft appeared, with approval of all interested bodies. As one senior planner remarked, 'the Plan is a product of group thinking and decisions. It represents agreement among a large number of interest groups, local, regional and national.'[1] Within the Commission itself each member examines the draft in its entirety and offers suggestions for revisions. Ultimately a collective product emerges. Even after the plan is approved dissent is not stifled, as in the case of Neogy whose

---

[1] To the author in New Delhi in February 1956, by a person who wishes to remain anonymous.

views on the public and private sector, at variance with those of his colleagues, were made public. Moreover, the planners are flexible, willing to make revisions in accordance with progress reports. This has been true of both plans.

Nehru's role in the planning process is crucial, despite the fact that he lacks expert knowledge of economics and finance. In fact, his influence spans the entire process, from the drafting stage to implementation. Firstly, he stands at the centre of the decision-making structure by virtue of his positions as Prime Minister, Chairman of the Planning Commission and Chairman of the National Development Council—and because he is Jawaharlal Nehru. He is the link between the planning agencies and the Government and is brought into any matter requiring Cabinet approval, notably broad decisions concerning targets, aims and priorities. Secondly, because of his multiple positions and personal prestige he is the central focus of attention for all pressure groups—the Commission itself and individual members, Cabinet Ministers with special projects, State Ministers seeking attention to their local needs, Congressmen anxious to please their constituents, trade unions and employer associations, and special interest groups or individuals like Vinoba Bhave and the *Bhoodan* (land gift) Movement, co-operative associations, community development officials, etc. He is, therefore, the pivot around which discussion and decision revolve. A constant stream of letters and verbal representations seek his intervention and approval. During the early years Nehru was inclined to depend on the Commission and not to busy himself with its deliberations. Since the autumn of 1954, however, he has devoted much of his time to planning problems. He attends and addresses all meetings of the National Development Council and its Standing Committee and expresses his views forcefully. Moreover, there is no doubt that these influence the planners and find expression in the Final Draft, notably his stress on heavy industry and on the proper relationship between the public and private sectors. 'Policy is made by the Prime Minister's public statements', according to one senior official. 'In other words, Mr. Nehru's "thinking out loud" on the subject of socialism sets the pace in the Leftward move, and Ministers and officials have to revise their plans periodically in order to keep up with him.'[1]

Not the least important is his role as liaison between the planners and the people. Nehru is the most effective salesman of planning in the country as a whole. Constant reference to the Plan in his speeches has helped to make the Indian people plan-conscious, indeed, has inculcated the belief that in planning lies the realization of their hopes for higher standards of living, education for their children, better health services and employment. This may well be his most important contribution, spreading the gospel that planning is the key to welfare. For with general acceptance of this view comes greater co-operation and a spirit of sacrifice, and with that the likelihood of a more rapid pace of development, other things being equal.

*   *   *   *

India's First Five-Year Plan (1951–6) was modest in scope and cautious in approach. Indeed, it could hardly be considered a plan in the accepted meaning of the term. It was, rather, an amalgam of specific projects drafted by the pre-Independence Planning Department and its successor, the Advisory Board on Planning. Many of them had already been introduced. The Five-Year Plan merely integrated these into a rational framework, established priorities, allocated additional funds where necessary, and provided further guidance for their speedy implementation. Planned expenditure of public funds underwent various revisions, but at no time was it ambitious or risky.

The Draft Outline proposed a public outlay of $3·6 billion divided into two categories: $3 billion designed to restore pre-war availability of essential consumer goods by fulfilling the goals of specific projects already under way and by extensions in agriculture, irrigation, power and communications; and $·6 billion for development if external funds were forthcoming. In the Final Draft the two categories were merged and appropriations increased to $4·1 billion. Further revisions raised the anticipated public expenditure to just short of $5 billion. The breakdown was as follows:[2]

---

[1] Reported by the Correspondent of the *Financial Times* (London), 23 May 1955.

[2] Based upon the table in Government of India, Planning Commission, *Second Five Year Plan*, pp. 51–52, at the rate of Rs. 1 = $.21.

	Millions of Dollars	Percentage of Total
Agriculture and Community Development ...	749·7	15·1
Irrigation and Flood Control	842·1	17·0
Power ...	546·0	11·1
Industry and Mining ...	375·9	7·6
Transport and Communications	1,169·7	23·6
Social Services, Housing and Rehabilitation ...	1,119·3	22·6
Miscellaneous ...	144·9	3·0
TOTAL ...	4,947·6	100·0

The most striking feature of the First Plan was its stress on agriculture. This was not unnatural in view of the central place of agriculture in the Indian economy. An added stimulus was the fact that famine plagued many parts of the country in 1950–1 and huge sums of foreign exchange were being drained away for food imports. Moreover, agricultural production was barely keeping pace with the annual population increase of about 4·5 million. Hence close on 40 per cent. of the total expenditure was earmarked for agriculture and related sectors (including a substantial part of the outlay for power). Until food production could be substantially increased and made less dependent on the uncertain monsoon by enlarging the area under irrigation, the static barrier could not be broken; foreign exchange would be 'wasted' on consumer goods; and plans for industrialization would be seriously retarded. The large expenditure for transport and communications was also geared in part to the need for meeting local food shortages. Industry was given a nominal sum in the expectation that once the food problem was overcome India could proceed to large-scale industrialization in the Second Plan period.

After a sluggish start the pace of public investment quickened. By the end of the plan period it reached approximately 83 per cent. of the anticipated outlay. The gap was due primarily to shortages in managerial personnel and administrative deficiencies, as well as the delayed start of certain major projects. Nevertheless, the Plan was an unquestioned success. National income rose by 18 per cent. over the five years whereas the population increased by 6 per cent. Food production reached a new high, some 5,000,000 tons above the target, freeing India of the spectre of famine in the short run and eliminating the costly drain on foreign exchange. *Per capita* annual income rose from $53.34 to $59.01, not spectacular but a step forward. Production of capital goods rose by 70 per cent., consumer goods and industrial raw materials by 34 per cent. Some 16 million acres of land were brought under some form of irrigation. Electric power increased almost 70 per cent., as did cement production. The planners had reason to be satisfied, even though the increase in food production was due in part to three favourable monsoons in succession.[1]

Perhaps the main achievement was to maintain the 'hope level' and to make planning more attractive by providing concrete evidence of its material benefits. Greater co-operation in the future would ease the planners' task. Nevertheless, the disturbing facts remained that India was still desperately poor, that unemployment was increasing and that agricultural prices were falling. The time had come for a bolder, more ambitious programme.

Nehru and others had reached this conclusion long before the end of the First Plan period. The pace of progress had to be quickened and the scope of development enlarged—such was the constant refrain of the Prime Minister and the Congress from 1953 onwards.[2] Equally important was the upsurge of 'leftism' in Nehru's pronouncements and the attempt to inject a stronger dose of socialism into India's economy. It began with a major policy debate towards the end of 1954—just after Nehru's return from China—and found expression in a series of 'radical' steps the following year. The central issue was the place of private and state enterprise in the Second Plan and, more generally, in the pattern of mixed economy to which the Government was committed. Broadly, the official view was that private enterprise has a rightful and secure place in the economy but is clearly subservient to the public sector. The business community claimed that private investors were inhibited by the

---

[1] Based upon *Second Five Year Plan*, pp. 2–3, and the *Review of the First Five Year Plan*, summarized in *The Hindu Weekly Review* (Madras), 5 August 1957.

[2] See for example *Congress Bulletin*, No. 5, May 1953, p. 156, and No. 8, 9, August–September 1953, p. 249. The Prime Minister conveyed this view to the author in March 1956.

implied threat of nationalization and that state enterprise was receiving preferential treatment.[1]

Nehru took the lead with an important address to the National Development Council on 9 November 1954. He spoke like an impatient man, eager for more rapid and more comprehensive economic improvement. He stressed the dynamic and continuous character of planning but he was also realistic in cautioning against an over-ambitious Second Plan. He was appalled by the blatant anomalies of the economy, illustrated by the crying need for engineers and the existence of large numbers of unemployed engineers. On the basic issue he came out clearly for a 'socialistic picture of society' though not 'in a dogmatic sense at all'. As for private enterprise, 'it is undoubtedly useful. . . . We wish to encourage it, but the dominance it exercised throughout the world during a certain period is no more. . . . There is plenty of room for private enterprise, provided the main aim is kept clear.' In the Second Plan, he added, the emphasis must be shifted from agriculture to industry. And so it was. Both Gandhians and 'Westernizers' could derive comfort from his remark that heavy industries and cottage industries should be developed simultaneously.[2]

Nehru stated these views frequently during the six-week debate that followed. While trying to reassure private enterprise he made it abundantly clear that he was determined to assert the primacy of the public sector. Throughout he was moderate in tone. He criticized Marxism as outdated, asserted that Communism was unsuitable to Indian conditions, and reaffirmed the 'middle way' in which both sectors of the economy could co-operate to mutual advantage. Nationalization of existing industry was not contemplated, he declared. The approach, he told Parliament, would be pragmatic, not doctrinaire, and India would follow the peaceful, democratic, non-violent way. As he remarked on another occasion, 'I believe in our capacity . . . in winning over people rather than fighting them. . . . We can bring about social changes and

---

[1] This view was expressed forcefully in a report by a seven-man committee headed by A. D. Shroff, Director of Tata Sons. Summarized in *Christian Science Monitor* (Boston), 14 August 1954.

[2] The text of this speech is to be found in Nehru, *Planning and Development*, pp. 15–20.

developments . . . by the friendly co-operative approach, rather than the approach of trying to eliminate each other. . . .'[1]

Notwithstanding his moderation, Nehru was trying, against considerable opposition, even within his own party, to take the country to the Left. The earliest indications came during the parliamentary debate in December 1954, when he gave notice of a proposal to amend the Constitution so as to remove from the Courts the right to determine the amount of compensation for nationalized property, and Deshmukh referred to plans to nationalize the Imperial Bank of India, the largest private commercial bank in the country.

Ideologically, the shift was given concrete form at the Avadi session of the Congress in January 1955. The road to socialism was charted, though what form it would take no one bothered to define: '. . . planning should take place with a view to the establishment of a socialistic pattern of society, where the principal means of production are under social ownership or control, production is progressively speeded up and there is equitable distribution of the national wealth'. With respect to economic policy, 'the public sector must play a progressively greater part, more particularly, in the establishment of basic industries'. The State would have to initiate large-scale power and transport projects, have overall control of resources, maintain strategic controls, prevent the development of cartels and the like.[2]

Indian reaction to the Avadi Resolution was mixed. All agreed that it was a logical outgrowth of Nehru's speeches during the preceding few months. But as to the meaning of 'socialist pattern' there was a wide range of views. One newspaper noted that no one bothered to define it and 'even Pandit Nehru . . . was brilliantly vague'. It was merely a play on words, remarked another, 'a distinction without a difference'. Some termed it realistic but not socialistic. One commentator remarked acidly that 'socialistic pattern' suited Nehru's 'all too flexible' approach, with its 'distaste for details and a penchant for soaring well above the earth, if not in the clouds'.

[1] Government of India, Planning Commission, *Prime Minister's Speech at the Meeting of the Standing Committee of the National Development Council on January 7, 1956*, p. 4.

[2] The text of the Avadi Resolutions is to be found in Fisher, Margaret W., and Bondurant Joan V., *Indian Approaches to a Socialist Society*, Appendix II.

Communists saw it merely as a catchy slogan. The newspaper founded by Nehru himself noted that while it might not mean socialism, 'it will help people to think socialism'.[1]

It was generally agreed at the time, and still is, that Nehru was the moving force behind the Avadi Resolution. Yet Nehru himself declared a year later: 'I might tell you I had very little to do with that Resolution. It was the new Congress President [Mr. Dhebar]. I approved, of course, heartily, but it was the new Congress President who took the initiative in the matter.'[2] As for the timing of the move to a 'socialist pattern' there was much speculation. Some believed it to be politically inspired, an effort to inject the governing party with much-needed enthusiasm, particularly on the eve of the crucial Andhra election where a powerful Communist Party threatened the Congress. Others saw it as Nehru's attempt to infuse new life into a flagging economy, for the pace of progress was disappointing. Many were struck by the fact that the shift occurred almost immediately after his China tour. Typical was the following comment: 'Informed circles would consider it less than fair to suggest that the idea caught on after Mr. Nehru's visit to China. But they would however not seriously demur to the observation that the China trip may have served to stir up his ever-impatient soul with a view to reassessing whether the purpose and direction pursued by the Congress corresponded with the declared objectives.'[3]

Nehru himself demurred. In response to a question about the possible link between his China tour and the Avadi Resolution, he said with some vehemence, 'absolutely nothing to do with it'. Further, 'we had talked about socialism throughout [the struggle for independence] and as long as twenty-five years ago the Congress said that the chief industries should be owned and controlled by the State [the Karachi Resolution of 1931]. After the coming of Independence it developed gradually and ultimately came out. Nothing special happened last year.'[4]

Be that as it may, there can be no doubt that Nehru was deeply moved by what he saw in China. He was impressed by

[1] Taken from Fisher and Bondurant, op. cit., pp. 9–16.
[2] To the author in New Delhi on 6 June 1956.
[3] 'Special Correspondent' of *The Hindu* (Madras), 18 January 1955.
[4] To the author in New Delhi on 6 June 1956.

the energy and discipline of Chinese workers, in contrast to Indians, particularly under the direction of an efficient centralized government which gave China 'terrifying strength'.[1] He admired the effective use of China's huge labour force in large-scale construction projects such as dams and hoped to emulate this in India—without the coercive mobilization of labour. He was comforted by the evidence that India was more economically advanced *at present* but must have been disturbed by the fact that China's *rate* of progress was faster. Upon his return he commented critically on the lack of free speech in China and extolled the virtues of democracy and parliamentary government.[2] According to some who accompanied him he felt proud of India's achievements after seeing the new China. Perhaps most important, he acquired added insight into the reality of Indo-Chinese rivalry, however friendly, for the ideologically uncommitted peoples of Asia. It may well be that subconsciously he was driven to the Left upon his return by the concern that China was winning this crucial contest.

Whatever the motive force, Nehru's speeches in the autumn of 1954 ushered in a new phase in Indian economic policy. First came the Avadi Resolution on a 'socialist pattern of society'. Then came the budget for 1955–6, termed by some (incorrectly) 'the first socialist budget' because of special taxes on salaried business executives, preferential rates for cottage industries, and the promise of substantial deficit financing to meet development costs.[3] Soon after, the Taxation Inquiry Commission recommended a statutory ceiling on incomes. Ironically, this 'socialist' proposal came from a group headed by Dr. Matthai, a prominent industrialist, and was rejected by a government pledged to a 'socialist pattern'. In the spring of 1955 Nehru secured parliamentary approval of the constitutional amendment which gave to the legislatures the authority to determine the amount of compensation for expropriated property, a right formerly held by the Courts, and authorized the legislatures to acquire any property deemed in the public

---

[1] To the author in New Delhi on 13 June 1956.

[2] For Nehru's comments on his return from China see Fisher and Bondurant, *Indian Views of Sino-Indian Relations*, pp. 107–9. For Indian press comment on Nehru's China tour, see ibid., pp. 110–19.

[3] For a detailed account of the 1955–6 budget see the *Times of India* (New Delhi), 1 March 1955.

interest. This, more than anything else, caused concern in the private sector.

On the heels of the constitutional amendment came the first major act of nationalization since Independence. The Imperial Bank of India, which had the largest network of branches in the country, was converted to the State Bank of India, giving the Government a major influence in commercial banking. Indeed, the primary intention of the move was to enable the Government to assist small-scale industry in town and village by easing loan conditions and stimulating economic expansion. This was followed by the Indian Companies Amendment Act aimed principally at the managing agency system, a unique Indian method of corporate management introduced by the British which created huge concentrations of economic power by means of interlocking management. Some managing agencies under the British *Raj* had controlled upwards of 100 companies ranging the entire spectrum of economic activity. Even by 1955 there were some agencies with forty companies tied together. Under this Act the maximum number of companies under one agency will be ten by 1960; the agencies will be non-inheritable; and the agency's remuneration will be limited to 11 per cent. of a company's profits.

These developments alarmed the business community. Nehru tried to smooth the troubled waters by a series of speeches clarifying the intent of the 'socialist pattern'. During the debate on the Avadi Resolution he remarked, 'all land in India is a private sector. . . . Probably all cottage industries will be in the private sector. . . . If the State cannot do something or does not want to do something, why shouldn't private enterprise start it? . . . As far as I can see the two [public and private sectors] must be seen as a whole. The main thing is to increase wealth in this country.'[1] To a gathering of Indian business leaders he said, 'do not be afraid of this phrase ['socialist pattern']. By adopting this ideal and working for its fulfilment, you will serve the country and benefit yourself. But you have to change your mental attitudes.'[2] As for the means of achieving the 'socialist

---

[1] Concluding speech on the 'socialist pattern' resolution at Avadi. Nehru, *Towards a Socialistic Order*, pp. 11–12.

[2] To the Federation of Indian Chambers of Commerce and Industry on 5 March 1955. *The Hindu* (Madras), 6 March 1955.

pattern', he informed his party colleagues: 'We shall do so in our own way, and that is a peaceful way, a co-operative way and a way which always tries to carry the people with us, *including those who may be apprehensive or even hostile to begin with.*'[1]

Three years later, in the spring of 1958, Nehru expressed his considered thoughts on Socialism.

I do not want State socialism of that extreme kind in which the State is all powerful and governs practically all activities. The State is very powerful politically. If you are going to make it very powerful economically also it would become a mere conglomeration of authority. I should, therefore, like decentralisation of economic power. We cannot, of course, decentralise iron and steel and locomotives and such other big industries, but you can have small units of industries as far as possible on a co-operative basis with State control in a general way. I am not at all dogmatic about it. We have to learn from practical experience and proceed in our own way.

On the question of nationalization he said: 'I think it is dangerous merely to nationalise something without being prepared to work it properly. To nationalise we have to select things. My idea of socialism is that every individual in the State should have equal opportunity for progress.'[2]

Nevertheless, the actions noted earlier raised doubts among the business community about the practical meaning of Nehru's assurances. Perhaps the most disquieting feature of the 'socialist pattern' in 1955 was the approval of Mahalanobis's 'plan-frame' by Nehru, the Planning Commission and the National Development Council. For Mahalanobis was a forceful exponent of enlarging the public sector at the expense of private enterprise, particularly with respect to basic industry. And the distinguished statistician had acquired considerable influence by arousing Nehru's enthusiasm and by reconciling his Western-type socialism with Gandhian economic views. Indeed, from the autumn of 1954 onwards Mahalanobis has been the Prime Minister's valued economic adviser, though his views have not always been accepted in full.

[1] Letter to the Presidents of the Provincial Congress Committees on 9 March 1955. *Towards a Socialistic Order*, p. 31. (Emphasis added.)
[2] Speech to the All-India Congress Committee in May 1958. Reproduced in the *Economic Review*, official Congress organ, and quoted in *The Hindu Weekly Review* (Madras), 26 May 1958.

Mahalanobis proposed a two-pronged attack on the problem of breaking through India's static economic barrier: the creation of a large machine-building industry as a basis for the expansion of secondary industries; and decentralized cottage industries to create jobs for India's army of unemployed and underemployed. The former was a pre-condition of dynamic economic growth, he argued. And the latter would have a number of advantages: the production of consumer goods at a low cost; the creation of employment; and a minimum of social dislocation. Once a machine-building industry was established the hand-loom would be replaced by the power-loom, and low-cost cottage industry would be able to compete with factory-manufactured goods. Other advantages would be a substantial saving on transport, electricity, oil and construction materials that would be needed for urban factories and housing. Urban industry would grow and would produce capital goods and all essential consumer goods, as well as those requiring know-how too complicated for the village peasant. But decentralization would be stressed and efforts would be made to utilize the vast pool of idle labour. Agriculture, irrigation and power were not ignored in the 'plan-frame'. On the contrary, the funds allotted to these three fields were considerably larger than in the First Plan, though they comprised a smaller proportion of total planned expenditure.[1]

The initial response to Mahalanobis's proposals was highly favourable. Gandhians welcomed the stress on cottage industries. Westernizers and socialists were drawn to the idea of heavy industry and the expansion of the public sector, for in Mahalanobis's 'frame' the machine-building industry and, indeed, heavy industry generally would, to a large extent, come under State control or direction. Nehru was impressed with the fusion of Western and Gandhian economic ideas for development and the emphasis on the public sector. Hence the Standing Committee of the National Development Council and the Council itself approved the 'plan-frame'.

The business community, however, was alarmed, both by the preferential treatment accorded the public sector and by the emphasis on cottage industries which could eventually compete on favourable terms with urban industry. Nor were they

[1] Based on an interview with Prof. Mahalanobis in London in October 1955.

enamoured of the professor's outspoken admiration for Soviet and Chinese planning methods. Within the Planning Commission and the Civil Service, too, there was opposition to the socialist tendencies in the 'plan-frame'. There was also some concern about the mysterious role of Soviet-bloc economists in its formulation, notably the role of the distinguished Polish economist, Prof. Oskar Lange, who had been a guest of Mahalanobis's Statistical Institute in 1954-5 and 1955-6.

Powerful pressure was brought on the Government with resultant revisions in favour of the private sector. This is evident from a comparison of the breakdown of public development expenditure in the 'plan-frame' and the Final Draft.[1]

| | PLAN-FRAME | | FINAL DRAFT | |
	Allotment in Crores of Rupees	Percentage of Total	Allotment in Crores of Rupees	Percentage of Total
Agriculture, Community Development, Irrigation and Flood Control	950	22·1	1,054	21·9
Power	450	10·5	427	8·9
Industry and Mining	1,100	25·6	890	18·5
Transport and Communications	950	22·1	1,385	28·9
Social Services, Housing and Rehabilitation	750	17·4	945	19·7
Miscellaneous	100	2·3	99	2·1
TOTAL	4,300	100·0	4,800	100·0

1 crore = 10 million = $2·1 million.

The most noteworthy change was the sharp decline in public outlay for industry and mining and a corresponding increase for transport and communications. Although total planned expenditure rose by Rs. 500 crores ($1 billion), the allotment for industry in the public sector fell by Rs. 210 crores. Almost 90 per cent. of the increase in expenditure went to transport which, among other things, would facilitate the growth of private investment in the countryside and would ease the flow of raw materials to the city and the reverse flow of urban-manufactured goods to the rural areas, reducing the cost advantage of cottage industries.

*   *   *   *

[1] The Final Draft figures are taken from *Second Five Year Plan*, pp. 51-52; the 'plan-frame' figures were made available to the author in New Delhi.

India's Second Five-Year Plan (1956–61) is designed to overcome the danger of economic stagnation and to place the country on the path of rapid progress. Like the First Plan its inspiration flows from the Directive Principles of State Policy in the new Constitution which embody the social and economic philosophy of the Congress. Broadly it aims at the creation of a Welfare State or, in Indian terms, a 'socialist pattern of society'. Four specific objectives are set out by the drafters: 'a sizeable increase in national income so as to raise the level of living in the country; rapid industrialisation with particular emphasis on the development of basic and heavy industries; a large expansion of employment opportunities; and reduction of inequalities in income and wealth and a more even distribution of economic power.'[1]

The main features of the Second Plan may be summarized briefly. The total planned expenditure of public funds is Rs. 4,800 crores (slightly more than $10 billion), more than double the outlay in the First Plan. Private enterprise is expected to invest an additional Rs. 2,400 crores (approximately $5 billion). The national income target is an increase of 25 per cent. in the five years, compared with a target of 11 per cent. in the First Plan. The goal for *per capita* income is an increase of 18 per cent., from $58.80 to $69.30 *per year*. To meet the challenge of rising unemployment the plan aims at 10 million more jobs—which barely covers the expected increase in the labour force during the five years; it also envisages special programmes for absorbing the educated unemployed and for producing the necessary skilled manpower.

In agriculture, the principal targets are an overall increase of 28 per cent. in production, including 25 per cent. for food grains, 31 per cent. for cotton and 25 per cent. for jute; an increase of 21 million acres under irrigation; and the extension of the Community Development Programme to all areas of rural India, covering 325 million people, compared with one-fourth of the rural population at the end of the First Plan. The targets for industry and mining are even more impressive: a 64 per cent. increase in net industrial production; a 150 per cent. increase in capital goods production alone; a 63 per cent. increase in coal production; iron ore from 4·3 to 12·9 million tons, aluminium by

[1] *Second Five Year Plan*, p. 24.

233 per cent., cement by 108 per cent., electricity by 100 per cent., and steel by 231 per cent., from 1·3 to 4·3 million tons. Railways are to be modernized and extended so as to carry 35 per cent. more freight and 15 per cent. more passengers at the end of the five-year period—and India possesses the fourth-largest railway system in the world. Enlarged transport and communications include the modernization of India's principal ports—Calcutta, Madras, Bombay and Vizagapatnam—and the construction of 19,000 more miles of surfaced road. Primary-school facilities are to be provided for 8 million more children, an increase of 23 per cent. The number of doctors is to be raised by 12,500, and there are to be some 3,000 new rural clinics. To achieve these goals the planners anticipate an investment of 11 per cent. of national income in the final year, compared with 7 per cent. in the last year of the First Plan period.[1]

The Second Five-Year Plan can hardly be considered ambitious in terms of India's needs. With a planned public expenditure of $10 billion, *per capita* annual income is expected to rise $10.50 to the dismally low figure of $69. Even if the steel target is achieved, India's output at the end of the plan would be 20 pounds *per capita*, which is lower than that of Spain, Yugoslavia, Brazil or Mexico. If the goal for new schools is reached, some 40 per cent. of all primary-school-age children would still not be able to receive a rudimentary education. The basic problem of unemployment is only touched, for even if the goal of 10 million new jobs is reached the task of drawing off the surplus millions from the land will remain.

While the current plan is modest in relation to India's needs it has proved itself over-ambitious in terms of existing financial resources. Indeed, the original estimates suggest optimism and a willingness to gamble, both on favourable domestic conditions and on foreign interest in India's future. Only 25 per cent. of the total planned outlay is covered by assured revenue—existing taxes, new taxation, railway profits, pension funds, etc. Another 25 per cent. falls in the category of loans and small savings which Indian planners do not consider deficit financing. Borrowing from the public is thought of as a diversion of existing purchasing power to public needs, without inflationary effects, and is differentiated from 'other credit operations', namely, borrowing

[1] Taken from *Second Five Year Plan*.

from banks which, by injecting new funds into circulation, may well produce inflation under certain conditions. This third category, deficit financing in the proper sense, accounts for an additional 25 per cent. Of the remaining 25 per cent. the planners anticipated two-thirds from foreign aid, that is to say, Rs. 800 crores or $1,600 million. The other Rs. 400 crores were to be covered by then unknown domestic resources. Realistically viewed, then, half the total public outlay depended on precarious or unreliable sources.[1]

Past experience and the conditions of 1956, however, offered considerable hope for the future. Approximately 21 per cent. of the First Plan expenditure was deficit-financed, only 4 per cent. less than the estimate for the Second Plan; price inflation was avoided; in fact, prices fell towards the end of the First Plan period. As for foreign aid, India entered the Second Plan with dollar credits of $357 million. Moreover, it planned to draw on its sterling balances to the amount of $400 million, giving it a total of $757 million. Thus the actual gap in foreign aid was $900 million, not $1,600 million. And $900 million was less than 10 per cent. of the total planned outlay. The planners were also fortified by the conviction that, at worst, if foreign aid was not forthcoming in sufficient quantities, the plan would be completed in six or seven years. They were certainly not unaware of the risks, either of deficit finance or foreign aid, as revealed in numerous statements and conversations with foreign visitors. But they felt that boldness was imperative if the 'hope level' was to be maintained. Nehru himself stressed this point on frequent occasions. Moreover, 'in the final analysis any effort is an act of faith. [For us, he told Parliament] that act of faith fundamentally is in the capacity of the Indian people. All I can say is that I have faith in the capacity of our people.'[2]

Before the Second Plan was formally inaugurated, the Indian Government announced a new industrial policy to reflect the emphasis on an enlarged public sector. The initial Industrial Policy Resolution in 1948, Nehru's 'retreat from socialism', had

---

[1] Taken from *Second Five Year Plan*, pp. 77–78. For a discussion of the financial aspects of the plan see ibid., ch. iv. One member of the Commission, K. C. Neogy, wrote a strong note of dissent on the grounds that the plan was over-ambitious in terms of financial resources. For a summary of his note see the *Times of India* (New Delhi), 10 May 1956.

[2] On 7 September 1956. *Times of India* (New Delhi), 8 September 1956.

confined exclusive State activity to six fields. Since that time, however, the Directive Principles of State Policy had been incorporated in the Constitution, the goal of a 'socialist pattern' had been proclaimed by the Congress, and the Second Plan proposed marked expansion in publicly controlled industry. Hence revision was necessary.

The Resolution of 30 April 1956 retained the form of three categories of industry. However, the scope of State enterprise was substantially increased. The list of reserved industries, the future development of which will be the exclusive responsibility of the State, was increased from six to seventeen and included 'all industries of basic and strategic importance, or in the nature of public utility services . . . and other industries which are essential and require investment on a scale which only the State, in present circumstances, could provide . . .' The most noteworthy additions were heavy plant and machinery for iron and steel production, mining, machine-tool manufacture, and heavy electrical plants. Moreover, in the concurrent list of twelve industries the State's dominant responsibility was clearly enunciated. And even in the third category, industries whose development will normally be undertaken by private enterprise, the State was not excluded. The only concessions to the business community were that existing private industrial concerns would not be nationalized and that the division into categories was not intended to be rigid; the door was left open for private entry into the list of industries reserved to the State and for joint State–private undertakings.

Despite the formal expansion of the public sector's sphere of development, flexibility was emphasized. The new policy also envisaged State trading as an instrument of planning and stressed the importance of small-scale and cottage industries which would continue to receive State support but would be expected to improve their methods of organization and production. Those who had been disappointed by Nehru's concessions to private enterprise in 1948 could take comfort from the shift towards some form of socialism. Businessmen could find compensation in the loopholes; no definite time-limit was set for the Industrial Policy Resolution.[1]

[1] The text of this resolution is to be found in the *Times of India* (New Delhi), 1 May 1956.

The business community had and has the added assurance that the road to a genuine 'socialist pattern' is likely to be very long. On the eve of the Second Plan State-owned *industry* comprised no more than 5 per cent. of the total; the bulk of publicly owned capital assets lies in railways, ports and irrigation works. Moreover, all land, upon which three-fourths of the Indian people depend for a livelihood, is privately owned. Although the ratio of public investment to gross national product rose in the Second Plan and will probably continue to grow, many more five-year plans will have to elapse before State enterprise constitutes a significant portion of the total—unless there is a drastic move towards nationalization of existing industry.[1] Furthermore, if the budget on the eve of the Second Plan were any test, the 'socialist pattern' did not seriously encroach on private enterprise. On the contrary, the bulk of new taxes, designed to raise about $70 million, was levied on consumer goods; a small share was to be raised from corporations with incomes above Rs. 40,000 per year and from individuals with incomes above Rs. 70,000 per year.[2]

India entered the Second Plan period with high hopes. The First Plan targets had been substantially achieved; the balance-of-payments position was satisfactory; the price level was stable; and, most important, the food position was better than it had been since the pre-war period. Before the first year of the Second Plan was over, however, this rosy picture was transformed and the plan was in grave jeopardy. By the middle of 1957 India was faced with the gravest economic crisis since Independence. Optimism gave way to gloom.

Nature dealt the first blow, in the form of widespread floods, hailstorms and drought during the autumn and winter of 1956–7. It was a cruel blow, indeed, causing human misery in many parts of the country, notably in the highly populated States of Bihar and Uttar Pradesh (U.P.). Food reserves which had been laboriously built up during the 'good years' of the First Plan period were rapidly depleted. And still the threat of creeping famine remained. This was not a unique situation; India has

[1] See Prof. Wilfred Malenbaum, letter to the editor, the *New York Times*, 25 September 1957.
[2] For a detailed account of the 1956–7 budget see the *Times of India* (New Delhi), 1 March 1956.

often known the grim reality of food scarcity, as recently as 1950–1 when famine plagued the southern States. But this time it came after three bountiful years when the monsoon, new fertilizers and irrigation works, and improved organization had combined to make India relatively self-sufficient in food, easing the burden on its precious reserves of foreign exchange. Agriculture had long been the 'Achilles heel' of India's economy. With Nature on the rampage once more it was necessary to meet this formidable challenge, with far-reaching consequences for the economy as a whole.

The planners had set an ambitious target for agricultural production including a 25 per cent. increase in food grains during the period 1956–61. This was necessary both for the anticipated population rise of 20 to 25 million during the Second Plan period and in order to provide a more balanced diet for the Indian people as a whole. Moreover, plans for industrial development were intimately linked to an adequate food supply, not only because of the perennial problem of foreign exchange but also because of the danger of inflation. A serious setback on the food front would retard general economic growth. And so it has during the early years of the Second Plan.

The increase in food production during 1956–7 was only half the target; in 1957–8 there was a decline of 2 million tons in overall food production.[1] One effect was a substantial rise in food prices—18·7 per cent. in rice and 15·2 per cent. in wheat, the two staples—during the first year. Another was to narrow the permissible scope of deficit financing for industrial development, a critical setback because no less than 25 per cent. of the Second Plan was to be financed by this method. The fear of runaway inflation has necessitated extreme caution. A third effect was to reduce the real value of Second Plan projects, estimated in 1958 to be of the order of 15 to 20 per cent. of the planned figures.[2] A fourth consequence has been increased pressure on India's foreign exchange reserves. Indeed, the severity of the economic crisis of 1957–8 was due precisely to the fact that the food crisis coincided with and aggravated a serious drain on foreign exchange.

[1] *New York Times*, 29 June 1957, and 5 May 1958.
[2] 'Touchstone' in the *Hindustan Times* (New Delhi), 29 January 1958, and *New York Times*, 5 May 1958. The decline in real value was due partly to inflation and partly to an underestimate of costs.

The programme of industrialization required the import of costly equipment, the products of which will not be forthcoming for some years. At the same time inflation weakened India's trading position. Thus during the first year of the plan India's balance-of-payments showed a deficit of $735 million, and its foreign exchange (mostly sterling) reserves declined to just over $1 billion, precariously close to the prescribed minimum of $840 million for currency backing. Moreover, the completion of industrial projects required a continued drawing on foreign exchange. As the Finance Minister remarked, 'we are riding the tiger of industrialization and can't get off'. In attempting to justify the gamble inherent in the Second Plan he added, 'we could not have taken a different course. In a democracy it's very difficult to get gratitude from people unless you do something substantial.'[1] Ironically, in view of the fanfare about an enlarged public sector, the bulk of the import excess was for projects in the private sector with a resulting cutback in State enterprise. According to Professor Mahalanobis, actual investment in the public sector during the Second Plan will probably be about 20 per cent. of the amount proposed in his 'plan-frame'.[2]

New Delhi's first response to this financial crisis was a draconian budget for 1957–8, designed to curb inflation and to increase domestic funds for development. Excise taxes were raised on thirteen items and customs duties on ninety others, most of them consumer goods. Railway fares were increased 5 per cent. to 15 per cent. and telegraph rates by 15 per cent. The income tax base was lowered from Rs. 4,200 to 3,000. The personal tax on bonus shares was increased from 12½ to 30 per cent., the tax on corporate income from 25 to 30 per cent., and that on excess corporate profits from 17½ to 20 per cent. In addition, two highly controversial taxes with a strong welfare bias were introduced, a tax on wealth and a tax on expenditure.

Both had been recommended by Professor Kaldor in 1956 as a means of broadening the tax base and of increasing funds for development. The levy on wealth would be applied to individuals with assets of more than Rs. 200,000, to undivided

---

[1] Quoted in the *New York Times*, 9 May 1957.
[2] To the author in New Delhi in January 1958.

Hindu families with assets above Rs. 300,000, and to companies with assets above Rs. 500,000; the rates for the first two categories would range from 1 to 1·5 per cent., for companies 0·5 per cent. Agricultural property, trusts and personal effects up to Rs. 25,000 were exempted. The expenditure tax was to apply to individuals and undivided Hindu families whose income for tax purposes is over Rs. 60,000, and was to begin in 1958–9.[1]

No section of the community was spared in this novel budget. The burden on the very poor was increased by higher customs duties on consumer goods; the middle class was affected by the lower income tax exemptions; and the well-to-do by the wealth and expenditure taxes. It was clear that the primary motive was to save the Plan. But the total expected yield from these new and increased levies was only Rs. 93 crores ($195 million). And while this would help to curb inflation it could not ease the foreign exchange crisis.

Drastic action was necessary, for the drain continued unabated. The initial act was to ban capital goods imports requiring foreign exchange unless sellers agreed to deferred payment. The Soviet bloc agreed at once, and at a low rate of interest, stealing a march on its ideological competitors. But this barely touched the problem. In September 1957 a drastic reduction in the import of consumer goods was announced; the expected saving was $210 million.[2] Even this, however, could not solve the crisis, for the foreign exchange gap was $1·4 billion for the remainder of the Plan, after certain cutbacks in industrialization. In an effort to raise this formidable sum by foreign loans the Finance Minister made a highly publicized tour of western Europe and North America while a lesser official went to Moscow. Nehru had already indicated that India would be grateful for American loans in the neighbourhood of $600 million to $800 million. The World Bank was expected to make available about $400 million, and the balance, it was hoped, could be raised from western Europe.

The approach to London was unsuccessful. West Germany was more helpful and eased the burden of payment on imported

---

[1] For a detailed summary of the 1957–8 budget see *The Hindu Weekly Review* (Madras), 20 May 1957. See also the *New York Times*, 16 May 1957.
[2] *New York Times*, 1 October 1957.

machinery for one of the steel plants. In the United States there was much sympathy. Dulles himself pledged favourable consideration. Former Ambassador Cooper, the *New York Times*, Walter Lippmann and others urged U.S. support, on the grounds that this was a small price to pay to ensure India's progress through democratic methods. The difficulty lay in the hostility of many Congressmen because of India's non-alignment policy and in the fact that such a large sum required Congressional approval. The Congressional obstacle was evaded at the beginning of 1958 by a smaller loan than that sought—$225 million—a much-welcomed but still inadequate amount. Some Indians surmised hopefully that loans of this amount would be repeated annually to the end of the Second Plan.[1] Others were less optimistic and remarked that the value of the loan was diminished by the fact that $150 million came from the Export-Import Bank which required the funds to be spent in the United States where the cost of machinery needed by India was considerably higher than in other countries.[2]

Amidst the negotiations for an American loan the foreign exchange crisis became acute. On 25 October 1957 India's reserves stood at Rs. 328 crores, perilously close to the statutory minimum of Rs. 300 crores. The danger of a total breakdown in India's international economic position was very real and with it the possibility of financial chaos at home. New Delhi took drastic action. At the end of October the Reserve Bank of India was authorized by Ordinance to draw sterling balances down to Rs. 85 crores and, if necessary, to draw even that amount, leaving a currency backing of gold and bullion to the value of Rs. 115 crores, a very slender base indeed. In this manner the danger of default was overcome—for eight months at least.[3] The U.S. loan eased the pressure further.

A disquieting feature of India's dependence on foreign aid, necessary though it may be, is the massive debt created for the future. At the beginning of 1958 its external obligations totalled

[1] See for example Prem Bhatia, Political Correspondent of *The Statesman* (Calcutta), 22 January 1958. Supporting evidence for this optimism was suggested by a resolution of the United States Senate in June 1958, expressing support for large-scale economic aid to India. *New York Times*, 7 June 1958.

[2] To the author in New Delhi in January 1958.

[3] The text of the Reserve Bank of India (Amendment) Ordinance is summarized in *The Hindu Weekly Review* (Madras), 4 November 1957.

approximately Rs. 600 crores ($1·3 billion).[1] Much of this represents dollar debts, and a considerable portion will begin to fall due in the early 1960's. If American loans for the duration of the Second Plan should meet Delhi's expectations, India's foreign debt by 1961 would be over Rs. 1,000 crores ($2·1 billion), a tremendous burden for the Third Plan period and beyond. The tragic feature of this foreign exchange problem is that much of the annual recurring debt arises from 'unnecessary' items: defence, which accounted for Rs. 120 crores in 1957–8, and is due in large part to the conflict with Pakistan over Kashmir; and food, which for a predominantly agricultural country should not be a drag on foreign exchange. The third principal item of foreign exchange outlay is capital goods, but these add to India's future capacity to meet its needs from domestic production. If the Second Plan targets are reached the foreign exchange problem will be less severe. Similarly, if India and Pakistan resolve their differences the burden of defence would be eased. The latter prospect does not appear to be very likely; and the former is not much more so.

In mid-1958 at any rate the Second Five-Year Plan was in serious trouble. Despite the U.S. loan, the use of its remaining sterling balances and deferred payment arrangements with various countries, India was still faced with a very large foreign exchange gap. Hence the long-delayed 'pruning' of the Plan took place. At the beginning of May, the day after Nehru yielded to the pressure of his colleagues to remain in office, the National Development Council postponed $630 million worth of development projects, officially until more funds are available, unofficially for the duration of the Second Plan period.[2] The 'core' remains: agricultural production; power projects; and the three steel plants designed to treble India's finished steel output, one being built with the aid of Russian capital and

---

[1] The breakdown of India's external obligations in 1958 is as follows:

The United States:	Rs. 270 crores
World Bank:	70 ,,
I.M.F.:	100 ,,
Soviet Union:	123 ,,
United Kingdom:	35 ,,
Total:	598 ,,

excluding debts related to the Rourekela steel plant.

[2] *New York Times*, 5 May 1958.

26. Greeting Mountbatten at Palam Airport, New Delhi, 1956

Press Information Bureau, Government of India

27. Nehru and Radhakrishnan receiving the Mountbattens at Palam
Airport, New Delhi, in 1956

technicians, another with British, and the third with German assistance. Yet even this core is not assured. The revised estimate of financial resources included a large amount of deficit financing. And the enormous foreign exchange gap remains. In July 1958 Delhi informed the United States, the World Bank and the International Monetary Fund that it urgently required $300 million before the end of the year. Total needs were estimated at $600 million by the summer of 1959 and $1,200 million by the end of the Second Plan period—this to achieve the reduced targets of the plan.[1] In the autumn of 1958 relief came in the form of a multilateral aid agreement. The United States, the United Kingdom, West Germany, Japan, Canada and the World Bank made available $350 million in loans to ease the foreign exchange burden. Nevertheless, the future seemed anything but bright.[2]

Perhaps the most notable casualty of the economic crisis in 1958 was the Community Development Programme, India's quiet rural revolution. Nehru was especially distressed, for this is at once the symbol and pillar of the new India he is attempting to fashion by consent. Community Development accounts for only 4 per cent. of the total public outlay in the First and Second Plans. But this is hardly the measure of its importance to Nehru and others. The Prime Minister has often spoken with pride about this aspect of planning. Typical is the following: ' I think nothing has happened in any country in the world during the last few years so big in content and so revolutionary in design as the Community Projects in India. They are changing the face of rural India.'[3] The main reason for his enthusiasm is evident in another comment:

For the first time, it may be said with truth, we tackled the rural problem in a realistic way. This was not merely from above but rather by inducing the people themselves to solve their own problems. Something life-giving went to them and their eyes brightened and their arms began to function and their muscles became stronger. A process of rejuvenation set in. This has spread already to carry the message forward to every remote village and hamlet.[4]

There is an aura of faith about Community Development in India. It began on 2 October 1952, the anniversary of Gandhi's

[1] *New York Times*, 21 July 1958.   [2] Ibid., 29 and 30 August 1958.
[3] Nehru, *On Community Development*, p. 36.   [4] Ibid., p. 43.

T

birthday, and was partly inspired by the Mahatma's aim of bringing dignity and progress to the village through active participation of the common man. The other major goal was linked to the broad objectives of planning, a substantial increase in agricultural production, income and employment. From modest beginnings—some 25,000 villages and 16 million people —it has grown rapidly. By the end of the First Plan period it embraced almost a fourth of rural India. The Second Plan target was the entire rural population, 325 million people living in almost 600,000 villages. But the foreign exchange crisis intervened and the programme's completion will be delayed.

The sheer scope of Community Development commands attention. So too does the organizational effort and the method. The basic unit is the Development Block of about 100 villages and 60,000 to 70,000 people. To each are assigned a group of specialists, for agriculture, animal husbandry, education, health, housing and the like, operating under the supervision of a Block Development Officer. All are specially trained for rural extension work. Direction from above takes place on two levels: activities within a District are co-ordinated by the District Officer, a civil servant appointed by the Centre; personnel and technical services are provided by the Development Commissioner of each State who works in co-operation with interested State ministries and administers broad policy laid down by the Ministry of Community Development in Delhi, formerly the Community Projects Administration. Within this seemingly cumbersome framework, however, the crucial fact is the wide degree of local initiative. Indeed, this is one of its most hopeful features. Day-to-day operation of the programme is in the hands of the multi-purpose village extension worker who is responsible for about ten villages and lives in one of them. Ultimately the success or failure of the experiment rests on his initiative and devotion, for to the villager he is the living symbol of the Government's desire to aid the process of change; and he is the carrier of new ideas and techniques.

The essence of the programme is self-help, democracy at the grass roots. Of necessity, the urge for change is induced (not coerced) from above, for the peasant in India as elsewhere is instinctively hostile to change. Field workers attempt to persuade the villager of the material benefits of new methods of cultivation, a health clinic, a new road, and of pooling their efforts in co-operatives. But decisions rest with the village acting through a local Council which the programme has tried to foster. The Block and extension workers cannot impose a set of projects; they advise and guide and stimulate interest in change, but they *act* only in response to a village or individual request. They offer improved seed, suggest methods of ensuring an adequate water supply by digging wells or tanks, stress the benefits of a new school, and the like. They stand ready to meet the village demands, but the village must show interest. In fact, no project is undertaken by the Block without active participation of the village. If a new school is sought, the programme provides part of the cost and the plans, the village contributes its labour and some of the money.

In this way it is hoped that the long-dormant peasantry will be moved to purposeful activity for its own benefit. Gradually, through example, it is believed that the abundant energy of rural India can be mobilized on the principle of self-help to transform the countryside and the social and economic outlook of the villager. In this way, too, a new sense of personal dignity may come to the peasant, and the 'dung-heap' in which he has lived for millennia may be slowly changed into a self-respecting community. But this takes time. It also requires an army of well-trained and devoted rural workers.

The material record thus far shows considerable progress but not of revolutionary dimensions: 15,000 new schools in the First Plan period; 1,000 health centres; 2 million acres brought under irrigation by local effort; 34,000 village councils formed; 250,000 acres reclaimed; and comparable figures for other aspects of the programme. Somewhat disappointing is the fact that average food production in Community Development areas is only 11 per cent. higher than in the rest of the country. There are undoubted weaknesses. General education has lagged. Rural employment has not noticeably increased. The administration tends to be top-heavy and extension workers are frequently lacking in skills. The gravest shortcoming, perhaps, is in the sphere of local initiative. The concept of self-help has yet to penetrate the bulk of the Indian peasantry. Aid is welcomed and has undoubtedly improved physical conditions, but local leadership is slow in developing. An official study remarked in 1957: 'Unless the Government deploys more resources in rural areas and the people in turn show greater initiative and self-help, a situation is being created in rural India which is bound to create serious difficulties.'[1]

Another weakness has resulted from the time-schedules originally set for development. Until 1958 there were three 3-year phases: National Extension Service, the same programme and goals as Community Development but with less funds and without the group of cadres and organization; intensive Community Development in which the bulk of the funds are poured into the area; and a post-intensive levelling-off period in which it is hoped that rural development can be continued by the villagers themselves. This has given way to a two-phase 10-year period with a relatively even annual rate of expenditure. The abandonment of 'shock tactics' for three years may well give the programme deeper roots.[2]

Notwithstanding these failings—and there are many others—the Community Development Programme has evoked the admiration of many observers.[3] On the extent to which the outlook of the villager is changing, one foreign expert remarked: '. . . it is my observation that villagers are no longer lethargic; that they are eager for any change that means progress in their production, in their amenities, and in their levels of living. It is my belief that they have changed more rapidly than have the concepts of some national leaders about villagers. I am convinced that changes in villages will accelerate so rapidly that the difficult problem will not be what kind of propaganda will induce them to change, but how can their rising expectations be fulfilled.'[4] Another expert, with fifty years of experience in rural extension work, commented: 'My admiration and enthusiasm for the programme as a whole, its vastness, its organization and its objectives is such that I can hardly express my judgment and opinions except in superlatives. In many aspects,

---

[1] From a report of the Programme Evaluation Organization, quoted in the *New York Times*, 28 April 1957.

[2] On this change in time-schedule see the *Times of India* (New Delhi), 22 January 1958.

[3] For thoughtful appraisals of Community Development see *Kurukshetra* (A Symposium on Community Development in India 1952–1955); Taylor, Carl C., *A Critical Analysis of India's Community Development Programme* (1956); and Wilson, M. L., *Community Development Programme in India* (1956).

[4] Taylor, op. cit., p. 57.

there has been nothing approaching its scope and objectives in the history of rural improvement and adult education throughout the entire world.'[1]

Others, without expert knowledge in this field, have also been impressed, this writer among them. A visit to villages touched by the programme and others still awaiting its introduction demonstrates the achievement. The paved road, linking a remote village to the outside world, built by village labour, has made possible the penetration of new ideas. So has the new village school, in which Untouchables sit side by side with caste Hindus. There is still a wide gap between them, and Untouchables are by no means fully accepted as members of the community, but the change is apparent. One sees, too, the new health clinic which has made the villager more aware of the importance of cleanliness and sanitation. In contrast to the dismal, windowless mud hut of the traditional village, there is evident the beginnings of a.housing programme which, in time, and with money, could transform the Indian village.

Most important, the villager has taken to the programme. He wants change; he is aroused and says that conditions are much better than before; his wife and children get better care; his land is more productive; new seed and more assured water have helped; he has a sense of satisfaction in helping to bring progress to his village and himself. Not all are pleased. Some are indifferent; others are still suspicious of townsmen and officials; still others find the pace too quick and the pressures too severe. On the whole, however, the impression is one of progress towards the attainment of the basic goal—revolutionizing the attitudes of the peasant and bringing to him the benefits of modern science.

In inaugurating the programme, Nehru termed it 'this sacred work'. On another occasion he remarked: 'If we succeed, and succeed we will, then we shall have done in our generation something worthwhile and something that will deserve permanent record.'[2] The setback in 1958 means only that more time will elapse before Community Development comes to all villages. It is, nevertheless, a welfare achievement which will also strengthen the roots of democracy in India.

*   *   *   *

[1] Wilson, op. cit., p. 2.   [2] *On Community Development*, p. 47.

In the closely related sphere of land reform the record leaves much to be desired. India is, and will remain for many years, a predominantly agricultural society; four out of every five Indians depend for their livelihood on the land. As in Asia generally, the reform of an antiquated agrarian system is the burning issue of the day. A comprehensive analysis of India's complex systems of land tenure and ownership is beyond the scope of this book. It is sufficient to note some of the major aspects of the problem: inequality of ownership; absentee landlordism; insecurity of tenants in wide areas of the country; an army of landless labourers, some 40 million at the time of Independence; fragmented, uneconomic holdings; layers of intermediaries between the State, theoretically the ultimate owner, and the actual tiller of the soil; exorbitant rents; very low per acre yields; primitive methods of production; and massive indebtedness.

The Congress had long pledged basic reform to remove the worst evils of the system. It was also committed to non-violent change and to fair compensation for expropriated property, a principle embodied in Article 31 of the Constitution. How was it to proceed? It was clear that the first step must be the abolition of intermediaries, notably the *Zamindari* (tax farming) system instituted by the British at the end of the eighteenth century. By the time of Independence this and related systems of ownership covered nearly half of India. Since land legislation falls under the jurisdiction of the States, uniformity in speed and scope is impossible. Gradually, however, enactments for the abolition of these systems were passed, with the result that by the end of the First Plan period this most parasitic of intermediaries had been eliminated throughout the country, with minor exceptions. This has been the most impressive aspect of Indian land reform, indeed, the only real measure of change on this front.

Even this was not accomplished without strong opposition, notably in the U.P. and Bihar where Zamindarism was strongly entrenched. Long delays ensued from frequent appeals to the Courts on the validity of the Zamindari abolition acts. Finally, in 1951, Nehru forced through the first constitutional amendment which had the effect of placing these acts beyond the purview of the courts and of giving them retroactive validity.

Many criticized this 'interference' with the Courts.[1] But Nehru had no patience for slow judicial processes when they affected something he considered vital to mass welfare. Moreover, he had enunciated the doctrine of parliamentary supremacy during the Constituent Assembly debate on compensation: 'No Supreme Court and no judiciary can stand in judgment over the sovereign will of Parliament representing the will of the entire community. If we go wrong here and there it can point it out, but in the ultimate analysis, where the future of the community is concerned, no judiciary can come in the way. And if it comes in the way, ultimately the whole Constitution is a creature of Parliament.'[2]

The abolition of the Zamindari system was a necessary first step. But it did not automatically ensure 'land to the tiller'; the tenant could purchase his land, in theory, but the cost is exorbitant, and the rent (land tax) now paid to the State is usually too high to leave any margin for the acquisition of ownership rights. Despite pressure by the Centre on the States to reduce rents, they remain high, ranging from one-sixth of total crop value in Bombay to one-half in Andhra, West Bengal and Kerala; the average is well above one-third. Nor has there been much success in reversing the trend to fragmentation of holdings, despite the urging of the Planning Commission. Protection against eviction of tenants has been improved, but cases crop up very frequently. This is particularly true when large owners, trying to minimize the loss which would arise from ceilings on land holdings, establish themselves as actual farmers and divide their holdings among members of their joint family. Thus far little has been done to ease the problem for evicted tenants though, in theory, they are among the first to benefit from redistribution of expropriated land, along with landless labourers. Ceilings on land holdings have been imposed in a few States—for the future—but the thorny question of ceilings on existing holdings remains unsolved.

The record is no more impressive in the positive aspects of agrarian reconstruction. Even if the goal of 'land to the tiller'

---

[1] See for example *The Statesman* (Calcutta), 15 May and 20 June 1951. The amendment Act was unanimously adjudged constitutionally valid by the Supreme Court in October 1951.

[2] *Constituent Assembly Debates: Official Report*, vol. ix, p. 1195.

were to be substantially achieved, there would remain the serious problem of how to improve management in order to increase production. Indeed, redistribution without subsequent reintegration (in a production sense) would result in a decline in overall output. One obvious need is to consolidate holdings, many of which are scattered, causing waste of time and manpower. More important is the urgent need to enlarge the cooperative movement—the pooling of resources so as to benefit from improved techniques and organization. Some progress has been made in both, but far from adequate to the demands of production. Similarly, in the area of rural credit facilities much remains to be done.[1]

There is ample evidence that Nehru, along with many others, is dissatisfied with the pace and scope of land reform. Apart from his initiative in 1951 to break the log-jam over the abolition of Zamindari acts, Nehru took the lead in 1955 to amend the Constitution further, with potentially far-reaching consequences. On the eve of his China tour he remarked, 'we have fallen into the hands of legal purists'.[2] Soon after his return he introduced a bill to amend, among others, Articles 31 and 31A relating to compensation. He noted that court decisions had given wide scope to the meaning of 'property' and urged that it was necessary to define more precisely the State's power to acquire and requisition property. Although the amendment was directed primarily to non-agricultural property, it included the right of the State to fix a ceiling on land holdings and to distribute excess lands. Most important, it removed from the jurisdiction of the courts the authority to determine the amount of compensation.[3] Nevertheless, the programme of land reform lags. And Nehru must bear much of the responsibility, even though it falls under State law.

India's land problem is seriously aggravated by a rapid and steady rise in population. This increases the pressure on land and absorbs much of the annual increase in gross national product—more than a third of the 3·5 per cent. increase in national

---

[1] For a comprehensive survey of land reform see Patel, Govindlal D., *The Indian Land Problem and Legislation* (1954). See also *Second Five Year Plan*, ch. IX, and Government of India, Planning Commission, *The New India*, Section I, ch. I, III and IV.

[2] *Hindusthan Standard* (Calcutta), 7 October 1954.

[3] For the text of the amendment bill see *The Hindu* (Madras), 21 December 1954.

income during the First Plan period. In 1956 India's population stood at 384 million. At present rates of expansion it will reach 408 million at the end of the Second Plan period and 500 million in 1976, at the end of the Fifth Plan period. While national income may be expected to rise at an ever-faster rate, this upward trend of population poses a serious problem. Yet Nehru and many others are still not population-conscious, certainly not as conscious as some economists believe necessary.

In 1956 the Prime Minister remarked:

I should like to limit the population of India or, if I may say so, to prevent it from growing too much. . . . Our Government has been helping, not in a major way, but in experimentation. However, the question of limiting the family is not the primary question. . . . We have to make economic progress much more rapidly and we cannot wait for family planning to bring results. . . . Also the rate of population growth in India is not high. . . . The point is that India can support a larger population given economic growth.[1]

The fact remains, however, that the population increase is a heavy drag on economic progress and that efforts to limit it can be undertaken simultaneously with developmental projects. The efforts thus far are puny compared with the need.

* * * *

Having said all this, it remains to be emphasized that India's progress is most impressive, measured both against its own previous conditions and against the record of any other underdeveloped country which has chosen the democratic route to social and economic change. No less vital is the point, which cannot be overstressed, that whatever progress has been achieved is primarily due to the efforts of the Prime Minister. Indeed, he is the heart and soul and mind of India's heroic struggle to raise the living standards of its 390 million people. There can be no doubt that he has been the prime mover in India's massive planning effort. He has also been the champion of the Community Development Programme, India's novel people's revolution. From the outset of independence he has striven valiantly, almost single-handed, to establish firm foundations for a secular order of society. He has waged a ceaseless one-man campaign against the evils of casteism, notably the

[1] To the author in New Delhi on 13 June 1956.

maltreatment of 50 million Untouchables. And he has set in motion a reformation of Hindu society through the Hindu Code Bills. By the same token, the numerous and serious shortcomings of these programmes, especially in the fields of land reform, population and the public sector, reflect in large measure the weaknesses of Nehru's policies and his frequent reluctance to act resolutely when forcefulness is necessary.

CHAPTER XIX

India and the World

INDIAN views on international affairs may be traced to a multitude of sources, some rooted in tradition and experience, others deriving from the contemporary world. Almost two centuries of foreign rule produced an instinctive antagonism to any form of Western (white) domination over Asian and African (non-white) peoples. Intimately related to this 'anti-colonialism' is an intense hostility to racial discrimination. Most Indian leaders have experienced the injury to pride and national self-respect arising from the exclusiveness of the British *Raj* and such trivial forms of discrimination as reserved compartments for Europeans on Indian trains. Moreover, the very fact of British rule—European rule and white rule—has created a genuine fear of renewed Western influence in Asia. It could not have been otherwise, for the twin experiences of colonialism and racialism have played an important part in moulding the intellectual and emotional responses of Indian statesmen.

The impact of 'anti-colonialism' and 'anti-racialism' on Indian foreign policy is amply illustrated by events of recent years. Western-sponsored alliances such as SEATO (1954) and the Baghdad Pact (1955) were opposed by Delhi on the grounds that they brought the Cold War to the very borders of India (Pakistan is a member of both) and thereby endangered India's security. But the extreme sensitivity of Nehru and others was largely due to the belief that these military pacts represented an indirect return of Western power to an area from which it had recently retreated.[1] Similarly, the sharp distinction which

---

[1] Nehru has termed SEATO an 'odd' and 'unfortunate' arrangement. Moreover, 'the Manila treaty rather comes in the way of that area of peace . . . and almost converts it into an area of potential war. All these facts I find disturbing.' To Parliament on 29 September 1954. *Indiagram*, No. 548, 1 October 1954. Krishna Menon has been much more blunt: 'this is not a regional organization. . . . It is a modern version of a protectorate . . .' *Daily Indiagram*, 30 August 1954. Similar views were expressed on the Baghdad Pact. For a typical comment by Nehru on military pacts in general see *Indiagram*, No. 647, 1 March 1955.

Indians make between West European colonialism in Asia and Africa and Russian control over eastern Europe and central Asia is due to the fact that India in particular and the rimland of Asia in general have never experienced Russian domination in any form. On the contrary, by championing 'anti-colonial' movements all over Asia, the Soviets acquired a large fund of goodwill which was diminished only by the Hungarian revolt of 1956.[1]

That episode and the simultaneous Anglo-French invasion of Egypt brought into bold relief the role of the colonial and racial factors in India's perspective. Nehru's immediate condemnation of the Western Powers and his initial rationalization of Russia's action suggest two subconscious responses: first, a continuing mistrust of Western actions because of the lengthy history of Anglo-French colonialism in Asia and Africa and a willingness to give the Russian case a fair hearing because of the absence of direct Russian penetration into South and Southeast Asia; secondly, an unstated belief that violence is bad but white violence against non-whites is worse.

The Korean War, too, revealed the depth of these emotions. The initial attack was accepted by Delhi, after some hesitation, as North Korean aggression.[2] Later events, however, strengthened the suspicion of America's motives, notably its flagrant disregard of India's advice about crossing the 38th Parallel and the bombing of the Yalu power plants. This mistrust had already been aggravated by the fact that while India's charge of Pakistani aggression in Kashmir led to leisurely discussions in the United Nations, military sanctions were voted against North Korea within forty-eight hours of the outbreak of hostilities.[3]

[1] Based upon extensive interviews in India in 1956 and 1958.

[2] India, then a member of the Security Council, accepted the Council's resolutions of 25 June 1950, calling upon North Korea to withdraw to the 38th Parallel and for a cessation of hostilities. On the Council's military sanctions resolution of 27 June, the Indian delegate delayed acceptance until 29 June because of 'lack of instructions'. Seven months later Nehru remarked: 'I think it is true that there was aggression there but it is also true that of the parties concerned none is wholly free from blame.' *Jawaharlal Nehru's Speeches 1949–1953*, p. 139.

[3] Typical of Indian sensitivity to Western policy on Kashmir and Korea is the following extract from the *Hindusthan Standard* of 26 July 1950: 'It is the United Nations and the Western Powers (not India, as suggested by the *New York Times* on 22 July 1950) who have applied two different yardsticks in calculating the aggression in Korea and that in Kashmir. . . . The contrast . . . is striking between the Security Council's boggling over Kashmir and rush for action in Korea. . . . It

Napoleon once declared that the foreign policy of a state derives essentially from its geographic position. While this is no longer entirely accurate, because of the revolution in technology during the past century, the bare facts of geography do limit a state's freedom of action in foreign affairs. No Indian statesman can ignore the compelling fact that the two Great Powers of the Communist world stand at the gates of the Indian sub-continent; indeed, that China rings a substantial part of its northern and eastern frontiers. It is true that the gates have traditionally been closed by the Himalayan mountain barrier, but the Chinese occupation of Tibet in 1950 shows that this 'natural' line of defence is not impregnable. Nor can it be forgotten by Nehru and his colleagues that in terms of sheer military and industrial power the Soviet-Chinese bloc is vastly superior to India. India does not anticipate an assault from the north. But this permanent feature of its geo-political landscape must occupy a key place in the calculations of India's policy-makers. Powerful neighbours must not be provoked or alienated, though vital interests must be protected, as in the case of the tiny border states. Friendship with Peking has, of course, other roots as well. But geographic contiguity strengthens the case for India's China policy.

India's geographic position also dictates a policy of intimate friendship with Burma, lest a powerful potential enemy stand at the gates of eastern India with consequences even greater than the Japanese thrust in the early 1940's. Moreover, India's position at the head of the Indian Ocean and its dependence on sea routes for the flow of goods and services give it an important stake in the power-political rivalries affecting all states in the region.

Closely linked with the geographic pressures on Indian foreign policy are those stemming from the structure of India's economy and the plans for large-scale development. An arrested economy, a low standard of living, a high rate of population growth, stagnant agriculture, the lack of heavy industry worthy

will not do to say . . . that aggression is aggression only when a power bloc declares it to be so.' A similar view was expressed by *Amrita Bazar Patrika* (Calcutta), 25 July 1950; *National Herald* (Lucknow), 27 July 1950; *Deccan Herald* (Bangalore), 26 August 1950; *Bharat* (Bombay), 3 September 1950.

of the name, an inadequate supply of capital—these were the cardinal features of the Indian economy at the time of Independence. Partition seriously aggravated the problem by making India dependent on substantial imports of food and by disturbing the natural economic links with the area of the sub-continent which now comprises Pakistan. The first few years had to be devoted to the formidable task of achieving internal political and economic stability, notably the integration of the princely States and the rehabilitation of five million refugees. When, in 1950, serious planning got under way, dependence on the outside world for capital and machinery assumed vital importance.

India's economic weakness and the basic goal of development provide powerful inducements to the policy of non-alignment. The doors must be kept open to all possible sources of aid, Western and Soviet, if the desired economic revolution is to be achieved. For these reasons, too, peace or war is an issue of paramount importance for India. The outbreak of war between the super-Powers would wreck the ambitious programme set in motion by Nehru and his colleagues and would make a mockery of the pledges for a better way of life which figured so largely in Congress propaganda during the freedom struggle. It is only in these terms that Nehru's efforts to mediate in international disputes and to localize conflict, as in Korea and Indo-China, can be properly understood. Indeed, all other factors which shape India's view of the world are subordinate to this overriding consideration, as Nehru has candidly stated on numerous occasions.[1]

These geo-political and economic factors derive added significance from the structure and dynamics of world politics at the present time. Bi-polarity, the Cold War, ideological crusades, the arms race, military blocs, the shrinking of distance as a result of technological change, and the relative weakness of India are basic features of the contemporary world to which policy must be adjusted. Theoretically, three courses of action were open to Nehru's India in the past decade: formal association with the Western bloc or the Communist world, or non-alignment. The choice of the last alternative gave rise to criticism and even surprise among some people in the West.

[1] See for example his speech in Peking on 26 October 1954. *Indiagram*, No. 566, 29 October 1954.

For has India not adopted democratic political institutions? Have its leaders not rejected the Communist philosophy and dealt harshly with Communism within India? And have they not proclaimed their devotion to individual rights and resorted to democratic planning? Why then the refusal to stand openly with the West?

Some of the reasons have already been noted. Non-alignment is considered essential to the fulfilment of India's economic revolution, for it maintains free access to the technical skills and capital of all the great industrial powers. Moreover, it avoids alienation of India's two powerful neighbours, China and Russia. Beyond that, however, is the conviction in Delhi that it contributes to the maintenance of peace and the relaxation of tension, the vital goals of foreign policy in a world where total destruction is a physical possibility. Indeed, the nature of world politics and the international balance of power impose a moral as well as a practical obligation on India to remain 'uncommitted'.

The argument advanced by Nehru and others is essentially simple. While India cannot play the positive role of balancer, because of its military and economic weakness, the existing balance between Communism and the West is such that if India allied itself openly with one of the two blocs the danger of world war would be increased. Moreover, an uncommitted India can perform, and has performed in some measure, the necessary task of building a bridge which otherwise would not exist between the two blocs. In doing so, it is serving not only its own vital interests, but also the real vital interest of all states. And India is happily situated to fulfil this role—an Asian state, traditionally friendly to China, without any legacy of conflict with Russia, yet friendly to the West, and following a 'middle way' in its programme of economic and social change. The wider the 'area of peace', that is to say, the area of non-alignment, the less the likelihood of war among the super-powers. Such is Nehru's oft-stated rationale for India's foreign policy.[1]

Non-alignment has the added merit of satisfying a deep, inner urge for recognition, a natural by-product of colonial

[1] See for example his speech in the House of the People on 25 February 1955. 'By enlarging the area of peace, of countries which are not aligned to this group or that . . . you reduce the chances of war.' *Indiagram*, No. 647, 1 March 1955.

subjection. And it enables a relatively weak, newly independent state to play a major role on the stage of world politics. There is, finally, a psychological barrier to full-fledged alliance with any bloc. Like the American 'founding fathers' in the early years of the Republic, Indian leaders are intent on guarding their recently won freedom from all possible encroachments. Membership of a bloc is equated with loss of freedom of action in external affairs. This, in turn, is identified with a return to colonialism, though in a different form.

Westerners who have exchanged ideas with Indians in recent years have been struck by a pronounced feeling of national pride—which sometimes gives the impression of arrogance and frequently involves sermonizing to other peoples. This is partly due to India's growing stature in the world community, as reflected in Nehru's prestige, in the courting of India by the super-Powers, and in India's leadership of the 'uncommitted' countries in South-east Asia. But this pride has deeper and more complex roots. First it provides compensation for the status of political inferiority during two centuries of foreign rule. There is pride, too, in the fact that Buddhism had its origins in India and attracted the faith of hundreds of millions beyond its borders. In the broadest sense it is the legacy of an ancient civilization with impressive achievements in the realms of religion, art and philosophy, the influence of which extends to much of East Asia.

This characteristic is common to the Indian intelligentsia and the political élite. What gives it special significance is the fact that pride finds its most acute expression in the personality of Jawaharlal Nehru. The consequences may be intangible, but they cannot be ignored. To cite but one example: the history of Indo-American relations bears ample testimony to the role of national and personal pride, notably in India's attitude to foreign economic aid, and most dramatically in Nehru's refusal to sacrifice what he considered to be a measure of independence for much-needed American food in 1950–1. The Victorian disdain for 'immature' and 'boorish' America, which Nehru imbibed at Harrow and Cambridge at the beginning of the century, also influenced the relationship, as did the general Indian contempt for 'materialism'. Pride was not the decisive factor, but it served as a defence mechanism against foreign criticism, influenced Nehru's outlook and, therefore, affected the content of India's foreign policy.

This influence has not always been beneficial, even in terms of Indian national interests. Nehru's frequent assumption of moral superiority has alienated friendly states, even some Asian states, like Indonesia. And an emotional response to international problems has sometimes distorted his judgement with obvious consequences for India's policies. The most notable recent example was his instinctive condemnation of Britain, France and Israel during the Suez War in 1956 and his vacillating attitude to Soviet repression in Hungary at the same time.

The legacy of India's religious and philosophic traditions also merits attention. No one has testified to this more cogently than Nehru, the most Westernized of Indian statesmen. Writing of Hinduism, he said: 'It has, indeed, often been remarked that Hinduism is hardly a religion in the usual sense of the word. And yet, what amazing tenacity it has got, what tremendous power of survival! One may even be a professing atheist . . . and yet no one dare say that he has ceased to be a Hindu. Hinduism clings on to its children, almost despite them.'[1]

More so than any other religion, Hinduism breeds tolerance of other faiths. The roads to truth and to an understanding of Brahma are infinite. No system of thought and belief is capable of comprehending the complete truth. Every approach to communion with God, from primitive animism to the most sophisticated metaphysics, represents but a different form of man's quest for the Good. On the road to truth some may advance more than others. But there is not one correct path. The rigidity and intolerance of some Western religions is totally alien to Hinduism. Indeed, it is possible to be a Christian, Muslim, Jew, Buddhist or devotee of any other faith, and still be a Hindu. Thus it was that Gandhi constantly invoked the teachings of other religions and paid tribute to their moral principles. Thus it was that Gandhi could be hailed as a great Christian.

Tolerance is not always practised by the followers of Hinduism, as revealed in the tragic history of communal riots. Nevertheless, it is embedded in the Hindu (and, therefore, Indian) way of thought. Imperceptibly, but inevitably, this flexibility in out-

[1] *Toward Freedom*, p. 105.

look conditions India's attitude to the ideological war of the mid-twentieth century. There is no messianic mission to convert the peoples of the world to one political or religious faith. There is, in fact, hostility to the ideological crusades being waged by Communism and the West throughout the 'uncommitted' world which affect India directly.

Another legacy of India's ancient tradition is the principle of *ahimsa* or non-violence. In the land where Buddhism had its origins, non-violence as a method of social action is deeply rooted. It is true that Buddhism in its institutional form has all but vanished from the Indian scene.[1] But the message of the Master penetrated the Hindu faith and was ultimately absorbed in that all-embracing religion. More recently, in the hands of Gandhi, non-violence became the creed of Indian nationalism and left an indelible mark on the generation which now rules the State. Although the purist Gandhian conception of *ahimsa* has been termed impracticable by Nehru and his colleagues, and though violence has been resorted to, notably in Hyderabad (1948) and Kashmir (1947–8), the principle has been accepted as an ideal to be sought and as a method to be pursued wherever possible.

There is, too, a conviction that non-violence is applicable to the international arena. Nehru is not unaware of the dynamics of power politics or of the depth of disagreement and distrust between Communism and the West. But the most compelling experience in his life was the struggle for freedom by non-violent means. He assumes, therefore, that this technique of political action can also serve to mitigate world tensions.[2] Perhaps the most striking example of its influence at the present time is Nehru's restraint on the problem of Goa. A show of force would terminate the conflict within a few hours; there is no physical barrier to invasion and annexation. Yet Nehru has consistently rejected this course of action, partly because of a desire not to alienate Western goodwill and the fear that Goa might become another Korea with the NATO allies of Portugal intervening;

---

[1] In the last decade, however, Buddhism has begun to attract increasing numbers in India, as evident in the proliferation of Friends of Buddhism groups. The *Buddha Jayanti* celebrations in 1956 strengthened this movement considerably.

[2] See for example his address to the U.N. General Assembly in Paris on 3 November 1948. *Independence and After*, pp. 318–24.

but also because of the strictures imposed by the principle of non-violence.[1]

No survey of the formative influences would be complete without reference to the profound impact of Indo-Pakistani relations on the thought and action of Indian policy-makers. From the upheaval which accompanied the Partition to the present day, Delhi's principal focus of attention in foreign affairs has been the wide range of unresolved disputes with its predominantly Muslim neighbour. A Cold War, sometimes not so cold, has raged incessantly, with grave consequences for both. Suffice it to note in this context that neither can escape from the imperatives posed by this tragic situation. What is more, neither can judge other, wholly distinct, aspects of foreign relations without being conscious of the implications for their relations with one another.

These, then, are some of the factors that shape India's distinctive view of the world. That outlook in turn moulds the character of India's foreign policy. The *pillars* may be summed up as follows: *anti-colonialism* or, in more positive terms, active support for all peoples in Asia and Africa who strive to eliminate the remnants of foreign rule; *anti-racialism*, i.e., a demand for *full equality among all races*, particularly recognition of equal rights for coloured peoples the world over; *non-alignment* with power blocs, not in the negative sense of neutralism, but an active, dynamic, positive assertion of independent judgement on all issues, taking each on their merits, but maintaining freedom of action in international politics;[2] *the recognition of Asia* as a new, vital force in the world arena and the right of Asian states to decide the issues of direct concern to them; *mediation* with a view to relaxing international tensions and to creating an atmosphere

[1] Agitation in India for the 'liberation' of Goa reached its peak in August 1955, on the eve of the eighth anniversary of Independence. Led by Socialists and Communists, persons from adjoining Bombay State launched a campaign of non-violence. About twenty were killed by Portuguese guards as they attempted to cross the border. Instead of yielding to the pressure for retaliation, Nehru sealed the Indian-Goanese border and prohibited a recurrence of *satyagraha*.

In his Independence Day speech he reiterated his decision to settle the problem of Portuguese possessions in India by peaceful means. See the *Times of India* (Bombay and Delhi), 16 August 1955. He has maintained this view ever since.

[2] The term to describe Indian foreign policy has undergone frequent change. It began with 'neutrality' or 'dynamic neutrality', later became 'neutralism' and then 'non-alignment'. Nehru prefers the phrase 'positive policy for peace', he told the author in New Delhi on 13 June 1956.

conducive to Indian economic development; the creation of a
no-war area in the 'uncommitted' part of the world, *a third
force* under India's leadership, which would reduce the possibility of world war and keep power-political rivalries away from
this area; and *non-violence* as the preferred means of settling international disputes, that is to say, the application of Gandhi's
principles to the conduct of international relations; *all other
features of Indian foreign policy are but refinements of these core elements.*

* * * *

The most articulate expression of Indian foreign policy since
Independence is to be found in the speeches of Jawaharlal
Nehru.[1] In Parliament and party caucus, in the village square
and at official functions, within India and abroad, Nehru has
hammered on these themes with remarkable consistency. The
broad lines of policy were outlined as early as September 1946,
in his first pronouncement as Member for External Affairs and
Commonwealth Relations in the Interim Government.[2] They
have not changed over the years. The emphasis may have
shifted but never the pillars of policy.

The influence of a Foreign Minister varies widely from one
state to another, depending on the form of government, the
relations between the chief executive and his Minister in charge
of external affairs, the personality of the Minister, the strength
of opposition parties and the like. In no other state does one
man dominate foreign policy as does Nehru in India. Indeed,
so overwhelming is his influence that India's policy has come to
mean in the minds of people everywhere the personal policy of
Pandit Nehru. And justifiably so, for Nehru is the philosopher,
the architect, the engineer and the voice of his country's policy
towards the outside world. This does not mean that he operates
in a vacuum, for the aspirations discussed earlier provide the
framework within which policy must be devised. Nor is he
entirely free from the influence of individuals and institutions in
India. It does mean, however, that he has impressed his personality and his views with such overpowering effect that
foreign policy may properly be termed a private monopoly.

[1] See *Independence and After* (a collection of Nehru's speeches from 1946 to 1949);
Jawaharlal Nehru's Speeches 1949–1953, and *Jawaharlal Nehru's Speeches* (Vol. 3, March
1953 to August 1957).
[2] See pp. 321–2 above.

Nehru prepared for this unique role long before the coming of independence. From the mid-'thirties onwards he was the acknowledged Congress spokesman on foreign affairs. In fact, it was he alone who made the party conscious of world politics during the struggle for independence. It was he who integrated the diverse strands of thought and emotion into a coherent policy and programme of action. It was he who provided a rationale for India's approach to international politics since 1947. It was he who carried the philosophy of non-alignment to the world at large. And throughout this period he has dominated the policy-making process. No one in the Congress or the Government, not even Sardar Patel, ever challenged his control in this sphere. In the country as a whole the voices of criticism are few, though they have grown in numbers during recent years.

The decision to remain in the Commonwealth was, in the last analysis, Nehru's, though he had the support of all his senior colleagues and though others helped to solve the technical problems.[1] India's Asian policy and the initiative for the Asian Relations Conferences in Delhi in 1947 and 1949 derive entirely from Nehru. So do the doctrine of peaceful coexistence (the *Panch Shila*) and India's policy towards China and the Soviet Union. It was Nehru, too, who intervened with an offer of mediation in both Korea and Indo-China.[2] Even in the execution of policy his role has been decisive—through his widespread travels which have taken him to China (1954), Russia (1955), the United States (1949 and 1956), South-east Asia (1950 and 1955), Japan (1957), almost every country in Europe, and Great Britain (annually since 1948, usually for the Commonwealth Prime Ministers' Conference). He is, then, Minister, chief policy planner and roving Ambassador, a combination of roles which has no parallel anywhere, with the possible exception of the United States in its Dulles period.

---

[1] See pp. 413–18 above.

[2] On 7 July 1950, a fortnight after the outbreak of the Korean War, Nehru addressed personal messages to Stalin and Acheson, the American Secretary of State. See the *Times of India* (Bombay), 8 July 1950. In the case of Indo-China there were two interventions. On 22 February 1954 Nehru appealed to the powers concerned to strive for a cease-fire. *Indiagram*, No. 399, 25 February 1954. On 24 April 1954, in another statement to the House of the People, Nehru presented a six-point peace plan for Indo-China. *Indiagram*, No. 440, 27 April 1954.

Nehru's approach to foreign policy was cogently stated in a letter to the Presidents of the Provincial Congress Committees during the summer of 1954: 'A policy must be in keeping with the traditional background and temper of the country. It should be idealistic . . . and . . . realistic. If it is not idealistic, it becomes one of sheer opportunism; if it is not realistic, then it is likely to be adventurist and wholly ineffective.'[1]

In the course of an interview two years later, India's Prime Minister spoke with the utmost candour about various aspects of Indian foreign policy. On the general question of motives in foreign policy he adopted a typical 'realist' position: 'Ideological urges obviously play some part . . . especially in a democracy because . . . no policy can go very far if it is quite divorced from the people's thinking. However, *in the final analysis, all foreign policy concerns itself chiefly with the national interest of the country concerned.*' As for the primary considerations in India's policy of non-alignment, he remarked: 'First of all, the background and conditioning factors are there. Secondly, apart from our desire for peace . . . is our feeling that peace is absolutely essential for our progress and our growth. And if there is war, big or small, it comes in the way of that growth which is for us the primary factor. Thirdly, with the coming of nuclear weapons, war seems to us—and seems to most people everywhere—as extreme folly, that is, it has ceased to promise what you want.'

Regarding the possibility of a threat to India, he said: 'I do not conceive of any kind of invasion or attack on India—not because of other countries' love of India, but because it will bring them no profit. India does not come into the picture. Any country attacking India merely adds to its troubles.' In case of attack, however, 'it is obvious that the people of India will fight that attack and defend themselves'. As for non-alignment, 'I would say that non-alignment is a policy which is nationally profitable for any country. But in some cases there is danger— because of the smallness of the country or because of its geographical position—that, whether it is aligned or non-aligned, it may suffer from the war.'

[1] On 4 July 1954. *Congress Bulletin*, No. 5, June–July 1954, p. 246. This letter (pp. 245–51) merits special attention because of its lucid exposition, its moderation, and because it is the only case in which Nehru has addressed himself to the foundations of foreign policy.

In reflecting on India's foreign policy goals, Nehru made a sharp distinction between a 'third force' and India's notion of an 'area of peace': 'a Third Force simply means you are trying to create another force to counter the [existing] forces or as a balancing factor but you are still thinking in terms of force. I think that this thinking in terms of force puts you in that vicious circle of force. I can understand an area which wants to keep out of war. That is a different matter.'[1] This distinction seems unreal, for a 'third force' merely denotes an additional area of *influence*, not necessarily resort to *coercion*. India's 'area of peace' is surely a 'third force' in this sense.

*   *   *   *

The content and conduct of any state's foreign policy are subject to various pressures operating on the government of the day. In a democracy there is the need to secure approval of policy in the Cabinet and in Parliament. There is, too, the attitude of the press, of other parties and of special interests, economic, social and religious. Finally, the foreign service must be taken into account.

In India's case most of these institutional pressures on the formulation of policy may be dismissed as of little consequence —not because India is not a democracy, but because of conditions peculiar to the Indian scene. The Cabinet may be dealt with first. Since Independence Nehru has held the External Affairs portfolio as well as the Prime Ministership. During the duumvirate with Patel from 1947 to the end of 1950 it was clearly understood that Nehru had exclusive jurisdiction over foreign affairs. Since that time no Minister other than Krishna Menon has concerned himself with the political aspects of foreign affairs, except in very special instances—Azad on Pakistan and the Middle East, and Azad and Pant on Hungary in 1956. And Menon has been Nehru's deputy for all practical purposes. In general it may be said that Nehru's word was and still is final in all Cabinet discussions on foreign policy.[2] This is equally true of the Congress Party. Year after year the party passes resolutions, almost invariably framed by Nehru himself,

---

[1] To the author in New Delhi on 13 June 1956. (Emphasis added.)
[2] Based on interviews with former Cabinet Ministers and prominent officials in India in 1956 and 1958.

which give full approval to the Government's, i.e., Nehru's, foreign policy.[1]

In Parliament, the overwhelming Congress majority (365 of 489 in the 1957 elections) assures approval for Nehru's policies. Criticism, sometimes virulent, comes from the Opposition benches—from Socialists, as on the Hungarian revolt in 1956 and Kashmir, from the Communists, on such topics as membership of the Commonwealth and 'colonialism', from the communalists, notably on Kashmir and Indo-Pakistani relations, and from a few Independents. Parliamentary sanction, however, is never in doubt.

In the press, too, there is widespread support for Nehru's initiative in world affairs, aside from purely party journals and a few independent national dailies like the British-owned *Statesman* and the *Times of India*. Yet even they do not question the basic principles of Indian foreign policy; their criticism is directed rather at the tone of Nehru's public posture towards the West. There are a few prominent commentators, such as A. D. Gorwala ('Vivek'), who call for a fundamental revision of Indian policy.[2] But these are voices in the wilderness. The country at large stands solidly behind the Prime Minister on foreign policy.

Within the industrial and financial community there has always been dissatisfaction, notably over the strained relations with America, but they have been unable to exert any significant influence on the formulation of policy. Neither have the career diplomats, on the whole. In those countries where the Minister is an expert himself (e.g. Dulles in the United States, Eden in Great Britain) the influence of the Ministry's officials is severely curtailed, certainly on the level of policy-making. So it is in India. This is not to suggest that they are ignored. During the first five years of independence, Sir G. S. Bajpai, Secretary-General of the Ministry, undoubtedly exerted a major influence on the *conduct* of policy. He was Nehru's technician and a valued counsellor, notably in the negotiations over Kashmir, both at the U.N. and in the sub-continent. His successor, Sir R. Pillai, also a former senior member of the I.C.S.

---

[1] These resolutions are reprinted verbatim in the party's official journal, *Congress Bulletin*, and frequently in *Indiagram*.

[2] See his collection of articles published as *India Without Illusions* (1953).

in the days of British rule, controls the day-to-day operations of the Ministry. Moreover, since 1956 his views appear to carry considerable weight with the Prime Minister. But there is no evidence to suggest that the Foreign Office has deflected Nehru from the path he laid down many years ago.

Thus far, then, the normal institutional pressures of a democratic state have had little discernible effect on the pillars of Indian foreign policy. This does not mean, however, that Nehru has imposed his views on a hostile political environment. On the contrary, his role on the world stage has called forth unstinted praise from the vast majority of politically conscious Indians. The reasons for this widespread support are many. For one thing, Nehru's policies have brought great prestige to India in the first decade of independence. His words are received with respect throughout the world community and his actions have a marked effect on the course of events, as in Korea, Indo-China and the Middle East. The growing recognition of India's prominence in international affairs satisfies a deep urge of his people; they share his triumphs and find compensation for past colonial subjection and present social and economic ills. For another, there is a mass faith in Nehru's leadership which extends to large sections of the intelligentsia. But most important is his capacity to express in words and deeds the basic feelings and aspirations of his people. He guides them as a teacher does his pupils, he knows their mood and channels their ideals into realistic policy, but he rarely goes too far ahead of them. Non-alignment, anti-colonialism and anti-racialism admirably reflect these emotions and objectives.

That Nehru has wielded supreme power over Indian foreign policy since 1947 is readily acknowledged by colleagues, critics and impartial observers. It should not be inferred, however, that he relies entirely on his own personal judgement of events. At different periods and for different issues the advice of a few people has weighed heavily in his decisions.

A striking feature of this select group is the absence of a professional diplomat. Another is heterogeneity. It comprises two English aristocrats (Lord and Lady Mountbatten), a member of Nehru's family (Mme. Pandit), a Hindu philosopher (Dr. Radhakrishnan), a Muslim divine (Maulana Azad), a talented intellectual who devoted many years to the service of the Indian

Princes (Sardar K. M. Panikkar), and a caustic, brilliant nationalist who spent half his life in Great Britain (V. K. Krishna Menon). Only one, Azad, was a Congress politician of long standing.

Lord Mountbatten occupies a unique position in this coterie of foreign policy counsellors, a foreigner and the last Viceroy of India yet an intimate friend and trusted adviser of the Prime Minister since the tumultuous days attending the Partition. Indeed, during the first year of Indian independence Lord Mountbatten exerted far more influence on Nehru's decisions than did his party or Cabinet colleagues. The two most noteworthy examples were the submission of the Kashmir dispute to the United Nations at the end of 1947[1] and, as noted earlier, the decision to remain in the Commonwealth. The Mountbattens' departure from India in the summer of 1948 naturally reduced the opportunities for influence in day-to-day decisions. However, their annual reunions in India and England and candid discussions between intimate friends undoubtedly affect the general outlook of Nehru and, therefore, the course of Indian foreign policy. It is, of course, a highly intangible factor, but important none the less. The Mountbattens' principal role has been to strengthen India's ties with the Commonwealth and to reduce its antipathy to the West as a whole.

During the early years Nehru's judgement on many issues appears to have been influenced by the views of his sister, Mme. Pandit. Having served as India's Ambassador in Moscow and Washington (and later in London and for a brief period as head of the U.N. delegation), she was a vital source of information and an invaluable link with most of the important diplomatic centres in the world. She was, moreover, a completely trustworthy aide and a person with more ready access to India's Prime Minister than any other member of the 'inner circle'. Her influence, primarily directed to friendship with the West, has declined during the past few years, especially since Krishna Menon came to the fore. But her special relationship with Nehru continues to give her views more weight than those of any other ambassador.[2]

[1] Campbell-Johnson, op. cit., pp. 251–2.
[2] Other Indian diplomats whose views probably carried much weight with Nehru are K. P. S. Menon (Moscow 1953), G. L. Mehta (Washington 1953–8) and R. K. Nehru (Peking 1956–8 and Cairo 1958–).

During the last years of Stalin's reign the most vital personal influence on Nehru's view of the Russian scene was Dr. S. S. Radhakrishnan, the most distinguished living Indian philosopher who served with great skill as Ambassador to the Soviet Union from 1950 to 1953 and then became Vice-President of India. In recent years he has been consulted by the Prime Minister on a wide range of problems. It seems reasonable to assume that foreign policy issues are not excluded from their discussions. In view of his strong intellectual affinities with the West, his influence would appear to strengthen his country's ties with England and with the non-Communist world in general. Yet Dr. Radhakrishnan is a firm believer in the policy of non-alignment, not only as best suited to India's interests, but as a positive contribution to world peace. To a private gathering some years ago he gave a spirited defence of India's policy and expressed the opinion that 'if Indian neutralism did not exist [as a bridge between the two ideological worlds] it would have to be created'.[1]

Maulana Azad never dabbled in diplomacy as such but his influence was wide-ranging. As the dean of nationalist (Congress) Muslims, he spoke for India's forty-odd million Muslims in the Congress High Command and in the Cabinet, of which he was a senior member from 1947 until his death in 1958. As an intimate friend and political colleague of Nehru for more than three decades, and one of the few party leaders with whom Nehru felt an intellectual comradeship, Azad was heard with the utmost respect by the Prime Minister. Azad's views were crucial on two aspects of foreign policy, Indo-Pakistani relations and the Middle East. The Muslim minority in India may properly be termed another basic source of India's world view, and Azad was its acknowledged spokesman.

In the perennial rivalry with Pakistan for the friendship of the Muslim world, the Maulana was India's most valuable asset. He was an ideal cultural ambassador to the Arab states, Turkey and Iran, a role which he performed with great success on various occasions. In this capacity he helped to offset the persistent Pakistani propaganda about the persecution of Indian Muslims. Moreover, India's staunch support for the Arab states in their conflict with Israel and its refusal to establish normal

[1] At McGill University in October 1954.

diplomatic relations with the Jewish state—a glaring violation of Delhi's oft-proclaimed view on the need to accept the 'political facts of life'—were largely due to Azad's advice.[1] The influence of Sardar Panikkar was felt notably in the sphere of India's policy towards China. As the first Ambassador to Peking (1950–3) and the only non-Communist diplomat on friendly personal relations with Chinese leaders, Panikkar laid the foundations for cordiality and trust between these two great Asian powers. His dispatches throughout the Korean War and his role as liaison between Communist China and the outside world won Nehru's admiration and contributed to India's growing prestige as a mediator. The Chinese occupation of Tibet in 1950 cast a dark shadow over Indo-Chinese relations for a brief period, but Panikkar assisted greatly in restoring friendly relations.[2] Nehru's insistence on the need to recognize the new régime in China flows logically from his assessment of the Asian scene and his past sympathy for the Chinese revolution.[3] Panikkar's views strengthened this attachment.[4] Since 1953 his influence appears to have declined sharply. His brief tour as Ambassador to Cairo in 1953 had no outcome of significance. Some of his recommendations in the *Report of the States Reorganisation Commission* (1955) did not endear him to the Prime Minister, notably that the U.P., Nehru's home State, should be divided into two units.[5] But the most important reason was the emergence of Krishna Menon as the right hand of Nehru in foreign affairs.

Menon's rise to prominence was meteoric. After many years as head of the India League in London, with no direct involvement in the struggle for independence, he was appointed the first High Commissioner of (free) India to London. His major achievement of the period (1947–52) was to assist in the negotiations leading to India's membership of the Commonwealth as a Sovereign Democratic Republic. It was not until 1953 that

[1] Based upon interviews with prominent Indian officials in 1956.

[2] For a valuable compendium of information on the Tibetan episode and Indo-Chinese relations in general see Fisher, Margaret W., and Bondurant, Joan V., *Indian Views of Sino-Indian Relations* (Indian Press Digests—Monograph Series, Berkeley, California, No. 1, February 1956).

[3] See his *China, Spain and the War*, pp. 11–53.

[4] For Panikkar's account of his tour of duty see his *In Two Chinas: Memoirs of a Diplomat* (1955).

[5] *Report of the States Reorganisation Commission*, pp. 244–52.

he achieved an international reputation as the controversial, tempestuous voice of India before the United Nations. Since that time he has led India's delegation to the annual sessions of the world organization and has served as Nehru's personal ambassador to many international conferences. After a brief spell as Minister without Portfolio in the Indian Cabinet, he became Minister of Defence towards the end of 1956.

There is no doubt that Menon occupies the position of chief foreign policy adviser to Nehru. Indeed, during the past few years he has been the Adjunct Minister of External Affairs. He has never had a personal political following and could count some Congress leaders among his many enemies. This has changed somewhat as a result of the barrage of publicity hailing him as the 'hero of Kashmir'—for his record-breaking eight-hour defence of India's case before the Security Council at the beginning of 1957.[1] Yet he exercised great influence before that dramatic episode.

The basis of Menon's influence is his personal relationship with the Prime Minister—which dates to the early 'thirties when Menon identified himself with the Nehru ideology in the Congress. He accompanied Nehru on his European tour in 1938 and the friendship blossomed. He also edited some of Nehru's books for publication in America. But the reason for his influence is more than friendship. Menon has the capacity to echo his leader's foreign policies, the ability to grasp Nehru's thoughts and objectives and to convey them accurately, always pungently, to the outside world. Sometimes he exceeds the bounds, as in his pro-Soviet vote over Hungary at the United Nations in 1956.[2] But these are exceptions which prove the rule. Menon is the carrier of Nehru's views the world over. In this sense he performs a function identical to that of Harry Hopkins for President Roosevelt. He is, however, more than roving ambassador and spokesman.

Menon is consulted on all issues of foreign policy by the

---

[1] Altogether Menon spoke for twenty hours on Kashmir during the Security Council debate in January 1957. At one point he collapsed in the Council chamber and had to be treated for what was described as a mild heart attack. He returned to the battle the same afternoon, apparently none the worse for wear.

[2] Menon opposed a resolution calling for U.N.-supervised elections in Hungary. He was under Nehru's instructions to abstain on all votes relating to Hungary, according to well-informed Indians interviewed by the author in 1958.

Prime Minister. And his views carry considerable weight, because of Nehru's respect for his intellectual ability and his knowledge of men and affairs. To what extent Menon shapes policy is a subject of widespread conjecture. Accuracy of a high order is impossible in the absence of more intimate knowledge about the policy-making process. Furthermore, it would be wrong to divide the formulation and execution of policy into two rigid compartments. The two aspects are inextricably intertwined, and the intent of policy is frequently altered in the course of implementation. Be that as it may, a broad distinction can and should be made between strategic and tactical decisions, and between general policy goals and the details of negotiation. Certainly in the case of India these distinctions seem valid.

The core objectives and guiding principles of its foreign policy are demonstrably Nehru's contribution. Long before Menon arrived on the scene, the policies of non-alignment, anti-colonialism, racial equality, non-violent methods, and a third force were formulated by Nehru. And these have remained unchanged. Similarly, the strategic decisions regarding Kashmir and Indo-Pakistani relations, China, Russia, the Commonwealth and Asian co-operation were made by Nehru. Menon has not altered these policies in their essentials. He has, rather, acted upon them to achieve specific goals, but always within the framework set by Nehru. Even with regard to Indo-U.S. relations it is doubtful that Menon's role has been crucial although he has alienated many Americans—both officials and the public. To some extent this has reacted upon Nehru's judgement, but not so as to shape his overall attitudes to the United States.

It has been in the capacity of 'trouble-shooter' that Menon has performed his distinctive role, negotiator with wide latitude, mediator between contending parties (often where Indian vital interests are not directly involved). Outstanding examples in recent years include the Korean armistice, the Geneva Conference on Indo-China in 1954 and the Suez imbroglio from 1955 to 1957. He has also relieved Nehru of the onerous burden of day-to-day decisions in many spheres, but he rarely acts contrary to the line laid down by Nehru. On the level of a cs, Menon's influence is considerable. Constant discussion results in a fusion of ideas and, very often, in Menon's suggestions being taken up by Nehru and unconsciously adopted as his own. Still another area in which Menon's influence is felt is in the drafting of specific policies. By all accounts he is a master technician, capable of setting down Nehru's aims in operative terms.

It would be a grave error, however, to exaggerate Menon's influence on the fundamental character and direction of Indian foreign policy. Nor does the evidence suggest that Menon would steer Indian policy into another course even if he had the authority to do so. He is, like Nehru, first and foremost devoted to Indian national interests, not the ideology or goals of any other part of the world. He appears to be as firmly convinced as Nehru of the merits of non-alignment and of the value of continued membership of the Commonwealth. Indeed, Menon has been among the staunchest Indian advocates of close ties with Great Britain.[1] As for his frequent denunciation of American policies and his more sympathetic tone to those of the Soviet Union, part of the explanation lies in his past political radicalism and the emotional legacy of the 'thirties.

One other personal influence deserves recognition. During the past few years Nehru's assessment of events in the Soviet Union and eastern Europe appears to have been affected by the views of Marshal Tito with whom lengthy visits were exchanged in 1955 and 1956. This is evident in Nehru's interpretation of the liberalizing trends in Soviet society since Stalin's death.[2]

*   *   *   *

A detailed account of Indian foreign policy since 1947 does not lie within the scope of this book. In any event, the historical record is readily available.[3] There are, however, certain key areas which merit discussion here.

A distinction can be drawn between Indo-Pakistani relations and those with the rest of the world. But the two categories are very closely related, and India's policies outside the sub-

[1] In 1956 Menon was responsible for founding a journal, *Envoy*, devoted to strengthening Indo-British friendship.

[2] See for example Nehru's remarks on Russia to *New York Times* correspondent, A. M. Rosenthal. *New York Times*, 19 May 1958.

[3] See Kundra, J. C., *Indian Foreign Policy 1947–1954* (1955); Karunakaran, K. P., *India in World Affairs 1947–1950* (1952) and *India in World Affairs 1950–1953* (1958); and Varma, S. N., *Trends in India's Foreign Policy 1954–57* (I.P.R. 1957).

continent are profoundly influenced by the 'permanent conflict' with its Muslim neighbour.[1]

The story of this tragic enmity between the successors to the
British *Raj* is too well known to require a lengthy exposition.[2]
Suffice it to note that India and Pakistan have been in a state
of undeclared war, with varying degrees of intensity, throughout
their brief history as independent states. A host of disputes
arose from the Partition, some political or economic, some technical, but all surcharged with violent emotion. Many minor
points of discord have been eliminated. The critical issues,
however, remain unresolved, notably Kashmir, the division of
the Indus Valley canal waters and compensation for properties
left behind by the ten million refugees. Together they represent
a Gordian knot which if not severed in the near future could
produce a catastrophe.

The price of discord during the past eleven years has already
been exorbitant. The constant threat of renewed military hostilities over Kashmir has compelled both states to channel a
large portion of their limited funds into 'defence'—an annual
average of approximately 80 per cent. for Pakistan and 50 per
cent. for India.[3] This, in turn, has had grave economic repercussions, notably the slowing-down of much-needed development programmes in both countries. Tension has also reduced
the flow of goods and services between their highly complementary economies, for some time eliminating it almost completely,
causing unemployment, inflation, use of precious foreign exchange, and increasing bitterness on both sides of the border.
Propaganda war has been endemic, contributing further to the
tension, heightening the sense of insecurity among minorities,
and stimulating a continuous migration, especially from East
Bengal.[4]

The strategic consequences have been no less severe. The
Indo-Pakistani sub-continent is a natural military unit whose

---

[1] This is, of course, equally true of Pakistan's foreign policy. See Callard, K.,
Pakistan's Foreign Policy: An Interpretation (I.P.R. 1957).

[2] See the author's *The Struggle for Kashmir* (1953); Korbel, J., *Danger in Kashmir*
(1954); Lord Birdwood, *Two Nations and Kashmir* (1956); and Sisir Gupta, *India's
Relations with Pakistan 1954–1957* (I.P.R. 1957).

[3] Brecher, op. cit., pp. 188–91.

[4] In the spring of 1956 the Minister in charge of refugees in West Bengal told the
author that no fewer than 3·5 million Hindus had fled East Bengal since 1947.

28. Dr. S. S. Radhakrishnan, Vice-President of India

Press Information Bureau, Government of India

29. Nehru, Vice-President Radhakrishnan and President Prasad

security depends on joint defence policies and co-ordination of their armed forces. The historic threat to the area came from the north-west, and any future invasion of Pakistan would inevitably affect India. Instead of military co-operation, however, the two states have been forced to prepare for a possible war with each other—a war which could destroy the stability of both and cause incalculable harm for the 450 million people of the area. One could enlarge this sombre picture by assessing the evil consequences of every dispute, but this is unnecessary.[1]

What makes the picture of Indo-Pakistani relations especially distressing is that few people in either country deny that the effects have been unfortunate for both, with no apparent compensation, yet all seem incapable of finding a way out of the impasse. Many are also unwilling to do so.[2] As for the relative importance of the individual disputes, there is some difference of opinion. Kashmir would appear to be the crux. This is so, not because of its material value *per se*—the canal waters problem is more significant in this sense—but because Kashmir symbolizes the root of the conflict between India and Pakistan. Here lies the last field of battle over the ideological cleavage which rent the sub-continent asunder in 1947. Here is the final test of the validity of the two-nation theory, the basis of Pakistan and its continuing *raison d'être*. Indian leaders still reject the theory, though they accepted partition on grounds of self-determination.

India's continuing struggle for Kashmir is largely due to the conviction that the future of its secular state and equality for its 40 million Muslims are at stake. The wounds of Partition are still deep. The secession of Kashmir and its inclusion in Pakistan, would, in the opinion of Nehru and others, lead to grave consequences for the internal stability of India. Among these would be a strengthening of Hindu communal forces, increasing distrust of the Muslim minority, a challenge to the secular foundations of the Indian Constitution, and a clamour for war with Pakistan. Most Indians remain convinced of the righteousness of their case, of Pakistan's aggression, of the U.N.'s dereliction of duty in not pronouncing judgement on

[1] See Brecher, op. cit., ch. ix.
[2] This conclusion emerged from extensive interviews in the sub-continent in early 1958.

U

their initial charge, and of their legal and moral right to include Kashmir in the Indian Republic. But it is the belief that powerful disruptive forces would be unleashed by a plebiscite and its accompanying propaganda, especially if a majority voted for Pakistan, that deters them from carrying out their pledge to hold a plebiscite under U.N. supervision.[1]

For Pakistan, the ultimate fate of Kashmir is no less vital. Ideological interests—the two-nation theory—underlie its attitude with perhaps greater force than in India. The actual danger of communal discord is less, for there are very few Hindus in West Pakistan, and the East Bengalis have no real attachment to Kashmir. But so much attention has been focused on Kashmir by the leaders and the press of Pakistan that it has become *the* internal political issue. No government could remain in office if it conceded India's claim, and the internal repercussions would be grave. This is less true in India in the purely political sense, though the overall effects would be severe. And for both the element of prestige now looms very large in their calculations.

Given these circumstances, it is inevitable that Indian foreign policy should be influenced by the struggle for Kashmir. A number of examples reveal this link with utmost clarity. On various occasions since 1948 Indo-British relations have been strained as a result of London's support for the Pakistani claim to Kashmir. A press tirade followed the Anglo-American resolution in the Security Council in 1950.[2] When the British openly criticized India for incorporating Kashmir into the Union early in 1957 and for refusing to implement the plebiscite, talk of leaving the Commonwealth reached serious proportions in Delhi. When India abstained on a U.N. resolution condemning Russia's suppression of the Hungarian revolt, the West was appalled. But India's vote had little to do with the question under discussion. On the contrary, when India opposed the proposal to send U.N. observers and the call for a U.N.-controlled election in Hungary, it was clear that Delhi wanted to avoid a precedent for Kashmir.

---

[1] Based upon interviews in New Delhi in January 1958. India is still officially committed to the plebiscite as embodied in agreements arranged by the United Nations on 13 August 1948 and 5 January 1949.

[2] See for example the *Times of India* (Bombay), 16 March 1950.

Reference has already been made to the link between India's Middle East policy—especially its championing of the Arab cause against Israel—and the rivalry with Pakistan for Muslim support on Kashmir. The outstanding example of Kashmir's impact on Indian foreign policy is to be found in the realm of Indo-U.S. relations. Nothing has done more harm to friendship between them than American arms aid to Pakistan since 1954. India considers this an indirect threat because it augments Pakistan's war potential. And Pakistan continues to proclaim its intention of 'liberating' Kashmir, by force if necessary. The Indian reaction to American aid was virulent in 1953–4.[1] It was expressed again in the autumn of 1957 when Nehru chided the United States for compelling India to increase its military expenditure, with serious consequences to the Second Five-Year Plan.[2] Moreover, American assistance to Pakistan has deepened Indian mistrust of U.S. motives in creating military blocs in South-east Asia and the Middle East.

The prospects for an amicable solution are no brighter now than at any time in the past. Indeed, they are even dimmer, as revealed by the failure of Dr. Graham's mediation mission early in 1958, the latest of a long series.[3] It is pointless at this stage to apportion blame for the dispute. One thing is certain: the wrangling has accomplished nothing thus far; and in the absence of a bold new approach, the future of India and Pakistan will continue to be plagued by the host of ills which flow from the impasse over Kashmir.

*   *   *   *

India's decision to remain in the Commonwealth occasioned much surprise both at home and abroad. As noted earlier, some critics termed it a 'betrayal' of Nehru's pledge of 'complete independence'. To others it was anathema because of

---

[1] See for example Nehru's speech at Dehra Dun on 11 December 1953, and his statement to the House of the People on 1 March 1954. In *Indiagram*, No. 350, 15 December 1953, and No. 403, 3 March 1954, respectively.

[2] *New York Times*, 10 September 1957.

[3] For a summary of Dr. Graham's (sixth) report to the Security Council see *New York Times*, 4 April 1958. In 1948 and 1949 there was a United Nations Commission for India and Pakistan (UNCIP) which submitted three reports; in 1950 General MacNaughton served briefly as an informal mediator and later in the year Sir Owen Dixon served as U.N. Representative for India and Pakistan. Between 1951 and 1953 Dr. Graham submitted five reports to the Security Council; and in 1957 Mr. Gunnar Jarring served briefly as a mediator. For an analysis of the U.N. role in the Kashmir dispute see Brecher, op. cit., Ch. IV–VII.

racial discrimination in various parts of the Commonwealth, notably in South Africa. To others still it implied an abandonment of non-alignment.

Some years after the event Nehru remarked: 'We decided that there was absolutely no reason why we should break an association which didn't come in our way at all, legally, constitutionally, practically, in any sense, and which merely helped us to co-operate in a measure, consult each other and maybe influence others and maybe to be influenced ourselves. . . . We are freer than two countries tied by an alliance.'[1] It was, in short, Independence plus, not Independence minus.

There were, however, more positive reasons for Nehru's decision. India could not risk total isolation in the aftermath of Independence, especially in an era of Cold War. Moreover, Commonwealth membership widened the stage on which India could play an important international role—without committing it to a bloc. Most important were strong material bonds which could be severed only at great cost. India's foreign exchange reserves were tied up in the sterling area, as was a major part of its trade. India's armed forces were equipped with British-made weapons. And its industrial development depended in large measure on the ability to use its sterling balances.

It is doubtful whether the decision was received enthusiastically, even by those who recognized the force of these arguments. In accepting it they were merely acknowledging faith in Nehru's leadership. To this day there is no genuine attachment to the Crown, however symbolic, or indeed to the Commonwealth as such. The link is tolerated because it serves India's interests. The tenuous nature of the tie is best illustrated by the frequent demands for withdrawal—whenever Great Britain acts in a manner which offends Indian sensibilities. This has happened over the Kashmir issue frequently. The greatest crisis, however, came over the Anglo-French invasion of Egypt in November 1956. A tremendous outcry followed, even amongst normally pro-Commonwealth groups. Only Nehru's firm refusal to countenance such a step prevented a break.[2]

As long as Nehru is at the helm of affairs it is virtually certain

---

[1] To the author in New Delhi on 13 June 1956.
[2] See *New York Times*, 21 November 1956.

that India will maintain the link. Thereafter it is an open question. The Communists are, of course, openly committed to withdrawal. So are many Socialists, as well as a substantial number of Congressmen who have remained silent thus far, in deference to Nehru's strong feelings on the matter.

India's foreign policy in the past decade has borne out Nehru's thesis that Commonwealth membership does not restrict its freedom of action. Nevertheless, the connection has exercised a subtle influence on Delhi's judgement of certain issues. There is, in the first place, a more restrained criticism of British colonial policies than of the French, Dutch and Portuguese variety, amply revealed by Nehru's words and deeds on Malaya, Kenya and British Guiana on the one hand, and Indo-China, Indonesia and Goa on the other.[1] The distinction may be intangible, but its existence is undeniable. Secondly, India's criticisms of the West, as a power bloc, are invariably directed at the United States, even though Britain is no less devoted to the Western alliance.[2] Thirdly, with the qualified exception of the Suez War, India is inclined to be more favourably disposed to the British case where it would normally be staunchly anti-West. An excellent illustration is the involved negotiations over the seizure of the Anglo-Iranian oil properties. In general the evidence suggests that as a result of the Commonwealth connection, the Prime Ministers' Conferences and the constant exchanges of information, India's attitude to many international problems is moderated by the British outlook. This, of course, is a reciprocal process, as exemplified by Nehru's plea for Commonwealth pressure to moderate American attitudes on the Chinese 'off-shore islands' crisis at the beginning of 1955.

* * * *

The record of Indo-American relations since 1947 reveals a deep and abiding friction between the two largest democratic states in the world. More frequently than not they have clashed on important international problems. Notable examples are the recognition of Communist China; the Japanese

[1] See for example Nehru's comment on Malaya on 10 April 1950 and his comment on West New Guinea on 7 July 1950, in Nehru, *Press Conferences 1950*, pp. 68 and 124 respectively.

[2] In part this is also due to India's conviction that British diplomacy is more mature.

Peace Treaty; disarmament and nuclear tests; Kashmir; the type and conditions of foreign aid; and the value of military blocs. Even where their policies were in substantial agreement, it was subject to qualification, as in the cases of Korea (1950), Hungary (1956) and the Middle East (1956–7). Indeed, one would be hard-pressed to find an illustration of a complete meeting of minds between Washington and Delhi in the realm of foreign policy.[1]

This divergence of policies on specific issues cannot be attributed to the whims of individuals, though the lack of personal affection, understanding or trust between Nehru and Dulles has certainly accentuated the friction. Rather, it stems from a fundamental difference in Indian and American Government views of the world and of the tasks confronting the statesmen of the mid-twentieth century. At the risk of over-simplification the basic disagreement may be stated as follows.

The United States State Department sees the contemporary world in a rigid black-and-white perspective, as a struggle between good and evil, between Democracy and Communism. The great issue of our time is freedom or slavery. There is no room for a 'middle way'. Non-alignment is immoral or, at the very least, amoral, for how can a state be neutral in a contest of this kind? Non-alignment weakens the 'free world' and serves objectively to strengthen the Communist bloc. Not only is it reprehensible in the American view, it is also sheer folly for the state concerned because international Communism will respect neutrality only as long as it serves Soviet interests. The vital task, therefore, is to forge an alliance of democratic and anti-Communist states and to negotiate from strength, for this alone can prevent Communist domination of the entire world and achieve a *modus vivendi* on the basis of which non-Communist states can survive and prosper. Not all Americans share this view. But it is clear that United States policy-makers think and act within this frame of reference.

Nehru rejects the premises and, therefore, the policy implications of this argument. To divide the world into rigid moral categories, he replies, is to indulge in fanciful self-righteousness.

---

[1] For a survey of Indo-American relations see Rosinger, L. K., *India and the United States* (1950); and Poplai, S. L., and Talbot, Phillips: *India and America: A Study of their Relations* (1958).

No state or way of life has a monopoly of truth or virtue, though one may be more admired. None is an absolute threat to peace and freedom. On the contrary, both East and West share the blame for international tension which hangs like a shadow of impending death over the entire planet. Both are guilty of provocative deeds and words. But both are firmly established in the present world and can only be eradicated by a contest on the battlefield. Since war is now capable of total annihilation, it is the absolute immoral act of our time. Indeed, the moral imperative is to rule out war and to concentrate on the difficult but essential task of relaxing tensions, to recognize the harsh realities of international life, and to search unceasingly for a negotiated settlement between the two blocs. The greater the scope of the bloc system, the greater the likelihood of ultimate war. Hence non-alignment is vital to peace, an ethical and practical necessity. As long as India and the 'uncommitted' countries of South-east Asia persist in this policy, they help to delay a catastrophe. And in positive terms they fulfil the historic role of maintaining a bridge between the hostile blocs.[1]

Beyond this world view, Nehru believes that national self-determination for all colonial peoples and racial equality are the most compelling immediate goals. The ideological conflict between Communism and anti-Communism only increases tension without any compensation. It is a luxury of advanced industrial powers which the recently freed states of Asia and Africa cannot afford, not the central issue of world politics. The task of statesmanship, in Nehru's view, is to moderate the conflict between Communism and the West, to press for national self-determination and to struggle for racial equality.

Given this enormous cleavage in basic outlook, the disagreement on a host of foreign policy questions is inevitable. Both India and the U.S. attach the utmost importance to peace, but they are poles apart on the meaning of peace and the methods to attain it. This does not mean, however, that they are enemies. Indeed, despite the fact that they adopt contrary foreign policies, they are akin in many respects. They share a belief in the dignity of the individual and the rights of man. Their political institutions derive from the same ideological

---

[1] For a typical statement by Nehru on India's role as a mediator and possible balancer see *Indiagram*, No. 364, 6 January 1954.

roots. They reject the theory and practice of Communism. Their way of life differs in that their historical experience and traditions have virtually nothing in common except the humanist ideal. But in so far as modern India has been influenced by non-Asian ideas and institutions, that influence has been overwhelmingly of the democratic West. Thus, to term India pro-Soviet is to mistake appearance (the frequent coincidence of Indian and Russian policies) for reality (non-alignment with both blocs).

It is true, nevertheless, that India criticizes the United States more frequently and more severely than the Soviet Union. The reasons are many and complex. For one thing, the hangover of emotional hostility to the West because of colonialism affects even a convinced rationalist like Nehru. With the departure of the British this feeling was transferred to the United States, the assumed successor to British interests in many parts of Asia. And American policies in Asia, such as the creation of military blocs and the continued alliance with Chiang Kaishek, strengthen the belief among Indians that the United States is, in fact, fulfilling this role. More specifically, these actions are taken to be an intrusion into an area of Indian vital interests to which Indians are no less sensitive than are Americans when non-American influences penetrate the Western Hemisphere. To the United States the Guatemala episode (1954) posed a dire threat to security. To Nehru and other Indian leaders the American-sponsored South-east Asia Treaty Organization is no less of a threat, magnified in Indian eyes because of the long experience of Western colonial rule. No such stigma attaches to the Soviet Union, partly because it has never controlled the rimland of Asia, partly because it has not *overtly* brought the Cold War to the area. Those cases where Soviet intervention obviously exists, such as Korea and Indo-China, are not clear-cut in Indian eyes, for they were enmeshed with nationalism or Chinese self-interest.

A second reason for the more virulent criticism of the United States is related to the racial factor. All politically conscious Indians are sensitive to any form of racial discrimination. The image of America held by many includes the inferior position of the Negro in the United States; this breeds hostility or at least mistrust of America's policies in the non-white areas of the world.

The Soviet Union, by contrast, is believed by most Indians to be a land of racial equality. It would be difficult to exaggerate the influence of this factor in moulding Indian attitudes to the U.S. and the U.S.S.R. The fact that the status and rights of the American Negro have improved steadily in the past generation is either not known to many Indians or is given little attention; much-publicized news of a lynching or of segregation nullifies this trend to racial equality in the minds of colour-conscious Asians.[1] By contrast, the realities of race relations in the Soviet Union are rarely examined by Indians; their general impression is a favourable one, and it is this attitude which influences Indian foreign policy.

Another reason for India's softer tone towards Russia's policy is its acceptance of India's non-alignment without apparent qualms. India refuses to 'stand up and be counted', and Moscow has never openly insisted on complete association with the Communist bloc. Moreover, the Soviet Union, alone of the Great Powers, has declared its support for India's claim to Kashmir, an issue which in Indian eyes is the supreme test of friendship or enmity.[2] The failure of the United States to match Russia's denunciation of South Africa's policy of *apartheid* has a similar effect. Furthermore, Indian leaders are acutely conscious of their geographic position, contiguous to the Soviet heartland and China. In their view it is wise to tread lightly when confronted with such powerful neighbours. Finally, there would seem to be a conviction among Indian leaders that a democratic state is less likely to be alienated by harsh criticism than an authoritarian régime, that is to say, the danger of alienating Washington is less because a democracy is accustomed to conflicting points of view.

Little need be added as to the sources of Delhi's comparative tolerance of Soviet deeds in the international arena. The analysis would be incomplete, however, without reference to certain elements which antedate the Cold War. First is the powerful attraction of Marxism for the Indian intelligentsia in the 'thirties. This created an initial climate of opinion favourable

[1] Typical was the hostile reaction to racial violence in Little Rock, Arkansas, in 1957. See *New York Times*, 8 October 1957.
[2] This was done by Khruschev during his visit to India at the end of 1955 and again in 1958 when the Soviet delegate to the Security Council vetoed a pro-Pakistani resolution.

to the Soviet experiment which affects the outlook of Indian leaders to the present day. The most noteworthy example is Nehru who acknowledged his debt to the Marxist way of thought in his voluminous writings. The infatuation has long since passed, but the intellectual influence remains.[1] It also instilled a faith in socialism as the 'wave of the future' and as a system capable of solving India's social and economic problems.

Intimately related to this ideological pull, indeed, giving it a material base of support, was the admiration of Nehru and others for the far-reaching changes effected by the Soviet revolution in the 'twenties and 'thirties, particularly because they concerned problems which were similar to those of India. Many Indian intellectuals in the inter-war period were impressed by the successful campaign against illiteracy, particularly in Soviet Central Asia, and the frontal attack on the land problem. The rapidity of industrialization in a 'backward' country, whose economic problems were basically the same as those confronting India after Independence, provided a hopeful precedent and, with qualifications, a guide to Indian economic thinking. Many Indians took at face value the Soviet claim of having solved the 'nationality problem' which is of such compelling importance to India. In the broadest sense the Soviet experiment 'proved' that an underdeveloped economy with seemingly intractable social and cultural problems could catch up with the advanced Powers of the West in a relatively brief period of time and could do so without excessive dependence on foreign aid.[2]

This does not mean that Indian leaders were ever enamoured of Soviet methods. Aside from dedicated Indian Communists —a tiny minority in the nationalist movement—there was outspoken criticism of the regimentation, the intolerance and the ruthlessness of Russia's 'way to socialism'. It was impossible to reconcile this with Gandhi's stresss on non-violence and on the prior importance of means. Nehru himself was profoundly troubled by this feature of Soviet policy and made known his reservations from the outset of his flirtation with Marxism.[3]

[1] See pp. 603–5 below for Nehru's views on Marxism.
[2] See pp. 116–20 above for Nehru's views in the 'twenties.
[3] See pp. 187–8 above.

With the passage of time his hostility to Russian methods became more strident. So too did his critique of Marxism as 'outmoded nineteenth-century thought'. Other Indian intellectuals preceded him in this personal disenchantment. Nevertheless, the emotional hangover remains and with it the belief that Soviet achievements can be reproduced in India without its repulsive methods. Finally, there is the practical consideration of Soviet economic aid. India has adopted the ways of democratic planning and the political institutions of the West. But it is anxious to keep the door open to both worlds in order to expedite economic development. Soviet aid has been comparatively small thus far, but any aid without strings is attractive. All these elements induce a sharper disagreement with American policy than with that of the Soviet Union. But it would be a serious error to infer that this places India in or even close to the 'Soviet camp'.

Indo-American relations have not been consistently strained, nor have Indo-Soviet relations been consistently friendly, in the past decade. During the first two years of Indian independence Delhi was more favourably disposed towards Washington than to Moscow, and the Soviets dubbed India an 'Anglo-American satellite'. Relations with the United States cooled after Nehru's unsuccessful bid for large-scale American aid without strings in the autumn of 1949. The period of greatest stress was undoubtedly 1953–4 when American arms aid to Pakistan seemed like a dagger pointed at India. As might have been expected, Delhi began to see more virtue in Soviet policy, while Moscow reciprocated by hailing India's neutralism.[1] Washington's support for Pakistan remains a barrier to complete trust. But the friction eased considerably in the autumn of 1956 as a result of America's pro-Egyptian stand during the Middle East crisis, at the expense of its chief allies. At the same time Indian trust in the Soviets received a rude shock with the undeniable evidence of brutal suppression of the Hungarian revolt. From that point onwards the scales were more evenly balanced in the mind of Nehru and others. The revival of Soviet hostility to Yugoslavia and the execution of the former Hungarian Premier, Imre Nagy, in the spring of 1958 tilted the balance away from

[1] This reached its peak in the very warm reception accorded Nehru on his visit to the Soviet Union in the summer of 1955.

Moscow.[1] So too did the U.S. Senate's expression of support for large-scale economic aid at a time when India's Second Five-Year Plan was in jeopardy.[2]

*　　*　　*　　*

Friendship with China has been an axiom of Indian foreign policy during the past decade, first with the Nationalist régime of Chiang Kai-shek, and since the end of 1949 with the Communist régime in Peking. India was the second non-Communist state to recognize the government of Mao Tse-tung.[3] Year after year it has taken the lead in pressing Peking's claim to China's seat in the United Nations. Nehru has been the most vociferous critic of America's non-recognition policy and has urged the West over and over again to accept the 'facts of political life' in East Asia. During the Korean War Delhi was Communist China's window on the U.N. and the non-Communist world. Largely through India's efforts, with noteworthy assistance from Chou En-lai's skilful diplomacy, Communist China has acquired a measure of respectability throughout Asia, highlighted by its successful début at Bandung in 1955.

In their direct bilateral relationships, warm friendship has been the keynote—with the notable exception of Tibet. Together, Nehru and Chou propounded the Five Principles of Peace, the *Panch Shila*, or the doctrine of peaceful coexistence, to which about a dozen states have subscribed as the basis of their foreign policy.[4] The two Prime Ministers have met

[1] Typical of Indian press reaction to the announcement about Nagy was the *Hindusthan Standard*'s exclaimer at this 'murder'. Further, 'Why should communism at the height of its power in two continents be afraid of anything and anybody? Yet it apparently is. Of whom? The free man? Of what? The free mind?' Quoted in the *New York Times*, 19 June 1958. The governing party of India was even more sharp. Shriman Narayan, Congress General Secretary (obviously writing with Nehru's consent) commented: '. . . the sudden news about the trial, conviction and execution of Imre Nagy has shocked the conscience of millions of people throughout the world. It is being felt the old methods of violence, hatred and terror are being revived in order to create a sense of fear and consternation.' Quoted in the *Montreal Star*, 26 June 1958.

[2] *New York Times*, 7 June 1958.

[3] Burma was the first. India followed a few days later, on 30 December 1949. According to Panikkar the Burmese requested India to allow them to be the first. *In Two Chinas*, p. 68.

[4] The Five Principles, first stated in the preamble to the Sino-Indian Agreement on Tibet on 29 April 1954, are as follows: mutual respect for each other's territorial

periodically to discuss a host of Asian problems.[1] Delegations of every conceivable description have flowed in both directions with increasing frequency. Nehru's tour of the Chinese mainland in 1954 was the occasion for public demonstration of mutual affection and trust before the eyes of the world. And the leaders of both countries never cease to proclaim their undying friendship, though India is more effusive in expressing the attachment.

It is a unique relationship—a neutralist, democratic India linked with the West by its choice of political institutions, economic system and social ideals, and an avowed Communist state deriving its inspiration from the Soviet Union. As the two most populous and potentially most powerful states in Asia, they are inevitable rivals for influence in the vast belt of 'uncommitted' countries in South-east Asia. Yet India persists in championing the cause of Peking in the chancellories of the world. To many Western critics Delhi is acting against its own vital interests. To Indian policy-makers, however, the case for friendship with China seems overwhelming, though some Indian intellectuals are beginning to have reservations.

The most compelling factor has already been alluded to—geography. India and China share a common border for approximately two thousand miles, some of it not clearly demarcated and most of it impenetrable until recently. With the Chinese occupation of Tibet their interests met in the heart of Central Asia. A conflict of interests in these circumstances might well lead to a direct clash, as it almost did over Tibet in 1950. But in its present position of weakness India is determined not to become embroiled in a dangerous conflict with its neighbour unless its vital interests are openly threatened, such as control over the Himalayan border states of Nepal, Bhutan and Sikkim.[2]

While geography has been a traditional barrier to enmity between India and China, history provides an inducement to

integrity and sovereignty; mutual non-aggression; mutual non-interference in each other's internal affairs; equality and mutual benefit; and peaceful coexistence.

[1] In Delhi in July 1954, December 1956, and January 1957, and in Peking in October 1954, as well as in Bandung in April 1955.

[2] Tibet was not considered absolutely essential by Nehru and his colleagues. Moreover, in their public view the Chinese legal claim was very strong. And in any event, they were not prepared to go to war with China.

friendship. Indians (and Chinese) constantly refer to the fact of two thousand years of peace between Asia's two greatest civilizations and the friendly cultural ties, notably the Indian contribution of Buddhism to China. In reality, the absence of war is largely due to nature, that is to say, the impossibility of physical combat, until recently, in the forbidding mountainous terrain. But the fact of peaceful relations is proclaimed a model in international affairs—and is an admirable point of reference in all public pronouncements on Sino-Indian friendship. It also creates a climate of opinion favourable to peaceful settlement of disputes.

In examining Nehru's attitude to China it is necessary to see the Chinese revolution through his eyes. Unlike many Westerners, especially American officials, Nehru views the establishment of the Peking régime as the culminating act in a century-old process of revolution and as a manifestation of Asia's political renaissance. The fact that the victor subscribed to Marxism is considered secondary, as is Soviet aid to the Chinese Communists. For most Indians the events of 1948–9 represented the rebirth of a united China after a lengthy period of disorder, something to be welcomed as part of the decline of Western colonial influence all over Asia. A sense of Asian solidarity takes precedence over divergent ideologies and social, economic and political systems. Moreover, Nehru is genuinely convinced that Chinese nationalism is a far more potent force in Chinese policy than Communism, that Chinese civilization is too old and too deeply rooted to succumb to Marxist dogma; or, to put it in other terms, that the Chinese Communists will adapt Marxism to suit Chinese needs and traditions.

Closely related is the belief that China is not inextricably tied to the Soviet Union, that the Western policy of 'containing' the Peking régime is forcing it to complete dependence on Moscow, and that acceptance of Communist China by the West would inevitably weaken the tie with Russia. Although it is never officially stated as such, this would seem to be the *raison d'être* of Nehru's role as champion of Peking's claims. Given his basic assumption—that the Peking régime is more nationalist than Communist—the logic of this thesis is unassailable. And it is clearly in India's interest to reduce China's reliance on the Soviet Union.

From a negative point of view this would ease the pressure flowing from the massive weight of a Moscow–Peking bloc surrounding India with enormous military power and 800 million people. From a positive viewpoint it would enhance Asia's prestige and power in world politics and might lead to an expanded 'third area of peace' based on Sino-Indian leadership. India and China together could then conceivably play the role of world balancer. In any event, a loosening of the Sino-Soviet link would reduce the threat of world war by adding another imponderable to the balance of world political and military forces. From India's perspective, everything is to be gained by its China policy.

Nehru is strengthened in this course of action by the conviction that Peking does not represent a threat to Indian interests in the foreseeable future, certainly not for a generation. China will be too preoccupied with internal problems, problems of economic development, social change, education and the like, to venture upon foreign aggression, argue Indian leaders in private. Hence there is no need for Delhi to take this remote contingency into serious account at present. Furthermore, if the Peking régime were brought into contact with the non-Soviet world, its Communist ardour would be reduced and, therefore, the likelihood of expansionism in the future.

It should not be inferred, however, that Nehru is dominated by these assumptions or that unqualified trust is the basis of his China policy. Indeed, he is disturbed by the evidence of Chinese penetration into the Himalayan border states and has made abundantly clear that he considers them to be in India's 'sphere of influence'.[1] Nor is he oblivious to the inevitable long-run rivalry between Democratic India and Communist China for the leadership of Asia. He knows full well, but never admits in public, that the ideologically uncommitted countries of the area are watching the contest between Delhi and Peking, particularly in the economic realm, to see which system can 'deliver the goods'. He knows that the fate of Asia hangs in the balance —and hopes that sympathetic Western statesmen will realize

---

[1] On 6 December 1950 he told Parliament: 'From time immemorial, the Himalayas have provided us with a magnificent frontier. . . . [They] lie mostly on the northern border of Nepal. We cannot allow that barrier to be penetrated because it is also the principal barrier to India.' *Jawaharlal Nehru's Speeches*, p. 176.

the implications of the contest before it is too late. Thus far he has been disappointed with the evidence of such imaginative understanding.

China undoubtedly occupies a key position in the thinking of many Indians about foreign affairs and economic development.[1] Prime Minister Nehru made the following observations in 1956: 'There is no competition as such, but it is, perhaps, inevitable for people to compare, from time to time, the progress made, because the two countries are alike in that they are big, with large populations, industrially underdeveloped, and also very ancient countries. [Their degree of success in economic development] is bound to influence other countries.' As for his 1954 tour, 'my major impression was one of the enormous basic strength of the Chinese people. They are amazing workers and they work together and that itself gives strength. And now, with a centralized government and all that, it gives them a really terrifying strength.'[2]

*   *   *   *

India's outstanding achievement in foreign policy has been to provide leadership in the political awakening of Asia after centuries of colonial rule. As the best-organized nationalist movement in the East, the Indian National Congress served as a model for the intelligentsia of South-east Asia and to a lesser extent of the Middle East. The attainment of Indian freedom in 1947 undoubtedly represented the major break in European control of vast portions of the Asian rimland and hastened the process of independence throughout the area—Ceylon and Burma in 1948, Indonesia in 1949 and Malaya in 1957. The withdrawal of British power from the sub-continent also influenced the course of events in the Middle East, for with the loss of its imperial bastion England could no longer retain its paramount influence in the Arab world. There were, of course, other factors responsible for the steady decline of colonialism— the devastating effects of the Japanese sweep through East Asia in the early 1940's, the rise of America to world power and the intervention of both the United States and the Soviet Union in

---

[1] Based on interviews in India in 1956 and 1958.
[2] To the author in New Delhi on 13 June 1956.

the area as a whole. But it was India's attainment of political freedom which set the process in motion.

Even before the completion of the freedom struggle, Nehru had proclaimed the objective of strengthening relations with all Asian states. And Nehru was the most articulate spokesman for a deep-seated urge to reassert Asia's rightful place in the world community. Although he has persistently denied any claim to Asian leadership, he is acutely conscious of a 'special position' which makes India pre-eminently fitted to play this role. In one of his speeches during the 1949 American tour he remarked: 'India's pivotal position between Western Asia, South-east Asia and the Far East made it the crossroads of that part of the world. India is the central point of the Asian picture. . . . India's role of leadership may not be so welcome to others although it may satisfy our vanity. But it is something which we cannot escape. We cannot escape the various responsibilities that arise out of our geography and history.'[1]

Acting in this belief, and with a view to restoring intra-Asian relations which had been shattered during the preceding two centuries, Nehru set out to give substance to the inchoate longing for some form of Asian co-operation. In doing so he was also motivated by the desire to create an 'area of peace' which could stand apart from the power struggle between the Western and Communist worlds. On the eve of Independence he took the initiative and summoned the peoples of Asia to the first Asian Relations Conference in modern history. Two years later this was followed by an emergency Conference of Asian states in Delhi to bring pressure to bear upon the Dutch and the U.N. in order to facilitate Indonesian independence. From 1950 onwards India has co-operated with its immediate neighbours in a loose grouping known as the Colombo Powers. And in 1955 Nehru's efforts culminated in the historic Afro-Asian Conference at Bandung, a gathering of twenty-nine non-Western states, most of whom had only recently emerged from a lengthy period of colonial rule.

It would be wrong to exaggerate the importance of Bandung in *contemporary* world politics, for little emerged of a practical value. The divisive forces—ideological, economic and other—

[1] To the Overseas Press Club in New York, on 19 October 1949. Nehru, *Inside America*, pp. 54–55. See also p. 190.

were sharp. No permanent organization was created. A third bloc did not ensue. None the less, the mere fact that these states gathered together symbolized a process which may ultimately have far-reaching consequences. Many individuals contributed to this organized expression of Asia's reawakening. But the principal contribution was undoubtedly made by Nehru over the past decade.[1]

While Nehru achieved marked success in focusing attention on Asian consciousness, he has failed to forge the kind of non-aligned Asian group which he considers necessary for world peace. Only Burma and Indonesia adhere to the policy of non-alignment. Ceylon is sympathetic, and the precarious states of Laos and Cambodia follow India's lead in so far as their freedom of action permits. But Asia is largely fragmented into blocs which are controlled from outside the area: Japan, South Korea, South Viet Nam, Formosa, the Philippines, Thailand, Malaya and Pakistan are closely tied to the Western bloc; China, North Viet Nam and North Korea are part of the Communist bloc. In the Middle East, India's 'middle way' has found more adherents, but the states of the area are weak and generally unstable. In the formal sense, then, Nehru has not succeeded in creating a materially significant third force.

And yet, the notion of an 'area of peace' has assumed increasing importance in world affairs, as the balance of power between the West and Communism approaches virtual equality. Regardless of what the smaller Asian states do, India's deeds and words are treated with respect. For in the last analysis the future of Asia rests primarily on the course of events in India and China. China has already made its choice. India remains 'uncommitted'. Barring some unforeseen shift in internal Indian politics, it will continue to plough this lonely furrow, certainly as long as Nehru dominates the Indian political scene. It will do so because of the firm conviction that in this way it will contribute to the basic objectives of Indian foreign policy— the preservation of independence and economic development— and to the goal of world peace.

[1] For an account of the Bandung Conference see Kahin, G. Mct., *The Asian-African Conference* (1956).

CHAPTER XX

Portrait of a Leader

Few statesmen in the twentieth century have attained the stature of Jawaharlal Nehru. As the pre-eminent figure in India's era of transition he bears comparison with Roosevelt and Churchill, Lenin and Mao, men who towered above their colleagues and guided their people through a period of national crisis. Only Gandhi inspired greater faith and adoration among the masses. Only Stalin, perhaps, had greater power. Like these outstanding men of the age he has also imposed his personality on a wider canvas. He is for many a symbol of Asia's political awakening and the outstanding spokesman of 'the middle way' in a world of ideological crusades. His name conjures up a host of associations, some praiseworthy, some critical —resolute fighter for national freedom, Gandhi's devoted aide, the Mediator, the neutral in a struggle between good and evil, the self-appointed guardian of morality in international affairs. Yet friends and foes alike recognize him as a leading actor on the stage of contemporary history.

Now approaching his seventieth year, Nehru stands at the pinnacle of fame. What enabled him to achieve this illustrious position? What are the sources of his power and popularity? A conclusive answer is wellnigh impossible, for the elements involved are varied and complex, some of them highly intangible. The most important are Nehru's personality, his relationship with Gandhi, the setting in which his leadership matured, the Indian tradition of hero-worship and the nature of his ideas.

The key to his extraordinary appeal would appear to be personal qualities which have long attracted people from all walks of life in India and in far-off lands. His physical courage is renowned. All who have known him have admired his integrity and selflessness, his sincerity of purpose and his devotion to the causes he holds dear, notably Indian freedom and world peace. Some have been drawn by his generosity and loyalty to colleagues, others by his honesty and apparent purity of motive. Few have failed to succumb to his inordinate charm. Many respect his detachment and intellectual tolerance, his idealism and abnegation of absolute power. For others still he is the epitome of the romantic hero in politics, the impulsive, youthful and daring leader of men, intensely human, fearless, and champion of the oppressed.

The range of persons who admire Nehru is best illustrated by two tributes, one from the most outspoken foe of Indian independence, the other from a political antagonist at the present time. In words attributed to Sir Winston Churchill, 'here is a man without malice and without fear'.[1] A leader of the Indian Communist Party referred to Nehru as 'the one romantic figure thrown up by the nationalist movement, a sensitive idealist with a broad vision, a politician with deep insight into national and international problems, a man with a fine aesthetic sense, a whole man in the Renaissance conception'.[2]

Most Indian intellectuals viewed Nehru in this light during the past thirty years or more, and with good reason. He was the most complete expression of a whole class—the young, Westernized intelligentsia which emerged after the first world war. Indian by birth yet Western by education, modern in outlook yet influenced by the heritage of his native land, a staunch patriot yet a man with international vision, he was the symbol of a new society—liberal, humanist and equalitarian. Indeed, he was the embodiment of an intelligentsia constantly in turmoil as it sought to reconcile its goals with the alien environment in which it grew to maturity.

The rare appeal of Jawaharlal Nehru arose precisely from his combination of contradictory elements. As one of his admirers remarked in the mid-1940's, he is explosive in speech, disciplined in action, impulsive in gestures, deliberate in judgement, revolutionary in aim, conservative in loyalty, reckless of personal safety, cautious about matters affecting Indian welfare. The same writer, Krishna Kripalani, unconsciously expressed the mood of many intellectuals in the following portrayal: 'He is

---

[1] Quoted in Rao, B. Shiva, 'Jawaharlal Nehru, Crusader for Freedom' in *The Hindu Weekly Review* (Madras), 18 November 1957.

[2] To the author in New Delhi in March 1956, by a person who wishes to remain anonymous.

at once personal and detached, human and aloof, with the result that now he appears fond, now cold, now proud, now modest. An aristocrat in love with the masses, a nationalist who represents the culture of the foreigner, an intellectual caught up in the maelstrom of an emotional upheaval—the very paradox of his personality has surrounded it with a halo.'[1]

Nehru drew the intelligentsia to the nationalist movement, as Gandhi mesmerized the peasantry. Yet Nehru appealed to the rural masses as well, in time acquiring a genuine popularity only slightly less than that of the Mahatma. During the 'thirties and 'forties he championed their cause more tenaciously than any other member of the Congress High Command. Not that Gandhi was averse to higher standards of living for 'the dumb millions', as he was wont to term them. But Nehru, with his constant broadsides on the iniquities of the land system and his pledge for a new order in the countryside, was their hope for the future. In 1937 he won the provincial elections almost single-handed by promising large-scale agrarian reform. They still believe in him to a large extent, partly because of their longing for an end to poverty, partly because of his unmistakable sincerity. But there are other reasons for this trust.

For many years Nehru was the Mahatma's acknowledged heir. This alone endowed him with enormous prestige. He had, too, the reputation of an indomitable fighter for freedom; even more, the halo of a modern prince who had sacrificed wealth and leisure in the struggle for independence. Many had served with equal devotion. Others had renounced as much, perhaps more. But none was so honoured as the aristocratic 'Panditji'. Along with his personal qualities, Gandhi's blessing, his renunciation and his articulation of their hopes, Nehru also benefited from the deeply ingrained tradition of hero-worship. No one was more suited to the role. And after the Mahatma's death it was but natural for India's peasants to transfer their attachment to his successor.[2]

---

[1] *Gandhi, Tagore and Nehru*, p. 73.

[2] Even among Indian intellectuals this cult of leadership is widespread. An extreme example is the following remark attributed to S. K. Dey, the driving force behind the Community Development projects and later Minister of Community Development in the central Cabinet: 'We *are* a country of hero-worshippers. Why not? If Panditji asked me to drown myself in that well tomorrow morning, I would do it.' Quoted in Lyon, Jean, *Just Half a World Away*, p. 251.

This, indeed, has been one of the pillars of his support since 1947, probably the most important source of his popularity. The effect has been to place him on a pedestal approached by none of his colleagues. Moreover, as the co-architect of independence, Nehru is the continuing expression of the freedom struggle. The only two conceivable rivals have long since passed from the scene—Subhas Bose in 1945 and Sardar Patel in 1950. Since that time he has been the last remaining hero of the Indian revolution.

In the broadest sense Nehru's influence derives from his role as the strategic link among diverse groups in Indian society. The older politicians in the Congress value his loyalty, the younger ones look to him for inspiration; the Right wing finds him indispensable, the Left wing has always considered him amenable; he was and is reasonable enough for capitalists, radical enough for most socialists; and the peasants view him as their main hope for land reform. Intellectuals, of course, see him as the bridge between tradition and the modern world. This unique role is enhanced by the blend of ideas which constitute Nehru's political philosophy.

*   *   *   *

In the realm of thought Nehru has always been a lonely traveller seeking answers to a myriad of problems, answers that seem to elude his grasp. To his keen and receptive mind almost all the ideological currents of the past half-century appealed at various stages in his growth to intellectual maturity: first in time was classical liberalism with its emphasis on individual rights; then, at Cambridge, he was drawn to Fabian Socialism; thereafter, he was influenced by the Gandhian stress on the purity of means and the message of non-violence; and in the late 'twenties and 'thirties by Marxist theory and the gospel of a classless society. He was also attracted to the ethical norms of Western humanism, and later, during his long war-time imprisonment, to the precepts of the *Vedanta*, the ancient system of Hindu philosophy, but stripped of its purely metaphysical and religious beliefs. Underlying all was a passionate devotion to the ideas of nationalism and racial equality. None of these dominated his outlook; all of them influenced his thought.

Indeed, the key to his thinking is a perennial scepticism about all claims to absolute truth and virtue.

Scattered throughout his voluminous writings are fragments of a world outlook, each reflecting the primacy of one of these strands at a given point in time. Nowhere is there a systematic effort to integrate them into a consistent personal and political philosophy—for Nehru is an eclectic in intellectual matters. Nevertheless, he did set down his mature reflections in the *Discovery of India*.[1] These merit special attention, perhaps, because as late as 1956, a dozen years after they were penned, Nehru termed them his most considered thoughts on 'Life's Philosophy'.[2]

As in all his writings there are moving passages. There are, too, candour and humility, intellectual tolerance and gnawing doubt about the right path. 'What was my philosophy of life [in the late 'thirties]?' he asked at the outset of these reflections. 'I did not know. Some years earlier I would not have been so hesitant. . . . The events of the past few years . . . have been confusing, upsetting and distressing, and the future has become vague and shadowy and has lost that clearness of outline which it once possessed in my mind. . . . The ideals and objectives of yesterday were still the ideals of today but they had lost some of their lustre. . . . They lost the shining beauty which had warmed the heart and vitalized the body. Evil triumphed often enough, but what was far worse was the coarsening and distortion of what had seemed so right.'

His constant dilemma over means and ends received poignant expression: 'What then was one to do? Not to act was a complete confession of failure and a submission to evil; to act meant often enough a compromise with some form of that evil, with all the untoward consequences that such compromises result in.'

Despite this uncertainty and occasional lapses into pessimism, faith in the future emerges from this philosophical self-analysis, faith in science and faith in man's upward march to a better life. There emerges, too, a portrait of a humanist and a pragmatist with a passionate interest in the welfare of men: 'The

---

[1] The following quotations are taken from the Indian edition of *The Discovery of India* (Signet Press, Calcutta), pp. 7–22.

[2] To the author in New Delhi on 13 June 1956.

real problems for me', he affirmed, 'remain problems of individual and social life, of harmonious living, of a proper balancing of an individual's inner and outer life, of an adjustment of
the relations between individuals and between groups, of a
continuous becoming something better and higher, of social
development, of the ceaseless adventure of man. In the solution
of these problems the way of observation and precise knowledge
and deliberate reasoning, according to the method of science,
must be followed. . . . A living philosophy must answer the
problems of today.'

Partly because of his preoccupation with material and social
problems, he was indifferent to religion as a guide to action.
Moreover, orthodox religion as practised in the modern world
repelled him because 'it seemed to be closely associated with
superstitious practices and dogmatic beliefs'. Mysticism irritated him because 'it appears to be vague and soft and flabby,
not a rigorous discipline of the mind but a surrender of mental
faculties and living in a sea of emotional experience'. Metaphysics and philosophy provided 'a certain intellectual fascination. . . . But I have never felt at ease there and have escaped
from their spell with a feeling of relief.'

Nehru also boldly proclaimed his agnosticism: 'I find myself
incapable of thinking of a deity or of any unknown supreme
power in anthropomorphic terms, and the fact that many people
think so is continually a source of surprise to me.' His only
concession in this regard was an expression of sympathy for 'the
old Indian or Greek pagan and pantheistic atmosphere, but
minus the conception of god or gods that was attached to it'.
Nevertheless, he felt strongly attracted to an 'ethical approach
to life' and acknowledged the profound influence of Gandhi
who applied ethical norms to the whole range of public affairs.

His intellectual debt to Marxism was also acknowledged.
However, 'it did not satisfy me completely, nor did it answer all
the questions in my mind, and, almost unawares, a vague
idealist approach would creep into my mind, something rather
akin to the *Vedanta* approach'. The basic reason for his dissent
was its rigidity and dogmatism: 'Life is too complicated and, as
far as we can understand it in our present state of knowledge,
too illogical for it to be confined within the four corners of a
fixed doctrine.' And while referring to Soviet society, some of

whose achievements he admired, he remarked: 'I am too much of an individualist and believer in personal freedom to like overmuch regimentation.' Although conscious of the powerful pressures limiting the scope of individual action, he also professed his belief in free will, within limits, and in the worth of the individual.

Perhaps because of the difficulty in resolving the many philosophical dilemmas, his attitude was not to think too much about fundamental intellectual problems, but rather to concentrate on the immediate, urgent and concrete problems of life. This is, indeed, the core of Nehru's approach, to merge thought and action in the achievement of social goals. 'The call of action has long been with me,' he wrote in 1944, 'not action divorced from thought, but rather flowing from it in one continuous sequence. And when, rarely, there has been full harmony between the two . . . then I have sensed a certain fullness of life and a vivid intensity in that moment of existence. . . . The old exuberance is much less now. . . . And yet, even now, the call of action stirs strange depths within me and, after a brief tussle with thought, I want to experience again "that lonely impulse of delight" which turns to risk and danger and faces and mocks at death. I am not enamoured of death, though I do not think it frightens me. . . . I have loved life and it attracts me still. . . . Without that passion and urge [to action], there is a gradual oozing out of hope and vitality, a settling down on lower levels of existence, a slow merging into non-existence.' The discourse ends on a typically ambivalent note: 'Whatever gods there be there is something godlike in man, as there is also something of the devil in him.'

Fourteen years have passed since Nehru itemized the elements that shaped his philosophy of life. The world has changed much, but the essentials of his outlook remain unchanged. The central fact is that he does not possess a systematic *Weltanschauung*; he does not have one basic premiss from which he constructs a logical system and derives a series of logical and rational deductions. Pragmatism looms very large in his thought, as it does in his approach to decisions. He does not cling to ideas *per se* but views them in a social setting. And he is brilliant in adjusting them to different circumstances.

The principal strain in his thinking is Western liberalism

which expresses itself in his firm devotion to political democracy and individual freedom. The evidence is overwhelming. Nehru is a genuine democrat, as revealed by his espousal of the parliamentary system, free elections, a free press, freedom of speech, of religion and assembly, political parties, and constitutional safeguards for individual rights. Socialism is also rooted in his thought, providing the stimulus to planning and the stress on social and economic equality. Evidence for his continued dedication to this idea is also abundant—the Five-Year Plans, the 'socialist pattern of society', the efforts to build up the public sector of the economy. Gandhism provides the basic approach to social, economic and political change, i.e., the method of morally sanctioned non-violent change—though many find his attitude to Kashmir a striking deviation from this attitude. And nationalism is the vital force behind the assertion of India's right to recognition, as well as the right to independence for all colonial peoples. Indian foreign policy since 1947 demonstrates this beyond doubt. In this significant practical sense, the four main strands in his social and political philosophy have been reconciled; each provides the stimulus to, and the rationale for, decisions in various aspects of public affairs.

At different times and in different spheres one or another will predominate in accordance with the needs of India during its period of transition. But they remain the broad guides to policy. Thus, for example, it is true that Nehru has not pressed forward with socialism at the same speed as he pledged before Independence. But this does not detract from his belief that India must go the way of socialism, in some form or other. Flexible on tactics, he is rigid on goals: socialism of the democratic type, achieved by planning, but within the framework of political democracy; secularism or, more correctly, equal rights for all communities in the Indian family; rising standards of living for the masses, to be achieved by peaceful change, not revolution; and the preservation of individual rights. These goals may, indeed, be termed Nehru's *idées fixes*. In the case of socialism his doctrinaire attitude of the 'thirties has become a pragmatic adjustment to circumstances and problems posed by events of the past dozen years. With age, too, he has become more cautious and conservative. Whereas before 1947 he was in favour of nationalization on a broad scale, he has come to the conclusion that top priority must now be given to production and that in this situation private enterprise has a valuable function to perform. Hence his willingness to tolerate, even encourage, private industry. The egalitarian strain is still there, but the principal object is to increase the total wealth to be distributed rather than to distribute poverty. Similarly, his penchant for radical and rapid social reform has been moderated by a variety of pressures since Independence. There is danger, of course, that tactical retreats may lead to strategic defeats. But the pillars of his thought are unimpaired.

Nehru is a convinced socialist but he is not a Communist. The record of word and deed is incontrovertible on this point. His earliest public statement on the subject is worth rescuing from obscurity. 'Bolshevism and Fascism are the waves of the West today', he told a Congress gathering in 1923. 'They are really alike and represent different phases of insensate violence and intolerance. The choice for us is between Lenin and Mussolini on the one side, and Gandhi on the other.'[1] This initial hostility later gave way to a prolonged flirtation. He drank deeply of Marxist literature from 1929 to 1939 but he *never* became intoxicated. This cardinal fact emerges clearly from his speeches and writings of that period, notably his Autobiography. Indeed, at the very height of his attraction to Communism, in the mid-'thirties, he remained the sceptic, impressed by certain Soviet achievements but repelled by their methods, influenced by the Marxist interpretation of history but unalterably opposed to its dogma, enamoured of Communist ideals but distressed by Communist practice. 'I am not a Communist,' he remarked in 1938, 'chiefly because I resist the Communist tendency to treat Communism as holy doctrine; I do not like being told what to think and do. I suppose I am too much of an individualist. . . . I feel also that too much violence is associated with Communist methods. The ends cannot be separated from the means.'[2]

The second world war proved to be a turning-point as far as his attitude to Indian Communists was concerned. Their

---

[1] Presidential Address to the United Provinces Provincial Conference on 13 October 1923. Bright, *Before and After Independence*, p. 41.

[2] To John Gunther. Quoted in 'Have you seen Jawaharlal?' in *Asia*, February 1939, p. 95.

'betrayal of the nationalist movement'—their co-operation with the Government after the 'August Movement' and the imprisonment of the Congress leaders—rankled deeply. In the autumn of 1945 he served on a special party committee which recommended the expulsion of all Communists from the Congress.[1] And since that time Nehru has been increasingly critical of the C.P.I. In the process he has made his position unmistakably clear on Marxism and Communism as well. 'Far from being revolutionary, the Communists are actually conservative', he declared in 1946.[2] By 1950 he had gone much further. At a press conference soon after the outbreak of the Korean War he said: '. . . huge monolithic States under Communist guidance [may] . . . answer an economic question, in certain countries but . . . at a tremendous cost. I don't like monolithic States, I don't like authoritarian States. . . . I do think that individual liberty, i.e., normally considered political liberty, does not exist in monolithic authoritarian countries.' As for Marxism, 'I am not interested in it. Why should I be? I am interested in finding a way out—not in interpreting Marxism or taking others' views. There are people who believe that whatever is in a scripture must be true. But my mind . . . is not made that way.'[3] Two years later he disassociated himself intellectually from Marxism: 'I think Marx is out of date today. To talk about Marxism today, if I may say so, is reaction. I think Communists with all their fire and fury are in some ways utterly reactionary in outlook.'[4] He has been saying this ever since.

His most pungent criticisms have been directed to Indian Communists. In one of his most scathing attacks, towards the end of 1954, he declared: 'They have no moorings in the land of their birth, but always look to outside countries for inspiration and guidance. They are of the opinion that internecine trouble, violence and bloodshed are the main things to be pursued.' He ridiculed them for clinging to the outmoded ideas of the Marxist

[1] The full text of the committee's report, which was acted upon without change, is to be found in *Congress Bulletin*, No. 2, 24 January 1946, pp. 24–34 and 36–37.

[2] To a press conference in Bombay on 27 February 1946. *Amrita Bazar Patrika* (Calcutta), 1 March 1946.

[3] On 7 July 1950. Nehru, *Press Conferences 1950*, pp. 124 and 130.

[4] To a press conference in New Delhi on 28 February 1952. *The Hindu* (Madras), 29 February 1952.

classics and for trying to apply them unchanged to India. He denounced them for maligning their country while abroad. And he noted, in public, that they had long opposed Indian foreign policy as a reflection of imperialism but began to approve it when the Soviet world did so.[1]

This charge of slavish dependence on Moscow was reiterated in the spring of 1958 when he assailed Indian Communists for their attitude to Yugoslavia. Nor was world Communism spared. Much had happened in recent years, he said. 'Sometimes it is called liberalization, sometimes democratization, sometimes "let a hundred flowers bloom". . . . Then the reverse process has taken place and all the flowers became weeds to be pulled out.'[2] An even more scathing indictment of Communism was penned by Nehru in the autumn of 1958: 'Its contempt for what might be called the moral and spiritual side of life . . . deprives human behaviour of standards and values. Its unfortunate association with violence encourages a certain evil tendency in human beings. . . . Its language is of violence, its thought is violent [and it seeks change] by coercion and, indeed, by destruction and extermination.'[3]

His actions since 1950 have corresponded to his growing verbal hostility. The Telengana rebellion, from 1948 to 1951, led to the prolonged detention of thousands of Communists. The C.P.I. was outlawed in four States, hardly likely without Nehru's consent. And although the detainees were released later, he indicated forcefully that any recurrence of violence would be treated harshly. It is true that he has not publicly rebuked the Soviet Union, but this is an issue of national interests, not ideology. As suggested in the discussion of India's foreign policy, friendship with the U.S.S.R. is considered a vital interest, and he does not believe anything is to be gained from an open split.

Nehru's attitude to Marxism, Communism and the Indian Communist Party could not have been otherwise, given his temperament, values and philosophy of life. He was influenced by the powerful anti-colonial themes of socialist theory and was

[1] To a public meeting in New Delhi on 28 November 1954. *The Hindu* (Madras), 29 November 1954. See also the *New York Times* and *The Times* (London) of the same date. [2] *New York Times*, 13 May 1958.
[3] 'Nehru on "The Tragic Paradox of Our Age"' in the *New York Times Magazine*, 7 September 1958, pp. 13 and 110.

acutely sensitive to the sufferings of the masses. But he has always been incapable of identifying himself wholeheartedly with a rigid body of doctrine. He was and is too much the nationalist to be a doctrinaire socialist and too much the aristocrat to be dominated by a proletarian party.

Where then shall we place him in the ideological spectrum? He is a liberal and a democrat, a socialist and an individualist. 'I suppose I am temperamentally and by training an individualist, and intellectually a socialist', he wrote just before the war. 'I hope that socialism does not kill or suppress individuality; indeed I am attracted to it because it will release innumerable individuals from economic and cultural bondage.'[1] Most of all, he is a humanist in the best tradition of East and West. His creed is best defined as democratic socialism and refined and humane materialism.

One discernible change in his outlook since the mid-1950's is a growing attraction to Buddhism. To an old friend he remarked: 'No orthodox religion attracts me, but if I had to choose, it would certainly be Buddhism.'[2] The explanation seems to be that he is drawn to its intellectual base, its stress on free will, its contempt for superstition, and its message of non-violence. Evidence of this attraction lies in his active role in the 1956 celebration of the *Buddha Jayanti* (the 2,500th anniversary of the Buddha's attainment of Enlightenment).

Nehru's admiration for Buddhism also emerges from an unusual incident during the visit of Soviet leaders to India at the end of 1955. A proud and enthusiastic Nikita Khruschev greeted him one day with the news that Soviet scientists had just perfected a terrifying weapon of mass destruction. The Indian Prime Minister listened politely to the bubbling and boastful tale and then reportedly responded in the following manner. 'You know, Mr. Khruschev, more than two thousand years ago a great warrior ruled over India. His name was Emperor Ashoka. Through frequent wars he extended his dominion throughout the land. His generals were victorious everywhere, and after every battle they would report thousands killed and many taken as slaves. Ashoka became troubled by this slaughter,

---

[1] Letter to Subhas Bose on 3 April 1939. Unpublished Nehru Letters.

[2] Related to the author in India in January 1958 by the person concerned, who wishes to remain anonymous.

and in time was converted to Buddhism. One day, after a victorious campaign, a general informed him that many more thousands had perished and untold destruction had been visited on his enemies. The Emperor could stand it no longer. Getting up from his throne, he removed his sword from its scabbard, broke it in two, and thundered, "Enough violence and carnage. There shall be no more. Peace will reign over the land."" Khruschev listened attentively, but as far as is known he made no comment.[1]

The true measure of Nehru's humanism, his tolerance and his liberalism, is perhaps best revealed in the following extemporaneous reflections on 'what constitutes a good society and the good life?'

Broadly speaking, apart from the material things that are necessary, obviously, a certain individual growth in the society, not only the corporate social growth but the individual growth. For I do believe that ultimately it is the individual that counts. I can't say that I believe in it because I have no proof, but the idea appeals to me without belief, the old Hindu idea that if there is any divine essence in the world every individual possesses a bit of it . . . and he can develop it. Therefore, no individual is trivial. Every individual has an importance and he should be given full opportunities to develop— material opportunities naturally, food, clothing, education, housing, health, etc. They should be common to everybody. The difficulty comes in about the moral aspect, the moral aspect of religion. I'm not at all concerned about the hereafter. It doesn't worry me; I don't see why it should worry people whether the next world is or is not there. And I am not prepared to deny many things. I just don't know! The most correct attitude, if I may say so, is that of the Buddha who didn't deny it and didn't assert it. He said 'this life is enough for me and when you don't know about something why talk about it'. I do believe in certain standards. Call them moral standards, call them what you like, spiritual standards. They are important in any individual and in any social group. And if they fade away, I think that all the material advancement you may have will lead to nothing worthwhile. How to maintain them I don't know; I mean to say, there is the religious approach. It seems to me rather a narrow approach with its forms and all kinds of ceremonials. And yet, I am not prepared to deny that approach. If a person

[1] Related to the author in India in March 1956 by a person who was present during the conversation.

feels comforted by that, it is not for me to remove that sense of comfort. I don't mind—I think it's silly for a man to worship a stone but if a man is comforted by worshipping a stone why should I come in his way. If it raises him above his normal level it is good for him. Whatever raises a person above his normal level is good, however he approaches that—provided he does not sit on somebody and force him to do it. That is a different matter. So while I attach very considerable value to moral and spiritual standards, apart from religion as such, I don't quite know how one maintains them in modern life. It's a problem.[1]

*   *   *   *

Individualist though he may be, Nehru does not live in a self-contained universe. The magnitude of his responsibilities compels him to rely on others. Who, then, are the persons who share(d) his confidence? Whose judgement does he respect? It is difficult to separate personal and political friendships and to measure the emotional attachments of any man. When that man is as moody, as lonely, as vain, as proud and as reserved about his private life as Jawaharlal Nehru the problem is complicated. An outsider has the added barrier of meagre acquaintance and approaches his task, therefore, with hesitation. In attempting to penetrate the intangible quality of friendship he must depend largely on the insights of others who have known Nehru intimately over the years and on the evidence of Nehru's associations.

For the period before Independence one is on reasonably sure ground. One man, Mahatma Gandhi, held Nehru's complete trust and confidence in matters both political and personal. A rare meeting of minds and hearts had developed over the years. Disagreements there were, of course, but never so keen as to affect the bonds that linked them in indissoluble friendship. With the Mahatma Nehru felt at ease. He could speak his mind freely, as a disciple to a master, though their relationship was not, strictly speaking, of that *genre*. With no one else has Nehru ever established that kind of rapport or attachment, not even with his father, the only other genuine confidant during the years of political struggle. Respect and affection were there, but Motilal Nehru could not draw out his son's emotional

[1] To the author in New Delhi on 13 June 1956.

30. At his desk

31. Ottowa, 1956

response to the same extent or in the same way as the Mahatma; perhaps because he was Jawaharlal's father and because the relationship forged in the younger Nehru's youth created a barrier, perhaps because of Motilal's personality. Certainly no Indian could emulate Gandhi's capacity to penetrate the depths of another's inner feelings and to draw them out in a mysterious, intuitive sense. Whatever the reasons, Gandhi's role as supreme confidant of Nehru was unique.

Since the Mahatma's death in 1948 Nehru has not shown complete trust in any man. He seems to rely on different persons for different purposes. A distinction must be made between the public and private spheres; and the former, in turn, must be divided into domestic politics, party affairs, economic matters and foreign policy. At a given point in time the persons who exert influence on Nehru in any of these categories can be readily determined. However, the structure of the élite groups around the Prime Minister changes through time in response to diverse pressures.

During the early years Patel held primary responsibility for internal politics and administration but he was hardly a confidant of Nehru, except in a formal sense. That function was performed largely by Rajagopalacharia, the south Indian elder statesman. At the end of 1950, immediately after Patel's death, he was brought to the Centre as Minister of Home and States and acted as Nehru's right-hand man in domestic politics. The period of direct collaboration was short-lived, however. Growing friction on sundry issues led to Rajaji's resignation towards the end of 1951. His successor in this role was Gopalaswami Ayyangar, the much-criticized U.N. spokesman for India in the early stages of the Kashmir dispute.

The gap created by Ayyangar's death early in 1953 was filled by Rafi Ahmad Kidwai, the second-ranking nationalist Muslim in India. A superb administrator, Kidwai was indefatigable and very successful as Minister of Food and Agriculture. He was, too, a nimble and shrewd political tactician with a brilliant sense of timing, qualities which he used with great skill in engineering the overthrow of Kashmir Premier Sheikh Abdullah in 1953.[1] Kidwai had one major advantage over both

---

[1] Kidwai's decisive role in this episode emerged from interviews with prominent Indian officials and politicians in 1956.

X

Rajaji and Ayyangar. As a close personal and family friend, an old colleague from the U.P. and one of the few senior Congress-men who shared Nehru's basic ideology, he had ready access to the Prime Minister; he was also one of the few Cabinet Ministers who spoke his mind fearlessly, and Nehru listened. His death in the autumn of 1954, while Nehru was in China, was a grievous personal and political blow and a great loss for the Congress. Since the beginning of 1955, as noted earlier, the position of key adviser on internal politics has been held by Pandit Pant, the Home Minister.

One other person whose views weighed heavily with Nehru was Maulana Azad, the late Minister of Education and leader of India's Muslims. At no time since 1947 was he the Prime Minister's principal counsel on domestic affairs. But at no time was his influence negligible. If there was one man whose posi-tion approximated to Gandhi's as the recipient of Nehru's com-plete confidence it was Azad. For thirty-five years they were intimately associated in the Congress. Others could match that record. But Nehru and Azad were intellectually akin, even though one was a Western-type agnostic and the other a Muslim divine. At the basis of their relationship was genuine affection and mutal respect which ripened into a mature friendship. Of all the Congress leaders, Azad was the most detached after Independence, free of the struggle for power and prestige, both of which he had by virtue of his earlier contributions and as dean of the nationalist Muslims. As a result Nehru used to consult him frequently about all manner of decisions. With Azad he could open his heart to an old comrade. While it is difficult to estimate Azad's influence on any particular decision, his overall effect on Indian politics was very great during the first decade of independence. Nor was it confined to domestic politics. The Maulana had the unique distinction of being a member of all but one of the Prime Minister's élite groups: his was a powerful voice in the party's High Command; on internal Indian politics his views were sought by Nehru; so too in foreign affairs, where he played a key role in shaping India's policies towards Pakistan and the Middle East; and in the private sphere he was the last of Nehru's comrade-in-arms for whom the Prime Minister felt a warm attachment. It is not surprising that when he died, in February 1958, Nehru reportedly wept as he delivered a moving eulogy.[1] Like Gandhi and Patel he was a giant of the nationalist movement.

The wielders of influence on Nehru's foreign policy have already been dealt with at length.[2] Suffice it to reiterate the changes in personnel over the years. From 1947 to 1952 the principal expert adviser—there was no dominant influence on policy—was Sir G. S. Bajpai, the Secretary-General of External Affairs. To some extent Mme. Pandit's views affected the outlook of her brother. On India's China policy, Sardar Panikkar played a key role from 1950 to 1953. A continuing, though intangible influence is being exerted by Lord and Lady Mountbatten. In recent years the advice of N. R. Pillai, the Secretary-General of External Affairs, has carried much weight. But overshadowing all these since 1954 has been Krishna Menon.

The composition of the Congress élite has changed little since the death of Patel. The key group is the Working Committee of twenty members. But of these only a half-dozen were and are involved in making important decisions. Other than Nehru and Azad, the dominant figures have been Pant, Morarji Desai, Dr. B. C. Roy, and U. N. Dhebar, Congress President since 1954. Approaching the inner group is Lal Bahadur Shastri of the U.P. In the central Cabinet, as already noted, it is much the same group. Following the Prime Minister, the unofficial ranking in 1958 was Pant, Morarji Desai and Shastri, with Krishna Menon occupying a special position in foreign affairs.

The position of economic adviser to the Prime Minister has been occupied by a succession of persons with widely diverging views. An important formative influence was Professor K. T. Shah, a professional economist of leftist convictions who directed the activities of the Congress's National Planning Committee from 1938 to 1946. In the aftermath of Partition the conservative ideas of Shanmukham Chetty and Dr. John Matthai, the first two Finance Ministers, tended to hold sway, as reflected in the Industrial Policy Resolution of 1948. Nehru's urge to introduce national planning received encouragement in 1949–1950 from Dr. Solomon Trone, an American engineer of wide experience who served as the Prime Minister's personal adviser on economic matters. Throughout the period of the First Plan

---

[1] For an account of Nehru's homage to Azad see the *Times of India* (Bombay), 25 February 1958.　　　[2] See pp. 569–75 above.

Nehru gave *carte blanche* to his very able Finance Minister, C. D. Deshmukh. Within the Planning Commission proper Deshmukh's views, supported by Nehru, generally carried the day. The Vice-Chairman, V. T. Krishnamachari, provided wise counsel and administrative guidance. The only serious discordant note was sounded by K. C. Neogy, who pleaded for greater caution. Deshmukh's successor, T. T. Krishnamachari, carried the private sector with him even though he introduced severe taxation. A man of extraordinary energy and drive, he fell foul of public morality in the notorious Mundhra episode and was compelled to resign early in 1958.

One other person, Professor P. C. Mahalanobis, must be noted in this connection. Indeed, his has probably been the most profound influence on Nehru's economic thinking since the autumn of 1954. A brilliant physicist who was honoured with membership of the British Royal Society as early as 1923, Mahalanobis later developed a keen interest in statistics and achieved further renown as Director of the Indian Statistical Institute in Calcutta. From that vantage point he became involved in high-level economic planning. The Left wing has applauded his role, for Mahalanobis is the most articulate spokesman for radical state planning using the lessons of Soviet and Chinese experience—though he is not averse to Western technical and capital aid. The business community and conservatives generally consider him the *eminence grise* who is steering the Prime Minister into dangerous waters.

Mahalanobis holds no official position, but his title, Honorary Statistical Adviser to the Government of India, does not represent a true measure of his influence. It was he who prepared the draft plan-frame for the Second Five-Year Plan which, if adopted without change, would have strengthened the public sector enormously at the expense of private enterprise. Only the powerful pressure of industrialists and financiers, supported by right-wing Congressmen, frustrated this move towards greater socialism. Nevertheless, he remains a key figure in Nehru's economic entourage with ready access to the Prime Minister, whose interest in science redounds to Mahalanobis's advantage.[1]

---

[1] For Mahalanobis's views on planning see his 'Science and National Planning', *Anniversary Address to the National Institute of Sciences of India*, January 1958.

The inner private circle around Jawaharlal Nehru has remained static since Independence. Two persons dominate the scene in the Prime Minister's Residence—which many Indians consider a modern version of the Moghul Court: Mrs. Indira Gandhi, Nehru's charming daughter, and M. O. Mathai, the little-known 'Special Assistant to the Prime Minister'. Both live in Nehru's official home and both are constantly by his side. Their influence is wide-ranging, though of an entirely different character.

Mrs. Gandhi is devoted to the care of her father, a widower for more than twenty years. By all accounts, she is an indispensable companion who helps to fill, in part, the deep void of loneliness which has long afflicted the Indian Prime Minister. Her functions are many and varied: official hostess at the Residence; Mistress of the Household; guardian of her father's health—in so far as his temperament permits—and travelling companion on almost all tours within India and abroad. Long overshadowed by her father, rather shy and retiring, and never in robust health, she has only recently emerged as a public personality in her own right. During the past few years she has been actively associated with a myriad of social welfare and women's agencies. In politics, too, she has become a force to contend with—a member of the Congress Working Committee since 1955 and of the powerful Central Election Committee of the party.

Her views on public issues are not too well known, but most observers would classify them as somewhat to the Left. One significant index is her expression of support for the Congress 'Ginger Group'. Her direct influence on the Prime Minister cannot be gauged accurately but in the nature of things must be considerable. She is, perhaps, the only person with whom Nehru can discuss most matters at ease, and the sheer amount of time which she spends in his company gives her a strategic position shared by no one else. She has also taken the burden of responsibility from her father in various secondary matters.

The position of M. O. Mathai is unique in contemporary Indian politics. Little is known about his background, except that he comes from Kerala and has been Nehru's devoted aide since 1946. Many are the stories of how Mathai joined the Prime Minister's staff. The most authentic one appears to be that he wandered in one day with his meagre belongings and offered his services to the future Prime Minister, indeed, beseeched Nehru to employ him in any capacity. He has been by Nehru's side ever since, first as stenographer, then as Private Secretary, and later as Special Assistant.

His functions are nowhere defined. In fact, his name appears nowhere, not even outside his lavish offices in the Ministry of External Affairs and in Parliament House, situated next door to the Prime Minister. Lacking an official post in the civil service—he is separate from, and clearly superior to, the head of the Prime Minister's Secretariat—he cannot deal directly with state matters. But his status as Nehru's trusted aide gives him great influence. All correspondence for the Prime Minister first crosses the desk of Mathai. Anyone who wishes to see Nehru, except for members of the family, senior Cabinet Ministers and a few other prominent officials, must approach the Prime Minister via Mathai.

The analogy of Sherman Adams in the Eisenhower Administration comes to mind, but this is inaccurate. Mathai does not exert any meaningful influence on policy decisions. Nor is the Chief Executive of India ill—or inclined to delegate authority to his staff. Mathai's power is, rather, of a negative character, namely, permitting or preventing access to the Prime Minister and, to some extent, determining the kinds of materials which come to Nehru's attention. Because of Nehru's trust, he is a man whom aspiring politicians consider it wise to flatter. It may also be that Mathai, through a carefully chosen word to the Prime Minister, can facilitate or hinder certain appointments. Many are surprised that he has succeeded in winning Nehru's confidence, for he is not an intellectual in any sense and does not appear to possess qualities that would attract a man of Nehru's stature.

Mrs. Gandhi and Mathai are the key figures in the 'court circle', but they are not alone. Mme. Pandit has ready access to her brother and lives at the Residence during her infrequent visits to the capital. So too does her younger sister, Mrs. Hutheesingh, though she has no influence on public affairs. Another member of the select group is Gopi Handoo, sometime personal bodyguard of the Prime Minister and a senior security officer of the Indian Government. Lord and Lady Mountbatten retain an intimate association with Nehru, a friendship that is cemented by annual reunions in Delhi and Romsey. A special position is held by India's distinguished philosopher—Vice-President Dr. Radhakrishnan, whose wise counsel is often sought by Nehru, both on matters of policy and personalities. Highly respected by Nehru, he has become an acknowledged elder statesman.

At the time of writing, the influential people around Nehru would seem to be as follows: Pandit Pant for internal politics and administration; Krishna Menon for foreign policy; Pant, Morarji Desai, B. C. Roy and Shastri for party affairs; Mahalanobis for economic matters; Mrs. Gandhi and Mathai in the private sphere; Radhakrishnan as an elder statesman; and the Mountbattens as personal friends. With the possible exception of Krishna Menon, Nehru no longer has close Indian friends.

*   *   *   *

Nehru's public life thus far has spanned a period of forty years. Almost thirty were devoted to the struggle for independence. And for more than a decade he has held the dual position of national leader and world statesman. What does the record reveal? What were his contributions to the nationalist movement? What are his achievements—and failures—as India's Prime Minister? More generally, what does the record suggest about his strengths and weaknesses as a political leader? And what is the likely legacy of his stewardship since 1947? Finally, what are the prospects for India after Nehru?

It would be foolish to pretend that conclusive answers are possible at this time, for we are too close to the events, notably those of his tenure as Prime Minister, to possess a quality of detachment. As for the future, one can offer only the most general type of speculation, particularly because so much depends on the date of his departure from the helm of affairs. Recognizing these problems does not, however, relieve a biographer from the challenge posed by such questions. Nor is he dissuaded by the knowledge that most judgements offered now will be subject to revision in the perspective of history. It is in this spirit that the author approaches the delicate task of judging Nehru as a leader.

We may begin with the nationalist phase of his career which

ended in 1947. We are on relatively sure ground here. We know that he was Gandhi's principal aide in the non-violent war for independence. We know, too, that he was beloved by millions. We know of his writings, of his years in prison and of his selfless devotion to the cause of freedom. Indeed, we are now in a position to appraise his contributions to Indian nationalism.

Perhaps his most distinctive service was to prevent the movement from becoming narrowly egocentric. None of his colleagues possessed either the talent or the outlook for this task, not even Gandhi or Subhas Bose. Most were so preoccupied with the Indian scene that events abroad were of little or no consequence—until the war compelled them to think about the world scene and its implications for the struggle at home. To the extent that they were aware of this link they were indebted to Nehru. Long before then he had stressed the need for an international outlook, beginning with his 'war danger' resolution in 1927 and continuing with mounting intensity through the mid-'thirties. In fact, he alone fashioned a Congress 'foreign policy' as expressed in the party's resolutions on international affairs from 1936 onwards. It is true that other members of the High Command were indifferent to this aspect of the struggle; some felt that they had to humour Nehru's pet interest, as they termed it; few appreciated his anti-fascist rhetoric or his emotional attachment to other freedom movements or, for that matter, his tears over the fall of Loyalist Spain and the rape of Ethiopia. Yet, imperceptibly, his relentless campaign penetrated their thought and widened their horizon. In simple words, Gandhi paid tribute to this contribution of his successor: 'Pandit Jawaharlal Nehru is Indian to the core but, he being also an internationalist, has made us accustomed to looking at everything in the international light, instead of the parochial.'[1]

Along with his international outlook was a vision of a renascent Indian society to follow independence, a land in which the timeless ills of poverty and disease would be eradicated or at least alleviated. In this vision, too, Nehru was alone among the senior Congress leaders. More specifically, his second vital contribution was to infuse a social and economic content into the meaning of *swaraj*, to give the movement a materialist and

[1] Tendulkar, *Mahatma*, vol. 7, p. 90.

socialist orientation. Independence, he argued time and time again, was the immediate goal but must be viewed as a prelude to the transformation of Indian society; and even during the political struggle a far-reaching reform programme should be enunciated. He hammered on this theme in his presidential addresses to the Congress in 1929, 1936, 1937 and 1946, in his writings and in innumerable speeches throughout the country. Despite strong opposition from the Right wing, he succeeded in getting party approval of his views in the Karachi Resolution on Fundamental Rights in 1931—the first step towards the goal of a 'socialist pattern of society'. His emphasis on social and economic reform also found expression in the Congress election manifestos of 1936 and 1946 which were drafted very largely by Nehru himself. Nothing could be done on a national scale until independence was attained, and little was done by the Congress provincial ministries in the late 'thirties. But the seed of socialist ideas had been planted. Nehru was not alone in setting forth this view, but his influence gave it special weight in the party.

The twin vision of Jawaharlal Nehru made him the voice of Indian youth and of a whole generation of intellectuals. This was his third contribution to the nationalist movement, to enlist the active support of the young, Westernized intelligentsia and young men generally for the Congress cause. He was, uniquely, the representative of a class and a generation, and in him their doubts and hopes found articulate and romantic expression, notably in his autobiography. In performing this role Nehru made another, indirect, contribution to the Congress: he offered the militant and radical youth a satisfying alternative to Communism and therefore weakened the Communist movement to the benefit of nationalism. Indeed, but for him there can be little doubt that young nationalists in the early 'thirties would have turned to the Communist Party in large numbers. Because of his pledge of far-reaching land reform and his magnetic personality he also attracted the rural masses to the Congress, supplementing the traditionalist appeal of Gandhi. Without Nehru they would have followed the Mahatma. But Nehru provided reinsurance of their loyalty to the nationalist movement.

Not only did Nehru make the Congress conscious of the outside world. Even more important, he made the world conscious of India and the struggle for independence. In a very real sense he was the Congress spokesman to people everywhere, a one-man antidote to the barrage of British propaganda extolling the virtues of the *Raj*. His autobiography became the authentic voice of Indian nationalism, and Nehru became the symbol of a people in revolt. To a large extent it moulded the attitude of the American intelligentsia in the early 'forties and created a real though intangible pressure on United States policy in favour of a rapid transfer of power. And in England it provided ammunition for those elements who favoured British withdrawal. Even among Tories it evoked a sympathetic response and raised doubts about the morality of continued rule over India. No better tribute to this role is to be found than the following letter to Nehru from C. F. Andrews, the Mahatma's closest English friend: 'You are the only one outstanding person who seems instinctively to know what the West can understand and follow easily. Bapu's [Gandhi's] writings had to be condensed and explained over and over again; and it was only . . . a genius of the first order such as Romain Rolland who could make him really intelligible. . . . Even Gurudev [Tagore] is very difficult when he gets away from poetry to prose.'[1]

Within India, Nehru provided still another link—between the Congress and the All-India States People's Conference, which espoused the nationalist ideal in the princely States. Nehru was not responsible for its creation but he played an increasingly active role in strengthening the bonds between the two groups, often in the face of staunch opposition from Gandhi and the Congress Right wing. The Mahatma held firmly to the view that the Congress should extend only moral support to the A.I.S.P.C. Nehru strongly urged active political support and guidance. Certainly to the militant popular leaders in the States, like Sheikh Abdullah of Kashmir, it was Nehru not Gandhi who provided the main source of inspiration.[2]

In the Congress proper Nehru rendered other services of note. Along with Subhas Bose he placed the issue of complete independence in the forefront of the party's deliberations as early as 1928. The following year he presided over the Lahore session which embodied the demand for independence in the Congress

[1] Unpublished Nehru Letters, 6 November 1935.
[2] For Sheikh Abdullah's tribute to Nehru's role in the A.I.S.P.C. see *Nehru Abhinandan Granth: A Birthday Book*, pp. 61–63.

Constitution. And throughout the 'thirties and 'forties he fought all efforts to whittle down the nationalist demand, though he was prepared to make tactical concessions. Moreover, through his writings and in his capacity as Chairman of the National Planning Committee, he made the Congress plan-conscious, another seed which bore fruit in 1950 with the establishment of the Planning Commission and the two Five-Year Plans that followed.

On the organizational side of party affairs Nehru's role has been deprecated in the face of Sardar Patel's administrative genius. Yet the older generation of Congressmen recall that the rudiments of a party organization were fashioned by Nehru during his long tenure as General-Secretary in the 1920's. Later he abandoned this aspect of Congress politics, not because of lack of talent but because of temperamental aversion to the party machine. From 1929 onwards he was, with Gandhi, the party's voice to the Indian masses. And as the elections of 1937 and 1946 revealed, he was the Congress's prize vote-getter, the salesman of its programme. He was also intimately involved in the shaping of that programme and shared with Gandhi the role of principal draftsman of resolutions and manifestos; after 1940 he performed this function alone. The Mahatma was the dominant influence on policy; Nehru translated the decisions into calls to action.

There remains one final contribution to the Congress, intangible but none the less important. Nehru's political, moral and personal integrity set an inspiring example to the rank and file and, with less success, to the leadership. The purity of his public life, his honesty, and his aversion to corruption served as a bastion in a movement which, like all movements, was affected by different motives and impulses.

Taken together, these contributions form an impressive record, perhaps without peer among political revolutionaries of this century. Gandhi's role in the attainment of Indian independence was undoubtedly greater, but Gandhi lacked Nehru's vision, both international and social. The Mahatma was no less interested in the welfare of the masses. However, in many respects his was an archaic conception of the ideal future. To one Westerner at least, it was illiberal, if not reactionary.

*   *   *   *

How shall we judge Nehru's record of leadership since 1947? Perhaps the best test is the extent to which he has succeeded in translating his ideas into reality. Nehru has long considered himself a revolutionary, by which he means a person who seeks fundamental change in society. He denies the necessity of violence and stresses the element of consent. For him, gradualism and mass participation are essential to the process, and the revolution must take place within a democratic framework.

That India is in the midst of a revolution is beyond doubt. That Nehru has been its philosopher and guide, its voice, indeed, its very spirit, is also unquestionable. That it has been non-violent, gradual, democratic and, in the main, supported by the bulk of the Indian people can be easily demonstrated. The price, however, will probably be judged severe by those who look back on this period of transition: the pace and scope of the revolution do not measure up to Nehru's own expectations and do not appear to be adequate to the needs of India at this critical juncture in its history.

A basic reason for this gap is the inauspicious circumstances attending its birth. The initial fruit of independence was bitter indeed: partition; widespread dislocation; millions on the march; communal tension; a vast refugee problem; danger of internal chaos and Balkanization; friction with Pakistan, and war in Kashmir. The revolution had to be postponed, for survival was the compelling need of the moment. Nehru was flexible enough to accept this challenge and he met it superbly. With the invaluable aid of Sardar Patel, he maintained the stability and unity of India against a formidable array of disruptive tendencies. This was his first major achievement after Independence. In a broader sense he has been the indispensable unifying force in Indian society since 1947. He has waged a relentless war against what he terms the three principal threats to stability and unity—provincialism, communalism and casteism—and has been relatively successful thus far. He has not eradicated these ills, but this has been impossible in so short a period. He has, however, created both institutions and a climate of opinion which have weakened their influence.

A long-term safeguard against the natural pull to provincial loyalties is the enormous power allotted to the central government in the Constitution. So great is the concentration of legislative, executive and financial authority in the Centre that while the Indian Republic is federal in form it is unitary in spirit. At the same time, provincialism was given a new source of strength by the reorganization of States along linguistic lines in 1956. To support the constitutional basis of unity against this fissiparous tendency he has used the power of his voice in constant personal appearances before his people. More than that, the Five-Year Plans provide a tangible attraction to national unity—as well as a hope for a better economic future. Similarly with communalism. Against strong opposition, Nehru has created a secular state in which, in theory, Muslims and other minorities have equal rights with the Hindu majority. And so far as possible he has tried to allay their fears. As for casteism, perhaps the most deep-rooted idea in orthodox Hindu thought, he has fought it valiantly, both in word and deed. The most tangible expression of his modest success is the formal abolition of untouchability.

These four elements, along with his role as the symbol of Indian unity, constitute Nehru's major achievements in domestic affairs since 1947: political stability and democracy; the Plans; a secular state; and social change. Together they represent substantial progress.

The Constitution was drafted largely by Ambedkar, but it was Nehru who provided the basic philosophy and goals in his Objectives Resolution. Moreover, it was Nehru who insisted that the process of constitution-making continue during the dark days following Partition in order that independent India might have a sound legal order at the outset. Equally important was his determination to hold elections as soon as the crises of the Partition were surmounted. His purpose was to provide the government with a basis of legitimacy, to bring politics to the village and to create the beginnings of a pattern of political democracy. Their success was impressive: the largest free election held anywhere in the world with an encouraging response from a preponderantly illiterate people; and the education of the masses in the meaning of the ballot. The second election was equally free. Although it cannot be said that a habit has been formed, India is well on the way to acceptance of the vital principle of periodic choice by the governed as to who should govern them. Along with these accomplishments, the central place of

Parliament in the political life of the nation has been deliberately fostered by the Prime Minister.

Within a decade of Independence, then, a democratic constitution has been enacted, two nation-wide elections have been conducted, and a parliamentary system of government has been established. Other persons certainly aided the process. But Nehru was the driving force behind this far-reaching innovation, superimposed on the Indian authoritarian tradition and British enlightened autocracy. The test of its durability, however, is yet to come, for the Congress has held a monopoly of power at the Centre and in all States of the Union but one since 1947. Nehru has planted the seed. Its growth has been encouraging —except for the fact, an important fact, that a genuine party system has yet to develop.[1]

The final accomplishment in the political sphere has been a strong, stable government. Against this, however, must be set inefficiency, maladministration and widespread corruption. Nehru himself has, on more than one occasion, criticized the central bureaucracy as 'an administrative jungle'. The blame for this state of affairs rests largely with him. One of his few outspoken critics put the issue bluntly: 'He who has power has responsibility. If having power he fails to discharge his own proper responsibility the least that can be expected from him is that he will refrain from complaining bitterly and loudly, as if it was somebody else's fault.'[2] The problem is not that Nehru does not discharge his responsibilities; he over-discharges them. Herein lies one of the Indian Prime Minister's grave weaknesses and failures since 1947.

The fact of the matter is that Nehru is an inept administrator. Decisions are concentrated in his hands to an incredible degree, not only because of objective pressures, but also because of his all-consuming interest in the pettiest of details. He lacks both the talent and temperament to co-ordinate the work of the various ministries. More important, he has never shown a capacity or inclination to delegate authority. The result has been the 'administrative jungle' which he bemoans. When Nehru is out of the country the decision-making process comes to a virtual halt. And even while he is in Delhi the bureaucracy

---

[1] For a study of the Indian party system see Weiner, M., *Party Politics in India.*
[2] Vivek (A. D. Gorwala) in the *Times of India* (Bombay), 8 November 1953.

functions only as rapidly as Nehru can handle the vast amount of paper that crosses his desk. The long-term implications are no less disquieting. The habit of dependence on Nehru, a veritable disease of Indian administration, has hindered the growth of self-reliance among those who will have to carry the burden of decision when 'Panditji' is no longer present. The experience of the last decade or more bodes ill for the future in this crucial matter.

The second broad area of achievement—and failure—has been economic affairs. National planning is a significant instance where an idea was translated into reality. And the credit belongs entirely to Nehru. The crises of Partition necessitated delay, but at no time did he cease to press for a national plan. Nor was it an easy task, for many persons, notably Patel, thought strictly in terms of administrative decisions for a day, a week or a month. It was Nehru and Nehru alone who made the Congress and the Civil Service aware that beyond today there is a tomorrow. Although he knows little about economics, he was the chief inspiration for planning.

The First Plan, modest in scope, was successful. The Second Plan ran into stormy weather in 1957–8, but the core remains. Perhaps most important has been the wide acceptance of Nehru's view that only through wide-ranging planning can India progress materially and socially. A closely related development for which Nehru is also primarily responsible is the ambitious Community Development Programme, an attempt to instil the concept of self-help into India's 325 million peasants. Psychological gains have been somewhat disappointing, but material progress thus far has been considerable. Within a few years the whole countryside will be covered by this pioneering scheme.

These achievements merit recognition, for they represent nation-building activities of the highest order. Against them however, must be set the woefully inadequate land reform programme since 1947. Nehru himelf has expressed dissatisfaction with its pace and scope.[1] Yet for more than twenty years he preached the necessity of revolution in the Indian countryside. He has not practised what he preached. It may be argued that agriculture is a State subject under the Constitution and that he

[1] To the author in India in March 1956.

does not bear direct responsibility for this aspect of the revolution. It is true that he still favours far-reaching agrarian reform. It is also true that powerful groups within his own party have frustrated his intent. And even among his closest colleagues there is opposition to change more drastic than that already achieved. There are, too, serious economic obstacles in various parts of the country. Nevertheless, this glaring weakness in India's economic revolution must be attributed partly to Nehru.

He has never controlled the Congress machine. But whenever he pressed his views with vigour, the Right wing ultimately gave way, as with the secular state and the Hindu Code Bill. On occasion he has fought for more radical land reform, as in the case of constitutional amendments regarding compensation; and when he fought he was invariably successful. By and large, however, he has not given land reform either the importance it deserves or the consistent support which one would have expected in the light of his pledges before Independence. Indeed, the slow progress in land reform must be adjudged the most striking failure in the economic sphere. More generally, social and economic change since 1947 have been less than that pledged—perhaps inevitable in the circumstances—and less than required if India is even to approach the goals set by Nehru in the past. The pace has also been less rapid than possible.

The inadequacy of land reform suggests one of Nehru's weaknesses as a political leader: the gap between words and deeds is often wide. Over the years he had denounced many unsavoury features of Indian public life, but the matter frequently rested there. He has criticized nepotism and corruption in the administration but has never acted against them. He has deplored the cesspools of disease and degradation that are the slums of Delhi and other major cities, but they remain. He has castigated black-marketeering and other nefarious aspects of Indian business life; in the earlier days, he even threatened to shoot or whip the guilty. But these practices continue. This is not to suggest that Nehru alone can solve all the problems of Indian society. But rhetoric alone will not improve the situation. By his constant verbal attacks on things which offend his sensitivity, often without following through with harsh deeds, he has tended to 'cheapen the coinage'. It is almost as if he has to get these sources of irritation off his chest. But the result, among the vocal part of the population at any rate, is to discount these threats as annoyances of the moment. The gap between words and deeds suggests something else. In some instances it is not the lack of time to follow through or the inability to change institutions overnight; rather, it is a tendency to shrink from radical deeds, partly because of the basic liberal make-up of the man, partly because of the experience of violence and disorder in 1947. Nehru is a social reformer; he is not a social revolutionary.

Perhaps his most notable accomplishment is the creation of a secular state. In the immediate aftermath of Partition, Hindu-Muslim tension was so great that only courage and resolution could safeguard the precarious position of India's largest minority. Nehru achieved this—against strong opposition, even within his own party. On the issue of Muslim rights he stood fast and literally forced his colleagues to accept his views, at least in principle. In this he was aided by Gandhi's teachings and the Mahatma's presence in the early months after Independence. But it was Nehru almost single-handed who held the extremist Hindu communalists at bay. He did so largely by force of personality but also by a clear indication that he would act decisively against communal violence.

Communal harmony has not yet been fully realized, but the wounds of 1947 are gradually being healed. To Indian Muslims Nehru is a rock and a shield. Wherever possible he has bent over backwards to give them special consideration. It is no mere accident that among all government ministries, the Foreign Office has the highest proportion of Muslim senior officers, except for the Education Ministry which was headed by a Muslim, Maulana Azad, until 1958. Even among his household staff Nehru has maintained a careful balance between the two largest communities. In private conversation, Muslims emphasize the vital protective role played by the Prime Minister. Of those who have spoken openly on this delicate subject the following remark is typical: 'Except the Prime Minister, Mr. Nehru, who enjoys the confidence and affection of Muslims in a remarkable degree, and one or two others . . . it is difficult to think of leading Hindus whose attitude towards the Muslims remaining in India can be said to be very friendly.'[1]

[1] Ismail, Sir Mirza, *My Public Life*, pp. 130–1.

Nehru's contribution in this regard has been twofold: to ease the transition to greater mutual trust between Hindus and Muslims; and to embody the secular ideal in the Indian Constitution, a bulwark of equal rights for all minorities in the future. He has also maintained a continuous onslaught on the ideas of communalism. If the election results are any guide, he has been very successful thus far. This does not mean that communalism has been vanquished. It has been forced to retreat, but it lies beneath the surface of Indian politics awaiting an opportunity to assert itself anew. With each passing year of Nehru's tenure as Prime Minister the forces of communalism are weakened. They will almost certainly come to the fore again, but the climate of opinion becomes less receptive. This achievement is largely Nehru's. It is likely to be his most enduring contribution to India, and it is the one of which he is most proud.

In the field of social reform proper the most noteworthy developments since 1947 are the abolition of untouchability and the enactment of the Hindu Code Bill. Few Congressmen could openly oppose the former because it had been one of the pillars of the Mahatma's creed. However, strong pressures were brought to bear on the reform of the ancient Hindu code; opponents could look to President Prasad and others for support. Nehru's efforts were frustrated for four years because the majority of his own party opposed the measure. He finally forced the issue and secured its passage through Parliament, though in the process he was compelled to make various concessions.

The record of Nehru's foreign policy has already been dealt with in ample detail. In this context it is sufficient to note an intangible contribution. For almost two centuries before Independence India's voice was inaudible; as a colony of Great Britain it acted in accordance with the wishes of London. In less than a decade, however, Nehru has brought India into the coterie of the Great or near-Great Powers. He has raised India's prestige and has enhanced the national pride as no Indian but Gandhi has done in centuries. A few Indians may question the wisdom of non-alignment and other aspects of his policy. But all bask in the glory that Nehru has achieved on the international stage. He has not resolved all sources of dispute, particularly with his neighbours, as the unhappy story of Indo-Pakistani relations, Goa and the position of persons of Indian origin in Ceylon reveal. But these pale into insignificance—as far as most of his countrymen are concerned—when set against India's and Nehru's stature in the world at large.

*   *   *   *

Some years ago Nehru set down his thoughts on the proper role of a leader: 'How is a leader of men to function? If he is a leader, he must lead and not merely follow the dictates of the crowd. . . . If he does so, then he is no leader and he cannot take others far along the right path of human progress. If he acts singly, according to his own lights, he cuts himself off from the very persons whom he is trying to lead. If he brings himself down to the same level of understanding as others, then he has lowered himself, been untrue to his own ideal, and compromised that truth. And once such compromises begin, there is no end to them and the path is slippery. What then is he to do? . . . He must succeed in making others perceive it [this truth] also.'[1]

How does Nehru measure up to his own conception of a leader? Some of his weaknesses have already been noted, especially his shortcomings as an administrator and the frequent gap between words and deeds. There are others. Perhaps his gravest defect is indecision. He vacillates in the face of alternative courses of action, all of which seem to have some merit. He is completely lacking in ruthlessness. But there are times in the affairs of a nation when ruthlessness is desirable, and with it a strong will to follow through the logical imperatives of a policy decision. It may well be that Nehru is an excessively pure democrat. Not only does he refuse to impose his will on the country—an admirable quality in a burgeoning democracy —but he seems to have a compulsion for universal consent. Partly this is due to his stress on mass participation; but in part it is due to an instinctive playing to the gallery, a desire to please the crowd, the ultimate basis of his political power. He is the supreme democrat who tries to please everyone, with the result that he arrives at decisions slowly. In extreme cases, too,

---

[1] Foreword to Tendulkar, *Mahatma*, p. xiii.

he will displease many. The outstanding example of these weaknesses in recent Indian politics, as noted earlier, was his action on States Reorganization.

Closely related to these defects is the tendency to yield to pressure. This was true in the years before Independence when Nehru frequently gave way to Gandhi and the Right wing, as in 1928 over complete independence versus Dominion status, and in 1940 and 1942 over civil disobedience. It has also been true since Independence. A notable example was the concession to the demand for a separate state of Andhra in 1952. Another was his concessions to private enterprise in the deliberations leading to the framing of the Second Five-Year Plan. For Nehru these are, perhaps, necessary tactical retreats in the continuing struggle to achieve his broad objectives. Yet these retreats have delayed their realization, certainly in the form and with the rapidity that he desires.

According to many who know him well, Nehru is a bad judge of character. He is also blinded by past loyalties and previous service of colleagues with the result that he retains them in high party or governmental positions after they no longer merit this trust and influence. Loyalty often outweighs sound judgement. He never thinks ill of an old colleague and rarely believes allegations of corruption. His normal response is to dismiss these charges as gossip or to question the accused directly and to accept his denial without further investigation. He has never openly forced the resignation of a colleague—though on occasion he has made it difficult for a person not to resign. Thus the highest echelons of party and government are filled with dead wood, old and tired men who have outlived their political usefulness to the country. They remain in power and prevent the training of younger men for the tasks of tomorrow.

With the passage of time one other weakness has become increasingly significant. During more than a decade in power Nehru has not trained a successor group, young men who are devoted to his programme and who can assure continuity in policy after he retires or dies. To many Indians this is the most disquieting feature of his leadership, the seeming lack of concern about tomorrow. The failure to gather around him men whom he can trust to implement his policies has not only resulted in distortions and delays in the execution of his decisions.

It may well mean that successors will freeze or try to undo some of his reforms.

At first glance this catalogue of failings seems formidable. But these weaknesses have to be viewed in perspective; they are the weaknesses of a giant. For Nehru is a giant, both as man and statesman. If political greatness be measured by the capacity to direct events, to rise above the crest of the waves, to guide his people, and to serve as a catalyst of progress, then Nehru surely qualifies for greatness. Almost single-handed he has endeavoured to lift his people into the twentieth century. He is, indeed, India's nation-builder. He has provided a focus of unity at a time of great stress. He has laid the foundations of a working parliamentary democracy. He has fashioned the machinery for planning and has instilled the idea that here lies India's path to material progress. He provided the philosophy for India's new Constitution with its emphasis on individual rights. He has succeeded in securing wide acceptance of the ideal of a secular and equalitarian society. He has restored India's faith in itself as well as its place in the family of nations. And he has begun the task of social reform.

In a wider sense Nehru has set in motion forces for long-term social, economic and political change. The abolition of untouchability and the ceaseless attack on casteism already show evidence of undermining the caste system, the hard core of the Hindu social order. The new Hindu Code may well alter fundamentally the social relations between the sexes in India's largest community and serve as a liberating force for Hindu women who for millennia have occupied a subordinate status. The Five-Year Plans and the Community Development Projects are breathing fresh air into the village, opening up vistas of economic improvement on a scale hitherto unimaginable. And the granting of adult franchise to the millions will probably alter the basis of power in future Indian society. Whether or not these forces will realize their potentialities depends on a myriad of factors. But Nehru has fashioned the elements out of which can emerge the new India that he spoke of before 1947. It is too early to be sure. The revolution is still unfinished; indeed it has barely begun. The loss of Nehru could be a catastrophe for India were it to occur before these elements are strengthened.

On the international stage Nehru speaks for a large part of

the Afro-Asian world. For many Westerners he is one of the few voices of sanity as the world hovers on the brink of disaster. Some disagree with his specific policies. But most recognize his sincerity and the vital importance of maintaining a bridge between the two hostile worlds. For many he is the genuine voice of peace. In nineteenth-century terms he may be compared to Cavour with an admixture of Garibaldi, i.e., a nation-builder with the dash of the romantic nationalist. To this might be added Wilson in the twentieth century, the spokesman for idealist internationalism. But all comparisons fail to convey the measure of any man. Nehru is Nehru, a man and a leader to be measured in the age in which he lives.

*　　*　　*　　*

'After Nehru who? After Nehru what?' These two questions have agitated the minds of Indians and foreigners alike since the early 1950's. As Nehru approached his seventieth year a sense of urgency about the future became increasingly felt. The Prime Minister was ageing quickly. He sought a respite from the gruelling pace of work and the oppressive burden of administrative responsibility which he had carried since Independence; but in vain. His colleagues implored him to remain at the helm of affairs; and he yielded to their cry. So it had been in 1954 also. But what would happen the third time, or the fourth, or the fifth? Some day Nehru would no longer be on hand to guide his people. A cloud of uncertainty hangs over his followers—and his opponents. For millions there is anxiety.

The problem of succession to the Prime Ministership is rarely acute in stable democracies. There, established institutions and conventions usually assure a smooth change-over. An Eden succeeds a Churchill, a Diefenbaker follows a St. Laurent. Policies may change; so too may the character and effectiveness of leadership. But society as a whole continues essentially along the same path. In India, however, such continuity is far from certain. Nehru has been no ordinary Prime Minister. And India is in a stage of transition.

Some of Nehru's roles will pass with him; they cannot, in the nature of things, be filled by any other person. And the institutions he has created, the forces he has unleashed—insufficient time has elapsed for them to become rooted in Indian society. What will happen to them after Nehru? The feeling of disquiet is heightened by the fact that Nehru has not trained a successor or group of successors.

Nehru himself *appears* to be indifferent to the succession problem. In public, at any rate, he has treated the matter lightly. Thus, in reply to a question about the safeguards for the continuity of his basic policies—socialism, democratic government, the secular state and non-alignment in foreign affairs—he said in 1956:

It's difficult for me to answer except to say that the policies I have encouraged, advocated, sponsored, have not been just individual policies. There are many people, and important people . . . who believe in them. What is much more so is that they have, vaguely and broadly speaking, the backing of the masses in this country. And, as step by step we give effect to those policies, well, that is a step confirming a certain direction of growth. It is very difficult to go back from these things. . . . My chief business, in so far as the people are concerned, has been . . . to try to explain things to them in as simple a language as possible. . . . For the rest, well, really, *one does one's best and one doesn't worry too much about the future.*[1]

It is difficult to believe that a man as sophisticated as Nehru and as dedicated to his ideals should be as unconcerned about the future as this comment suggests. Indeed, those who know him contend that he has many deep and anxious moments about the succession, not in the sense of who will become Prime Minister but what will be the fate of his policies. One can only speculate on his line of reasoning and his concrete response to the problem. The following hypothesis may provide an explanation.

Nehru is genuinely concerned about the succession. The most logical method of ensuring continuity would be a moderately leftist Congress led by a group devoted to his policies. Either he is incapable of training such a cadre because he is too much of an individualist or he has tried and has failed. In any event, he may well have come to the conclusion that the Congress of the future will be a conservative force. Certainly the Right wing of the party dominates the machine in the twilight of his career, as it has during the past thirty years. There

---

[1] To the author in New Delhi on 13 June 1956. (Emphasis added.)

is ample evidence that most prominent Congressmen do not share his ideology. They pay lip service to the 'socialist pattern of society', for example, because they know how strongly he feels about socialism and because it would be imprudent to show disloyalty. They do not oppose his policies openly because Nehru is the assurance of Congress victory at the polls. But in his absence their opposition might well lead to a reorientation of policy. Nehru knows this, though it would be impolitic to say so. There is, then, one feasible alternative to the conservative Congress leaders of the future. This is to make a compact with the Indian people at large, to appeal above the party to the masses, to create a level of urges and expectations which will compel his successors to follow the basic policies laid down by him, in their own self-interest, namely, the retention of power. Here lies the insurance of continuity, the general will, as directed and expressed by Nehru since 1947. Regardless of who assumes the Prime Ministership, the forces set in motion by Nehru and the ideas instilled in the people will act as a formidable restraining force on deviation from Nehru's policies.

This hypothesis would seem to be in accord with Nehru's essentially Marxist view of the relationship of a party to the mass. Its validity is certainly strengthened by his continuous personal contact with the masses and by his incredible number of tours to the countryside. On every possible occasion he stresses the essentials of his programme and ideology, thereby creating powerful areas of pressure for continuity. Most important, Nehru himself has suggested that he considers the masses the key to the succession: 'All this trains, educates people, makes them think in a particular way and drives all of them forward in a particular direction. Now, some of them [successors] may stop the pace, not going in that direction, or they may make it faster. *But I don't think it is possible in the future for the mass of the people to be taken away, far away, from their moorings.*'[1]

If this is an accurate explanation of Nehru's approach to the succession it suggests two other observations. Nehru's compact with the masses is a gamble fraught with grave possibilities, for he may be creating urges and expectations which no democratic party will be able to satisfy in the future, thus paving the way for some kind of authoritarianism, either Communism or a form

[1] To the author, in New Delhi on 13 June 1956. (Emphasis added.)

of Hindu Fascism. If Communism should triumph, future historians will be tempted to call Nehru 'the Kerensky of India'. Moreover, the masses may provide insurance for continuity but they are no substitute for positive leadership by a group devoted to his image of future Indian society. This weakness of his leadership will continue to cause anxiety among those who try to anticipate an India without Nehru.

The question of *who* will succeed Nehru is less important than *what* will follow his death. (Even if he relinquishes the Prime Ministership he will remain the dominant figure in Indian politics.) Furthermore, any speculation depends on *when* the change-over takes place. As of 1958, the line of succession within the Congress High Command is clear. First in order is Pandit Govind Ballabh Pant, the seventy-one-year-old Minister of Home Affairs who was elected Deputy Leader of the Congress Parliamentary Party during the resignation crisis in the spring. A long-time Chief Minister of the United Provinces, the most populous State of the Union, Pant is considerably to the Right of Nehru on economic and social matters. His views on foreign affairs are not well known, but it is reasonable to surmise from his intervention during the Hungarian revolt in 1956 that he is more inclined to the West—though a believer in non-alignment as best suited to India's position in the world.

Second to Pant is Morarji Desai, the sixty-two-year-old former Chief Minister of Bombay who came to the Centre at the end of 1956 and was elevated to the Finance portfolio early in 1958. Partly because of Pant's advanced age, Desai is the leading contender for the succession. But there are other qualities that endear him to the Congress, especially to the Right wing and the traditionalists. Like his hero, Sardar Patel, he is considered to be an able administrator. His integrity is above reproach. He is firm in action and free from the gnawing doubts of India's Prime Minister. In outlook he is, if anything, more conservative than Pant and much more rigid. A fanatic on prohibition, he more than anyone else has been responsible for its retention—in the face of a large economic burden. A staunch defender of private enterprise, he has never shown any enthusiasm for the 'socialist pattern of society'. And he is the most orthodox in social outlook among senior leaders of the party. He makes no secret of his pro-Western views, though it is doubtful that he would abandon non-alignment in principle. An ascetic, deriving his strength from Gandhi and Patel, he is utterly devoid of that magnetism which lies at the root of Nehru's power. Few people are enthusiastic about Desai, but most respect his incorruptibility and decisiveness. He is the unquestioned choice of the Right wing in the Congress and the business community, two levers of power which make his selection very likely should a successor become necessary in the next decade.

Nehru is very fit, however, and may well outlive both Pant and Desai—or the Congress may be defeated at the polls. The latter contingency need not concern us at the moment. The former is well within the realm of possibility. Should Nehru remain active for another decade the question of succession assumes a totally different perspective. It is impossible to foresee who will emerge from obscurity. The Congress President since 1954, U. N. Dhebar, has the advantage of relative youth —he was forty-nine when he assumed the post. But he has not yet revealed the necessary stature nor has he acquired a powerful following within the party. The one other person who stands in the wings of the party is Lal Bahadur Shastri who ranks fourth in the hierarchy in 1958, immediately after Desai. Highly respected for his administrative ability, a middle-of-the-roader ideologically, a native of the all-important United Provinces, like Nehru and Pant, and young compared to other senior leaders—he was born in 1904—he has a growing following among the rank and file.

Krishna Menon, well known in the West and recently popular in India because of his filibustering tactics on the Kashmir dispute at the United Nations, has little strength in the party as of 1958. Even should the need for a successor come within a few years, it is difficult to conceive of Menon being acceptable to powerful conservative leaders. He might be retained because of his skill in international affairs, but his political influence rests almost entirely on his personal friendship with Nehru. In the long-run, however, he looms as a possible successor, by virtue of his growing links with the armed forces and his strength on the non-Communist far Left.

Among the non-Congress democratic leaders two persons merit attention. The first is Jaya Prakash Narayan, founder of the Congress Socialists in the early 'thirties and the leader of the Socialist Party (later the Praja-Socialist Party) until his formal withdrawal from politics in 1956. Even before that year he had become the right-hand man of Vinoba Bhave in the *Bhoodan* (land gift) movement. Narayan is the only political figure other than Nehru who commands the affection of the Indian masses, and his reputation for devoted service to the cause of independence is second to none. Until the early 1950's he was considered by many to be Nehru's heir, even though he was no longer in the Congress. He is, perhaps, the only person in this select group who is ideologically akin to Nehru, though he has recently espoused more Gandhian ideas about how to solve India's problems; and he has serious doubts about the efficacy of reform through legislation as well as about centralized planning. On such issues as secularism and democracy he is still close to Nehru. The fact that he has retired from formal politics does not, however, exclude him from the succession. On the contrary, Narayan has followed the time-honoured Indian path of renunciation and is strengthening his attachment to the peasantry. As Vinoba Bhave's stature grows so too does that of Narayan. Vinoba himself is inconceivable as Prime Minister, but a combination of Narayan and Bhave, like Nehru and Gandhi, heading a mass movement—such an eventuality cannot be ruled out.

A possible alternative to all of these is the highly respected C. D. Deshmukh. His gravest liability is that he was not associated with the Congress during the struggle for independence. However, he is admired by the business community; is the acknowledged dean of India's civil servants; is respected by the Congress Centre and Left because of his support of the Five-Year Plans; and was somewhat of a hero in his native Maharashtra because of his struggle over Bombay City. After leaving the Government he became Chairman of the Universities Grants Commission. But he is, at sixty-two, still young enough to have a future in Indian politics.

Whichever person succeeds to the Prime Ministership, no one can succeed to Nehru's position in modern India. He has towered over his colleagues and the nation at large as no one can in the foreseeable future. He is, uniquely, the leader of the transition period. His successors will have to be men of a different stamp and stature. Where Nehru has inaugurated certain ventures, they will have to consolidate and expand them. While Nehru has stifled initiative they will have to foster it. While Nehru has ruled by force of personality, they will rule by more traditional political practices. The age of the heroic, charismatic leader will give way to a period in which the administrator will govern.

There has been the assumption, thus far, that the successor will probably come from the Congress. This is likely if the need arises before the elections of 1967 and is possible thereafter. What then does the future portend for India's governing party? On the surface, disintegration seems very possible, for Nehru has been its unifier. Certainly its hitherto-dominant position in Indian politics will pass with him, for he was the most potent factor in the party's previous electoral victories. However, his absence certainly does not presage its doom.

One must distinguish between the Congress at the Centre and in the States. The State branches are the core of the party and they will not disintegrate after Nehru. The machine which Gandhi built and Patel consolidated has deep roots in the countryside and in certain cities. Moreover, the party will be able to capitalize on Nehru's lengthy leadership for some years. Nor should it be taken for granted that the struggle for the succession will destroy the party as an effective political force. Greater decentralization seems inevitable, but the Congress leaders are ideologically flexible. In the interests of power, pragmatic adjustment of conflicting views is likely, at least in the short-run. The real struggle within the party will be between the (minority) Nehruite Left wing and the more orthodox, more traditionalist, more conservative group led by Pant and Desai. Total disintegration is possible, but not probable. Rather, the Left wing may bolt the party and possibly join forces with the Praja-Socialists to form a stronger left-wing democratic party. The remaining members of the Congress would then refashion their policies along more conservative lines, not breaking with Nehru's programme, but slowing down the process of change.

Whether or not the Congress proceeds along these lines, one thing is certain. The party in 1958 is in the throes of a severe crisis, greater than any in its history. It is likely to be returned to power at the 1962 elections, especially if Nehru remains active in politics and devotes more time to party matters. Even then, its majority will almost certainly be sharply reduced. After that one can only surmise. But it would certainly not be a surprise if the Congress is removed from power within a decade.

What of the longer-term prospects for Indian politics after Nehru? To take national unity first. Among the positive elements are the following: unlike its neighbour, India is geographically integrated; its constitution has a strong bias in favour of centralization and gives the Centre overriding powers to deal with any serious threat of secession; Hinduism provides a common way of thought and behaviour for the vast majority of Indians; the internal schism deriving from the Muslim struggle for Pakistan was eliminated with the Partition; the Plan creates a sense of national unity, permeating as it does the entire country; so too does the continuing influence of Gandhi and Nehru; and the ideal of nationalism, having triumphed so recently, is not likely to be discarded easily. There are, however, serious sources of concern: the mentality of casteism which leads to parochial loyalties; communalism, particularly among Hindus, which has only retreated in the face of Nehru's massive personal onslaught; a persistent pull to regional cultures, which may be enhanced by the reorganization of States in 1956; the closely related fact of linguistic diversity, the absence of a real national language and the continuing friction arising from the attempts to impose Hindi on the country as a whole; and the still-sharp division between village and urban attitudes, ways of life and standards of living. Nehru's passing will certainly put a serious strain on Indian unity, but it is not likely to be catastrophic. On balance, the forces for unity seem sufficiently strong to prevent a reversion to the chaos which preceded the coming of the British. The fundamental source of unity is not Nehru; rather, it is the fabric of Hindu society and the stability of the peasantry. The consequences of the death of Gandhi and Patel were negligible in this regard. Of course, Nehru was present at the time. But the continuing factors for unity, along with Nehru's own contributions since 1947, would seem to ensure essential unity in the future.

The future of parliamentary government in its present form

is less certain. There are many favourable features: the constitutional provisions for a parliamentary system, periodic elections, an independent judiciary and the standard democratic freedoms; a working parliamentary system since Independence; two free general elections; the acceptance of defeat at the polls by the governing party (Kerala in 1957); the existence and unhindered operation of opposition political parties; the tradition of civilian control over the military services; and a decade's experience of a Head of State who has not attempted to exert his wide-ranging formal powers. Against these must be set the prevalent corruption in the Congress and the Administration; the tendency of the Executive to assert its power over the Judiciary and to treat court decisions with something less than respect; the frequency of constitutional amendment, which detracts from the permanence of the constitutional order; the tradition of authoritarianism in Hindu society and the lengthy experience of the British *Raj*; powerful opposition to the parliamentary system as unsuited to India's traditions and conditions, notably by Vinoba Bhave and many orthodox Hindus; and the weakness of the democratic alternative to the Congress, namely, the Praja-Socialist Party.

Perhaps the most important source of concern is the reliance on one man during the formative period of the experiment in parliamentary government. Nehru has made a conscious effort to foster the idea and practice of parliamentary decision, and this has strengthened the institution. But he has a dual role. By virtue of his pre-eminent position he has delayed its acceptance by the population as a whole. The basic problem is to substitute loyalty to institutions for loyalty to a man. This must await Nehru's departure from active politics.

The ultimate test of democratic government to survive will be its capacity 'to deliver the goods'. The attachment to democracy *per se* is not yet sufficiently rooted in Indian soil to ensure its acceptance indefinitely. Widespread unemployment, particularly among the growing army of young university graduates, does not augur well for the future. If democracy is unable to press forward with Nehru's programme of reform more rapidly, many will turn to other creeds which offer hope of more rapid and far-reaching improvement in their way of life. And as the English language declines in importance, the nourishment for a

Western-type parliamentary system is sapped. Finally, the example of Chinese success makes more attractive the alternative method of achieving social and economic reform.

The prospects of Communism have been implied throughout this discussion. Since 1951 the Communist Party has made substantial inroads into the electorate and by 1957 it had become the second-largest organized political force. The gap in votes and legislative seats between the Congress and the C.P.I. is still very large. But whereas the Congress is in decline, the Communists are devoted, well organized and imbued with a mission. They have established a beach-head in Kerala. They benefit from the growing discontent with the Congress, particularly because of the weakness of the Praja-Socialists and the trend to polarization in Indian politics. They are aided, too, by the example of China and the blandishments of the Soviet Union, as well as its economic aid and its support on the Kashmir issue. They have also been strengthened by the respectability flowing from India's friendly relations with the Communist world. And more recently they have adopted the cloak of purely peaceful methods of attaining power, by changing their constitution in the spring of 1958. Nevertheless, the road to Communism will not be easy in India. Non-Communist and anti-Communist forces are still powerful, as represented by the Congress and orthodox Hinduism. Its success will be in direct proportion to the Congress's failure to mend its ways. Even more, its future will depend upon the capacity of the Congress or a more leftist democratic party to continue the revolution which Nehru has set in motion.

In the short-run the danger to constitutional democracy is more from the extreme Right than from the Left, some form of Hindu authoritarianism rather than Communism. The Congress will probably retain power for some time at least; and if conservative forces are in control, they will certainly slow down the process of social and economic change. They will probably not be able to freeze it entirely. But even slowing the process may strengthen the challenge from the Communists. Unless a non-Congress democratic party can take over after Nehru, a conservative Congress may drift or move deliberately to an authoritarian régime, with the backing of Hindu orthodoxy and possibly the armed forces. Such a course would be fatal for

Indian democracy; henceforth, the contest for political power in India would be between a form of Hindu Fascism and Communism; and Communism, with its pledge to complete the revolution initiated by Nehru, would be the likely victor.

For all of these reasons the next decade is crucial to the future of India—and therefore of Asia as a whole. If Nehru remains at the helm of affairs and the Second and Third Five-Year Plans fulfil their goals, then India will have broken through the static barrier and will be well on the way to realizing the pledge of a better life for its people. At the same time, the democratic political framework will have the necessary time to demonstrate its effectiveness as an instrument of reform, not only in India but throughout Asia. Hence Nehru's continued leadership is indispensable for some years to come, whether as Prime Minister or as elder statesman.

Some years ago, in a pensive moment about the future, Nehru proposed the following epitaph for himself: '. . . if any people choose to think of me then, I should like them to say: "This was a man who, with all his mind and heart, loved India and the Indian people. And they, in turn, were indulgent to him and gave him of their love most abundantly and extravagantly." '[1] They will indeed say this of Nehru. And much more. And it will be deserved.

[1] *The Statesman* (Calcutta), 21 January 1954.

SELECT BIBLIOGRAPHY

A. Official Records and Reports

Before 1947:

Cmd. 9109, 1918. (Montagu-Chelmsford) *Report on Indian Constitutional Reforms.*

Cmd. 681, 1920. *Report of the* (Hunter) *Committee appointed to Investigate the Disturbances in the Punjab.*

Cmd. 1586, 1922. *Telegraphic Correspondence regarding the Situation in India.*

Cmd. 3568-9, 1930. (Simon) *Report of the Indian Statutory Commission.*

Cmd. 4147, 1932. *Communal Decision.*

Cmd. 6121, 1939. *India and the War.*

Cmd. 6219, 1940. *India and the War.*

Cmd. 6350, 1942. *Lord Privy Seal's* (Cripps) *Mission. Statement and Draft Declaration.*

Cmd. 6652, 1945. *Statement of the Policy of His Majesty's Government.*

Cmd. 6821, 1946. *Statement by the Cabinet Mission and His Excellency the Viceroy.*

Cmd. 6829, 1946. *Correspondence and Documents connected with the Conference between the Cabinet Mission and His Excellency the Viceroy and Representatives of the Congress and the Muslim League, May 1946.*

Cmd. 6835, 1946. *Statement by the* (Cabinet) *Mission dated 25 May . . .*

Great Britain. House of Commons: *Debates.*

Great Britain. House of Lords: *Debates.*

Government of India: India and Communism (unpublished, 1935).
   History of the Civil Disobedience Movement 1940-41 (1942, for official use only).
   Correspondence with Mr. Gandhi, August 1942-April 1944 (1944).

Home Department (Political Section) Fortnightly Reports (from the Chief Secretary of each Province to the Home Department, New Delhi, 1919-1943. Unpublished).

After 1947:

Constituent Assembly Debates: Official Report (New Delhi, 1947-1950, twelve volumes).

Government of India, *The Constitution of India* (1949 and reprinted with amendments to 1956).

White Paper on Indian States (1950).

Report of the Press Commission (1954).

Report on the First General Elections in India, 1951-52 (1955).

Y

Report on the Second General Elections in India, 1957 (1958).
Report of the States Reorganisation Commission (1955).
Report of the Official Language Commission (1957).
Government of India, Planning Commission, *The First Five Year Plan* (1953).
Second Five Year Plan (1956).
The New India (New York, 1958).

B. Books and Pamphlets

All-India Satyagraha Council, *Report of the August Struggle* (Allahabad(?), n.d. *circa* 1945).
Anup Singh, *Nehru: The Rising Star of India* (New York, 1939).
Lord Birdwood, *Two Nations and Kashmir* (London, 1956).
Bolitho, Hector, *Jinnah: Creator of Pakistan* (London, 1954).
Bose, D. R. (ed.), *New India Speaks* (Calcutta, 1947).
Bose, Subhas Chandra, *The Indian Struggle* (Calcutta, 1948).
Bourke-White, Margaret, *Halfway to Freedom* (New York, 1949).
Bowles, Chester, *Ambassador's Report* (New York, 1954).
Brailsford, H. N., *Subject India* (London, 1943).
Brecher, M., *The Struggle for Kashmir* (Toronto, 1953).
Bright, J. S. (ed.), *Before and After Independence* (Collection of Nehru's Speeches 1922–1950) (New Delhi, 1950).
Brown, Ermine A. (ed.), *Eminent Indians* (Calcutta, 1946).
Brown, W. N., *The United States and India and Pakistan* (Cambridge, Mass., 1953).
Campbell-Johnson, Alan, *Viscount Halifax* (London, 1941).
Mission with Mountbatten (London, 1951).
Coupland, R., *Indian Politics 1936–1942* (London, 1943).
The Cripps Mission (London, 1942).
India: A Re-Statement (London, 1945).
Cousins, Norman, *Talks with Nehru* (London, 1951).
Dutt, R. P., *India To-day* (Bombay, 1947).
Dwivedi, R. (ed.), *The Life and Speeches of Pandit Jawahar Lal Nehru* (Allahabad, 1930).
Fischer, Louis, *The Life of Mahatma Gandhi* (New York, 1950).
Fisher, Margaret W. & Bondurant, Joan V., *The Indian Experience with Democratic Elections* (Berkeley, 1956).
Indian Views of Sino-Indian Relations (Berkeley, 1956).
Indian Approaches to a Socialist Society (Berkeley, 1956).
Gandhi-Jinnah Talks (New Delhi, 1944).
Gledhill, A., *The Republic of India* (London, 1951).
'History of the Freedom Movement' (New Delhi, Collection of Unpublished Papers 1919–1947).

Hutheesingh, Krishna Nehru, *With No Regrets* (London, 1946).

'Nehru and Madame Pandit' in *Ladies' Home Journal* (Philadelphia, January 1955).

'Independence for India League' (New Delhi, unpublished file in A.I.C.C. library).

Indian Annual Register (ed. by Nripendra Nath Mitra, Calcutta, 1920–47).

Indian National Congress, *Congress Bulletin* (bi-monthly, Allahabad, later Delhi, 1930–).

The Indian National Congress 1920–1923, Being a collection of the resolutions of the Congress and of the A.I.C.C. and of the Working Committee of the Congress from September 1920 to December 1923 (Allahabad, 1924).

Reports of the Annual Sessions (Allahabad, later Delhi, 1918–).

Report of the Linguistic Provinces Committee (1949).

Press Clippings on Nehru (Delhi, 1946–).

The Constitution of the Indian National Congress (Delhi, 1953 and with amendments to 1957).

Ismail, Sir Mirza, *My Public Life* (London, 1954).

Jennings, Sir W. Ivor, *Some Characteristics of the Indian Constitution* (London, 1952).

Karaka, D. F., *Betrayal in India* (London, 1950).

Nehru: The Lotus Eater from Kashmir (London, 1953).

Karunakaran, K. P., *India in World Affairs 1947–1950* (Bombay, 1952).

India in World Affairs 1950–1953 (Bombay, 1958).

Keith, A. B., *A Constitutional History of India 1600–1935* (London, 1936).

Khare, N. B., *Nehru as I Know Him* (Bombay, 1957).

Khosla, G. D., *Stern Reckoning* (New Delhi, n.d.).

Kogekar, S. V. & Park, Richard L. (ed.), *Reports on The Indian General Elections 1951–52* (Bombay, 1956).

Kripalani, K. R., *Gandhi, Tagore and Nehru* (Bombay, second edition, 1949).

Krishnamurti, Y. G., *Jawaharlal Nehru: The Man and his Ideas* (Bombay, 1942).

Kundra, J. C., *Indian Foreign Policy 1947–1954* (Gröningen, 1955).

Kurukshetra (A Symposium on Community Development in India 1952–1955) (Delhi, 1955).

Lal, Ram Mohan (ed.), *Jawaharlal Nehru, Statements, Speeches and Writings, With an Appreciation by Mahatma Gandhi* (Allahabad, 1929).

Lumby, E. W. R., *The Transfer of Power in India* (London, 1954).

Mahalanobis, P.C., *Science and National Planning*, Anniversary Address to the National Institute of Sciences of India (January 1958).

Majid Khan, Abdul, *Jawahar Lal Nehru and his Ideas* (New Delhi, 1951).

Malaviya, K. D., *Pandit Motilal Nehru: His Life and Speeches* (Allahabad, 1919).

Masani, M. R., *The Communist Party of India* (London, 1954).

Mehta, Ashoka, *The Political Mind of India* (Bombay, 1952).

Mende, Tibor, *Nehru: Conversations on India and World Affairs* (New York, 1956).

Menon, V. P., *The Story of the Integration of the Indian States* (New York, 1956).

The Transfer of Power in India (Princeton, 1957).

Moraes, Frank, *Jawaharlal Nehru* (New York, 1956).

Morris-Jones, W. H., *Parliament in India* (London, 1957).

Narayan, Jaya Prakash, *Towards Struggle* (Bombay, 1946).

Narendra Deva, *Socialism and the National Revolution* (Bombay, 1946).

Nehru, J.

(a) *Books*

Soviet Russia (Bombay, 1929).

Letters from a Father to his Daughter (Allahabad, 1929).

Recent Essays and Writings: on the Future of India, Communalism and other Subjects (Allahabad, 1934).

Glimpses of World History (Allahabad, 1934–5).

India and the World (London, 1936).

Eighteen Months in India 1936–1937 (Allahabad, 1938).

China, Spain and the War (Allahabad, 1940).

Toward Freedom: The Autobiography of Jawaharlal Nehru (New York, 1941).

The Unity of India (Collected Writings 1937–1940) (New York, 1941).

The Discovery of India (Calcutta, 1946).

Nehru on Gandhi (New York, 1948).

Independence and After (Delhi, 1949).

Visit to America (New York, 1950).

Press Conferences, 1950, 1951, 1952, 1953, 1954 (New Delhi).

Jawaharlal Nehru's Speeches 1949–1953 (Delhi, 1954).

Nehru on Africa (Delhi, n.d. *circa* 1954).

Jawaharlal Nehru's speeches (Vol. 3, March 1953 to August 1957) (Delhi, 1958).

A Bunch of Old Letters (Bombay, 1958).

(b) *Pamphlets*

Prison Land (Allahabad, 1933).

The Question of Language (Allahabad, 1937).

Report to the All-India Congress Committee in 1938 (Allahabad, 1938).
Nehru-Jinnah Correspondence (Allahabad, 1938).
Where Are We? (Allahabad, 1939).
Nehru Flings a Challenge (Bombay, 1943).
Youth's Blunder (Bombay, 1945).
Report to the All-India Congress Committee in 1951 (New Delhi, 1951).
Letters to the PCC Presidents (New Delhi, n.d. *circa* 1955).
Report to the All-India Congress Committee in 1955 (New Delhi, 1955).
Towards a Socialistic Order (New Delhi, 1955).
Planning and Development (Delhi, 1956).
On Community Development (Delhi, 1957).
Nehru Visits U.S.A. (Washington, 1957).

(c) *Articles, Speeches and Miscellaneous not Reprinted*

'The Solidarity of Islam' in *The Modern Review* (Calcutta, vol. 58, November 1935).
'His Highness the Aga Khan' in *The Modern Review* (Calcutta, vol. 58, November 1935).
'Orthodox of All Religions, Unite' in *The Modern Review* (Calcutta, vol. 58, December 1935).
'Before India is Reborn' in *Asia* (New York, vol. 36, June 1936).
Foreword to Masani, M. R., *Soviet Sidelights* (Bombay, 1936).
'Guidallo Ranee' in *Living Age* (New York, April 1938).
'Anxious India' in *Asia* (New York, vol. 39, May 1939).
'India Can Learn from China' in *Asia and the Americas* (New York, vol. 43, January 1943).
'Colonialism Must Go' in *New York Times Magazine* (3 March 1946).
'A Cable' in the *New Republic* (New York, 4 August 1947).
Foreword to Menon, K. P. S., *Delhi–Chungking: A Travel Diary* (Oxford, 1947).
'Immersion of the Ashes' in *United Nations World* (New York, May 1948).
'The Question of Language' in *Indian Information* (London, March 1949).
'Swamiji's Teachings and Political Awakening' (tribute to Ramakrishna) in *Hindusthan Standard* (Calcutta, 10 April 1949).
Foreword to Tendulkar, *Mahatma* (Bombay, 1951).
Presidential Address, Indian National Congress, Fifty-seventh Session (New Delhi, 1951).
Preface to *The Ajanta Caves* (UNESCO, 1954).
Foreword to Aiyar, N. Chandrasekhara, *Valmiki Ramayana* (1954).
Asian-African Conference (Delhi, 1955).

Foreword to Sinha Dinkar, R. D., *Sanskriti Ke Char Adhyaya* (Four Phases of Culture) (Delhi, 1956).

'A Deep Malaise' in the *Times of India* (New Delhi, 15 January 1958).

Nehru Abhinandan Granth: A Birthday Book (New Delhi, 1949. Presented to Nehru on his sixtieth birthday).

Overstreet, Gene D. & Windmiller, Marshall, *Communism in India* (Berkeley, 1959).

Panikkar, K. M., *In Two Chinas: Memoirs of a Diplomat* (London, 1955).

Parikh, Narhari D., *Sardar Vallabhbhai Patel* (Ahmedabad, 1953).

Parkin, Raleigh, *India Today* (Toronto, 1946).

Prasad, Rajendra, *India Divided* (Bombay, 1946).

At the Feet of Mahatma Gandhi (New York, 1955).

Pyarelal, U. N., *Mahatma Gandhi: The Last Phase* (vol. i, Ahmedabad, 1956).

Rosinski, *The World of Jawaharlal Nehru* (n.d.).

Roy, M. N., *Jawaharlal Nehru* (Delhi, 1945).

Sahgal, Nayantara, *Prison and Chocolate Cake* (London, 1954).

Saiyid, M. H., *Mohammad Ali Jinnah* (Lahore, 1945).

Shah, K. T. (ed.), *Report (of the) National Planning Committee* (Bombay, 1949).

Sharma, Jagdish Saran, *Jawaharlal Nehru: A Descriptive Bibliography* (Delhi, 1955).

Shelvankar, K. S., *The Problem of India* (New York, 1940).

Sitaramayya, B. Pattabhi, *History of the Indian National Congress* (vol. i, 1885–1935, Bombay, 1935; volume ii, 1935–1947, Bombay, 1947).

Spear, T. G. P., *India, Pakistan and the West* (London, 1949).

Spencer, Cornelia, *Nehru of India* (New York, 1948).

Srinivasan, N., *Democratic Government in India* (Calcutta, 1954).

Talbot, P., 'The Second General Elections: Some Impressions' (New York, 1957).

'The Second General Elections: Voting in the States' (New York, 1957).

Tandon, P. D. (ed.), *Nehru Your Neighbour* (Calcutta, 1946).

Taylor, Carl C., *A Critical Analysis of India's Community Development Programme* (Delhi, 1956).

Tendulkar, D. G., *Mahatma: Life of Mohandas Karamchand Gandhi* (eight volumes, Bombay, 1951–4).

The Earl of Halifax, *Fulness of Days* (London, 1957).

Thompson, Edward & Garratt, G. T., *Rise and Fulfilment of British Rule in India* (London, 1934).

Tuker, Lieut.-General Sir Francis, *While Memory Serves* (London, 1950).

Unpublished Nehru Letters (1917–48; 210 to Nehru, 30 from Nehru).
Unpublished Nehru-Mahmud Correspondence (1921–54. 150 letters).
'Vivek', *India Without Illusions* (Bombay, 1953).
Weiner, Myron, *Party Politics in India* (Princeton, 1957).
Wilson, M. L., *Community Development Programme in India* (Delhi, 1956).
Wint, G., *The British in Asia* (London, 1947).
Woodruff, Philip, *The Men Who Ruled India: The Founders* (London, 1953).
  The Men Who Ruled India: The Guardians (London, 1954).
Zinkin, M., *Asia and the West* (London, 1951).
Zinkin, Taya, *Changing India* (London, 1958).

C. JOURNALS AND NEWSPAPERS

Amrita Bazar Patrika (Calcutta).
Bombay Chronicle.
Christian Science Monitor (Boston).
Eastern Economist (New Delhi).
Economic Weekly (Bombay).
Express (Bombay and New Delhi).
Far Eastern Survey (New York).
Harijan (Ahmedabad).
Hindustan Times (New Delhi).
Hindusthan Standard (Calcutta).
India Quarterly (New Delhi).
Indiagram (Washington).
Manchester Guardian.
New York Times.
Shankar's Weekly (New Delhi).
The Hindu (Madras).
The Hindu Weekly Review (Madras).
The Statesman (Calcutta and New Delhi).
The Times (London).
Times of India (Bombay and New Delhi).
Tribune (Ambala).
Young India (Ahmedabad).

D. SELECT LIST OF PERSONS INTERVIEWED

In England:
Horace Alexander (prominent member of the Society of Friends).
Earl Attlee (Prime Minister of Great Britain 1945–51).
Thomas Balogh (Fellow of Balliol College, Oxford).
Alan Campbell-Johnson (Press Attaché to Lord Mountbatten in India, 1947–8).

N. C. Chatterjee (President of the Hindu Mahasabha).
Malcolm Darling (prominent writer on Indian agrarian problems).
E. M. Forster (novelist).
P. N. Haksar (Counsellor, Indian High Commission in London and
    later Head, External Publicity Division, Indian Ministry of
    External Affairs).
Sir Frederick James (former member of the Viceroy's Executive
    Council).
Sir Evan Jenkins (Governor of the Punjab, 1946–7).
Philip Mason (former member of the I.C.S.: author of *The Men Who
    Ruled India*).
Andrew Mellor (*Daily Herald* Correspondent in India in 1947).
Sir Walter Monckton (Constitutional Adviser to the Nizam of
    Hyderabad, 1947–8 now Lord Monckton of Brenchley).
Professor W. H. Morris-Jones (University of Durham).
The Earl Mountbatten of Burma (Governor-General of India,
    1947–8).
Mme. Vijaya Lakshmi Pandit (sister of Nehru).
Professor C. H. Phillips (Chairman, Department of History, later
    Director, School of Oriental and African Studies, University of
    London).
Sir George Schuster (former member of the Viceroy's Executive
    Council).
Percival Spear (Bursar of Selwyn College, Cambridge University).
Professor N. Srinivasan (Head, Department of Politics, Andhra
    University).
Ian Stephens (Honorary Fellow, King's College, Cambridge Univer-
    sity, and former editor of *The Statesman*, Calcutta).
Dr. Solomon Trone (Personal Industrial Adviser to Nehru 1949–50).
Lieut.-General Sir Francis Tuker (G.O.C., Eastern Command,
    India, 1945–7).
Sydney Walton (noted publicist).
Guy Wint (leader writer for the *Manchester Guardian* and Fellow of
    St. Antony's College, Oxford).
Woodrow Wyatt (Private Secretary to Sir Stafford Cripps during the
    Cabinet Mission in 1946).

In India:

Anup Singh (M.P. and author of a biography of Nehru).
Aruna Asaf Ali (prominent Congresswoman, later member of the
    Communist Party's Central Committee, later Mayor of New
    Delhi).
B. P. L. Bedi (writer and politician).

Freda Bedi (professor of English and prominent social worker).

Prem Bhatia (Political Correspondent of *The Statesman*).

Professor P. C. Chakravarti (Jadavpar University, Calcutta, and sometime acting Director, History of the Freedom Movement project).

Renu Chakravarty (Communist M.P.).

Diwan Chaman Lall (M.P. and former Ambassador to Turkey).

Sachin Choudhury (Editor, *Economic Weekly*).

Eric da Costa (Editor, *Eastern Economist*).

Morarji Desai (Chief Minister of Bombay; later member of the Union Cabinet).

U. N. Dhebar (President of the Indian National Congress).

Faiz Ahmad Faiz (Chief Editor, *Pakistan Times*).

Professor D. R. Gadgil (Director, Gokhale Institute of Politics and Economics).

N. V. Gadgil (M.P., prominent Congressman from Bombay and former member of the Union Cabinet).

Feroze Gandhi (M.P., and Nehru's son-in-law).

S. M. Ghose (M.P. and former President, Bengal Provincial Congress Committee).

A. D. Gorwala (prominent publicist; former member of the I.C.S.).

G. K. Handoo (Deputy-Director, Intelligence Bureau, Ministry of Home Affairs; sometime officer-in-charge of Nehru's security).

Shaukat Hayat Khan (Pakistani politician).

Azim Hussain (Ministry of External Affairs).

Raja and Krishna Hutheesingh (brother-in-law and sister of Nehru).

Mian Iftikharuddin (Pakistani politician and owner of the *Pakistan Times*).

H. V. Kamath (M.P.).

R. K. Karanjia (Editor, *Blitz*).

Khushwant Singh (novelist and journalist).

Dr. Saif-ud-din Kitchlew (prominent nationalist Muslim and President, All-India Peace Council).

J. B. Kripalani (former Congress President and leader of the Praja-Socialist Party).

Krishna R. Kripalani (Private Secretary to Maulana Azad and Secretary of the National Academy of Letters).

Mrs. Sucheta Kripalani (M.P. and former prominent member of the Praja-Socialist Party).

V. T. Krishnamachari (Deputy Chairman, Planning Commission).

A. Krishnaswami (prominent Independent M.P.).

Professor Oskar Lange (economist).

Dr. P. S. Lokanathan (Director-General, National Council of Applied Economic Research; former Executive Secretary, ECAFE).

Professor P. C. Mahalanobis (Honorary Statistical Adviser to the Government of India and Director, Indian Statistical Institute, Calcutta).

Dr. Syed Mahmud (former Minister of State for External Affairs).

H. K. Mahtab (Governor of Bombay; later Chief Minister of Orissa).

K. D. Malaviya (Minister of State, Union Cabinet).

D. R. Mankekar (Editor, *Times of India*).

Minoo Masani (M.P.; former Executive Assistant to J. R. D. Tata; a former leader of the Congress Socialists).

M. O. Mathai (Special Assistant to the Prime Minister).

Dr. John Matthai (Minister of Finance, 1948–50; later Director, State Bank of India).

Ashoka Mehta (M.P.; a leader of the Praja-Socialist Party).

V. K. Krishna Menon (Minister of Defence).

V. P. Menon (Constitutional Adviser to the Viceroy, 1942–7; Secretary, Ministry of States, 1947–51).

Penderel Moon (Adviser to the Planning Commission).

Professor Hiren Mukherjee (Communist M.P.).

Brijlal Nehru (cousin of Nehru).

Jawaharlal Nehru.

K. M. Panikkar (Ambassador to France; former Ambassador to China and Egypt).

Pandit G. B. Pant (Minister of Home Affairs).

S. K. Patil (President, Bombay Provincial Congress Committee; later member of the Union Cabinet).

N. R. Pillai (Secretary-General, Ministry of External Affairs).

Sri Prakasa (Governor of Madras; former member of the Union Cabinet and later Governor of Bombay).

Dr. S. S. Radhakrishnan (Vice-President of India).

Keshu Ram (Principal Private Secretary to Nehru).

Escott Reid (High Commissioner for Canada to India, 1952–7).

Chester Ronning (High Commissioner for Canada to India, 1957–).

Dr. B. C. Roy (Chief Minister of Bengal).

P. B. Sitaramayya (Governor of Madhya Pradesh and author of *History of the Indian National Congress*).

C. R. Srinivasan (Private Secretary to Nehru).

K. Srinivasan (Editor, *The Hindu*).

Y. N. Sukthankar (Secretary of the Cabinet, and Secretary of the Planning Commission, later Governor of Orissa).

Saumyendranath Tagore (leader of the Revolutionary Communist Party of India).

Tarlok Singh (Head, Plan Co-ordination Section, Planning Commission).

D. G. Tendulkar (biographer of Gandhi).

S. D. Upadhyaya (former private secretary to Pandit Motilal Nehru and to Jawaharlal Nehru).

Mohammed Yunus (Ministry of External Affairs).

Maurice Zinkin (former member of the I.C.S., author of *Asia and the West*).

Taya Zinkin (correspondent for the *Manchester Guardian* and the London *Economist*).

INDEX

A.I.C.C. (All-India Congress Committee), see Congress, Indian National

A.I.T.U.C. (All-India Trades Union Congress), see Trades Union Congress, All-India

Abdullah, Sheikh, former Prime Minister of Jammu and Kashmir, 618; tried for treason, 1946, 312; overthrown, 1953, 609

Abell, Sir George, Private Secretary to the Viceroy, 1945–7, 359, 360 f.

Adams, Sherman, Assistant to the United States President, 614

Adult Suffrage, demand for, 130, 176, 197

Advisory Planning Board (formerly Planning Department), 514, 524. See also Economic Planning, Congress, s.v. National Planning Committee, Planning Commission

Africa, see Bandung Conference, Kenya, South Africa

Afro-Asian Conference, 1955, see Bandung Conference

Aga Khan III, 180; detention of Gandhi in his palace, 1942, 288

Agra, Nehru family at, 35, 36

Agrarian reform, Congress demand for, 130, 169, 226, 229, 237 f., 239; agitation for, U.P., 181 f.; Nehru's interest in, 69, 70, 169, 226, 229, 358, 390, 597; Lucknow resolution on, 238, cf. 495; implementation of, 550 ff.; inadequacy of, 623 ff. See also Zamindari

Ahmad, Muzaffar, Member of Central Committee of Communist Party of India, 166

Ahmadnagar Fort, Bombay Province, Nehru imprisoned in, 81, 288

Ahmedabad, site of Gandhi's ashram, 79, 288, 485

Akali agitation, see Sikhs

Akali Dal, see Sikhs

Alexander of Tunis, Field-Marshal Earl, 46

Alexander, A. V., later Lord Alexander of Hillsborough, member Cabinet Mission, 1946, 305

Alexander, Horace, friend of Gandhi and Nehru, 392 n.

Ali, Asaf, Indian Ambassador to the United States, 295, 307

Ali, Chaudhuri Mahomed, member of Steering Committee of Partition

Ali, Chaudhuri Mahomed, contd. Council, 1947, Prime Minister of Pakistan, 1955–6, 350

Ali, Maulana Mohammed, Khilafat leader, 67, 73; President of Congress, 1923, 92, 93

Ali, Munshi Mubarak, Nehrus' family servant, 44

Ali, Sayeed Fazl, Chairman of States Reorganization Commission, 1954–5, 482

Ali, Shaukat, Khilafat leader, Mohammed's brother, 67, 73

Aligarh Muslim University, dispute over, 399

Alipore Central Jail, Calcutta, Nehru imprisoned in, 81, 201, 202

All-India Congress Committee, see Congress

All-India States Peoples' Conference, Congress affiliate in princely States, 91, 345, 406, 407

All-India Federation Proposal, see Federation

All-India Radio, 357, 365 n.

All-India Trades Union Congress, see Trades Union Congress, All-India

All-India Volunteer Organization, 92 f. See also Civil Disobedience Campaigns, Congress

All-Parties Conference, 1928, 129; 1929, 140. See also Nehru Report

Allahabad, U.P., A.I.C.C. meeting at, 1942, 284; All-Parties Conference at, 1929, 140; Congress H.Q. at, 151, see also Swaraj Bhawan; Home Rule League Branch at, 55; Kumbh Mela satyagraha at, 94 f.; Nehru defies Salt Act at, 161; Nehru family home at, 35, 36 ff., 52, see also Anand Bhawan

Almora District Jail, U.P., Nehru imprisoned in, 81, 208 f., 301

Ambedkar, Dr. B. R., Untouchables' leader, 443; demands separate electorates for Untouchables, 1932, 189, see also Poona Pact; represents Untouchables at Cripps Talks, 1942, 277; Chairman of Drafting Committee, Constituent Assembly, 423, 454; Minister of Law, 423, 454; resigns from Cabinet, 423 f.; conversion to Buddhism, 455; death, 423, 455

Amery, L. S., Secretary of State for India and Burma, 1940–5, 301

Kaul, Kamala, *see* Nehru, Kamala
Kaul, Raj, Nehru's ancestor, 35
Kaur, Rajkumari Amrit, Minister of Health, 1947–57, 449
Keith, Professor A. B., *A Constitutional History of India*, 216
Kellog-Briand Pact, 1928, 119 f.
Kerala State, formerly Travancore-Cochin (*q.v.*), State elections, 470; Congress Provincial Branches in, 480; Dravidian languages spoken in, 489; Communists in power in, 22, 475, 478 f., 638, 639; land tax in, 551
Keynes, J. M., influence on Nehru, 48
Khadder, home-spun cloth, 70, 72, 125, 176, 226. *See also* Constructive Programme
Khaliphate, the, *see* Khilafat agitation
Khan, Bahadur Sarfaraz, 98 n.
Khan, Ghazanfar Ali, Muslim League minister in Interim Government, 323, 324
Khan, Khan Abdul Ghaffar, Pathan leader, leader of Redshirts (*q.v.*), 155, 157, 305; imprisoned, 1931, 180; resigns from Working Committee, 1940, 269; opposes Partition, 181 n.; proposes Pathanistan, 351. *See also* Khan Saheb, Dr.
Khan, Sir Khizar Hayat, Premier and Unionist leader of Punjab, 1946, 338 f.
Khan, Liaquat Ali, 1939 talks with Congress representative, 264; pact with Desai, 1945, 300; Finance Minister, Interim Government, 320, 343; opposes Mme Pandit's appointment to Moscow, 349; Mountbatten's discussion with, 343, 344; Premier of Pakistan, 1947, 353; and Punjab boundary question, 361; pact with Nehru on rights of refugees, 428 f., 452, 454
Khan Saheb, Dr., Pathan leader, 180, 181 n., 305, 350 f. *See also* Khan, Khan Abdul Ghaffar, Redshirts
Khilafat agitation, 1920, 67 f., 78; Congress support for, 67 f., 73, 85, 97 f.
Khizar, *see* Khan, Sir Khizar Hayat
Khruschev, Nikita, 585 n., 606 f.
Khudai Khidmatgars, Servants of God, *see* Redshirts
Kidwai, Rafi Ahmad, Muslim Congressman, Minister of Food, 1952, 449, 451 f., 609; resigns from Congress, 1951, 433 f.; friend of Nehru, 24, 223, 610
Kisan Mazdoor Praja Party, formed, 432; in 1951 elections, 441, 443;

Kisan Mazdoor Praja Party, ii merges with Socialist Party, 432. *See also* Praja-Socialist Party
Kisan Sabhas, Peasant Leagues, 181, 203, 217; relationship with Congress, 219, 237 f., 250, 391, 393; declared illegal, 184
Kisans, peasants, 69 f., 76, 78, 125, 517, 518; discontents of, 33, 128 f.; support Congress in 1937 elections, 227 ff., *cf.* 393; in 1951–2 elections, 440
Kitchlew, Dr. Saif-ud-din, Congress leader, arrested, 1919, 62, 93 n.; and Delhi Pact, 140. *See also* Amritsar Tragedy
Kohat, communal riots at, 1924, 97, 98
Korea, North and South, 594. *See also* Korean War
Korean War, 556, 558, 565, 569; Panikkar and, 572; Krishna Menon and, 574; India's role in, 588
Kripalani, Acharya J. B., Congress General-Secretary, 1934–46, 267, 430 f.; abstains on Poona Offer vote, 1940, 269; exempted from satyagraha, 1940, 273; imprisoned, 1942–5, 295; withdraws in favour of Nehru in Congress Presidency elections, 1946, 314; attends Mountbatten Plan conference, 347; Congress President, 347, 378; hope of reuniting India, 378; attitude to Partition, 349, 378 f.; resigns Presidency, 1947, 381; candidate for Presidency, 1950, 430 f.; forms Congress Democratic Front, 432, 433; resigns from Congress, 433; joins K.M.P.P., 433; defeated in 1951–2 election, 443; co-operation talks with Nehru, 464, *see also* Praja-Socialist Party; and Travancore-Cochin elections, 1954, 471
Kripalani, Krishna, *Gandhi, Tagore and Nehru*, 596 f.
Krishikar Lok Party, peasant party, Andhra Assembly, 473
Krishnamachari, T. T., Minister for Commerce, 1952–6, 456; Minister of Iron and Steel, 1955–7, 456; Finance Minister, 1956–8, 450 n., 612; resigns over Mundhra Affair, 21, 460 ff., 612. *See also* Mundhra, Haridas
Krishnamachari, V. T., Deputy Chairman of National Planning Commission, 520, 612
Kumbh Mela festival, and satyagraha, 94 f.
Kunzru, H. N., member of States Reorganization Commission, 482

Z

Date Due

	PRINTED	IN U. S. A.	